The Rugged Staircase

by

Cherry-Anna D. Law

First Published September 2021
by
Budding Authors Assistant
www.help2publish.co.uk

Cover design by Mary Rowlands

KDP ISBN: 9781919625409

DEDICATION

"For Anna"

CONTENTS

ACKNOWLEDGEMENTS

I owe the creation of The Rugged Staircase to the tireless efforts of my husband, sons and daughters, who have been my continual technical support, endured delayed and/or burnt dinners while their distracted mother loses track of time.

Special thanks go to my publisher Deb Griffiths, for practical support and professional input, to fellow writer Kate Nicholas for advice and encouragement, and to Shannon Finlayson and Sarah Gerrard, the social communications assessors, who diagnosed my Autism and encouraged me in creative writing.

I would also like to thank all the people I have ever met, who have shaped my life path, character, and decision-making, inspiring me to translate my experiences and observations into story form.

Finally, I would like to mention my mother, herself a gifted and unsung storyteller, who taught me to read and write, shared her own stories with me, and inspired me to become a writer at the age of four.

1: Edencroft

A solitary seagull mewed, breaking the silence of a warm September morning. On the Westcombe hills, the sun was shining. Deciduous forests and emerald-green fields of lazily grazing Guernsey cows, whitewashed cottages, high-hedged lanes, and red-tiled roofs painted a vibrant scene. Along the valley floor, meandered the river Helmer, a golden ribbon under a dome of benign protection. In this quiet corner of England, nothing of significance ever happened.

The stertorous rumble of a car engine signalled the presence of human activity. A green Morris Traveller emerged from a tunnel of foliage, snorting along the potholed road like a determined bulldog, past a disused railway, pumping station, and playing fields. The sleepy seaside town of Westcombe-on-Sea shimmered in heat-haze. The car stopped beside a pair of identical red-bricked bungalows, where the lane widened to smooth tarmac, marking the boundary between rural and urban.

At the wheel of the car sat a slender, greying gentleman in his late forties.

'Goodbye, Lucy,' Albert Wylie said. He stubbed out a smouldering cigarette and snapped the ashtray shut. 'Have a good day. See you here at four o'clock.'

Hunched in the passenger seat, a small girl stared apprehensively at the box-like buildings lurking behind a flimsy line of silver birches. The playing fields, daisy-speckled swathes, contrasted starkly with the prison-like edifices of Westcombe Grammar and Beechwood Secondary Modern.

'Bye, Dad,' the child whispered, the sharp features of her young face betraying raw angst. Fifty yards up the road, big green buses were stopping, disgorging hordes of youngsters in dark blue. Lucy cowered behind her briefcase, inhaling the mellow smell of new leather. Her mind was blank, her emotions numb. She got out of the car and secured the navy-blue beret, pulling it over one ear. The freshly-starched blouse and tunic were stiff and uncomfortable. A brief, backward glance at the tiny red triangle on the distant hillside boosted her morale. Home was in sight.

The school entrance was ungated; a tarmac path divided by a low, wooden fence. Lucy walked down the empty side of the path. Through a thick, hawthorn hedge she discerned a whitewashed house with sky-blue window frames, wondering who lived there. Lucy paused at a row of black bollards, startled by a jingling bell and screeching brakes. 'OUT OF MY WAY IDIOT!'

Lucy hurtled sideways, the briefcase and the beret skittered under the fence into the path of two teenage boys.

'Watch where you're going, little squirt!'

'Who's she? Not seen her before.'

The cyclist towered over Lucy, growling, 'This path is for cyclists only!'

Red-faced, Lucy snatched up her briefcase and hat, and merged in the surge of walkers on the right side of the divide, resolving to put this humiliating experience behind her. The cyclist sailed unscathed to the cycle sheds and nudged his friend, smirking and pointing. Lucy felt all eyes on her. Everyone else was hatless, so she stuffed the beret into her briefcase, silently disappointed, as it was stylish, unlike the pudding-basin hat of her last school.

Lucy kept to the tarmac path. Some students scuffed defiantly across the grass like errant sheep. At the junior girls' entrance, a group of girls leaned against a wire fence – a redundant measure against trampling feet. Lucy checked her wristwatch. Three minutes to nine. Three long minutes. Lucy stood as straight and tall as her four feet ten inches would allow, counting slowly, in her head, from one to sixty, killing another minute. From the corner of her eye, she detected movement. A gawky girl sidled towards her, shoulders hunched and head askance, a sweep of raven-black hair revealed well-defined eyebrows, a sullen face and receding chin. Eyes stared wide as saucers, grey-green, and snake-like.

'Are you the new girl for form 2D?' The girl's voice was cultured and strangely malevolent.

D? Lucy's heart sank. You're the clever one, Lucy! Your sister has the looks, but you have the brains. Work hard, and you will go far...

'I – I don't know,' Lucy stammered. 'It's my first day. I don't know what class I'm in.'

The others crowding around like spectators at the scene of an accident. They introduced themselves, but Lucy instantly forgot their names, except Abigail Leuchars – the dark-haired ringleader.

On the dot of nine o'clock, the bell shrilled. The double doors were flung open, and the girls escorted Lucy to the art room on the second floor.

'This is our form room,' explained a freckle-faced girl with a tidy chestnut bob. 'Most of our lessons will be next door, in room eleven, and our book lockers are at the top of the stairs.'

Lucy nodded. The art room was messy and cluttered and smelt heavily of paint and turpentine. There were surprisingly few windows, and Lucy wondered how anyone could work in such poor natural light. In the hubbub

2

of laughter and multiple conversations, Lucy felt lost and alone. The noise went over her head like the din at a crowded railway station. She opened her briefcase and rummaged pointlessly.

Nobody reacted when a dishevelled young man mooched into the room, leaned on the front desk, picked up the register, and stared tiredly through an unkempt blond fringe. 'Can I have your attention please, class?' he mumbled.

The noise abated. The speaker slouched in a posing stance. Brown velvet jacket, avocado-green shirt and baggy corduroy trousers testified to Hippie inclinations.

'I'm Mr Smith, your form tutor and art teacher for the next academic year.'

'Anything you say, Sir!' The sarcastic remark from the back row raised a flurry of snickering. While the register was called, students resumed talking, until the noise level was as before. Mr Smith rapped the board rubber on the desk and bellowed, 'ATTENTION PLEASE!'

The hubbub ceased.

'A brief announcement,' Mr Smith added, 'we've a new member of the class today, so please welcome Lucy Wylie from London.'

Ominous silence. Lucy sat stiffly, her briefcase on her lap. The bell rang again. Chairs scraped, students stood up, flocked to the door, and trooped downstairs, along a labyrinth of corridors to the assembly hall. Lucy followed, diminutive and vulnerable, easily the smallest in the class. At the hall door, each pupil was handed a pristine hymn book with a blue linen cover.

In a brief address, the headmaster welcomed everyone to the new academic year, emphasising the importance of good behaviour and conscientious study. Craning her neck, Lucy discerned over the sea of heads the gaunt form of the school's ageing principal. An Oxford don, Mr Kingsley wore a black gown, laser-like stare, chiselled features, and deep, even-toned voice that conveyed an aura of respect. A Bible passage was read, and a short prayer said, by a man in a brown, military uniform. Then a hymn was sung in dirge-like tempo. The words and tune were unfamiliar, and the singing feeble. Lucy stifled a yawn.

Afterwards, Lucy was allocated a locker in an adjacent classroom and a seat in room eleven, smack-bang in the centre of the room, offering nowhere to hide.

The first lesson was History, with Mr Edgington – a wizened, weasel-like man with no hair and a voice like a droning bluebottle. Each student was issued a dog-eared copy of *Time and Mankind* – an archaic textbook with small print and very few pictures. Lucy looked out of the window at the terracotta-tiled homes and neat gardens, thankful her wild garden at home was bigger and more interesting.

Mathematics was next, with Mr Jenkins, the lean, grizzled soldier from morning assembly. Heavy tomes entitled *Logic and Progress* were distributed.

'Take good care of these books,' Mr Jenkins advised. 'They're valuable, educational tools and school property. They must be treated with respect. Your parents will pay for any damage. Open your books to page three. The first topic is Sets.'

A fluttering of pages and veiled snickering.

'Sex,' someone whispered in the back row.

One stern glance from Mr Jenkins and all eyes were on the figures, symbols and brackets on the printed page. Lucy tried hard to concentrate, but the view was too distracting. Blue sky, red tiles, a verdant, well-stocked garden of the white house epitomised the perfect home, the likes of which Lucy imagined she would one day own, though not right beside a school.

The class was asked to draw brackets and circles and inserting lists of figures. Lucy used her compass and a sharp pencil, ensuring neatness, although she hadn't a clue what it was supposed to represent. At the sound of the bell, the class clumped into ready-made cliques and trooped downstairs for morning break. As second years they all knew their way around. Downstairs, girls and boys separated, the girls headed for the same door they had entered earlier. Apprehensively, Lucy dogged the footsteps of Abigail and friends, half relieved nobody spoke to her.

There was no schoolyard, just landscaped lawns with spindly saplings, flowering shrubs, and three tennis courts surrounded by high, chain-link fencing. Students congregated in small groups on the tarmac, snacking on crisps and fizzy drinks. Lucy wondered if there was a tuck shop, but since she had brought no money, she didn't bother asking. She chewed on her apple and wandered around the perimeter of the tennis courts, trying to look as if she belonged.

Two forty-minute lessons followed break: Religious Education and English. The RE teacher shuffled into the classroom ten minutes late and thudded a battered, black briefcase on the table. The dishevelled man with a shock of grey hair and smudged, dark-rimmed spectacles didn't introduce himself.

'CHEWING-GUM IN BIN – NOW!' he growled. A freckle-faced lad loped to the front and flung the offending article into the metal bin.

'Open your Bibles at the beginning, at the book of Genesis,' the teacher said, in lilting tones that reminded Lucy of Margaret Pritchard – her closest friend at her old school.

A fluttering of pages like light rainfall on leaves.

Lucy opened her copy of the Authorised Version, the same Bible her mother had bought for her a year before, for starting at Wordsworth Grammar School. The Bible was a cloth-bound edition with gilt lettering, neat illustrations and columns of small print in old-fashioned language.

'"In the beginning God created the heaven and the earth. And the earth was without form and void, and darkness was upon the face of the deep." In your own words, write your interpretation of the Creation theory.'

The teacher's speech was slow and slurred.

Exercise books were distributed. Someone at the back yawned protractedly.

In her best writing, Lucy wrote:

Monday, September 9th, 1968.
The Creation Theory.

Minutes passed. Heads down, students were scribbling their responses, maintaining a level of noise not tolerated in the two lessons before break. Then, in a flash of inspiration, Lucy continued writing.

Creation must have happened because it's in the Bible. Scientists and astronomers believe the universe has a beginning. It's not known how God managed to make it in six days. It is said planets, plants, and animals were made first, and people last. Human beings are made in God's image, which means God must look like an ordinary man. We don't know what Jesus really looked like, as pictures of Him vary considerably, and even if cameras had been invented back then, the photographs could be fakes. In the world, things keep changing. A lot of things are bad. My home is called Edencroft. The garden, like Eden, is very beautiful but there are stinging, scratching plants that make me allergic, and bugs that bite...

'Stop now. Put your pens down and listen.'

Chairs creaked, pens clattered, pencil-case zippers opened and closed, in an exaggerated symphony of corporate impatience. Lucy put her cartridge pen in the groove at the top of the sloping desk lid beside the empty ink well, irritated by the interruption.

'Mr Jones's shirt is hanging out,' someone whispered.

'The Bible is thousands of years old,' Mr Jones droned, 'and there are many different translations of it, some of them dating from... um...'

Lucy closed her jotter and studied the lines and whirls on the wooden desktop. Ingrained with decades of grime, it boasted an array of graffiti: names, initials, triangles, stars, and asterisks, each mark assiduously scratched into the oak. In the top right-hand corner, someone had painstakingly carved,

R.I.P. Me. DYING of BOREDOM 12/1/1961

DENNIS Woz Ear 1966

Mr Jones's voice was monotone, lulling her to sleep. Swaying, Lucy gulped in air to stay awake, bothered by a peculiar, sour odour. Others whispered and fidgeted. At the sound of the bell, Mr Jones picked up his briefcase and swayed out of the room.

'Old Jonesey was a bit worse for wear today,' someone said.

'It's only the first day of term. What's he going to be like by the end of it?'

'His problem, not ours. Good thing he only teaches RE, which isn't important.'

'He should quit teaching and get another job.'

'No one would have him. He should get on the wagon first and deal with his demons.'

Hardly had Mr Jones left the room when a small, balding gentleman in a grey suit appeared and placed two hessian bags on the front table. With a hasty scraping of chairs, every student in the class rose respectfully to their feet.

'Good morning everyone, I'm Mr Hargreaves, your English teacher for this academic year. Since you are a select group, I expect a high standard of work, all year. Please sit down.'

Lucy bristled with apprehension. English was once her best subject, until the January exams at Wordsworth Grammar, and Miss Montague's damning report after Lucy misread an exam question. The wall clock rumbled. The room was so quiet Lucy could hear the others breathing. Mr Hargreaves took handfuls of brand new paperbacks from the bags and counted out six books for each of the five rows of desks, instructing the person at the front to hand them back.

'Write your name, in pencil, inside the front cover of your books,' Mr Hargreaves said. 'These books are school property and are to be respected as such.'

The book's front cover was simple but inspiring, its title at the top, in block letters: *A SCHOOL ENGLISH PRIMER Book 2*. [Editied by Quentin R. James, M.A. Cantab.]

Underneath, a series of blue, vertical lines above a trellis of tessellating triangles against a white background. Lucy opened it at random, glanced at an excerpt from *Moby Dick* and a list of comprehension questions which she didn't bother reading. She touched the smooth pages, inhaling the pungent smell of new paper and ink.

'Turn to the first chapter, page five.'

Lucy hurriedly inscribed her name inside the front cover.

'A volunteer to read the passage please?'

A modest show of hands and Mr Hargreaves nodded to a robust-looking girl near the front who looked much older than her twelve years. The girl read with fluency and confidence:

6

'In the cold morning light, smoke curled lazily from a thousand chimneys, forming a pall of gloom above the waking town. Lights winked from grimy windows as lamps were lit. Along the terrace, street doors were opening. Men and women shuffled tiredly to factories to begin another working day.

In the cottage at the end of the street, no lamps were lit. A solitary candle guttered miserably on the mantlepiece, shedding its feeble light in the austere parlour.

"Hurry up and finish the chores!" The old woman's voice was ragged and weary.

"First, fetch enough coal, then light the fire."

"I'm too tired, Mam," the small boy moaned, tracing patterns in the cold ash with the poker. A forlorn figure, the lad crouched pitifully at the flagstoned hearth, shivering with hunger and cold.

"We have fresh bread and milk. I can make us breakfast."

A sudden shout sounded from below the window, accompanied the clattering din of a falling dustbin lid.

An irate tirade followed. 'These lazy stay-at-home folk that do nothin' all day long should know better! Leavin' their bin in the alley-way with no thought for others. No man to rule the roost, they sponge off the state while some of us turn out every day, rain or shine, to do an honest day's work! It's a disgrace! Send 'em back to the gutter, I say. It's where they belong."

The neighbour's voice rang against hard stone walls, her footsteps clacking on cobbled stones, the sound growing gradually fainter.

Mother and son were silent, while the mantle clock ticked on until the half-hour chime.

Then the boy spoke, his voice a hoarse whisper.

"I hate it 'ere, Mam. When are we goin' home?"

From: *Finding Our Way* by Annette MacGregor"

'Thank you and well done,' Mr Hargreaves said. 'Your name, please?'

'Janet Ford, Sir,' the girl replied.

'What kind of story is this?'

A show of hands crept up.

'An old fashioned story,' said a boy in the back row.

'Slightly Dickensian,' said the girl behind Lucy.

'It's about every day life for people struggling in difficult circumstances,' Janet added succinctly.

'Indeed,' Mr Hargreaves nodded, then nodded to a boy near the front with a Beatle haircut. 'Read the first question, please.'

'When and where is this story set, and how do we know?' The boy spoke with adolescent huskiness. Lucy found it strange being in a school with boys again, after a year at an all-girls Grammar school. Another show of hands went up, and a petite girl with doll-like features answered,

'Probably in the north country, because of the way the characters speak.'

'Yes, a good answer. Your name, please?'

'Alison Rodgers.'

The girl smiled, and her picture-perfect face lit up.

'Next question?' Mr Hargreaves asked, picking another pupil.

'List FOUR adjectives which tell us about the characters, and find FOUR adverbs which tell us about the setting.'

I like him better than Miss Montague, Lucy thought, still too shy to put up her hand. The exercise was followed by a discussion on post-war, provincial poverty in Britain, and the struggles facing working-class families. The contrast between urban poverty and the abundant beauty of Edencroft was incalculable.

At lunchtime, Lucy followed the crowd to the dining-block and sat at a table with Helena McDonald, the dark-haired girl with freckles, and quiet Megan Griffiths who was almost as petite as Lucy. Table by table, pupils formed a queue at the servery. At Wordsworth Grammar School, students had remained seated and were handed meals from a trolley. Things were different here, even the food tasted different. The meat was cold and leathery, the gravy thicker and the carrots and peas sweeter. On the bright side, real potatoes were served, not powder from a packet. Scarily popular, Helena joked with the older girls at the table, while Megan sliced her food into small pieces and ate like a programmed robot, without once looking up. Lucy studied the neat parting on Megan's greasy hair, hoping Megan would speak to her, but she didn't. Below the window, a burst of faded hydrangea blooms framed a view of the red-bricked edifice of Beechwood School. Big windows with cream-painted frames were wide open in the sultry afternoon. Lucy wondered what lessons were going on in the classrooms, and what it was really like in a Secondary Modern school. Her sister had gone to one, and had by all accounts enjoyed it, mainly because of the social life. *Social life?* Lucy didn't care much for that. Two or three good friends were enough, like Melanie and Margaret at Wordsworth Grammar. Melanie and Margaret didn't get on, but they both liked Lucy, and that's what mattered. Lucy struggled to finish her lunch, most of it now cold and fatty. Dessert was stodgy sponge pudding and custard, the alternative of chocolate ice cream having been taken by earlier tables.

'Table nine, you are dismissed!' A stocky teacher was yelling in a foreign accent. All at Lucy's table stood up, returned their plates to the hatch and left the hall.

Lucy tagged behind Megan.

'How long until the bell?' Lucy asked pointlessly since she already knew.

'Half an hour,' Megan answered curtly.

They had reached the lawns and tennis courts.

'Where do you live?' Asking questions seemed to be the sole inroad into a meaningful conversation.

'Randolph Crescent.' Megan's soft voice was barely audible.

'Oh,' Lucy said, noticing that two others had joined the troupe. She hadn't a clue where Randolph Crescent was, and nobody enlightened her. Megan's friends sparked a conversation about a forthcoming equestrian event. Lucy had never once sat on a horse and felt distinctly left out.

She looked at her watch, raised her arm to her ear, listening to the silvery ticking that reassured her the watch was still working, not that there was any reason to suppose it wasn't. A present from her parents for having passed the Eleven Plus, the watch had broken twice in the first year of its life: once when the buckle on the strap worked loose and the watch fell onto the hard schoolyard, and another time when Lucy over-wound it. Each time, for twelve weeks, Lucy saved her pocket money to fund the repair, suffering the lack of a watch and pocket money.

The bell was due to ring in twenty minutes. Girls swarmed the area like busy beetles, with apparent purpose. A hundred yards away, scores of boys darted about the lower tennis courts with youthful energy. The combined noise of two hundred teens added to the raucous squawking of seagulls.

On the edge of countryside, the school buildings sprawled greedily over swathes of green, unlike the London conurbation that engulfed Wordsworth Grammar School's meagre precincts. It had been Lucy's lifelong dream to live in the country, beside the sea. Westcombe's golden shore lay beyond the houses, tantalisingly out of sight. Lucy longed to be there, to hear the crashing surf upon rattling shingles, and feel the gritty warmth of sand between her toes. Visits to the beach had been few and far between since the move. There was always too much to do in the house and garden, and her parents were rarely free to take her. Living in a place wasn't the same as being on holiday in it.

The welcome rattle of the bell summoned multitudes of blue-uniformed minions back into the building. Lucy joined the throng but didn't belong. Students jostled to their respective destinations like disgruntled, rush-hour commuters. At the top of the stairs, Lucy was denied access to her locker by an irate teacher shaped like an over-sized pumpkin.

'No, you may *not* come in here to get books! My lesson has started. Go away!'

'You'd better learn right now *never* to annoy Miss Hawksworth!' a gawky, redhead remarked disparagingly.

Lucy said nothing. Miss Hawksworth trumped even fearsome Mrs Grierson of Macadam Primary School in grumpiness.

'I only wanted to get my French dictionary,' Lucy said.

'You should have come earlier to get things from your locker,' the ginger-haired girl said.

The French teacher was young, vivacious Madame Mantes, English by birth and married to a Frenchman. Lucy answered the questions easily and read aloud fluently from the new textbook – *Bonjour la Classe!* – a colourful paperback with plenty of pictures.

After the lesson, Lucy summoned the courage to ask why the class was named 2D.

'We are the clever ones,' guffawed the ginger girl proudly. 'We all got the highest marks in the summer exams. Everyone else didn't make the grade, so they're all beneath us.'

'You must have had a pretty good report from your last school,' drawled a large, pale-faced girl peevishly.

'W – well, I suppose I must have done,' Lucy stammered. The reverse was true, since she had failed two of her end-of-year exams had struggled to keep abreast of the work throughout the whole year. She crumbled inwardly at the memory of over-anxious parents shaking their heads over her poor reports.

A few puzzled looks were exchanged, which Lucy failed to notice. She muddled through the next lesson, which was Geography with Miss Hawksworth. Lucy hoped her neatly drawn map of South America would meet the teacher's approval, but the bell rang before it could be finished.

Bursting with impatience, Lucy snatched up her briefcase and edged her way downstairs and out of the building. The green Morris Traveller was in the promised place, Lucy scuttled towards it, flung open the door and flounced into the passenger seat.

'Well? How was it?' Albert Wylie enquired through a veil of cigarette smoke.

'Okay,' Lucy answered. 'By the way, what's for tea? I'm *starving.*'

'Sausages.'

'Oh, goody!'

School was quickly forgotten. As the car rumbled over the brow of the lane, and the whitewashed bungalow and unkempt garden came into view, Lucy's spirits soared. She dashed to the back door, kicked off her shoes, and burst into the kitchen. Her mother sat at the table peeling vegetables.

'Hi, Mum!' Lucy panted. 'When's food ready?'

Hilda Wylie's care-worn face creased into a smile.

'Soon enough. Cup of tea first? Then you can tell me all about your day.' The sounds of chinking crockery and the whistling kettle were music to Lucy's ears. The kitchen door nudged open and in scampered a Dalmatian, snorting and snuffling, head-butting Lucy with excitement. The briefcase thudded to the floor, and Lucy submitted joyfully to the attentions of her boisterous pet. The navy blue uniform was smothered in hundreds of tiny, white hairs.

'Don't spoil that uniform,' Hilda warned. 'I'll take a photo of you in it now, then you can get changed.'

Camera-shy and un-photogenic, Lucy stood in the garden with her blazer and cap brushed and straightened. She forced an awkward smile, her mouth closed, concealing crooked, buck teeth.

'Say Cheese', Hilda coaxed, fiddling with her treasured Box Brownie camera, then clicked the button, a cameo captured on camera, against a backdrop of Appledore Down's distant silhouette, misty and mysterious against azure sky.

'One more shot please, keep still.'

Lucy's eyes narrowed in the sun's glare. She adjusted her beret and shuffled her feet, blindly optimistic about her future in this remote near-perfect place. She pictured herself in a few years' time, tall and grown up, leaving school to begin life as a responsible adult. Ideally, she would marry and have four children, spend her days in her seaside home, writing stories and painting pictures of nature's cornucopia of beauty. Or might she change her mind, live in London, and work in an office, like her sister Marion? Would there ever be a time when she wouldn't want to run and play?

The years stretched ahead, like blank pages in an unwritten book.

A future awaited, both thrilling and terrifying.

One school day followed another, novelty became routine. At home, Lucy was the captive bird released into new-found freedom. Edencroft's vast, unkempt grounds never failed to entice and enthral – a jungle of secrets in a rural paradise. Hilda flapped in a constant flurry of activity, often too busy to ask Lucy about school, for which Lucy was grateful. Albert spoke of a recurring dream about having more garden than he could manage, but he still hoped to open a market-garden. New tools were bought, making a noticeable impact on two acres of dense, tangled undergrowth. Lucy was taught to weed and hoe, and to wield a sickle and scythe.

Albert smoked endlessly, Hilda complained about the price of cigarettes.

'Cigarette smoke keeps the midges away,' was Albert's excuse. He patched up the dilapidated greenhouses and hacked back the overgrown privet hedge bordering one side of the plot. Using an electric hedge cutter, Albert shortened the hedge by three feet and declared the top wide enough to drive an Austin Mini along. Curiosity led Lucy to climb the step-ladder and discover that truth for herself, musing at the notion of a vehicle being stuck atop a hedge that couldn't possibly support her own weight, let alone the weight of a car. Soon, an electric lawnmower and a petrol-driven rotavator were needed, to keep lawns tidy and break up untamed ground. Hilda expressed concern at the rapidly diminishing bank balance, but Albert quietly assured her everything was under control. Eager to make a difference, Lucy decided one Saturday to paint the front hall, a small area of faded Anaglypta wallpaper in the lobby spanning conservatory and the living-room. She found a tin of white paint in the shed and daubed the hall walls, standing on a chair to reach the top. A picture rail at the level of the door tops enabled her to finish with a straight line. She proudly surveyed her work, tidied up and disappeared to her bedroom. When her parents came in for lunch, an indignant shout resounded through the bungalow.

'WHAT ON EARTH IS THIS?'

Lucy's bedroom door was flung open.

'Have you taken leave of your senses, child?' Hilda's face was ashen with anger. Lucy stood trembling, bracing herself for the inevitable tirade. A lengthy lecture followed about how wicked, disobedient and sneaky she was. She hid at the bottom of the garden, engulfed in guilt and shame, numb inside, her hands blue with cold. Albert found her two hours later. He quietly explained gloss paint isn't supposed to be put on wallpaper, then invited Lucy to help him paint the front gates instead. Lucy agreed and spent an hour helping her father prime the tubular steel gates with a wire brush and paint them with gun-metal gloss. The day ended well, after all. Her father had praised her for her efforts, and her mother's anger had abated. After supper, as shadows lengthened, Lucy escaped through the back gate and sat on the stile, contemplating the view. Agricultural land stretched to the distant outline of Westcombe shrouded in sea mist. The shaded hills of Combe Ridge rose darkly against a sunset sky. It was such a privilege to live in this beautiful place, far from the noise and bustle of London. Lucy pinched herself to ensure this wasn't a dream.

This is second best to Heaven alone, Lucy mused, *I'm the MFG – the world's Most Fortunate Girl.*

Dusk was falling. Roosting rooks chittered overhead. Lucy jumped from the stile, scrambled up the sandy bank by the big ash tree, ran through the orchard, where ramshackle outbuildings were swamped in rampant Russian vine. Tomorrow, she would explore more. Supper first, then an evening of television and toys.

The next morning, Lucy's euphoria remained. At breakfast, she looked longingly out of the window at unsettled skies.

'Those trees in the copse make the shape of a big creature, crouching on the hill,' Hilda remarked.

'And the ash tree looks like the monster's head,' Lucy said. 'A gap in the branches even looks like an eye.'

A sudden shower descended, drenching the window pane and obscuring the view.

'Rain is forecast all day, so I'll make that sign for the gate,' Albert said.

'Edencroft is a much better name than Foxes' Chase,' Lucy said, 'it reminds me of the Garden of Eden and a Highland croft.'

'We named it after Edencroft Drive, where Uncle Charles lived,' Albert said.

'We wouldn't want to be called the Wylie Foxes of Foxes' Chase!' Lucy laughed. All morning she watched her father work on the new sign. First, a length of oak was sandpapered and lightly oiled with linseed, and left to dry. Next came the exacting task of drawing each letter on white, sticky-back plastic and cutting it out with a sharp penknife. Albert drew a line on the board, peeled and stuck each letter to form the name *Edencroft*, in white, plastic letters.

'Is it finished?' Lucy asked. 'Won't the letters come off in the rain?'

'It's not finished,' Albert said. 'Watch.'

Using a sharp pencil, he carefully drew around each letter and peeled off the plastic. Afterwards, he took a fine squirrel-hair brush and painted around each letter with perfectionist precision, in black oil paint.

'When the paint's dry I'll varnish it,' Albert said. 'Then, it'll be ready.'

EDENCROFT

'It's really good,' Lucy said, wishing she shared her father's patience.

The sign took four days to dry. When it was installed on the front gate, Lucy felt her parents had put their personal stamp on their new territory. Edencroft was home.

One afternoon, Lucy arrived home from school to find the bottom of the garden full of hens. She changed into jeans and an old sweater, then hurried to investigate. The near-derelict hen-house had been repaired and filled with chickens. Orange crates and tea-chests used for the house move served as nesting boxes. A four-foot high mesh fence surrounded the coop, the derelict pig-pen, and the ramshackle hut. It was rumoured that long ago, a mad artist had used the hut as his studio, and Lucy wanted to do likewise. Tangled vines obscured the hut and invaded the sweet chestnut tree like a robe, trailing into the unkempt wilderness into which two dozen Rhode Island Reds were making enthusiastic inroads.

'Have they laid any eggs yet?' Lucy whispered.

'Actually, yes. When we unpacked the sacks, there were a few smashed eggs inside. They were probably laid from shock!'

A sudden raucous clucking sounded from the coop, and an agitated hen flapped out.

'Goodness! That hen just laid three eggs!' Hilda exclaimed. 'You won't find eggs as fresh as this in the shops.'

Lucy touched the eggs, feeling their warmth. 'They're all slightly different,' she observed. 'They must have been laid by three different hens.'

'Hen-keeping is fun,' Hilda said, 'but we must keep a firm hold on reality.

I'm keeping a log of every penny spent on feed and equipment against income generated from eggs used or sold. In winter, there'll be fewer eggs and hungrier hens, so expenditure will outweigh income.'

Lucy glazed over. Country life was heaven on earth, and that's what mattered.

Dull, wet days were far from idyllic. One rainy afternoon, Hilda stood at the stove, musing aloud. 'My hand is on the plough. There's no turning back, but what on earth are we doing here? Perhaps we should never have come?'

Nobody spoke. Albert clung doggedly to the dream he had nurtured for twenty years, while the spectre of economic ruin lurked in the deepest recesses of Hilda's mind. Lucy listened silently from the next room, her arms curled around the dog. *I never want to leave this place*, she sighed, wishing with all her heart her parents would *never* leave their beloved Eden.

After three weeks at school, Lucy was still friendless. She missed musically gifted, fashion-conscious Melanie, and gentle, unassuming Margaret, who had the fashion sense of a scarecrow. The two could hardly be more dissimilar. They vied for Lucy's friendship, boosting her confidence. Westcombe Grammar School offered no such encouragement, all cliques seemed firmly closed. Lucy kept herself to herself, hoping that eventually, someone – just one person – would be a friend. *Maybe it's because I'm new? Or too small?* Lucy wondered. A very tall, African girl in the year below – the only black girl in the school – stood out as being different, but she was popular. Lucy longed to be taller and fatter. Perhaps then, she would fit in?

She wasn't unduly concerned, until it was clear she was making enemies rather than friends. Games lessons were the worst. Westcombe students seemed more athletic, doubtless due to the fresh sea air and a wider choice of outdoor pursuits. Might Lucy's skills and stature eventually measure up? Until then, mockery, disdain and contempt must be endured. From the pungent odour of perspiration pervading the changing-rooms to the last snide remark from buxom bullies, each games lesson was an ordeal. Nevertheless, Lucy was determined to make things work. One October afternoon, she resolved to walk tall, look cheerful and take every discouragement that came her way with a smile.

'HOCKEY TODAY!' Miss Forbes strode through the changing-room, booming like a sergeant major. Respectful hush fell. The tall, flame-haired Scotswoman had power and charisma to terrify every arrogant teenage girl. Lockers were flung open, students rummaged for kit. Eagerly, they shrugged off their uniforms and donned their games gear. Voices clamoured, bodies wobbled. Lucy noted with disappointment that even tiny Megan Griffiths had breasts the size of tennis balls under her child's cotton vest. Lucy wondered why Megan wasn't wearing a bra but didn't dare ask. Lamenting her own lack of curves, Lucy took comfort her mother was flat-chested and her sister a late developer. While ribald remarks were exchanged among the figure-flaunting well-endowed, Lucy bent to tie her laces. The black, canvas hockey boots, size two, still fitted perfectly after more than a year. She tied the laces tightly, biting her lip. The ambient noise went over her head.

'I'M SO SEXY!' someone bellowed.

Another voice responded, 'Yeah, stop showing off, Sandra, we all know you were in the front row when they were given out.'

Ironically, Hilda often joked about being in the back row when "they" were given out – a reference Lucy usually found amusing. But not today. Lucy hunched her scrawny shoulders and tried to hide.

Fortunately, with hawk-eyed Miss Forbes presiding, there was little time for chat or banter.

'Pick your stick and line up at the door!' Miss Forbes ordered. This time, Lucy was quick enough to find one of the new ones. Last lesson, Lucy actually managed to hit the ball, but the sharp tap jarred painfully along a fissure in the wood, pinching the flesh between her thumb and wrist. But that was nothing compared with the humiliation when teams were selected. Lucy was always the last to be picked.

Today might be different? Lucy mused optimistically. As usual, Miss Forbes appointed two team captains, names were called, the two teams swelled. Alison Rodgers was petite but was always picked early, probably because she was pretty, popular and good at sports. The overweight, bespectacled, and vertically challenged remained – and Lucy, twirling her hockey stick absent-mindedly on the soft ground.

'STOP THAT AT ONCE!' Miss Forbes's voice thundered across the pitch, echoing against the wall of the science block. It took Lucy a while to realise she was the person being addressed. The crowd rippled with amusement.

'Yes, YOU! Look at me when I am speaking to you!'

Lucy raised her head and caught Miss Forbes's steely stare.

'In this school, manners and obedience are in order! Stick and pitch are to be respected!'

Lucy cowered under a tide of terror and shame. Predictably, she was last to be picked, welcomed by the rest of the team with a unanimous groan.

'Not her again,' someone muttered. 'She's useless.'

Lucy's inward pain clearly showed on her face. At the whistle-blast, the game began. Enthusiastic shouts of the eager players and the sharp clap of the hardball on wooden sticks broke the calm afternoon. Lucy was neither cheerful nor calm, her thoughts in turmoil.

The next games lesson coincided with heavy rain.

'Country dancing today, girls!' Miss Forbes announced. 'No need for full kit, just change into your gym shoes.'

In the hall, a rousing tune resounded from a reel-to-reel tape recorder in the corner. The line of dancers led on. Lucy tried to figure out what to do, but the others were taller, obscuring her view. She tried to copy the person in front but couldn't remember what move came next. Everything was happening too quickly. One mistake or hesitation could prove disastrous. Lucy's actions were untimely and inappropriate, and more than once, she trod on someone's toes. Amid the din of the music, her feeble apologies weren't heard. Afterwards, nobody commented, and Lucy assumed all was well.

During break, she was approached by pasty-faced Shirley Johnson, whose tired-looking, bespectacled eyes looked friendly enough. Perhaps Shirley would be a friend, like Margaret?

But Shirley's arms were folded, her words as a bucket of ice-cold water.

'Why don't you try with dancing?'

Lucy stared blankly. The question sank in, working like poison. A small group had gathered. Floundering in an abyss of personal failure, Lucy protested.

'B – But I am trying!'

'Yes, you are trying all right – very trying,' Abigail leered sarcastically.

Lucy didn't answer. *At least Miss Forbes hasn't said anything,* she reasoned.

The shrill note of the lesson bell was a welcome sound. Lucy followed the others to the science block. *Biology* she thought, cheered at the prospect of another lesson on the structure and function of plants.

Stocky, greying Miss Hughes stood at the laboratory door, counting heads, then lumbered to the front and greeted the class indifferently. Unfurling a poster, she said, 'Look carefully at this cross-section diagram of the broad bean plant. Copy and label it, on your next blank page.'

Lucy sat up straight, pencil poised. There was a rustling of pages and the occasional clatter of a dropped pencil on ceramic tiles. The wooden cupboard door felt hard, against her knees, so Lucy quietly opened the door and stretched her legs out into the empty space under the bench. She began her drawing, meticulously copying its intricate detail. Miss Hughes paced around the room, her hands clasped behind her back, silently inspecting pupils' work. She paused beside Lucy, and Lucy looked up, anticipating praise for her drawing.

But that wasn't what happened.

'Who do you think you are, child? You cannot sit with your feet in the cupboard! Whatever next?'

A murmur rippled through the room. Lucy felt the blood rush to her face. She slid off the stool and closed the cupboard door. At Wordsworth, pupils were permitted to perch with their legs tucked comfortably inside the laboratory cupboards. Lucy fought back tears of humiliation, having made yet another mistake.

Home time couldn't come quick enough. Lucy rushed back to her locker to collect her homework. Turning around, she sensed an atmosphere. Two figures hovered uncomfortably close – Jodie Maitland, the class extrovert, and her side-kick Jessica Hoare, the hyperactive, toothpaste-commercial smiler from 2C. No one else was in the room. Jodie sat on a desk and crossed her legs, showing silver-grey nylon stockings. Briefcase on lap, Jodie leafed lazily through her homework diary.

'French, Maths, Geography...' she drawled.

Suddenly Jessica sprang into action, flinging open Lucy's locker.

'*Och aye*, Wylie, let me help you tidy your *weeee* locker,' she crowed in a mock Scottish accent. Awaiting the start of an hour's detention, Jessica was in no hurry. Lucy watched helpless, as books flew past like demented pigeons, pages flying and covers ripping as they landed on and around desks and chairs. Jodie snatched Lucy's open briefcase, scattering its contents to the floor, and Jessica held the plastic raincoat triumphantly aloft, cackling gleefully, 'Come and get yer weeeee packamac!'

Lucy stared numbly at the chaos around her, then scuttled on all fours, feverishly retrieving the misplaced items, dreading chastisement for damaged books issued in her name. Tired of their sport, Jodie and Jessica sloped off laughing like jackals, their shrill voices echoing mockingly down the stairwell. Seething with annoyance, Lucy lamented the loss of fifteen minutes of her precious time. Time she could have spent at home doing the things she loved. But what could have provoked such an attack? Lucy hadn't a clue. Arriving home, she went straight to her room, knowing better than to mention anything to her parents. She was in no frame of mind to be told to *get along with everybody*, and *school is such a wonderful opportunity for education*.

Lucy ploughed through her homework, then went outside, Dotty following closely at her heels. In the tranquil garden, Lucy wondered how beauty and peace could exist just two miles away from such noise and hostility. She rested on the lower bough of her favourite apple tree. Edencroft was a haven of safety, where she could be herself, and no one could hurt her.

The next day would be another opportunity to start afresh, but again, Lucy's optimism was short-lived.

After assembly, lower school girls were detained for unspecified notices. Lucy was pleased to be missing part of the maths lesson, oblivious of an advancing tsunami.

'My attention has been drawn to a matter of considerable concern,' Miss Hawksworth droned in caustic tones. 'A gross act of vandalism took place in the junior girls' toilets yesterday afternoon. Evidently, *someone* thought it would be a good idea to unravel toilet rolls and paper towels, block the sinks, turn on the taps, and flood the floor!'

So what, Lucy thought. She stopped listening. Suddenly she was nudged into action by the girl beside her. The trial of potential suspects had narrowed to 2D. Miss Hawksworth's brows knit in a glowering grimace.

'Well? I am waiting! Someone is responsible for this despicable act.

Whoever you are, you cannot hide any longer, so own up!'

Seconds ticked by.

Then Miss Hawksworth asked, 'Was it you, Lucy?'

Stony silence. Lucy's blood turned to ice, her mind frozen in shock and disbelief. Had someone told lies about her?

Lucy shook her head and said, 'It wasn't me.'

With serpentine smoothness, Miss Hawksworth said, 'I cannot imagine that any of these girls here would be capable of such an act. Because I know them, and they are well behaved. Therefore it has to be you, Lucy Wylie, for I do not know you and therefore I cannot trust you. You're also a Londoner, which gives me further reason to believe you're responsible.'

Suspecting some kind of warped joke, Lucy forced an awkward smile.

'There! You see!' Miss Hawksworth exclaimed, 'She even looks guilty. Come, confess!'

Lucy had always been brought up to be scrupulously honest.

'But I didn't do it,' she protested quietly.

A ripple of excitement passed among the others. Lucy stood trembling, ashen, the hollow ticking of the wall clock as a countdown death-knell. Miss Hawksworth sighed heavily and dismissed the group. As the line filed out, nobody saw the satisfied smirk on the face of Abigail Leuchars.

The evening, likewise, was far from fun. Mother was in a bad mood, and Lucy brooded in silent misery behind her homework.

'I'm sick to death of the bloody country!' Hilda spat, lugging a tub of damp laundry into the kitchen. 'A line of washing nearly dry, and then a gust of wind blows it over the hedge into a field full of Biddlecombe's dirty old cows!'

Hilda rarely used expletives. Lucy's parents had problems of their own, managing the household and wondering where money for the next bill was coming from. Lucy battled on with the maths assignment, every answer complete guesswork. She hated school. *If only I had just one friend*, she mused miserably. With half term fast approaching, she was hoping for a miracle. Getting a word in edgeways in any conversation was nigh impossible. Small talk was invariably about horse-riding, pop groups, bra sizes, or boyfriends – all of which left Lucy no scope.

Common ground must to be found. *Music, perhaps?* After Marion left home three years ago, Lucy's window on the modern world had closed. Many a night, she lay awake listening to her father's home-built stereo. Borodin's "On the Steppes of Central Asia", Tschaikowski's "1812 Overture", Elgar's "Enigma Variations", Mussorgsky's "Pictures at an Exhibition", and Holst's "The Planets" were Lucy's favourites. Ironically, the only person interested in Classical music was Abigail Leuchars.

The next morning, Lucy fetched her books for first lesson and sighed wearily. Janet Ford was a few steps ahead. Lucy thought *Janet's so clever, so grown up. If only I could be more like her...*

Janet turned around briefly and held the door open for Lucy.

'Thanks,' Lucy mumbled quietly, detecting the ghost of a smile. The first lesson was Latin with Mr Kingsley. He instilled fear into everyone. Today's chapter was about Roman military campaigns, and the homework was to copy and label a picture of a Roman soldier in full armour – a welcome break from the usual grammar drills.

History was next. As usual, Mr Edgington dictated copious notes.

'In ancient times,' he began, 'people believed the earth was flat...'

I remember learning that in Mr Jolly's class in primary school, Lucy thought.

'Afterwards, scientists proved the Universe was sun-centred, or heliocentric.'

Mr Edgington paused to spell the word aloud. ' h – e – l – i – o – c – e – n – t – r – i – c.'

Lucy liked big words.

Mr Edgington continued, 'and this new theory caused much controversy, c – o – n – t – r – o – v – e – r – s – y, among politicians and church leaders. Galileo Galilei was imprisoned in his own home. His belief contradicted the teaching of the Roman Catholic church.'

Lucy glanced at Janet, who was busy writing. Janet was a loner but was everything that Lucy was not – tall, confident, a high achiever, popular with teachers.

At lunchtime, Lucy stood behind Janet in the dinner queue. Janet turned around and said, 'You live in the country, in a house called Edencroft.'

'How do you know?'

'I read your address inside your briefcase, whenever you open it.'

Lucy swelled with pride. 'Edencroft is between Helmstone and High Lea. All on its own, with gorgeous views.'

'I live three miles outside Combe Ridge,' Janet said. 'I like the country better than the town. What are your hobbies?'

'Art and craft, reading and writing, exploring my enormous garden, walking my Dalmatian, playing with my ginger-and-white cat,' Lucy gabbled enthusiastically.

'So you never get bored.'

'Not at all. What about you?'

'I walk my King Charles spaniel, Jasper, and I enjoy reading, especially stories about travel and adventure.'

'Do you write?'

'Actually, I do. I keep a diary. Not every day, just for special things like holidays. I went on a road trip with my parents to five European countries this summer. I could bring the diary to show you, if you like?'

'I'd love that –' Lucy began, then someone pushed her from behind and growled, 'Get a move on! We want lunch!'

19

The conversation with Janet continued over sausage, mashed potato, and beans.

'My parents own a smallholding too,' Janet said. 'In the mornings I help feed the ducks and chickens and collect eggs while my Mum sees to the pigs. We also have a donkey and a Shetland pony in our paddock.'

Lucy was ecstatic. 'We have a field next to our garden too, and we might get a donkey. My Mum looked after pigs in the Second World War, when she was in the Land Army in Wiltshire.'

'My parents were still children during the war, and they were sent to places in the country, which is what gave them a taste for rural life.'

The table was dismissed, and Lucy and Janet continued their exchange of life-stories. Janet told of her early childhood in Bristol and the move to Westcombe three years ago. Lucy described her childhood pets, the garden, family holidays, and picnics with her parents in the Chiltern Hills. She deliberately glossed over the subject of school and was thankful Janet didn't ask about it. Faithful to her promise, Janet brought the diary the next day. Each neatly logged entry covered pages of narrative, detailing the Dormobile's repeated breakdowns in the Austrian Alps and the family's rescue in a freak blizzard. At first, Lucy thought Janet was making it up, believing such things only happened in stories. Lucy wished for a more interesting life. The move to the country had been quietly idyllic, but hardly a rip-roaring adventure.

'Wake up!' Lucy heard Janet's voice penetrate her train of thought. 'Don't you like my diary? You haven't said a word.'

Lucy blushed. 'It's really very good,' she said wistfully.

Janet scowled and snapped the diary shut. Mr Jenkins had entered the room, and the lesson began. Lucy sighed. It was impossible to concentrate. She clock-watched through forty minutes and wasted no time collaring Janet after the bell.

'I've been thinking,' Lucy asked Janet. 'Would you like to come and visit me on Saturday?'

Janet didn't answer. Lucy speeded up her speech. 'My Dad could come and pick you up, and we could have tea outside in the garden if the weather is fine. I'll show you the hens, we can explore –'

'I'll think about it,' Janet replied.

Two days passed. Lucy's contact with Janet lessened. They were in different groups for various lessons, and at break time Janet always had something else to do – a meeting with a teacher, an errand to run, or a spell in the nurse's room because she had a headache. When Friday afternoon came, Lucy could wait no longer.

'D – did you ask your parents if you can come to Edencroft tomorrow?' Lucy asked tentatively as the class filed out to lunch. Janet looked down, disdainfully at the small, scurrying figure beside her.

'We'll be going out,' Janet replied coldly. The words stung Lucy like a whip, awakening suspicions that the embryonic friendship was dead. All morning, the cold reality of rejection slowly sank in. Earlier that week, Janet had sat beside Lucy, but not today. Lucy entered the room to find Janet seated next to Megan, talking and laughing, her back to Lucy. Hovering nearby, Lucy hoped to be invited into the conversation, but Janet carried on talking to Megan. She neither sat beside Lucy nor spoke to her again.

Half term had begun. The lid tightly shut on the evil Pandora's box of school, Lucy threw herself whole-heartedly into arts and crafts and exploring outdoors. She was glad she had said nothing about Janet to her parents. Edencroft was a completely different world, another life. In the mad artist's hut, Lucy played the pioneer explorer, carving wood by candlelight, making a makeshift home, safe from wild winter storms. Alone in her bedroom, she played the puppeteer, enacting scenes in dolls' homes and schools, creating scenes with plastic animals, walls, fences, and trees. Toys were her friends. They would never abandon her or call her rude names. They did exactly what she wanted, except when they fell down, spoiling her neat arrangements. But that was a mere, mild irritation compared with the agony of humiliation from humans.

On Saturday afternoon, Lucy set off with Dotty, down the footpath to the lower lane, revelling in freedom. The puppy crashed through tangled undergrowth, snuffling and snorting in pursuit of rabbits.

'Come on, Dot!' Lucy called. The eager Dalmatian shot out of a thicket and wriggled underneath the stile, almost knocking Lucy down. Lucy laughed aloud, uninhibited, happy, and herself. She loved her dog – a creature so beautiful, entertaining, and affectionate. Lucy climbed the stile and landed smartly on thick meadow grass. Across a field of stubble, a third stile was just visible. Lucy ran to it, paused for a moment, legs astride the stile, surveying the sun-dappled pasture, checking there were no cows in sight. Thankfully, the way ahead was clear.

Or was it? A hundred yards ahead, beneath the trees, something was moving – too small to be a bull. *Oh no, not humans*, Lucy thought. But Dotty had spotted intruders on the scene and was racing ahead. Two figures were walking, side by side. Lucy tensed, fearing an unfriendly encounter if her dog jumped at strangers and muddied their clothes.

Lucy looked again at the approaching walkers.

Could it be... Marion and Paul!

Lucy hurtled forwards, lighter than air, and dashed wildly into her sister's open arms.

'Hi, kid! How are things?' Marion asked, lifting her little sister high up in the air. Hugging her briefly, Marion set Lucy down gently on the grass.

'Things are wonderful!'

Lucy began, then the words came tumbling out incoherently – a jumbled

21

rendering of events since the move.

'But why are you two here anyway?' Lucy panted. 'Mum and Dad didn't mention you were coming.'

'We didn't tell them, but – er – well, um –' stammered Paul.

'We have a little surprise for you,' Marion cut in.

'Oh?' Lucy asked, looking at the rucksack on Paul's back and the shoulder bag at Marion's side – the black, leather one with zips and tassels, a birthday gift from her parents, years before.

'What surprise? It's not my birthday or Christmas.'

'You'll find out soon, after all, it wouldn't be a surprise if we told you now, would it?'

'I suppose not,' Lucy said, surprised at her own eagerness at seeing her sister again. Whilst they had been living at home together in the cramped, suburban family home, they had often quarrelled fiercely. It was different now. It was good just to hear Marion's voice again after so long. Lucy walked between them, holding Paul's and Marion's hands, skipping like a lamb.

'I can't wait to show you everything – the garden, the dog, the house, the hens – our home is nothing like our old home in Ash Farm. Here there are real farms and real ash trees. See those woods over there? They're part of Biddlecombe Farm, where we get fresh milk delivered. There's so much to do here and to explore. Edencroft is such a wonderful place!'

'Yeah, Sis,' Marion said softly, 'I'm sure it is.'

At the top of the hill, the footpath sliced through a hawthorn hedge and Albert's eighty yard stretch of trimmed privet, too high even for Paul to look over.

'That's our hedge!' Lucy panted. 'The garden's enormous, just wait and see!'

'It's big,' Paul agreed. 'The garden's more like a park. It must be a lot of work for your dad?'

'He doesn't mind, Dad loves gardening.'

A gap in the hedge revealed a low, wooden gate with the Edencroft sign.

'Come on!' Lucy dragged Marion by the hand. 'Mum and Dad will be thrilled to see you.'

Dotty bounded through the dog-flap, greeting the guests with a sharp bark, then hurled herself at Paul. Marion looked aghast. 'Your new jeans, Paul! They'll be ruined!'

'It's okay,' Paul said. 'Denim can cope with dogs, and this pup reminds me of Skipper when he was small.'

'Who's Skipper?' Lucy asked.

'My dog. I got him when I was your age,' Paul said.

'Is he a Dalmatian, too?'

'No, just a mongrel. Heinz fifty-seven varieties, from Battersea Dogs' Home.'

Lucy burst into the bungalow, yelling, 'MUM! DAD! Guess who's here!'

Albert and Hilda were as surprised as Lucy was. Paul, it seemed, was still Marion's boyfriend after a year, which was a record for Marion.

'I expect you're hungry, so I'll rustle up some grub,' Hilda said. She clucked and flapped about the kitchen, opening and closing the cupboard doors, muttering to herself and wondering what on earth to make for dinner.

'I'll put the kettle on,' Albert said.

Lucy invited the guests to the breakfast room. 'You can sit down at our new little table and look at the garden. All of it's ours, right up to those woods.'

'Yes, Lucy,' Marion said tiredly.

Paul perched on a chair facing away from the window, resting his elbows on the table. Marion pulled out a chair and sat beside Paul.

'Nice Formica-top table, very modern,' Marion remarked, seemingly more impressed with the furniture than what was outside.

'It's brand new,' Lucy boasted. 'So are the chairs. They have padded seats. Mum got the set so we could sit in here and look out at the garden. It's like being in a posh tea-room.'

Marion leaned closer to Paul and sighed. Over a pot of tea, the conversation was quiet and very ordinary, mostly about Uncle Peter's family, Marion's job, and what clothes she had bought in the summer sales. Lucy wasn't listening. She sprawled on the floor, head and shoulders in the dog basket, her arms around the puppy. She studied the length and growth direction of Dotty's hairs: the ones on her head were very short, twice as long on her back, and longest of all at the tip of her tail. The fur below her neck was of medium length – probably just under an inch from root to tip and grew symmetrically, meeting in a swirl above her chest that Albert called the true-lovers'-knot. Dotty wriggled free from Lucy's eager embrace and sat beside Paul, ears square with curiosity.

'More tea, anyone?' Hilda asked.

Marion shook her head.

'No thanks, Mrs Wylie,' Paul mumbled quietly. He fondled the dog's ears absent-mindedly, his thoughts elsewhere. He looked intently at Marion, at the curve of her cheekbone and the sweep of honey-blonde hair. He glanced at Albert and Hilda as if trying to attract their attention. Then he boldly announced, 'I would like to request your daughter's hand in marriage.'

The words were spoken quickly as if they had been rehearsed many times.

A deep smile broadened across Hilda's tired face. Albert's cigarette dropped by half an inch, his eyebrows raised imperceptibly behind dark-rimmed spectacles. Marion smiled, her hands clasped on her lap, while Lucy sat on the floor, hugging her knees and grinning. For a moment, no one spoke. In the quietness, a solitary robin trilled its autumnal melody from the rose trellis outside the window.

Hilda broke the silence. 'Well, darling, that's wonderful news. I really don't know what to say... I'm delighted! Congratulations to you both!'

The expression of relief upon Paul's face was clear to all but Lucy, who was looking out of the window at the view.

'This calls for celebration!' Hilda exclaimed, serving another round of tea. To Paul, she said, 'when you're married you may call me Mum.'

'Thanks, Mrs Wylie.' Paul sipped his tea, failing to notice his future mother-in-law had forgotten his usual three sugars.

The evening passed happily, with not a cloud on the horizon. Marion proudly showed her engagement ring – a simple band of gold with a delicate coronet, clasping a glittering diamond. Marion's mood was mild and sweet, every past disagreement forgotten. Now there were wedding plans to be made. A date was agreed, almost a year away, for a Saturday in September – dove-tailing with Albert's fiftieth birthday. A happy future lay ahead. The last train had left. It was a given Marion and Paul would stay the night, in separate rooms, of course. A staunch moralist, Hilda offered Paul the spare room and made up the camp-bed for Marion in Lucy's room.

In a quiet moment before bedtime, Marion placed a small object in Lucy's hand.

'Here, Lucy – I'm giving you this. I wish you the very best for the future.'

Lucy opened her hand and gazed in amazement at her sister's most treasured possession – a sterling silver ring encircled with four pairs of bells.

'Why – Marion – thank you!' Lucy's voice was faint with wonder.

'It's okay, Sis. This ring brought me luck, and now it's yours for keeps. I've another ring on my ring finger now.'

Forgetting her troubles, Lucy basked in the happiness of her family and immersed herself once more in the magic of Edencroft.

2: THE DIARY

Winter came early to the Westcombe hills. Temperatures nose-dived, prevailing gales swept mercilessly across exposed hillsides, bending stunted trees, turning lush landscape to barren wilderness. Edencroft ceased to be a balmy Shangri-La. The flowers were gone, the garden a morass of dead vegetation. Wild winds whistled around the eaves of the bungalow, stripping bare the plunging boughs of the great ash tree, exposing spidery branches, gaunt and forlorn against grey skies.

Cycling to school, Lucy faced powerful squalls that taxed her strength and hurled thousands of icy darts into her face. One morning, Lucy arrived at school fresh-faced and tousled, her socks and shoes spattered with mud. Before registration, she went to the girls' toilets, ran a comb through her hair and did her best to clean her socks and shoes, uncertain which would annoy Miss Hawksworth more – a dishevelled appearance, or the improper use of paper towels. At the start of first lesson, noise levels in the room dropped to the sounds of creaking chairs, pencil-case zippers, and faint sighs. Textbooks were shut and quietly put away.

Miss Hawksworth handed out sheets of lined paper.

'Draw three columns, with the headings Country, State Capital, and Port. Then list all the countries of South America, their capital city and principal port, remembering some countries are landlocked and therefore do not have a port.'

In the stillness of the airless room, pens scratched, heads bowed in silence, arms curled protectively around answer sheets. Lucy remembered all the names bar the capital of Ecuador, until a serendipitous reminder via Megan's clearly visible answer sheet across the aisle. Quito, of course, as in mosquito – a mnemonic which, Lucy, ironically, had forgotten.

At break, Lucy sat alone to eat the picnic her mother had packed, bridging the long gap between breakfast and lunch. Hilda had increased Lucy's mid-morning snack to a full packed lunch – two slices of bread with a rich protein filling, an apple, and a slice of home-made cake. You're are growing girl, Hilda insisted. Lucy found the sandwiches stodgy, her hunger appeased after just a few mouthfuls. Looking over Lucy's shoulder, a girl said,

'That's a lot of food for break-time, didn't you eat breakfast?'

'Yes,' Lucy answered, 'a bowl of porridge and two slices of toast and Marmite.'

'Gosh, where do you put all that food? There's hardly anything of you!'

Lucy shrugged her shoulders.

'What's in the sandwich?' someone else asked.

'Meat,' Lucy answered, not caring what the meat was.

Nobody else spoke to her all day. On the way home, the wind was behind her, for now. Around the hairpin bend, gale force gusts hurled shards of freezing rain into Lucy's face. On the gruelling one-in-five gradient, she taxed Marion's old bicycle to its limits, crashing the gears, determined never to set her foot down. Her chest tight with exertion, she battled defiantly to the top and felt cool air buffeting her face. Surely her leg muscles were getting stronger? Physically, she felt fitter than ever before. Arriving home, she tossed the left-over sandwich to the hens before her mother would notice.

The next day Lucy was less lucky with the weather. Halfway up the big hill, light drizzle turned to a sudden downpour. Lucy stopped to forage in her briefcase for her raincoat. Sheets of water tumbled out of the sky, running in rivulets behind her collar and trickling down her back. It wasn't worth putting on the coat. Already, her clothes clung to her chest, her legs were drenched and her shoes full of water. Streams gushed like mountain cataracts down the hill, dragging mud and gravel in fractal courses. Lucy pressed on, gritting her teeth until she reached home. She parked the bicycle in the garage, unstrapped her sodden briefcase and dashed up the slope, eager for dry clothes, and a fireside mug of hot tea.

The wild weather continued all night. Lucy did her homework at the fireside. Her workbooks were damp, some of the pages smudged. It was hard to concentrate. Chewing her pen, Lucy started on a comprehension exercise on Thomas Hardy's *Far from the Madding Crowd*. The noise and the crowds of London now seemed a million miles away. Sounds of crackling logs on the open fire and the clatter of dishes in the kitchen were comforting competition to the raging storm outside, where wild wind whistled, rattling the slate roof.

'Albert! Batten down the hatches!' Hilda called from the kitchen.

'Yes, dear.' Albert stoked the fire lazily, warming his chilled feet on the sleeping dog's back. He stood up stiffly, secured the panelled double glazing and drew the curtains.

Two days later, Lucy went down with a streaming cold, but it was school as usual. At the start of first lesson, she sat quietly, fountain pen and blotting paper ready. Mr Kingsley was never late, and today there was a test. Lucy took out a Kleenex and blew her nose as unobtrusively as possible, pre-empting excessive snuffling through the next forty minutes.

'My goodness, dear! I'm sure you feel better now, don't you?'

The voice startled her. Fiona Jarvis, the class brain-box, was as near perfect as could be, never a hair out of place. Abigail lurked nearby. Escape wasn't an option. Mr Kingsley was less than a minute away, but in that time a lot could happen. Lucy withered inwardly.

'What's that on your pullover?' Abigail asked.

Lucy saw nothing amiss.

'All those white things?' Abigail asked.

'I don't know what you mean,' Lucy said.

Then, mercifully, Mr Kingsley's arrival sent students scurrying to their seats.

'Porto, portas, portat!' The venerable schoolmaster strode through the room his long, black academic gown flowing behind him.

'Portamus, portatis, portant!' Textbooks were hastily shut, and all eyes were upon the awe-inspiring disciplinarian.

'Amo, amas, amat. Amamus, amatis, amant.'

As regular verbs were recited in unison, Lucy's head felt like a bundle of compressed cotton wool, her voice vibrating against her eardrums. At last, Mr Kingsley paused before the class and raised his hand, the signal for the customary two minutes' recitation to stop. Silence reigned. All copies of *A School Latin Primer; Book One,* duly lay closed in front of each student. Then, a brief nod from the teacher, and all books were put away. The wall clock gave one hollow click. Pens poised, every student sat statuesque, all eyes on the awe-inspiring figure at the front. The room was so quiet one would have heard a feather touch the floor.

'Facsimile!' Mr Kingsley intoned, striding up and down the aisle, handing each pupil a sheet of crisp, lined paper. 'Write the vocabulary list, with conjugations, in the exact order it appears in your text book. You have precisely five minutes. You may commence.'

A faint rustling, then pens flew across paper. Under Mr Kingsley's tutelage, emphasis was on accuracy and speed. In the surrounding hush, nought was heard but the scratching of nibs on paper and the occasional muffled cough. Evidently, Lucy wasn't the only person in the room with a cold. Breathing anxiously through her mouth, mechanically writing, marking time, she completed the required task. The minute hand on the wall clock edged its way to half past nine, the appointed time for Pens Down.

Then Lucy noticed the clusters of tiny white hairs on her clothes. *Dotty's hairs! Why are animals so much nicer than people?* Lucy dragged herself doggedly through the day, her limbs heavy with fatigue. Home time couldn't come quickly enough. At the sound of the bell, she suddenly revived, pedalled home as quickly as she could, raced up to the porch door, and breezed breathless into the bungalow. Bursting into the living-room, Lucy flopped onto the sofa, feeling the heat of the open fire warming her damp clothes.

'Hi, Dad. Where's Mum?' Lucy asked.

'In the bedroom, getting changed.'

'Getting changed? Why? Did she go out today?'

The door to the bedrooms suddenly swung open, and Hilda emerged, wearing her usual baggy jumper and nylon slacks. Her blue eyes twinkled merrily.

'I've PASSED!' Hilda exclaimed, triumphantly tearing a pair of cardboard L-plates to shreds. For almost a decade, Hilda's love-hate relationship with driving had once almost shipwrecked her marriage. Driving will give me more independence, Hilda had said, but the mistake was allowing her husband to give her the lessons. One of Lucy's earliest memories was of her distraught mother tearing up a red booklet, which she later learned was a driving licence. Hilda vowed she would never again sit behind the wheel of a car, but in time, a new licence was obtained and the lessons resumed. Hilda's first failure at the test was attributed to nerves, as were numerous subsequent attempts.

'You m – mean the – Driving Test?' Lucy stammered in disbelief.

Hilda winked happily. 'I'll now make a trunk call to London – never mind the expense. I must tell Marion, and Peter and Rose!'

On Saturday, hearing the postman's van snorting to a halt, Lucy ran to collect the post. Ignoring the usual shower of earwigs from the mailbox lid, she snatched the letters – both for Hilda – and ran indoors.

'From Marion and from Peter,' Hilda smiled proudly. 'I'll put them in the Trophy Cabinet, as they deserve a place of honour. Passing that dreaded test is a major milestone for me.'

Hilda put the cards into the wall-mounted display cabinet between the two living-room windows overlooking the garden. This quirky piece of furniture, left behind by the previous owner of the bungalow, was now a showcase for memorabilia – Uncle Charles's silver golfing cup, a gaudy plastic gondola – a Venetian holiday gift from Peter and Rose, a painted plaster-cast model of a Caribbean mama made by Marion, and a clay chicken Lucy made at Wordsworth Grammar. Arriving home on Monday, Lucy learned fresh news.

'I've got a job,' Hilda announced brightly. 'Just three days a week, starting tomorrow, with Maverick and Co. Solicitors, in Wellington Parade, Westcombe. And Dad has agreed to let me use the car!'

For a while, there was no more talk of financial hardship, and Lucy's weekly pocket money of one shilling was re-instated, having been stopped just before the move. However, the house wasn't the same when Lucy came home from school on Tuesdays, Wednesdays and Thursdays. The fire was unlit, the rooms reeked of stale cigarette smoke, and dinner was hours away. Albert was usually in the tool shed, where he had installed lights and a heater. Lucy made a jam sandwich and retreated to her room to play with toys. Hilda came home between five-thirty and six, too tired and harassed for conversation. Dinner was cooked, eaten and cleared away by half past seven, then Lucy and her parents huddled around the fireside, tantalised by memories of the old house with its creature comforts. Lucy hunched over her homework, while her parents stared at a third-rate show or low-budget thriller. *Surely life was better now?* Lucy clung stubbornly to the notion that it was.

Many a night, Lucy lay awake, restless and bored. Often, the low buzz of her parents' voices drew her from her bed. Crouching silently in the darkness, she pressed her ear to the door, catching the gist of tempered conversations.

'He ignored my letter and refuses to answer the telephone...'

'We're placated with excuses...'

'That solicitor is a crook...'

'Mercurial Mr Morton promises prompt results, but he's just dragging his feet...'

Lucy pictured a fat, jolly man wearing a waistcoat and pocket-watch, scuffing his shoes on the ground. Words like probate, legacy, and codicil sounded poetic but meaningless. Lucy couldn't be bothered looking them up in the dictionary. Weary and aching with cold, she crept back to bed, taking comfort from teddies and toys, until sleep carried her to the next dismal day.

In the cold light of morning, Hilda had other things on her mind.

'Dotty is in season', she said, spreading an old sheet across the floor.

Lucy looked blank.

'For female dogs, a season is like a period – except it lasts for three weeks, and more importantly, unlike human women, it's a time to become pregnant, so we must be vigilant. Dotty must stay in the lounge and kitchen, where floors can be wiped, and outside she must be kept on the lead at all times. If a dog gets to Dotty, we'll end up with a litter of unwanted mongrel pups. '

'Okay,' Lucy nodded slowly. 'I understand.'

'Might we still let Dotty have Dalmatian puppies?' Lucy asked. 'You were thinking about opening a kennels.'

'We'll have to see. Looking after one dog is difficult enough, and I'm not sure we could manage lots of them, especially other peoples' dogs. It's a tremendous responsibility and would entail astronomical insurance costs.'

'Why?'

'Because if anything went wrong, we'd be legally responsible. Dotty is primarily a pet. Dalmatians are highly strung, plus Dotty is sensitive to loud noises and doesn't always come when called. I wanted to apologise to Mr Biddlecombe when she escaped into his field and barked at his cows, but that man is never about when you want to speak to him. When sour milk was delivered to our doorstep I considered it an act of revenge.'

'What about dog training classes?' Albert suggested quietly.

'I doubt that would do any good, but anything's worth a try.' Hilda agreed.

Dotty was duly enrolled at Clarissa Mainwaring's Canine Academy, to start when her season was over. On the evening of the first lesson, the Wylies arrived late, delayed by a diversion caused by a burst water main on the potholed road.

Twelve dogs and their owners walked sedately round the room, overseen by a tall woman in country tweeds. Order reigned, each dog held on a short leash. Suddenly the door opened, and Dotty burst onto the scene with resounding bark, Albert in tow, struggling to maintain balance. The tidy circle was thrown into immediate disarray. In chaotic cacophony, all the dogs whined, barked, and howled in unison, while their embarrassed owners did their best to regain decorum.

Clarissa Mainwaring drew herself to her full five feet eleven inches and yelled, 'ORDER!'

The scuffling continued. One ear-splitting whistle-blast and every dog was still.

Without further ado, Dotty was welcomed in to the canine class, and within the hour had been shown the rudiments of walking on a short leash, and responding to three simple commands: Sit! Stay! and Lie-Flat!

The instructions were practised at home. The second visit was on Call and Reward, which Dotty did badly. There was no third visit. Hilda's brave face at Maverick's finally fell. Twice in the same week, she had come home with a blinding migraine and taken to her bed for the rest of the evening.

'Old Maverick lives up to his name,' Hilda admitted. 'He's a hot-tempered taskmaster, pays paltry wages, and the work is one big headache, figuratively and literally.'

Deemed ineffectual and expensive, the dog-training classes were no longer an option. On November 5th there were no fireworks, no bonfire and no Guy. Dog walks and beach trips seemed a lifetime ago, Christmas was too far off to be excited about, and daily life was engulfed by a bog-standard, British winter. Lucy pondered past winters, when Mother had given her quality time, reading stories or playing Snakes and Ladders or marbles. There was spontaneity and laughter, but now, the long months of winter stretched ahead like a jail sentence. One evening, a comedy show was on television, but nobody laughed even once. Monochrome images flashed across the screen, accompanied by monotonous dialogue and canned laughter. In feeble lamplight, Hilda sat slumped in an armchair, shielding her eyes. Albert stared vacantly into the fire, warming his stockinged feet around the dog's flanks. Coals hissed and spluttered, flames leapt brightly in the grate, their reflections dancing on the ceiling. Lucy clasped her chilled hands around her mug, feeling the warmth of scalding hot tea. Her parents always made a good pot of tea. She remembered her own attempts to make tea: it had always turned out too weak, too cool or with leaves floating on the top.

At school, break-time conversations were heated with rumours of exams.

'They'll be before Christmas, like last year,' Shirley declared stoutly.

'I need more time to revise,' Janet moaned.

'It doesn't matter what you want, Janet,' Joanna argued, twirling her strawberry-blonde ponytail.

'I'd rather get exams over with now. I don't want to spend the Christmas holidays revising, because I have my private piano and clarinet exams in January,' Abigail said.

Lucy stood in the background, lost in a cloud of gloom. In assembly, Mr Kingsley announced exams would be in January.

The inevitable was merely postponed. Lucy wavered between worrying about school work and lamenting the lack of friends. As a distraction, she decided to keep a diary, using an empty, hardback notebook.

Sunday, December 1st

Christmas is coming! In less than three weeks, the holidays begin. Two whole weeks of freedom! After breakfast, I set off in sunshine down winding country lanes on my bicycle. At school, things are starting to feel Christmassy. In Art, I designed a Christmas card and decorated it with glue and glitter. Also, I got a Christmas card, from Jodie Maitland, who also gave everyone else in the class a card. At least someone is feeling festive! Jodie sits in front of me in class and seems friendly, but she doesn't speak to me often. Thankfully, there's been no more trouble since that afternoon, months ago, when Jodie and her friend Jessica from 2C threw my books around. In fact, I haven't noticed Jodie talking to Jessica at all lately, so maybe they're not friends anymore.

After school, before dark, I made a course of jumps in the garden with Dotty. She kept knocking them over, and I realised I had placed the jumps too close together, so I moved them further apart and gave Dotty a big hug after telling her off. Later, Dad and I took Dotty down the lane, and we looked at the stars. Dad pointed out the Plough, which looks like a giant saucepan with the dots not joined up. There were millions of other stars. It was a wonderful sight...

Hearing her mother's footsteps in the hall, Lucy hastily put down her pen and hid the diary under the bed.

'Come in the lounge where it's warmer,' Hilda said. 'There's cocoa and chocolate biscuits.'

Lucy jumped up immediately and sat at the fireside for supper.

That week, cards were exchanged daily, but there were no more for Lucy. Every day, bawdy jokes were told, and raucous laughter rang. Lucy felt isolated and distant, ghost-like. On Friday morning, she sat at her desk, rummaging in her briefcase, when a voice behind her said, 'Have you received any Christmas cards at all, by any chance?' Turning to face Abigail, Lucy bristled, sensing more than mere idle curiosity.

'Actually, I have,' Lucy answered truthfully. Then, the timely arrival of the teacher curtailed the conversation. Later, Lucy wrote:

Today at school, everyone was being very loud, telling silly jokes and bursting into song. They sing We wish you a Merry Christmas or Jingle Bells, but no traditional carols, except "While Shepherds Washed their Socks by Night", which is just another silly joke.

At break, someone suggested a game of five-a-side netball. Because there were ten of us, there was no problem about anyone being picked last or being left out of the game. However, when the game was about to begin, along came show-off Rosemary Richardson. The crowd decided someone had to go, to keep the sides even. Everyone pointed at me. I argued I was there first and I really did want to join in, but they wouldn't listen. They were like a pack of wolves. They choose their victim, go in for the kill. I stood still. They surrounded me, little beings, piercing hate with sharp, blazing eyes...

Lucy hesitated, wondering if she should tear the page out. She re-read the entry and decided she rather liked it. It seemed more realistic to include bad things – like shadows contrasting with sunshine. If there were no Downs in life, there would be no Ups, as her mother often said. When Hilda called Lucy for supper, she placed the diary spine facing inwards on the shelf. With thirty-one daily entries, the diary could almost become a short novel. Each day, Lucy disappeared into her room on the pretext of doing homework. The narrative swelled, and after two weeks, the notebook was half full.

Friday, December 13th.

Today is supposed to be unlucky, but it wasn't in the least. The morning was dreary and grey, but I was happy to face whatever might come my way. Nobody at school was particularly friendly, but at least they left me alone. I'm just going to enjoy the things I love: the countryside, the beautiful garden, the sea and my pets.

'It's the weekend!' I yelled on arriving home. Nobody answered. Mum was in the chicken house and Dad somewhere else in the garden. Then I noticed post for me on the kitchen table – a little brown paper package from Melanie and a Christmas card and letter from Margaret. What joy! Two old friends remembered me!

I tore open the letters immediately. Melanie said lots of news about school, which did make me feel a bit homesick, but then I see the beautiful countryside and think it's probably better here after all.

I'm keeping the present from Melanie until Christmas Day.

Margaret is leaving Wordsworth Grammar School too. Her parents are moving house, not anywhere nice though. Far from it. They're moving to Catford, in South East London, where it's very built up and busy. I would hate that – unless there are cats there. That would be nice. Margaret has a cat called Charlie. Margaret has looked at her new school and it says it's nice. I hope she's right.

Now for a cosy evening by the television with mince pies and Christmas nibbles! This weekend, we will put up the decorations. I'm so excited!

Saturday, December 14th.

In the morning, I went with Mum and Dad on the weekly shopping trip to Westcombe town. I did some Christmas shopping. I've managed to save one pound, nineteen shillings and eleven pence pocket money – just enough for a few stocking fillers. At Westcombe's Woolworth's, I bought Dad gardening gloves, a diary and a pair of woollen socks, and for Mum, a mustard pot shaped like a miniature teapot with the words 'Souvenir from Westcombe' painted on it.

I also bought a thicker, fibre-tip pen for me, and I'll try it out now.

When we got home there was a fat envelope with a German postmark in the mailbox. Mum opened it and said it was from her cousin Martha – the only cousin in Germany (or anywhere else for that matter) who bothers to keep in touch. The envelope contained a paper decoration of a Father Christmas with his arms raised and holding a tiny card, on which Martha had written 'Very Good Christmas 1968'. Mum put the German Santa on top of the television where everyone can see him.

(This pen is awkward to write with, so I'll change back to the other one)

'Look!' Mum laughed. 'He's famous – he's on the telly!'

After lunch, we took advantage of the sunshine and went for a long walk over the downs – the first decent walk for weeks. Dotty startled some pheasants and barked at a distant herd of cows but was otherwise quite well-behaved, for a change. We went the long way up High Lea Down, along the chalky ridge, with its brambly thickets and stunted, windswept trees. On top of the hill, the views of the sea and countryside were breathtaking.

Then Dad began to prune a yew bush with his secateurs.

'What are you doing that for?' I asked.

'It's for the Christmas Tree,' Dad replied.

'That's right,' said Mum, 'because we're not allowed to trespass on Forestry Commission land, or to cut down a proper tree, so we'll tie these branches together to look like a real Christmas tree. Once it's decorated, you would hardly know the difference.'

'Why can't we just buy one in the shops?' I asked.

'Because we can't afford one. Perhaps next year we'll get an artificial tree, which will last for many years.'

I think real trees are better, even if they're only sprigs tied together.

An enjoyable evening was spent at the fireside, watching television. There was news about the Apollo 8 journey around the moon, showing the astronauts' photo of Earth as a complete ball. Absolutely fascinating!

Weekday entries were shorter, listing school lessons, meals, and television programmes. Term ended like a damp squib, cold, wet and miserable – dull, but relatively painless, with no obvious bullying, apart from being ignored. On the last Friday afternoon of term, Lucy was glad to be home. The next entry marked the start of the school holidays, when Christmas had truly begun, albeit with a hint of sadness.

Saturday, December 21st

Today is the anniversary of Uncle Charles' death. I still find it hard to believe we will never see him again. He was always a kind, gentle person.

I spent the morning wrapping presents and making gift tags. Then I polished the silver for Mum – a job I always enjoy. It's rewarding to see dull, tarnished metal shining bright again, adding to the sparkle of Christmas. When I went into Mum and Dad's bedroom to get the silver-plated candlesticks, I noticed a bag of parcels wrapped in brown paper. Mum said she couldn't afford fancy wrapping paper this year. I took a quick peek and discovered four small packages labelled 'To Lucy'. I squeezed them, sniffed them, and guessed I was going to get soap, sweets and socks on Christmas morning. The last parcel intrigues me. It's flat, possibly a book? Then I heard the dog bark and Mum and Dad come in, so I quickly put the packages back and acted as if nothing had happened.

The sideboard is now full of goodies. I can almost forget there is supposed to be a major economy drive this Christmas. At least we have a few of the usual dates, figs, tangerines, nuts and sugared almonds to look forward to. I still wonder about that book-shaped present. I hope it isn't anything boring or educational. If it's another notebook, I'll write another story!

Sunday, December 22nd

We went for a lovely walk on the downs after lunch, working up an appetite for home-baked mince pies and sausage rolls – another family favourite at Christmas.

After a cosy fireside evening, I turned in at ten o'clock – a little later than usual, as it's the holidays. Unfortunately, I couldn't sleep. Thoughts were racing through my mind, as I lay tossing and turning, wondering about my presents. At last, I fell into a fitful slumber, and when I awoke, it was morning.

Monday, December 23rd

Today it was drizzling, and heavy fog clung to Biddlecombe Copse, draping the crouching monster in what looked like a fluffy raincoat. I didn't feel like going out, so I stayed in making paper snowflakes and sticking them on my bedroom window with Sellotape. But the windows were misted up, and the snowflakes kept falling off. Mum wouldn't let me put any on the lounge windows, saying it was too much clutter. I don't agree. The best part of the day was spent in the lounge, enjoying good food, television and listening to Christmas music on the radio. I'm so excited I can hardly breathe!

Tuesday, December 24th

IT'S CHRISTMAS EVE!!

Today dawned crisp and clear, with tiny crystals of frost in the corners of my bedroom window–pane. There is little hope of it being a white Christmas, but who needs snow, when there is so much frost? The hills, fields and woodlands looked simply beautiful.

I sprang out of bed and dressed hurriedly in my jeans and thick jumper. Dad was on his hands and knees, busily lighting the log fire. Mum was in the kitchen making breakfast, and Dotty was still asleep in her basket, tucked under Mum's old Land Army overcoat. Marmie, the marmalade cat, was rubbing against Mum's legs, purring loudly.

'You're up early,' said Mum, 'I wish I could get you up as early as this on a school day.'

'It is after eight o'clock,' I answered, 'I don't want to miss any of Christmas.'

'No presents until tomorrow, mind,' said Mum firmly. 'And remember, no snooping!'

There was a twinkle in her eye. Did she suspect anything? Perhaps I didn't put all the parcels back exactly as she had left them? I said nothing.

After breakfast, Dad drove to town to stock up on cigarettes and get one or two things like bread and extra milk and cream. Mum stayed at home to prepare the dinner.

By lunchtime the weather was foggy, but it's still Christmas. We went on a walk along the two-mile circuit past farms, fields and cottages and finishing up on my usual cycle route up the long hill. It was dark when we got home, so we put on the tree lights immediately.

After tea, we sang carols by the light of the Christmas tree. We sang 'Silent Night', 'Once in Royal David's City', 'In the Bleak mid- Winter', and 'Hark, the Herald Angels Sing'. I played a few tunes on the recorder, and Mum and Dad kept making me laugh and play wrong notes, which made me laugh even more. It was a superb evening.

December, 25th – Christmas Day!!!

I opened my eyes and found it was already light. I needed no reminding what day it was. Quick as a flash, I jumped out of bed and raced to the window from where I could see the bare, wintry hills covered in thick, grey mist. There was neither frost nor snow, but that didn't matter. It is our first Christmas at Edencroft, and that is simply wonderful.

From the living-room came the sounds of Dad raking the ash and banking up the fire, Dotty whimpering excitedly and Mum walking about briskly on the wooden floor. Seconds later, I joined them for a quick cup of tea and some toast.

Then we opened our presents. Nobody minded the brown paper wrappings. In some ways, it was more exciting – a bit like being self-sufficient in the wilderness. There were no big presents, but again it didn't matter, as it's often the small things that please the most. Mum and Dad were delighted with the bits and bobs I bought them, and as for me – I fared far better than I expected. In my stocking were gloves, socks, sweets, slippers, a 1969 diary, another smaller diary from Melanie, a sewing kit, a tin of watercolour paints and squirrel-hair artist's paintbrushes, writing paper and envelopes. Last but not least, the "book" present! I opened it nervously, slowly tearing away the brown paper to reveal a coloured cardboard package with a cellophane window. Inside was a handsome set of pens and pencils: a wide-nibbed fountain pen, a narrow-nibbed cartridge pen, a retractable ball-point pen, and a propelling-pencil. Spare leads, cartridges and a bottle of ink were included. Trying out the new pen to write this journal is just the start, as someday I'll write so much I'll need a typewriter – but that's a thought for the future.

Finally, Dotty the Dalmatian wasn't forgotten. Eagerly she pounced on her package and ripped it open to reveal a pack of dog chews which she devoured in seconds and most of the paper with it. Mum put aside a tube of Dog Chocolate Buttons for her to have later.

After a traditional Christmas dinner of roast chicken with all the trimmings, and a small plum pudding with custard, we all felt so stuffed that we decided to go for a long walk in the hills.

There were no telephone calls, and we phoned nobody. The only reminder of our friends and relatives was the long line of cards hanging above the fireplace. It was Christmas to ourselves, and one we would doubtless always remember.'

December 26th – Boxing Day.

Boxing Day always seems a bit of an anti-climax. All the presents have been opened, and the excitement is over. There is no logical reason for feeling down in the dumps, for all the presents are still there to be enjoyed, and the tree and decorations are still up. It is said that Boxing Day is the time when people put presents they don't want into boxes and give them to the poor people who have nothing. That makes more sense than the sport of boxing. There wasn't even any boxing on the telly.

Mum phoned the family today. Marion was supposed to be at

Uncle Peter's today, having spent yesterday with her fiancé Paul and his family. (I still haven't quite got used to having a telephone in the house. It is a big black thing in the hall. It stands on the small wooden table with a drawer, and when it rings, the sound is like a fire-alarm and always makes me jump out of my skin.)

I sat on the hall carpet, listening as Mum picked up the receiver. First, came the deep, soft purring noise which Mum said was the dialling tone. Mum dialled 'O' for the Operator and asked for a trunk call to London. When the call was connected, I could hear Uncle Peter's voice quite plainly, though it was a little crackly, and then my sister Marion speaking softly, but I couldn't hear much, except that all was well, and they were having a happy Christmas.

Lucy found little else to add. The next day, wind and rain swept in from the west, and the remaining entries were mostly about television programmes, meals, and the weather. On Saturday, Lucy didn't bother going with her parents on the weekly shopping trip to Westcombe. Instead, she stayed indoors reading, sewing and rearranging her toys. The Wylies weren't in the habit of celebrating New Year's Eve, and during that day, nothing out of the ordinary happened. The post-Christmas atmosphere anti-climax had given way to a strange sense of calm.

After supper, in the seclusion of her bedroom, Lucy wrote the final paragraph of her diary.

At the end of this magical month of December I can honestly say this has been a wonderful Christmas — with everything I could wish for; brilliant presents, a wild, exciting garden, lovely pets, and the peace and beauty of the best countryside in the world. This year — 1968 — has indeed been the most exciting and eventful year of my life.

Lucy put down her pen, pleased to have completed what she proudly considered a real book, with a hardback cover. She covered the diary in a pink paper drawer-liner, and carefully penned its title, using a ruler and black felt-tipped pen.

DECEMBER DIARY

She gift-wrapped it brown paper and attached a label, a brief message inscribed in her best handwriting:

To Mum and Dad. Happy New Year. Love from Lucy xxx

Lucy hid the package under her pillow, and after supper, when her parents had settled at the fireside, she crept into the living-room bearing the gift.

'This is just a little home-made present for you. I hope you like it.'

'That's nice of you dear,' Hilda said, not taking her eyes off her knitting. Albert put the newspaper down and glanced at the slim package on the coffee table.

Hilda looked up.'You don't usually give us anything for New Year. We weren't expecting any more presents, were we Albert?'

Albert drew on his cigarette and looked bemused.

'I would've given it to you for Christmas, but I couldn't, but it wasn't finished until now,' Lucy said.

'Can we open it now?' Hilda asked.

'Oh, yes, please do!' Lucy answered excitedly.

Hilda untied the ribbon and peeled back the wrapping. Lucy watched with mounting apprehension. The diary mirrored her innermost feelings. Suddenly, with the prospect of her soul being laid bare, she sat down, trembling with apprehension.

Hilda adjusted her spectacles and said, 'So you've been writing a diary! So this is what you've been doing in your room, in secret?'

'Yes, but it isn't just about boring, everyday things –'

'And I really thought you were putting in extra hours of homework,' Hilda interrupted. 'Don't you remember how you fell behind last year, when you were at Wordsworth Grammar? All due to your lack of concentration because we were moving house. You really must adopt a more adult attitude towards your school work. Life isn't all about playing!'

Hilda paused, realising that tonight was perhaps not the right time for a lecture on the merits of self-discipline. 'All right then,' she continued calmly, 'We'll get around to looking at it after you've gone to bed.'

At ten o'clock, Lucy went to bed and lay awake, hearing the usual sounds of footsteps, the fire being poked, the dog snoring, and low voices, deep in conversation. It was tempting to eavesdrop, but the fear of being caught was a powerful deterrent.

After a restless night, Lucy awoke to the sound of the grate being cleared in the next room. She went into the breakfast room, trying to act normally.

'Morning, Mum,' she said, attempting a modicum of cheerfulness. Inwardly, she was petrified, heart thumping and legs like jelly. She sat facing the window. The view was seasonally bleak: a thin mist hung over the garden, bare branches in Biddlecombe Copse stark against stony sky.

Behind her, the sounds of clanking pans and crockery, the brisk scraping of the butter knife on crisp toast, even the steady thump-thump of the dog's tail on the rug seemed harsher than usual. Hilda placed a bowl of steaming hot porridge and a mug of tea in front of Lucy.

'Thanks, Mum,' Lucy said.

Hilda said nothing. In the ominous silence, Lucy prickled with anxiety, her fingers twisting nervously around the spoon. Telling herself not to worry, she ate her food, placed the empty dish in the sink, and went into the lounge. Albert was at the newly-lit fire, warming his feet on the hearth. The diary was on the bookcase, her mother's spectacle case beside it. Lucy picked up a magazine and pretended to read it. Her mother's quick-cadenced footsteps echoed like a Gestapo march.

'Looks like the mist is going to lift later,' Lucy began, attempting to sound upbeat. 'Perhaps we could try that long route over the chalk ridge with Dotty this afternoon?'

Hilda sat down. 'Yes, maybe,' she answered flatly.

Albert cleared his throat and said nothing.

The suspense was overpowering.

Lucy could wait no longer. 'By the way, did you have time to look at the diary?' she asked, trying with all her might to sound relaxed.

'Yes, we've read it,' Hilda answered abruptly.

Lucy froze.

'Sit down, love. We need to talk,' Albert said, gently. Lucy sat down stiffly on the edge of the sofa, quaking.

'I really don't know what to say,' Hilda began, her voice charged with emotion. 'After all you father and I have done for you – bringing you here – it was what we all wanted wasn't it? You are well fed and cared for, with a comfortable home, a good education...'

Was this a bad dream?

'You're not very happy, are you?' Hilda said bitterly. 'You have so much to be thankful for, but all you can think about is yourself and worrying about what people think of you. You have a lot to learn. When I was your age I did not have even a quarter of what you have. We lived in just two rooms in a London tenement block, with a shared toilet with four other families, down three flights of stairs, in the back yard. I had nowhere to play. No garden, no room of my own, hardly any toys, no new clothes, and barely enough to eat. But I was happy. I walked tall and looked life straight in the eye. I enjoyed being your age.'

All of this had already been said, countless times before. Lucy sat motionless, stupefied, listening to her mother's embittered tirade, each word a venomous dart in her frozen heart.

'Self-pity is such an ugly thing. I never had time for such nonsense. You never think of others. No wonder nobody likes you at that school! You don't deserve to have any friends.'

Wave after wave of horror and despair swept over Lucy, vicious words sinking into her very soul.

Without further word, Hilda stood up and walked out – where to she did not know. It didn't matter. All she wanted to do was walk, for as long as it took until she dropped with exhaustion. Anything was better than remaining incarcerated in that little box of a bungalow on the hill with a laconic, work-shy husband who smoked like a chimney and an estranged, demented daughter whom she now viewed as good as dead.

Albert stood staring out of the window, saying nothing.

Lucy spoke first.

'It wasn't meant to sound that bad,' she said weakly, 'Really it wasn't. I just thought – and well, anyway, I did say lots of good things about you and Mum and about being at home, here, didn't I? Of course I like it. It's just that school is a bit difficult sometimes –'

'You've upset your mother very badly,' Albert cut in, 'You're well and truly in her black books now. I just hope she'll come round.'

In a deluge of despair, Lucy stood rooted to the spot. Giving the diary as a present had been a mistake, after all. But it was too late now. Lucy had truly failed to do anything right in the mystifying world of other people, none of whom wanted to be her friend. And now, apparently, she had lost the trust of her parents.

Desperate, she fled to her room and flung herself on her bed, burying her face in the pillow, sobbing with pent-up tension from months – and years. Of course, she felt sorry for herself, of course, she would far prefer to be happy and contented.

After all, who wouldn't?

Angry with herself for having believed in the magic of Edencroft, Lucy faced the new year with nothing to aim for, hope for – or even live for.

3: CHILDHOOD'S DEMISE

L ife went on because it had to.

'You have drawn a wedge beween us,' Hilda told Lucy at lunchtime when Lucy finally emerged from her bedroom.

'I'm sorry,' Lucy said in a monotone, sensing a lost cause.

'It doesn't matter how sorry you are, the damage is done. From now on, things can never be the same.'

This wasn't the first time Lucy had deeply offended her mother. The last big row had been over bad grades at her last school – an episode Lucy preferred not to recall. That bad atmosphere slowly dissipated like melting ice, so this time would doubtless be the same.

Meanwhile, the pain had to be endured. For a whole week, a dark cloud of hostility hung over the household. Hobbies held no charm, ordinary tasks were arduous, the pleasurable dog walks now a chore. Home no longer felt like home. Somehow, Lucy dragged herself from day to day, like a pre-programmed android.

But this wasn't the time to give up. It was 1969 – a year pregnant with promises. The so-called big, bad world out there was burgeoning with opportunities. Advances in technology, the Space Race, changing trends in fashion, music, and the whole of life itself was filled with new things waiting to be discovered. Twenty years post World War Two, the human race seemed hooked on peace.

Peace, Love and Far Out Man was the Hippies war-cry – or rather peace-cry. Lucy secretly wanted to be a Hippie, like the crazy artist who, once inhabited the hut. Hilda had always said Hippies were drop-outs – sad losers, too lazy to work, steeped in the evils of sex and drugs. Lucy neither understood not cared about what other people did if she wasn't in the picture. From her perspective, the outside world was unknown territory, a closed shop.

Term began on the first Thursday in January. Despite being friendless, Lucy was glad to get back to school. At nine-thirty on that dismal, overcast morning, it was still dark. In the lower school library, fluorescent lights buzzed and flickered, doing nothing to improve the attention span of thirty unmotivated pupils. Water gushed and gurgled in the pipes, radiators belted out heat. In the stuffy classroom, chairs creaked, noses sniffed, students sighed, and someone at the back was snoring.

'Sack the government for changing the clocks,' Mike Fidler hissed under his breath.

Crispian Cowley responded with a yawn. Mike suppressed a smirk, his eyes darting surreptitiously towards Sandra Bright's generous curves. Lucy chewed her pen. January was, without doubt, the worst month of the year – perpetually wet, cold, and dark. Lucy stared blankly at the hazy reflection on the misted window-pane – a thin barrier between the airless room and an opaque wall of freezing fog.

Mr Hargreaves was talking about verbs and adjectives. Nobody was paying attention, not even Janet Ford, whose eyelids were drooping. An atmosphere of post-festive anticlimax prevailed.

'Turn to page forty,' Mr Hargreaves droned, his voice barely rising above the hum of the electric lights. 'From the adjective beautiful, we derive the verb beautify, from courageous we have encourage, and so on. Now we will attempt the first exercise. Any offers for rich?'

A few hands went up. Mr Hargreaves chose a boy at the back.

'Enrich, sir,' Jimmy Murphy replied boldly.

Someone muttered, 'That was easy-peasy – much too easy for us!'

Perhaps they were expecting Jimmy Murphy, the class clown, to entertain everyone with a deliberately silly answer?

'Any offers for the next word, poor?' Mr Hargreaves peered over the top of his spectacles. 'This one isn't quite so easy, perhaps. Anyone brave enough to volunteer an answer?'

'I haven't a clue, Sir,' Jimmy mumbled tiredly.

'Enpoor',' suggested Joanna, with a trite smile.

Pooren!

Make poor!'

Rip off!

Voices clamoured in a weak attempt at levity, while more studious individuals fumbled feverishly in their pocket dictionaries. Mr Hargreaves shook his head slowly.

'Oh, no, no,' he said solemnly, 'No, think – all of you. Think!'

A sudden flash of insight fell upon Lucy, a familiar word emerging to the forefront of her hibernating brain.

She slowly raised her hand. In the suspended silence, all eyes were upon her. With a smile and a nod, Mr Hargreaves invited Lucy to speak.

'Impoverish,' she said quietly.

Silence. There were a few blank looks and puzzled expressions. A dropped pencil rattled on the tiled floor.

'That's a big word for little Lucy!' Rosemary Richardson gasped in mock surprise. In recent eavesdropping sessions, Lucy had heard Hilda use the word repeatedly and with conviction. Its meaning was obvious. For one awful moment, Lucy feared her mother might have invented the word.

'Correct! Well done Lucy. You are doubtless an avid reader,' Mr Hargreaves said.

Lucy felt a flush of pride. *But didn't everyone's parents use the word impoverish?* Lucy didn't share her mother's financial fears, for what did she know about household bills and making ends meet? Her chief concern was that if the money ran out, her parents would leave Edencroft and move somewhere unbearably cramped and urban. Lucy even toyed with the idea of getting a weekend job to help with the bills, but being still a child and looking much younger than her twelve years, Lucy imagined no one would want to hire her.

Lucy's moment of glory was soon forgotten. She plodded through the rest of the school day, speaking to no one. At home time, she trudged off to the misty hills, taking a short cut through the fields, where low fog hugged the rising slope, ghost-like gossamer decked denuded hedgerows, and spindly trees stretched bare branches aloft like emaciated waifs awaiting rescue. The wind moaned eerily through telegraph wires. A fragrant whiff of wood-smoke from the freshly-lit fire drew her onward.

Albert was in the lounge, in his usual fireside chair. An inch-long finger of ash dangled precariously over an unfinished cup of tea.

'Tea's in the pot, love, help yourself,' he said.

'Thanks,' Lucy mumbled, her brow furrowed with anxiety. Graphs, velocity, vectors, something about plotting speed against time? Visions of a lofty, Victorian classroom, and stern-faced, silver-haired Mrs Grierson deflated all motivation.

'Did you have a good day at school?' Hilda called from the lounge.

'It was all right,' Lucy answered in monotone, idly leafing through the *Westcombe Herald*.

'Your father and I were in town shopping today,' Hilda continued, 'I got the paper, so I can look for another job. It's so important to have a decent job. And you have every opportunity to have a fantastic career that'll pay well and last you a lifetime.'

'Yes, Mum,' Lucy replied. She went to her room, spent five minutes staring at a page of meaningless shapes, facts and figures, then escaped to a fantasy world of plastic animals and dolls.

Revision week had begun. At least there were no games lessons during exams, so hopefully less bullying. In the English paper, Lucy was careful not to misread the question, as she had done to her cost in the past. French was easy, and Lucy knew she had done well. In all the other papers she just muddled through. Maths, Geography, and Environmental Science offered the opportunity to draw neat diagrams, and the history paper included a question on the ancient astronomers. Perhaps she had not done badly, after all?

On Monday morning, the class waited with bated breath at the start of the first lesson. Seconds after the bell, Miss Hawksworth lumbered into the room with pile of exam papers, her face drawn and haggard. Picking up the first paper, she said, 'An excellent result for Janet Ford. Eighty-nine percent!' Janet beamed proudly, and there were a few low groans around the room.

'Also scoring eighty-nine percent – Fiona Jarvis.'

Fiona breezed forward to collect her paper. More names were read out and papers handed back in descending order of achievement. Half the pile was left. Lucy gripped her seat. Three more papers were handed back. Lucy felt she would suffocate – and then, her name was called.

'Lucy Wylie. Fifty-three percent'.

Lucy's heart pounded. Why hadn't she done better? Her maps and drawings were neat, careful and accurate. Glancing at other students' papers, Lucy didn't think their efforts to be any better. Scoring above half marks, she hadn't failed the exam, but the overall mark was a mystery. Why so low? She hadn't the nerve to protest.

By Thursday, Lucy was pleased to have gained passes in Latin, History, Music and RE. On Friday morning, Lucy was optimistic. First lesson was French. Predictably, top of the pile were Fiona and Janet, who scored ninety-six and ninety-five percent respectively. Then Madame Mantes picked up two papers simultaneously. Lucy sat rigid, choked with fear.

'And now, we have another excellent result – ninety-three percent – another tie, between Jonathan Whitmore –'

How unsurprising, Lucy thought, as did everyone else.

'- and Lucy Wylie.'

Shock delight! Lucy pricked her finger on the tip of her compass, feeling its sharpness. This wasn't a dream.

With a tight-lipped smile, Jodie turned around and handed Lucy her paper. A stifled snort sounded from somewhere behind, but Lucy didn't look round.

At break, students discussed the remaining results and the overall class positions. Bets were made, who would be top of the class – Janet, Fiona, or Jonathan? Lucy made herself scarce. At the start of the maths lesson, she sat at her desk, lost in a welter of worry, barely noticing a small commotion outside the classroom door. Mr Jenkins stood at the front desk, his briefcase bulging, and his face like thunder. Some of the girls were visibly unsettled, and Lucy shuddered with apprehension. *Were the exam results that bad?*

The truth of the kerfuffle soon became apparent.

'Poor Alison!' Joanna protested. 'It really wasn't her fault. *Logic and Progress?* Fat chance of that! Those stupid books are far too big, and it's time someone applied a bit of logic and made them smaller.'

She didn't mean it...
There's not enough room...
Those lockers should be somewhere else...
'SILENCE!' Mr Jenkins roared.

Hush fell. Mr Jenkins never lost his temper!

All eyes were on polite, well-behaved Alison, trembling in her seat.

'I- I'm s- sorry, Sir. It was an accident. There was nowhere else to my books, and I just left it on the ledge for a second – 'Alison stammered, her usually cheerful face puckered, close to tears.

'A word of warning to you all,' Mr Jenkins intoned, 'never to place books – or indeed any object – above the stairwell. That falling book missed me by a millimetre – any closer and the outcome could have been very different. You are the intelligent class, so you should at least exercise a little common sense!'

Outside the window, a seagull squawked. Mr Jenkins opened his briefcase.

'No doubt you're all keen to know your exam results,' he said quietly. Without announcing names, he handed back papers individually, in descending order of achievement. The pile ever-dwindling, Lucy tried to stay calm. She fixed her gaze on the teacher's dun-coloured army uniform. Mr Jenkins ran two clubs: Army Cadets and Christian Union, neither of which interested her in the least.

An answer sheet was thrust unceremoniously on her desk. At the top, in bold red Biro, was the score. For an instant, Lucy hoped it wasn't hers, but denial gave way to stone-cold truth. Lucy swallowed her disappointment: – forty-eight percent – a fail.

The teacher explained the questions at the blackboard, talk-and-chalk that went way over Lucy's head.

Next was Environmental Science. Lucy was dealt a second blow. Unimpressed by neat drawings and imaginative embellishments, Miss Hughes awarded Lucy a meagre forty-five percent. Another fail. In the exam, Lucy had felt sorry for the formaldehyde-soaked bean, so instead of dissecting and drawing it, she took it home and planted it. Disappointingly, the bean never germinated.

One more result to go. English – the all-important subject Lucy had flunked so abysmally at her last school. As the last lesson bell rang, Lucy's stomach did backflips. Mr Hargreaves arrived punctually and dropped a pile of papers brusquely on the desk. Students rose nervously to their feet.

'Good afternoon, Mr Hargreaves,' the class chorused unenthusiastically.

Mr Hargreaves was one of few teachers who insisted on such formality. He stood still, tapping his fingers pensively on the hardwood, giving his usual benign, grandfatherly stare. He lowered his spectacles and his expression darkened.

He's in a bad mood, Lucy thought, terrified.

'A few of you are not going to have a pleasant weekend,' Mr Hargreaves warned, in a low, menacing tone. 'Students of your academic calibre must think! Some of you are becoming complacent.'

In airless silence, thirty pupils sat motionless. Lucy gripped the sides of her chair, her hands cold and clammy on the varnished wood. Mr Hargreaves lifted the first paper and handed it to the hitherto unsung Hilary Masters, who received her result with modesty and gratitude. The top result was seventy-nine percent, which didn't bode well. The usual high-flyers were next, scoring only in the high sixties.

Lucy visualised being among those facing an unpleasant weekend.

Suddenly she sat bolt upright. Her name had been called out, and her paper was being passed back to her by a smiling Jodie. Lucy stared incredulously at her score. Sixty-seven percent – written in bold, red ballpoint pen. She found the compass point again, reassuring herself this wasn't a dream.

However, on hearing Lucy's results, Hilda and Albert shook their heads in dismay.

'You promised faithfully you'd do well!' Hilda snapped. 'Well, you're just going to have to try even harder.'

'I know,' Lucy answered meekly, feeling neither dejected nor elated.

She clung to the positives. *I may not be good at everything*, she reasoned, *but at least I'm good at something.*

The weekend passed by with routine mediocrity, and on Monday morning the final class positions were read out in assembly. Six hundred students stood motionless, all ears. Lucy hung on every name, every word until she heard her own status: nineteenth in a class of thirty. Her feelings were mixed, but she was determined to persevere.

The dark days of winter dragged on. Lucy resented her parents staying at home, while she had to get up early every morning and go to a place of toil and torture and no friends. One day Lucy arrived home, tired and hungry and in no mood for anything. Albert was in his fireside chair, smoking.

'Hi, Dad. Where's Mum?'

'In the bedroom, getting changed.'

Suddenly the door swung open. Hilda stood in the doorway, wearing dark blue office clothes. *She's got another job*, Lucy thought, then a piercing whistle-blast sent the dog scampering wildly about the parquet tiles, scattering cushions and rattling the glass panes of the double glazing and trophy cabinet.

'PATROL LEADERS – ATTEN-TION!' Hilda yelled. 'Finally, my Guiding skills are being put to use. The High Lea Guide company needed a new Lieutenant – and here I am, and you, Lucy, are invited into the company!'

'Guides? Wow – that's amazing!' Lucy had often heard her mother boast affiliation to two uniformed organisations – the Women's Land Army and the Girl Guides' Association.

'I've got you a hat and shirt at Dawson's in Westcombe, and you already have a dark blue skirt. Guides is fun, you'll love it,' Hilda said.

Meetings were Friday evenings, at High Lea Methodist chapel hall. Hilda and Lucy arrived early. The kingfisher-blue Guides' shirt was baggy, allowing for growth. It was scratchy and uncomfortable, but Lucy liked the colour and the indigo, military-style hat with the Girl Guides logo at the front. The chapel was built on a steep hillside, the hall in the basement. At the door, Lucy heard the clatter of chairs on floorboards and saw a tall figure in a navy blue uniform setting up a trestle table. The hall smelt musty and dank.

'Lucy, meet Captain Merryweather!' Hilda beamed, introducing Lucy to the figure in blue – a vivacious dark-haired woman in her forties.

Captain spoke hurriedly and distractedly, barely looking at Lucy. 'Hello Lucy, we're a friendly bunch, you'll be able to help the Guides learn new skills, and they're such nice girls, so I'm sure you'll get along fine. Here they come now! Lieutenant Wylie, help me get the tables and chairs.'

Hilda frowned. Lucy felt like a fish out of water.

Hearing pattering footsteps and piping voices on the concrete steps, Captain fussed and flapped like a demented hen. A dozen uniformed girls spilt into the room, some of them very young. Some hats were worn lopsided, others not at all. A few Guides had badges stitched to their sleeves, all of them wore a polished, brass badge pinned to a maroon necktie.

A sharp whistle-blast drew the troops in line.

'Guides! Meet Lieutenant, Mrs Wylie and her daughter Lucy, so let's give them a good Westcombe welcome.'

There was a feeble round of applause, then silence. Lucy squirmed, looking at her shoes and staring at an ink stain on the floorboards. The party dispersed into smaller groups for hands-on activities. Today's task was a wildlife project on birds. Lucy shared her knowledge, helped find pictures in magazines, reading aloud to those with poor reading skills. Not one Guide attended the Grammar school; consequently, none of them had heard of Lucy. They welcomed her with unbiased charm.

'What's it like, in the Grammar school?' asked a small girl with lively, brown eyes and a mop of cropped, blonde hair.

'It's okay, I suppose,' Lucy answered. 'What's your name? Do you live in High Lea?'

'I'm Valerie. I live in the cottages by High Lea station.'

'What school do you go to?'

'Beechwood. I'm in class 1A. Do you have brothers and sisters?'

'A sister, she's twenty, lives in London and is engaged to be married. Actually, my mum says she might be getting married in this church.'

'Wow! There hasn't been a wedding here for years! But isn't High Lea a bit far from London?'

'Mum says a lady must be married near her parents' home. And guess what? I'm going to be bridesmaid,' Lucy bragged.

'That's nice. I've never been a bridesmaid. I have a brother who's eight. My dad's disabled and doesn't have a job, and my mum's a dinner lady at High Lea Primary School.'

'Oh,' Lucy said, then added, 'my parents don't have jobs at the moment.'

A game of musical statues was next. Everyone was friendly and refreshingly simple. Lucy found she fitted in. Being with younger children reminded her of games with the children next door, at the old house. The meeting concluded with a group circle. Lucy was officially enrolled and presented with a Girl Guide handbook, a maroon necktie, and a gleaming brass Girl Guide badge. It didn't matter that she'd never been a Brownie. Lucy had wanted to join the Ash Farm Brownies, but Hilda wouldn't hear of it, due to a personal disagreement with the Brown Owl, whom Hilda described as opinionated riff-raff.

In the cosy circle, "Kookaburra" and "London's Burning" were sung in a round, as were a few songs Lucy didn't know. She particularly liked "Land of the Silver Birch" – a Canadian campfire song, evoking the beauty and mystery of a land wild and distant, like the Westcombe hills.

As the Girl Guide flag was lowered, prayers were said, and "Taps" was sung:

> Day is done.
> Gone the sun.
> From the lakes, from the hills, from the sky.
> All is well.
> Safely rest.
> God is nigh.

The group exchanged quiet goodbyes. Lucy felt she truly belonged. On the way home, she said, 'That was wonderful, thanks, Mum!'

'I'm glad you like it,' Hilda replied, 'Tonight's meeting took me back to the days of my youth. Hikes, camping, a good sing-song, and a congenial sense of belonging.'

Later, Hilda handed Lucy a small, oblong box. 'I'd like you to have this.'

Lucy's eyes widened. 'What is it?'

'It's my old pocket-knife, the same one I used many years ago, when I was a Guide,' Hilda said.

'Thanks, Mum,' Lucy whispered, opening the box to reveal a knife the size of a tea-knife, but wider, with a tortoise-shell, patterned handle. Under the leather sheath, the blade was pitted with rust and wasn't particularly sharp.

'It'll be useful for hikes and outdoor activities badges,' Hilda said. 'It's sharp enough to cut through twigs and hessian string.'

'I look forward that,' Lucy said, cherishing a new hope that would carry her through the rest of the winter.

The following Friday, Lucy and Valerie were appointed respective leaders of the Blackbird and Robin patrols. They helped the younger Guides with activities and games.

Inviting Valerie to Edencroft was easy.

'I bet you love living in the country,' Valerie said.

'I love it,' Lucy replied. 'How about you come to tea tomorrow? I'm sure we can arrange a lift.'

'I'd love that, thanks!'

'Great, I'll just ask Mum.'

Hilda agreed, taxi service included.

Saturday afternoon was an extravaganza of childhood bliss. Lucy and Valerie climbed trees, discovered old birds' nests, and converted the ramshackle hut into a clubhouse. Wooden planks and orange crates, and a metal milk crate made makeshift furniture. Lucy sequestered a bag of swag from the house – old curtains, cushions, matches and candles, adding a homely touch.

Lucy closed the door and lit a candle. They sang "Land of the Silver Birch" pretending they were pioneer explorers stranded by snows.

In truth, the hut was damp, the still air dank and chill. Blooms of rust-coloured fungus sprouted from the boards.

'This is like being at camp,' Valerie said. 'Camp's fun. Captain took us on a weekend to Tullington Cove last year. It rained the whole time and we got soaked, but it was warm around the camp fire.' Valerie's enthusiasm was infectious. In her piping voice, Valerie sang a different song. The words seemed made-up, but the tune was jolly and easy to remember.

> Ging gang gooli, gooli gooli watcha ging gang goo ging gang goo. Ging gang
>
> Hayla, Hayla Shayla, Hayla Shayla Hayla ho!
>
> Shallywally shallywally shallywally shallywaly, Oompah, oompah, oompah.

'I don't know that one, but I like it,' Lucy said.

'It's another Guides song. We sing it in a round. You'll get to sing it soon.'

'What do the words mean? '

'I don't think they mean anything. Captain said the song was made up by Guides meeting in India or Africa or somewhere, when Lord Baden Powell was there with a load of Guides from different countries who spoke different languages. It's just about Guides getting together and having a happy time.'

A few favourite songs later, Lucy said, 'Let's do some drawing.'

'Okay.'

Valerie shared Lucy's penchant for arts and crafts. Lucy folded sheets of plain paper and sliced them in half with her hiking knife.

'Enough here for us to draw some nature pictures for next week's meeting.'

Lucy drew a blackbird and Valerie a robin. The wooden crate wobbled, spilling blobs of candle wax on the paper. Lucy wrote *SURVIVAL TIN* on a card and taped it to an empty Bisto tin.

'Looks good, don't you think? Quite professional.' Lucy was fishing for compliments, but it somehow didn't matter that she didn't get them.

'Hmmmm,' mumbled Valerie, who was fixing a net curtain to the window. 'Curtain looks good, too – like in a real house.'

Lucy emptied a bag of sweets into the Survival Tin, took out a sherbet lemon and said, 'These are our emergency rations!'

'All this fresh air is making me hungry,' Valerie said, helping herself to a handful of Dolly Mixtures.

This all seemed too good to be true. Lucy prodded her finger gently with the pocket-knife, reassuring herself this wasn't a dream. Then, suddenly, she remembered school. Seeing the pocket-knife lying on a crate, she thought how easy it would be to pick it up and hurt somebody with it. She gave an involuntary shudder and said nothing.

Valerie broke the awkward silence.

'Shall we go back in the garden?'

'Good idea,' Lucy agreed. 'before it gets dark.'

She puffed out the candle, plunging the hut into sudden gloom.

Dotty stood at the hen-run gate, tail wagging. And then, a welcome shout from the back door. 'Tea's ready!'

The girls raced into the porch and kicked off their boots.

'Wash your hands!' Hilda ordered, but Lucy was already in the bathroom, running the taps and boasting to her guest.

'This is the new bath suite my dad installed. Look! There's also a shower.'

'Very nice,' Valerie said, 'and it's indoors. Our bathroom is in the yard.'

'Come, let's eat, I'm starving!' Lucy said, rushing ahead.

Hilda had laid a spread of ham, cheese, egg salad sandwiches, and slices of wholemeal bread and butter, cut into triangles. The best, blue-ringed, patterned china was out. Four cups of tea stood waiting on the table, curls of steam rising into the reddish glow of lamplight.

Hilda switched on the main light and closed the curtains.

'That looks lovely!' Valerie exclaimed.

'Eat up, you growing girls!' Hilda urged. 'Help yourselves.'

'Thank you, Mrs Wylie,' Valerie replied, wide-eyed.

'Help yourself to seconds, Valerie, we have plenty.'

Lucy gobbled greedily, but Valerie's table manners were restrained. She unfolded her serviette, took small mouthfuls, and sipped her tea slowly.

Lucy had finished her salad and was impatient to get onto the bread-and-jam stage.

'Do you have any pets, Valerie?' Hilda asked.

'No. My little brother's allergic to fur. He's asthmatic and has a heart condition. He's very thin, because he has to take breaths often and doesn't have enough time to chew food and swallow.'

'That must be very difficult for you, and for your mother,' Hilda said.

Valerie's eyes danced. 'Yes it is, but we manage. I have to help my mum a lot.'

'I don't have any brothers or sisters at home to keep me company,' Lucy said, her mouth full. Hilda glowered. Lucy swigged her tea.

'My brother doesn't play much because he gets tired, but I read him stories, and he smiles lot,' Valerie said.

'Where do you go for your holidays?' Lucy asked.

'We've never been on holiday.' Valerie's voice showed no resentment or bitterness. 'But I did go to London once, for a weekend.'

'That's nice,' Hilda said, smiling.

Valerie ate heartily, doing justice to Hilda's High Tea. Afterwards, as promised, Hilda took her home to the council cottages by High Lea Station.

Driving off, Hilda said, 'Valerie's a bright little spark, and so pleasant!'

'She's really nice,' Lucy answered, convinced she'd found a friend for life.

'A lovely child,' Hilda said, 'but we'll wait a while before asking her back, as I think she was a little overwhelmed. And I suspect her family wouldn't be able to reciprocate.'

Lucy said nothing, suspecting her mother was probably right.

In the following fortnight, Lucy and Valerie sailed through their Hospitality, Handcrafts, and Flower Arranging badges, which they proudly sewed to their uniforms. Mr Hargreaves and Mr Smith agreed to assess Lucy's Writer's and Artist's badges, during morning breaks. It was good to have a valid reason to spend time in the warm building, safe from bullies. In the art room, Lucy was working on a painting of a stagecoach escaping a blazing town at night.

'Not too much black,' Mr Smith advised. 'Black is a negative colour and can swamp other colours. Try mixing green, indigo and brown to obtain a dark, near-black effect.'

Lucy crumpled her unfinished work and threw it in the bin. She started again, applying the advice, with a much-improved result.

Mr Hargreaves seemed impressed with Lucy's collection of short stories and plays.

'Do you write these for children?' he asked.

'No,' Lucy replied, 'but I used to make up stories for neighbours' children at my old house in London.'

Mr Hargreaves rubbed his chin thoughtfully.

'They're really quite good, and definitely good enough for your Guides badge.'

Lucy glowed with pride.

However, the swinging pendulum of Lucy's luck was about to change. At the start of the next lesson, she sat in her usual seat, idly doodling in her homework jotter.

'What on earth is all that?' Abigail asked, peering over Lucy's shoulder.

'Nothing!' Lucy retorted, closing the book.

'I saw what you wrote! Bubbles, Patch – Sindy!' Abigail scoffed, gaining the immediate attention of Jodie, Fiona and Joanna.

'SINDY? Would you believe it? She's made lists of toys! And she still plays with dolls! How old are you, Wylie?'

Lucy didn't answer. Fiona and Jodie laughed like jackals.

'I got rid of my Sindy doll when I was eight!' sneered Joanna.

Alison and Rosemary were smirking and sniggering. Lucy squirmed with embarrassment, deeply regretting having disclosed her secret indulgence. *So what? Does it matter if I play with toys?* she thought defiantly. *Mum and Dad haven't said I can't, so it can't be wrong!*

That evening, Lucy stuffed every doll and soft toy in the bottom of the wardrobe. She hadn't the heart to throw any of them away. They had been her friends for most of her life. Doubtless, there would be a Guides' jumble sale soon, and then they could all go to decent homes. From that day onward, Lucy barely gave the toys a thought. A significant milestone had been passed on her long and arduous climb to adulthood.

4: BRAVERY

On the first Saturday in February, Lucy reluctantly attended her twice-yearly dental check. Health checks were potentially embarrassing and painful, therefore best done quickly. The Westcombe dental surgery was on the ground floor of a Victorian villa, just off the High Street. It had a neat front garden with rose bushes and looked just like an ordinary house. Lucy followed her mother up a short flight of steps into a gloomy hallway filled with the tell tale smell of antiseptic. The bay-windowed waiting-room was empty. There was barely time to sit down and look at magazines, for a nurse appeared immediately and ushered Hilda and Lucy into the room across the hall. White walls and bright lights shone on a black, reclining seat in the centre of the room. Instruments of torture lay ready on a steel trolley. The windows were fitted with cream-coloured Venetian blinds, half-closed. Lucy wondered if anyone outside could see in.

During the brief consultation, the dentist solemnly declared Lucy's mouth to be too small, and four of her back teeth must be removed under anaesthetic. An appointment was made for the following Saturday. Exactly a week from today, while her parents shopped on the High Street, Lucy would be in this very room, exposed to unprecedented pain. She swallowed hard and said nothing.

On the way home, Hilda told Lucy she would be put to sleep by gas, and wouldn't feel a thing under the anaesthetic. It seemed a veiled threat, suggesting animal euthanasia or a wartime atrocity. Lucy silently processed the information. Ordinarily, the prospect of such an invasive procedure would terrify her, but this time, a strange, morbid fascination outweighed apprehension. For the rest of the day, Lucy went about her homework and solitary pursuits with fresh serenity. Hilda interpreted Lucy's silence as stalwart courage, in the face of impending adversity.

After supper, Lucy sat at the dining-table, immersed in homework, listening through the half-open kitchen door.

'She's taken the news very bravely,' Hilda said to Albert. 'Many a child of her age would be petrified at the thought of having teeth pulled.'

'That's true,' Albert agreed, quietly.

The dog grunted sleepily, as if in agreement.

Lucy basked silently in her mother's praise. She wasn't afraid of the promised ordeal. In fact, she was secretly hoping it would be the first of many painful trials. Wasn't she, after all, worthless and stupid? Everyone at school told her so. A recent string of insults from teachers and pupils had undermined her confidence to a new nadir. Miss Hughes called her unteachable, Miss Hawksworth declared her deliberately disrespectful, and classmates called her ignorant, retarded, selfish, and a useless piece of rubbish.

It was all too much. The time had come for radical change. A harsh dose of suffering would doubtless help her become a better person – stronger, more independent and mature? Lucy looked forward to the quadruple molar extraction with masochistic zeal.

On Saturday morning, she entered the dental surgery with a tight-lipped smile. While her mother fussed and fretted, Lucy remained calm and resolute, silently embracing this opportunity to suffer. Without a word, she sat back in the hard leather chair and glanced at the glossy white walls and the menacing array of stainless steel instruments. She inhaled the pervading smell of antiseptic, thrilling with excitement. A large cylinder stood nearby, with a tube and mask attached. Fear suddenly gripped her – but cowardice wasn't an option. She had to be brave. A recent memory rescued her from the abyss of terror. One of the Guides, Fenella Dawson, had said that having a tooth pulled was nothing to worry about.

I had this funny dream, Fenella had said, in her thick, country accent.

What did you dream? Lucy had asked inquisitively.

I dreamed that the doctor was taking my tooth out.

Dentist, you mean?'

Yes.

A rubber cone was placed over Lucy's nose and mouth. Immediately she was assailed with a strong smell of rubber. What exactly had Fenella meant by a dream about something which was obviously happening? Didn't the anaesthetic work? Lucy panicked. There was a faint hissing sound. Lucy gulped a sour draught of cold air and struggled for breath. Suddenly the stifling sensation was gone, she felt comfortable and relaxed.

Another millisecond of memory:

You feel yourself going to sleep, a classmate once said of her tonsillectomy experience.

Was this it? Feeling yourself fall asleep?

In black depths of oblivion, Lucy wrestled with torment, something truly dreadful, worse than anything she had ever known.

I can't stand it any longer...

The glare of a circular lamp shone directly into her face. Someone was patting her gently on the cheek, saying, 'It's over, you can wake up now.'

Lucy surfaced into consciousness as quickly as she had slipped out of it. She saw before her the stark surgery walls, the big bay window screened by blinds and the blurred, swimming faces of two people standing over her. There was no pain, just a dull, throbbing sensation in her jaws. She bit down hard on two cotton swabs on each side of her mouth and felt tingling numbness.

'Can you stand up?' the nurse asked.

Lucy nodded, took a deep breath, and rose slowly from the chair. That dreadful, unbearable feeling was gone. Hilda took Lucy by the hand as they left the building, and held it tightly as they walked the marble steps and mosaic path to the wrought-iron gate. The chill February air struck hard on Lucy's face. She marked each step carefully, trying not to stumble. The last thing she wanted was to be considered weak.

'You were very brave, Lucy,' Hilda said, 'undergoing such a terrible ordeal. Most folks would be quivering jellies at the thought of having one tooth out, let alone four.'

'It was nothing,' Lucy said.

The car was parked nearby, Albert at the wheel, smoking his third successive cigarette. Lucy sat in the back, wrapped in thoughts about becoming a better person. As the effects of the anaesthetic wore off, she took comfort in the persistent, dull ache, believing every measure of pain would add to her overall debt to the Universe, toughen her into a new Lucy – caring, capable, likeable and strong. All weekend, she re-lived the dentist experience and enjoyed her mother's attentiveness. There was none of the usual badgering to do school work. Lucy recovered well, and on Monday morning was deemed fit for school.

No one knew what Lucy did on Saturday, and neither did anyone ask. Buoyed up with pride at having withstood a trauma, which might have reduced her peers to snivelling wrecks, Lucy walked the corridors with confidence, cherishing the desire for more and greater physical pain.

'Does having my teeth out count as an operation?' Lucy asked Hilda that evening.

'No, dear.'

'But what about Marion? She had teeth removed too, last year.'

'She was in hospital It was an operation because a cut was made, under a stronger, general anaesthetic.'

Lucy was disappointed. She hadn't been especially brave, after all. A serious illness or accident, however, would definitely rack up the pain-bank. Perhaps she would be hit by a vehicle, or fall from her bicycle? How wonderful it would be to break a leg on the school hockey pitch and have her enemies witness directly how Lucy Wylie could deal with pain! Serious injury would mean extended absence from school. No bullying, no boring lessons, and plenty of time at home to do what she wanted. More importantly, she would become a better person, inwardly purified, free from unworthiness and guilt? Lucy spent much time brooding over these ideas, sharing them with no-one.

Her parents, meanwhile, were preoccupied with other concerns. Hilda was searching for work, and Albert busy with repairs and maintenance. Using his skills as an electrician, Albert re-wired the entire bungalow, but Hilda still feared mice might nibble the underfloor cables.

'I can't stand mice,' she said. 'They're such detestable creatures and a threat to health and safety. That cat of ours will have to make himself more useful.'

'I don't think so,' mumbled Albert. 'He's too old.'

Albert was reluctant to jettison the old, round-pin electrical plugs and suggested they might be of use to the school science department. Lucy couldn't have cared less, but she took the plugs to the physics lab anyway, where they were gratefully received, the teachers surprised by the sudden thoughtfulness of their least proactive student.

Albert dug up the concrete floor in the kitchen, leaving a gaping hole and a heap of rubble. Apparently, Hilda noticed a peculiar smell in the house and suggested there might be a problem with the drains. A fine layer of white dust covered every surface and was trodden all round the house. Lucy took the mess and upheaval in her stride. It wasn't her problem. Ironically, Albert only noticed an odour after Hilda had mentioned it, and Lucy never noticed it at all. She arrived home from school one day, to discover the cooker beside the sideboard, looking absurdly out of place. The big aluminium kettle thumped on the hob, sending puffs of steam into the room. Saucepans and crockery occupied the table, where a space had been left for Lucy to do her homework. Hilda poured Lucy a cup of tea.

'Thanks, Mum,' Lucy said quietly. She sat down and made a reluctant start on Maths and Geography but couldn't focus. So far, Albert's excavations had revealed nothing untoward, but Hilda was adamant the bad smell was still there. Lucy was advised to move to the spare room for health and safety reasons. The spare bedroom was a simple, box-like extension attached to the north side of the bungalow, and it did have a peculiar smell – a vague whiff of damp woodwork and lavender-scented beeswax. Marion's old bed and Uncle Charles's antique chest were large and cumbersome, occupying valuable space. Lucy pinned magazine cuttings of horses, dogs, the Beatles, and Elvis Presley on the walls, covering as much as possible of the ugly yellow-and-brown, floral wallpaper. Nothing could be done to hide the polystyrene-tiled ceiling and the stained sag in the corner where the flat roof had leaked.

Ironically, after ten days of disruption, it was concluded the strange smell was nothing to do with the drains. Everything was put back in its place, and

Lucy returned to her own bedroom.

'You'd better remove those pin-ups!' Hilda ordered. Without arguing, Lucy did as she was told. The source of the mysterious smell was never discovered, but the silo at Biddlecombe Farm topped Hilda's list of suspects, along with Edencroft's septic tank, which was duly emptied the following week.

At half term, the Wylies were invited to spend a weekend with the Hills, in the Sussex village of Fordham. Albert's old army friend, Arthur Hill, was keen to hear all about Edencroft, first-hand. Lucy loved visits to the Hills. There was always good food and a cheery welcome in the rustic, rambling bungalow with its wild garden overrun with hens and cockerels. Arthur's wife Joan was a comely countrywoman, and their children Anne and Anthony had known nothing but rural life.

On Friday, Lucy was collected straight from school at the start of the long road trip.

'A pity I can't go home and get changed,' Lucy complained.

'We need to get as far as possible while it's light. Your father doesn't like night driving, so you'll just have to change when we get there. Your bag's in the back.'

As usual, her mother had everything organised.

'Where's Dotty?' Lucy asked.

'In kennels. We can't bring her, because of Arthur and Joan's dogs. They might fight. Mrs Daly from down the road is going to feed Marmie.'

Guides wasn't even mentioned. Tonight's meeting would be missed, but a trip to Fordham was more than adequate compensation.

This time, however, the thrill of Fordham had lost its edge. Compared to the environs of Edencroft, the conglomeration of cottages, post-office-cum-general-store, and the parish church seemed almost urban. But the happy hospitality in the homely, weather-boarded bungalow was unchanged. A hot meal was waiting, blackened pans and kettles steaming on the kitchen range. Arthur sat in his fireside chair, telling jokes, the Jack Russell terrier on his lap, the collie at his feet. Homely Joan waddled like a Christmas turkey and laughed like a drain. Appetising aromas filled the bungalow, as pots bubbled and newly-baked cakes cooled on the kitchen windowsill, out of reach of the dogs. Lucy clasped her hands around her mug of tea, studying the red-check pattern on the table cloth. It seemed strange to find a favourite childhood idyll so curiously jaded.

For two hours, voices clamoured, and laughter pealed, as the past year's news was exchanged. Lucy kept mostly out of the conversation, replying in monosyllables. Arthur wanted to know all about Edencroft. Hilda said it wasn't a market-garden, as such. Arthur and Albert discussed horticulture, Joan and Hilda talked about hen-keeping, baking, and knitting. The younger generation amused themselves. Seventeen-year-old Anne sprawled on the sofa, watching television, and ten-year-old Anthony played in the corner with toy cars. Lucy was bored, wishing she'd brought knitting or a book to read. She opened her school bag and idly doodled a flower pattern on the cover of a jotter.

'Come and see the night sky,' Albert said. Lucy followed her father outside. The clear night air struck hard, but stars were visible, the constellation of Orion, and a faint whisper of the Milky Way. Somewhere in the trees, an owl hooted.

'The Plough is clear tonight,' Albert said, pointing up to the saucepan-shaped asterism that reminded Lucy a huge white-on-black join the dots puzzle.

'Those stars must be very far apart,' she said.

'They're light-years apart.'

'It's hard to grasp how big space is. And we get so bogged down with the affairs of Earth.'

'True, the night sky goes way over our heads. Star-gazing puts everything in perspective.'

'It does,' Lucy sighed. 'This is the most meaningful conversation of the evening.'

Albert lit a cigarette and said, 'In some ways, your'e right.'

'I'm going inside now though. It's freezing cold out here,' Lucy said, shivering.

Lucy was to share Anthony's bedroom. The threadbare carpet was littered with shoes, odd socks, toy cars, and a mud-caked football. Model aeroplanes hung from the ceiling, and Meccano models and books were arranged haphazard on the dusty shelves. The camp-bed was clean and comfortable. It was after eleven o'clock when everyone retired to bed. Lucy wriggled contentedly between crisp, cool sheets and was delighted to find a hot water bottle. Anthony turned out the light but still talked.

'What's your school like?' he asked.

'Boring.'

'No boyfriends then?'

'Definitely not.'

'What lessons do you do?'

'Same ones as in any other school.'

'What's your favourite subject?'

'I don't have one.'

'You like everything then?'

'No, I like nothing.'

'Oh. Who's your best friend in school?'

'I don't have one. Anyway, I'm tired and want to sleep.'

Lucy was relieved nothing more was said. Anthony was soon snoring softly, but Lucy lay awake, hearing the melancholy hoot of an owl and the distant barking of dogs. At last, she turned over, pulled the eiderdown over her head and slept.

Anthony was awake before Lucy.

Yanking back the curtains, he yelled, 'It's SNOWING! Yippee! Let's go sledging and build a snowman!'

Reflected light from newly fallen snow invaded the room. Lucy jumped up and rushed to the window. A white blanket spread across rolling fields to matt-grey woods.

'GREAT! That's just WONDERFUL!' The child within her revitalised, Lucy dressed quickly and burst into the parlour, eager to inform everyone it was snowing – a fact they had already observed for themselves.

'A good job you travelled yesterday,' Arthur remarked over breakfast.

'Indeed,' answered Albert. 'I wouldn't attempt to drive in bad weather'.

'Bad weather?' retorted Lucy with a smile, 'Not bad for Anthony and me. We're off out to enjoy the snow!'

'Rain is fine weather for ducks, snow is fine weather for children', Joan said, 'so get some hot porridge inside you, then wrap up warm and go and enjoy yourselves'.

After breakfast, Lucy borrowed gloves and Wellington boots and helped Anthony built a big snowman outside the kitchen window. Using pieces of coal and a fat carrot for a nose they put a cheerful face on it that grinned back at Joan when she was busy in the kitchen. In the wan sunshine, woods and fields glittered like a Christmas card. Lucy was young again, happy, laughing, and absorbed in the simple pleasure of playing in the snow.

Anthony asked Lucy about the new home. Lucy told him about the pets, the hut, the countryside, and the beaches. Anthony didn't say much and Lucy wondered if he was jealous. In the afternoon, the snow was still hard and frozen. Anthony and Lucy took makeshift sledges to the slopes of a nearby meadow, where children gathered with a motley collection of toboggans, some of them home-made. Sledging was an all-new experience for Lucy. The thrill of whizzing down an icy slope and feeling the keen air in her face was an exhilarating high, with a hint of danger. After several turns, Lucy and Anthony swapped sledges with Anthony's friends and were handed a metal sheet with two holes drilled through the front and a rope attached.

'I'll drive,' Anthony said, 'and you sit behind and grab me round the waist. Try not to fall off!'

Lucy sat down on the cold, hard metal rectangle and linked her hands around Anthony's waist. The sledge sped away swiftly. Seconds later, they were at the foot of the slope. Anthony failed to stop. They hurtled towards a dense hawthorn hedge. There was no time for fear. The dark mesh of thorny thicket was upon them. Instinctively, Lucy ducked. In a nanosecond, she tasted the thrill of real risk – the immediate danger of being badly hurt, or – killed? At the moment of impact, Anthony and Lucy shielded their heads with their hands, and suddenly they were through to the other side, tumbling down a steep bank into a narrow lane.

Icy wind sharpened Lucy's pain of multiple cuts and scratches.

Anthony got up stiffly and brushed his clothes.

'Phew, that was a narrow squeak. But, what a great ride!' he puffed.

Breathless with excitement, Lucy was eager to try another run.

'Let's do it again!' she panted.

'Oh, no! Not me.' Anthony shook his head resolutely. 'Besides, we have to give this sledge back now and go back to using mine.'

Lucy had the impression Anthony was looking for an excuse not to try again. For her part, she longed for another risky ride. She borrowed Anthony's sledge and made repeated attempts to experience another thrilling crash through the thicket, but failed to gather sufficient momentum. The snow was melting, excitement turning to Doldrum-like disappointment.

It rained that evening and the next day. Lucy continued to re-live the sledge ride, day-dreaming of a more dramatic result, such as breaking an arm or leg. She dwelt again on her experience at the dentist. If only life would bring her more pain and suffering! Surely that would make her a better person, strong and brave in the face of adversity? Then, people would look up to her and admire her courage, and she would never lack friends.

5: THE TEENAGER

The cold snap was over. The Westcombe hills had seen no snow all winter, just a few flurries that didn't settle. Lucy spent the rest of half term hunkering down in her room on the pretext of studying. She stared miserably out at the mist-shrouded view, yearning for summer. On Monday morning, the same view was decked in glittering frost. Lucy cycled to school cautiously, scanning the tarmac for icy patches, dreading the prospect of double science followed by double games. During registration, nobody spoke to her. The physics class on electrolysis didn't interest her, so she spent most of the lesson staring out of the window at the dormant buds on the cherry trees, wondering when summer would come. At break, she sat alone in the sun trap between two laurel bushes, catching up on homework. When the bell rang, Lucy waited for the crowd to disperse, then dawdled to the girls' changing room.

Entering the building, Lucy was jostled from all sides, overwhelmed by noise. She wished she could time-travel, and for the next ninety minutes to be over. But by then, things could be even worse. Miss Forbes emerged from her office in a garish purple tracksuit.

'Go immediately to the cloakroom and fetch your coats, hats, gloves, and scarves!' she yelled with military gusto. 'Pick up every stitch of clothing you brought with you to school this morning and report back here immediately!'

Good, thought Lucy, *a clothes inspection*. She breathed easily at the thought of ten minutes off double hockey. Minutes later, thirty girls stood waiting, arms encumbered with winter apparel. But there was no expected clothes check.

'Right!' barked Miss Forbes. 'Put everything on. We're going for a walk.'

Even better! Lucy thought. There were low whispers of speculation about the route.

'I hope we're going to the beach,' Rosemary said, sparking enthusiasm among her friends.

'Yeah – so do I!'

'We might get a suntan?'

'I didn't bring sun cream.'

'A route-march on the old railway?'

'Or maybe –'

'Silence!' roared Miss Forbes. 'You'll find out soon enough where we're going. Onward! Quick march!'

There was not a breath of wind. In the brilliant sunshine, frost-sprinkled trees stood motionless, and hills basked in a quality of light unseen for months. As the crocodile of walkers stretched out, tongues were loosened, fresh country air stimulating tired brains. At the disused railway crossing, Miss Forbes gave the order to continue straight ahead.

Lucy looked wistfully at the distant downs and the tiny, terracotta roof peeping above the woods. It was tempting to shout out and tell the world what a wonderful place she lived in.

Half a mile from Edencroft, and drawing ever closer!

Lucy quickened her pace. At the junction with Helmstone Lane, the order was to turn left. It was odd walking past familiar landmarks: the white house with red gables, the modern bungalow half-hidden behind a row of conifers, and the ramshackle cottage with the tiny enclosure with five white hens. Behind the hedge at Westcombe Riding School, startled horses tossed their heads and whickered softly at the sound of approaching voices. Joanna stopped to pet her favourite pony and received a quick rebuke from Miss Forbes.

'Looks like we'll be going through Helmstone and back along the old railway,' someone said. It seemed a given. The route would bring them back to school in good time.

However, at the next corner, Miss Forbes shouted, 'Turn right!'

The line snaked around the hairpin bend and up the steep hill. The group would now definitely pass beside Edencroft.

Someone was walking close to Lucy's personal space. Then a friendly voice asked, 'You live somewhere up here, don't you, Lucy?'

Lucy bristled, then turned to face a smiling Alison Rodgers.

This was probably the first time Alison had ever spoken to Lucy in a positive way. Weeks earlier, Alison remarked upon a doodle in Lucy's jotter. *Potty Dotty?* Alison had sneered, *a good name for you – it suits you.*

Dotty is my dog, Lucy had protested. *I call her Potty Dotty because she's so playful. She's a Dalmatian.*

'Yes, I live up here,' Lucy answered cautiously. 'A bit further along. I come this way on my bike.'

'I know. I've seen you on a green bike. It's too big for you.'

'It was my sister's. She's grown up now.'

'But you're not.' Alison smiled again. Lucy didn't know if she was mocking.

'I'll be thirteen in April,' Lucy argued defensively.

'I won't be thirteen till June,' Alison said.

'Do you have brothers and sisters?' Lucy ventured.

'My sister Sandra's in 3A – she's eleven months older than me. I've also a ten year old brother, Charlie. What brothers and sisters do you have?'

'A sister called Marion who's getting married this summer. She's twenty and lives in London, and I'm going to be a bridesmaid.'

'How lovely ! I've never been a bridesmaid.'

Lucy stalled with embarrassment, wondering if she should say more about Dotty. Alison seemed to read her mind.

'I've got a dog too, a black Labrador called Cedric. He's also very lively and gets in in the way at my parents' restaurant. We've only a small back yard, so Cedric doesn't get enough exercise, except when Dad takes him to the beach, which isn't often. Maybe we could take our dogs on a walk together, sometime?'

Alison's words echoed in Lucy's auditory memory like music. *Am I dreaming? Is this really happening?* Lucy was speechless. An overture of friendship was the last thing she would have expected from someone as popular as Alison.

'I'd love that,' Lucy said quietly. 'Dotty is very excitable. She jumps up at strangers.'

'Cedric's playful too. He's eight months old, so still a puppy. We give him old shoes to chew. He likes my dad's best because they smell of cheese.'

Lucy sniggered. They'd made good headway up the hill, and Lucy had hardly noticed the climb. By this time, she and Alison had overtaken most of the group and were near the front. Miss Forbes was pacing back and fore, chivvying stragglers at the back. As they crested the next hill, a distinctive white bungalow came into view, nestling among trees on a hilltop.

'There's my house and garden!' Lucy exclaimed.

'Wow!' Alison sighed enviously. 'It looks lovely.'

'Yes, it is' Lucy boasted. A few heads turned. 'The garden runs all the way along that field to the woods over there, and that field at the side is ours, where we keep our hens.'

The double gates were open, and the green Morris Traveller was parked on the drive.

'I helped my dad paint those gates,' Lucy said, 'and that's our car!' Lucy jumped up and down, waving, hoping to catch sight of her mother or father and prove what a wonderful place she lived in.

'Look, chickens! Cluckety-cluck!' Someone was laughing and pointing to three plump hens scratching in the grass.

'Those are my mum's chickens, and this is where I live,' Lucy said again.

More heads turned. Miss Forbes was up and over the brow of the hill by now, unaware of the small flurry of excitement fifty yards behind.

'I bet you love living there,' Alison said, wistfully.

'Maybe you'd like to bring Cedric here on Saturday?' Lucy asked.

'Actually, I'd like that,' Alison said.

'Come at about two o'clock?'

'Better make it half past as I'm working in the restaurant until two.'

'Okay, and then we –'

'GET A MOVE ON, BACK THERE!' Miss Forbes yelled.

Alison broke into a brisk run, and Lucy kept pace, no longer caring if she was on the receiving end of Miss Forbes' wrath. It no longer mattered that six lessons and two breaks stretched between now and home time. In friendship there was safety.

On Saturday, Alison arrived as promised. Ecstatic, Lucy ran out to greet her. 'Alison! You're here! You came!'

Fresh-faced and tousled, Alison unleashed her dog and said, 'If Cedric's too lively, I'll put him back on the lead.'

At the end of a brisk, two-mile, uphill walk, Alison wasn't out of breath.

'You're very fit,' Lucy observed, resisting the urge to say, I wish I was as good at games as you. It was too soon to jeopardise this embryonic friendship. Cedric greeted Lucy with a lively leap, then Dotty gave a sharp bark and bounded through the dog-flap and began frolicking with Cedric. With unbridled enthusiasm, Lucy rolled on the grass, exclaiming, 'Alison, welcome to Edencroft!'

Alison stifled the urge to laugh. In the brilliant sunshine crocuses and snowdrops were in full bloom, and the hedgerows rang with the lively melodies of calling birds.

'Let's go and look at the hens!' Lucy gabbled. 'There's a sort of summerhouse in the hen run, which I'm using as a den –'

Hilda appeared in the doorway. 'Alison has just walked all that way up the hill, so how about some biscuits and a drink first?'

Alison's face lit up. 'Thank you, Mrs Wylie. That would be lovely.'

In the breakfast room, sunshine streamed through the windows, and the budgie chirped shrilly.

'Please excuse the mess', Hilda apologised. 'We're still decorating.'

The gaping hole in the kitchen floor had been filled, but bare concrete floor and chipped paintwork remained.

'That's all right, our flat is always untidy, but I really love your garden. It's beautiful – and so big!' Alison gasped.

'It's hard work, though,' Hilda said, offering a plate of biscuits and two glasses of lemon squash.

'Thank you, Mrs Wylie,' Alison said.

Lucy guzzled her drink, revelling in the praise of her beloved idyll. After refreshments, she wasted no time showing Alison around.

'I like your art hut,' Alison said. 'Do you spend much time in it drawing and painting?'

'Oh yes, nearly every day,' Lucy said, whereas, in fact, she had barely been in it since Valerie's visit, due to bad weather and general lack of motivation. Inside the hut, dust-laden fabrics flopped forlornly in the gloom, and the net curtain draped miserably in the cobweb-strewn window like Miss Havisham's wedding veil.

'It's a bit of a mess,' Lucy admitted, 'but now the weather's better and the evenings lighter, it's time for some spring-cleaning.'

'I could bring some stuff from home,' Alison offered. 'Some old curtains and table cloths, perhaps? My mum's always getting new things for the tea room and throwing out the old.'

A sudden, agitated clucking from behind the Russian vine interrupted the talk.

'Cedric's chasing your hens! I'd better put him back on the lead.'

'I'll put Dotty on the lead and we could walk up High Lea Down, there's a fantastic view from the top,' Lucy said.

'I know,' Alison said.

'Have you aways lived in Westcombe?' Lucy asked.

'I was born here, but I also lived in America for two years.'

'How exciting! Where abouts?'

'California. My dad had a job working at his cousin's hotel in Sacramento.'

'What was it like living there? Did you have to go to school?'

'Of course we went to school. My brother was just a baby but my sister and I went to school.'

'What was it like?'

'It was okay. Pretty much the same as school here. We learned, we played games in the yard, the teachers were cool.'

'Cool? Oh, you mean they were nice?'

'Yes. They gave us more freedom and hardly ever told us off.'

Alison's accent was sounding more American.

Eager to know more, Lucy fired questions like bullets.

'What was the weather like? And the landscape?'

'It's warm and sunny all year, the beaches are super and the waves fit for surfing. There are mountains – high ones and tropical fruits growing all year round.'

Lucy was reminded of Janet Ford's holiday diary of colourful European adventures. By comparison, Lucy's life seemed incredibly dull.

'So why did you stay only two years?'

'Dad's job at the hotel didn't work out.'

'Oh. But you don't mind being back here?'

'We miss the good weather but Westcombe's a good place. How about you? Tell me your story.'

'Not much to tell. I was born near London and lived there all my life until last summer. Ever since I can remember, my parents planned to move to the country, near the sea, and now here we are.'

At the top of the hill, the dogs were unleashed on open heathland. Lucy stood mesmerised by the view: a panoramic sweep of land and sea, chalk and sandstone cliffs, a veil of cotton-wool cloud hugging the hilltops of Combe Ridge. Westcombe town seemed a fuzzy blob, small and still, and in the opposite direction, the blurry outline of the Nyehaven harbour just visible in sea mist.

'On a very clear day you can see as far as Salton,' Alison said.

'This really is a wonderful place,' Lucy sighed, 'I wish to stay here for ever.'

Alison didn't stay for tea, saying she had to be home by five to help in the restaurant. All week, at school, Alison, remained amicable but preferred the company of extrovert, fashion-conscious Rosemary. Lucy tried not to worry. When the bell rang at the end of Friday afternoon, Lucy was first on her feet, ready to dash off and beat the crush. On the stairs, Alison caught up with her and said, 'I'm taking Cedric up High Lea Down tonight. He needs a good walk. Maybe you and Dotty could join us?'

Lucy was thrilled. 'Yes, that sounds a great idea! Just come to the gate. I'll be looking out for you.'

An hour later, the girls were sitting on the hilltop heath, the dogs snuffling nearby on the trail of rabbits.

'You and Rosemary are very different,' Alison said. 'Do you like Rosemary?'

'I've nothing against her, but whenever she's talking, I don't know what to say, and I can't get a word in edgeways.'

'You're not interested in the same things.' quipped Alison. 'You see, I like lots of things. I enjoy dog-walking, hiking, rambling, exploring the countryside, but I also like sports, fashion, pop music, and ... boys.'

The last word sounded like an accusation. Lucy considered herself too young for boyfriends, and Alison didn't seem the type of girl to be interested in going out on dates.

'M – my sister likes all those things.' Lucy floundered, 'but I have friends in the High Lea Girl Guides, and my mum helps run it. She's the Lieutenant.'

'I was in the Girls' Brigade once,' Alison said. 'But I left after two weeks. I didn't like it because it was too religious.'

'Guides isn't religious.' Lucy argued. 'Well, not preachy, anyway. We say a prayer at the end of a meeting, and there's a church parade once a month, but mostly we do interesting things, we learn new skills, have quizzes, play games, go on hikes, camps and treasure-trails, and work for badges. Recently I got my artist's and writer's badges, so I've got five badges now.'

Alison looked bored. Lucy guessed she wasn't going to persuade her to join the Guides. Lucy couldn't picture Alison feeling at ease among the uncomplicated little village girls.

'What do you think of Bob Dylan's music?' Alison asked. Lucy hesitated, her ignorance undisguised. Alison gave an exaggerated sigh, then mumbled an excuse about having to be back early for tea. She leashed Cedric and walked away. Lucy was crestfallen, fearing the final curtain had fallen on the fragile friendship.

In fact, Alison neither rejected Lucy, as Janet Ford had done nor did she drift away, like Valerie. After school on Monday, Alison collared Lucy again and suggested another dog walk on the beach.

On the beach! This opportunity was unmissable. Lucy raced home, lied to her parents about having no homework, then sallied forth with Dotty on the two-and-a-half-mile walk to Westcombe pier. She arrived, panting and dishevelled, delighted to find Alison and Cedric already there.

'Do you come here often?' Lucy asked.

'Every day, rain or shine. Cedric needs the exercise.'

'Don't you mind?'

'Not at all! I love the beach!'

'I do, too.' Lucy drew a deep breath, tasting the fresh, salt tang in the air. The dogs frolicked on the shore, kicking up showers of damp sand beside the ebbing tide. Towering chalk cliffs were bathed in sunshine, the sea a restless rug of shimmering sapphires, the wide sky a calm canopy of milky-blue. It was a golden moment – a scene that filled Lucy with irrepressible joy. On a sudden burst of energy, she exclaimed, 'Let's go paddling! The water looks so – inviting.'

'Sooner you than me,' retorted Alison, 'Nobody goes in the water in March. It takes months for the sun's heat to warm it up. The holiday season doesn't properly start till May.'

Lucy stared defiantly at the ice-blue water, removed her shoes and socks and stepped into the foaming tide. Instantly, the icy water struck hard and sharp, shocking yet stimulating.

'This is really good! Not cold at all. Why don't you try?' Lucy strode further, feeling the biting chill rise to her ankles, penetrating nerve and sinew. Thrilled by the challenge, she waded until the water was knee-deep.

The dogs followed, paddling in the shallows.

'I'm looking forward to summer,' Lucy said airily, trying not to let her voice quaver. 'In summer it'll be w- warmer.'

Alison was beside her now, shoulders hunched and teeth chattering.

'It's t – too c – c – cold for me. I've had enough. I'm going b – back.'

'Nonsense, it's not that b- bad!" Lucy insisted. Icy water lapped round her kneecaps, tightening its grip around her sensation-starved legs.

This was enough. She turned around and waded back to shore. Minutes later, in the Rodgers' family flat above the Merry Teapot, Lucy hugged frozen fingers around a mug of hot tea. The dogs were settled on the hearthrug, Alison was talking about teachers and homework, but Lucy's attention was on the intrepid paddling experience.

Then she noticed the time.

'It's six o'clock! Dinner will be ready, and my mum will wonder where I am.'

Lucy left hurriedly, feeling flustered. It had been a brilliant visit, but too short. Dotty pulled her most of the way home. She arrived whilst her parents were still eating.

'Sorry I'm late, Mum. I was at the beach with Dotty. Alison and Cedric were there. We had a great time but I lost track of time.'

'Your dinner's in the oven,' Hilda said, 'Eat up, then you can do your homework.'

'Thanks, Mum.'

Relief flooding her tired limbs, Lucy fetched her food and joined her parents at the table.

'What are the homework subjects tonight?' Hilda asked.

Lucy chewed and swallowed. 'French, History, and Latin.'

'I didn't make a dessert today, so I'll clear the table and you can get started. Cup of tea and slice of cake when you've finished.'

Lucy nodded, mouth full of chicken pie. Now that school was bearable, hobbies were more fun, food tasted better, and even homework had ceased to be a chore. The tide had truly turned. From now on, life would be wonderful again.

Marion and Paul came for Easter. The school holidays had begun, and the mood at Edencroft was happy and bright. Marion brought a long-playing record of the film "The Sound of Music". Lucy recognised the song about the cuckoo clock, which had been sung at Guides.

'What's the film about?' Lucy asked.

'It's a love story,' Marion said, 'about a young, Austrian nun who looks after seven children, teaches them songs. The children's mother is dead, but the nun falls in love with their father and they get married.'

'I thought nuns don't get married?'

'They don't. Maria leaves the convent. She had to give all that up.'

'So a happy ending?'

'Yes and no, because that's not how the story ends. The Second World War starts, and the Nazis drive them out, so they have to hide and escape.'

'A romance, and adventure, and a musical.'

'More or less.'

'Sounds interesting. I wish I could go and see it.'

'You will, one day.'

As the vibrant melodies rang through the open windows into the spring sunshine, Lucy sang along uninhibited, twirling with wild abandon around the garden. Through the open window, she caught snatches of conversation.

'We must book the church...'

'And order the flowers...'

'White roses and red carnations...'

'Cornflower-blue bridesmaids' dresses...'

Lucy dashed indoors, eager to hear more. Hilda and Marion were at the table, poring over glossy magazines.

'Marion, you will look wonderful in a full length, white satin gown overlaid with lace, and of course, a white veil and white shoes.'

'You'll be going to the dressmaker's, Lucy dear, to be measured,' Hilda said.

'Yes, Mum,' Lucy scowled, then sloped off, sunshine and birdsong drawing her back outside. She ran to the bottom of the garden and climbed the low, mesh fence into Biddlecombe Copse. Under a thickening canopy of foliage, vines sprawled over oaks and alders, gnarled tree roots lay exposed in sandy hollows. Lucy was wondering where to start building a den when she heard her mother's shrill voice calling 'There's a friend here for you!'

She raced to the back door, where Hilda stood holding a tumbler of orange squash.

'Who is it?' Lucy asked.

'What do you mean?'

'The friend.'

'What friend?'

'B – but you said there was a friend here for me!' Lucy protested.

'I think you misheard me. I said, There's a cold drink here for you. Now drink this and come in and wash your hands before lunch.'

Lucy's heart sank with disappointment.

Easter Sunday was another day of golden sunshine, Lucy spent the morning traipsing back and fore from the hut, furnishing it with cloths and trinkets from her room. Then, on the porch step, she found a small box labelled, *to LUCY*. Inside was a posy of primroses, snowdrops and violets, and wrapped in tissue paper were ten tiny foil-covered chocolate eggs. A crumpled note read,

Hi Lucy,

Just passing by with Cedric· Sorry to have missed you·

Happy Easter, Alison·

Lucy scouted around the footpath but saw no one. Delight outweighed disappointment. Lucy never received gifts from a friend unless it was Christmas or birthday. She was deliriously happy for the rest of the day, even when Hilda asked her to help with the chores.

'How about a coming of teenage party?' Hilda suggested over tea.

'A what?' Lucy asked.

'You'll be thirteen very soon. You could invite friends – girls and boys – play records, dance, play a few games. Nothing babyish, of course.'

'But I don't know any boys.'

'What about the boys in your class at school?'

'Can't I just invite a few girls? A few Guides, and Alison, but definitely no boys.'

'But you can't have an all-hen party.'

Lucy pictured hens bobbing about, enjoying plates of layers' pellets. She hid her face in her sleeve, stifling a laugh.

'It'll be a teenage party,' Hilda continued. 'It's time you started mixing with boys. Nothing immoral, of course, but you're growing up now and must learn to take your place in society. One day you'll be married, and who knows, you could meet the right man before the end of your teen years? Marion was nineteen when she met Paul, and I first met your father when I was fifteen. He was a friend of Uncle Peter's and no more than an acquaintance. We didn't fall in love until the war ended. You must get to know boys respectfully, allowing friendship to develop first, before romance.'

Lucy's future yawned before her, a cloud-filled chasm. Lucy stared resentfully at the cruet, recalling her mother's oft-repeated tale of Uncle Peter inviting friends to the tiny London flat to play darts. One of the lads was Albert Wylie. World War Two intervened, and a chance meeting, seven years later, at a Regent Street bus stop sparked their lifelong bond. Much as Lucy wished to be grown up, she was still a child, in a child's body. Far from her thoughts was the adult world with its shackles of responsibility and the forbidding realm of sex.

'You could invite Nigel Daly, the farm labourer's son from down the road?' Hilda suggested.

'I don't think so.'

'Why not?'

'Because he wouldn't fit in with my friends.'

'I don't see why not,' Hilda argued. 'Invite Nigel and ask him to invite some of his friends. I'd also like his advice on hen-keeping.'

'All right then. There's nobody else,' Lucy reluctantly agreed.

Nigel Daly was a strapping lad of fourteen, who lived with his parents and grandmother in a rented cottage down the lane. Lucy hailed Nigel the next time she saw him walking his dog.

'Good afternoon, Nigel. Mum was asking if you could come and give some advice about the hens.'

'Give me a minute,' Nigel said, 'I'll put Jasper in the shed and come straight up.'

Five minutes later Nigel stood in the chicken house, pressing loose, rotting planks, while Lucy cowered nearby, fearing the whole structure would fall apart. She stared at Nigel's close-cropped reddish-brown hair, fleshy face and thick, calloused hands. Lucy felt dwarfed in his presence yet not intimidated.

'You'll have to get these holes blocked,' Nigel warned, 'or the foxes will be in. Maybe you've had a visit from them already?'

'I don't think so', Lucy replied, 'we still have twenty-three hens. One died during the winter, because it had no tail feathers, and the other hens kept picking on it.'

'Yeah, we've had one or two of those', Nigel replied casually. 'They don't lay, so we wring their necks and put them in the stew pot.'

Nigel missed the shocked expression on Lucy's face.

'I'm having a few friends round Saturday after next,' Lucy said, changing the subject.

Nigel threw Lucy a quizzical look.

'I'll be thirteen, and my Mum suggested a coming-of-teenage party with both girls and boys. Would you – er – like to come?'

'You are thirteen?'

'I'm still twelve until my birthday,' Lucy replied, feeling the blood rush to her face. She fumbled nervously in the nesting boxes in search of eggs.

'Four eggs in this box,' she muttered, 'but I've nothing to carry them in.'

'Yes please, I would like to come.' Nigel answered.

'The trouble is,' Lucy continued, 'I don't really know any other boys to invite, and I just wondered – if – if you could bring a couple of friends?'

Nigel paused.

'All right,' he grinned.

'No more than about five or six though,' Lucy added, quickly.

'No worries. Just leave it to me. Tell your parents the hens are good, but the coop must be mended for their safety.'

Hilda appeared with an empty basket.

'Good afternoon, Mrs Wylie,' Nigel said gruffly. 'That's a fine lot of hens you have.'

'I'm glad you think so,' Hilda smiled proudly.

'Well I'd best be on my way,' Nigel said, and with a nod and a wink he swaggered off.

'Nigel said he will invite some of his friends,' Lucy said, 'so I don't need to worry about inviting any more boys.'

'Nigel can invite just two or three friends, that's all. I will speak to him about that. We can't afford to entertain large numbers of hungry visitors, not with Marion's wedding to pay for!'

'What games will we play at the party?' Lucy asked.

'We could play Postman's Knock, Charades... and Operations.'

'What's Operations?'

'It's a hilarious game I played at parties when I was young. It'll have you in fits of laughter. Each guest is blindfolded and invited to assist in a make-believe operation. Someone hands them pieces of warm, moist fruit or vegetable, saying it's a bodily organ. The peeled grape is the best one. I really thought it was someone's eyeball.'

Lucy pulled a face. 'Okay,' she agreed.

The Easter holidays passed in glorious sunshine. Lucy revelled in endless hours of freedom. She tried her hand at woodwork, constructing a small table from scraps of wood and hardboard. It wobbled and looked odd, but looked better when covered with patterned curtain. Alison donated two folding camping-stools and a sheepskin rug to the hut, completing the make-believe domestic scene. Lucy and Alison sat at the rickety table, dining on soup from a flask, and cheese and pickle sandwiches, sharing crusts with the dogs. Lucy persuaded Alison to help build a brushwood den in a hollow, below a beech tree.

'Looks good, wouldn't you agree?' Lucy boasted, stepping back to admire their handiwork. 'We would watch birds. I often hear woodpeckers but I've never seen one.'

'Shall we give the den a name?' Alison suggested.

'We'll put names in a hat and pick one out,' Lucy said.

'Okay.'

Lucy scribbled eagerly.

'You pick,' Alison said when they were ready.

Lucy picked a chit and read it.

'The Bush House.'

'I thought of that one,' Alison said, needlessly.

'Let's pick another,' Lucy said.

Alison took the next one.

'The Squirrel's Dray.'

'Let's have that one,' Lucy said. She painted a sign and attached it to the den.

'I'll have to be going soon,' Alison said. 'I have to help at the restaurant tonight, and all day tomorrow.'

'Okay.' Lucy replied, unfazed.

The next day Lucy was ready for another day outdoors, but Hilda had other plans.

'This morning, you're coming with us to meet the church minister, after which we'll go to the dressmaker,' Hilda said at breakfast.

'All right,' Lucy agreed. 'Alison's working today, so she won't be coming.'

'Family before friends, in any case!' Hilda retorted.

Arriving at the church, Hilda said, 'The church office is in the main building, above the Guides hall.'

A faded sign outside the doors read:

WHAT IS MISSING FROM THIS CH--CH?

Lucy didn't think this attempt at humour would attract anyone to church. Albert stubbed out a cigarette-end with his foot, asking, 'How long will this meeting take?'

'Not long,' Hilda replied curtly.

Inside the cramped, dusty office, Lucy sat with her parents, sister, and brother-in-law-to-be, day-dreaming about The Squirrel's Dray, relieved she didn't have to say anything.

'I look forward to this happy occasion – the first wedding here for twenty years!' the wizened cleric concluded joyfully.

Lucy was glad to get out into the warm sunshine.

'Right,' Hilda announced. 'We're off to the dressmaker's.'

'I'll wait in the car,' Albert said.

'And I'm going to the paper shop,' Paul mumbled quietly.

'This place reminds me of Arthur and Joan's,' Hilda said, jabbing the buzzer at the door of the dressmaker's corrugated-iron bungalow overlooking the village. A bird-like elderly lady answered the door, introduced herself as Mrs Bailey and invited her clients into the chintzy parlour. A tray of tea, cake and biscuits was offered, helping Lucy through the half-hour of what she considered unnecessary fuss. Lucy lingered over her tea and devoured the dainty plate of Garibaldi biscuits, while Marion stood to be measured. Her mother's shrill voice, Marion's soft treble, and the dressmaker's quavering tones wafted over her head like discordant birdsong.

Then it was Lucy's turn.

'Come along, dear,' the old woman beckoned. 'Let's get your vital statistics.'

Lucy was familiar with the euphemism popularised by faddy females who worried about their chest, waist and hip measurements.

'Lucy will be thirteen next week,' Hilda chuckled. 'By September she'll have shot up a couple of inches and grown in other directions too, no doubt.'

Lucy frowned. Her mother clearly had more faith than she did.

Marion and Paul left the next day. The house was quieter without them. Lucy was sitting at the table, writing to Melanie, when Hilda sat down beside her.

'How do you feel about becoming a teenager? How do you think you'll cope with growing up?'

Lucy doodled in the margin of her letter. As far as she was concerned, her thirteenth birthday would be just another day, at the end of which she would still be the same person. She would wake up in the morning, and be no taller, no fatter, and no different, inwardly or outwardly. So what was there to cope with? She said nothing, absent-mindedly chewing her pen.

'Don't do that!' snapped Hilda, 'Act your age, for goodness sake! I know what thirteen-year-olds can be like.'

Her mother's sudden change of mood was puzzling. Lucy recalled the stormy scenes between Hilda and Marion, years before.

Hilda clicked her tongue. 'I never had the chance to hurt my mother and – God only knows – she was so loving, so kind, so gentle. Too good for this world.'

'But I'm not Marion, Mum,' Lucy said, quietly.

'You had better not turn out like her. I couldn't take it a second time. I was happy until my mother died. At your age, I kept a diary. I wrote how wonderful it felt to be thirteen, my whole life before me and so much to live for. Uncle Peter and I never had new clothes, nor even enough food, but we had each other – and Mother...' Hilda's voice faded to a whisper.

Lucy said nothing.

'You have your life before you, Lucy, so live it to the full,' Hilda concluded, getting up from the table.

Lucy's thirteenth birthday dawned dry and fine. On waking, she crept out of bed and crept into the living room, where a small pile of white envelopes and wrapped gifts lay on the dining-table. Lucy felt a ripple of excitement. Hilda appeared from the kitchen, saying, 'Many happy returns of the day, Lucy. Sorry there aren't many presents, as funds are still short.'

'It doesn't matter. Thanks, Mum.'

Lucy opened the presents – a white, imitation leather handbag and white gloves from Marion, and from her parents two pairs of school socks, a box of chocolates, pens, pencils and notepads.

'I like simple, useful things,' Lucy said, 'I don't need anything big and expensive.'

Lucy spent the morning helping prepare sandwiches, stuffed tomatoes, and fruit salad. After lunch, she waited eagerly for the guests to arrive. Nigel came first, with three boys Lucy had never met. The lads were happy to chat among themselves and look around the garden. Then Valerie and Paula from Guides arrived, and Megan from school. By half past two, everyone had arrived, except Alison. Lucy thanked her guests for their cards and gifts of sweets, flowers, note pads and pens. Lucy counted twelve cards in all, including those from family and friends elsewhere. Lucy was hoping for a thirteenth card to perfect her thirteenth birthday.

The guests wandered around the garden in twos and threes, like visitors to a public park, exchanging pleasantries, petting the dog, and admiring the view. Lucy felt like an ignored outsider, Great-Gatsby-like, alone in a home-grown crowd. It was a relief when Hilda invited everyone into the house for games. Everyone behaved politely, but the group didn't gel. The girls sat and talked in one corner of the room, and the boys congregated in the other, occupying the settee and the armchairs. *But where was Alison?* Lucy had a hunch something was wrong. She tried to be happy, but her dark cloud of despondency didn't lift. Even the operations game, which raised a few smiles and polite laughs, wasn't hilariously funny.

After the games, Hilda put on "The Sound of Music" record, hoping the guests would dance, but nobody did.

'When's the grub going to be served?' mumbled one of Nigel's friends.

'I'm starving!' one of the lads said.

'Food in five minutes!' Hilda called from the kitchen.

The group instantly relaxed. The boys asked Valerie and Paula what they liked to watch on television, closing the divide in the middle of the room. The sexes slowly mingled, and even mouse-like Megan chatted with one of the lads.

The buffet was enjoyed by all, the plates quickly emptying. By half past four, Alison still hadn't appeared, and Lucy concluded she wasn't coming. With mixed feelings, Lucy watched the sausage rolls, stuffed tomatoes, crisps, peanuts, vol-au-vents and ham sandwiches disappear. At least everyone else was happy.

Happy Birthday was duly sung, Lucy extinguished all thirteen tiny candles on the cake with one puff, and everyone cheered Hip-Hip-Hooray!

The cake was one of Hilda's special, two-tier Victoria sandwich sponges, baked with extra free-range eggs, filled with strawberry jam and buttercream, and topped with vanilla icing. Hilda divided the cake equally, and there were lots of compliments. Lucy demolished her slice in seconds. Strangely, after eating plenty, she felt no fuller. In fact, she seemed to be perpetually hungry of late.

One by one, the guests were leaving, expressing their thanks and appreciation.

'I've put some food aside in case Alison turns up,' Hilda said. Lucy didn't answer, wavering between anxiety over Alison's wellbeing and disappointment at her absence. There hadn't even been a telephone message. Lucy stared at the pile of used plates and the scattering of crumbs on the floor.

'I'll help tidy up,' she said.

The doorbell buzzed faintly in the background.

Lucy raced to the door.

There stood Alison, in jeans and T-shirt, Cedric at her side, on the lead.

'Sorry I'm late,' Alison panted, 'I had to bring Cedric. I hope you don't mind – he hasn't had a walk all day. It's just that – there wasn't time to take him out...'

Alison's voice quavered. Lucy suddenly felt stupid wearing the pink floral frock with frilled sleeves – the same dress she had worn on her tenth birthday. It had been too big, back then. Now it fitted perfectly, as a long blouse over her blue jeans.

'Anyway, happy birthday,' Alison said, handing Lucy a package and card.

'Thanks,' Lucy said. She opened the package, revealing a necklace of brightly-coloured beads and a matching bracelet.

'Thanks, Alison – they're lovely.'

'You're welcome,' Alison said, forcing a smile.

'I'm glad you came I'm also glad you brought Cedric. He's always welcome here. Come on in, we've kept some food for you.'

In the breakfast room, Hilda offered Alison a plate of goodies and a cup of tea.

'Thanks, Mrs Wylie,' Alison replied. She picked daintily at the food.

'Aren't you hungry?' Lucy asked.

'Not especially – sorry, it's just not been a good day.'

Hilda closed the kitchen door. Out of earshot of the remaining guests, Alison explained, 'Today we had some very bad news – my Granddad – he died suddenly. We're all in a state of shock. He is – er- was – quite old I suppose at sixty-four...'

'Oh dear, I'm sorry,' Lucy said, trying to sound sympathetic. She'd never known her grandparents.

'I wanted to come,' Alison said, 'but I felt a party wouldn't be right thing at this time, but in the end Mum said I might as well go. I'm glad I came.'

When all other guests had gone, Alison stayed to help with the dishes, then left at dusk.

That night, as Lucy settled for bed, she reflected happily on the day. Alison had come after all, and with thirteen cards, the celebration was complete.

However, Lucy felt no different. *Being a teenager isn't such a big deal* she thought, drifting into a deep sleep.

6: THE SCHOOL OF LIFE

Early in May, on her forty-fifth birthday, Hilda awoke with a feeling this would be a good day. In the morning, Lucy handed her a home-made card with a colourful drawing of fruit, flowers and teacups, and gifts of hand cream and chocolate peppermint creams. Lucy set off for school at half past eight, humming tunes from "The Sound of Music".

After a hassle-free school day, Lucy came home to an atmosphere of intangible joy. Hilda was in the kitchen making tea, singing 'O Dan – ny Boy, the – pipes, the – pipes are ca – al – ling...'

Hilda paused.

'I have good news,' she said.

'What?' Lucy asked, recalling the day of the Driving Test victory.

'I have a job!'

'Where?'

'Assistant wages clerk at Mayfield Electrics, Nyehaven.'

'Nyehaven? Isn't that a bit far?'

'Not really, just twenty minutes by car.'

'When do you start?'

'Monday morning. At today's interview, I was offered the job, a fitting birthday gift,' Hilda chuckled. 'They asked me about my education. I told them I had a very good school. What school? they asked. The school of life, I told them, which made them laugh. Mr Underwood lives in a modern mansion beside the factory. He treats his workers with respect, so it'll be a step up from working for that old codger Maverick. It's full time and the pay's better, so we'll be more financially secure. Still not a penny from Charles's estate! I don't think much of that solicitor who's supposed to be handling everything. I couldn't trust him further than I could throw Big Ben.'

'Mr Morton was Charles's friend,' Albert said.

'I don't care who he was! With friends like that, who needs enemies?'

'Any post today?' Lucy asked, hoping for a letter from Melanie or Margaret.

'I don't know, unless the postman came when we were out.'

Lucy went to check the mail, returning a minute later with one letter.

'Sussex postmark,' Lucy said.

'Joan's handwriting. I wonder what she has to say?' Hilda mused.

'You open it, dear,' said Albert, stubbing out a cigarette.

Hilda tore open the envelope.

'Well, well, well...' she gasped, 'Anne is getting married! Two weeks before Marion! Joan writes, Anne was swept off her feet, but she's sure she's found the right man...'

'Another wedding!' Lucy exclaimed. 'Can we go?'

'I think we can manage a trip to Fordham a fortnight before Marion's wedding,' Hilda insisted. 'It would be a shame to miss Anne's wedding. They'd be offended if we didn't come.'

Albert lit another cigarette. 'These young women,' he mumbled. 'Always in a rush to race to the altar.'

'Anne's man must be quite a guy to sweep her off her feet so suddenly,' Lucy said.

Hilda's eyes narrowed. 'Haven't you any homework to do?'

It was a rhetorical question. Lucy went to her room, smiling. Homework was no chore when life was this interesting. Last winter's dark, miserable days seemed a lifetime away. Hilda's new job meant dinner was later – a mad rush on Fridays, before Guides.

One Saturday Captain Merryweather organised a hike on Appledore Down. Watching Lucy enjoy barbecued sausages and camp-fire songs, Hilda suspected Lucy's studies might be figuratively on the back burner. Hilda's suspicions were correct. The next day, Lucy spent the afternoon with Alison in Biddlecombe Copse.

'You're wasting too much time at that Kaffir hut in the woods,' Hilda snapped when Lucy arrived late for tea.

'What's a Kaffir hut?'

'Don't you know what a Kaffir is?'

'I don't know, that's why I asked.'

'A Kaffir is a south African tribesman. Everyone knows that, and so should you. You don't read enough. You're always out playing like an irresponsible child.'

Lucy munched silently on her salad. *Alison's parents aren't strict*, she thought. Lucy didn't engage in backchat, and Hilda thought Lucy looked suitably repentant, so the conversation ended there. However, Lucy's exam results weren't outstanding. She marginally failed Mathematics and Environmental Science, so Hilda insisted Lucy spend extra study time in the evenings, to which Lucy quietly acquiesced.

School life was improving. As Alison's friend, Lucy was gaining respect among her peers, but her guard was down. Games lessons were tolerable now, with summer activities of tennis, athletics and swimming. Since the move there'd been little opportunity for swimming practice, just a couple of summer beach trips, never the lido. 'I can't stand public baths', Hilda said, 'because you catch verrucas, and the chlorine gets up your nose'. Westcombe Lido was a far cry from the modern, indoor pool where Lucy had learnt to swim, a year before. In the dank, cavernous changing-room, she endured the cold, gritty feel of sodden wooden slats underfoot. The windowless space reeked of a single, malodorous toilet, but nobody grumbled. Within minutes, twenty giggling girls were ready in caps and costumes and hurrying out into the brilliant June sunshine.

The pool's azure surface was mirror-smooth, awaiting the intrusion of a score of thrashing bodies. Lucy surveyed the cold, blue rectangle with apprehension. Miss Forbes drew the group to attention. Competent swimmers were ordered to the deep end, everyone else told to spend time usefully in the shallows. Staying close to the edge, Lucy swam halfway up the pool and back again, pausing briefly to rest. Nobody bothered her. When the whistle sounded, everyone climbed out and stood dripping at the water's edge. Miss Forbes commended each pupil for their efforts, and Lucy was pleasantly surprised to hear she had earned a certificate for swimming twenty-five yards. *So she was watching me swim!* Glowing with pride, Lucy was totally unprepared for the hostility awaiting her in the changing room.

'What's wrong with you?' Abigail asked. 'No girl of thirteen is that flat chested.'

'Girls are supposed to develop a bust,' Rosemary added, fastening her size 34A Lucky Check bra. 'I'm not particularly big, but she's way too small.'

A barrage of voices chimed in unison.

'She – I mean it – isn't normal!'

'It will probably grow a willy...'

'Yeah – Lucy Willy!'

'Weird!'

'Freaky!'

'A les!'

'Yeah – a lesbian!'

Gales of laughter filled the stagnant air. Lucy had no idea what a lesbian was, but she was sure it must be something quite dreadful. She resolved secretly to find out. She would do chest-developing exercises, eat more protein, buy a bra and pad it with cotton wool. Later, Lucy spoke with her mother alone. Hilda had gone to bed early, complaining of a headache, but Lucy crept into the darkened room and sat at the foot of the bed. Hilda lay motionless, a cold compress over her forehead.

'What is it you want, dear?' Hilda whispered.

'I – I just wondered if you – er – needed anything.'

'No thanks, I don't need anything. But what is it you really want?'

Lucy cleared her throat. 'Mum, how old were you when you started wearing a bra?'

'I suppose I must have been about fourteen. It was after I'd left school and started work. There was no way I could afford one before then.'

'But when did you actually need one?'

'I'm not even sure if I even need one now! But I think I was about thirteen when I first started getting a bit bigger up there.'

Lucy's heart sank.

'But you don't need to wear one yet, do you?' Hilda asked.

'No, but when do you think I will?'

'All in good time.'

'How old was Marion when she needed one?'

'Fourteen or fifteen? But you honestly needn't worry.'

'But everyone at school is much bigger than me, and they say there's something wrong with me.'

'Someone has to be the smallest. You'll grow, soon enough. I know, we'll go to Nyehaven to buy you new clothes in the summer sales. By then you'll probably have grown an inch or two.'

'Thanks, Mum, I'd love that.'

Lucy was appeased, for now. She had food for her stomach and food for thought. Her appetite was good, and in her mother's kitchen, there was never a shortage of healthy meals and satisfying snacks. Upper body strengthening exercises were needed. Swimming was good. Horse-riding? Girls at school were horse-mad, a few privileged enough to own a horse, including Abigail, whose parents owned a farm near Nyehaven. Alison and Joanna went to Westcombe Riding School. However, riding lessons were prohibitively expensive, a course of twelve lessons costing six guineas. Lucy faced a wall of despondency.

Suddenly she had an idea. *I'm thirteen now, so maybe I can get a job?* Alison boasted about generous tips from waiting on tables in The Merry Teapot, but she was the proprietor's daughter, so maybe that was different? But the idea didn't go away.

Lucy found her mother seated in the lounge, quietly shelling peas from the garden. Lucy hovered behind the wing of the armchair.

'What is it, dear? I can tell you want to talk.'

'I've been thinking – about – looking for a little part time job in the holidays – serving teas, cleaning, fruit-picking?'

'Lucy, that's a wonderful idea! I'd far rather you spent time working than idling at home. And you can start saving money.'

'Thanks, Mum!' Lucy threw her arms about her mother, sending the colander of peas scattering across the floor.

'Don't forget your studies!' Hilda warned.

'I won't, Mum, I promise.'

On Saturday, Lucy cycled to town, determined to find work within the hour. Several inquiries at restaurants, tea rooms and shops yielded polite refusals. *I only need one job* Lucy told herself. Then she saw a notice in a tea room window.

WANTED

WAITRESSES

Apply Within

Lucy parked her bicycle and marched boldly through the open door. A mature woman in white cap and apron stood at the counter, polishing chrome teapots.

'Excuse me – I've come about the advertisement in the window.' Lucy's voice sounded small and insignificant. The counter loomed. Shelves with cups, jugs, and teapots towered behind it.

'I'll tell the manageress. She could do with extra help. She's not been well lately.'

Lucy tried to look sympathetic. 'I'm sorry to hear about that.'

Moments later a shrew-like, elderly lady appeared, wearing a sagging navy blue suit and horn-rimmed glasses.

'I don't want you, you're too young,' she said crisply.

'B – but, I'm thirteen –' Lucy protested.

'I said, you're too young,' the old woman repeated, showing Lucy the door.

The sharp rebuff spurred Lucy on to the esplanade. Half a dozen fruitless inquiries later, a rotund supervisor in overalls showed her an ice cream parlour that rocked with noise from the jukebox in a greasy, steam-filled cafeteria. The pay was minimal, with no tips or perks.

'We need dish-washers. You can start right away if you want,' the woman said.

The offer took Lucy by surprise.

'Er – I'll um- think about it and let you know,' Lucy answered, then cycled home, her disappointment masked by hunger and exhaustion.

'You could try the local farm?' Hilda suggested over lunch. 'It would be much closer than going all the way to town.'

'You might be right,' Lucy answered.

'There's a documentary tonight about the lunar mission,' Albert said. In all the recent distractions Lucy had almost forgotten about the Space Programme.

'Pleeeease can I stay up and watch it?' Lucy looked imploringly at her mother.

Hilda nodded. 'Of course you can.'

Absorbed in the Apollo Eleven mission, Lucy shelved her search for work. In the wee, small hours of the last Monday of term, she was woken to witness Neil Armstrong and Buzz Aldrin's first faltering steps on the Moon. The footage was blurred, hazy, and apparently in slow motion. No scintillating music, just the astronauts' blurred voices, a series of bleeps, and fuzzy, live commentary from Houston, Texas, United States, Planet Earth. Two humans in cumbersome-looking space suits galumphed semi-weightless, in the low gravity of another planet – at this very moment! History in the making – an iconic moment in Space and Time.

'It looks like a badly made science fiction film,' Lucy mumbled from the depths of the sofa.

'Not science fiction – science truth!' Albert said.

'An unprecedented achievement for mankind!' Hilda added.

'Truly wonderful,' Lucy whispered, trying to retain as much as possible of those monumental events, which for every other spectator on Earth would soon be mere memory.

'Space travel has begun' Lucy said. 'One day, people might go on holiday to Mars? Or maybe other galaxies, like on *Dr Who* or *Star Trek?*'

'Don't be ridiculous,' Hilda said.

The next day, Earthly affairs seemed on hold. Sleep-deprived and stupefied, students moved at snail's pace, mimicking the slow manoeuvres of astronauts. Lessons were as usual.

'Avez-vous vu les hommes, qui marchaient sur la lune?" Madame Mantes asked jovially.

'Oui, oui, Madame!' Rosemary guffawed. Her friends grinned. The atmosphere of jollity continued. At break, students opened their lockers, revealing favourite pictures stuck on the doors.

'Oh, Neil!' Sandra Bright, sighed ecstatically at a magazine cutting of her latest heart-throb. 'You're my hero!"

Rosemary and Joanna sniggered at the image of Neil Armstrong. Sandra slammed the locker door.

'But he can't be your boyfriend, he's married,' Megan said quietly.

'I don't care – he's just so dreamy,' Sandra crooned.

'I prefer George Harrison myself,' Joanna said.

'That's a first for you!' scoffed Jodie, 'I always thought you prefered horses!'

'Joe Cocker is my hero,' Rosemary drawled, 'but what about Lucy? Who does she fancy?'

'No one would fancy her, that's for sure,' Joanna sneered.

Fortunately, Abigail wasn't nearby, or the outcome would doubtless be worse. Lucy slammed her locker door, but it was too late. Joanna had noticed a photo of Dotty.

'She's got her dog in there!'

'It must be a very small dog...'

'Her pin-up is a dog?'

'Hey man – that's really weird!'

'She fancies dogs?'

'Always knew she was a screwball.'

Fighting back tears, Lucy hurried to class. Word had already spread that Lucy Wylie was ripe and ready for ribbing. On her desk was a folded scrap of paper with unfamiliar handwriting. Assuming it to be someone's lesson notes, Lucy was about to take the note to the teacher's desk, when Abigail rose cobra-like from her seat.

'What's that?' Abigail asked.

Lucy shuddered. Abigail snatched the note and said, 'Read it out loud so we can all hear.'

'No,' Lucy replied firmly.

'Why not?' demanded Abigail, 'You wrote it, didn't you?'

'I'm not saying anything,' Lucy whispered, floundering in fear.

'Just as I thought,' Abigail sneered, turning to her supportive audience. 'Either she can't read or she's lying.'

Alison made no attempt to defend Lucy. Joanna laughed loudly, obscuring a timid voice at the front of the room.

'Come on, girls, sit down now, please.'

The Latin teacher, Miss Hipp, a new arrival since Easter, had entered the room. Said piece of paper fluttered to the floor under the desk of one of the boys.

'Page twenty, exercise four,' Miss Hipp continued softly. Students slouched and yawned. No one took notice of this newcomer in a purple mini skirt, and red-and-yellow paisley blouse – a young teacher as relaxed and modern as Mr Kingsley was strict and old-fashioned. Nobody believed Hipp was a real name. It was rumoured she changed it by Deed Poll because she was a Hippie, but Lucy checked the telephone directory afterwards and found the name Hipp did exist.

'Today, I'd like you to do the translation, *The Augean Stable*,' Miss Hipp announced, her voice swallowed in conversations about the lunar landings. Lucy stared at the printed page, noticing how few letters with tall stalks were in the Latin passage – hardly any 'b's 't's or 'd's.

'The orgy in the stable!' chortled Rosemary, raising a few laughs.

Lucy's mind wandered. Something had to be done about her body size and shape. She envisaged the bridesmaid's dress hanging sack-like on her bony shoulders, and everyone staring at her, laughing. Perhaps there actually was something wrong with her? A serious handicap – or a fatal disease?

Lucy was very quiet for the rest of the school day. That evening, she sat for a long while on the hilltop stile, beyond the garden, contemplating the sunset over Westcombe Bay. Inventing lamenting lyrics, she sang in a low voice,

Goodbye, goodbye!

Dare I raise a hand to wave the world goodbye?

The sun sets on the shimmering sea,

Nature's beauty surrounds me, but sad and all alone,

I sit and watch that Golden Ball go down.

Concluding the swan-song of her youth, Lucy stood up and walked away.

At High Lea Farm, a five-minute walk away, Lucy knocked on the door of the stone-gabled farmhouse.

The door was opened by the farmer's round-faced wife.

'Well now, you're the little girl from up the road, aren't you? What can we do for you?'

Lucy resented being called little, but at least she wasn't being told to go away.

'I was wondering if you need any help with strawberry picking?' she asked.

'We could use an extra pair of hands. Just go to the barn, Mr Wilson's in there and he'll show you what to do.'

Thank you,' Lucy replied, scarcely believing how easy it had been to net a job, virtually on her doorstep. In the barn, she was handed a wicker basket.

'Allow half an inch of stem when you pick the strawberries, and pick only the ripe ones,' Mr Wilson instructed.

'I'll pick as many as I can,' Lucy said.

She worked swiftly. Breaking the stems with chewed fingernails was difficult. Lucy longed to conquer her life long habit of nail-biting. With dusty knees and aching back, she lost track of time, filling baskets and leaving them with Mr Wilson at the edge of the field.

Finally, she stopped. 'Um, I've picked eight baskets,' she mumbled nervously.

'That's two hours' work,' Mr Wilson said, handing Lucy four half-crown coins. 'We're always here, so just come and ask. When the strawberries are finished there'll be potatoes to lift.'

'Thank you, thank you very much,' Lucy responded ecstatically.

Ten shillings! The reward mercifully eclipsed the day's painful scenes at school. Having a paid job was as thrilling as learning to swim or passing the Eleven Plus. Lucy raced home to tell her parents.

'Well done,' Hilda said, and Lucy basked with pride at being part of the world's workforce.

The school year almost over, affairs were winding down. Proud to be included in the swimming gala, Lucy swam one length of the pool, earning one point for her house. Doubtless, her aura of serenity was noticed, for no one bothered her, and on leaving the changing-room, Lucy was in for a pleasant surprise. Alison tapped her on the shoulder and asked,

'Hey, Lucy! Are you still looking for a holiday job? My dad says he can give you a job if you're still looking.'

'I would love that,' Lucy gabbled, almost choking with excitement.

'Come round after school and Dad'll sort something out for you.'

Lucy saw herself in a white cap and apron, serving teas, waiting on tables, earning good money and generous tips. She dreamed of saving up for horse-riding lessons, a telescope, a reel-to-reel tape recorder, even a typewriter.

The Merry Teapot resembled a modest shop with two display windows and a single door up a flight of three mosaic steps. A spacious dining area filled with Formica tables and wooden chairs extended to the back of the building, where one small sash window gave light to a raised area with four more tables. At the tea servery, white china gleamed, aluminium urns bubbled. Mrs Rodgers and her daughter Sandra served families, elderly folk, and happy tourists with home baking and afternoon tea.

'Afternoons are quiet, as are the mornings,' Mr Rodgers explained. 'It's the mid day slot we need help with, when we serve hot meals.'

Lucy was led through the kitchens to the scullery and introduced to Mr Henderson, a stout, balding man in a striped butcher's apron, his arms submerged to the elbows in a sink full of pans.

Mr Rodgers towered over his ageing employee and said, 'Lucy will be your new lunch time assistant.'

To Lucy, Mr Rodgers said, 'Mr Henderson will keep you on track. Your hours will be midday to one-thirty-two-o'clockish, depending how busy we are and how fast you work. You will be paid one guinea in cash at the end of each shift, plus a free hot dinner and a dessert.'

'Thank you,' Lucy said, feeling a tad disappointed. She wasn't to be a waitress like Alison, which seemed unfair, since Alison was younger, albeit by a few weeks. *Perhaps everyone starts off working in the scullery?* Lucy wondered.

Mr Henderson dried his hands on his apron and gave Lucy a polite, firm handshake.

'It gets very busy in here,' Mr Rodgers warned. 'You'll need to work fast. It can be busy at the tea servery too, so you might also work there. Do you have any questions?'

'Er – no, I don't think so at the moment.'

'That's settled, then. You can start on Saturday.'

'Congratulations,' Alison smiled, 'you're one of the team now!'

Lucy's self-esteem rocketed.

'Hey – Dad!' Alison caught her father's attention. 'I was about to ask Lucy if she wants to try the Combe Ridge to Tullington Cove walk with me, on Saturday.'

'I'd like that,' Lucy said.

'Please say yes!' Alison persisted. 'Cedric will be out from under your feet all day.'

Mr Rodgers shrugged his shoulders. Winking at Lucy, he said, 'A fine thing, I must say. The minute you're offered a job, you ask for the day off. Go on then, I'll let you off. You can start on Sunday instead.'

7: THE ROARING SEA

On Saturday, Lucy awoke to bright sunshine and the lowing of cattle. Her eyelids flew open, a tide of excitement engulfed her. *Tullington Cove!* The very name conjured up visions of a beach bursting with beauty and secrets. Lucy sprang out of bed and rummaged in the chest of drawers for clothes.

Hilda brought in a pink, roll-neck sweater. 'It's breezy today, so dress warmly. How about this?'

'But that's yours. It'll be too big.'

'Try it on.'

Lucy pulled the sweater over her head. As expected, it was baggy and reached her hips, and the sleeves were too long.

'Roll the cuffs over, that's it – it suits you.'

'Thank, Mum.' The colour was vibrant and conspicuous, but Lucy liked it. Hilda prepared a packed lunch and persuaded Lucy not to bring the dog on such a long, unfamiliar walk. After breakfast, Lucy set off down the cross-meadow footpath towards the town. The school campuses were silent and still in morning mist that rose wraith-like above trees and rooftops, disappearing into azure skies. Ring-necked doves hooted in unison, competing with squabbling gulls on the station roof. A two-carriage train rumbled into the station, a few tourists alighted. Breathless with excitement, Lucy dodged traffic and pedestrians, until she reached the esplanade. Alison was sitting barefoot below the pier steps, trainers and rucksack at her side. Of Cedric, there was no sign. Lucy loped down the steps as fast as her legs would carry her.

'Alison! Have you been waiting long? Sorry I didn't bring Dotty.'

'No worries,' Alison said, 'I only just got here. I changed my mind about bringing Cedric. Dogs can run faster than us, but they don't have the strength to keep walking all day in hot weather. Today's going to be a roaster, so we'd better get going!'

Lucy doubted she had the stamina to cope with a long walk planned by athletic Alison, who even barefoot, dwarfed Lucy by four inches. A sharp breeze whipped up the waves, the ebbing tide left smooth sands soft and springy. Lucy took off her sweater and tied it round her waist. She removed her shoes and felt the warm sand underfoot.

Passing a group of holidaymakers in deck chairs Alison whispered,

'Let's pretend we're French! We'll recite one of those dialogues we learned with Madame Mantes!'

Lucy nodded. 'Okay!'

'C'est bien la semaine prochaine qu'on va partir en vacances?' Alison began in her best accent.

'Oui, les billets et les passeports sont dans la valise.' Lucy responded fluently.

A few heads turned.

'Well, that worked,' Alison sniggered. 'People always stare at foreigners.'

Beyond the town, the strand bordered towering sandstone cliffs. Gulls wailed overhead, and tiny wavelets lapped on the glistening shore.

'By the way, I've always meant to ask what your middle name is,' Alison asked, suddenly breaking the silence. 'What does the R stand for?'

Lucy had an answer ready.

'Rena,' she replied, giving an abbreviated version of her middle name, Renate – a German name chosen by her mother, meaning born again.

'That's an old-fashioned name,' Alison replied, 'but middle names often are, and our parents pick them. Shirley Johnson's middle name is Emily, and that's really out of date.'

'Some names come back into fashion,' Lucy commented prophetically. 'What's your middle name?'

'June.'

'That's nice. It makes me think of summer.'

'My birthday's in June.'

'Is it? I missed it,' Lucy said, feeling guilty and excluded.

'I didn't do much. I just went to Tiffin's tea-room for coffee and doughnuts with Rosemary and Joanna. We had a laugh and then went horse-riding.'

'That's nice,' Lucy repeated, surprised Alison's parents hadn't organised a party.

A longer pause in conversation. Below sheer cliffs, the beach was practically deserted. Two miles distant, the crowd of sunbathers on Westcombe Beach appeared as a colour-sprinkled flower border.

'Combe Point can only be crossed at low tide,' Alison said.

Doubtless, Alison knew this walk well, or did she?

Alison seemed to read her thoughts. 'The tide's coming in. People have been known to be stranded here, and currents are very strong around the headland.'

Alison's tone was almost casual. Torn between fear of drowning and being dubbed a weakling, Lucy said, 'I have my first swimming certificate and took part in the gala.'

Alison sniffed. 'Anyone can swim a length of that pathetic little fish tank. I've done my Bronze Medallion, and now I'm working on the Silver. We dive in, wearing clothes over swimming costumes, and pretend to rescue someone.'

They approached the headland in silence. Lucy's toes clung tightly to shifting shale. In six inches of water, she felt the sea's bracing chill and the disquieting tug of an unseen current. Her courage wavered. This wasn't like the time they waded out from Westcombe shore in March. This time Alison had the edge.

A brisk breeze swept strands of hair across Lucy's face, obscuring her vision. The sun was high in the sky, the cliff face rose dramatically, casting a dark shadow on the rippling waters. Out on the open sea, waves were cresting. The current grew stronger, rocks and sand more slippery. Lucy leaned on a low outcrop of seaweed-strewn rocks, to maintain balance. A vast body of azure sea surrounded her, drawing her towards its quaking maw of indigo gloom. Petrified, she wished with all her being she hadn't come.

'Get ready to swim through fifty yards of freezing currents around the corner,' warned Alison. 'There's no beach at the other side. The cliff goes straight down into the water.'

Lucy froze. 'B – but –' she began.

'Ha! That had you worried for a minute!' Alison laughed aloud above the slapping waves. At that moment, they rounded the corner to brilliant sunshine. Lucy felt a comforting eddy of warmer water swirl around her feet. There was no sign of the promised deep waters. Instead, a wide swathe of smooth, yellow sand stretched ahead to the yellow curve of Tullington Cove.

Lucy gave a false, nervous laugh, and kept walking, feeling the sand soft and warm between her toes. Tiny, white cottages on the shore were slowly drawing closer.

'Not far now. Soon we'll be sitting comfortably, enjoying our cream tea,' Alison said, with a smile showing a line of perfect teeth.

'Yes, we will,' Lucy answered, tight-lipped, comforted by the grainy feel of shell-rich sand underfoot. She feasted her eyes on the picture-postcard-perfect scene of golden sands, red cliffs, green hills, and pastel-blue skies. She wanted to capture the moment and regretted not having a camera. She began filling her bag and pockets with shells and pebbles, drawn by every colourful stone and pretty shell.

'I must tell my parents to come here,' she said, 'They'd love it. It's so quiet, and so beautiful.'

'We could make a sand castle?' Alison suggested. 'Or make a model of Cove Cottage tea rooms?'

'But I don't know what it looks like.'

'I do, though. I've been there thousands of times. It's a quaint, thatched cottage. I'll start.'

Alison knelt on the sand and began shaping a house, drawing forming a roof, chimney, windows and doors with the ease and expertise of a sculptor. *Alison's good at everything*, Lucy thought. Together they added tiny shells and stones and draped the roof with seaweed, then left their handiwork to its inevitable destruction by the incoming tide.

'A pity we can't take pictures of it,' Lucy said. As they left, she stooped to scrawl a message, adding her own touch of humour.

COVE COTTAGE

This model was built by Alison Rodgers & Lucy Wylie

(who are at this moment having lunch at Cove Cottage)

'You've a nerve!' Alison said. 'This isn't a sand castle competition. Do you expect people to come and find us and pay us?'

Puzzled, Lucy said nothing. Lunch at Cove Cottage was every bit as idyllic as she imagined. Cream tea served on a tray with a chrome teapot, white cups and saucers, and freshly baked scones with jam and fresh cream. They sat at an outside bench, overlooking the shore.

I'm going to eat my picnic, but we need to be discreet because it's not tea-room food,' Alison said, popping a small sausage roll in her mouth. She sipped her tea.

'Me too,' Lucy said, surreptitiously nibbling a sandwich.

They weren't caught. Lucy recalled the time Melanie coerced her to discard a fish-and-chip wrapping into a posh suburban garden.

'You look like you're enjoying this,' Alison remarked, 'and you've caught the sun – you're quite brown.'

Lucy looked at her freckled arms. 'I suppose so,' she replied, pleased to be complimented by someone unquestionably prettier.

'I wish I had your looks,' Lucy confessed.

'Perhaps you'll be better looking when you're older,' Alison replied.

Lucy stared at the shimmering sheet of sparkling diamonds, where yachts bobbed, white sails fluttering in the breeze.

'More tea?' Alison asked, filling the cups with the expertise of a seasoned hospitality worker.

'Please,' Lucy answered, shivering with apprehension at the thought of starting work the next day.

'It's good tea,' Alison said. 'It tastes better in the open air.'

'It does,' Lucy agreed. 'My mother says that every time we go on a picnic. We have a little meths stove and make the tea fresh. It tastes much better than from a flask.'

'It's a pity we don't have a tea urn at school. The teachers have one in their staff room. It's not fair. From some of the classrooms you can look across and see them all guzzling.'

'What do you think of the teachers?' Lucy asked.

'Most are okay. Mr Edgington's an old fuddy-duddy, Mr Jones a drunkard, Miss Hipp too soft, and Mr Kingsley too strict.'

'Agreed. I think Miss Hawksworth is an eccentric old biddy who has favourites.'

'I hate that too. It's clear she likes Janet Ford best. You were friends with Janet for a while, weren't you?'

'I was, but not for long.'

'That's no surprise. Janet's an insufferable swot. I don't like her at all, nor Jodie Maitland, who's an outrageous weirdo. So is Susan Schofield. I find her very rude and she uses far too many swear words.'

'You like Rosemary and Joanna, though?'

'Rosemary's always cheerful and Joanna's a good egg, if a little horse-mad.'

'Who's your best friend?' Lucy inquired, boldly.

'Rosemary, but I've plenty of other friends. You're included, along with Joanna, Helena, Fiona, and Abigail.'

Lucy shuddered. 'Am I a good friend?' she asked.

'You're a bit odd sometimes. You're okay, once people get to know you. It's hard for anyone coming new to a school. I didn't like you when you first came, because you were new.'

'You've got friends in other classes too, like Barbara Davies?'

'She's not really a friend. Her parents own a guest house and my mum gets on well with her mum. Barbara's far too snooty.'

'But she's grown up and sophisticated.'

Alison sniffed disdainfully. 'She likes to think so. She goes to that Christian Union. Anyone who goes there must think they're perfect, or at least better than everyone else.'

'I absolutely agree. You'll never find me at one of their meetings,' Lucy answered emphatically.

'Barbara was showing off the other day, and I thought Christians weren't supposed to do that.'

'What did she do?'

'She and Rosemary were boasting about periods and being grown up enough to have babies. I still can't.'

'Neither can I,' Lucy said, pleased to have found an ally in the league of late developers. Alison was taller than Lucy, but equally skinny and lacking in womanly curves.

'Come on,' urged Alison, 'Let's finish the scones and cream. Who knows? We might even put some weight on!'

Lucy grinned impishly, feeling full, but happily cramming the rest of her scone. She felt weary and unready for the long walk home and starting a new job the next day. Alison strode along effortlessly, but Lucy struggled on, weary and footsore. True to her pledge for self-improvement, she soldiered on uncomplaining.

The next day, at five to twelve, Lucy duly presented herself at the Merry Teapot. The working atmosphere in the scullery was congenial and brisk, and Lucy soon earned the sobriquet Little Lucy – the elf-like figure who zipped to and fro carrying piles of dirty dishes to Mr Henderson for washing, then ferrying a pile of warm, clean plates to Mr Rodgers, who toiled tirelessly over seething saucepans and bain-Marie meat trays. Lucy washed, rinsed and stacked plates, while Mr Henderson dealt with the heavy pots, pans and utensils. If shelves looked empty, Lucy replenished them. Soon she became adept at transporting towers of saucers stacked on plates, surprising everyone that such a small girl could be so strong and dexterous. At two-thirty, Lucy was rewarded with a hot lunch and her wages. Lucy ate the food, banked the money, then made for the beach.

Each day merged into the next. Lucy found she could carry a dozen cups – one cup hooked on each finger and thumb, plus an extra one between thumb and forefinger. Time management was crucial. Rush hour began at one o'clock, earlier on wet days, and reached its peak by two. Mr Henderson and Lucy redoubled their efforts, pre-empting the waitresses' complaining about nowhere to put dirty dishes, and Mr Rodgers demanding clean plates. Lucy helped with the arduous task of scrubbing huge aluminium pans. One was so enormous Lucy felt sure she would fit inside it. At shift end, she devoured steak-and-kidney pudding and a heavy dollop of treacle pudding and custard. Then, an afternoon alone in the beach crowd, a cycle ride home for tea, a quick shower, and a relaxing evening of TV. Thankfully, Hilda rarely asked her to do chores.

In the first fortnight, Lucy's reputation of being a thorough, efficient worker remained untarnished. Mr Rodgers' favourite command was, 'Faster, slaves!' It took Lucy a while to realise he was joking. She smiled at the notice on the kitchen wall:

QUICK LOOK BUSY - HERE COMES THE BOSS!

Lucy wasn't taking any chances. She took her work very seriously. On busy days, she worked an extra hour after lunch, tidying and cleaning the restaurant area, for which she was paid an extra ten shillings. Six days a week at the restaurant and one day at the farm was almost an addiction.

'Don't squander your hard-earned cash on trivia,' Hilda advised. 'Now you're older, you'll need to save for important things.'

'I've banked most of it and want to get a typewriter,' Lucy said.

'Excellent! That'll help you with your homework. A decent typewriter costs at least twenty pounds.'

'I'd also like a course of horse-riding lessons,' Lucy added quickly, 'and I'll need to buy wedding gifts for Marion and Paul, and for Anne.'

'And not forgetting your father's fiftieth birthday, the same day as Marion's wedding.'

'No, Mum. I hadn't forgotten.'

'Good, although I'm not too sure about the value of horse-riding lessons.'

Lucy didn't comment, having already set aside six guineas for horse-riding. After supper, she escaped unnoticed to the stables. Across a gravelled yard was a low, whitewashed building. Through the half-open door, Lucy glimpsed the proprietor Miss Crawford, in tweed jacket, check shirt, beige jodhpurs and mud-spattered leather boots.

'Come in, dear, we don't stand on ceremony here!' Miss Crawford sat at her desk, telephone receiver in one hand and a smouldering cigarette in the other. The airless room smelt heavily of leather and horses, its grimy, whitewashed walls festooned with cobwebs and faded rosettes hanging like forgotten Christmas decorations. Three girls slouched on a grubby settee in the corner. An overweight golden Labrador lay on the flagstones, snoring heavily.

Miss Crawford spun around on her swivel chair, a strand of greying auburn hair trailed across her aristocratic-looking face.

'So how may I help you, young lady?'

'I – I'd like to book a course of six l – lessons,' Lucy stammered.

'Have you ridden before?'

'No,' Lucy answered, blushing. There were muffled sounds of sniggering from the couch.

'Very well. I'll book you for six beginners' lessons. That will be six guineas, please.' Lucy placed the money on the table and was handed a booklet of yellow tickets.

'The beginners' hack meets here at ten o'clock sharp, every morning during the summer holidays, seven days a week. You must arrive fifteen minutes early to tack up. Use the tickets for whichever days you choose.'

'Thank you,' Lucy answered quietly.

Without looking back, she ran all the way home and presented her mother with a fait accompli.

'I've booked my horse-riding lessons,' Lucy said, trying to sound casual.

'WHAT?' Hilda's jaw dropped. 'What about the family presents? And your typewriter?'

'I'll still have enough money for all those things by the end of the holidays.'

Hilda shook her head. 'I sincerely hope so.'

Lucy was finding it increasingly hard to sleep. She lay awake for ages, listening to her parents going to bed, the Dalys' dog barking, and the sound of passing vehicles in the lane. Looking at the clock made things worse. *In eleven hours' time*, she thought fearfully, *I'll be at work again!* In fitful dreams of dirty dishes, foaming pans and cutlery trays, Lucy continued working, believing herself to be actually there, in the stifling heat of the scullery.

Her performance began to fall. One day, her clean record for never having broken a plate was ruined. Within two hours, she broke three plates and knocked the handle off a cup. At first, Mr Rodgers seemed forgiving, but Lucy was uneasy. She lived for afternoons at the beach, where she would doze off in the warm sunshine. It seemed to be the only time she had any proper rest. She regretted booking the riding lessons. Though the rides were pleasant, they added one more activity to her busy agenda. Alison was rarely at the beach, preferring to go out with friends or rest at home before the evening shift. After three weeks of washing dishes, Lucy hoped for the offer waitressing work, but that didn't happen. One day, half the restaurant was cordoned off, owing to staff shortage. Mrs Rodgers was at the hatch, serving teas.

'I could stand in for one of the waitresses?' Lucy suggested.

'You're needed in the kitchen,' was the abrupt reply. At half past twelve, she was faint with hunger. It was Mr Henderson's day off, so there was more to do. Stifling a yawn, Lucy leaned on the drainer, surveying the massive pile of waiting plates toppling precariously on the hatch. Business was booming, there were at least forty dishes and plates to be collected, doubtless requiring at least three or four trips. Lucy's legs felt like lead.

Her thoughts were broken by a harsh voice.

'Come on, buck up over there! You're not paid for standing around doing nothing,' Mr Rodgers growled. The words stung like whipcords. Mortified, Lucy defied every nerve and sinew that cried out for rest, ploughing on doggedly on a tide of self-deprecation, hunger, and fatigue. Such a small yet justified remark couldn't be ignored. Chastisement must be taken with dignity. Lucy longed for the stiff-upper-lip attitude which her mother so frequently preached. The masochistic wishes resurfaced. Furiously, she plunged her hands deep into the sink of scalding hot water, scrubbing, scouring, secretly hoping for an injury from submerged cutlery and an excuse to have time off and gain sympathy from others. At three o'clock, she sat alone to eat her lunch. Mr Rodgers paid her as usual, and nothing more was said about the slacking incident. Lucy left quickly, not wanting to come across Alison. She sought out a different part of the beach and lost herself in the crowd.

'Does bullying stop when you're grown up?' Lucy recalled asking her mother. 'Of course not', Hilda had said, in many ways it gets worse.' Lucy sighed. If life became any harder, it would be unbearable. The next day, all the waitresses were back on shift. At one o'clock, when Lucy was returning a dozen cups to the servery, she noticed Alison sitting on the stairs, sipping a cup of coffee and reading a magazine. Mrs Rodgers was nearby serving teas. Lucy wondered why waitresses were allowed breaks and dish-washers weren't. Perhaps there were different rules for the proprietor's daughters?

Lucy found it hard not to speculate and harder still, not to be angry.

In the afternoon, the beach was deserted, the sky overcast with chilly blustery showers. The tide was high, leaving little sand. In the lee of the sea wall, Lucy watched the tossing waves. Restless, grey waters leapt up to meet lashing rain, angry breakers thundered their wrath upon on the stony shore, reaching the pebbles below the promenade. Lucy sat transfixed, then stood up and stepped into the shallows, wading slowly. Each wave was a unique formation of energy, a spectacle worthy of her full attention. She observed from a distance of twenty yards, as a new, shadowy wave took shape, the slowly swelling, dark wall of water rising higher, its menacing crest tipped with quivering foam.

Poised carefully on her inflatable body-board, Lucy was ready. The wave plunged forward in a sweeping cascade, its energy catapulting her forward, the shock of cold water a threat of destruction. Then the exhilarating, rapid ride to foaming shallows – a thrill more exhilarating than the toboggan ride months before, and quickly over. Now a harsh rasping sound on sand and gravel that bit deep into her unprotected knees. The foaming tongue of the dying wave raced up the shingled slope, its angry hiss blending with pounding surf. Knee-deep in the cool, choppy shallows she felt the sharp sting of sand on her legs. Wind and current drew the waters into a sidelong flow. Carefully gauging distance and trajectory, Lucy stood poised as the next wave approached, its dark, menacing form gathering momentum for a predatory pounce. Lucy looked over her shoulder and took a deep breath. The wall of water rushed up, engulfing her. In one terrifying moment, all sense of direction was lost. Then Lucy felt herself buoyed up and pitching forwards, the sting of sharp stones tearing at bare flesh. Undaunted, she struggled to her feet, feeling the receding drag of undertow.

Alone on the deserted, turbulent shore, Lucy continued her argument with the elements for a further hour, then went home at the usual time, exhausted but refreshed. Under the shower, she washed off the sand, enjoying the gentler feel of cool spray in her hair, silently reliving her long session in the surf.

'Dinner in an hour!' Hilda called through the door.

'I won't be that long in here,' Lucy called back. Showered, dried and changed, she lounged on the sofa, ready to lose herself in the next episode of *Hawaii 5-O* – an apt and relaxing choice.

Sleep came quickly that night. The events of the past weeks crystallised into a strange sense of satisfaction and indomitable optimism. *Hard tasks and hard work will surely make me into a better person?* Lucy wondered, then dozed into oblivion.

8: SUMMER WEDDINGS

I n the rolling fields of High Lea Down the clanking of combine harvesters invaded sleepy summer days. In Edencroft's abundant garden, fruit and vegetables ripened under golden sunshine. Hilda had time off during the firm's summer shutdown, and Lucy reduced her working week to five days. As promised, Hilda took Lucy to Nyehaven for new clothes and essential wedding items. Lucy was excited, especially after her mother's passing remark that she was 'getting taller by the minute'.

The night before the shopping trip, Lucy couldn't sleep. The hours ticked in the greyness of her room, punctuated by the dog's rhythmic snores next door. Imaginary scenarios tantalised Lucy's overtired brain. She pictured an exhausting trail round stuffy, crowded department stores with her anxious, money-conscious mother clucking at her side, being seen and teased by bullies from school, losing her purse in the crowded street... Awake again, Lucy tried thinking about "The Sound of Music", pets, garden, and gently foaming surf on golden sands. She screwed her eyelids tight shut, but they immediately sprang open again. Long night hours stretched before her. The boredom of lying in bed doing nothing was insupportable. She tossed, turned, and scanned the gloom for a glimmer of dawn, thoughts tangling with the strange sensation of falling and having already fallen.

The sound of her mother's rapid footfalls heralded daybreak. The bedroom door opened.

'We must set off soon to beat the traffic and the crowds,' Hilda chivvied. 'Make sure you're ready by half past eight.'

Lucy hauled herself out of bed, longing for a completely free day in which to simply unwind.

Nyehaven nestled in the lee of the Westcombe hills, boasting salubrious seafront hotels and a pier twice the length of Westcombe's. A popular destination since Regency times, the town had since grown threefold, maintaining its original esplanade and tasteful architecture, its inland streets blending with low-rise businesses and modern homes. The steep High Street ran in a straight line from the town hall to the shore. Lucy guessed that beach time wouldn't be on her mother's schedule, so she didn't bother asking.

By nine o'clock the crowds were out, narrow pavements packed with strolling pensioners and harried housewives with wicker shopping-baskets. *Humanity's pageant*, Lucy recalled from a school poetry class. Nyehaven was far too busy for her liking.

'That van's just pulling out. Squeeze in there, and we'll be nice and near the shops,' Hilda told Albert.

'Yes, dear.' Albert said.

Good, Lucy thought *less walking, more time saved.*

The shops comprised popular chain stores and local businesses. Hilda insisted on traipsing through all the clothes shops, trying on outfits until she was fully satisfied she had good value for money. For the mother-of-the-bride outfit, she bought a beige, crimplene suit and a dark brown hat, and for Anne's wedding a high-necked, nylon shift dress in lilac satin. Lucy chose a pink crepe mini-dress with long, gathered sleeves and lace-up neckline with a pointed collar, which she assumed was the latest fashion.

The Nyehaven branch of Dawson's the Drapers was a vibrant Aladdin's Cave of clothes, fabrics, and needlework requisites.

'And now, Lucy, you can choose your lingerie – a bra, stockings and suspenders,' Hilda announced.

To Lucy's immense relief, the shop was empty, bar the assistant and two elderly ladies. Small bras were in stock, and Lucy was furnished with white lace nylon stockings, a broderie anglaise suspender belt, and a matching bra, in the smallest size, 30AA. Lucy purchased a white lace table cover for Marion and Paul, cushion covers for Anne, and a woollen scarf and gloves for her father, which totalled five pounds ten shillings and eleven pence, which Lucy duly paid, feeling immensely grown up.

Back home in the tranquillity of Edencroft, Lucy went into the garden and lay on her back, staring up at the summer sky. The evening air was filled with the perfume of roses, mingled with woody whiffs of burning vegetation from a nearby bonfire. Albert had made a fire near the hen run, and Hilda was hurrying down the garden to add a pile of paper and cardboard to the brazier. Lucy went indoors and found her new outfits spread out on the bed. She heard her mother come back and rummage noisily in her bedroom, apparently in ill temper. Lucy tried on the dress and stockings with her old open-toed slingback sandals, which still fitted after two years. The pink crepe dress felt stiff and uncomfortable and had a peculiar oily smell. The sleeves were slightly too long, so she rolled the cuffs over.

Then Hilda appeared in the doorway and said, 'Lovely! Give us a twirl.'

Lucy pirouetted distractedly and asked, 'Where's the bra, Mum?'

'Well, that's just the problem,' Hilda muttered vaguely. 'I can't find it anywhere. I know it wasn't left in the shop, as I distinctly remember seeing it in the bag.'

House, garden and car were thoroughly searched, and eventually, it was concluded the ill-fated garment had been scooped up with the rubbish and burned in the brazier.

'Never mind, dear,' Hilda said sheepishly, 'that makes you a liberated woman! However, I will buy you another bra.'

Lucy smiled through her disappointment.

On the next visit to Mrs Bailey, Lucy stood statue-like for the dress fitting. The soft crepe fabric tickled her skin, and the occasional tiny pin-prick sent shivers up her spine. Was it her imagination, or was the dress a little tighter than before? While the old granny fussed and tugged at the folds of the unfinished garment, Hilda smiled approvingly. Two small tucks in the bodice allowed for Lucy's non-existent bust. Lucy pouted and looked out of the window. Later, in the privacy of her bedroom, she tried on the suspender belt – upside down around her chest, linking the clasps on her shoulders, pretending it was a bra. It fitted neatly, although it seemed to serve no purpose. Lucy tried hard to imagine how it would look and feel to have breasts. She had heard startling stories about drastic changes in a girl's body during puberty, dramatic mood swings, and the desire to be near boys and men. Lucy took the suspender belt off, shrugged back into her child's T-shirt, and sighed. The notion of being physically attracted to another person was unimaginable. A while ago, Hilda had tried explaining to Lucy about love, marriage, and sex – the subject everyone at school seemed so obsessed with.

'Marriage is a sacred bond', Hilda said. 'Sex before marriage is a violation you would deeply regret'. The words echoed like a legal edict. Besides, the idea of sex seemed totally repugnant. Lucy couldn't imagine ever being close to anyone, emotionally or physically. A life of peace and harmony with nature was far more appealing than a life shared with another human being.

Though glad of a break from working, Lucy found Friday's long road trip to Fordham immensely tedious. By evening she was tense and tetchy.

'We're in Sussex now. Can we stop for a break soon?'

'Act your age!' Hilda snapped. 'Enough of your peevish wheedling! We already stopped once. You father wants to get there before dark.'

Lucy bit her lip and stared out at the twilit scene. They arrived at ten o'clock. Lights blazed from every window of the bungalow which rocked with the sound of voices and clumping feet. The night air heavy with fluttering insects and hooting owls. Only the dogs came out to greet the guests, everyone else indoors otherwise preoccupied. Joan had the usual pot of tea ready and waiting on the kitchen range, but there was no cooked meal, just snacks. While everyone else laughed and chatted, fretted and fumed, Lucy sat in a corner of the living room, nibbling on crackers and cheese. The magic of the Hills' rural idyll was gone. Compared with Edencroft, their bungalow was cramped and scruffy, the garden small and boring, the environment bland and lacking panoramic views. Shortly after eleven, the two youngsters were ordered to bed. The air in Anthony's room was stifling and faintly musty. A good night's sleep was wishful thinking.

'You're thirteen now, Lucy,' Anthony announced knowledgeably. 'That means you can still just about share a room with me, because you haven't got any private parts yet, but next time, we'll be put in separate rooms.'

'That's fine by me,' Lucy answered, fearing she may never acquire the private parts which Anthony seemed so eager to mention. He switched off the light, plunging the room into pitch darkness. Soon the sound of steady, rhythmic breathing assured Lucy that her inquisitive roommate had fallen asleep.

Lucy had never attended a wedding ceremony before. Years before, she had been to the wedding receptions of two of her parents' acquaintances. At one, Lucy had worn a yellow cotton frock and was photographed beside the bride – a tall brunette wearing a white gown and holding a bouquet of red roses. Lucy didn't like the photo. It showed her close-cropped hairstyle with a fringe that was too short, and her puckered, pouting face with the usual tight-lipped, false smile.

'Is getting married as exciting as going on holiday to the seaside?' Lucy had asked.

'Much more exciting than that!' Hilda had replied, but Lucy wondered what on earth could be better than a bucket-and-spade holiday by the sea?

In the next room, Anne was wide awake too, arguing with her mother about the buffet food and the guest list. Suddenly Anne shrieked, 'THERE'S A SPIDER, A BEETLE AND AN EARWIG IN HERE, AND IT'S NOT FAIR!'

Joan muttered a rebuke. Abrupt shuffling and clattering sounds followed, then all was quiet, but for the chirping of crickets below the open window. In the stifling heat, Lucy pulled off her pyjama top, leaving the bra, her upper body outside the covers. She slowly began to drift off. Something thudded on her bare arm. Lucy's flesh crawled. She sprang out of bed, groping in the darkness for the light switch and stumbled over a chair leg, triggering an avalanche of objects off a shelf.

Anthony snapped on the bedside lamp. 'What's up?' he demanded. 'It's not time to get up, it's still dark!'

'S – something landed on my bed – on my arm!' Lucy stuttered, torn between fear of the mysterious object and being seen by Anthony in her ill-fitting bra. She grabbed her top and held it close to her chest, trembling.

'Something was on the bed – it came from up there!' Lucy pointed to the dusty electric heater on the wall above the bed. Anthony looked around the room but found nothing.

'Nothing!' he declared firmly. 'Now we can get some sleep?'

Whatever it was that Lucy felt had disappeared – for now. Lucy was convinced a large spider had dropped from the redundant wall heater. Every muscle taut, she lay as stiff as a board, petrified, dreading a subsequent arachnid encounter. She lay awake for what seemed ages, then finally fell asleep.

In the morning Hilda was first to wake, roused by the raucous crowing of a cockerel. She yawned and stretched, sending a spent candle on a brass dish clattering to the floorboards, waking the household.

'What's that racket?' Albert demanded gruffly, stumbling out of bed, searching for his cigarettes. Dogs barked, doors opened, footsteps echoed down the hall, Joan's strident tones merged with yapping and clucking – a cacophony that reverberated through the bungalow. Anthony was snoring, adding to the dubious symphony. Lucy cowered under the covers, then dressed cautiously.

Predictably, the morning was a flurry of activity. Lucy felt she was in the way, so she retreated to the garden seeking solitude on the rope-swing and in the summerhouse. She was glad when lunch was ready. Afterwards, it was time to get changed and set off to the church, arriving as the village clock struck two. In the cool gloom of the medieval chapel, forty well-dressed wedding guests sat waiting. Ladies fanned themselves with hymn-sheets, stiff-shirted gentlemen sat awkwardly, and children whined and fidgeted. Lucy sat between her parents, looking around. Floral sprays decked stone plinths and window sills, reflected sunlight bounced off diamond-latticed panes, casting irregular pools of light on stone walls. White-noise whispers wafted beneath the vaulted ceiling. Minutes passed. The groom waited nervously at the front of the chapel, facing the altar, hands clasped behind his back.

Finally, the organ struck up the rousing strains of a well-known wedding march, and the assembled group fell silent. *Here comes the bride, all fat and wide...* Lucy thought, with a smirk, recalling a playground ditty from years before. Hilda threw Lucy a sidelong glance, and Lucy sniffed into her handkerchief, feigning an attack of hay fever. She turned slowly, looking behind her. Arm-in-arm with Arthur, Anne was walking down the aisle, resplendent in a flowing, white gown, her rosy face hidden beneath a veil of white lace – the perfect entrance for an idyllic, rural wedding. As the music faded, the quietly spoken clergyman announced something about a joyous occasion and treasured moments, the soft voice drowned by poor acoustics, inappropriate whispering, and untimely noises from infants. Lucy's attention wandered along the shafts of golden sunlight, her thoughts turning to Westcombe, London, and school. Quickly, she forced herself to focus on something else. She wondered how the dog was doing in kennels, and if Nigel Daly had remembered to feed the chickens and the cat.

The congregation rose and sang feebly to the dirge-like tempo of the out-of-tune organ. Hardly anyone seemed to know the hymn. Maybe they didn't enjoy singing? Weren't weddings supposed to be happy occasions? After the service, the mood changed dramatically. Amid shouts and peals of laughter, the guests spilt into the gravelled yard. Like rough-and-tumble schoolchildren newly released into the yard after harsh hours of lessons, the newly-weds screeched with glee, throwing flowers, ducking under a deluge of confetti and crazy-foam. The couple composed themselves briefly for the photographs. The peaceful, pastoral setting with its golden chestnut trees and fields of ripening corn seemed oddly out of place.

Slowly, everyone drifted across the car park to the timber-framed hall, where a sumptuous buffet lay spread upon rows of trestle-tables decked in pristine linen. The lofty, oak-beamed hall was filled with the babble of voices. Alcohol flowed freely, tongues were loosened and inhibitions cast aside. Lucy was offered a sip of sherry from Hilda's glass and was later allowed to finish it since Hilda was complaining of a headache. Her hunger appeased, Lucy waited impatiently for the reception to be over. The speeches came next, delivered in slurred tones, and then someone got up to sing a silly ditty and dance a drunken dance, triggering more roars of laughter. Lucy yawned and fumbled with the cord on her lace-up neckline, longing to be back home, in her everyday clothes, far away from this stifling, smoke-laden sweat-box of intolerable heat and noise. As the feast finished, guests dispersed, reeling and staggering past untidy tables, conversing garrulously. Lucy and her parents mingled with the crowd, watching from a safe distance, as cans of baked beans and jars of mustard pickle were emptied over the beribboned wedding car – a light blue Austin Mini. Then someone daubed the bridal car with Crazy Foam and tied old boots and tin cans to the rear bumper. Anne and her husband tumbled into the car and drove off noisily, cheered on by the cries of well-wishers.

That evening, Arthur and Joan expressed disappointment over Marion and Paul's absence from the wedding. Joan felt particularly slighted, as she was also Marion's godmother. Hilda did her best to explain Marion was busy trying to juggle a full-time job and preparations for her own imminent wedding. Joan just sniffed and carried on with the dishes. Lucy sat at the table, drinking tea, half listening.

'We'd better get an early night,' Hilda said. 'We have to be up early in the morning to beat the worst of the traffic. We've important things to do tomorrow.'

'Okay, I'll turn in now,' Lucy said, too tired to even be bothered by big spiders.

At seven o'clock, Lucy awoke from a deep sleep, taking a while to remember where she was. Events around her seemed tied up with a vivid dream – fragments of which kept surfacing, then vanishing.

At eight o'clock, they were on the way to London. Strangely, the journey seemed both short and long, the edges between dream and reality still blurred. Lucy recalled three dreams, each apparently unrelated. The first featured Albert taking a specific alternative route on today's trip, the second was about

Hilda forgetting to pack a jar of Joan's home-made jam, and the third was about a cemetery being unexpectedly closed. Lucy tried thinking about the weddings, but her thoughts drifted, marred by a nagging headache.

The car lurched to a halt at traffic lights.

'I forgot that jam,' Hilda said, sounding irritated. 'I doubt Joan will remember to bring it to Marion's wedding. At least we remembered the flowers for the graves.'

Lucy blinked hard and said nothing. Minutes later, Albert signalled to turn left down a particular road, only to find a road works sign positioned in the middle of it, redirecting traffic elsewhere.

'Hmph!' he snorted. 'Road works! This'll add half an hour to the journey.'

The scenario was exactly as it was in the dream. Lucy quietly wondered if she might be losing her mind.

Five miles further on, the approach to the cemetery where her grandparents were buried was drastically altered. A row of terraced houses had been demolished, replaced by a building site and boarded fences displaying posters and graffiti. A few dishevelled youths loitered by a public house. All around, diggers were in operation, their noise deafening.

'It looks like they're going to build something over the cemetery!' Hilda exclaimed. 'Whatever is the world coming to?'

A police car drew up alongside. Hilda opened the car door and said, 'Good morning, Officer! Please tell us the cemetery is open? Is it safe to walk about in this neighbourhood?'

'Don't worry, Madam. The cemetery is open for visitors. My colleague and I will keep a close watch on your vehicle in your absence.'

'Thank you, Officer,' Hilda replied gratefully. 'Thank you, very much.'

The tall, heavy wrought iron gate groaned, and the gravel scrunched underfoot. The once well-kept gate lodge was deserted and boarded up. No one was in sight. Hilda glanced apprehensively over her shoulder. The graveyard was a jungle, the chapel at the end of the path forlorn and derelict. Hilda placed roses from the Hills' garden on her the graves of her parents, Gregor and Theresa Wester, was silent for a moment, then said, 'Life is short, we must move on, but not forget those who have passed.'

Safely back in the car, Hilda said, 'Next, we'll go to Morton and Gordon-Smythe's Solicitors in Camberwell Green and hopefully get some answers from that crook of a solicitor.'

The short journey was worsened by heavy traffic.

'The directions that man gave make no sense. It's as if he didn't want us to find his office,' Hilda growled.

And then, as if in answer to prayer, Lucy said, 'Look, that sign over there says Morton and Gordon-Smythe – Solicitors. There's even a car park!'

Hilda hadn't made an appointment and was hoping to simply catch the solicitor unawares. To her chagrin, the spinsterly-looking secretary informed her Mr Morton was on holiday, and Mr Gordon-Smythe was busy with clients all day.

'Very well,' Hilda responded icily, 'but tell Mr Morton he will be hearing from us again, and from others.'

With a curt nod, the gaunt, hawk-like woman closed the door, and the Wylies withdrew wearily.

On the onward journey, Lucy covered her ears and tried to think of other things, while her mother moaned, and her father smoked cigarette after cigarette. Eventually, they reached Ash Farm, where Lucy had spent her early childhood. In the quiet suburban churchyard, Hilda placed dahlias in the small urn beside her mother-in-law Catherine Wylie's marble gravestone, shook her head, and sighed. Nobody spoke. Lucy knew cancer had claimed her grandmother in middle life, and Hilda had cared for her in her final months. Albert's father had sustained serious injury in the Great War, from which he never recovered. The whereabouts of his grave was unknown. 'He was a peculiar character', Hilda said, 'Miranda couldn't stand him. The story goes he punched an Italian ice cream vendor in the face, and he brought a barmaid home, so your grandmother left him.' Lucy had the impression her grandfather had been a man of bad character. No one spoke well of him. As a child, she once referred to him as that bad man, which drew a sharp rebuke from her mother, and left Lucy guilty and confused.

Finally, they were on the way home, westwards to the setting sun. Three graves had been visited, and three random dreams had come true, a peculiar phenomenon which Lucy kept to herself. After a three-day absence, Lucy found Edencroft strangely unfamiliar in the long day's fading light. For no apparent reason, it no longer felt like home. The next day Lucy returned to work and resumed her routine, taking a day off before the wedding. On that morning, Lucy went horse-riding. She was greeted by Miss Crawford's surly assistant, Doris.

'Come and help tack up Lone Ranger!' Doris ordered. Lucy took up the weighty leather saddle in her arms and heaved it up onto the smooth, oily contour of the capricious colt's back. Then she pulled the girth tightly under Ranger's firm, round belly until the coarse, spiky hairs protruded through the stout chrome buckles.

Doris pulled a face. 'This will not do!' she shouted, tugging the girth tighter, while Lucy stood wondering how on earth the poor pony was expected to be able to breathe.

'Right! That's better!' Doris declared. Turning to Lucy, she growled, 'Now you can get on.'

Lucy mounted carefully. Once in the saddle, she patted Ranger's neck stroked his forelock. The pony tossed his head, and snuffled cheerfully. Lucy was growing rather fond of this temperamental but graceful animal. The hack followed the tree-shadowed lane through Helmstone, passing by the history teacher's house – an instant reminder of school. 'Can you rise to a trot?' Joanna had asked. At the time, Lucy wasn't sure what rising to a trot meant.

Just then, the riding party broke into a trot. Lucy jiggled in the saddle like a sack of potatoes, her teeth chattering. The hired riding-hat tipped forward slightly, obscuring her vision. Then she copied the graceful, swaying motion of everyone else, resulting in a more comfortable ride. The party slowed down, the sound of hooves clattering lazily on the tarmac. Lucy stared through the leafy curtain of overhanging branches at the milky blue sky and wondered when she might buy her typewriter.

'You there! Stop star-gazing!' bellowed Doris. Lucy almost fell out of the saddle. She tightened Ranger's reins and said nothing. On an open stretch of road, Ranger suddenly lunged towards a patch of green. Lucy pulled the reins as hard as she could, but the pony's powerful neck muscles were as strong as steel. She sat powerless, as the pony tugged mouthful after mouthful of meadow grass. Other riders looked on smugly. Doris rode up to Lucy and promptly attached the leading rein to the bridle. Humiliated, Lucy bit her lip and said nothing.

That evening, Hilda was tense and irritable, struggling to fit in as many jobs as she could.

'How am I suppose to cope, with Marion living and working in London? The invitations, photographers, reception, car hire, and the flowers... it's all been left to me and it's been one big headache. Arthur and Joan will be here soon, and Marion's supposed to be on the first fast train from Paddington, but she still isn't here!'

'Trains are often slow on Fridays,' Albert said quietly. He sat in the armchair, waiting for the telephone to ring, while Hilda flitted back and fore to the kitchen, checking on the dinner.

'There's so much to do,' Hilda twittered, rummaging feverishly in the top sideboard drawer. 'It feels like I'm getting married myself.'

'You're already married, dear,' remarked Albert dryly. His attempt at humour fell unnoticed on Hilda, who flurried about on a tide of nervous energy.

The Hills arrived first. Lucy showed them to their room. Albert and Hilda were to sleep in the spare room, having given up their bedroom for Arthur and Joan, squeezing a camp-bed in the corner for Anthony. A second camp bed was made up for Marion in Lucy's room. In spite of past quarrels with her sister, Lucy sensed Marion's last night as a single woman would be different.

Dinner was hurried and fraught with tension. Hilda fretted and fussed, Joan laughed loudly, Albert and Arthur conversed quietly, lingering long over tea and cigarettes. Marion sat pale and drawn, saying little. After the meal, Lucy and Anthony went into the garden with the dog.

'LUCY!! Get in here at once and help with the dishes!' Hilda yelled.

Lucy sloped inside and grudgingly set about her task.

That night, Lucy lay awake, feigning sleep. In the thickening gloom, Marion's huddled form was visible. Marion turned over, and the rickety old camp-bed creaked alarmingly.

'Are you awake?' whispered Lucy.

'Yes.' Marion's whisper was barely audible.

'Are you nervous?'

'Not really, at least, I don't think so.'

'Are you excited?'

'I was, and I still am, but I'm too tired to think any more.'

'How does it feel, I mean, what's it like, getting married?'

'I'm not married yet, and I won't be until tomorrow. Look, can we stop this conversation. I'm tired and I want to sleep.'

Lucy concluded her sister was suffering from pre-wedding nerves. It puzzled her that neither Anne nor Marion seemed particularly excited about their weddings. Lucy lay still, listening to Marion's light, erratic breathing, and the sounds of footsteps and lowered voices in other rooms. At last, all was quiet.

The next morning was a series of muddled scenes, as one activity followed another, Hilda darting from one task to another like a bee in a flower border. Lucy thought it best to keep out of the way. It still seemed like an ordinary day. The sun shone warm and hazy on the golden hills, the postman's van had trundled by at half past nine, the cattle were lowing in the meadows, and Mr Biddlecombe delivered the milk at the usual time, whistling tunelessly to the soughing of the wind in the oak trees. At eleven o'clock, Hilda called her in from the garden to get changed.

But this was no ordinary day. In the bedroom, Lucy took off her jeans and sweater, put on the suspender belt and white stockings, and wriggled into the crisp, sky-blue crepe bridesmaid's dress. Lastly, she put the curved comb with silk flowers in her hair and slipped the silver ring on her ring finger.

Marion came in and started to get ready. She sat on the bed, wearing just a waist slip and bra, staring at the cellophane-covered wedding dress hanging on the wardrobe. Lucy had never noticed Marion develop such generous curves, since she had never seen her in just her underwear. 'Will I look like that when I'm twenty-one?' Lucy wondered. She pulled her sandals out from under the bed and fiddled with the buckles, trying not to stare. With eight years between them, the two sisters had never been particularly close. Lucy had always been Marion's kid sister and the butt end of her jokes, but Marion was good-hearted, generous with presents, cast-off clothing, and unwanted bric-a-brac. Marion's marriage would be a final cutting of apron strings – properly leaving home.

The bedroom door opened and Hilda swept in, the nylon lining of her new dress rustling noisily. She assisted Marion with the folds and fastenings of her wedding gown, then attached the veil and tiara. The process of primping and preening seemed to take forever. Lucy sat on the edge of the bed, squirming with impatience.

'Where's Paul?' she piped up suddenly.

'On his way, I expect,' Hilda replied.

'Is he coming all the way from London?'

'No. He's been staying with relatives in Dorchester, meaning a shorter journey and hopefully no delays. There now, Marion, dear, take a look at yourself in the mirror.'

Marion turned and glanced shyly through the cloud-like curtain of white voile at her reflection in the glass – the flawless face of a young woman in her prime, radiant and beautiful, on the threshold of a life of new joys and responsibilities. Marion's lower lip trembled imperceptibly.

'I can't believe this is really happening,' she whispered. 'It's like a dream.'

'You'll be fine. You'll only have one wedding day, Marion, so enjoy it!' Hilda said.

In the mirror, Hilda regarded the face of her oldest child, fresh and unspoilt as a rose about to be plucked. Gone were the days of boisterous games of tag and hide-and-seek, when Marion would hide Lucy's favourite toys and chase her round the three-piece-suite in the cherry-carpeted parlour.

Lucy stared speechless. Her sister's beauty was enhanced by a light tinge of shell-blue eye shadow, peach-coloured face powder and silvery-pink lipstick, her honey blonde hair stiff and lacquered behind a pearly tiara, framing her graceful neck. Lucy had always envied Marion for her looks, and now, on her wedding day, Marion was more beautiful than ever. Lucy wished she had been born blonde, well-proportioned and with fine, regular features and a soft, angelic face. Sadly, Lucy seemed destined to remain mousey, odd, and unattractive.

At half past twelve, the group set off serenely, blessed by blue skies and sunshine. Outside the chapel, a small crowd was gathering. At five feet eight inches, Uncle Peter was dwarfed by Paul's parents and older siblings. Paul's eight-year-old brother Robert was almost as tall as Lucy. Three-year-old Tracey, golden-haired and cherubic, was the youngest Clements sibling and the smallest of the three bridesmaids. Lucy's seventeen-year-old cousin Sarah, Peter and Rose's daughter, was the oldest. Sarah looked stunning in the long, pastel-blue gown, her smiling face framed by a tidy thatch of chestnut-brown hair. Lucy looked around, wishing the ground would swallow her up.

Inside the church, floral displays adorned plain white walls. Well-dressed guests whispered in polished pews. Lucy sat at the front, beside Sarah, twirling her posy. As the organ struck up Mendelssohn's "Wedding March", Lucy's heart leapt. This was Marion's moment! As Albert and Marion passed close by, arm-in-arm, Lucy felt tears prick her eyes. From the corner of her eye, Lucy observed the Clements clan, who far outnumbered the Wylies who occupied just three pews. She longed for a larger family. Would there be nieces and nephews? Dare she even wish, one day, for children of her own?

The first hymn was "Praise My Soul the King of Heaven", which Lucy remembered well from primary school. She sang heartily and sat patiently through the prayers and the minister's short address. As the marriage vows were declared, Paul's resounding I do was audible to all, but from Marion a mere murmur. Lucy saw her sister mouth the words but heard nothing. *Is Marion unsure?* If so, it was too late now. Rings were exchanged, and Marion and Paul were solemnly declared man and wife. "All Things Bright and Beautiful" was sung, and the final blessing announced. The organ struck up a rousing melody, the congregation rose. Hand-in-hand Marion and Paul walked smiling down the aisle. Lucy was reassured; her sister had done the right thing. Hilda however, viewed the scene through a veil of tears, her mask of happiness dutifully worn for the last hour, was melting. With a gloved hand, she discreetly wiped away a stray tear, then sat up straight, regaining composure. No one must, on any account, detect a chink in the armour of the indomitable Hilda Wylie.

The formal ceremony over, the wedding breakfast, with its promise of rich food and alcoholic beverages, was tantalisingly close. On the rough ground between the church and the police station, guests were forming small groups, chatting and smoking. As far as the Clements family was concerned, weddings were occasions to get together for a good laugh and plenty of free food and drink. Hilda found the proximity of the police station reassuring, since the reputation of the Clements was less than pristine, and one of the guests was absent at Her Majesty's pleasure. As Lucy stood between Sarah and Tracey, waiting for the photographs, an equestrian party passed by, clip-clopping on the tarmac. A girl from school hailed Lucy with a cheery greeting, and Lucy waved back, delighted at the unexpected friendly gesture. Being a bridesmaid was wonderful. *This'll boost my reputation at school*, she thought hopefully.

'I shan't ask you where you'd rather be,' Arthur remarked wryly. Lucy smiled and twirled her posy.

The venue of the reception was a hundred yards down the hill, in the village hall overlooking a small, cobbled square, where five roads branched off in various directions. Lucy would have gladly walked the short distance, but tradition required her to be chauffeur-driven in the shiny Bentley, along with the other bridesmaids and close family members. The lofty hall milled with guests, stained lath-and-plaster walls festooned to the rafters with fragrant flower garlands and wide banners displaying, Congratulations Marion and Paul, and Happy 50th Birthday Albert. Trestle tables were decked with white cloths, floral sprays, gleaming cutlery, and starched linen napkins folded into fan shapes. A splendid, three-tiered wedding cake dominated the centre of the bridal table. The building was filled with the smells of food and fresh flowers, soon to be tainted with the odours of cheap perfume, after-shave, perspiration, and tobacco smoke. Food and drink were plentiful, the speeches succinct and devoid of lewd humour, and there was no disorderly behaviour. Hilda sighed with relief. Most importantly, Marion radiated happiness.

One detail puzzled Lucy. Aunt Rose was wearing odd shoes. Lucy looked again. She wasn't imagining things. Rose's high-heeled, slingback sandals didn't match, each a different design and shade of beige. Lucy considered pointing out the inconsistency, but someone started speaking to Rose, and the opportunity was lost.

Hours later, at dusk, Lucy and Hilda attended to the hens. Marion and Paul had set off on their honeymoon, and Arthur, Joan, and Anthony had gone straight home from the reception. The bungalow was in disarray: dishes unwashed, the floor unswept and the bedroom carpets strewn with fluff and crumbs. Arthur and Joan's room was the messiest. For once, Hilda didn't fuss. After a short dog walk, Albert made a pot of tea, and Hilda sank into her favourite chair, sighing heavily, declaring the tidying up could wait until morning. Lucy went to bed early, closed her eyes, and relived what had been a unique and unforgettable day.

9: THE VICAR PLOT

On Monday morning, Lucy laced up her school brogues, as usual. The thick, black leather felt strangely tight about the toes. The shoes were too small. Two years before, Lucy had outgrown her size one shoes and was fitted for a new pair, size two. Lucy felt a thrill of excitement. *If my feet are growing, maybe the rest of me will grow too?* So far, there was no evidence of that, since the bra still hung ludicrously around her child's chest. Lucy wore the shoes to school, feeling them tight all day. In the evening, she complained of sore, blistered toes, and Hilda admitted it was time for a size larger. Temporarily, Lucy was obliged to wear a pair of Marion's old sandals, size three, in crinkly, blue leather, with brass buckles and pointed toes. Lucy found them both comfortable and stylish.

Meanwhile, another priority occupied Lucy's horizon. Albert met her from school, and together they caught the train to Nyehaven. Lucy didn't care who saw her out and about with her dad, for soon she would have something to boast about. In the warehouse-like office equipment store, Lucy was faced with rows of filing cabinets, far-reaching shelves of shining, new typewriters. Lucy chose a compact, middle-of-the-range, Japanese model with white keys and metallic grey casing. At twenty-three pounds, nineteen shillings and eleven pence, the machine was deemed good value for money, a valuable tool for work and leisure. Lucy felt on top of the world.

'You must look after it,' Albert advised. 'Remember, it's not a toy.'

'Yes, of course, Dad.'

They walked to Mayfield Electrics and met Hilda in the car park. Lucy sat on the back seat, the treasured typewriter on her lap, its case tightly zipped up. Arriving home, she placed her new acquisition on the dining-table and rolled in a sheet of white paper.

'The last time I tried typing was two years ago, on Sarah's typewriter,' Lucy said. 'I managed with two fingers.'

'You'll have to learn to touch-type, like Marion,' Hilda said, demonstrating the correct fingerings, encouraging Lucy to rely on memory and not look at the keyboard. Lucy experimented happily for a while. She was given a cup of tea, which she sipped thoughtfully, whilst surveying her efforts. Though peppered with errors, the typewritten sheet looked pleasingly professional. Further attempts to touch-type her name resulted in Luct or Lucu, and rarely Lucy, which was amusing at first, then highly irritating.

Scrutinising the flawed script, Lucy reached for her cup and felt the handle slip from her grasp. Instinctively, she flashed her hand forwards – a fraction of a second too late. Hot, sweet tea flooded the side of the machine, spattering the working parts and forming a widening brown puddle inside the base.

Lucy sprang to her feet. Her parents came to the rescue with cloths and paper tissues. Lucy flapped nervously, desperately trying to undo what had already been done, boiling with embarrassment, fearing a rebuke and the likelihood her hard-earned savings were lost to one unguarded moment of carelessness.

'I'm sure it'll be fine,' Hilda said reassuringly, after all visible evidence of the tea had been removed. 'Go on – give it a try.'

Happily, the typewriter still worked, although the keys seemed a little stiffer than before.

With a twinkle in her eye, Hilda said, 'you've christened it!'

In the morning, Lucy complained there was something wrong with the blue sandals. Hilda examined the shoes and found no fault.

'Put them back on and stop fussing,' she ordered, crossly.

Lucy did as she was told.

'The toes pinch,' Lucy insisted.

Hilda probed, prodded and declared, 'They're too small.'

'Maybe they shrank in the rain?' suggested Lucy.

'Don't be ridiculous! Shoes don't shrink. Marion got them wet plenty of times and nothing happened. No, your feet have grown.'

'Again? But they've only just gone up one size last week.'

'Well, I can only deduce they've gone up another size. I'll lend you a pair of mine, size four.'

Hilda fetched a pair of flat-heeled walking-shoes. 'Have these, as I hardly ever wear them now. They're too smart for the garden, and I wear court shoes to work.'

Lucy regretted relinquishing the sandals. She feared becoming a freak of nature with a tiny, underdeveloped body and enormous feet. The next day Hilda collected photographs from the developer's. The pictures showed Lucy looking small and tomboyish in the garden with Dotty earlier that year, and more recently at Anne and Michael's wedding, standing between her parents, gawky and gangly in the pink crepe dress, her bony, stockinged legs ludicrously stick-like in the white sandals. Lucy loathed the sight of her sullen, pinched face and thin curtain of wispy hair. The photos of Marion and Paul's wedding weren't yet ready. Lucy hoped they would be more flattering.

On Saturday, Lucy slept in. She surfaced slowly after half past ten from a deep sleep, heavy-eyed and limbs like lead. Hilda left a cup of tea on Lucy's bookcase, where it steamed tantalisingly out of reach. Lucy emerged slowly from the warmth of the eiderdown, feeling the sharpness of the autumn morning envelop her like a cold bath. She dragged a favourite jumper over her head and pulled on her blue jeans. The rough denim felt cold against her bare legs, so she hurried to fasten the zip. She tugged harder at the unyielding waistband, but button refused to connect with buttonhole. Breathing in, muscles taut, Lucy yanked harder, breaking the zip. The trousers were simply too tight.

But they fitted yesterday! Have I got bigger? Lucy pulled her jumper down over the open trousers, drank her tea, then crept into the living-room.

'Did you sleep well, Lucy?' Hilda chirped.

Shoulders hunched, Lucy stared out of the window.

Hilda turned to Albert and said, 'Typical teenager you know, dear. They need their sleep, these youngsters. It's all the growing they have to do.'

'Probably,' mumbled Albert.

How did she know? Lucy wondered. She was about to mention the trousers when an overwhelming apathy swamped her. A shame about the jeans – Lucy had bought them only a week earlier, for horse-riding. After breakfast, Lucy pierced holes in the denim and threaded a bootlace through the holes, forming a lace-up fastening. The result looked hideous, so she pulled her jumper down, but it no longer covered her hips. Seething with frustration, she took the jeans off and tossed them aside.

Since the summer weddings, life had lost its sparkle. The new school year had begun a month ago, form 2D, now 3D. Students seemed confident and carefree, boasting, 'we're no longer two-dimensional and we won't be continually flattened, we're three-dimensional now, so we'll stand out and be noticed...'

The classroom was in room twenty, on the top floor. Lucy's desk was at the back, where she sat alone and friendless. For no apparent reason, Alison was ignoring her and had returned to Rosemary's clique. Homework was harder, and Lucy skipped through most of it. Each school day was an ordeal, every lesson torture, except French and Art. Gloom engulfed Lucy like dense fog.

Guides and horse-riding were the highlights of the week, although the latter would soon stop now that summer jobs were finished, and money was needed for Christmas gifts. Recently, Lucy had progressed to longer, cross-country rides. Cantering gave her a feeling of freedom and movement, although she was still a long way from becoming an experienced equestrian like Abigail or Joanna.

'I'd like a riding hat for Christmas,' Lucy announced, at dinner.

'We'll see, dear. How much are they?' Hilda asked.

'About six pounds.'

Albert snorted over his sausage and mash.

'It's for safety reasons, not just to look nice,' Lucy said.

'Very well, if that's what you want. That reminds me, one of my colleagues, Marjorie Mayfield has a daughter your age, who you might like to meet. She likes horse-riding too.'

Lucy sat up straight.

'Her name is Georgina,' Hilda continued. 'She also struggles to make friends at school and would like to get to know you. Perhaps you could write her a letter, introducing yourself?'

'Is Marjorie Mayfield the owner of Mayfield Electrics?' Lucy asked.

'No. Mayfield is a common name in Nyehaven, apparently. Georgina is a pupil at the expensive convent school for girls.'

'Convent? Is Georgina a nun?'

'No, the teachers are nuns.'

After dinner, Lucy wrote to Georgina, introducing herself and listing her hobbies and interests, without mentioning school. Two days later, she received a reply, with an invitation to Sunday tea, during half term. Lucy accepted. More notes were exchanged. Georgina described her bedroom and her school time table. She had no pets. Lucy wrote back about Guides, suggesting Georgina might want to join, but Georgina politely declined, describing instead an absolutely ghastly essay question on the subject of abortion. Lucy was horrified and very glad she wasn't a pupil at that school.

On the Sunday before half term, Lucy went horse-riding. She was given her favourite piebald pony, the Lone Ranger, and anticipated an interesting ride. The sky was filled with scurrying clouds, trees bowing and bobbing in the brisk autumn breeze. On the springy turf, Ranger broke into a swift canter, and Lucy felt free as a lark, borne up and away by wild winds of approaching winter.

Suddenly the ride stopped, in a clearing on a leafy descent. The horses tossed their heads, whinnying softly. A few riders allowed their horses to graze, and since Doris wasn't there, Lucy didn't deny Ranger the privilege of enjoying a few mouthfuls of fresh grass.

'There's been an accident,' someone said, 'a rider has fallen.'

Lucy overheard talk of injury and hospital, and that someone had gone to the nearest farm to telephone for help. The group edged closer to the scene of the accident. A woman lay on her back, moaning, semi-conscious on the ground, a leader at her side, offering reassurance. The victim wasn't getting up. All but two riders were advised to turn back. On the way back, Lucy scarcely noticed the stunning beauty of the countryside.

All evening, Lucy dwelt morbidly on the incident, wondering what injuries had been sustained and how bad was the pain. *This should have happened to me,* she mused melodramatically, revisiting the notion of suffering, being purged of her selfish, evil nature. It had to happen. She felt sure that one day it would.

'Ready for tea, love?' asked Albert, softly. Hilda was serving boiled eggs and ham salad, and the table was spread with a white linen cloth and bone china plates laden with tempting delicacies – miniature pork pies, green salads, crusty bread rolls with poppy seeds, iced fairy cakes, and fruit sundaes in stem glasses.

'You must be hungry after all that fresh air,' Hilda said.

Curiously, the more Lucy ate, the hungrier she seemed to be. After tea, she sat on the sofa, trying to forget a full school week loomed ahead. She leafed through magazines, feeling strangely tense. An article about the film *Ring of Bright Water* caught her attention for a while. On the next page was an article about women who wanted to get married, to each other. Discovering what a lesbian was, Lucy hoped her bullies weren't right. So far, she sensed no attraction to boys or girls. In fact, she disliked everybody. She put the magazine away and tried reading a library book. It was impossible to concentrate. She shifted her position on the sofa and sat with her legs curled up, ignoring a vague ache, somewhere inside. She shuffled about, stood up and walked around, concluding she must be suffering from indigestion. Lying on her side only added to the discomfort. Tendrils of pain searched her insides until, unable to keep still, she went to her room. The pain grew sharper, angrier, tightening its grip. Lucy thought of the riding accident and her wish to feel pain. It seemed her wish had come true. Pain was a tangible presence, blurring the edges of reality. This wasn't mere imagination. She recalled a time years before when she had been alone in the old house at half term. The pain had begun as a dull abdominal ache, worsening until it was unbearable. Lucy had crawled up the stairs, burying her face in her hands, hoping with all her heart that someone would come home and help her. And then suddenly, the pain had lifted, leaving Lucy wondering if she had dreamed it. In the light of her recent growth spurt, Lucy suspected this episode might be a period, which wouldn't however, explain similar episodes in her childhood. Lucy refused supper, and went to bed early, writhing under the covers, fighting the pain's ragged edges. She drifted into a fitful sleep, and in the morning, the pain was gone, its unexplained source a mystery.

At home, Lucy deprived herself of pleasures, spending more time doing things she disliked. She figured the more she invested in the pain bank, the richer she would become in character. Her parents discovered a different Lucy, who offered to do the dishes, tidy up, mop floors, feed the animals, without being asked. This new Lucy no longer lounged around watching television or pestered for sweets. In fact, she appeared to be every parent's idea of a model child, but sullen and subdued. Hilda decided she preferred the old Lucy to the new one but decided not to confront Lucy about it.

On November the Fifth, there were again to be no fireworks. Hilda reiterated that they were expensive, noisy, childish trivia that spooked the dog. Hilda didn't even give her garbled rendering of the historical events of the Gunpowder Plot. The date in the diary and the talk at school of a fireworks party – to which Lucy wasn't invited – were sole reminders what day it was. Alone with her homework, Lucy felt a twinge of regret. Self-pity hovered uncomfortably close. Then a random page in a textbook altered her perspective:

"A vicar is a church minister, a person who helps others, but the adjective vicarious means helpful, selfless, and charitable – virtues anyone can display if they wish, irrespective of their association with the established church."

'...if they wish,' Lucy whispered, deciding upon a name for her self-improvement project – *The Vicar Plot.* In her diary, she penned the caption, *"Never mind the Gunpowder plot... I have the Vicar Plot!"* She sketched a burning Guy crossed out, beside it a glowing dog-collar.

Now, Lucy reasoned, she would endure suffering, and would miraculously morph into a better person.

An opportunity to put plan into practice soon presented itself. On Friday evening, Captain Merryweather announced a Bob-a-Job fundraiser, inviting Guides to spend their Saturday working for charity. In the morning, Lucy awoke to the sound of wind and rain and remembered her resolve. At nine o'clock, she donned waterproofs and cycled off, working her way round the five-mile circuit, offering help at every house. She fed chickens, swept sheds, dusted parlours, washed dishes, peeled potatoes and polished silver, before arriving home, drenched and exhausted at six o'clock. She had collected the princely sum of four pounds, nine shillings and seven pence halfpenny for Oxfam.

'You've done well,' Hilda remarked. 'No doubt Captain will be pleased with your efforts.'

Lucy felt too tired for personal pride. Hilda took Lucy's soaking wet clothes and hung them in the porch. Then she ordered her into a hot bath. On Monday morning, Lucy awoke with a streaming cold. At school, she received neither sympathy nor criticism. By the weekend, remarkably, she had already outgrown Hilda's size five shoes.

'It looks like you'll be the giant of the family,' Hilda said, 'There's tallness on your father's side of the family. Your grandfather was very tall, as were your father's cousins, so I'm told. Maybe it's the fresh country air and good food? My goodness, you were such a shrimp of a child when we came here, and now you're turning into a great, strapping lass just like the big country girls I used to work with in the Land Army.'

Lucy sat at the dining-table, immersed in homework. She looked at the hem of her jeans that now reached halfway up her wide calf muscles. Her wish to grow bigger was finally coming true, not that she particularly cared.

'On Saturday I'll buy you a new pair of shoes,' Hilda promised.

'Thanks, Mum,' Lucy answered, not looking up from her books.

Hilda smiled, reflecting how studious Lucy had become of late. At last, she appeared to be taking her education seriously.

Lucy's choice on Saturday's shopping trip was a pair of black leather lace-up brogues with a decorative pattern leather fringe at the front. However, at school on Monday, Lucy regretted her choice.

'I like your new shoes,' drawled a familiar voice from behind. Lucy froze. If Abigail Leuchars began a conversation with a pleasant remark, she was unlikely to end it with one. Lucy turned around stiffly.

'I'm so glad you like my shoes and admire my taste,' Abigail smirked. Lucy noticed Abigail's shoes were identical to hers. Lucy said nothing, and Abigail sidled off.

By break time, news of Lucy's choice of footwear had filtered through the class clique.

'What a copy-cat!'

'Fancy trying to suck up to someone by getting the same shoes.'

'How pathetic!'

'She's such a moron.'

The voices floated menacingly around the landing, where students loitered around the lockers. Lucy tried to ignore them.

The next lesson was double physics, with student teacher Mr Finnegan, whom everyone teased mercilessly. Today's topic was prisms, which Lucy might have found interesting if there hadn't been so many distractions. As small, cuboid glass prisms were handed round, the conversations became a cacophony of catcalls.

'Sir! You spelt prison wrong!' Jimmy Murphy yelled from the back row.

'Hey – skinny Finny, your shirt's hanging out!' Rosemary shouted audaciously.

'I haven't got a prison, sir!' protested Mike Fidler mockingly.

The volume of noise in the room was deafening. The teacher tried in vain to keep control.

'SILENCE!' Mr Finnegan roared, but everyone ignored him, apart from Jonathan Whitmore and Shirley Johnson, who cowered in the front row, wincing and cupping their ears.

Lucy held her prism up against the light from the window and looked through it, admiring the refracted light and rainbow colours.

'It's really pretty,' she said.

'It's really pretty,' Alison mocked. In the ear-splitting din, Lucy had the beginnings of a headache, compounded by the fact that Rosemary and Joanna had started a chorus of high-pitched dog-barking noises, adding to the pandemonium.

'All the dogs can get out, please,' Mr Finnegan begged lamely, but no one took any notice.

'This noise is making my headache worse,' Alison said.

Lucy had no idea Alison also had a headache.

'In fact – I think I might be getting the 'flu,' Alison added tiredly.

'Don't give it to me,' smiled Lucy, attempting to sound humorous. In truth, she wanted to catch an illness so that she could miss school.

'That's not a very kind thing to say to someone who isn't feeling well!' Alison sniffed into her handkerchief.

Remembering *The Vicar Plot*, Lucy reflected on its failure so far. The forty-minute lesson bell buzzed faintly in the background, indicating the double lesson was only halfway through. Lucy looked out of the window at the stream of students crossing the yard to their next class, most of them talking and laughing together. Nobody looked unhappy or left out, not even the dwarf girl from the year above. In spite of her obvious disability, she never seemed to lack friends. Lucy's throat tightened. She fought back tears, taunted by unanswered questions: *Will I ever be happy? Will I ever have friends? Why am I even here?*

Nobody spoke to her for the rest of the school day. On arriving home, Lucy was shown the latest photos of Marion and Paul's wedding. Hilda had placed a framed, monochrome print of the happy couple in the Trophy Cabinet. Lucy agreed Marion looked incredibly beautiful. She flicked through the other photos, silently despising the pictures of herself.

That night, Lucy couldn't sleep. Wide awake in the thick darkness of her room, she placed her pillow over her head and held her breath, counting.

'Thirty, thirty-one...' Gasping, Lucy drew breath. She inhaled deeply and tried again, this time reaching fifty-nine seconds. Remembering what she had read about Maori pearl divers who could hold their breath for over a minute, Lucy concluded she was physically fit, in spite of being appallingly poor at school games. Might oxygen deprivation cause brain damage? In a wave of masochistic zeal, she repeated the breath-holding exercise, until her chest ached and her head throbbed.

Now, she thought, *I will learn to be a good person, like everyone else...*

Sleep soon stole over her, until cold, grey light invaded her room at the start of another miserable day.

10: SHADOWS

'We're going to London on Saturday.'

Hilda's voice betrayed a hint of anguish. 'Albert, you must check the car, and I'll prepare everything the night before, ready for an early start. We'll have to bring the dog. There's no time to book kennels.'

Albert mumbled a quiet response. Hilda had just arrived home at the usual time. The customary cup of tea to help Lucy through her homework didn't come. Lucy closed her books and listened hard through the bedroom door. *Hilda must have received bad news whilst at work. But what?*

Lucy tiptoed into the living room and asked, 'Why are we going to London?'

Hilda caught Lucy's eye.

'It's Aunty Rose – she's very ill. We're going to visit her in hospital.'

Lucy stared blankly. 'B – but, how? I mean – she was at the wedding a few weeks ago and looked fine.'

Hilda shook her head and sighed. 'You're too young to understand.'

Still wearing her coat, Hilda went into the kitchen and began preparing dinner. Lucy remembered Rose had been wearing odd shoes at the wedding. Was this relevant? Rose was from Newcastle, with an honest, down-to-earth, no-nonsense approach to life. It didn't make sense.

Hilda woke Lucy at six thirty on Saturday morning. Sleep-fogged, Lucy remembered what day it was. She dragged herself out of bed, got dressed, and slouched heavily into the breakfast room, every fibre of her being crying out for rest. One sidelong glance from her mother drew Lucy to her senses. On the long car journey, Lucy lay curled up on the back seat and tried to sleep.

'Just look at the autumn sunrise!' Hilda exclaimed. 'Little woolly lambs scuttling across the sky.'

In moments of thoughtfulness, Hilda could be remarkably poetic.

Lucy looked up at cotton-wool clouds high in the sky tinged with golden-pink, wintry sunrise. 'Yes, it's very beautiful,' she whispered.

An uncanny emptiness hung in the air.

'Red sky in the morning, shepherd's warning!' Hilda added solemnly. 'A good day for travelling. A pity this is such a sad errand.'

Hilda had arranged to visit Marion and Paul at their one-bedroom flat in Neasden in time for lunch. Unfortunately, Paul's directions were vague and failed to factor in one-way streets.

'Look out for street names, Lucy,' Hilda said, fumbling in the glove compartment for the well-thumbed, London A-Z. She put on her sunglasses to ward off a gathering headache.

'Yes, Mum.'

It was past one o'clock, and she felt lethargic and light-headed. Lucy did as she was asked, and finally, the car drew up outside a box-shaped block of modern maisonettes. Sunshine streamed warmly on yellow brick walls and plain, rectangular lawns. In a wide, uncurtained window Lucy recognised a few familiar objects: a blue vase and a set of three carved wooden storks.

'Typical!' muttered Hilda. 'The milk is still on the doorstep, and in the sun. It'll be turned to cheese by now. My goodness, that girl's got a lot to learn about being a housewife.'

'Perhaps the milkman has only just come?' Lucy suggested quietly.

'I hope you're right,' said Hilda, 'And I hope they've remembered we're coming. For all we know, they might have gone out, or still be in bed.'

Lucy sighed, longing for the promised roast dinner. Hilda jabbed her finger on the doorbell, which buzzed tiredly. Seconds later, Marion appeared, wearing a yellow frilly apron, rubber gloves, and a happy smile. Lucy thought she looked a typical homely housewife. It was hard to believe the same sister who'd teased her and thrown soft toys and cushions at her two years ago was now a married woman. The fleeting thought crossed Lucy's mind that Marion could be pregnant, meaning little Lucy, would be an aunt – a role for which she felt totally unprepared.

Marion and Paul's living-room was sparsely furnished but homely. Marion darted in and out of the kitchenette like an excited canary.

'Dinner's on – and I'm just making a pot of tea,' she said.

'That's good.' Hilda gave a nod of approval.

Five minutes later, the tea was served in mugs, not traditional cups and saucers. It was weak and very milky. Albert and Hilda smiled politely and stood the mugs on the tiled floor, as there was no table. Lucy didn't mind at all. Marion's home reminded her of the hut at Edencroft, where she and Alison had played at houses earlier that year. Lucy sat cross-legged on a floor cushion and smiled.

'I like this,' she said. 'It's really Hippie-like, rather like my hut.'

Hilda threw Lucy a stern glance.

Marion returned to the stove, Paul absorbed in yesterday's *Daily Mirror*. Lucy didn't like the look of the cumbersome, grubby looking sofa-bed and was reluctant to sit on it, especially after hearing it had been crawled on and soiled countless times by babies and toddlers in the Clements' family home. She wisely kept silent.

Meanwhile, tantalising smells emanated from the kitchenette, but the promised meal was a long time appearing. It was almost seven hours since breakfast, and Lucy wondered how on earth adults managed to go so long without food. She sat with her arms around Dotty, fussing with the dog's collar and true lovers' knot. Predictably, conversation was about Marion and Paul's newly-wedded status and the health of Aunt Rose.

'An impressive little home, you've made here,' Hilda said. 'Very cosy.'

'We like it,' Marion said.

'A shame about dear Rose,' Hilda sighed, 'She's been a good friend to me over the years.'

Marion nodded.

'But you two are happy aren't you?' continued Hilda.

'Very happy. Paul's just popped out to the paper shop. He won't be long.'

'So, they've decided not to operate?' Hilda continued.

'They're trying some treatment first. Rose will to tell you more this afternoon.'

Paul returned with six cans of lager and another tabloid newspaper.

'Put these in the fridge will you, love,' he told Marion, then slumped on the sofa and hid behind his paper. Marion returned to the kitchen to attend to the vegetables.

'Do you need a hand, dear?' ventured Hilda.

'No thanks, Mum,' Marion replied. Minutes later, the meal was finally ready, and everyone shuffled into a more comfortable position.

'Sorry there's no table,' Marion said, bringing in two plates piled with roast lamb and vegetables. 'Paul and I usually sit on the sofa with trays on our laps.'

'Not to worry, dear. We'll manage.' Hilda perched on the edge of the sofa, smoothing her skirt. Just as she was about to pick up her plate from the floor, she exclaimed quietly, 'Dotty! No, that's not for you!'

Lucy glimpsed the Dalmatian's ears dangling in her mother's dinner, and a succulent slice of meat entering drooling jaws.

'You little rascal!' laughed Hilda.

'Dotty's dinner bowl is always on the floor,' Lucy explained pointlessly.

'Let her eat it,' said Marion. 'I'll get you another dinner, Mum. There's plenty more.'

Lucy launched gratefully into her meal, savouring every mouthful.

'I must say, you've done us all proud,' Hilda said. 'This meal is every bit as good as a mature housewife could produce.'

Marion blushed modestly. 'Sorry there's no pudding,' she added apologetically.

'It doesn't matter, dear. We'll have to be going fairly soon anyway, as we don't want to miss visiting hour.'

As a child, Lucy had often visited great-uncle Charles or great-aunt-Miranda in hospital. Lucy's enduring impression of hospitals was mausoleum-like buildings, labyrinths of concrete corridors, echoing footsteps, hushed voices, and strong-smelling disinfectant. Today was no different. Arriving at the forbidding, grey edifice, she followed her parents through double doors into a shock of warm air laden with smells of cooked meals and antiseptic. Through an open door, she saw a polished floor flanked by two long rows of high, steel-framed beds, each one doubtless containing a frail, elderly person awaiting death.

Hilda strode onward, up a flight of stairs, down a long corridor to a ward with cottage-like windows and pretty floral curtains, through which low afternoon sunshine filtered brightly. Aunt Rose was in a room on her own. She was sitting up in bed, propped up with pillows and looking her usual, cheerful self. Her hair was neatly permed, and she greeted her visitors with a beaming smile. Hilda placed a bouquet of chrysanthemums and a punnet of red grapes on the faded, green counterpane. Albert went to fetch some chairs.

Rose put down her pen and crossword. 'You've come all that way. You must be very tired.'

'Not at all,' responded Hilda, ignoring the nagging headache which had settled over one eye. 'What about you?'

'Oh, they're slowly getting me sorted out. I'm feeling much better now.' Rose's eyes were dark and sunken behind her fancy spectacles.

'Marion says you weren't well when you went to the wedding.'

'That's right. Peter and I had just got back from a week in Cornwall. I wasn't able to enjoy the holiday. I felt dreadful, like nothing on earth. I knew there must be something wrong, but I'm glad we came to the wedding...'

Rose's voice trailed off. Hilda caught Rose's eye. Lucy looked out of the window. Unanswered questions, unspoken fears hung in the air.

'I'll be going home in a few days, after I've had a good rest,' Rose said.

Another silence followed. Lucy stared at the patterned curtains.

'How are Marion and Paul settling in their new flat?' Rose asked.

'They're very well. Marion cooked us a splendid lunch, didn't she, Albert?'

Albert cleared his throat, 'Yes, dear. It was very good.'

'That's good', Rose continued. 'Tell me more about your new place in the country.'

'It's beautiful, so picturesque, the air is so fresh. You must come and see us when you're on the mend. Edencroft is always lovely, but in April and May it's absolutely wonderful.'

'Oooh, that'd be grand,' Rose replied.

Hilda was silent for a moment, then asked about John's apprenticeship as a motor mechanic and Sarah's job as a trainee hairdresser. Lucy wasn't interested. However, Rose's concluding remark hit home: 'I don't mind what job my children do, as long as they're happy.' Lucy wished her mother was as relaxed and easy-going about careers as Rose evidently was. *Perhaps,* thought Lucy, *I might not after all be the academic high-flyer Mother thinks I am?*

However, the thought of an ordinary Monday-to-Friday job appealed to Lucy much less. So did the idea of marriage. In fact, she couldn't imagine being stuck with anyone or anything for the rest of her life. The future stretched terrifyingly before her, like an unlit highway into the unknown.

Soon, the silvery tinkle of a small hand-bell indicated the end of visiting hour. Through the open door, Lucy saw the rotund figure of the ward sister striding purposefully down the corridor. On the journey home, Lucy felt deflated and downcast. Hilda however, appeared to be in better spirits for having seen Rose.

'Look!' Hilda exclaimed suddenly, 'Pyestock! What a funny name! Doesn't it make you feel hungry? Someone is cooking a pie and making the stock!'

Lucy stifled an unexpected snigger.

'And there's also a house called Retirement Roost,' she added, giggling hysterically until Hilda told her to stop.

Everyone was glad to get home. The cat was eagerly awaiting his evening feed, rubbing affectionately against Albert's legs at the pantry door. Hilda went to close the hen-house door, first checking for eggs. She groped in nesting-boxes, ignoring trilling notes of protest, but found no eggs. Turning towards the bungalow, she saw the golden rectangle of an uncurtained room, Albert making tea and Lucy jumping happily with the dog. Hilda paused, regarding the crouching silhouette of the ridge against indigo-black sky, feeling strangely detached, as an outsider looking in on an uncomplicated domestic scene. Then she shuddered, and hurried indoors.

In the weeks that followed, Lucy assumed Rose was making a satisfactory recovery. One evening after supper, Hilda was sitting at the dining-room table lingering over her cup of tea, drumming her fingers absent-mindedly on the tablecloth.

'It's time to get ready for Guides, Mum,' Lucy whispered. Hilda said nothing. Perhaps she had a headache? But tonight was Guides night, which Lucy had been looking forward to all week.

'I'll go and get my uniform on,' Lucy said.

'Yes, dear,' Hilda answered, with a vacant frown.

That evening, the church hall buzzed and quaked with a score of energetic youngsters. Captain was working on a poster advertising a jumble sale, scrawling the information with indelible ink on white wallpaper. The letters of the last word were crowded to fit in. Lucy knew she could have made a far better job herself.

Suddenly Valerie piped up, 'Captain! Guides is spelt wrong!'

Everyone crowded to view the alleged error:

GIUDES JUMBLE Sale

Lucy felt stupid for not having immediately spotted the mistake. Even Fenella, who regularly muddled her letters and spelt practically every word wrong, recognised it.

'Oh, it doesn't matter!' snapped Captain defensively, ushering the Guides to their tables. Hilda winced. Lucy went to the Blackbird patrol table, where Guides were clamouring for paper and crayons. She helped them with their drawings and soon forgot about the botched poster.

After the meeting, the short drive home started off in stony silence, Hilda staring at the road ahead.

'Village idiots!' Hilda hissed.

Lucy was tempted to laugh. 'Pardon, Mum?' she inquired quietly.

'Village idiots! All of them! Stupid people in this backward, uncivilised place. Fancy not being able to spell the simplest of words? And I'm not just talking about Captain Merryweather. It's that Biddlecombe man too. They're all so inefficient, so disorganised. They're like it at the office too. And as for that Merryweather woman – she couldn't even organise a bun-fight in a bakery! I've had more than my fill of Guides. I'm going to resign.'

Lucy bit her lip and said nothing. In Lucy's opinion, Captain Merryweather was far nicer than anyone at school. The next Guides' meeting seemed an eternity away, but at the moment, it was all Lucy had to look forward to. Throughout the week she kept herself busy with chores, homework, handcrafts, and random writing on the typewriter, marking time.

The next Guides' meeting was Hilda's last. Captain was in an upbeat mood, demonstrating the principles of hand and nail care and providing manicure sets for the girls to try out in their respective groups. Lucy was both inspired and disheartened, for she was an incorrigible nail-biter. *I've bitten my nails for as long as I can remember*, she thought sadly, hiding her ugly, ragged fingertips.

When the group gathered for Taps at the end of the meeting, Captain made a brief announcement.

'Tonight is Mrs Wylie's last evening with us as Lieutenant. Let's wish her well, and give her a round of applause to show our appreciation for all the work she's done for us.'

There were a few gasps of surprise. Lucy stood open-mouthed and clapped mechanically along with the others.

On the way home, Lucy said, 'I thought you were joking when you said you were giving up. I mean, I thought you would stay a bit longer.'

Hilda shook her head. 'When the writing is on the wall, you just have to leave. I can't wait to get home and get this monkey-suit off.'

Lucy felt cold and numb. Her mother was in no mood for discussion. Lucy wisely remained silent.

The next day, it was too wet for a walk, the kind of day when the mist never lifts and it never quite gets light. Lucy helped Hilda chop a basketful of

Seville oranges and stir them into a huge, aluminium tureen, to make a year's supply of marmalade. Hilda was hoping to save a few shillings on the grocery bills. However, making marmalade proved unexpectedly difficult, and she regretted buying the large saucepan. Mrs Mayfield's hand-written recipe didn't include instructions to leave the lid off during boiling and simmering. Consequently, Hilda spent two hours stirring and fretting over the seething mixture, which seemed to take forever to thicken. The result was a rich, dark, treacly substance, which Albert appreciated, although far fewer jars were filled than Hilda had hoped. Lucy made decorative labels and carefully wrote on each one, using her favourite felt-tip pen:

Best Edencroft Marmalade

(AUTUMN 1969)

Lucy found a pink crayon to colour a background for the labels and thought the result looked very professional. She wrote to Georgina about the marmalade, and about Albert's new hobby of wine-making with apples and wild blackberries from the garden.

'Clear the table when you've finished,' Hilda said, 'I'm going to tidy the pantry and make a space for all those jars.'

Alone in the breakfast room, Lucy stared at the three thick glass demijohns in the corner of the room, each one containing enough wine to fill several bottles. Albert's home-made wines were well on the way to being ready by Christmas, and Lucy looked forward to designing more labels. Each demijohn was sealed with a wide cork, a delicate glass fermentation lock at its centre. Every few seconds, a bubble slowly formed, then escaped into the air, exuding a sharp, fruity fragrance. Lucy placed her finger over the trumpet of one of the locks, watching the bubble grow bigger, then released it to give a louder pop and a stronger smell. Through the thick glass wall of the demijohns, myriads of tiny bubbles were rising as the yeast did its work. It was a weeks-long process that no one could hurry.

Lucy decided to watch one more bubble. Unluckily, this time, the unit fell onto the tiled floor, shattering the delicate glass into fragments. Surveying the disarray, Lucy was reminded of the tea and typewriter incident. Time could not be turned back, what was done was done. However, her parents were furious and insisted she pay for the damage. Lucy crumbled inwardly – recalling the time three years ago when she was made to pay for a can of enamel paint she had taken from the garage to smarten up her bicycle. Her parents had called her a thief. The memory turned like a rusty knife. Burning with anger and shame, Lucy revisited the *Vicar Plot*, determined to improve herself at any cost. For the next week, she buried herself in homework, refused luxury foods, and chastised her body by wearing insufficient clothing in worsening weather. Insomnia returned with a vengeance. On weekday nights, Lucy's bedtime was at half past nine, irrespective of whether or not she felt tired. Through the thin walls, she would hear the ten o'clock news start and finish and still be wide awake, often until after eleven, when her parents were preparing for bed.

On Saturday, Lucy met Georgina, the visit having been postponed due to the trip to visit Rose. Lucy imagined Georgina would be old-fashioned and bespectacled, like Margaret Pritchard, and she wasn't far wrong. Both Georgina and her mother were dressed in thick, woollen cardigans, nylon slacks and fur-trimmed carpet slippers, in spite of their house being centrally heated. Georgina's pale face was framed by a thick mop of tight blonde curls. Myopic eyes stared from behind heavy-rimmed glasses.

The Mayfields' chalet bungalow was ultra-modern and carpeted throughout, with a distinct smell of newness. Georgina's bedroom was open-plan, with neatly filled shelves like the interior of a shop. Books, toys, ornaments and folded clothes were a colourful feast for the eyes.

'We could play Scrabble?' Georgina suggested.

'Okay,' Lucy nodded.

Georgina was slow and ponderous and chose short, simple words. Lucy quickly became bored and sleepy in the dry heat, her mind wandering to the homely disarray of her rustic bedroom at home. In a practically perfect house, there was nothing left to do. Also, Georgina wasn't much of a talker. Tea was served at six o'clock, in the long, clinical-looking dining-room. Mr Mayfield, a small, balding man in his fifties, briefly acknowledged Lucy's presence, then sat down to a pot of tea and scrambled eggs on toast. Scarcely anyone spoke, every little sound seemed exaggerated. Chinking cups, pouring tea and the gentle clack of spoon on china filled funereal quietness. Georgina smiled pleasantly across the table, and Lucy returned the gesture with a wry grin. She reached nervously for another salmon and cucumber sandwich.

'That's right, dear. Help yourself!' Mrs Mayfield said. Lucy blushed nervously. The grandfather clock ticked solemnly from the corner, looking out of place in such a modern house. Lucy ate in silence and was glad when it was time to leave.

'Well – what was it like?' Hilda asked later.

'It was all right,' Lucy answered, suspecting her mother was angling for a detailed description of the house, but she couldn't be bothered giving one. Lucy wondered what to do with the rest of the winter evening. She knew now Georgina would never become a close friend. Sighing, she wandered into the kitchen, where her mother stood, apron-clad at the sink, her arms submerged to the elbows in a bowl of dishes. Hilda frowned and was muttering under her breath.

'You know the Dawsons' cat has had kittens?' Hilda asked.

Lucy nodded. 'Fenella told me last Friday.'

'I saw Mrs Dawson when I was out walking Dotty this afternoon,' Hilda continued. 'One of the kittens has gone missing.'

Lucy was staring blankly at the hinges on the pantry door, worrying about next Thursday's maths test.

'A tiny, sandy coloured ginger kitten, like our Marmie used to be when he was younger, but ginger all over and without any white patches. Mrs Dawson asked us to look out for it. It might be sheltering somewhere in the undergrowth.'

Hilda shook her head and sighed deeply. 'I don't give much hope for the poor little mite. It'll be... God only knows where... perhaps, tonight, you could say a little prayer for it?'

Lucy found the request strangely disquieting.

'All right, Mum,' she agreed quietly.

Later that night in the dark silence of her room, Lucy remembered the kitten. Cowering under the bedclothes, she tried to pray, in the same way she had done as a small child, 'Dear Lord Jesus, please help that kitten...'

The words seemed to fall on hollow emptiness, swallowed in silent oblivion. But she had done what she had been asked to do, believing nothing would change.

The next day, on her way home from school, Lucy scanned the hedgerows, parting brambles, peering deep into bushes, but found nothing. The Dawsons, friends, and neighbours continued their search, but the little kitten was never found.

11: LACK AND LOSS

Against all the odds, Lucy decided to write another December diary. She hadn't the heart to throw away last year's disastrous December diary but had kept it well hidden. She certainly wasn't going to tell her parents she planned on writing another one, nor that she had convinced Georgina to write one also. On the First of December, Lucy wrapped gifts: socks and gloves for her parents, a box of Quality Street chocolates for Marion and Paul, a 1970 diary for Uncle Peter, and two packages for Aunt Rose, a home-made tag on each one.

For Auntie Rose: A special Christmas gift and get-well
wish from LUCY xxx

Inside the gaudy wrappings were lavender-scented bath cubes, and a set of writing paper and envelopes. *Aunt Rose has been ill and should have an extra present*, Lucy sighed, putting the parcels away.

In her diary, she wrote:

Wrapping the presents and hiding them in the drawer gave me great pleasure. It was the last remnant of childhood like cobwebs left unnoticed in the corners of a room. I thought I had swept away the things of childhood long ago, but at Christmas time there still remains a vestige of the magic of childhood – a thrill which fills me with joy and hope...

'Are you ready, Lucy?' Albert asked, through the closed door. Lucy quickly hid the diary under the bed.

'Just coming, Dad!' Lucy hurried to get her coat. Albert had agreed to take Lucy to Guides and spend the hour in a local pub, where dogs were welcome and Dotty had befriended a chocolate Labrador called Towser. Albert enjoyed the opportunity to get out of the house to drink a pint of bitter and share cigarettes and gardening tips with Towser's owner, a retired farmer called Jim.

Lucy entered the Guides' hall with fresh hope. She was looking forward to an evening of carol singing and artwork, and the meeting lived up to her expectations. Since Hilda's resignation, Captain Merryweather had hurled herself enthusiastically into planning the Christmas concert and seemed to be coping well without a Lieutenant. It was decided the Guides would stage two puppet shows; a typical family Christmas, and the Nativity. The decision who was to do what was made with the toss of a coin. Lucy's patrol was assigned The Birth of Jesus. Initially disappointed, Lucy soon got used to the idea. At home, she found materials and props and started writing the script. She sat on the sofa, feeling the warmth of a roaring fire, and hearing the gentle tap of a line of Christmas cards on the wall.

'That's convection, you know,' Albert explained. 'A warm current of air rising from the fire, lifting the cards.'

Lucy wasn't listening.

Suddenly the telephone rang.

'Who on earth could that be?' Hilda muttered, rushing into the hall.

'Hello! Peter!' Hilda cried a note of hysteria in her voice. 'She's back in hospital? No... oh no...'

Lucy strained to listen, regretting the words she had written in a get-well card to Rose, only last week. *I'm so glad you're feeling better and back home again. They think of clever things nowadays to make people better, so we all look forward to seeing you in the new year.*

Hilda emerged from the hall speechless and ashen. Albert and Hilda exchanged glances. On the hissing fire, a log crackled.

'Peter's going to need all the help he can get – and as for the children? God only knows how they will cope,' Hilda sighed, her voice barely a whisper. Lucy found it strange, hearing her older teenage cousins being referred to as children.

All week, a dark cloud of despondency hung over the household. Lucy shut herself in her room, trying to fool herself nothing was wrong. At school, she stood outside the social bubble of frivolity. Festivities were in full swing, reflecting a tinselly, artificial happiness that continually evaded Lucy's grasp. Everyone was in a festive mood. Janet Ford, a length of gold tinsel around her head, leaned out of a window and yelled, 'MERRY CHRIMBLE, EVERYONE!'

Failing to share the merry mood, Lucy felt utterly empty and alone. *If only I could be like other people*, she thought desperately. Confusion culminated in raw self-pity. *The Vicar Plot had failed. Stuff self-improvement!* Lucy seethed, wallowing in bitterness and resentment. Her life was hard. She was denied Christmas fun. Last year, bullies had ruined her Christmas, and doubtless, they would do the same again – and now this! Someone in the family just had to get seriously ill and be at death's door at Christmas, of all times!

Emerging from her room that evening, Lucy tried to sound cheerful.

'Shall I put up the cards that came today?'

'You needn't bother,' Hilda said.

'But I could just stand them up on the shelf, couldn't I?'

Lucy sensed a storm brewing.

'Put them up if you like, I suppose,' Hilda answered in monotone.

'All right!' Lucy answered brightly, her voice betraying an angry edge.

Hilda gave a muffled, choking sound. 'I just can't face the thought of celebrating Christmas this year,' she sobbed, 'not with our dear Rose so terribly ill. It just isn't right.'

The paper Father Christmas and gaudy animals with bulging tissue-paper bodies suddenly seemed ludicrous and absurd. Something inside Lucy snapped. One by one, she tore each of the decorations down and cast them in a sad heap on the floor, completing the meltdown with an irate tirade.

'Oh well, if that's what you want, we might as well take all this lot down and have done with Christmas – AND the tree! That'll have to come down too. If we're not going to celebrate Christmas, then what's the point of having any of these stupid decorations?'

Albert snorted behind his cigarette, and Hilda stood stock still, open-mouthed, the double-edged sword of grief turning mercilessly within her. Tormented by the impending loss of a sister-in-law, and the sudden rebellion of a beloved daughter in one fell swoop, she could take no more. Was this ranting, raving tirade of total selfishness truly coming from her sweet, darling little Lucy, whom she had always believed in and trusted?

Hilda was mortified.

In ominous silence, Lucy felt her heart thumping.

The anguish of last year's diary debacle was back.

Lucy rued writing another diary. Why would this December be better than last? It was probably worse. A chapter title for the day –Decorations Down – flashed across her mind. She bit her lip until it drew blood.

Albert spoke first. 'You don't care a jot about Uncle Peter! All you ever think about is yourself. Me, me, me – every time. Never mind about anyone else. As long as you've got your nice, easy little life everyone else can go and take a running jump, as far as you're concerned. For God's sake, why don't you at least try and put yourself in someone else's position for once!'

Hilda turned slowly, revealing a tear-stained face. 'That's right! You heard! 'Now – go! Out of my sight!'

Cold and numb, Lucy went quietly to her room and took comfort in homework. But her concentration failed, her father's words resounding in her ears: your nice, easy little life. Stifled by anger and frustration, Lucy craved happiness, security, friendship, and – dare she even say – love?

But what did she know about life, love and death?

With a heart as heavy as stone, Lucy knew she knew nothing of these things. Three days passed. Lucy and her parents exchanged only the necessary words and went about their daily routines. Lucy found the short days and long, dark nights curiously comforting.

The phone call everyone had been dreading came at six on Friday morning.

The shrill bell-tone pierced the darkness of the draughty hallway, shattering the silence of the pitch-black midwinter night. Lucy heard her mother stumble into the hallway, pick up the phone and speak briefly, in stifled sobs.

Twelve hours later, Hilda was back home, seated at the square dining-room table, her hands cupped around a steaming mug of tea. Her coat still on, the collar turned up, she related snatches of the day's events. Albert sat listening, a cigarette smouldering lazily in his hand. Lucy sat facing the fire, ostensibly doing homework.

'The early morning express train to London was practically empty,' Hilda began. 'I got a hot drink and a snack in the buffet car, as there'd been no time for breakfast, not even a cup of tea. I just had to get to Peter as soon as humanly possible. The train was fast. I sat huddled in the empty buffet car, clasping my hands around a paper cup. The tea kept spilling every time the train went over a bump.

I don't know what time I arrived – it was just getting light, so I suppose it must have been about nine o'clock. Peter, John and Sarah were wandering about the house in a daze. Peter told me they all stayed up, all night, with Rose, until the end. Just like Peter, Dad and I, when we lost our dear mother when we were young. When Peter greeted me this morning, he put his arms around me and said nothing. No need for words. Besides, what could we say?'

Hilda paused in her narrative, struggling to fight back the tears. The orange glow of the fire flickered on the ceiling. Lucy stared at the cheerful colours on the cushion covers and fumbled absent-mindedly with the tasselled fringe.

'If I hadn't been there,' Hilda continued, 'they'd have sat there all day, not touching a morsel of food or drink. But I got them to face reality. Rose would've wanted it that way. "Life goes on", I said, so I made them all a pot of tea and rustled up a bit of lunch, just a few bread rolls and some soup.'

Hilda stopped, her voice heavy with emotion. 'Whatever are they going to do, now that she is gone? Rose was such a good wife and mother! One of the world's best, with a true heart of gold. Only yesterday John asked Rose if she could sew a button on his shirt, but she was too weak to hold the needle. When she was taken to hospital they all went with her and never left her side. The end came in the early hours – the coldest, darkest part of the night, before it begins to get light and when the body is at its lowest ebb...'

Hilda buried her head in her hands and sprawled onto the table, tears flowing unchecked into the tablecloth, her small frame racked with silent sobs and exhaustion. Albert sat down beside her and gently put his arms around her, saying nothing. In the grate, damp logs hissed and crackled, firelight flickered. The Christmas tree stood unlit and forgotten in the corner by the television. The fluorescent light in the kitchen buzzed faintly in the background, casting a harsh pool of light through the half-open door.

Lucy felt nothing. She couldn't believe Rose was dead. Uncle Charles had passed away peacefully at the ripe old age of ninety-one, but Rose had been barely half as old, with her children still living at home. Lucy had never felt close to Aunt Rose, a feeling which served only to widen the gulf between herself and her mother.

In the days that followed, Lucy didn't feel like doing anything. *What's the point?* She asked herself dismally. But she went to school, simply because she had to. Also, she knew she was committed to going to the Guides' concert and helping organise her patrol's puppet show. On the evening of the concert, Albert agreed to give her a lift, and reluctantly, Hilda agreed to go and watch the show. The little hall was crowded, and Hilda sat near the back, huddled in her overcoat and headscarf, hoping nobody would speak to her. With a scraping of chairs and customary chorus of coughing and throat-clearing, the audience prepared themselves for an hour of dubious entertainment.

First on the agenda was The Bloggs's Family Christmas. Hilda heard an annoying babble of children's voices and saw toys falling into a decorated cardboard box, into which small hands continually darted. Hilda yawned and stared at the skirting board. In a brief interlude, carols were sung, and the Guides played "The First Nowell", "Once in Royal David's City" and "Silent Night" on the recorder – an enthusiastic but badly executed performance. Then Lucy's piping voice announced, 'The Birth of Jesus'.

Hilda looked up. Across a sea of heads, she saw a makeshift puppet theatre at the front of the hall. Hilda braced herself for disappointment but was pleasantly surprised. Each scene was easily identified, and the words clearly spoken. Hilda even recognised some of the decorations from home: the little wooden donkey Uncle Charles had given Lucy several Christmases ago, and the cardboard angel with the tissue-paper dress, which had been up on the wall a few days ago.

'The Nativity was a nice little play,' Hilda told Lucy on the way home, 'The story came across very clearly. It was much better than the other puppet show. I recognised our wooden donkey and that angel I bought in Woolworth's last year.'

Lucy thought she detected an edge of humour in her mother's voice. For an instant, her heart leapt with hope, but she said nothing. Lucy secretly continued with her December Diary, her frozen heart beginning to melt. She described the concert, the presents she had bought for the family, and the letters exchanged with Georgina. She wrote nothing about school or about Aunt Rose. Christmas Eve was the day of the funeral. In her diary, Lucy merely mentioned a trip to London to visit her uncle and cousins.

The truth was quite different. In the kitchen of the small, suburban house, mourners gathered round the square table where the familiar, glass sugar-basin with its chipped edges stood in the middle, teaspoons lay scattered on the plastic cloth, leaving brown, sticky stains which no-one bothered to wipe away. The same frilly net curtains hung at the window, draped dismally over the bowl of artificial fruit, each item bearing a visible layer of dust and grime. Lucy recalled the day Rose had come home from the market, saying 'I thought this bunch of fruit looked nice and realistic – and it'll last a lot longer than the real thing!' Ironically, the plastic apples, oranges and bananas had outlasted the person who had bought them. It seemed odd that such banal, inanimate objects should still be there and not their owner. Why is man's mortal frame so weak it cannot outlast a few pathetic, lifeless man-made objects? Lucy kept expecting Rose to appear through a doorway at any moment, her curlers in, wearing her floral apron and greeting her guests with twinkling eyes and winsome smile. Strange it seemed, family and friends gathered here, in Rose's house, without Rose, in crowded rooms, many a moist eye and tear-soaked handkerchief, all struggling with grief. Dark clothes matched midwinter skies that never got properly light. Marion sat serious and sullen, her face hidden behind the dark lace veil of a pill-box hat. In a black, circular skirt, black tights and pullover, Lucy sat hunched by the window, staring out at fogbound suburbia.

The front door swung open, admitting in more mourners and icy blasts. Lucy envied the mothers with babies and toddlers, whose innocent infant cries broke through hushed, tempered conversations. A young man burst into tears, comforted by his wife. Lucy overheard someone say he was Rose's first son from a previous marriage – information Lucy had never been privy to. Feeling like an intruder, Lucy longed to be invisible.

John stood by the fireplace, hands in pockets, staring at the floor, Sarah sat sullenly by the window staring vacantly the frost-encrusted grass. Hilda said, 'I hear you passed a diploma in hairdressing last week. Well done, Sarah.'

'Yeah, that's right, Auntie Hilda,' Sarah replied, neither moving her head nor averting her gaze from the stunted rose bush in the middle of the garden. Hilda moved away discreetly, ignoring Lucy, who leaned against the wall, staring at the floor.

Mourners filed through sliding doors to the backroom, to pay their last respects. Rose's lifeless body lay in an open coffin between two tall, white candles. The air was heavy with the perfume of incense and the fresh fragrance of floral tributes. Peter looked very different in a black suit, his eyes downcast.

This wasn't the Peter Lucy knew.

'Do you want to see Auntie Rose?' Peter asked. Momentarily, Lucy fought with her thoughts. Part of her was morbidly curious, wanting to see a dead person for the first time, but that would be disrespectful. Rose had been a kind, loving person who had led a good life, and Lucy had scarcely even got to know her.

Peter read the confusion in Lucy's face.

'Or would you prefer to remember her as she was?'

'Yes, I would rather remember her as she was.'

Lucy felt comfortable with that choice.

She hid incognito, among strangers. Passing by the open door, Lucy inadvertently caught a glimpse of the curve of Rose's face and the stillness of her dark eyebrows as she lay still and cold in the open casket. Lucy averted her gaze, feeling awkward and embarrassed. She didn't want to see her aunt in death, clinging instead to the memory of that cheerful, vibrant person who was always smiling.

When the hearse arrived, Lucy went upstairs and watched through the net-curtained window of Sarah's room. Was this Christmas Eve, supposedly the most exciting and joyful time of the year? The notion was ridiculous. It seemed Christmas no longer existed, and perhaps it never had? Snowflakes fluttered from leaden skies, vanishing as they touched the ground. Four pall-bearers in top hats and black swallow-tail suits walked to the front door, reappearing minutes later, bearing the flower-decked, oak coffin to the waiting hearse. Lucy stayed behind with all the children, of whom she was probably the oldest. She sat in a corner by herself, doodling on the cover of her diary. When the party returned, Lucy stood beside her uncle in the empty lounge. Someone had extinguished the candles, the lingering smell of molten wax a poignant reminder this was supposed to be Christmas. Only then did Lucy notice there was not one single Christmas card or decoration in the house.

'Hard times,' said Peter, shaking his head slowly, 'Hard times, Lucy. But life goes on.'

Lucy nodded silently and looked at the floor. For a brief moment, she was tempted to wish her uncle a happy Christmas but thought it best to stay silent. Then her mother beckoned her to the door, saying it was time to leave.

The long journey home began in silence. Hilda shook her head and sighed. 'The good die young. Rose certainly knew how to live, and she also knew how to die. She was so dignified, so brave. Poor John and Sarah. They're the ones who'll have to be brave now. They're bearing up so well, those kids, and dear, dear Peter,' Hilda's voice quavered. 'He needs our prayers now more than ever.'

The sense of finality struck Hilda afresh, tears welled up, silently spilling down her face, onto her tightly-clasped, gloved hands and black patent leather handbag.

She would need time. Lots of time – years, decades, perhaps the rest of her life?

Albert said nothing, his eyes fixed intently on the road ahead.

Lucy sat motionless in the back seat, staring numbly at the blackness of the midwinter's night. The desire for suffering no longer satisfied her. No amount of physical pain would appease her callous conscience and hurting heart. She began to harbour a secret fascination for death itself.

12: Hopes

'Why didn't you tell me?' Alison asked. 'You always keep things to yourself. People never know what you're thinking. Nobody at school had any idea what you were going through.'

In the undulating meadow, Dotty and Cedric frolicked in the crisp January sunshine. Lucy hadn't expected Alison to be so sympathetic, nor for her to attribute her pre-Christmas melancholy solely to the death of her aunt. She frowned and said nothing, leaving Alison with the belief she was still grieving. Lucy knew her sadness was for herself alone. She cast her mind back to last year's birthday party when Alison had arrived late, subdued and tearful after the death of her grandfather.

'Suzy Munro also died of cancer this Christmas,' Alison said.

'Yes. On Christmas Eve, the day of my aunt's funeral.' Lucy's voice was monotone. She didn't share Alison's interest in popular music celebrities. With cold reflection, Lucy contemplated her lack of sentiment for others.

'Suzy was so young, and with so much to live for,' Alison said.

Lucy said nothing. She felt like an outsider, inwardly numb, brooding about her own shortcomings. Sometimes she wondered if she was even human.

The dogs burst in and out of dense hedgerows, barking excitedly on the trail of rabbits.

'Come on, Cedric!' Alison's call echoed against the chalk ridge, but the lively Labrador had disappeared from view.

'Time will heal, I suppose,' Lucy answered dully, 'I've got to accept that losing a relative is part of life. Everyone dies eventually.'

Deep inside yawned an empty, aching chasm. Lucy looked at the silvery-blue horizon of Westcombe Bay.

'Where are the dogs?' Alison asked.

'Dottyyyy!' Lucy screeched, clapping her gloved hands and twirling the lead around her wrist. Suddenly both dogs hurtled through the hedge and onto the meadow, flashes of black and white upon the frost-speckled ground.

'Exams start, week after next,' Alison said.

'Yes. I'm not looking forward to it.'

'Nor me.'

'Done any revision yet?'

'Yeah, but not much.'

Lucy was past caring, or so she thought.

Watching the dogs frolicking in the frost was a cheering sight, but the exam challenge loomed like the sheer cliff of an unclimbed mountain. Swallowing her fears, Lucy took a deep breath. Then from deep within sprang a defiant desire to begin again, to excel. She stood tall, silently vowing to make every effort to attain the best results ever – results that would amaze everyone.

Later that day, she pinned a typewritten notice on her bedroom door:

PLEASE KNOCK BEFORE ENTERING

STUDENT PREPARING FOR EXAMINATIONS

It wasn't long before Hilda knocked, armed with tea and biscuits. Lucy sat on the bed, surrounded by books, an open science jotter on her lap. Hilda smiled approvingly.

'Thanks, Mum. You don't think the word student is too grown up?'

'Not at all. A student can be any age.'

Lucy felt a flush of encouragement. She set aside a study plan for weekday evenings, full days at the weekend, and kept to it. She approached each exam calmly, answering questions as thoroughly and relevantly as she could. By the end of the week, she had no reason to doubt she had done well.

As a reward, Hilda took Lucy to see the school production of *The Teahouse of the August Moon* – a modern play set in war-time Japan. The lead actress was Gloria Wisdom, a dynamic redhead and academic high-flyer, studying for four A-levels. Lucy dreamed of owning a well-stocked Japanese tea garden, its visitors ever pleasant-mannered and calm, a life of serenity and joy.

On Sunday, Georgina came to tea. Hilda had insisted on reciprocating. Before tea, Hilda dropped the girls at the smaller riding school at High Lea, preferring it over Miss Crawford's down-at-heel establishment. Creosoted ranch fencing surrounded well-maintained stables pungent with disinfectant. The young instructor helped Lucy tack up her pony, as she had apparently been shown incorrectly by Doris. Georgina rode confidently, but Lucy was uneasy in the saddle of a pony who wasn't Ranger. When the horses broke into a gentle canter, Lucy's new riding hat felt tight, and the visor obscured her view. She adjusted the brim – an action she quickly regretted. The pony jerked its head upwards, Lucy tightened the reins, pressing her knees against the horse's flanks, striving to stay in the saddle. Instantly she was projected into the air and landed on soft ground, embarrassed but unhurt.

'Are you all right?' someone asked.

Lucy stood up and brushed herself down. 'I think so.'

'Firefly can be unpredictable sometimes,' the instructor explained apologetically.

Back in the saddle, Lucy thought no more of the incident. Georgina didn't tease her, and no one at school would know what happened. The afternoon in the fresh air helped Lucy and Georgina do justice to Hilda's spread of salad, boiled eggs, triangles of wholemeal bread and butter, and plates of home baking. Georgina behaved impeccably.

'Georgina's a pleasant-mannered girl, and rather quaint, just like her mother,' Hilda said later.

'Am I like you?' Lucy asked.

'You and I are very much alike, Lucy. We're honest, decent, upright citizens, energetic and hard-working. You also have a creative streak, from your father.'

'Yes, Mum.' Lucy agreed. It was a hard benchmark to measure up to.

Two days later, Lucy sat on the science laboratory stool, rigid as a taxidermied bird on its perch, hoping to wake from a bad dream. In her hand, a paper scored with vivid red, an abysmal grade. All around, students surveyed their papers with smugness or indifference. *What went wrong?* Neat diagrams of electrical circuits count for nothing, if every calculation is incorrect. Her father would be bitterly disappointed at such a poor result in his beloved subject! But what's the point of holding a post-mortem on something that's clearly dead? And Mother? Lucy dared not speculate on her reaction, especially having pledged to do better than ever this time. No, she's done worse than ever – failed five subjects – the worst results yet. Stray tears spilt through clenched fists, smudging her answer sheet. Mr Finnegan's voice was barely audible above ambient chatter. Lucy watched the second hand of the wall clock jump to eleven thirty, reminding her of a television jingle.

At half past eleven, I will be in heaven, with a nice cup of tea...

A mocking parody sprang to mind.

But I will be in heaven when I'm in class 3C!

A move down to 3C would mean easier work, less pressure. Fresh thoughts fell like raindrops after drought: *In 3C, I'll be able to learn German! That'll really please Mum!* Lucy was good at French and would doubtless be good at German. Then she could write to and visit the cousins in Germany! In 3C, she would escape from class bullies, but be more exposed to Jane Haslett and her sporty cronies. Nevertheless, Lucy's mind was made up. She looked forward to her proposal being approved and presenting her parents with a fait accompli at the end of the day. At break, she headed straight to Mr Kingsley's office. In the foyer, she felt her legs weaken, and her knees tremble.

Supposing he said no?

The yellow, gloss-painted door with the copper plaque bearing the one word HEADMASTER seemed a parsec away. Lucy kept walking, looking down at the streaked patterns on the polished, grey-and-yellow floor tiles, her light footsteps swallowed by scores of voices in the corridor. Trembling with apprehension, she rehearsed potential phrases:

Please, Sir, I would like to discuss an important matter concerning...

Because of my exam results think it would be best if...

I know I did really badly in the exams, so if I am put in 3C I will do better...

She knocked timidly. No response. She knocked again, a short, sharp rap that hurt her knuckles, reminding her of the time Mrs Pygge beat her with wooden blackboard pegs at Macadam Primary School for looking out of the window.

'Come in!'

Lucy took a deep breath and opened the door. The office smelt of ink, new paper, and strong coffee.

Mr Kingsley looked over the top of his spectacles.

'Ah, Lucy! What brings you here?'

Lucy twisted her hands behind her back. 'Sir, um – it's about –'

'Sit down, Lucy. Take your time.'

Lucy sat down. 'It's the work, Sir, I m – mean – the work in 3D. It's just that I'm finding it rather difficult, and my exam results were a bit disappointing.'

The headmaster looked at Lucy and said nothing. Infused with nervous energy, Lucy began to gabble. 'Maths and Science I find especially hard, and I failed even though I revised lots and tried really hard, and I failed both History and Geography. Five fails, so I thought if I could be put down into form 3C, I could learn German instead of Latin, and I'd be able to do the other subjects properly...'

Lucy's voice faded.

Mr Kingsley raised his eyebrows. 'Others too, are discouraged by their results. Examinations in third year are not meant to be easy, they serve as strict guidance to a student's progress leading up to Ordinary Level public examinations. At this time, everyone finds it harder to achieve the grades they attained last year. If you are struggling with Maths and Sciences, these are the subjects at which you need to work harder. This doesn't mean that in a year or two you won't achieve a pass at O-level. In certain subjects, I note, you've done quite well – French, especially.'

'Then, can I start to learn German? In 3C?' Lucy asked excitedly.

'You can learn German, Lucy, by all means, when the time is right, and doubtless you will do well. But for now, your place is where you are, in form 3D, where, like everyone else you will be stretched to the limits of your ability and beyond. Furthermore you will have opportunity to gain more certificates and better grades.'

'Then you're not going to move me to 3C?'

'No, Lucy. This may be hard for you to accept, but it's for the best in the long run. You were chosen for the D stream on the basis of your academic record from your previous school, and on the work you've done since. I have no reason to doubt your ability – and neither should you.'

Brief eye contact was made.

'Then I do absolutely have to stay where I am?' Lucy asked, but as she spoke, her desire to change classes evaporated.

Mr Kingsley concluded, 'While I'm in authority over you as your headmaster, it is my responsibility to act in accordance with your best interests. I cannot bring myself to allow you simply to throw away your chances of a bright future, because of a mere whim. Therefore, Lucy, you can stay where you are.'

'Yes, sir. Thank you.'

Outside the office, Lucy's head whirled. *I'm not that bad, after all!*

Then fears flooded in. *What should I tell Mum and Dad? Will they believe me if I tell them what Mr Kingsley said?*

Lucy was so distracted she scarcely noticed the bell, nor the stream of jostling students charging up the concrete stairs.

'Move over, Wylie!' someone yelled, elbowing her in the ribs. Lucy trudged upstairs to the customary cuboid of doom on the top floor. More boring lessons, more maths she didn't understand, and yet another homework task she couldn't even begin. How was she to work harder if she couldn't do any of it? All day, Lucy rode the roller-coaster of her active imagination, culminating in the idea of eloping to Paris to be an artist.

That evening, Hilda's reaction was predictable.

'You must face facts,' Hilda said coldly, 'You're just going to have to pull your socks up and work a jolly sight harder. You'll just have to cut down drastically on leisure, and concentrate on your studies!'

'B – but that's just what I did before the exams!'

'Evidently not enough! Shame on you for wasting such a wonderful opportunity for education! And with your gifts and abilities! Listen, this is what we'll do. Every evening, after you've finished your homework, you will recount a detailed summary of everything you've learned in school that day. We simply cannot have you falling behind!'

Lucy didn't see fit to retaliate. Mr Kingsley was probably being polite and saving himself paperwork. It seemed nobody cared, and there was nothing left worth living for. Lucy viewed herself as a freak of nature, a mistake – a useless baggage in everyone's way, occupying valuable space. It occurred to her that her absence would make the world a tidier, happier place. The concept of suicide lurked enticingly – a last-ditch exit from misery, a one-way ticket to the unknown. What alternative was there, if everyone demanded the impossible and nobody liked her? At school, Lucy remained sullen and withdrawn. At home, she talked, laughed and acted as she always did, masking the dark and sinister.

Hilda worried about Lucy's lackadaisical attitude and offhand manner. No doubt, Lucy wasn't telling her everything. 'Was Lucy all right after her fall?' Mrs Mayfield had asked. *What fall? What else was that deceitful daughter of hers hiding?* Alarming scenarios flashed through Hilda's mind. *Shoplifting? Drugs? A clandestine love affair? An illegitimate child?*

Lucy had been an unruly child, often wandering off to play in places frequented by disease-ridden rats and evil people. Hilda sighed heavily. Enough for one evening.

The next day Hilda confronted Lucy over the horse-riding incident.

'Mrs Mayfield said you fell off a horse on Sunday. Is that true?'

'It was nothing, I landed on soft grass,' Lucy said flatly.

Hilda sighed. 'What did you learn in school today? Show me your notes.'

'I aready showed Dad my physics book. It was about electrolysis. We also did French, English, games and art today.'

'Nothing else?'

'Geography.'

'Show me.'

Lucy opened the jotter at a double page of writing with no maps or diagrams. Hilda studied it for thirty seconds and said, 'Tell me, in a few words, what the topic is about.'

'Economy and land use in Scandinavia. Forestry, fishing, smallholdings, and tourism, in Norway – and hydro-electric power,' Lucy answered in monotone. Lately, she had grown to hate Miss Hawksworth and her copious dictated notes. 'Could we stop now, please? I'm so tired.'

By now, it was past bedtime, and her tired brain wasn't functioning.

'Very well', Hilda said. 'It's after eleven o'clock. Tomorrow is another day.'

The next day, Lucy's subdued mood didn't fall unnoticed on her classmates. The bullying intensified, with snickering jeers and taunts at every available opportunity. Lucy found comfort in no one and nothing. The *Vicar Plot* now seemed ludicrously childish. Lucy was convinced she would never become a better person, however hard she tried. With every passing day, things only grew worse. Outside the music room, the din in the corridor was deafening. Nobody talked to Lucy. She stood with her back to everyone else, studying a bronze plaque on the wall.

IN MEMORY OF ALL OUR HEROES WHO MADE THE
SUPREME SACRIFICE DURING THE GREAT WAR 1914-1918 AND
WORLD WAR II, 1939-1945

Below the embossed inscription, fifty fallen warriors were listed, behind every name, a life. A person who had lived and died at another time, for a noble cause. If today's boorish youths had been born decades earlier, they would have been warriors, dying heroically on a battlefield.

The doors opened, and students jostled to their seats. Lucy sat at the back, lost in thought. Why would anyone make the supreme sacrifice – give their life – for anything? She applied the same question to herself. Did she really want her life to end – for nothing? Simply opting out of life because of poor achievement and lack of popularity was tantamount to desertion.

'Which do you think is worse – physical or mental suffering?' the teacher asked.

A few hands went up. The teacher picked Rosemary.

'Mental suffering, Sir,' Rosemary answered.

Rosemary said THAT? Then why does she bully me?

'Yes,' the teacher replied. 'Mental pain is deeper, and can be relieved in the expression of music, by listening to music, playing an instrument, or by composing music.'

An interesting observation – but irrelevant, from Lucy's perspective. She had given up playing the recorder and couldn't remember when she last spontaneously sang a happy song. The contrast between joyful and melancholy was marked – an unbridgeable gap. Lucy viewed herself as two distinct personalities: one light, one dark. She named her lighter side Goody – peaceful, submissive, and kind. Her darker side Genie – aggressive, daring and unscrupulous would strengthen her in adversity, protect her from bullies, and weave an aura of mystique.

Alone in her room that evening, Lucy toyed with the pocket-knife, running her finger across the blade and feeling the point, imagining it would be difficult to penetrate skin. The knife seemed a valuable asset to Genie's tough image. With a sardonic smile, Lucy put the knife back in its sheath and hid it under her pillow. As Goody, Lucy was an optimist, ready to develop her natural abilities. She responded to a magazine advertisement for an art correspondence course. As Genie, Lucy was curious to explore secrets of the supernatural and responded to an advertisement for a personal horoscope. Rekindling her love of music seemed a good idea, so perhaps the clarinet would be the next step up from the recorder? It would also please her parents and boost her self-esteem. But there was one distinct barrier. Abigail Leuchars also played the clarinet. If Abigail discovered Lucy was copying her again, there would be consequences. Surely, Genie would shield Lucy from the fiery darts?

Lucy approached her mother boldly. 'I'd like to start learning the clarinet.'

'Clarinet? Well, I must say, that sounds a good idea, provided it doesn't take the place of homework.'

'It won't. Thanks, Mum,' Lucy said.

Lessons were arranged for a modest fee, including the loan of an instrument. Tuition was one-to-one, on Thursday mornings, during assembly, with a private tutor who let Lucy learn at her own pace, encouraging her to practise at home. The instrument was cumbersome, the fingerings difficult, but Lucy persevered, drawing comfort from the clarinet's low, mellow tone. Her favourite tunes were "We three Kings of Orient are", and "He who would valiant be". The silent listener at Lucy's bedroom door, Hilda concluded Lucy was coping well.

Ever restless, Lucy scanned the school notice board for more extra-curricular activities. Sports, debating, and church meetings were out of the question. Sadly there was no Art club. Drama Club? Lucy remembered Gloria Wisdom's recent stellar performance in *The Teahouse of the August Moon* and decided to attend tomorrow's Drama Club meeting. *You were so convincing,* teachers had said of Lucy's performance as the grandmother in Wordsworth Grammar's production of *The Snow Queen* two years before. *Might acting be a wise career choice?*

'What I really want to do with my life is become an actress,' Lucy declared boldly, over dinner.

Hilda's response was explosive. 'DON'T BE RIDICULOUS! An actress? Whatever next! That is one thing you'll never be.'

Lucy's expression dropped. She whispered feebly, 'Why?'

'Because the world of show business is closed to anyone who isn't already rich or famous, and since we, the Wylies of Edencroft, are neither well-known nor have enough money to live on, you can forget the whole stupid idea.'

The meal ended in silence, and Lucy briefly mourned the loss of another cherished hope.

The next morning was bright and frosty. Hilda dropped Lucy at school on the way to work. Lucy went to her clarinet lesson feeling optimistic, but the new piece of music was challenging and the tune unfamiliar. The tutor was patient, but Lucy grew despondent. Any tune she played sounded wooden and lifeless, not at all like the rippling melodies of woodwind instruments on her father's records. She left the lesson dejected, ready to resign. The clarinet had done little to alleviate her dread of school. At the end of the afternoon, she walked home feeling more cheerful. The sun was shining, sparrows chirped in the hedgerows, and green shoots were peeping above the ground. After the brisk climb up the hill, Lucy burst rosy-cheeked into the breakfast room, where her parents sat drinking tea.

'Hi, Mum and Dad, I'm starving, what's for tea?' Lucy gabbled, dropping her bag and clarinet case on the floor.

Something was different. Hilda sat in the armchair, looking pale and drawn, her face marred with dark streaks.

'Did work finish early today? Have you been gardening?' Lucy asked.

'Sit down, Lucy.' Albert said. 'Your mother met with an accident this morning. The car skidded on ice on the bend between Westcombe and High Lea and went over the hedge. Mum's lucky to be alive.'

'H – how?' Lucy asked.

'I said a quick prayer because I really thought my last moment had come,' Hilda said. 'The car flipped over and landed in a field. I thanked God for preserving me, and concluded He must have more work for me to do in this life! I crawled out of the wreckage, beside a herd of Jersey heifers chewing the cud, as if seeing a car fly over the hedge and land in front of them happened every day. Black ice is invisible, on the point of melting, and extremely dangerous. If you hadn't had to carry your clarinet today, you'd have cycled to school, I wouldn't have given you a lift, and this wouldn't have happened.'

The last remark wasn't intended to sound like an accusation. Lucy felt guilty but had found an excuse to give up the clarinet.

'Are you okay?' Lucy asked.

'Just a few bumps and bruises, that's all.'

'Did you go to hospital?'

'I went to Casualty. Nothing broken, just a few superficial cuts and bruises. They let me home after an hour. But the car's a write-off.'

'What do you mean?'

'The insurance company won't pay for repair costs if they're higher than the vehicle's value. If the the car is scrapped, we get the money to replace it.'

'Oh,' Lucy said, saddened at the news of the green Morris Traveller's abrupt end. She stared out of the window, wondering when new leaves would appear on the monster shape of the trees of Biddlecombe Copse.

'I've decided I don't want any more clarinet lessons,' Lucy said. 'It's very difficult, and I have too much homework.'

'Very well, dear, if that's what you want,' Hilda said.

It was so easy. A done deal in less than a minute.

Lucy's next new project was learning German. Her mother's faded copy of *Teach Yourself Modern German* was far from modern, the Gothic print devilishly difficult to decipher. Lucy was captivated by the current Geography topics on the industrial region of northern Germany, and the below-sea-level polders of the Netherlands. Lucy hoped one day to meet her mother's cousins, learn their language, and experience their way of life. Cousin Martha lived in the textile-producing town of Kochendorf, and Lucy's grandfather hailed from a humble farmstead, twenty kilometres away on the Dutch border. Lucy decided to buy a German dictionary and phrasebook, determined to learn German immediately.

However, by a twist of fate, Lucy was quarantined by mumps, a childhood illness which had previously passed her by. The prospect of three weeks without bullies was welcome, but losing points from missed assignments would significantly lower her overall term grade. No option existed for work to be sent home. If lessons were missed, they were missed. Lucy said nothing to her parents. During her imposed isolation, Lucy enjoyed sunnier, warmer days, spending long hours outside, sketching and painting flowers and landscapes.

The reply from the horoscope advert arrived first.

Astroguides Ltd.
13b, Fanchurch Street,
LONDON EC5

March 25th, 1970.

Dear Miss Wylie,

Thank you for your enquiry and your interest in Astroguides Ltd. In accordance with your request, I am pleased to present you with your detailed, personal Horoscope.

You are a strong, determined woman with immense potential and a great deal to offer. Life's path isn't always easy for you, but you have the strength of character and the courage and fortitude to persevere through the toughest of trials, both personal and financial.

Because you are surrounded by people who are willing to help, you will have every opportunity to support your family and friends. You have the ability to offer comfort to your colleagues and deal with turbulent working relationships. Younger folk will respect and admire you because...

Lucy didn't bother reading further. No doubt the exact same letter had been sent to thousands of girls and women the length and breadth of the country. Disappointed, she tore the letter up and threw it away.

The next day Hilda got to the mailbox first.

'Letter for you, with a London postmark,' Hilda said, handing Lucy a drab, brown envelope.

'Oh, yes, that,' Lucy said, trying to sound indifferent.

She ripped open the envelope, revealing a glossy flyer with a picture of Van Gogh's Sunflowers and a hand-written letter. Lucy gasped and handed the letter to her mother.

Hilda adjusted her spectacles and frowned. 'You realise what this means?'

Lucy looked blank.

'They want you to begin a correspondence course, which means expensive, private tuition.'

'No, it doesn't,' protested Lucy. 'It says the art school principal is coming to see me personally next Saturday, because he's really interested in the sample drawings I sent...'

'Oh, I don't doubt he's interested! Interested enough to come all the way to the back of beyond, because of some starry-eyed little girl willing to part with money she doesn't have. The conniving shark! Do I really have to spell it out for you, Lucy? This is just one big con-trick! Ten pounds registration fee? What a nerve! I've a good mind to write to this Mark Worthington person myself, and give him a piece of my mind!'

'But you can't –'

'Can't I? Well I'm not having him come here on any pretext, and that's final. I will write to this man and make it perfectly clear that my thirteen-year-old daughter responded to his advertisement, unaware of the financial requirements. I'm sending the letter without a stamp. Let him pay for the postage! And if he shows up here I'll get the police,' Hilda said coldly.

Lucy looked shocked. 'But the letter won't get there without a stamp!'

'It'll get there, all right,' Hilda growled.

Saturday came and went, and of the dubious art club and its zealous proprietor nothing more was heard.

Lucy returned to school a week before the Easter break. Everyone was curious about her absence.

'Did you have the 'flu?' Alison asked.

Lucy said nothing. *Let them believe what they want*, she thought. Abigail and the gang crowded round, suggesting more reasons for her absence.

'Chicken-pox?'

'Morning sickness?'

'Nah – she was prob'ly skiving off – lazy bitch!'

'I thought you'd left!'

'Or been put in the looney-bin!'

Raucous laughter followed, and then mercifully, the bell sounded.

On the last day of term, Lucy woke to the merry chirping of sparrows in the privet hedge, her mood marred by the dreaded Class Positions, to be read in afternoon assembly. Her hopes of being placed anywhere higher than last had dwindled to nil.

Lessons began with French and the option of a French penfriend. Lucy completed an application form, giving animals, art, fashion, and music as her favourite pastimes. Chat between lessons took her mood down a notch.

'Who do you think will be top?' drawled Fiona.

'You, probably,' simpered Janet.

Other voices chimed in.

'My money's on Jonathan Whitmore.'

'I think it'll be Hilary Masters – she's a dark-horse, always swotting quietly at the back.'

'What about Megan?'

Maybe, but hopefully not Janet, she's such a know-it-all...

Janet sat her desk, her nose in a book. Tension hung in the air like evil ether. Afternoon assembly hovered over Lucy like an executioner's axe. At lunchtime, bets were made on who would be top of the class. Lucy made herself scarce, not risking hearing her name mentioned as the class dunce.

At last, the dreaded time came. Mr Edgington, now head of lower school, stood sphinx-like on the stage, above a sea of expectant faces.

'This is the moment you've all been waiting for. Your class positions for this term.'

Silence. Somewhere at the back of the hall, a sneeze was stifled.

'Form 1A. First, Anthony Harrington, second, Amanda Griffiths, third,

Margaret Hawkins...'

Mr Edgington read the list of names in slow, laconic fashion, like a bad sports commentator giving late football results. Second-year lists were next, followed by forms 3A, 3B and 3C. As the first name of 3D was read out, Lucy adjusted her hair-band, surreptitiously sticking a finger in each ear. She counted slowly, in her head, from one to thirty. Then she looked up with a calm half-smile, in time for Mr Edgington's customary pep talk about using time wisely during the holidays, staying safe on the beach, and not acting irresponsibly. The bell rang, and students were dismissed. In the foyer, Lucy dodged the crowd and hurried home, where her parents were too preoccupied to remember that such a thing as Class Positions even existed.

The next day, against initial expectations, the green Morris Traveller was returned – shining and bright as new, after extensive repairs and panel-beating. Hilda was pleased to have her own transport again, as weekday walks to and from High Lea bus stop had eaten significantly into her working day.

'I think my migraines are due to the perpetually flickering fluorescent lights in the office,' Hilda complained. 'So I'm looking for another job.'

Hilda's decision prompted Lucy to do likewise. On Saturday, Lucy embarked on her quest. Enquiries in Westcombe's boutiques and souvenir shops yielded polite refusals, but at Woolworth's, Lucy was immediately offered an interview in the office at the back of the shop. The bespectacled manager in suit and tie asked for her name and address, date of birth, and details of previous work experience. Based on her fruit-picking and dish-washing work of the previous summer, Lucy was offered a Saturday job, nine to five, starting next week. It had been so easy. Lucy left the store euphoric, not caring a jot what her mother would say. She needn't have worried in any case.

'It's a step up from the Merry Teapot,', Hilda said, 'although you mustn't neglect your studies!'

Lucy was to start at Woolworth's, a few days shy of her fourteenth birthday. Life was full again. Goody reigned supreme, Genie had shrunk into the shadows.

Lucy came home to another pleasant surprise. In the mailbox was a blue airmail envelope with a French stamp and Bordeaux postmark. Inside was a flimsy sheet of squared paper, a handwritten letter in good English, from a girl called Martine – an only child, living with her parents, dog, and three cats in a house with a large garden. Lucy was thrilled with a new friendship, albeit a long-distance one.

The next day, Lucy wandered about the garden, discovering by chance a clutch of seven eggs in the derelict pig-pen. One of them was practically weightless, the shell intact. Lucy prodded it with a stick and was assailed with an overpowering stench reminding her of the time a high-spirited schoolboy dropped a stink bomb on a London bus. Lucy took the remaining eggs to the kitchen, where Hilda tested them in a bowl of water.

'If an egg floats in water, it's past its best, and if it sinks, then it could still be fresh,' Hilda said. 'Let your nose be your guide; an egg tells you if it's bad.'

Lucy searched for more secret nests and found Hilda's favourite hen, Little Blondie, in a clump of butcher's broom. The startled hen stood up, conveniently dropping an egg. It was the first and only time Lucy ever saw a hen actually lay an egg, and as it happened, it was Easter Sunday.

The following Saturday morning, Lucy arrived at Woolworth's at ten to nine. The sign on the door read CLOSED, but lights were on, and assistants in pale blue overalls were busy filling shelves. Lucy pushed the door, and it swung open suddenly. Lucy stumbled forwards, her foot struck something hard. A metal pail lay on its side, a pool of soapy water spreading speedily across the marble floor.

'I'm sorry –' Lucy began, embarrassed at such a dramatic entrance. A young assistant approached. Heavily mascaraed eyes smiled behind a strawberry blonde fringe.

'I know you're keen to start your shopping, but there's no need to kick the bucket! We open in ten minutes,' the girl laughed merrily. Other assistants hovered nearby, a couple of them of them smirking. Goody viewed the brash stranger with mistrust, while Genie feasted on the remark about kicking the bucket – a ludicrous reminder of Lucy's dormant interest in death.

'I'm here to work as a Saturday assistant, and it's my first day,' Lucy said.

The girl guffawed heartily. 'What a way to start a new job! I'm Sally. And you are?'

'I'm Lucy.'

'Come in, Lucy, and watch your step!'

A middle-aged woman in a dark blue overall was hurrying towards her.

'Ah! You must be Miss Wylie. I'm Mrs Hancock, the staff supervisor. Come with me, and I'll issue you with your uniform.'

Lucy was led through a heavy fire door, marked STAFF ONLY, and up a narrow flight of concrete stairs to the rooms above the shop. She was given a quick tour of the kitchen, staff canteen, cloakrooms, and upstairs stockrooms. She was issued with a light blue, nylon check overall with the embroidered Woolworth's logo. She put it on, trembling with pride and apprehension.

'Right, Miss Wylie, follow me,' Mrs Hancock ordered crisply, leading Lucy through another fire door and back downstairs to the shop. The manager, Mr Doyle, was strolling round, hands behind his back, in a relaxed, jovial stance.

'Top of the morning, Lucy! Are you ready for action?'

Lucy nodded nervously. 'Yes, I am. What area will I be working in?'

Mr Doyle gestured to the confectionary counter.

'Sweets,' he said, with a smile.

Lucy was quietly disappointed, as she had hoped for the clothing counter. A dark-haired girl with buck teeth stood behind the well-stocked displays. Lucy was introduced to full-time assistant Pamela. Mrs Hancock showed Lucy how to operate the manual cash register and where extra supplies were kept under the counter. The working space was long and narrow, and there were no seats.

'We're running low on treacle toffees. I'm just going upstairs to get more from the stock room,' Pamela said after Mrs Hancock had gone. 'You can serve any customers while I'm up there. I'll only be a few minutes.'

'Okay,' Lucy agreed. Her first customer was an elderly lady requesting a quarter of mint humbugs from the Pick-n-Mix selection. Lucy carefully weighed and wrapped the sweets, giving a shilling change from a two-shilling piece. At the till's cheerful Ker-ching, a shilling sign popped up in the display. Lucy thanked the customer and watched her put a sweet into her mouth and hobble off. *This is much better than slaving away in a steaming scullery,* Lucy thought, *but it's just a casual job, and I wouldn't want to do just this for the rest of my life...*

The rest of her life? Lucy bit her lip and began replenishing the baskets of sweets.

Pamela had returned. 'You're filling them too full!'

Lucy stopped, feeling awkward. 'What shall I do, then?'

'Just stand here and wait for customers to come.'

Lucy waited for trade to pick up, which it eventually did, and by the end of the morning, her legs were aching. Tea break at eleven o'clock provided a welcome, ten-minute rest. The workers were down-to-earth, ordinary folk, like older versions of the Guides, uncomplicated and unpretentious. They talked about home, family, food, and friends. There was more to life than school. At closing time, Lucy collected her wage packet, stuffed her overall into her bag and cycled home in the hazy sunshine of a warm April afternoon, filled with hope.

13: BLUE DAYS

Monday morning coincided with the first spell of summer weather. In morning assembly, students stood stiffly in their crisply-laundered uniforms, grudgingly facing a week of school in beach weather. In the corner of the hall, the piano cheerfully pounded out the familiar tune of Mr Kingsley's favourite hymn.

> So here hath been dawning
>
> Another blue day.
>
> Think, wilt thou let it
>
> Slip useless away?

Lucy hated the hymn. The sky outside was the same rich shade of summer blue as the hymn book.

Another blue day?

An early summer's day with clear skies and optimism? Blue also means sad and melancholy. Doubtless, this day would indeed slip useless away.

School's set routines were as regimented and unyielding as prison. Seven unbearable hours stretched before her. Notices were read out by a new teacher. Lucy's attention drifted. Then a sudden buzz of excitement caught her attention.

'Everyone in favour of introducing sex education to the school curriculum raise your hand!'

Instantly a sea of hands went up. *That's got nothing to do with me*, Lucy smouldered, *I'll never marry or have children*. Her hand stayed down. Nobody noticed.

Lucy went through the day speaking to nobody. Goody dreamed of a bright future with a career, a handsome husband, beautiful children and a lovely home, Genie dwelt morbidly on pain and suffering and an untimely, violent death.

In the afternoon English class, excerpts were read from a modern play about unplanned teen pregnancy. The class displayed avid interest, but Lucy kept quiet and was thankful Mr Hargreaves didn't request her input.

Homework was to write a three-page dialogue between a distraught parent and their fourteen-year-old daughter, pregnant by a boy in her class. *I can't do this*, Lucy groaned, but in the evening she tackled the task quickly and objectively. She handed it in the next day, more fearful than hopeful. To her surprise, she received a good grade.

The new History teacher was Mr Mosey – an inexperienced college graduate who couldn't control the class. Jimmy Murphy and the usual class clowns sniggered through lessons. Practically everyone did as they pleased – homework in other subjects, reading anything from Tolstoy's *War and Peace* to the *Daily Mirror*. Barely anyone listened. The young schoolmaster quickly earned the nickname Dozy Mosey – Dozy for short.

'Homework for this week will be to imagine you are Martin Luther!' Mr Mosey shouted feebly over the noise. 'You are to write a letter to your father about the Diet of Worms.'

'I prefer spaghetti!' Rosemary yelled from the back, raising a few laughs, and then someone turned on a transistor radio, releasing a brief blast of Radio One. Mr Mosey ignored the misdemeanour and explained that Diet was a kind of church tribunal and Worms was the name of a German city. Only the studious pupils at the front were paying attention. Exasperated, Dozy Mosey wrote the instructions on the board, and was struck by a paper dart as he turned his back on the class. Lucy doodled swirly patterns on her pencil-case. She copied the details into her homework diary, without the faintest idea what to write. After two days of worrying, she persuaded Jodie to lend her jotter, from which Lucy painstakingly paraphrased Jodie's answer. Dozy didn't notice.

Maths was an uphill struggle for almost everyone. Mr Jenkins was increasingly absent due to illness, and after a series of ineffective supply teachers, mild-mannered, greying Mr Conway was appointed as a temporary replacement. His explanations were vague, and he set far too much homework, none of which Lucy could do. Everyone was required to buy a slide rule – a useful, mathematical tool that didn't come cheap. Lucy told her parents, and Hilda rushed out to buy a slide rule the next day, but the gadget failed to improve Lucy's failing maths skills, and she was left far behind. Friendless and alone, she alone at her desk, sliding the cursor back and fore, while the rest of the class worked quietly in pairs. More excluded than ever, Lucy despaired of everything.

Days were mixed, light and shadow, Goody and Genie. Bright sunshine one day, rain the next. Georgina wrote about the school prayers for the safety of the crew of the ill-fated Apollo Thirteen spacecraft. Lucy thought the idea of saying prayers was stupid and was disappointed there were no lunar landings, although she was relieved to hear of the endangered crew's safe return to Earth.

'How's Dotty these days?' Alison asked Lucy, one morning. This was the first time Alison had spoken to Lucy in weeks.

'She's fine, thanks! Lively as ever. How's Cedric? We could take them on a walk soon if you like?' Lucy's eager response was probably a mistake.

'I'm rather busy at the moment, but I'll think about it,' Alison declined politely. Lucy wasn't giving up. She hoped to sit next to Alison in the next lesson.

'Where's Alison?' Lucy asked nobody in particular.

'With Helena, of course,' Joanna sneered. 'Helena is Alison's friend, in case you hadn't noticed.'

Helena nudged Alison, sniggering furtively. Stocky, dark-haired Helena reminded Lucy of a chimpanzee. *What does she have to offer that I don't?* Lucy wondered, doubting Alison would remember it was her birthday tomorrow. Unaware she was staring, Lucy inadvertently caught Helena's attention.

'Lucy, do you smoke?' Helena asked.

'Of course!' Lucy lied emphatically.

'Of course!' mocked Alison. 'Why of course?' Why not just simply say, yes?'

'How about no, if you can bother being honest,' quipped Fiona.

Lucy was cornered. In truth, she despised her father's tobacco habit and had no intention of adopting it.

'She's gone beetroot red,' leered Abigail, winning approving glances. Renewed references to Lucy's lack of womanly curves were voiced, which Lucy chose to ignore, but comments kept coming, like rocks at a public stoning.

'Have you started?' Abigail scoffed. 'I bet you haven't. I doubt you ever will. You're a freak of nature and you'll never be able to have kids!'

'Do you fancy girls?" Joanna jeered. 'Keep away from us, because we don't fancy you!"

As venomous darts, the words worked their poison. Fighting back tears, Lucy sat rigid and expressionless, gazing at the wall clock above the blackboard. Home-time was aeons away. The day passed by in a nightmarish blur, one unpleasant incident following another. After lunch, Abigail lurked in the classroom doorway, smirking. A folded note with her name on lay on Lucy's desk. It was doubtless a prank, but she opened it anyway. The typewritten note was peppered with errors.

```
Daarrrling Lucy!

This is a genyouwine love letter to you from a devoted
fan who has been watching and admyring you from a
distance for a long time now. You are sooooh clevver
and soo very verry beeeeauuutiful!!
I sincerely hope you will reply to my letter of love
and declare your undying loove for me.
Yours truly and adooringly,

ALAN GRAHAM XXXXXXXXXX
```

Alan Graham was a small boy who sat at the front. He was often absent from school due to poor health and was also a target for bullies. Lucy crumpled the note, appalled that anyone would bother making other people's lives a misery.

'You'd better reply soon,' Abigail told Lucy, 'or at least thank Alan. Go over and thank him now, before the lesson.'

'I have nothing to thank him for,' Lucy answered.

'Of course you do. Alan is nuts about you, and you should tell him how you feel about him, too, or he'll be very sad.'

'Alan didn't write the letter, and he's not in love with me, nor me with him,' Lucy hissed.

'It's wicked to tell lies, you know,' Abigail drawled.

Lucy shrugged her shoulders and unpacked her books.

'Don't ignore me when I'm talking to you,' Abigail retorted. 'You're what's commonly known as ignorant.'

Lucy floundered, dropping a book. It landed open, pages downwards on the dusty floor.

'You vandal – that's school property! You pathetic, filthy piece of rubbish, it's time someone put you in the bin and closed the lid!'

Abigail's tirade was halted by the timely arrival of the teacher. Lucy stared out of the window at the distant hills, wishing she was far away from the mob.

'Abigail is always so unreasonable with me. I don't know why, but she just seems to enjoy having a go at me,' Lucy told Alison later.

'Having a go?' sniffed Alison. 'That's not very good English.'

Joanna sidled up and said, 'Why don't you like Abigail? She's a lovely person, and you've no right to keep running her down.'

Lucy regretted having trusted Alison. *Of all the injustice – why can't they just believe me for once?*

The day's troubles were far from over. She returned to her seat to find someone had scratched LUCY THE LES LAZES HERE on the desk lid.

And then, if that wasn't enough, Jimmy Murphy was at the blackboard, chalking a post-script to a message for the janitor.

ALL PAPER TO BE BURNED
including WYLIE

Lucy hated being referred to by her surname, like a criminal.

I am a criminal, after all, Lucy thought, adding Genie to her list of bullies. It was time for a reality check. Goody must be put to death!

After school, Lucy trudged home through rain-sodden fields. Over and over again, she asked, what on earth is wrong with me? She tried to think rationally, seeking a solution, a way out. Leave this world in which she clearly didn't belong? Death would be a sure-fire means of escape – the ultimate, drastic last resort. Lucy could think of nothing else to stop the pain.

Ignoring her homework, Lucy took refuge in the sandy hollow, below the big ash tree in Biddlecombe Copse. She twirled the pocket-knife, its point on her fingertip. It didn't break the skin. She placed the point on her chest, above her heart and wondered how hard she would have to push it to kill herself. She looked up at the curtain of spring foliage, imagining the hollow to be the jaws of a giant beast and that the ground would swallow her. Tomorrow was her fourteenth birthday. Birthdays, like Christmas, had lost all the charm of childhood, and tomorrow promised to be every bit as bad as today.

At dinner time, Hilda and Albert exchanged glances, watching Lucy idly prodding her food.

'Her hair looks greasy, don't you think, dear, and her face is getting spotty,' Hilda remarked to Albert.

Albert made a sound of agreement, his mouth full of food. There was a vague, indifferent flicker on Lucy's face. Hilda continued talking. 'A sure sign of hormones working. See how rapidly she's growing? She'll be a woman soon, you know.'

Lucy once cared a great deal about body development, but not any more. She wanted to destroy her body, along with its flawed, dysfunctional brain that made her say and do all the wrong things.

'Come on, Lucy,' Hilda coaxed. 'Eat your dinner. You're a growing girl. And don't forget what day it is tomorrow!'

Hilda winked saucily, and Lucy braced herself for the usual jokes about the calendar being altered and her birthday being cancelled this year, or about what terrible belly-ache her mother had so-and-so-many years ago. Lucy stared glumly at the cruet in the middle of the table and said nothing.

'You're still thirteen for another twenty-one hours,' Hilda droned like a well-worn gramophone record. 'I loved being thirteen. I can remember writing in my diary about how happy I was. And then, of course, at fourteen I was off to work. We all had to work in those days if we wanted to survive.'

At this moment, Lucy didn't even want to survive. There seemed no point in doing so. Her childhood was gone, banished behind a barred and bolted door on a forbidden garden, the future unspeakably bleak. That night Lucy tumbled into her bed without bothering to undress. She tossed and turned, got up, and paced feverishly around the room like a caged animal, muttering, 'why am I even here?'

Suddenly the light snapped on. Hilda stood in the doorway, white with rage.

'Whatever do you think you are doing?' she hissed. 'Your father and I are trying to sleep! Have you taken leave of your senses? You're acting like a thoroughly spoiled brat! I know what these teenagers can be like nowadays. Your sister made my life hell, and I'm not – I repeat NOT- standing for it a second time! So don't you think you can get away with anything, my girl, you mark my words!'

'I'm mad,' Lucy said, 'quite insane, and not normal...'

'STUFF AND UTTER NONSENSE!' Hilda exploded, pushing Lucy onto the bed. Lucy lay on her back, her school blouse unbuttoned and the padded bra showing. She felt humiliated, stupid, worthless. The harsh glare from the hundred-watt bulb dazzled her eyes like a Gestapo light, unmasking her tear-stained face.

'There's nothing wrong with you,' Hilda spat, 'nothing that a good hiding and a few home truths wouldn't cure! You've got ten times what I had at your age. Just look at yourself! You're a disgrace! Pull yourself together for God's sake, and let's all get some sleep.'

'Sleep? I can't sleep. That's just it. I'm mad!'

'You ungrateful minx! God above! He can see you for what you are. You're insulting Him, who made you, coming out with such dreadful nonsense! Shame on you!'

Lucy doubted very much God made her and doubted He even existed. She used to believe in God once, long ago, at Sunday school, when life was easier – easy enough to believe in a benign creator somewhere in the clouds. But Lucy knew she would never be good enough for a distant, aloof Supreme Being wielding a big stick. Schoolmates, teachers, parents, and now, apparently, even God had become Lucy's enemy.

When morning came, Lucy surfaced from a dreamless state, the memory of yesterday's events flooding back with stark reality. With leaden limbs and heavy heart, she went to the kitchen. It was a dismal, overcast morning. The fluorescent light buzzed, its cold glare striking hard on Lucy's tired eyes.

'Your presents are on the kitchen worktop,' Hilda said stonily. 'After you've finished your breakfast, you can open them.' Lucy felt a flicker of emotion. She shovelled down her cereal and chewed the toast, staring at the small pile of packages wrapped in re-used gift paper. Lucy opened the cards first. There were just three – from her parents, from Marion and Paul, and from Uncle Peter, John and Sarah.

Lucy stood the cards on the sideboard. 'Thanks,' she said quietly.

Hilda silently brushed away a tear, noting the absence of Rose's name from the last card. There was nothing from Lucy's London friends. She opened the presents: cerise-pink nylon socks, writing paper, chocolates, a striped plastic pencil-case, and a pair of paper scissors with orange, plastic-coated handles.

'I wasn't expecting anything, so, thanks,' Lucy said.

At school, she went stoically from one lesson to the next, ignoring everyone. Everyone ignored her. Nobody acknowledged her birthday. Returning home, Lucy found nothing had come in the post, nor the next.

On Saturday morning, Hilda woke Lucy at seven-thirty, bringing a cup of tea. Lucy surfaced slowly, recalling fragments of a strange and vivid dream.

She wrote down what she could recall.

I stood alone beside the level-crossing by Westcombe station. In bright sunshine, all was strangely quiet and still, not one person in the street nor in the school playing fields. I stepped forward. Suddenly a train appeared, from the left, as if from nowhere and silently. Before I had time to think or blink, the train was upon me. No fear, no pain. In the instant before my death, I caught a glimpse of the train driver. It was Miss Hawksworth. And she was smiling.

In a disembodied state, I saw my bloodied, motionless corpse on the track. The school uniform I was wearing was different – not the usual dark blue gymslip and grey, pin-stripe shirt, this uniform was a white shirt and navy blue tie and navy blue blazer, and a skirt with two pleats at the front...

Lucy stopped. It was time to go to work. Her parents were going shopping, so they gave her a lift. Arriving at work, Lucy buttoned her overall, feeling a strange sense of satisfaction. Wearing it, she could be someone else, serving customers, wiping Pick-n-Mix trays, filling shelves. Her co-workers didn't bother her. Lucy barely spoke to them and failed to notice Pamela's glowering glances. Absorbed in the work, Lucy kept her distance. When Mrs Hancock appeared, Lucy was at the till, and Pamela filling the basket of raspberry ruffles on the Pick-n-Mix display. Lucy noticed Pamela slip a sweet wrapper into her pocket.

'Will you make the tea today, Miss Wylie?' Mrs Hancock asked.

'Yes, Mrs Hancock,' Lucy said. Pamela stood nearby, scowling.

Just then, Hilda appeared.

'Hi, Mum!' Lucy squeaked. The supervisor directed a gimlet-like stare.

'See you later, Mum.' Lucy scurried to the staff door and disappeared.

'A quarter of peppermint creams, please,' Hilda requested.

Pamela served her in silence.

'Lucy's my daughter, you know,' Hilda said, unwrapping a peppermint cream and popping it into her mouth.

Upstairs Lucy filled two big aluminium kettles and put them on the stove, pleased to have found the matches and worked out how to light the gas. At home, she had only ever used an electric cooker, as Hilda hated gas appliances, ever since she singed her eyebrows on a rogue water heater in a holiday caravan. Lucy lined the cups and saucers and filled the milk jug and sugar bowl. A simple task, like making tea at home, but with more people to cater for. The big kettles were taking a long time to come to the boil, and Lucy grew impatient, wondering what to do next. She put three tea bags into each of the two large teapots. Perhaps the gas was on the wrong setting? She adjusted the dials, and a flame went out. Frantically, she grabbed the matches and relit the jet at the third attempt. A faint smell of gas hung in the air.

Suddenly, the door downstairs banged. Footsteps and voices echoed in the stairwell. Quickly, Lucy lifted a kettle and filled both teapots with hot water. She stood nervously at the hatch, as thirsty workers trooped into the dining-room.

'Oh my gosh, my poor legs are killing me,' Sally sighed.

Lucy began pouring the teas.

'Thanks, ducks,' grinned Sally. 'Hey, wait a minute – that tea's a funny colour. What did you put in it? Floor-sweepings?'

A burst of laughter followed, Lucy squirmed with embarrassment. At that moment, Mrs Hancock swept into the kitchen, grabbed Lucy by the arm, then emptied half the water from each kettle.

'For enough water to boil on time, kettles must be half full,' she said, then emptied both teapots into the sink.

'Right! We'll start again. Seven tea bags are required for each pot – one tea bag for each person and one for the pot. Then, you make sure the water is boiling, before filling the pots, and stir the tea before pouring.'

Lucy nodded and watched, and when all was done, Mrs Hancock asked, 'Now then, do you think you remembered all that?'

Lucy nodded.

'So next time you are asked to make the tea, you'll know how to do it properly, won't you?'

'Yes, Mrs Hancock,' Lucy answered, too overwhelmed to feel guilty or embarrassed. Happily, nothing more was said, and the working day continued without further ado.

'Who was that crab-apple of an overseer giving orders this morning?' Hilda asked that evening.

Lucy suppressed a smirk.

'You mean Mrs Hancock, the staff supervisor? She's all right really. It's a nice job, better than the Merry Teapot'.'

'I should jolly well think so! And you'll save money, too.' Hilda said stoutly.

Lucy said nothing. She was thinking about what to save up for next, but her ideas were conflicting. Goody wanted a modern bungalow behind the conifers on the edge of Westombe Park. Such homes were expensive, none under ten thousand pounds, a long-term dream. Genie had a less expensive, but infinitely more terrifying idea. If Lucy was indeed as useless and expendable as she was led to believe, then a basic funeral must in all fairness be paid for by herself. Nobody at school would care if she disappeared off the face of the earth. How delighted Abigail Leuchars would be! Probably. But perhaps not?

Lucy envisaged a scenario after her suicide: a solemn announcement in morning assembly, a devastated Rosemary Richardson, mortified with remorse for her inane, cruel teasing. And her parents? What would they really think? Lucy tried to imagine, but her mind was blank. She continued to entertain her secret like an illicit love affair, drawing from it dubious comfort.

Arriving home on Monday, she emptied her bag lethargically and started on her homework. Then, she discovered the slide-rule shattered across the middle in jagged, diagonal fractures. A valid excuse for evading tonight's homework was one thing, telling her mother was another. Hilda's reaction was predictable.

'You haven't had that thing five minutes, and now look at it! Smashed beyond repair! Someone must have vandalised it. I'm writing a letter of complaint to the school!'

Finally, her mother believed there was bullying at Westcombe Grammar School.

This time, however, Lucy wasn't sure bullies were to blame. On the cycle ride home, the bag had been momentarily trapped between wheel and mudguard, so Lucy feared the damage might be her fault. 'No need to do that, Mum. I don't actually need a slide-rule any more. There are some at school that we can borrow,' Lucy said.

'Well, that was a complete waste of money!' Hilda snorted. The matter was soon forgotten. There were spare slide rules at school, but Lucy didn't bother borrowing one, as she still hadn't a clue how to use it. She neither did maths homework nor cared about the consequences.

By mid-May, verdant meadows and trees burgeoned under azure skies. Arriving home one day, Lucy found a parcel with foreign stamps on her bed.

'It's from Martine!' Lucy exclaimed. 'I thought she wasn't going to write any more.'

The package had been delayed. It contained a newsy letter, a net of foil-wrapped chocolate mini-eggs, and a cobalt-blue necklace of wooden beads wrapped in white tissue paper. Lucy was ecstatic. She offered her parents a chocolate egg, but they declined. Hilda said chocolate gave her migraines, and Albert said French chocolate was horrible, having tasted some during the Second World War. Lucy ate all the chocolates herself and found them delicious. She read Martine's description of her house, garden and pets with avid interest, but was sad to read about five kittens being destroyed because nobody wanted them.

The next day, post came from Melanie and Margaret, and they both wanted to visit Edencroft. And then, Albert announced Arthur had telephoned with an invitation to spend Whitsun weekend at Hills' new home.

'Arthur and Joan never mentioned last summer that they were planning to move house,' Hilda said.

'Arthur told me he wanted to live somehwere quieter,' Albert said.

'I bet they were jealous, because of our new place,' Hilda scoffed.

'Their new home is in a tiny hamlet, across the border with Kent: it has a big garden with shrubs, plants and greenhouses.'

Lucy tried looking forward to the trip, but the next fortnight was an ordeal. It seemed everyone was her enemy, nobody her friend, each day a minefield of misery. On the last day, Miss Hawksworth humiliated Lucy in front of the class, for using the wrong pen to outline a map, calling her work slipshod trash. Lucy silently endured the rebuke, jealously guarding her dark secret, but her contorted expression was as a red rag to a bull. Cowed, submissive Goody crumbled, while defiant Genie revelled in the spectacle, vowing never to let her attackers see her cry. After the lesson there were whoops of triumph, jokes cracked like bad eggs, spearheaded by Abigail, Joanna and Fiona. Jimmy Murphy sprang in front of Lucy and spat in her face, and Crispian Cowley extended a Doc Marten boot, causing her to stumble, drawing more guffawing from the mob. Lucy dragged herself to the next lesson, where she sat silent, hunched and swollen-eyed, until the final bell. Walking home, she stared at the ground, marking her footsteps, slowly counting from one to four hundred and eighty, all the way up the hill to the stile by Biddlecombe Copse. Soon, she would be home, and everything would be different, like turning a page in a book to a new chapter. A chapter about Goody.

Twenty-four hours later, a hundred miles away, Lucy reclined on the terrace of a rustic, weatherboarded bungalow, basking in sunshine. Arthur and Albert were in the greenhouse, Hilda and Joan chatted cheerily on the terrace. Cups chinked on saucers, honey bees buzzed in the overhanging jasmine, the air resounded with calls of nesting birds – a scene too peaceful to be real. Anthony raced across the lawn with a fishing net, chasing a butterfly. Suddenly he threw down the net and huffed into the house.

'Why do you always stick your nose in that stupid diary?' Anthony asked Lucy.

Lucy didn't answer. She was tired of his childish chatter and incessant bragging about being accepted at the Technical High School, twelve miles away. At least she didn't have to share a bedroom with him. Instead, she slept – or attempted to sleep – on the living-room couch, an arrangement which suited her well, since her wakefulness disturbed no one and no one disturbed her.

During the day, Lucy went for lone walks and spent long hours lounging on the terrace, hiding behind a book of horror stories. Thoughts of school overshadowed everything. Lucy picked a random day in her diary, marking it with a black swastika. December 8th would be the day she would end her life if circumstances hadn't improved by then. In her heart of hearts, Lucy wished she could forget the whole idea. All weekend, an intangible gloom hung over the household, which Lucy imagined she had brought with her. It seemed safer to assume everything was her fault.

You are your own executioner! Her father's words from years before were small comfort in the face of her mother's continual lectures. *You must fit in! To have friends, you must be a friend to others. Treat others as you would be treated yourself.*

However, this never worked, no matter how hard Lucy tried.

'That's a pretty blue necklace you have on,' Joan remarked, 'and a nice ring, too? It looks like an engagement ring, with all those bells on it.'

'The beads are a gift from my French penfriend. Marion gave me the ring, and no, it's not an engagement ring.'

Joan glanced at the cover of Lucy's diary.

'Oh, Lucy, you must have plenty of secret boyfriends! Just look at all those bleeding love-hearts with arrows through them.'

'Language, dear!'' exclaimed Arthur.

'No. No, no,' protested Joan innocently, 'The hearts are actually bleeding, like injured love-hearts.'

Lucy let Joan think whatever she liked, that she was a normal teenage girl with hopes and dreams of falling in love. For Lucy, the broken hearts symbolised heartbreak and death.

Playing cricket with Anthony, strolling along picturesque lanes past distinctive oast-houses with conical roofs, and braving a quick dip in the ice-cold water, Lucy appeared happy and carefree. No-one guessed her dark, sinister secret.

Lucy noticed Anne was home again, scarcely venturing out of her room. There was no mention of her husband. Even Joan was a little less jolly than usual, in spite of the nice new home and Anthony having got into a good school. It was said Anne was unwell. Lucy suspected pregnancy, until passing by Anne's half-open door, she saw an open pack of tampons on the bed. Lucy wondered what on earth could be wrong.

On the way home she found out.

'I feel sorry for Anne,' Hilda said to Albert.

'Yes, it's a shame,' Albert said.

'Why?' Lucy asked.

'Anne's home again because the marriage didn't work out.'

'Why not?'

'Her husband was violent. He beat Anne up more than once, and then the police were involved. Anne's still in a state of shock. Apparently, he said and did things to her that she can't forget. Anne was so distraught that she took an overdose of sleeping pills. A dreadful thing to do. Such a silly girl, rushing into marriage to someone who turned out to be an absolute rotter!'

'But what did he do?'

'I can't tell you, you wouldn't understand. He was – I mean the two of them weren't – compatible, and things went from bad to worse.'

Lucy didn't reply. She spent the rest of the long journey brooding over the news, wondering what could have caused Anne so much suffering. If Lucy had known Anne was so unhappy, she might have wanted to talk to her, which may or may not have been helpful, but it was too late now. Lucy marked off the days in her diary, which she kept safely wedged among books where her mother was unlikely to look. Lucy guessed her parents had her best interests at heart, which was worse, as she would only disappoint them, whatever choice she made. In the dark stillness of the rural night, Lucy put the notebook and a torch under the pillow. Sleepless, she drafted a short story, then typed it up the next day after school.

EXCLUSION

```
    There's little room left in our world. The planet
is too small to contain all its people. Only the
cleverest survive in our society.
I, unfortunately, am not among them. Success is based
on achievement and usefulness. Because I have failed
in these things, I am restricted to a form of
accommodation like a prison block. I do not go
outside. My room is a small cell; grey, metallic and
sparsely furnished. No one visits me, and no one
speaks to me. Silence surrounds me. Others in the
block have places to go and jobs to do. They are
recognised because they are superior.
    Above the cold, steel door an orange light flashes
on. I open the door. They have left food and water
for me. They expect nothing in return, for there is
nothing I can give. I am of no practical use to them.
I take the tray and eat and drink. There is no
purpose in my being here. I once hoped to be part of
the people of this place, but now I know this is not
possible. They have rejected me totally. There is no
escape, except by death. There is no reason to wait
for death. It is the next and the only way forward.
    In this world, there is no room for love. No room
to live, no room for me. Therefore I must leave.
```

Hearing her mother's approaching footsteps, Lucy quickly hid her manuscript, rolled in a fresh sheet of paper and began typing out notes from a school book.

'Tea's ready Lucy,' Hilda smiled. 'Nice to see you busy with your studies.'

At school, nothing changed. Lucy encased herself in self-imposed armour, masquerading as the impervious Genie, actively welcoming the attacks that fed the furnace of her self-destructive desires. The more dominant Genie became, the more Goody receded into the background. Lucy took long-suffering Goody to her Saturday job, a strategy which worked. A day spent serving customers, enduring backache, sore feet, and Pamela's increasingly offhand manner was a welcome challenge.

'I don't like your attitude. I'm going to report you to the supervisor,' Pamela said, storming off. Lucy watched from the corner of her eye as Pamela spoke with Mrs Hancock at the haberdashery counter. Lucy continued serving customers. Nothing was mentioned afterwards, and the matter was taken no further. Lucy later learned Pamela herself was in trouble. A visiting inspector had caught her red-handed, stuffing her pockets with handfuls of sweets in the stock-room. After the incident, Pamela seemed a changed person, less tetchy, and more polite to customers and colleagues alike, including Lucy. A brief storm in a teacup, the disagreement with Pamela was soon history. If only people at school were as simple, Lucy thought.

Lucy's latest craze was horror stories – paperback editions of short, cleverly written tales. It was almost an addiction. In lessons, Lucy read them behind textbooks and was never caught, until Miss Meadows, the notoriously strict science teacher spied an open book on Lucy's lap and confiscated it forthwith. That same afternoon, Dozy didn't turn up. Amid a flurry of paper darts, the din from the unsupervised class could be heard down the corridor. Lost in a book of ghost stories, Lucy was oblivious of the commotion, until the room suddenly went quiet. The striking form of a tall woman in a matching red ensemble stood before the class.

'SILENCE!' The order was roared with unexpected authority. 'My name is Mrs Hogg, and I am your supply teacher for today. You all have exams to revise for. Use your time wisely.'

With subdued whispering, students quietly found something to do. Lucy carried on reading. Presently, she felt someone nudge her shoulder. Alison was handing her a crumpled scrap of paper. Lucy expected another billet-doux of insults, but this time, the eccentric supply teacher was the object of Alison's attention.

Mrs Hogg is wearing red lipstick, rouge on her face, red earrings, red bead necklace, red blouse, red jacket, red skirt, red stockings, and her handbag and shoes are... you guessed it... RED!! I wonder what colour her bra and knickers are?

Alison gave a sly grin. Lucy scrawled a post-script reply:

Red, I suppose. It's enough to make you see red!

Alison smirked, and Lucy returned to her reading. Around the room, chairs creaked, and feet shuffled. Mrs Hogg paraded silently round the room.

'What are you drawing?' she asked Jonathan.

'A steam-engine, Miss. It's part of my science project.'

'I see.' Mrs Hogg moved on, leaving a trail of heavy perfume and an obtrusive rasping of nylon stockings. Jimmy Murphy was drawing motorbikes, and Sandra Bright was writing an erotic letter to her latest boyfriend, but Mrs Hogg stopped beside Lucy. 'What are you reading?' she asked.

'She means you, Lucy!' hissed Alison from across the gangway.

'Oh – um, it's a b-book of short stories of mystery and suspense,' Lucy stammered, fearing a second confiscation.

'Show me, please.'

Lucy handed the teacher the book. Mrs Hogg flicked through a few pages, then asked, 'Would you mind if I read one of these out?'

'No, Miss,' Lucy answered, feeling a curious thrill.

Mrs Hogg read the first story, and the class was enthralled. The spine-chilling tale filled with tragic irony was a far cry from the *Saddle Club Pony Stories* – Lucy's former favourite reading material, recommended by Georgina – a brief interest quickly curtailed when Jane Haslett caught her reading *Ginny's Gymkhana* during lunch break.

Mrs Hogg read, "The girl waited anxiously in pitch darkness. A hinge creaked. The shutter rattled..."

The class sat spellbound. Lucy swelled with pride. Better yet, Alison was amicable again. Finally, would everyone else start showing her some respect?

On the way home, Lucy's footsteps were light.

That evening, Hilda had another surprise in store for Lucy.

'Would you like to learn to drive?' Hilda asked. 'Just starting slowly, getting used to the controls and manoeuvring the car on the driveway.'

Lucy's eyes widened.

'When?'

'Tonight, when you've finished your homework. Since your father acquired the Vauxhall Viva, the Morris Traveller is mine to do what I please with.'

'All right. I'm nearly finished,' Lucy said.

She had paid little attention to the car her father had bought a week earlier. Minutes later, she was seated at the wheel of the Morris. Hilda talked her through the controls, her explanations clear, and concise. Turning the ignition key and operating the accelerator was easy. The engine roared like a faithful lion. Lucy learned to use first gear and reverse gear, shunting the car backwards and forwards.

'You did well, Lucy,' Hilda said. 'I'll just straighten the car up...'

Hilda paused, noticing Albert standing at the top of the slope. Flustered with embarrassment, Hilda revved harder, the car listed into soft ground, the engine emitting a high-pitched whine. The rearview mirror was speckled with mud.

Albert shook his head. Defeated, Hilda got out of the car and said, 'I'll get back in the car and you and Lucy can push from behind.'

Their combined efforts did nothing.

'It's no use, we can't do this on our own.' Hilda said. 'Lucy, get help.'

At the Dalys' cottage, Lucy collared Nigel and three of his friends, but despite their best efforts, and planks under wheels, the car stayed put. Finally, Mr Wilson was summoned with his tractor and hauled the car from its muddy furrow in seconds. Hilda thanked him profusely and offered him two ten-shilling notes for his time and trouble, but the gesture was politely declined. Hilda blushed scarlet, while the three boys stood nearby, looking hopeful. Hilda considered they deserved tea and biscuits, so she invited them into the kitchen.

Lucy felt nervous in the boys' presence. She sat at the breakfast room table, dunking her biscuit. One friend was tall and skinny, the other small and ferret-like with sharp features and a mop of blond hair. Nigel smirked smugly, eyeing Lucy up and down and reaching greedily for the biscuits.

'How are your hens, Nigel, are they laying well?' Hilda asked.

'Not bad, we're getting about fifteen eggs a day.'

'Do you sell any?'

'Nope, we use them all. Mum does a lot of baking and we freeze the cakes for winter, when the hens are off lay.'

Lucy sat stroking the cat, wondering when – or whether – her mother would give her another driving lesson. As polite talk drifted around her, she reflected on the afternoon's events. *If it wasn't for school, life wouldn't be bad.*

14: HIRONVILLE

In balmy July sunshine, holidaymakers explored, shopped, and relaxed on the cross-channel ferry. Trade was brisk in onboard restaurants, bars, coffee-cabins and gift shops. The upper decks offered fresh air, and views of the cornflower-blue Solent and the emerald-green western tip of the Isle of Wight, where white cliffs towered and chalk pillars rose sheer into summer skies. The boat chugged on through sun-sparkled waters, while tourists clicked cameras, captivated by the scene. The iconic red-and-white striped lighthouse stood sentry-like beyond the last chalk-stack.

Without warning, calm waters morphed to plunging waves. The vessel pitched and tossed through heaving seas of grey-green. Passengers swayed and staggered, seeking safety. The port of Cherbourg still hours away, there was no promise of respite. Cruel gusts buffeted braver tourists away from open decks. Massive waves battered the ship's sides like unbridled beasts, sending clouds of spray surging over decks, drenching empty wooden seats.

Lucy stood alone, bracing the stiff breeze blustering against her small frame, flattening her dampened clothes and threading her hair into dishevelled knots. Lucy gripped the railings, her hands white with cold. Detached and free, on life's turbulent sea, she relished every moment, her thoughts rising and crashing with the waves. *At one with nature, at odds with man*, she mused poetically, *if only the crowd at school could see me now!*

This was the longest boat trip she had ever made. A crossing from Portsmouth to the Isle of Wight seven years ago on waters still as a millpond didn't compare. Neither did an earlier voyage to Lundy Island, curtailed mid-ocean by heavy seas. On that day, Marion had carried Lucy down steep stairs to an engine room where huge machinery thundered. Lucy covered her ears and buried her head in Marion's red-and-green woollen dress, the one Hilda later cut up to make cushion covers. Lucy said she was cold, so Marion wrapped her bottle-green suede jacket around her, and then, disappointingly, everyone was told the ship was turning back because the waves were too big.

Today, there would be no such disappointment. Lucy scanned the southern horizon, where hazy spray hovered above seething white-grey waters. After a sleepless night fraught with excitement, she was hyper-excited at the prospect of a week's holiday in France – her first time abroad. The trip was another of Mother's surprises, a reward for good grades in French, plus an opportunity for a family holiday. Lucy wished she had known about it earlier. The joy of anticipation would have been a buffer against the trials of school.

A massive wave smacked the side of the ship, crashing over the deck, drenching Lucy's feet. The sense of danger was intoxicating – Lucy imagined the terror of tackling turbulent waters, armed with just an inflatable body-board. A death wish suddenly seemed foolish. She doubted she would ever go ahead with her dark agenda, not that she even had a proper plan. At the moment, life was good. It was summer, filled with long, sunlit hours and the promise of happy times. Seven days of bliss stretched before her, a short future undiscovered, unwritten, unknown.

Lucy returned to the covered deck, where her parents sat sandwiched between two French nuns and a family of scantily dressed, shivering Brits. Albert pulled out his cigarettes and then put them away again, noticing the nuns on one side of him, and green-faced holidaymakers on the other. The nuns seemed oblivious of their surroundings; one reading a book, the other knitting, miraculously managing not to drop any stitches.

'We were wise to have just a light picnic before the boat trip,' Hilda remarked, noticing a nearby tourist with their head in a paper bag. Lucy stared fascinated at the jagged horizon, the English coast now vanished from view. From time to time, she got up and walked around, enjoying the challenge of keeping her balance and seeking a glimpse of French shores. All around, dozens of ailing passengers lay stricken, sprawled across seats and on floors – a scene of devastation akin to a great plague. Lucy smiled smugly. Gradually the wind and waves subsided, the ship's foghorn resounded with the slow, rhythmic throb of engines. At last, a solid line appeared on the horizon, subtly changing contours etched against the peachy glow of a sun-soaked sky. Lucy stood mesmerised at her first sighting of foreign shores. The distant forms of trees and buildings emerged from the mist, a bell tolled, deep and melancholy, resonant with the church bell on the "Sound of Music" record. Lucy caught her breath. 'So this is France', she murmured, enthralled.

'France is just like England', Georgina had said, 'with houses, trees, shops and the same things as us'. Lucy thought otherwise. France was different from England. Vehicles drove on the right, horns blared, drivers seemed impatient. Cherbourg had buildings, certainly, stone structures neater and grander than in British towns. Lucy already decided she liked France. French countryside was vast. Hedgeless fields of golden corn sprawled under wide skies. So much empty space – endless acres of agricultural land, sliced by arrow-straight lanes and neat villages, clusters of grey-slated roofs. By comparison, England seemed cluttered and overpopulated.

Hilda moaned about Mrs Mayfield's misleading map and suspected Albert had taken a wrong turning. Lucy wasn't worried. Doubtless, they would shortly arrive at their destination – the coastal village of Hironville, on the Breton peninsula.

The car suddenly stopped. 'Go on, Lucy!' Hilda urged, 'Let's hear you practise your French. Ask that man over there the way to Beaumont – that's the town Mrs Mayfield mentioned in her directions.'

Archetypally, an elderly man was wheeling a bicycle, a string of onions slung over the handlebars. The man stopped and looked suspiciously at the foreign car and its occupants.

'*Savez-vous la route à Beaumont, Monsieur?*' Lucy asked quickly, in her very best French.

The old onion vendor's face creased into a broad smile.

'*Ah, Beaumont! Ah, oui!*' A torrent of incomprehensible French followed. '*Merci beaucoup*,' Lucy replied, having understood virtually nothing.

'Well?' asked Albert.

'Translation, please, Lucy?' Hilda asked impatiently.

'I think we need to turn back and go the way we came.'

Several kilometres further, past endless swathes of ripening corn, a village appeared. It was extremely small and was not called *Beaumont*.

'Stop here, and we'll ask someone else,' Hilda said.

Two men in boiler suits were working on a garage forecourt. Albert and Lucy got out of the car. The mechanics glanced mistrustfully at the two strangers.

'*Où est Beaumont?*' Albert mumbled, his distinctive London accent undiminished. This was embarrassing.

Lucy lost her shyness and asked, '*Savez-vous la route à Beaumont?*'

'*Ah, Oui!*' exclaimed one of the men, and another rapid torrent of provincial French followed.

'*Merci, Monsieur – merci beaucoup*', Lucy answered.

Back in the car, Albert asked, 'Well? Where to now?'

'Okay, Dad. We're to go left – that's all I understood,' Lucy said, shrugging doubtfully. However, the next cluster of grey-slated roofs and pointed church spire was indeed *Beaumont*. Hilda scrunched up Mrs Mayfield's handwritten directions, handed Lucy a twenty-franc banknote, and sent her into the nearest *librairie* to buy a map.

Inside the bookshop a young girl stood behind the till, looking bored. She was red-haired and fair-skinned and didn't look particularly French.

'*Avez-vous un carte de France, s'il vous plaît?*' Lucy asked tiredly.

'*Un carte de France?*' the girl echoed with a faint note of sarcasm. Lucy bought a road map of Normandy and Brittany, and soon headway was made, but not enough to reach Hironville by nightfall. Street lamps flicked on, and pairs of amber headlights twinkled in the twilight like eyes of hunting felines.

Suddenly Hilda grabbed Albert's arm. 'Stop!' she yelled, 'What on earth are you doing?'

The angry cats dazzled sharply, horns blared, tyres screeched. The Vauxhall Viva veered sharply to the right and halted.

'You nearly had us all killed,' Hilda hissed, teeth clenched.

Albert said nothing.

'You're not fit to drive!' snapped Hilda. 'We'd better stop somewhere for the night, or you're going to crash the car and at best ruin the holiday.'

Lucy was unfazed. Soon afterwards, she was standing with her parents in the dimly-lit foyer of a small boarding house.

'Come on, Lucy, let's hear some more French!' Hilda chuckled.

A short, balding man, a dead ringer for Hercule Poirot, stood behind the oak-panelled reception desk, shouting loudly on the telephone, behind him a board of hooks with keys, and a large set of pigeonholes crammed with letters. Noticing guests were waiting, the man put down the phone.

Lucy reeled with tiredness.

'*Nous sommes perdus. Nous voulons une chambre, pour une nuit, seulement*,' she said, trying not to yawn.

The man listened with interest.

'*Demain*,' Lucy continued, trying to remember the future tense.

'*Nous irons,'* Lucy felt quite pleased with herself, and then her mind went blank.

The man repeated, '*Oui, Nous irons...*'

Lucy stared past the man's face at the board of keys, noticing the word clefs above it. Ah, yes, *clefs*, that means keys, Lucy trawled her tired brain for more French.

'*Demain, nous irons à l'hôtel en Bretagne, à l'hôtel 'Au Lapin Blanc' à Hironville... Nous n'arrivons pas aujourd'hui. Il est trop tard. Il faut rester ici, une nuit. Il faut téléphonner...*'

'*Ah, oui! D'accord!*'

'Translation, please, Lucy!' Hilda requested.

'I said we wanted to go to the White Rabbit Hotel in Hironville, Brittany, tomorrow instead of today, because we were too late to arrive today, so we'd need to stay here tonight and phone the White Rabbit –'

'Good work, Lucy. Here – give the man the details,' Hilda said, handing Lucy the *Pension au Lapin Blanc* flyer.

After that, everything went smoothly. The hotel proprietor phoned the Breton boarding house on his guests' behalf and provided them with a comfortable room for the night. The Wylies trudged wearily up the curved wooden stairs to a room on the third floor, where Lucy tumbled thankfully into a neatly made bed with a striped cotton duvet and a bolster shaped pillow. The sheets were crisp and cool and enveloped her into instant slumber.

What seemed a moment later, a vehicle rumbled noisily up the steep hill outside, shaking the wooden shutters. The large, airy room smelt of polished wood and fresh linen. White shafts of daylight penetrated through the slats, shedding brightness into the room. Lucy remembered where she was and trembled with excitement.

Downstairs in the restaurant, the traditional French breakfast was everything the school textbooks had led Lucy to believe, except the bowls of milky coffee had handles. Lucy broke off a piece of croissant and dipped it into her coffee. Hilda threw her a stern glance.

'It's okay, Mum – you're supposed to dunk.'

Hilda smiled and winked. 'Eat up! We've a long journey ahead of us.'

Early mists gave way to rich, blue skies. The sun climbed high, hedgeless, rolling fields extended forever, shimmering in golden haze. The road seemed endless, straight as a dart and table-top flat, with quivering puddles that curiously vanished on approaching.

'Mirages,' Albert explained. 'We saw them often in the Sahara desert, during the war. They're caused by heat on the ground and refracted sunlight.'

'Fascinating,' Lucy said. Though reminded of school physics lessons, she had to admit science was still interesting. During a picnic stop, Hilda brewed a pot of tea on the Primus stove, Albert smoked two cigarettes and studied the map, while Lucy sketched vast, unfenced cornfields.

'We must move on now,' Hilda said. 'There are no toilets here, so we need to get to our destintion soon.'

After a hundred kilometres of undulating, agricultural fields of varying shades of yellow, green and russet brown, a navy-blue ribbon finally appeared on the horizon, with glimpses of rugged, black rocks and ivory-white sands.

'That's the Armorican coastline!' Lucy exclaimed, suddenly finding relevance in one of Miss Hawksworth's lessons.

'America?' Hilda asked, 'I don't think we've come that far.'

'No, *Armorica*. It's a region of Brittany. I remember learning about it in school.'

'Good. Anyway, it can't be far now, so start looking out for a signposts to *Les Moines, Mantes*, or *Hironville*.'

Hilda, who had never been taught a word of French in school, pronounced the names the English way: *Les* as the shortened form of Leslie, *Moines* as Moynes, and *Mantes* as Manties, rhyming with panties. Lucy sniggered, recalling her mother's jocular attempts to read from her French jotter. Hilda had read *maintenant* as maintenance, *poisson* as poison, and *lit*, the French word for bed, as lit in the context of the fire was lit. At least she pronounced *Hironville* correctly since Lucy had spoken it aloud many times.

Three kilometres from the main road, Hironville was easily found. A Norman church dominated the village, the hotel *Au Lapin Blanc* situated immediately opposite. Whitewashed houses dazzled in the sunshine, with painted shutters and wrought iron grilles across the windows. The hotel was low and L-shaped, with slate cladding and tall windows on the first floor. There was no garden. A terraced forecourt was ablaze with colour: apple-green tables and chairs, rainbow sunshades, gift stalls, and an attractive array of hanging baskets. Lucy liked it instantly.

'Well, this is it,' Hilda declared, sounding a trifle disappointed.

The hotelier, Madame Miget-Bonnin was in the foyer to welcome her guests. In broken English, she asked if they'd had a pleasant journey.

'*Oui, oui, Madame*,' Hilda returned the greeting, and Madame helped carry bags to the first floor. The room was clean and simply furnished, with polished wooden floorboards and colourful fabrics.

'Let's get some air in here, it's stifling!' Hilda gasped, flinging open the windows – windows that opened inwards and overlooked the church. Sounds and smells floated up from the street below – gabbling voices, revving engines, and the dubious odours of garlic, tobacco, exhaust fumes, and inadequately functioning drains. There were no en-suite facilities. Hilda was horrified to discover the shared toilet was at the end of the corridor, but at least it was a proper toilet and not just a hole in the floor.

Lucy's bed was a narrow divan by the window, her parents to share an iron-frame double bed beneath a large fan suspended from the ceiling. Both beds were decked with bright jacquard print counterpanes. The walls were plain white. The simplicity was refreshing, like a blank canvas ready to be daubed with something exciting and new. Lucy shivered with excitement. A warm breeze wafted the net curtains apart. Lucy glimpsed the cycle sheds by the church and a faded billboard bearing the slogan *JOIE DE VIVRE* – The Joy of Life.

The days passed happily, filled with walks, picnics, and visits to villages, picturesque chateaux, and white, sandy beaches with shell-studded coves. Lucy thrived on the discovery of new things, living the experience with childlike zeal. Breakfast was fresh rolls, *croissants*, and milky coffee in large bowls, without handles. Albert and Hilda insisted on tea in cups with handles.

'Ask Annette what that is,' Hilda asked Lucy, suspiciously scrutinising a dish resembling fish in white sauce. The waitress was gawky, freckle-faced and pleasant mannered.

'*Qu'est-ce que c'est?*' Lucy asked.

'*C'est du blanquette de veau.*' Annette replied, with a toothy smile showing braces.

Hilda looked worried. Lucy leafed hurriedly through her dictionary.

'It's veal, not fish.'

'Thank goodness it's not horse meat,' breathed Hilda.

Afterwards, Hilda asked Lucy to request a pot of tea with proper cups and saucers. Annette did her best. The cups were small, and the tea a tad too weak, but Hilda was loathe to complain.

The next morning, a different waitress appeared and introduced herself as Brigitte.

'*Où est Annette?*' Lucy asked.

'*Chez le dentiste.*' Brigitte replied, pointing to her teeth.

'Ah, yes. Dentist. Well, I hope she gets on all right. Could we have a pot of tea, please?' Hilda asked.

'*Oui, oui, Madame!*' Brigitte said and returned after five minutes with teapot, milk jug, and three breakfast bowls on a tray. She poured insipid-looking tea, with hot milk into the bowls.

Hilda looked aghast, then asked, 'What's that?'

Part of a garlic clove protruded from the dribbling teapot spout. The embarrassed waitress whisked the teapot away and returned with a fresh pot of warm water and one solitary tea bag. Lucy suppressed a smile, remembering her first tea-making attempt at Woolworth's.

Hilda had a headache and didn't protest. 'It'll be good to get home and have a decent cuppa,' she grumbled quietly.

Lucy, however, was in no hurry to go home. She wanted the holiday to last forever. On Tuesday evening, she sprawled on her bed, writing postcards to family and friends. When she finished, she asked, 'Can we go out somewhere in the car?'

'No,' Hilda answered from her bed, where she lay horizontal with a damp flannel over her eyes.

Albert sat in the wicker chair by the window, smoking.

'We're tired and just want to spend a quiet evening at the hotel,' he said.

'I'm going for a walk,' Lucy announced, failing to understand why grown-ups were so boring.

'All right, but be careful and mind the roads!' Hilda warned.

'Of course I will,' Lucy said.

She headed straight for the local beach, a beauty spot yet undiscovered. Lucy had asked to go there, but her parents were against the idea. You can't go swimming there, the water's too shallow, her father had said, while her mother shook her head and warned there might be quicksands. Drawn by the beauty of a summer sunset sky and the thrill of mystery, Lucy quickened her pace. Beyond a line of fishermen's cottages, the village ended abruptly. The lane led down to the estuary, where flowing tide shimmered silvery-grey in the evening light. All was calm, but for the high-pitched screech of swallows overhead and the erratic buzzing of a small motorcycle. The irritating noise gained pitch, drawing ever closer, then stopped. Lucy kept walking.

Then a gruff voice behind her said, '*Bonjour, Mademoiselle!*'

Lucy looked round. A teenage boy sat astride his motorcycle, regarding Lucy through a mop of thick, black hair. It was like a scene from a film. Lucy wished she'd worn different clothes. The light blue jeans were tight, and the padded bra under her turquoise tank top was uncomfortable. She sensed the boy looking her up and down. Nervously twirling her bead necklace, Lucy said, '*Je suis en vacances.*'

The boy responded with a phrase of colloquial French and sped off noisily, leaving a trail of petrol fumes. Lucy wondered if she had offended him. What was wrong with saying she was on holiday? Along the shore, a few fisher folk stooped on the sprawling sand flats, gathering shellfish under vibrant sky. The sun had set, purple and indigo clouds trailing across the flame-gold horizon. Lucy paused, transfixed by the beauty of the tranquil scene, then turned back up the hill.

Up ahead, motorcyclists were approaching. The purring engines stopped in front of Lucy, followed by a burst of voices, '*Bonsoir!*'

The boy was back, with three friends – two boys and a girl. The cheery greeting was followed by torrents of rapid French. All four lit cigarettes and talked excitedly. The dark-haired boy swaggered up to Lucy, offering an open pack of *Gitanes.* Lucy sensed a gesture of friendship, and politely took one.

'*Merci.*' she said. A second lad struck a match. Lucy put the cigarette into her mouth and sucked in slowly, tasting fragrant, acrid smoke in her mouth and nostrils. She didn't inhale.

'You like?' the first boy asked in English.

'*Oui,*' Lucy replied politely, mildly annoyed the boy wanted to speak English. Suddenly, she no longer cared about smoking and its possible consequences. The moment was spellbinding. Welcomed into a group of young people of her age and being the centre of attention, Lucy was ecstatic.

Questions were fired at her in both languages.

'You are on holidays?'

'*Quel âge as-tu?*'

'What is your name?'

'*Où habites-tu?*'

In her best school French, Lucy answered, thrilled at her ability to converse in a foreign language. Across the bay, shadows were falling fast, and under the cloud-studded, crimson sky, Lucy's happiness levels hit a new high.

'*Le ciel est belle!*' she exclaimed excitedly.

Someone laughed quietly, and the dark boy said, 'Le ciel est beau.'

'*Ah, oui! Le ciel est beau.*' Lucy realised her mistake.

The group ambled back up the hill. Lucy made her cigarette last, hoping not to be offered another. In the course of conversation, she learned the dark-haired lad was called Philippe and was from Paris. She wondered if he had ridden his motorcycle all the way, or if he'd moved house and was living locally, but she didn't ask. Lucy wished she knew enough French to tell him more about herself, but it was getting dark, and she worried about the time. She understood the group would meet on the hotel terrace tomorrow afternoon.

The clock struck ten.

'*Au revoir*,' Lucy said and hurried back to the hotel.

Madame Miget-Bonnin was in the hotel foyer to greet her.

'*Ah, vous voilà, Mademoiselle!*'

Behind her stood Albert, puffing on a cigarette.

'Am I glad to see you, Lucy!' he exclaimed quietly. 'Your mother and I have been frantic. We were about to send out a search party!'

'But I wasn't gone that long,' Lucy argued lamely, following her father up the wooden stairs.

'Your mother's already gone to bed,' Albert said. 'She has one of her headaches.'

The reprimand quickly over, it was time for lights out. Lucy wriggled between cool sheets and drew the thin duvet over her ears. She lay awake and alert. From the church belfry came the chittering of roosting swifts, and at eleven o'clock, the church clock struck its solemn notes, then repeated them minutes later, as it always did. The window was open, a gentle breeze ushering in a symphony of sounds: happy guests leaving the restaurant, throbbing engines, and the distant barking of dogs. It was magical. If only time would freeze and she could stay here forever.

The next day, after lunch, Lucy sat alone on the terrace, twirling her blue beads and hiding behind her sunglasses. It had been a quiet morning: a leisurely breakfast, followed by a drive to the countryside for a picnic under a wayside walnut tree. Her parents were tired, now upstairs resting. The church clock struck three. Disappointed, Lucy walked around the village, bought a pair of sunglasses she didn't really need and returned to find Philippe and the others waiting on the terrace. They invited Lucy to a game of snooker in the bar. Philippe rubbed a small cube of turquoise powder on the end of the snooker cue and said, '*C'est du maquillage!*' Philippe smiled.

Maquillage – makeup, Lucy smiled, noting the resemblance to her mother's eye shadow. It didn't matter that Lucy wasn't good at snooker, it was just good fun. She understood little of what the young people were saying but had the impression she was accepted. Lounging on her bed in the evening, she wrote in her diary:

I took one puff on the cigarette. It tasted dreadful, but that didn't matter. The sunset over the estuary was magnificent.

'Le ciel est belle,' I said, like an idiot. The tall, dark boy turned to me and said...

Tiredness stole over her. Yawning, she pushed the pen and notepad under her pillow. Outside the window, swallows and swifts screeched and swooped. Albert stubbed out his last cigarette of the day, and Hilda muttered something about missing a cup of proper English tea. Then, noticing Lucy had fallen asleep, she tiptoed across the room and switched off the bedside lamp.

Three more idyllic days merged together in blissful trips to local towns, villages and beaches. In St Brieuc, Lucy bought a net of six plastic-coated balls, in pairs of primary colours with a small wooden red ball – a simple game of bowls for three players, ideal for playing on the smooth, white sands. Having been a keen cricket player in his youth, Albert won hands down every time, Hilda did reasonably well, and Lucy was invariably the loser. But it didn't matter, it was just fun. Like the flocks of swallows, the French teenagers came and went as they pleased. Relying on happenstance, Lucy loitered around the hotel terrace, waiting for them to appear, then tagged along like a mascot. She followed them to the beach, lounged on the warm sands. The girl, Claudette, had moved to Hironville from Paris when she was four, and the boys, Alain and Marc, had lived locally all their lives.

The sands of time were slipping. On the last day of the holiday, nothing seemed to lift Lucy's dark cloud of despondency. In her diary, she wrote,

This has truly been the holiday of a lifetime – a window of sunshine in a wall of rain.

A short tour to a sandy beach and a game of boules on the beach helped pass the time. Lucy dreaded going back. She still wanted to elope, start a new life here, be someone else. The day was hot and humid. There was sand in her hair, and her clothes clung to her sunburned skin. There was no bath or shower, just a hand basin in the room for washing, but Lucy didn't care. After supper, she sat on the hotel terrace, twirling her beads and silver bells ring. A small girl appeared and admired Lucy's ring and necklace. Lucy was about to give up hope of seeing any of the gang, when they suddenly appeared, with rumbling mopeds and a chorus of happy shouts.

'*Bonsoir, Lucy! Viens! On joue au snooker!*'

Lucy jumped up and followed them. She adored the atmosphere of the little café with its round tables and red-and-white check cloths. The jukebox pounded out Mungo Jerry's *In the Summertime*, a song already associated with this holiday. But disappointment and tiredness stole over her, and she had difficulty staying awake. At ten o'clock, she went upstairs to bed and slept heavily.

In the morning, after breakfast, Madame, Brigitte, and Annette stood on the terrace to wave off their English guests and wish them safe travels.

'It wasn't a posh place, but they treated us well,' Hilda said.

As Lucy waved, she caught sight of Phillippe dodging between tables. He caught Lucy's eye and smiled. Lucy waved frantically as the car pulled away.

That was the last time Lucy ever saw him. They had exchanged neither addresses nor surnames. Their meeting had amounted to the mere shadow of a friendship. Lucy felt regret, but also a sense of wonder. It was a privilege to have made so many memories in just a few days, connecting with people from another culture, another land. Later, as the ferry left the harbour, Lucy stood alone on the deck, watching the coastline slowly disappear into the mist, wishing with all her heart she might one day return to France.

15: The Goth

On September 7th, Westcombe Grammar School and Beechwood Secondary Modern merged into one huge, so-called forward-thinking Comprehensive school. Under the new regime, the school was re-named Westcombe High School – an establishment promising equal opportunity – in theory, at least. Mr Kingsley was the Headmaster, the former head of Beechwood having retired. Mr Edgington remained head of Lower School, and a new deputy head had been appointed from elsewhere, a Mrs Keane, whose husband was Lucy's new form tutor. Lucy paid little attention to the hype about fairness and progress. Forms four to six were based in the former Grammar school building, so Lucy wasn't expecting the school day to be any different. The uniform, however, had changed. Gone were the royal blue colours of Beechwood and the Grammar school's navy blue twill and grey pin-stripe shirts. The new uniform was a white shirt, striped tie, dark blue V-neck pullover, and matching skirt for girls, trousers for boys. Uncannily, it was identical to the outfit in the dream about Miss Hawksworth and the train.

During morning registration, a strange tension reigned. Students sat quietly, some looking nervous, others indifferent. Lucy sat awkwardly in her seat, smoothing the creases of her new skirt.

A balding, grey-suited man stood at the front. 'Good morning, class, I'm your new form master, Mr Keane,' the man announced in monotone.

Nobody responded.

'Form assembly today. There will be no assembly in the big hall. Trusting you all had a good holiday?'

A few mumbles of assent sounded from around the room. Lucy stopped listening, daydreaming about France. A sudden ripple of surprise passed through the class, then a cascade of comments.

'He wasn't even old...'

'Forty-something – I think...'

'Cancer is a dreadful thing...'

'Mr Jenkins was nice...'

'He didn't deserve to die...'

'Who will we get now for maths?' Janet asked.

'Mr Conway will continue as your maths teacher,' Mr Keane said.

A few groans followed, and someone muttered, 'That idiot doesn't teach us anything.'

Ironically, the first lesson was maths. Grey-haired, rubber-faced Mr Conway greeted the class in lilting, light-hearted tones.

'You're all going to have to work very hard this year. Today, we'll begin with algebra, and get straight into the homework swing.'

Swing? As far as Lucy was concerned, a swing was a piece of rope tied to the ash tree in the hollow in Biddlecombe Copse or a plaything she was never allowed as a child because the garden was too small.

'4K stands for Klever, Sir!' Jimmy Murphy piped from the back row.

Mr Conway stared through his thick spectacles and said nothing. Someone at the front was sniggering furtively.

'Whoever is making that noise can stop immediately,' Mr Conway said evenly. 'This isn't the time for tomfoolery.'

Red-faced and shaking uncontrollably, a new boy cowered behind his bulging briefcase on his desk. The class stared. Mr Conway chalked an equation on the blackboard. Lucy lost the thread from the start. The new boy stopped laughing and sat hunched over his books, a mop of dark, unkempt hair obscuring his face. He glanced at the board, answered the teacher's questions swiftly and accurately, inviting curious stares.

'May I have your full attention please,' Mr Conway warned the class, 'you are in form four, and you cannot afford to fall behind.'

Too late for me, Lucy thought dismally.

The next lesson was French. The class swarmed over to the old Beechwood block, heading for the new, state-of-the-art language laboratory. The once invisible barrier between the two schools was gone. Although a stone's throw away, Beechwood had always been out of bounds, and any liaison with the other school had been strictly taboo. Today was different. Merging with the stream of navy-clad students, Lucy felt safe and anonymous. In the crowd, she hoped to find a familiar face from Guides, but the clamour of voices and footsteps in the maze of corridors filled her head with confusion. She walked stoically, her mind frozen.

The language laboratory was designed to help students learn languages quickly and efficiently. Each cubicle was furnished with a headset with an attached microphone, and a concealed reel-to-reel tape recorder operable via an array of levers and switches. Seated between Hilary and Megan, Lucy was relieved not to be flanked by show-offs.

A bald, stocky gentleman in a grey suit introduced himself in fluent French. '*Bonjour la classe! Je suis Monsieur Leblanc.*'

'Is his name really Leblanc?' Crispian whispered.

'I am indeed Monsieur Leblanc,' the teacher responded in a faint French accent. 'I am from *Alsace*. This academic year, I will be sharing your French time table with Mr Ross.'

Yet another new teacher, Lucy thought. It was all too much to take in.

'*Alsace?*' Crispian nudged Jimmy. 'That means this guy is an Alsatian!'

'So we'll call him Old Dog,' Jimmy scoffed quietly.

As it happened, the name stuck. Unaware of his newly-dubbed sobriquet, Mr Leblanc continued giving instructions how to operate the machines, glorifying the merits of modern technology. Lucy was nonplussed.

'If anyone damages the equipment, the bill will be sent to their parents!' Old Dog growled.

'No one's going to touch my equipment,' snickered James, and Rosemary sounded as if she was going to explode. As instructed, Lucy put on the headset and pressed the switch marked PLAY. What she heard next took her completely by surprise.

Der Winter ist kalt...

In a year, Mr Kingsley had promised, Lucy would finally start German. Too long.

After a quiet crackling, the anticipated French exercise began. A tinny, hyper-cheerful, female voice inquired, *Aimez-vous le chocolat?*

Lucy pressed the RECORD switch and spoke into the microphone, *Oui, J'aime beaucoup le chocolat.*

Tape reels screeched faintly in the background, Lucy responded to a series of mundane questions. Talking to a machine was redundant, dead. Lucy re-lived the magic of Hironville, wondering what the young folk were doing now. She regretted not one of them had asked to be her pen-friend.

At lunchtime, the class discussed the benefits and drawbacks of what was largely considered an overrated invention.

'That was fun, I like the fancy equipment...'

'I prefer a normal lesson with a teacher explaining things...'

'It's hardly a laboratory – French isn't science...'

'What's the point of doing this, just to play it back and listen to it yourself?'

'Better than boring normal lessons...'

'The sound quality was rubbish...'

In the dinner queue, students squabbled like starlings at a bird-table. Lucy was jostled forward by a bunch of boys she'd never seen before. She took her food and sat at a table of complete strangers. Nobody spoke to her. After lunch, another change was in evidence – all pupils were permitted to stay inside the building. Gone were the days of being thrown out by stern-faced teachers and pompous prefects! Lucy wandered around, trying to look as if she knew where she was going. There was nowhere to sit, nothing to do, and no one to talk to. Afternoon lessons were Latin with Miss Hipp and Geography with Miss Hawksworth. Lucy yawned, doodled, and counted the minutes till home time. Finally, the bell rang at the new, earlier time of half past three.

On Saturday, Lucy bought a German dictionary and phrasebook. As days went by, homework piled higher, as did litter in classrooms. At the start of afternoon lessons, Lucy would invariably lift her desk lid to the unwelcome sight of someone else's packed lunch left-overs. One day, she found a chocolate wrapper, orange peel, two apple cores, and an empty can of cola dribbling its dregs into the pages of *Caesar's Gallic War, Book V*. Then, to her horror, she discovered her new German dictionary was missing. Last week, Janet Ford reported a stolen cartridge pen, others reported sweets or crisps mysteriously disappearing from their desks. With classrooms open to nine hundred students, thefts and vandalism had become the norm. Tracking down thieves was impossible, so Lucy didn't bother reporting her loss. She trudged from lesson to lesson, her head in a perpetual fog. It was late September, and since the start of term, scarcely anyone had spoken to her.

The next morning, Mr Keane introduced a newcomer.

'Good morning, class! This is Julie Fawkes, just moved from Hounslow, West London.'

A gawky girl slouched at the front of the classroom, smirking slyly behind a forelock of blonde hair. The failed friendship with Janet Ford long forgotten, Lucy hurled herself at the unsuspecting Julie Fawkes, regaling her with details about her home and garden, her pets, the holiday in France. All day, Julie quietly endured Lucy's perpetual chatter and allowed herself to be chaperoned around the school buildings like a child. The next day, Julie decided she'd had enough of limpet-like Lucy, so she ignored her and befriended Jodie instead. Jodie was good fun, self-assured and always ready with side-splitting jokes and spicy gossip. In addition, Jodie was practically a neighbour, just three streets away in Nyehaven and was Julie's travelling companion on the train. The switch was predictable and practical.

In the afternoon Lucy sat in defiant denial, hiding behind her history book, glancing in Julie's direction, watching how well she and Jodie were getting on. The teacher was late, and the class was chirpy. Lucy stared at the clock above the blackboard, waiting for plump Mrs Pilkington to arrive and drone on about the Agrarian Revolution.

'Hello, there – wakey, wakey!' Julie called, waving her hand across Lucy's face. Briefly, a flame of hope leapt. Perhaps the friendship was still alive?

'Oh – Julie! Yes – er – sorry, what did you say?'

'What on earth were you thinking about just then?' Julie asked, 'Your face looks like a wet dish-rag.'

Three girls within earshot burst out laughing. Lucy stared blankly at her open book and swallowed hard. It was high time to put Goody away and resurrect long-forgotten Genie. After school, Lucy took refuge in Biddlecombe Copse. Seated on the ground, in the hollow of the ash tree,

Lucy immersed herself in her mother's old teach-yourself German book. The archaic, Gothic style type-set was difficult to decipher, but Lucy persevered, slowly devouring new words and phrases that fuelled her fascination for all things sinister and dark. She learned that Tod is Death, tot is dead, and sie ist tot means she is dead. There were many ways to die, but for each individual, only one death. Lucy wondered how she would die. With the rope swing she had often leapt from the sandy bank, flying through the air for enjoyment, but now she could do the same, imagining she was plunging from a cliff. Or she could climb the tree and hang herself. She looked up at the breeze-stirred branches that moved like curling lips of a hungry beast. She imagined gigantic teeth slowly closing, trapping her inside the monster's jaws.

Every waking moment was spent dwelling on the macabre. Lucy filled her notebook with sketches and coded messages, and bought more horror stories and devoured them avidly. She watched television thrillers, revelling in morbid, tragic storylines. She bought a second German dictionary, replacing the stolen one and guarded it safely. She spent an entire maths lesson daubing the cover of her homework diary with a large, black swastika and scratched DECEASED with a compass point after her name on her ruler. Mr Conway set homework, and Lucy didn't even bother copying it down.

Hilda noticed the swastika.

'Do you know what that means?' she demanded, her brows darkening in disapproval.

'It's the sign Hitler and the Nazis used in the Second World War,' Lucy answered.

Hilda clicked her tongue. 'We don't want to be reminded of that, thank you very much!'

Lucy wanted to know more about the war. Library books taught her that Nazis favoured a master race and meritocracy – a society of superior people rewarded according to personal input. All who failed to conform were hunted and exterminated. The bullies were right. If I am incapable of conforming to this world, then I will leave it, Lucy reflected. She had missed the benchmark at school and had disappointed her parents. Suicide was the next logical step. But how on earth was she supposed to kill herself? Hanging was one option. Perhaps an overdose of over-the-counter pills? Or the romantic option of shooting, like in stories and films? However, obtaining a gun would be nigh impossible.

In her next lunch break at Woolworth's Lucy bought a toy cap gun, which she kept with the pocket-knife. Alone in the hut and the copse, Lucy toyed hungrily with her killer tools, counting the days until the dreaded ultimatum. In the sandy hollow of the Monster's Head, Lucy held the gun against her chest, imagining this was her last moment. As she pulled the trigger, a small pocket of gunpowder exploded with a sharp crack, releasing a smell of sulphur and a faint trail of smoke. Dotty whimpered, cowering close by. Lucy felt nothing. There was no sense of satisfaction. All she had succeeded in doing was terrifying the dog. She wondered what to write in a suicide note. She could present her case for being a completely useless, meaningless blot on society. She would apologise to her parents for disappointing them. Perhaps her demise would even make headline news? As far as Lucy knew, she was the youngest person alive entertaining such thoughts – thoughts that marked time, offering brief relief from a living hell.

A teen magazine posed the question: What do you think you will be doing in ten years' time? Readers had written in with their views:

I see myself happily married and with a family.

I want to travel the world.

I hope to start my own business.

I'd like to be rich and famous.

Lucy unzipped her typewriter and considered writing two contrasting letters: Goody the happy mother with a satisfying career, and Genie the decaying body of a young girl who had died with a smile on her lips – a smile that welcomed release from an existence devoid of hope. Lucy scrapped the idea without typing a single word. It was too much bother.

Reading the local newspaper, Lucy was struck by the high incidence of suicide in Westcombe and Nyehaven, victims all adults with health, unemployment, or family problems. Coroners' reports invariably attributed their deaths to the balance of the mind being temporarily disturbed. Lucy wondered what could have gone so badly wrong in the lives of these unfortunate people. Perhaps she wasn't so alone, after all?

At home, the evening winter routine was unchanged. Hilda came from work at six, dinner was at seven, then homework, television, and bed at ten-thirty. Hilda reminded Lucy it was her twenty-fifth wedding anniversary in December.

'Your father and I were married at Christmas,' Hilda spun the oft-repeated yarn. 'It was the end of the war, when times were hard. We had a simple ceremony in the register office and a honeymoon weekend in Bournemouth. Cheap and cheerful, and good enough. But this year, for our silver wedding, we're going out to dinner. I'll leave you some casserole, and you won't mind looking after the animals for one evening, would you, Lucy? We'll be back by ten.'

'Yes, Mum.' Lucy's answer was automatic.

Will they want to celebrate if I go ahead with the plan?

Lucy stalled, her heart pounding.

At school, Lucy's sole consolation was Thursday's art class. The latest project was calligraphy, and Lucy was working on Gothic script, a skill she incorporated into an anniversary card for her parents. *Pity I probably won't be alive when they get this*, Lucy thought darkly.

'That lettering looks really professional,' Susan Schofield said, staring through heavily made-up eyes and a glossy fringe of raven-black hair.

'Thanks,' Lucy answered, sensing commonality. Susan was a misfit and not particularly popular. She liked heavy metal and motorbikes, had few friends in school, but associated with the Combe Ridge Greasers. Lucy didn't imagine she would be accepted in Susan's circle of terrifying friends. After finishing the card, Lucy painted an array of dark silhouettes, pistols and revolvers. She used black paint for the guns and didn't care what anyone said.

The feedback was unexpected.

'It looks like a poster for a spy thriller,' Rosemary remarked. 'Quite impressive.'

'I used my left hand,' Lucy boasted.

Others gathered round, and Lucy revelled in compliments from those who normally mocked. Unconsciously she relaxed, lowering her guard.

The next day, Lucy discovered her private notebook missing from the bottom of her desk. Observing Lucy's frantic rummaging, Abigail strolled up and asked, 'Looking for something?'

'Um – nothing. It doesn't matter,' Lucy mumbled.

'Oh, I think it does. Why do you even bother lying about it?'

'I left some notes in my desk and just wondered where they were. That's all.'

'What were they? Bank notes?' drawled Fiona.

'Anyway,' Abigail continued, 'I hear the boys had a great RE lesson this morning while we were all at games.'

Lucy preferred not to think about the morning's games lesson, in which Jane Haslett had called her useless garbage.

'Jimmy Murphy took your little stories to the boys' RE class and persuaded boozy old Jonesey to read them out,' scoffed Joanna.

'What's all that stuff about the KGB and an embassy at Vladivostok?' Abigail asked.

'The story about the prisoner was really interesting,' remarked Alison. 'Where do you get your ideas from?'

Lucy didn't answer.

'You're always going off on your own and won't talk to anyone. We didn't know you were planning to kill yourself,' Jodie said, with a puzzled frown.

Lucy's heart was thumping.

'I always thought you were a bit odd, so what's all this about nine o'clock in the morning, on December 8th?" Alison asked.

'A quarter to nine, actually.' Lucy corrected. 'It's one of my stories, just – oh, well you might as well know, I get my ideas from reading horror stories and from things I watch on the telly.'

'You are a horror, after all, Lucy!' quipped Rosemary, raising a few sniggers.

Goody didn't share the amusement, but Genie was enjoying the banter. Lucy had now clearly earned the reputation of being the class freak, but at least she was making people laugh, even if it was for all the wrong reasons.

On Friday afternoon the French teacher was late, due to discipline problems in another class. No work had been set, and pupils were at a loose end. Only Shirley Johnson and the eccentric Arthur Long were studying, Shirley learning vocabulary and Arthur immersed in *Lipsey's Positive Economics*. Everyone else was enjoying the teacher's absence. The din was deafening.

'What a relief! I hate French,' snorted Jimmy.

'It's so boring!' added Mike Fidler, opening a copy of *The Sun* and gloating eagerly over page three.

'I just can't understand French,' Jimmy groaned tiredly. 'But I suppose it's really easy if you can do it.'

Lucy glanced over her shoulder at Jimmy's freckled face leering in her direction. She quickly buried her nose in a book, disappointed the teacher was late. She was secretly growing fond of dark-haired forty-something Mr Ross.

'That's a stupid thing to say, Jimmy,' Mike replied. 'Anything is easy if you can do it!'

James sniffed and said nothing. Few noticed the door open, and a sixth form boy enter the room and tell the class to be quiet. The chattering didn't stop. The prefect sat down at the teacher's desk and tried to read a book.

'Oi! You!' Jimmy shouted to the front. 'Can you teach us anything?'

The boy looked at his watch. The class hurled suggestions and requests.

'We could have a quiz?'

'Pop music of course, not school stuff.'

'Or football?'

'Tell us a few jokes!'

'Or we could come to the front and tell some of our jokes!'

'Some of us are quite talented, you know.'

More whistling, hooting and raucous laughter swelled the charged atmosphere. The prefect rose wearily to his feet, tapping his pen thoughtfully on tightly shut lips. A paper dart floated onto the front table, and the room was filled with the trilling of plastic rulers vibrating under desk lids.

'Come on, Rosemary! Give us a song!' Mike and Crispian were on their feet, gesticulating. Jimmy led the class with a slow clap.

Rosemary blushed coyly. 'Are you sure your ears could stand it?'

'Jonathan could show us his stamp collection!' jeered Joanna.

'I haven't brought it to school today,' replied Jonathan, 'I don't want my prized collection ruined, thank you very much.'

Then Abigail whispered something in Joanna's ear. Immediately, Joanna jumped to her feet, her eyes bulging with excitement.

'I know what!' Joanna bellowed above the din. 'Ask Lucy Wylie to do something. She's really weird!'

There was a brief hush, and the class began chanting in unison.

'Lu-cy! Lu-cy! Lu-cy!' tapping rhythmically on their desk-tops with pens, rulers and bare knuckles, hungry for entertainment.

Lucy froze. Her heart was hammering so hard she could scarcely draw breath. She thought desperately for ideas. Perhaps she could impersonate a teacher? The very strict English teacher, Miss Menzies? Or maybe Miss Hawksworth? The prefect signalled for quiet and beckoned Lucy to the front. Every nerve taut and poised, Lucy stood up.

Just then there was a knock at the door, and a small boy entered the room and handed the prefect a piece of paper.

'A message from Mrs Jenkins in Lower School,' muttered the boy.

'Well, how bizarre,' said the sixth-former, reading the note and scratching his head. 'Lucy Wylie is standing up. Off you go, Lucy. Mrs Jenkins would like to see you in her office immediately.'

Never before was Lucy so relieved to be spared in the nick of time – but she felt a whisper of disappointment. A golden opportunity to prove herself to the class had been missed. Besides, what could Mrs Jenkins possibly want with her? Did she even know her? Minutes later, Lucy was face-to-face with the stout, motherly schoolmistress, who had no reputation for being frightening.

'Yes, it was you,' Mrs Jenkins said.

Lucy looked blank, her heart still pounding. She scarcely believed how much trouble she was in – just in one afternoon.

'It was Mrs Taylor who saw you,' Mrs Jenkins began. 'Mrs Taylor, the assistant art teacher. She was with me in the car. She recognised you and told me your name and form. Otherwise I wouldn't have known who you were.'

Lucy was mystified.

'You were on your bicycle at the crossroads with Hillcrest Road and Central Drive, after school last Wednesday, weren't you?'

Lucy quickly cast her mind back. Yes, she had gone into town after school to buy another book of horror stories but recalled nothing unusual. Nor did she even remember having taken that particular route.

'That's right. I was in town last Wednesday afternoon,' Lucy answered quietly.

'Then surely you will recall your narrow escape?'

Again, Lucy looked blank. 'I'm not sure what you mean.'

'You rode your bicycle straight into a main road without even looking. Mrs Taylor and I had an awful fright. I had to slam on the brakes. You're supposed to stop at that junction.'

Lucy was speechless. Would she be banned from cycling to school? She quaked at the possibility of further public humiliation.

'I – um – I didn't know. I mean, I didn't mean to do anything wrong,' she stammered.

'Then you obviously need to learn some basic rules of road safety. As a cyclist you are particularly vulnerable and must act responsibly on the roads – bearing in mind that there are other road users, apart from yourself. Otherwise, you are putting your safety and the safety of others at risk. Just think how dreadful it would have been, for everyone concerned, if you had been hurt.'

There was an awkward silence.

'Yes, Miss,' Lucy answered.

Mrs Jenkins was the well-respected leader of the Christian Union –further vexation to Lucy's troubled conscience. She had offended a good person and would doubtless never be good enough for God, if He even existed? She suddenly sensed irritation at being treated like a child, and at what she saw as an invasion of her private life. *How dare these busybodies interfere! And what would have happened if she had performed her hastily prepared impersonation of Miss Menzies?* Lucy bit her lip and scowled at the floor.

'Have you nothing more to say for yourself?' Mrs Jenkins asked.

'I'm sorry.'

'Well, I hope you'll at least be more careful in future!' Mrs Jenkins sighed wearily. She had done what she'd felt burdened to do. Soon she would face a weekend with her children, comforting them in the aftermath of their father's untimely passing, weeks before.

'I will be more careful,' Lucy concluded.

'Very well, then. You may go.'

All eyes were on Lucy when she returned to class. A barrage of questions followed.

'What was that all about, then?'

'What did Mrs Jenkins want?'

'Are you in trouble?'

'What did you do?'

'You managed to get out of that nicely, didn't you?'

'We were looking forward to having a good laugh.'

Lucy ignored them. It was half past three. The bell rang insignificantly into the din. Desk lids banged, chairs scraped on the tiled floor. Students spilt out of the room and clattered down the stairs, shouting and laughing.

'SILENCE!' roared Miss Hawksworth from an open doorway.

Lucy darted unnoticed through the crowd and disappeared.

The weekend passed without mishap. Trade in Woolworth's was slack, and the only interesting moment was when Miss Crawford came into the shop and bought half a pound of Raspberry Ruffles from the Pick-n-Mix. She gave Lucy a big wink. Lucy was glad Miss Crawford didn't begin a conversation, as Lucy was disinclined to tell her she was tired of horse-riding and wouldn't be booking any more lessons. During lunch break, Lucy bought dark grey eye shadow and black mascara and eyebrow pencils. Later in the privacy of her bedroom, she applied heavy layers of makeup and was pleased with her enhanced Gothic image. Hearing her mother's footsteps, Lucy hurriedly put the makeup in the drawer and rubbed her face with a paper tissue.

On Monday morning, Lucy dared to apply a little of the makeup and wear it to school. Nobody commented. At the start of the games lesson, Miss Forbes gathered the group in the main hall to select new hockey and netball teams. Alison and Jane were appointed as team captains. Everyone had a place in a team or reserve team and was commended for their contribution to the school sports programme.

Everyone but Lucy.

'And then, we also have Lucy Wylie,' Miss Forbes declared coldly. 'She never says anything, never does anything, and in fact she might as well not be here.'

Might as well not be here.

'Yeah, Wylie is just a useless waste of space,' Jane Haslett sneered, winning the crowd's approval. A flood of despair swept over Lucy, icy fingers searching out every part of her soul. Every vestige of hope had vanished in one fell swoop. Mortified, she hid her face. Silent tears flowed, smudging the black mascara. Lucy rubbed her face with a tissue, hoping nobody would notice. Furiously, she fixed her attention on the moment she would cease to exist.

Lucy counted the days. Seventy-four remaining – far too many. Might circumstances miraculously improve before then? Lucy doubted it. In the meantime, practical arrangements would have to be made: a suicide method, a note, and funeral expenses to be met. Lucy had no idea how much a funeral would cost, but she set a target of one hundred pounds, of which she had already saved eighty-seven, from Woolworth's and fruit-picking. If she wasn't going to be there at Christmas, there would be no need to buy presents. Alone in her room, Lucy fed her morbid fantasies by writing, drawing, and reading shocking things, and by scoring deep scratches on her arms and hands, watching the blood well forth and trickle in crimson rivulets on her pale skin. At night, awake and alone in the dark, she lay motionless, placed the pillow firmly over her unflinching face. She counted, slowly, for a minute or longer – determined to hold her breath for long enough to experience the intoxicating thrill of hypoxia – hoping to induce harm – even death. Part of her clung desperately to the notion there were others who thought, felt, and suffered as she did. But what hope was there of ever finding them? Much less a way out of this living hell. Day and night, Lucy took silent refuge in her dark imaginings. A horror story referenced the words of Friedrich Nietzsche, laughing at me, they still hate me.

Hate was the operative word. Not love. Love was for the privileged alone. Everybody hated her. Therefore Lucy hated her life, her soul, her self.

16: Distractions

'Wake up, Lucy! It's half past ten. Melanie's coming today!'

Hilda's strident morning call was enough to wake the dead. Lucy blinked hard, slowly identifying the candy-striped pattern of her pillowcase. A mug of tea steamed lazily on the bedside table, inches away. Suddenly, today's agenda invaded her sleep-fogged brain like shutters opening into sunshine, dispelling shadows of sleep. Hauling herself upright, Lucy rested on her elbows, her head reeling with the sheer effort. How she hated sleeping in, missing half the day, in the holidays. Annoyingly, after nearly twelve hours' sleep, she still felt exhausted.

Revived by the tea, Lucy got up and went to the wardrobe to choose clothes for the day. She pulled out her favourite lilac-coloured Ben Sherman shirt and the light blue jeans with rows of coloured buttons which she had sewn on the pockets and seams. She dressed tiredly, applied a thick layer of makeup, and paused at the dressing-table. The girl reflected in the glass was not the same person who had said goodbye to Melanie in London two years before. Gone was the impish, freckle-faced child. A serious, square-jawed face of someone much older stared back at her. It could be the face of a film actress or someone in a magazine – not a particularly pretty person – but someone else. Lucy put on her chain belt, her favourite turquoise mini-jumper and a floppy, wide-brimmed black felt hat, pulling it at different angles, trying different facial expressions.

Has Melanie changed, too? Lucy wondered.

A sharp rap on the door made her jump.

'Lucy! Whatever are you up to in there?' Hilda demanded. 'Breakfast is on the table!'

Lucy pushed the hat under the bed and hid the makeup in her underwear drawer. 'All right, Mum, I'm coming.'

Lucy went to the kitchen and sat facing the window. Surely Melanie would be impressed with the park-like lawns and shrubbery ablaze with autumn colours? Melanie had always boasted about her leafy, suburban home with its half-a-dozen-or-so songbirds' nests in the back garden. Now it was Lucy's turn to show off. She would give Melanie a guided tour of Edencroft's extensive gardens and unnumbered birds' nests. Or maybe Melanie wasn't interested in wildlife any more? It had been a while since she had mentioned such things in her letters.

Lucy finished her porridge, and Hilda asked the usual question, 'marmalade or Marmite?' Lucy gave the usual answer, 'I don't mind.'

As usual, Hilda chose the healthier option and spread two slices of toast with Marmite.

'Thanks, Mum.' Lucy said.

Hilda sighed happily. Lucy seemed much more cheerful this morning.

Lucy's jeans were tight. She hadn't worn them since the French holiday, and now, a roll of fat overhung the waistband. She didn't care, she was just glad it was half term.

Melanie arrived an hour late. Hearing the scrunch of car tyres on the drive below, Lucy and Hilda went to greet the guests. Mr Stewart rolled down the window of his well-polished Mercedes. 'Sorry we're late! We got a bit lost en route.'

'Will you come in for a cup of tea?' Hilda asked.

'That's very kind of you Mrs Wylie, but we'd better not,' Mrs Stewart replied. 'We're on our way to visit friends in Cornwall, and we're already running late.'

Melanie jumped out of the car.

'That garage is a bit of a shambles,' she remarked rudely.

'I know,' Lucy said. 'My dad hasn't got round to pulling it down and building a new one yet. Come on, I'll give you a guided tour of Edencroft.'

'Give your poor friend a chance,' Hilda said. 'She'll be tired after the journey.'

Melanie loped up the slope, carrying her small case. Her short, cropped hairstyle was still the same, but she had grown significantly taller.

'Your garden's enormous – and there's even a view of the sea!' Melanie exclaimed.

After lunch, Lucy showed her round the garden.

'Tell me about your school,' Melanie demanded.

'Not much to tell. It's comprehensive now, and pretty awful – too noisy and crowded.'

Melanie smiled smugly, showing braces and yellowed teeth. 'Wordsworth's still a grammar school, thank goodness.'

'I miss Wordsworth,' Lucy sighed. 'I had friends there. People here are so strange.'

'So you keep mentioning in your letters. We have peculiar people too, and bullying. There's a new girl in my year who gets bullied. She's too quiet and doesn't stick up for herself.'

'Come on girls! We're going out for a drive,' Hilda called from the back door.

In the fine weather, a sightseeing tour seemed reasonable, but Melanie was sparse with compliments.

'What do you think of the scenery?' Lucy asked.

'It's okay,' Melanie sniffed.

Lucy found comfort on Combe Ridge cliffs, where angry waves crashed seventy feet below, hammering ragged rocks with timeless strength. The sound of pounding surf on clattering boulders filled the chill air. Lucy watched an advancing wave swamp a wrack-clad rock, far below.

'Just think, Melanie!' she shouted above the deafening roar, 'We were standing down there just a few minutes ago.'

'Yeah, so what?' Melanie yelled back.

'If we were there now we would be swept away!' Lucy shouted, her voice drowned in the din of wind and waves. On the narrow path, Lucy almost missed her footing, caught a fleeting glimpse of jagged rocks, scores of feet below. Regaining balance, she relived the moment of tension, resolving to preserve its memory for the next unbearable moment at school.

On the way home, the setting sun cast shafts of light over the bay. Dark clouds hovered ghoulishly on distant hills.

'A typical Westcombe view, with changeable weather,' Lucy said. A break in the clouds shed reflected sunlight on wet tarmac. The road stretched ahead like long, golden ribbon rising to the next ridge.

'Look – over there! That's a road!' Lucy exclaimed.

'Yes, of course it's a road. I can see it is,' Melanie said. The rest of the journey was spent in silence.

Lucy sat morosely through supper, while Melanie boasted about her musical achievements. With a shudder, Lucy remembered school and her own dark agenda that lurked hungrily in the deepest recesses of her mind. Was the once vibrant friendship with Melanie over? As eleven-year-olds they squabbled over trivia, but now there was mutual coolness, as between two strangers. Perhaps they'd never really been friends at all?

After the meal, Melanie sat on the settee with her legs curled up, staring at the television.

'What's that book you keep scribbling in?' she asked.

'Nothing you'd find interesting.' Lucy closed her diary.

Melanie sniffed. 'Tell me about Woolworth's.'

'It's okay. The money's useful.'

'Saving up for anything?'

'Not really.'

'Daddy got me a Saturday job in the solicitor's office. I do filing, and I'm learning shorthand typing.'

'My sister does that,' Lucy answered, remembering her typewriter lying neglected in its case at the bottom of the wardrobe.

'I get a clothes allowance from my parents,' Melanie continued. 'I have so many outfits now, I'm using the spare room as a dressing-room.'

Lucy didn't answer. She was glad when it was bedtime and Melanie had gone to the spare room.

The next morning, it was pouring with rain. Albert gave the girls a lift to town, where they looked around the shops. Passing by the Merry Teapot, Melanie said, 'Is this where your friend Alison Rodgers lives? What a dump!'

Lucy noticed the peeling paint, and the darkened windows displaying the sign, CLOSED.

'She's not my friend,' she said, staring blankly up the rain-drenched street.

'Isn't there any social life around here?' Melanie inquired disparagingly.

'Not much.'

'I don't want to hear any more about Guides – too stuffy and institutionalised.'

'I'm finished with that now. It was good for a while, but now it's too babyish.'

'I should think so too! Anyway, how about a midnight feast?'

'Never had one. I've only read about them in stories about boarding schools.'

'I've had plenty. They're good fun.' Melanie grinned impishly. 'We'll buy our own stuff, of course, or it won't be a secret. Your parents need never find out.'

In the supermarket, they bought a selection of snacks and sequestered them back to Edencroft. As the day wore on, Melanie's sullen demeanour softened, and Lucy saw more of the fun-loving friend she remembered.

'Do you wear a bra?' Melanie asked.

'Yes, I do, actually,' Lucy replied.

A year ago, the whole business of growing up had been extremely important, but now it seemed dull and irrelevant.

'What about periods? Have you started yet?' Melanie asked.

'No.'

'It's very uncomfortable, feeling like you've wet yourself all the time. It's especially bad every time you get up. You can feel it –'

'Can't say I'm looking forward to it, then,' Lucy interrupted.

'What about Margaret Pritchard?' Melanie asked. 'She moved away, too. Do you still write to her?'

'Yes.'

'Can you show me some of her letters? She always was a bit odd. Remember how we used to laugh at her?'

Lucy still valued Margaret's friendship, but it was hard not to be swept along by Melanie's charisma.

'Okay,' Lucy agreed reluctantly. She picked two letters containing news of Margaret's school, and a family holiday in Wales. Melanie glanced through the letters and tossed them aside.

'I bet she's still got acne!' she sneered.

'Do you want to see my diary of the holiday in France?' Lucy asked.

'Okay, show me.'

Lucy took the thick exercise book off the shelf. Melanie glanced briefly at the colourful postcards on the cellophane-decked front cover and flicked through Lucy's hand-written narrative and neat drawings.

'There aren't any photographs!'

'My Dad's got those. I can show you them, if you like.'

'Nah, don't bother. Your diary is too personal and very boring. It's only about what you did. You haven't said much at all about France.'

Lucy silently concluded that Melanie was jealous.

At five minutes to midnight, Lucy's pocket-sized alarm clock rattled unobtrusively under her pillow. She pressed her finger on the silencer button, got up and crept down the hallway to the spare room. She tapped softly on the door.

'Melanie, are you awake?' Lucy hissed through the keyhole. A muffled groan. Lucy opened the door. A floorboard creaked.

'Shhh,' Melanie whispered, 'Come on, let's get started!'

Lucy switched on her torch and scrambled under the bed to retrieve the picnic. The food tasted good, especially the mushroom soup, still hot from the Thermos flask. How unnerving it had been to prepare it quickly without being seen! The girls guzzled in silence, grinning like pirates gloating over stolen treasure. So far, so good. Lucy was reminded of picnics with Alison in the art hut, but this was more exciting because it was clandestine and vaguely illicit. Then Lucy remembered her parents' propensity for sniffing out suspicious smells.

'What's wrong?' whispered Melanie.

'Nothing. But what if there's is a draught, and my parents smell the soup.'

'Don't be daft! Eat up and enjoy it. You're such a wimp. We've every right to do this, we paid for it with our own money, remember?'

The food was filling, and there was plenty left over. Lucy wrapped the remaining cheese and pickle sandwiches and chocolate biscuits and hid them under the bed.

'I suppose we'll have to go and brush our teeth,' she yawned.

'Don't be ridiculous!' Melanie grinned, revealing yellowed teeth.

Lucy bit into an apple.

'I've an idea,' Melanie hissed wickedly. 'Let's compare bust sizes!'

'If you want,' Lucy agreed tiredly.

Melanie took off her pyjama top, revealing breasts big enough to wobble. Lucy removed her top, revealing the padded bra she'd been wearing all weekend. Melanie wasn't fooled.

'Take that off, or I'll never see what size you really are.'

Lucy removed the cotton wool first, then the bra. 'Hmmm.' mumbled

Melanie. 'You always were very small. Now, turn round.' Lucy turned round.

'You look much older from the back,' Melanie said, 'you'll grow yet, and probably not far off.'

'Far off what?' Lucy asked apprehensively, still with her back to Melanie. 'Periods, of course.'

'Fat chance of that. Mum's been saying it'll be soon, but it still hasn't happened. Anyway, it's freezing in here. I'm putting my top back on.'

'What about hair?' inquired Melanie.

Lucy looked blank.

'Body hair.' Melanie raised her arms, showing shady armpits, dark with a fuzzy growth of hair. Then she pointed to her briefs, and more dark hairs sprouting through the holes in the lace.

'Well, I don't have as much hair as you.' Lucy gave a short, nervous laugh.

'What's funny?' quipped Melanie. 'You're laughing.'

Embarrassed silence.

'This is the E.L.C,' Melanie said.

'The what?'

'The E.L.C. The Edencroft Lesbian Club. '

Lucy looked at the clock and feigned a yawn. 'It's late, so I'm off to bed now.'

'You're a cowardly-custard,' Melanie muttered.

'Good night,' Lucy whispered, silently opening the door and disappearing into the dark corridor. In the morning, she smuggled the left-overs outside and gave them to the hens. Her parents said nothing. In the afternoon, Melanie was collected by her parents, and Lucy was both wistful and relieved.

'She's still a bright little spark, isn't she?' Hilda said as the Stewarts' car disappeared down the lane.

'I suppose so,' Lucy replied.

On the Saturday after half term, Lucy noticed a dark stain on her underwear. She went to tell her mother, who was waxing the linoleum floor in the spare bedroom.

'It's happened,' Lucy said.

'What's happened?' Hilda asked, fearing something dreadful. Lucy told her. Hilda gave a gasp of surprise as if she were already grandmother to Lucy's child. Mother and daughter embraced briefly, sealing a future unwritten, unborn. Lucy was strangely light-hearted. Gone was the puny, irresponsible child, and now, she must start living as an adult. She told nobody at school. Nobody asked about her half term holiday. Lucy continued the double life of Goody and Genie, marking each day in her diary – a countdown to the dreaded ultimatum. Deep down, Lucy longed for miraculous escape.

One evening, as Lucy sat on the sofa, poring pointlessly over physics homework, Hilda said, 'I've been thinking about your social life – or lack of it. There's not much here, is there?'

'I'll give Guides another try?' Lucy suggested.

'If that's what you want, dear.'

On Friday evening, Lucy found her uniform fitted better than ever. Humming the tune to "Bring me Sunshine", Lucy was hopeful. Albert dropped Lucy at the church, pleased with a reason to have a drink and reconnect with Farmer Jim.

'Welcome back, Lucy,' Captain Merryweather said politely. The hall was full, but Lucy was disappointed to find Valerie, Fenella and Paula had all left, and there wasn't one Guide over the age of nine.

'I'm a bit old for all this, now,' Lucy said to the new Lieutenant.

'Never mind, dear, it's really nice to have you back,' the chatty lady said. 'I hear you did a lot for last year's Christmas concert. We need someone who's good at art. That's nice eye makeup you are wearing. It makes you look very grown up.'

'Thanks,' Lucy said, vaguely flattered. She looked across the room at the knot of giggling Guides at the table where Captain was folding paper cards. She decided there and then she wouldn't be coming back.

'Isn't there anything else you could go to?' Hilda asked later. 'A sports' group or country dancing club?'

Lucy pulled a face. 'There is a youth club,' she said, 'In the old Beechwood hall. I could find out more about that.'

Lucy recalled only bad reports about the club. Alison had said, 'they smoke like chimneys, swear like troopers and drink like fish. Mr Jones calls it a den of iniquity, and that's rich coming from an alcoholic!'

Lucy figured she had nothing to lose. On Friday evening, at seven o'clock, Albert dropped her by the entrance.

"Bye, Dad – see you at half nine,' Lucy said, without a backward glance. Inside the building, the noise was deafening and the air dense with second-hand smoke. Surrounded by strangers, Lucy felt a curious sense of security. The jukebox in the corner pounded out Freda Payne's "Band of Gold" – a song Lucy was soon to associate with this episode of her life. The pink crepe dress was uncomfortably tight and far too short. Other girls wore long skirts or flared jeans. Lucy found an empty seat and idly traced patterns on the Formica table with a spent match stick.

'Can I get you a Coke?' Beside her stood a scrawny boy with furtive eyes and sharp features, in his hand a gently smouldering pipe exuding a rich, fragrant aroma. The lad looked familiar.

'My name's Clive. What's yours?'

'Lucy. You were at my thirteenth birthday, with Nigel Daly, also helped push my Mum's car out of the mud.'

'Of course. It's been a while.'

Clive pulled out a pack of tobacco, refilled his pipe and took a quick puff, clouding his face with billows of grey smoke.

'Let me get you a drink. What'll you have?'

'Um – I'll have a Coke, please.'

Clive swaggered to the bar, jingling coins in his jeans pocket. He returned a minute later with two tumblers of cola with ice.

'Thanks,' Lucy said.

'You look older – I mean, more grown up,' Clive said.

'Thanks.'

'I left school last year,' Clive continued. 'I couldn't stand it. I couldn't wait to get out and find a job. I'm a butcher, in Nyehaven.'

Much as she hated school, Lucy couldn't imagine anyone wanting to spend their life working in a butcher's shop.

'Really?' Lucy sipped her drink. The ice cubes were cold against her teeth.

'I'll be sixteen in a few weeks!' Clive proudly puffed his pipe. 'And then I'll have finished my year's apprenticeship, and the boss says there'll be a permanent job for me. With the pay rise I should be able to save up for a new motorbike. You could have a ride on the back if you like?'

Lucy suppressed a nervous yawn. 'Hmmmm,' she agreed dubiously.

Clive put down his pipe. 'Okay, enough about me. Tell me about you.'

'I'm fourteen, still at school, I hate it. I work in Westcombe Woolworth's on Saturdays and in the holidays, but I wouldn't want to spend the rest of my life working there.' Lucy shouted above the noise. *What was she saying?* According to one plan she had in mind, she certainly wouldn't be working at Woolworth's and going to school for the rest of her life. *The other plan?* Lucy teetered on the edge of an abyss of doubt.

'I moved from London two years ago.'

'London,' mused Clive. 'I've never been there. You like it here?'

'The scenery is beautiful.'

'You like astronomy?'

'How did you guess?'

'Dunno. On clear nights I spend ages looking out of the window, and if it's cloudy, then I just look at my books. I keep them under the bed. Sometimes I spend half the night studying the stars. I only need a couple of hours' sleep.'

This was reassuring. *He neither needs much sleep nor worries about it!*

'I know the constellations,' Clive went on, 'There's Great Bear, Little Bear, Andromeda, Cassiopeia... I expect you know them.'

'My Dad showed me some, on evening walks with the dog.'

'I can identify planets in the Solar System too, without a telescope. Perhaps, one night, I can point them out to you?'

'Yes,' Lucy agreed, then realised the suggestion was tantamount to a date. Suddenly she remembered the time.

'I have to go in a few minutes. My dad's coming to pick me up.'

Clive's face fell. 'Club finishes at half ten, but it's nearer eleven, by the time they get everybody out.'

'It's my first time here, and I wasn't sure if I'd like it.'

'Will you be here next week?'

'I think so. Thanks for the Coke. 'Bye.'

Lucy left the club, her mind reeling. Might Clive be a potential soul-mate?

The following Friday, he was there again, sitting at the same table. Again, he bought her a Coke. The music was loud, conversation a challenge. A song came on the jukebox – a song with powerful lyrics:

"Drown my hopes of staying alive... through all this... I will survive..."

Clive's smouldering pipe lay neglected on the table. Then he got up and said, 'Let me introduce you to some of my friends.'

In the games room, Lucy met Maurice and Wendy, Edward Teddy Grantham, and Philip Bonzo Monkhouse, and Hector the Hedgehog – a lanky, feisty skinhead who sported the best denims, braces, Doc Marten boots, and unbreakable self-image. Nigel Daly needed no introduction. All were former Beechwood pupils, many with full-time jobs. The club leader, a tall, wiry figure with thick, Ronnie Corbett spectacles and baggy, corduroy trousers was called Robin Banks, affectionately known as Robber by club members.

Lucy was invited to join in a five-a-side hockey game in the old Beechwood gymnasium. The mood was relaxed, and it didn't matter two hoots who was on which side, nor who won. Caught up in excitement and laughter, Lucy didn't miss the opportunity to strike the ball. The aim was to keep sticks low to reduce the risk of injury or of smashing a window. Miss Forbes's rule about not dragging the stick along the ground was non-existent here. It was a different world. Flushed and breathless, Lucy joined the others afterwards for more cold drinks. It had been tremendous fun. The only bad thing was an accidental blow on the shin from someone else's stick. *Nothing compared with pain inflicted by bullies*, Lucy reflected, recalling the music teacher's maxim about mental pain being worse than physical.

'You played well,' said Wendy. 'Are you in the school team?'

'Not a chance,' replied Lucy. 'Miss Forbes can't stand me.'

Petite, pint-sized Wendy tossed her head back and laughed. 'I know just what you mean. That woman has the knack of making you feel this small.' Wendy closed her thumb and forefinger together with less than a millimetre between them. Finally, Lucy had found an ally in someone Miss Forbes disliked. Wendy looked diminutive and vulnerable, potentially a target for bullies, but she possessed a feistiness Lucy lacked.

'Try one of these!' Clive pulled out a pack of cigarettes. Lucy hadn't seen the pipe for nearly an hour.

Lucy recalled the evening walk with Philippe and his friends.

'These are menthol,' Clive said, 'They're less strong.'

'Thanks.' Lucy took one. Clive took one, too, clicked his lighter and lit Lucy's cigarette first. She sucked in the smoke, feeling a cold, sharpness on her tongue. Clive inhaled deeply and blew smoke out through his nostrils. Lucy wondered how he managed to do that, but she didn't ask.

The next day, Hilda took Lucy to Westcombe to buy a new winter coat. Lucy chose a forest-green, woollen midi-coat with a satin lining. It was a trifle short, so Lucy carefully lengthened it by half an inch. On Friday night, she wore it over the bridesmaid's gown, which now fitted very well. She dabbed a touch of Californian Poppy fragrance behind her ears, daubed a thick layer of mascara and crimson lipstick, and regarded her striking image in the mirror. Long hemlines were fashionable and appealed to the theatrical side of Lucy's nature. Arriving at the club, she swept confidently through the doors.

Clive was reclining at the usual table.

'I'm going to talk to you about nuclear physics,' he began, proceeding to bombard Lucy with facts, figures, and rocket science. He didn't mention Lucy's clothes and appeared not to notice. Between puffs of his pipe, he described the nature of the atomic bomb and its awesome potential.

'Following a nuclear blast winds are so strong they would send a blade of grass right through a person.'

'Our physics teacher said a molecule is so small it could drop through the wooden workbench,' Lucy added, feeling knowledgeable.

'If the earth were to spin backwards on its axis fast enough, we'd travel back in time, and if the earth continued spinning in the same direction millions of times faster we'd be transported into the future,' Clive explained.

'Really?' Lucy tried hard to listen above the jukebox bass and the ambient chatter.

'I know what,' declared Clive, standing up. 'Let's go outside and I'll show you the sky at night.'

Outside, the air was sharp with frost and a biting, northerly wind. Shivering, Lucy pulled her hat over her ears.

'Are you cold?' asked Clive. 'Here, let me put my arm around you.' Lucy didn't object. As far as she was concerned, Clive was just a friend.

'That's Orion,' said Clive, pointing in one direction. 'And that one over there – the W-shape is Cassiopeia.'

Lucy gazed up at the myriad of tiny white dots in the black blanket of the winter's night. The infinite expanse, the awesome beauty were lost on her. Earthly concerns were closer. Bitter cold penetrated her coat, her teeth chattered, inwardly she battled a raft of insecurities. Suddenly, Clive locked Lucy in a tight embrace, the light from the doorway casting amber glow on his immature features.

'Look at me,' Clive said. His mouth closed over hers. Lucy tasted stale, acrid tobacco and felt a wet, slippery tongue, touching, tasting, exploring inside her mouth. So this was what kissing was supposed to be like? Was this, bizarre, revolting activity supposed to provide enjoyment and be an expression of romantic love? Repulsed and mortified, Lucy wondered why she felt so cold towards a boy who clearly found her attractive. Perhaps there was something wrong with her after all?

Recently, Hilda had taken Lucy aside and given a brief description of sexual intercourse, which she called married love, leaving Lucy shocked and confused. In addition, Hilda had bought Lucy a boned corset with suspenders attached. Now you're a woman, you must wear this, to keep your tummy muscles under control, Hilda insisted. The corset was torture.

Clive pulled away slowly, with a pleased, satisfied expression on his face. Lucy said nothing. Clive relit his pipe and took a determined puff.

'How about if I come up and see you on Sunday? About two o'clock?'

'If you like. Could we play table tennis now?' Lucy was eager to make a diversion. Together with Wendy and Maurice, they made a foursome. Lucy found the long dress awkward to move in, and the boned corset dug painfully into her ribs. She was glad when it was time to stop.

Sunday was a bright, cold day. Early winter sunshine streamed boldly into the little bungalow, highlighting dust and smears on walls and windows. Hilda bustled busily with her cleaning-cloths, eager to make the house presentable for a new guest. Clive arrived punctually at two o'clock. Lucy welcomed him into the living room, where the fire was lit, and Albert sat with his stockinged feet around the snoozing dog. Hilda made tea, and Clive procured his pipe, which he lit with panache, asking Albert, gentleman-to-gentleman, whether he too smoked a pipe.

'Oh, no, not me, I'm a cigarette man,' Albert shook his head, needing no excuse to pull out a pack of filter-tips and light up.

Conversation was pleasant and formal. The favoured topics were astronomy, television documentaries, and the weather. After tea Albert and Hilda withdrew, and Lucy and Clive sat side by side on the sofa. Lucy stared at the flickering logs and said nothing. She felt Clive's arm extend around her back, and his fingers explore.

'You're nice and firm in the breast,' Clive remarked.

'No, Clive,' Lucy said, wincing with embarrassment. 'You'd better stop. You're getting too – personal.'

Clive shrank back, then picked up his pipe.

'You know so much about science and the stars, so why did you leave school so early?' Lucy asked.

'Like I said, I didn't like it. Didn't suit me. Couldn't wait to get out and get a job.'

'What was Beechwood like?'

'Boring.'

'Did you have friends?'

'Yeah – a few.'

'Were you ever – bullied?'

'Never really noticed.'

Clive filled his pipe and snapped on his pocket lighter. Lucy focused on the little orange flame and the coils of blue-grey smoke. She was glad when her father came in and switched on the television.

'He's so quaint, so... comical!' Hilda exclaimed later.

'I suppose so,' Lucy said, grateful her mother approved of the friendship. Feeling free to express herself, Lucy daubed her canvas shoes with the words, *I love Clive.*

It didn't take long for Hilda to notice.

'You're not in love with that boy, I can tell,' Hilda said firmly. Lucy didn't listen. She liked Clive, and perhaps, in time, she would grow to love him too. She scrawled *I love Clive* on her bag and pencil-case and awaited inevitable reaction. *So you have a boyfriend, now? Who's Clive? Do we know him? Tell us about him!* Lucy would keep everyone guessing.

By late November, Lucy's sinister schedule was on hold. Egged on by Georgina, she began writing yet another December Diary. She went Christmas shopping and wrote cards. Unexpectedly, after a silence of almost two years, a Christmas card came from Susan Quinn, a primary school friend, who apologised for having mislaid Lucy's address. Christmas post arrived from Melanie and from Margaret, the latter requesting a short visit after Christmas, to which Hilda agreed. Life was definitely looking rosier. The notion of putting an end to herself now seemed utterly absurd.

Awaking to the cold, grey light of December 8th, Lucy felt no different. It was just another ordinary day – a day on which the sun was yet to rise – a day Lucy had neither created nor was able to destroy. At a quarter to nine, she was sitting quietly on her bed, dressed and ready for school, her bag on her lap. The empty silence was both comforting and disturbing. The time for her so-called appointment with Eternity had come, the long-awaited moment she had planned to end her life. In recent weeks that plan seemed to have fallen apart. In fact, Lucy had barely given it a thought. She no longer wished to die.

The door opened quietly.

'Lucy, are you ready?' Her father stood in the doorway. Casting her closely-guarded secret upon the ocean of infinity, Lucy stood up and followed her father to the car.

The school day passed smoothly. Nobody remembered the date in Lucy's desecrated notes, discovered in Mr Jones's lesson, weeks earlier. At break, blowsy Bridget Barker of 4C approached Lucy, with a toothy grin and said, 'I hear they've been threatening to beat you up after school?'

'Who have?' Lucy asked.

'Oh, you know, that lot in your form – Rosemary, Joanna, Fiona – to name but a few. They're all too stuck up for their own good. You need to stick up for yourself.'

'Okay.'

Clenching her fist defiantly, Bridget caught Lucy's eye and said, 'Don't be their punchbag. Don't let 'em get away with it.'

This unforeseen gesture from a seasoned tough-cookie was encouraging. After school, Lucy walked boldly up the path, looking neither to the right nor the left. Nothing happened. A milestone had been passed.

Arriving home, Lucy found Georgina had sent a Christmas card by post.

'Mrs Mayfield wasn't at work today. What does Georgina say?' Hilda asked.

'They're down with 'flu, so no visits,' Lucy said.

'Well, they can keep their germs to themselves,' Hilda said.

'Georgina says a man came to fix the phone and trod dog mess on the hall carpet, and Mrs Mayfield had to get out of bed with a high temperature, and clean it up.'

'She keeps that house far too warm,' muttered Hilda. 'She invited me over there one lunch time and it was like walking into an oven. These centrally-heated houses are a health hazard. Besides, those wall-to-wall carpets must have cost a fortune. In a place that smart, they can't keep pets. I'm told they used to have a budgerigar but got rid of it because it messed on the curtains.'

Lucy stifled a laugh.

'Georgina is a funny looking girl, isn't she?' Hilda went on. 'Like an African albino. There must be a touch of the tar-brush somewhere.'

Lucy winced. Some of the nicest people she had known in London were black. Suddenly, the lights went out, leaving a flickering, orange glow from the open fire.

'Bother!' exclaimed Hilda, 'Another power cut! They're at it again – people who go on strike should be made to get up off their backsides and get on with life! Albert – where did you leave the matches and candle?'

Lucy went to her room and wrote her diary by torchlight:

Another power cut tonight. The electricity workers are still on strike. Mum blames the greedy people, but perhaps wages should be higher? I'm thankful we've a log fire and candles, and that at the end of this day I am still alive...

'Cup of tea, Lucy!' Hilda called, opening the door. 'Your father managed to get the Primus stove working.'

'Thanks, Mum,' Lucy answered, pushing the diary under the bed.

On the last day of term, a Christmas party was held in the old Beechwood hall. Lucy arrived early, having arranged to be collected at ten. At eight o'clock, Robber unlocked the doors, and the teens swarmed in, heading straight for the buffet table.

'Dancing first, food in half an hour!' Robber shouted. Lights dimmed and flashed, amplified music filled the building, masking the sound of a dozen motorbikes. Suddenly the doors swung open and in marched the Combe Ridge Greasers, intent on making trouble. Robber ordered them out, but Hedgehog and his entourage of ten Skinheads were snatching paper plates and hurling them like frisbees at their opponents. Within seconds the hall was in turmoil. Serviettes became paper darts, sandwiches and vol-au-vents missiles. Most of the guests backed away, others joined the fray. Hairy Mike, the Greaser grabbed Hedgehog by the collar, but the burly Skinhead tripped Mike with his boot, sending him hurtling face-first into a quiche Lorraine. Someone yanked the table cloth, pulling plates of sandwiches and sausage rolls to the floor, where they were trampled to pulp by hobnailed boots.

Robber blew his whistle and bellowed, 'EVERYBODY – OUT!!'

Guests stood in dumb disbelief. Mr Banks was emphatic. 'Yes, I mean it! The party's off!'

"You can't call off the Christmas party!' someone shouted. There was a chorus of agreement. Skinheads sneered, and greasers guffawed. A mince pie whizzed past Robber's face, closely missing his glasses.

Robber roared at the top of his voice.

'I MEAN IT! I WANT EVERYONE OUT OF HERE IN THIRTY SECONDS OR I'LL CALL THE POLICE! All of you – every single one of you... out!'

Stunned silence fell. Slowly the crowd moved towards the open doors.

'What are we going to do?' protested Lucy. 'It's only ten past eight and my Dad won't be coming till ten.'

Clive put his arm around Lucy and said, 'Don't worry, there are plenty of things we can do.'

'We'll go on a pub crawl,' boasted Nigel, heading the group across the rugby field and towards the town.

The north wind chased cruelly through the narrow streets. Excited and apprehensive, Lucy tightened her coat. The first pub was small and friendly, with a cheery red carpet, beamed ceiling and roaring, log fire. A large, artificial Christmas tree stood in the corner, and the bar was festooned with garlands of tinsel and sprigs of holly and mistletoe.

'What are you having, Lucy?' Clive asked.

'The usual, I suppose,' Lucy answered nervously.

'What's that?' teased Nigel. 'A triple Scotch?'

'Do they sell Coke here?' Lucy inquired anxiously.

'Of course they do,' grinned Clive, as he and Nigel made for the bar.

It was early evening, and business was slack.

'Try to act grown up,' whispered Clive in Lucy's ear. 'We're under age, remember.'

Lucy trembled. Clive slurped his lager, and Nigel grinned over his pint of Guinness, flecks of foam clinging to the hairs on his upper lip. Lucy sipped her drink slowly. She hadn't any money with her, which could prove embarrassing. Would she be thrown out onto the freezing streets or be arrested for being in a public bar? Clive seemed to read her thoughts.

'Just act naturally,' he said, puffing on his pipe, 'and people won't bother us.'

Lucy wasn't reassured. Clive reminded her of a small boy who played an aristocrat at a primary school play, years before.

'Come on, Lucy! Give us a kiss!' Clive pulled her towards him.

Nigel obligingly held out a sprig of mistletoe. Clive kissed Lucy, on the mouth, in public – in a public house. Lucy was aghast. She wasn't in love with Clive, and even if she was, she would never make such a bold public statement.

Maurice bought the next round of drinks. One of Nigel's friends nudged him in the ribs.

'Don't look now,' he said in a low whisper, 'But I think we're being watched.'

The middle-aged bartender glared at the unlikely crew of youngsters in the corner of his tavern. The teens finished their drinks and left.

'We'll eat now,' said Maurice. In the nearest fish and chip shop, they joined the queue, spending more time in the warm. The boys shared their fish and chips generously with Wendy and Lucy.

'Time for liquid refreshment,' Nigel said, heading the group to the next pub, which was crowded, loud, and smoky. Lucy accepted another Coke, while the boys drank more beer and became more talkative, telling jokes Lucy didn't understand. She laughed along with the others. At ten o'clock, Clive walked Lucy to the school entrance. Mercifully, Albert was already there. Lucy was glad to be spared another of Clive's revolting kisses.

'Well, then?' Albert asked. 'How was the party?'

Lucy described the initial fiasco, but her version of the story included a much later end to the party and a much shorter walk around the town.

Christmas came and went. The weather was bright and frosty, the mood at Edencroft cheerful and relaxed. Albert and Hilda enjoyed their evening out, and Lucy binged on Radio One at full volume in their absence. Marion and Paul came for four days, which was probably as long as either they or Albert and Hilda could tolerate. Albert enjoyed listening to Classical music, while Paul preferred a steady background of Radio One. Whenever the noise became too unbearable, Albert disappeared into the garden. Likewise, when Paul was exposed to too much Classical music, he would slink off into the breakfast room with a newspaper and can of lager. Lucy blended quietly into the background, enjoying what was unarguably the best Edencroft Christmas yet.

Marion and Paul were still there when Margaret came to stay, and for one night, the little bungalow was crowded, with two people in each of the three bedrooms. On Saturday evening, the younger generation occupied the lounge, while Hilda and Albert stayed in the kitchen and breakfast room. An X-rated horror film was on the television, about a man who conjured up demons that pursued him through dark woodlands at night. Lucy watched with vague interest.

'Nasty,' remarked Margaret, regarding the unconvincing screen monster with contempt.

Marion looked away, trembling. 'I can't stand that sort of thing,' she muttered.

Lucy said nothing, feeling sheepish for having entertained such self-destructive thoughts.

After Marion and Paul had left, Hilda took Lucy and Margaret on a visit to the underground caves. Margaret didn't say much. Was she scared? Lucy recalled the time Margaret complained of feeling faint in a biology lesson at Wordsworth Grammar when a real skeleton was used to demonstrate human bone-structure. Lucy was transfixed by stalagmites and stalactites, the timelessness of nature. Below the narrow footbridge, a sheer drop to black oblivion. *How easy it would be to slip and fall – and cross the fine line dividing life and death!* Lucy's terror remained unspoken.

'I think we've seen enough. Let's go to the cafeteria,' Hilda said.

Margaret stared at the stalactites, the floodlights reflecting in her spectacle lenses.

'Good idea,' Lucy said. 'I need tea!'

In her dowdy, baggy clothes, Margaret was as shy and reserved as Melanie was assertive and brash. After tea, Margaret and Lucy drew silly pictures of teachers and laughed together.

'Our maths teacher is Mr Wellington, and we call him Old Boot,' Margaret said.

'How old is he?'

'Over fifty – he must be – he has no hair.'

'We have a French teacher called Old Dog, because he's an Alsatian.'

Margaret sniggered like a six-year-old.

'Our English teacher for this year is Miss Menzies,' Lucy went on. 'She's old and wrinkled and very strict. No-one dares give her a nickname.'

'We have a strict English teacher, too. She's really old and is called Miss Winterbottom!'

'Is that a real name?'

'Yes. We call her Frosty.'

'My Latin teacher is called Miss Hipp. She's very young and wears modern clothes, so her nickname is Hippie. Last year we had Dozy for history and now the Pilchard.'

'Why? Does she like fish?'

'No idea. Her name's Mrs Pilkington.'

Margaret sniggered, and her glasses slipped down her nose. Lucy found Margaret's unattractive appearance and poor fashion sense reassuring.

'Did you mind starting a new school?' Lucy asked.

'Not once I'd found my way around and learnt people's names.'

'Did anyone bully you?'

'Sometimes. I was called Speckly-Four-Eyes because of my glasses and my spots.'

'Didn't it bother you?'

'No. I just ignored them and eventually they all shut up.'

Lucy wished she could be as confident and calm.

The evening finished with a game of table tennis. Margaret admired Lucy's drawing of the countries of the world on the ping-pong ball. Unfortunately, Lucy accidentally hit the ball into the fire, where it vanished in a brief yellow flash.

'*The Day the Earth Caught Fire!*' Hilda laughed wryly, referencing a science fiction film from weeks before. Lucy stared at the glowing coals, recalling Clive's theory that one day the earth really would catch fire.

Margaret left in the morning. Albert drove the girls to the station, while Hilda stayed at home to tidy up. As the train pulled away, Lucy stood on the platform, waving frantically, watching Margaret's friendly face slowly disappear.

Later, Hilda was unusually quiet.

'What's the matter, Mum?' Lucy inquired in a small voice. Hilda tugged off her rubber gloves, emptied the washing up bowl, pulled open the drawer and tossed the cutlery into it.

'Ignorant!' Hilda spat like an irate cat. 'Just plain, pig ignorant!' The last teaspoon went in, and Hilda slammed the drawer shut.

'What do you mean, Mum?'

'That dreadful, awful girl!'

'What dreadful girl?' Lucy hadn't seen her mother so angry since she left Guides.

'That so-called friend of yours! Crass ignorance! Her parents couldn't have taught her one iota of common, down-to-earth decent good manners! Pigs on the farm grunt when they're fed, but she – she didn't even bat an eyelid nor breathe a word of thanks for anything, the whole time she was here. She practically used your father and me as doormats, and as for congenial conversation – I could have been talking to a lump of lard!'

Lucy stared through the misted window at the fog-bound garden and said nothing.

17: The Motto

January 1st 1971 was a normal working day, with one distinct difference: decimal coins had just become legal tender.

Lucy stood at the sweet counter, watching her first customer hobble towards the Pick-n-Mix section.

'I'd like a quarter of chocolate limes, please dear,' the elderly lady said.

Lucy scooped the sweets, weighed them, and tipped them into a white paper bag, deftly twisting the top.

'Twelve new pence, please.'

The customer handed Lucy a half-crown coin.

'Half a penny change,' Lucy said, placing a freshly-minted copper coin in the customer's hand.

The old woman stared suspiciously. 'It's too shiny and not heavy enough. It's toy money!'

'It's a decimal coin. They're new. You can ask the manager if you like.'

The lady looked around. Everyone was counting their change more carefully than usual.

'I don't know what the world's coming to,' she muttered, shuffling off.

Trade was brisk all day. Arriving home, Lucy tipped a handful of coins on the kitchen table and said, 'Look at the new currency!'

Hilda looked nonplussed. 'Mark my words, there'll be a massive rise in inflation. The day of the three-shilling loaf will soon be upon us.'

Lucy wasn't worried. She had bought a new diary and resolved to write in it regularly.

Friday, January 1st

Today, decimal currency was introduced. The coins are small and light, like toy money, but it's much easier to do money sums. Working at Woolworth's was an honour and privilege – being part of this historic day.

<u>*Saturday, January 2nd*</u>

Another busy day at work. People are still getting used to the new coinage. I haven't decided yet what to save up for this year. Mum and Dad can't afford another foreign holiday, but I'm sure I'll think of something.

<u>*Sunday, January 3rd*</u>

I hate Sundays in Winter. Through my bedroom windowpane, I see a cold, grey and cheerless scene. Buried in the depths of the country, I am lonely and bored.

In a moment of distraction, Lucy left the open diary on her bed. Hilda saw it and lectured Lucy on the merits of gratitude and self-discipline. Lucy took the advice on board and was careful where she left her diary. In fact, she didn't write anything in it for a while.

The next morning, before the first lesson, Lucy found Alison, Abigail, and Fiona gathered around Joanna, who sat subdued, head in hands. Lucy caught snatches of conversation.

'Why Maureen?'

'It's unfair. A tragedy...'

'So much to live for...'

'Such a shame. She was so nice.'

Lucy vaguely knew Maureen, a regular visitor to Miss Crawford's stables.

'What happened?' Lucy inquired quietly.

'Haven't you heard?' screeched Joanna.

'Heard what?'

'She's dead!'

Lucy froze, speechless.

'Maureen had a seizure, she often had them. An ambulance was called straight away, but this time she didn't make it,' Alison sighed.

Lucy was confused. *Why Maureen and not me? Maybe fate took her instead of me?*

Maureen never said a bad word about anyone. She was probably the nicest person at the stables. Lucy recalled the time Maureen swung a full bucket of water over her head without spilling a drop.

The bell rang. Arthur Long stood at the blackboard, chalking the word

xenophobia.

'Ex-enophobia! Nice one, Arthur,' Rosemary said, 'very clever. It means fear of exercise. It applies to lazy people.'

'No, it means fear of extroverts!' Jodie said. 'That's why Arthur keeps his distance from me.'

Lucy looked in her dictionary, discovering xenophobia meant a fear of strange people and new things.

Miss Menzies arrived, and Arthur scuttled to his seat.

'Xenophobia. That's an interesting word,' Miss Menzies observed. 'I shan't ask who wrote it, but would anyone like to tell us all what it means?'

Nobody responded. Lucy couldn't be bothered sharing her new-found knowledge. On her copy of *SHORT STORIES OF OUR TIME*, she doodled over the second S.

'No volunteers?' Miss Menzies enquired again.

Silence.

'For your information, it means fear of strangers. No doubt whoever wrote the word is either ignorant of its meaning or afraid to speak up. Now we'll proceed with the test. Have a pen ready, and close all books.'

Sheets of paper were handed out.

'You have twenty minutes to write a succinct summary of *Through the Tunnel*, and a paragraph describing how the author engages reading.'

The minute hand on the wall clock jumped.

'You may begin.'

Nothing was heard but the faint scratching of pens on paper. Lucy completed the task with confidence and ease. English remained one of her best subjects, despite Miss Menzies' authoritarian approach.

After the lesson, Joanna noticed the amendment to Lucy's book cover.

'Short Tories of our time? Very funny, some clever wisecracker must have thought of that!'

Lucy shrugged, flattered by Joanna's appreciation of her wit.

Monday, January 11th

It's the Winter of Discontent. Countless endless strikes. The current (pun intended) electricity workers' strike in Britain means unpredictable power cuts. Another outage tonight, another dark evening cheered by candlelight. Mum asked me what I'd learned in school. I mentioned William Pitt's window tax — a stupid idea, as people blocked windows rather than pay the government, uglifying houses and undermining health.

The postal strike is unbearable! Long weeks with no mail, pillar boxes overflowing, rain-drenched letters blown away by the four winds. I'm writing to distant friends, each letter growing to many pages.

<u>Tuesday, January 12th</u>

There's zero respect for school property these days. Books are defaced with obscenities, teachers too busy to notice. Graffitiying the blackboard is the latest craze: Rosemary's unflattering caricature of Mr Conway, Jodie's horse wearing spectacles with the caption "loonettes", and Arthur Long's random words in Russian and Chinese.

Arriving home, I made the grisly discovery of two severed chicken heads in the garden. Mum suspects hooligans, but I fear Miss Crawford's dogs could be the culprits. According to rumours, the stables are going downhill.

<u>Wednesday, January 13th</u>

Mum reported the chicken incident at High Lea police station, convinced it was sabotage. The officer listened patiently to her tirade and said, 'I'm afraid to tell you, Mrs Wylie — that you have been foxed!"

The eerie, nocturnal barking of foxes is evidence of that.

<u>Monday, January 18th</u>

Exams began today. History and Maths. Remembering Mr Kingsley's advice, I did my best, taking things in my stride.

<u>Monday, January 25th</u>

My exam results are mixed. Most of the class failed maths. Mr Conway sets too much homework and doesn't explain things properly. In front of the class, he said I was very good at certain other subjects and could be good at maths if I had more faith in myself. Afterwards, he suggested one-to-one breaktime tuition.

<u>Tuesday, January 26th</u>

Naturally, Mum and Dad approved the maths tuition. I sat through the first tutorial, listening to Mr Conway's long-winded rambling, watching the pencil dance across the page.

Confused as ever, I still can't do the homework.

Monday, February 1st

Today was a good day. In Art, I copied a postcard from Hironville – a breaking wave reflecting sunlight. Rosemary said it was so good it took her breath away.

Finally, we have post! A fat, newsy letter from Margaret, enclosing a thankyou letter for Mum, from Margaret's mum, saying Margaret was "bubbling over with enthusiasm" after her visit.

Better yet, I'm invited back this summer, and Mum says, Yes!

Tuesday, February 2nd

I received A+ for a French essay – a huge morale boost. I really like Mr Ross, not because he gives me high grades, but because he's good looking – tall, dark, and handsome. I can't place his accent and wondered if it was Welsh, but Jodie says it's Scottish.

Friday, February 5th

At lunchtime Dozy Mosey made everyone laugh, saying, "For what we are about to receive, may the Lord protect us."

Jodie and I served the teachers' dinners and were first in the dinner queue. Jodie served Dozy, and I served the Dog (Monsieur Leblanc). The dog is vegetarian, so I gave him cheesy vegetables, which he refused because I'd put gravy on. I got him another dinner and ate the other dinner myself. As I sat down, my tie draped in the gravy, and Jodie and I laughed until our sides ached. Jodie's drifted away from Julie and is practically my friend now. Also, I'm invited to Jodie's birthday tea at half term!

Saturday, February 13th

I've bought a cotton-lined, decorated shopping basket for Mother's Day, which I'll fill with gifts and flowers. I also bought two long-playing records: TOP TEN HITS 1969 and 1970, smuggled them home and played them when Mum and Dad were out. Disappointingly, the songs sound different. Reading the small print, I discovered they're not by the original artists. I secretly listen to Radio One. Infuriatingly, Mum discovered my list of this week's Top Twenty, threw it on the fire and gave me a row.

<u>Wednesday, February 17th</u>

I woke with a bad cold, but still went to Jodie's since she already has the cold and nobody else was coming. Dad gave me a lift. Jodie's home is a ground-floor, Victorian flat in Nyehaven. It's very austere, with polished linoleum, no carpets – totally unlike the Mayfields' opulent bungalow. The visit was refreshingly low-key. We had tea and Marmite toasties in the galley-style kitchen. Jodie liked her present – a book – Quantum Star Quest. Jodie's parents were at work, so was her new boyfriend, Alfie. Jodie said he asked her to marry him, and showed me the dress she was making. Like the flat, it was plain and small, probably too tight around Jodie's ample curves. If I ever marry, I'll make a flouncy dress with lots of frills. We played Beatles and Bob Dylan records, also Joni Mitchell's Woodstock and Les Crane's Desiderata. Amazing!

<u>Monday, February 22nd</u>

Back to school, and alas, more bullying. Wet weather, so indoor games. Miss Forbes wasn't there, and the student teacher failed to keep order in the synergy of scores of teenagers. Outside the hall, the boys waited noisily, Jimmy Murphy yelling the loudest. Shouts were fired like pistol shots. I blocked my ears. A crumpled scrap of paper fluttered to the floor. Someone handed it to me, smirking. The note read, "Dear Juicy Lucy! Will you come out with me for a bit tonight. This is a TRUE love letter From ARTHUR LONG."

Arthur didn't write the note. He's bullied, just like me. I showed Mum the note, and she was aghast and told me to stick up for myself or people would walk all over me. Mum said, "In my day such an outrage would be quashed by a few lashes of the birch!"

Encouraging words, but how do I fix this?

<u>Friday, February 26th</u>

Reports are out, and Mum isn't pleased. Miss Hawksworth described me as "erratic". Predictably, Miss Forbes wrote I was "a *passive member of the form". So much for being quiet, trying to stay out of trouble! Whatever I do, is wrong.*

"The men teachers – Mr Ross and Mr Keane – say you'll do well," Mum said, 'so don't let the catty women get to you. Have more faith in yourself. You're a human being like everyone else.'

Though I sometimes doubt if I'm even human, the words of DESIDERATA ring true, especially the bit about having A RIGHT TO BE HERE. Also, Mum actually IS on my side. The old Grammar School motto PER ASPERA AD ASTRA finally makes sense. Loosely translated "a rough road to the star of glory", Mr Kingsley explained it years ago. The motto was retained when the two schools merged, but the noble words emblazoned beneath the school crest in the hall and on every student's blazer were practically ignored.

I resolve to persevere, however hard the road ahead may be.

Unbeknown to Lucy, Hilda had made a private appointment with Mr Kingsley to discuss Lucy's insecurities and future prospects. Hilda was quickly reassured that Lucy would overcome her present difficulties, as student develops at different rates and in different ways. She told Lucy about the conversation.

'I'm so glad you're in a good school, with strong leadership,' Hilda said.

18: SHAKY RELATIONSHIPS

Sunday, February 28th

Went rabbiting with Clive and Nigel. A fascinating experience.

Lucy sank back on the bed and closed her eyes, too tired to write any more.

In fact, it was a long while before she bothered writing anything in the diary again.

That Sunday had begun wet, low cloud settled over the hills – the kind of drizzle that soaks everything. But that did nothing to dampen Lucy's spirits.

"Bye Mum, see you later,' she said airily, setting off, fresh-faced and smiling.

'Stay safe – and don't be late for tea!'

'Don't worry, Mum. I'll be fine.'

The lads were waiting on the lane, Nigel in a boiler suit and Clive wheeling a motorcycle and wearing blue jeans and bomber jacket. Hilda watched them disappear over the brow of the hill and sighed heavily.

Up on the chalk ridges of High Lea Down, rabbits abounded deep in their burrows.

'We're doing our bit for British farmers,' Nigel said, fondly lifting two ferrets from the sack. 'We're protecting our crops and getting a tasty bunny or two for the stew pot!'

Clive took out his pipe and puffed importantly, sending rings of smoke floating into the damp air. Lucy disliked the idea of animals killing animals. I'm still a townie, she thought. Bunnies were innocent, cute creatures, the idea of killing them abhorrent. Nigel released the ferrets into strategic holes and spread nets across others. Seconds later, a rabbit blundered into a net. Nigel quickly lifted it and clubbed it smartly on the back of its neck, killing it instantly. He held it aloft by the back legs and boasted, 'That'd fetch a quid or two at work!'

'Check it for myxomatosis,' Clive added seriously.

'That was a female, so one less breeding machine,' Nigel smirked. Saddened by the animal's abrupt and violent end, Lucy hoped it hadn't been pregnant. Within ten minutes, three more rabbits were netted and killed, the ferrets still underground. Lucy preferred not to think what might be happening inside the warren. She walked around, keeping Dotty on a tight leash.

'That's another three!' Nigel exclaimed. 'We'll head back now and prepare them for the pot.'

The trio split up, Nigel the pillion passenger on Clive's new secondhand motorbike.

'See you later!' the boys chorused.

'Where are you going to end up?' Lucy asked.

'In a bush!' laughed Nigel, grinning wickedly. 'Well, no, not really. We'll meet up at my place. Come and join us.'

'Okay, see you later,' Lucy said. Clive pulled the throttle, engulfing bike and riders in a pall of grey smoke. The purr of the motorcycle engine faded into the mist. Lucy choked back the fumes, her eyes smarting. She stood still, gazing at the cloud-shrouded hills, strands of dark hair clinging to her face. The weather was closing in fast, thick clouds enveloping the hillside. On the rain-soaked ground, Lucy tried hard not to slip. Arriving home, she hurried indoors. Hilda was in the porch, holding the dog towel. 'Thank goodness you're home,' she said.

Lucy stood in the doorway, her anorak hood up, water dripping on the floor. 'I'm just going down to Nigel's to help with the rabbits,' she panted.

'What rabbits?'

'The rabbits they caught with the ferrets on the walk.'

'Very well. Tea at six, don't forget.'

'I won't,' Lucy said.

Lured by thoughts of sheltering in the warm – perhaps with tea and Mrs Daly's home baking – Lucy hurried through torrential rain to the Dalys' whitewashed cottage, where Clive's motorcycle was parked on the drive. No lights shone from the cottage parlour, and the car was gone, but voices sounded in the creosoted outbuilding, and a faint light burned in the window. Lucy pushed the door open.

'Come in! We're at the skinning and gutting stage. Are you okay with that?' Nigel asked.

'Yeah, fine.' Lucy nodded, noting the dank odour of fresh kill mingled with oil, tar, and ferrets. It didn't disgust her. In the indifferent glow of the hurricane lamp, the lads were dissecting a second rabbit, observing body parts with interest and amusement. Lucy stood redundantly in the background. What a medieval way of life, she thought, wondering what the fashion-conscious crowd at school would make of such barbarity.

In the wake of the rabbiting trip, Clive made a last-ditch effort to win Lucy's affections.

'By the end of the summer,' he said, puffing pipe smoke into the thick air of the youth club lounge, 'I'll be a qualified butcher, earning more, and looking for that lucky lady to marry me and share the flat above the shop.'

Lucy huffed into the din of the disco. Clive never talked about science or astronomy any more. Lucy ensured there were no opportunities when Clive might try to kiss her.

'Are you free this weekend?' Clive asked.

'You know I work Saturdays, and Sunday is spoken for.'

'By whom?'

'Um – a friend is coming, and I'll have homework.'

'Oh.'

So ended the conversation. Lucy felt guilty, having lied about a friend coming, but the lie gave her an idea. She would phone Jodie and invite her instead.

Fortunately, Jodie accepted, and Sunday was sunny. Lucy suggested a dog walk, but Jodie was a slow walker, puffing and panting, all the way to the top of High Lea Down.

'If we had a telescope, we could probably see your house,' Lucy said, pausing to admire the sprawling panorama.

'If anyone had a telescope, he'd be in for a real treat!' Jodie laughed. Lucy turned, startled by the spectacle of Jodie stripped to the waist, flaunting her ample cleavage over a low-cut bra.

'Are you hot?' Lucy asked innocently.

'Daft question! Of course I'm hot – extremely hot, and soon I'll have the hots for a nice young farmer if there's one about.'

Lucy glanced around, embarrassed, fearing the close proximity of Nigel and friends, or worse yet, the quiet, decent Mr Wilson.

'We'll go back now, all this fresh air's making me hungry,' Lucy said.

'Fresh, and hungry – that's me,' Jodie chortled, as they set off down the hill.

Tea was served punctually at six, in the breakfast-room. Hilda had prepared cucumber sandwiches cut into triangles and home-made Victoria sponge cake oozing with jam and buttercream. The table was laid with the white lace cloth and the best cutlery. Jodie replied politely to Hilda's questions; her mother was a health visitor, her stepfather an accountant, and her biological father lived in America.

'What does he do for a living?' Hilda enquired.

'Search me? Sowing his wild oats on the plains of Texas, no doubt.'

'I see,' Hilda answered with a visible grimace.

Jodie appeared nervous. She spilt tea into the saucer and on the white tablecloth. The bone china cup rattled precariously, and Hilda sprang up and rescued it from certain death upon the tiled floor.

'Never mind, dear,' Hilda said reassuringly. 'I'll pour you another cup.'

'Sorry – I'll get a cloth,' Jodie replied, rising from the table and banging her head on the base of the budgerigar cage hanging from the ceiling.

'BALLS!' Jodie exclaimed.

Balls? Lucy found the response amusing. Jodie said that word often, and Lucy assumed it was just one of her silly expressions. There were polite remarks about the weather, and uncomfortable silences. When Jodie's stepfather came to collect her, Jodie handed Lucy a slim package in a W H Smith bag.

'Here – an early birthday present for you. Have fun!'

'Thanks,' Lucy said, 'I'll wait till my birthday.'

'She's quite a character,' Hilda said, later. 'She's well-spoken, but sadly lacks common decency and refinement.'

'What do you mean?' Lucy asked bewildered.

'Her language!' retorted Hilda. 'Fancy being invited to someone's house and shouting out the word for a man's sexual organs!'

Lucy was shocked by her mother's graphic response and her own ignorance of common slang.

'I bet that girl has the morals of an alley-cat,' Hilda muttered disgustedly.

Lucy left the room. Jodie gave no explicit details about her liaisons with boys, and Lucy saw no reason to pry. She opened the package – a paperback edition of DH Lawrence's *Women in Love*. The title gave Lucy the impression it could be about lesbians, but reading its graphic portrayal of heterosexual love, Lucy appreciated how it might appeal to Jodie.

Walking home from school the next day, Lucy noticed a wild rabbit cowering in the grass, its movements slow and spasmodic. Matted fur and moist eyes encrusted with white scales were telltale signs of myxomatosis. Without hesitation, Lucy found a heavy stone and clubbed the rabbit sharply on the back of its neck. Putting the rabbit out of its misery gave her no pleasure. The next day, she cycled to school, avoiding the likelihood of finding another ailing rabbit. However, in the lane by the stables, Miss Crawford's dogs dashed out, barking and snapping at Lucy's ankles. She waved a thick twig, fending them off, then above the snarling, Lucy heard enraged shouts and glimpsed the gaunt form of Miss Crawford.

Lucy sped from the scene as fast as she could.

Sunday, March 24th

Mother's Day. Mum was delighted with the shopping basket filled with a potted, purple primula, toiletries, sweets, tea towels, rubber gloves, and a box of the biological washing powder.

Friday, April 16th

My fifteenth birthday. Mum and Dad gave me notelets, luxury soap, chocolates, and a pair of black velvet Hot Pants – the latest fashion bib-and-brace shorts. I wore them to Youth Club, a pair of nylon tights underneath. Boned corsets are a thing of the past, thank goodness.

Monday, May 10th

We're entered for English Language, French, History and Geography O-levels. Thankfully, Maths is postponed until form five, because we've missed so much work.

Miss Hipp dismissed us just before the 3:30pm bell. I think she was glad to get rid of us!

Tuesday, May 11th

More disastrous news. I arrived to find people whispering, apparently upset. Again, Joanna screamed at me when I asked what had happened, saying I was ignorant and selfish. Then Susan Schofield remarked casually, a girl in form two was run over after school yesterday. In assembly, Mr Edgington gave a lengthy lecture on road safety. The victim had run into the road without looking, was hit by a bus, her life marred by one unguarded moment. Such things shouldn't happen to someone so young and with so much to live for.

Friday, May 14th

Finally, Clive realises I don't want to be his girlfriend. He backed off graciously, like a gentleman. However, mingling with others attracted the attention of someone else – a quiet, unassuming boy twice the size of Clive. He bought me a Coke, introduced himself as Steve. I'm glad I wore my light blue jeans and white cricket jumper (and not the Hot Pants). Steve sat close to me, smelling of onions and stale sweat. He said he was a trainee butcher in Nyehaven. Did Clive engineer this? I thought angrily. Then Steve said he'd like to visit me on Sunday afternoon, and I was too polite to refuse. I don't want another boyfriend. I just want friends.

Sunday, May 16th

Steve arrived in his Morris Minor saloon. Mum served boiled eggs, bread-and-jam, and home baking. We talked about the weather, Steve's job, and the car, which he'd borrowed from his dad. After tea, Steve showed me the car. It looked old and rusty, and I'm glad he didn't offer me a ride. We went for a walk instead, to Biddlecombe Copse, where summer foliage and birdsong filled me with happiness. But Steve had other things on his mind. Without warning, he held me close and kissed me on the mouth, like Clive did, but there was something hungry and carnal about the kiss. I shrank back and said nothing. Steve didn't persist, and we went back to the house.

Two days later Lucy received a bouquet of red and white roses, delivered to the door by Interflora. Inside the bouquet was a simple, handwritten message:

To Lucy my love, from your boyfriend Steve XXX

Hilda's expression was stern and serious. 'He's very taken with you, Lucy dear,' she said suspiciously.

'Yes, I suppose so,' Lucy said lamely.

'How do you feel about him?'

'I'm not sure. I don't really know him.'

'But he must know you, if he sends you roses and a message like that!'

There was an anxious edge in Hilda's voice. 'You must never let him kiss you, for if you do, he will get the wrong idea and want to go further. I've told you before, you must not get too involved with boys. It may lead to something you'll later regret.'

Lucy couldn't imagine herself being an unmarried mother. Since Christmas, two pregnant girls had dropped out of school, one of them just thirteen.

'Clive kissed me once or twice,' Lucy admitted, 'but it didn't mean anything.'

'That's not the point!' snapped Hilda. 'Steve is different. He's more – how can I put it – rough and ready. I don't like the thought of you being alone with him.'

Lucy realised Steve might prove difficult to get rid of.

'Anyway,' Lucy said, leaving the room. 'I've got homework.'

Hilda was shocked. This business was far from over.

Over supper, she asked, 'There's something you're not telling me about you and Steve, isn't there?'

'What makes you think that?' Lucy answered evasively. 'I've told you all there is to tell.'

'I don't believe you! I smell a rat and I'm determined to get to the bottom of it.'

'I don't tell lies, Mum.'

'You are lying, if you refuse to tell me everything. Remember, I am your mother.'

'As if I could forget that,' Lucy muttered under her breath.

Hilda heard. Weeks of pent-up anger, tension and frustration welling up, she grabbed the shopping-basket and flung it at Lucy's feet.

'I'm not speaking another word to you! You can have that basket back – I don't want your gifts any more. They mean nothing to me.'

Hilda marched out, slamming the door. Lucy stared at the basket, wondering what to do with it. Finally, she picked it up and hung it in the lobby, behind the winter coats. Perhaps her mother would simmer down in a few moments and ask for it back?

But the wall of silence between mother and daughter continued for three days.

Friday, May 21st

Mum is speaking to me again. She let me go to Youth Club as long as I keep Steve at arm's length, which I am happy about. I mingled with everyone, played hockey and table tennis, enjoying the jukebox music.

Saturday, May 22nd

I've bought two singles. Don MacLean's American Pie, and George Harrison's My Sweet Lord. They're great songs, in the hit parade, but I don't know much about them. I played them when I got home, and Mum said the lyrics were political, or about drugs, and told me not to waste my money on things I knew nothing about. Mum says Hippies are sad, insecure drop-outs. "When I was young, everyone had to fight in the War," Mum said. "So we grew up very quickly."

Sunday, May 23rd

Steve showed up again like a bad penny. I never invited him and told Mum so straight away. We offered him tea and biscuits from politeness, that's all. Steve was his usual taciturn self. I just sat in the chair and said little. He got bored after half an hour and left.

'He's a right glue-pot,' Mum said afterwards, 'just like a boy I knew years ago. He used to follow me round like a little dog.'

And then, from the corner of my eye, I noticed the shopping basket back in its usual place on the hook behind the pantry door.

19: PAST AND FUTURE

Marion and Paul came for Whitsun weekend. Lucy arrived home from Woolworth's on Saturday to find the couple sprawled on the sofa, Marion asleep and Paul gawping the television. Lucy went to her room.

Sunday lunch reminded her of old times at the family at home in London – roast dinner and serious talk.

'So, you're saving up for a down-payment on a house?' Albert asked.

'That's right, we've both been working overtime. It's very tiring,' Paul said.

Hilda nodded. 'Hard work brings rewards.'

'Yeah, we got married to have a good time, didn't we?' Paul nudged Marion. 'When we get home I'll play my favourite Monkees and Rolling Stones records and liven things up.'

Marion nodded, smiling. Lucy recalled Susan Quinn had been an ardent Monkees fan and still was, according to her last letter.

'T Rex are overrated,' Paul went on. '"Hot Love" only got to number one because all the kids bought it.'

Lucy cringed. Marion's fork slipped, and she pulled a face. 'Mum, you know I can't stand sprouts.'

'But you cooked a lovely meal for us, with sprouts, at the flat,' Hilda said, looking tense.

'We don't have a roast dinner every day, Mum.'

'Of course not, dear. Meat's expensive, especially after all this decimalisation, and you're saving up for your house.'

Cutlery clattered, and the dog snored. Nobody broached the subject of Marion and Paul starting a family. After dessert, Marion and Paul went for a walk while Lucy helped her parents clear up.

'They look relaxed,' Albert said. 'I think married life suits them well.'

Hilda raised an eyebrow and said nothing. Lucy stared out of the window at the patio wall, where Marmie the cat sat sprawled in the sunshine.

Marion and Paul came back and sat on the sofa. Paul dozed off, gaping like a beached porpoise, today's copy of *The Daily Mirror* falling apart at his feet. Albert turned up the volume of Beethoven's fifth symphony, and Marion went into the bathroom for a shower.

'Paul's a simple soul, but he's a good sort,' Hilda remarked, patronisingly. 'At least he rolls his sleeves up and does an honest day's work. He has a steady job as a plumber, and Marion's found a nice job as a shorthand typist at British European Airways. With a secure income they'll soon enjoy the comforts of a small house.'

Lucy made a pot of tea, then sat at the table to read *The Westcombe Herald*.

'Why don't they make newspapers smaller, like magazines?' she grumbled. 'Holding open these big newspapers makes my arms ache.'

Hilda was absorbed in last week's giant crossword and didn't answer.

Then a short article caught Lucy's attention:

Quiet man found dead

Police were called to a Nyehaven flat last week, following the discovery of a body at 33, Quay Street. Landlord Mr Philip Jefferson reports using his key to enter the flat, intending to speak to its occupant regarding rent arrears since last November and two ignored written reminders. Mr Jefferson found the body of his tenant Mr Paul Newton on the bed, a suicide note beside him, dated December 8th, last year. Evidence suggests that unemployed Mr Newton, 37, had been dead for several weeks. Neighbours described Mr Newton as a quiet man with no known friends or relatives. His death is not thought to be suspicious, its cause yet to be confirmed, pending Coroner's report.

Lucy felt strangely responsible for the fate of a complete stranger who had apparently died in her place. She read the short report over and over again, wondering what had gone so dreadfully wrong for Paul Newton.

Monday, May 31st

Marion and Paul left this morning.

Seeking a change of scene, I went to Westcombe Park, found a quiet corner, let Dotty off the lead and sat down to read. In JACKIE magazine was a picture of David Bowie with his wife and baby son. Soon, Marion will have a child, and so, one day, might I? Beside the park, half-hidden by trees are beautiful bungalows. I'd like to live there when I'm older, if I don't buy Edencroft from Mum and Dad, depending if they move somewhere smaller.

Leaving the park, I was greeted by Rosemary Richardson. We had a good chat. On her own, she's quite friendly and polite.

Tuesday, June 1st

The park was practically deserted. Doubtless, everyone's at the beach in the good weather, but I prefer to sunbathe and read undisturbed. I'm reading a science fiction library book about the sun's radiation, causing mass suicides, leaving not one sane, normal person on earth. I would probably survive such a disaster, but I wouldn't wish such a fate on anyone — nor be part of a world of disorganised, immoral and corrupt weirdos.

Noticing Dotty was missing, I called her, disturbing a flock of pigeons that flapped and scattered twigs and debris on the seat below. Then I noticed a young man, sunbathing bare-chested on the grass. Dotty appeared, scampering with a golden Labrador. Someone called the Labrador, and it ran off. Disappointingly, the sunbather wasn't the owner, as I wanted an excuse to talk to him.

Wednesday, June 2nd

The sunbather was there again. Under cover of trees, I watched him until he got up and walked away. I crept past the rhododendrons, following him to the park's edge. Dotty barked, and the man turned round and probably saw me. Realising, with horror, I was stalking him, I hurriedly leashed Dotty and went home.

<u>Thursday, June 3rd</u>

Rain all day. Mum let me cut up my childhood red velvet dress to make other things. I sewed a pouch for my playing cards, patched the threadbare knees of my red corduroy trousers and stitched a heart shape on the front of my shorts. Mum told me to remove it because it looked vulgar and would give men the wrong idea, so I unpicked it.

It's time to revise for the O-levels. I feel calm about English Language and French but less sure about history, geography and science.

<u>Friday, June 4th</u>

Marmie, the cat, is missing. A nine-year-old rescue kitten and a keen hunter of mice, rats, and rabbits, we assumed our beloved pet would soon appear. Lately, however, he seems less lively, and his fur looks matted. I searched his favourite spots in the garden and finally found him lying stiff and awkward in the corner of the shed. At first, I thought he was dead, but when I touched him, his back felt warm. I carried him to the kitchen, where Mum coaxed him to take a few drops of milk from a teaspoon. I suggested taking him to the vet. Mum said we'd see how he was in the morning.

I forgot all about Youth Club and probably won't bother going back anyway.

<u>Saturday, June 5th</u>

Marmie seems better, but still not eating. Work was busy, the store packed with tourists. Arriving home, I noticed cans of baby food in the pantry. I wondered if Marion was pregnant, but Mum shook her head and said the cans were for the cat.

Mum mentioned a letter from Arthur and Joan. They're decorating and unable to invite us, but they're visiting Edencroft in August. Also, Anne is divorced and has a new job.

Sunday, June 6th

Marmie is no better. This morning I carried him in his basket and tipped it gently on the lawn, so he could climb out, but he flopped out with plaintive mewing and limped to his favourite spot under the hedge. Last year there was an epidemic of cat flu at the farm. I still recall the haunting sight of a dead kitten, lying in a disused dog kennel, its mouth and eyes wide open in defiance and despair. Mum says Marmie doesn't have cat flu, which she'd observed among farm cats in her wartime Land Army days. Mum told of the sad day she found her favourite kitten, Daisy Belle, dead in the ashes on the hearth, where she'd tried to keep warm. Whatever's wrong with Marmie, he'll definitely need to go to the vet.

Monday, June 7th

This morning, a pair of swallows swooped down and tried to attack Marmie. I chased them off and told Dad what happened, begging him to take Marmie to the vet, even if it meant having him put to sleep.

At school, the first exam was science, which I've probably failed. Arriving home, I found a cardboard box on the chair. Trembling, I opened it, dreading what was inside. Marmie lay curled in an attitude of fireside contentment, like the time I drew a picture of him and won the junior art prize at Wordsworth Grammar. For an instant, I was hopeful, but touching his back, I found it cold and unresponsive. Part of me wanted to cry out and plead for another chance, but it's too late. Earlier, I spoke in haste, now I bitterly regret not having wished my old friend goodbye. Dad said Marmie didn't suffer, but I still can't believe I'll never see him again. When Mum came home, we buried him in the centre of the lawn, and Dad planted a white rose bush, marking Marmie's grave. Strangely, I feel sadder at the passing of a pet than any human.

Tuesday, June 8th

Today was the French-speaking test. Being at the end of the register, I wasn't needed at school until the evening. Uniform wasn't obligatory. Wearing my white dress with the red brocade, and white leather clogs, I strolled into the exam room feeling confident and secure.

Mr Ross was the examiner. He also made a tape recording of the test to be submitted to an independent examiner for final grading. I was asked a selection of simple questions and did a five-minute talk on a chosen topic: Le village D'Hironville. Having practised it many times, I remembered every word and relived the fun of last year's holiday. I left the exam room feeling on top of the world.

Wednesday, June 9th

Mum and Dad were mad at me today for reading a library book instead of revising when I got back from the beach. I was reading AJ Cronin's Hatter's Castle, lost in its tragic plot when I didn't hear Dad asking me about the exams. Mum told me not to be rude and warned me not to fail English like I did at Wordsworth Grammar – YEARS AGO! No mention of the good marks I've had since! Mum lectured me about not throwing away my education and ruining my chances for the future. Dad agreed. As usual, Dad was smoking like a chimney, and I could hardly breathe. I felt stupid in the pink bikini top, pale skin, untouched by the sun, showing at the edges. I felt like an empty-headed dolly-bird, all body and no brain. Perhaps I'm not cut out for the academic life after all?

Thursday, June 10th

Mum says she's reached the end of her tether at Mayfield Electrics, due to the heavy workload and constantly flickering fluorescent lights that give her migraines. Dad's advertising for freelance electrical work to fill the dent in the bank balance after buying the Vauxhall Viva. There's still talk about the delayed inheritance from Uncle Charles, and Mum called the solicitor dealing with the case "a rogue and a charlatan".

Friday, June 11th

The English Language O-level is over! It wasn't difficult, but I think I went a bit mad writing a dramatic, tragic ending to the picture essay of some people on a train.

After school, I took Dotty to the beach and met Alison and Cedric. The beach was crowded with picnicking holidaymakers, but we found a small space to squeeze in to eat our packed lunches. A stray, black dog kept sniffing at Dotty for no good reason since Dotty isn't on heat. As we were leaving and I put Dotty's lead on, the black dog suddenly snarled and bit my hand. We left quickly. I washed the shallow graze in the sea's saltwater and hoped for the best.

Alison invited me on a sponsored walk, Sunday after next, to raise funds for the lifeboats. I jumped at the opportunity.

Tuesday, June 22nd

Exams are over a last! It's a wonderful feeling to be free of the shackles of revision, even with normal time table having resumed. Mrs Pilkington was absent this afternoon, and in the din of the unsupervised lesson, I read the WHOLE of AJ Cronin's THE SPANISH GARDENER — a compelling, tragic story. At home, I started reading Cronin's ADVENTURES IN TWO WORLDS. My reading was interrupted by a phone call from Nigel Daly, asking me out for a drive in his Dad's car, to celebrate passing his Driving Test. I congratulated him but declined the invitation.

Wednesday, June 23rd

A good job I didn't go out with Nigel in the car! Mum said, 'That stupid Daly boy took his father's car to Combe Ridge last night and drove it into a tree. As with my accident on the ice last year, the car went off the road and was written off, its driver escaping with minor injuries.'

I mentioned the phone call, and Mum clicked her tongue and praised me for my prudence.

'If you'd gone with him, Lucy, you might not be here to tell the tale,' she added in a serious tone.

Sunday, July 4th

Today was the Sponsored Walk. The circular route was along twenty miles of country lanes, and easier than expected. Dozens of people were there, mostly adults and teenagers, but no children. I kept up with Alison all the way, finishing back at Westcombe. Then I walked another three miles to get home. Today was fun, but I'm exhausted. School tomorrow!

Monday, July 5th

This morning I awoke stiff and aching, so Dad gave me a lift. Hobbling into class, I discovered Alison and a few others who'd taken part were suffering the effects of yesterday. First lesson was games. Miss Forbes wasn't there, and the student teacher allowed us to sit and watch the others play tennis, pretending we were at Wimbledon. A shame there were no strawberries and cream!

At break, Jodie showed her pack of tampons and recommended them to us all, saying they were a wonderful invention. Mum calls them "tampoons" and says they're only for married women who've already had a baby.

Saturday, July 10th

Work was busy. After a morning on my feet, my back and legs were aching, so I was glad when it was lunch hour. On Jodie's advice, I tried using a tampon, taking a while working out exactly how and where to put it, and it was fine, so I went swimming. Mum doesn't need to know.

Arriving home, I found Mum has bought twenty point-of-lay pullets and put them in my old art hut. I complained at first, then realised it didn't matter, as I spend more time in town these days and can't remember when I was last even in the hut.

Monday, July 12th

Miss Hawksworth took us on a field trip today, along the coast. At the picnic area above Combe Ridge, we all spilt out of the mini-bus, armed with clipboards and pencils. Instructions were to sketch the rocks, listing their different properties. Nobody listened. Pupils swarmed to the picnic tables, disturbing tourists, and flocking round the ice cream van. I sketched the picturesque panorama of rugged cliffs and sea. The next stop was a beach. Miss Hawksworth told us to find stones and fossils and write about them, but we had other plans. Half the class took off their outer clothing, revealing previously donned swimwear and made straight for the glittering sea. Splashing happily in the waves, I noticed Miss Hawksworth standing on the pebbled shore, glowering powerlessly at the garrulous teenagers indulging wildly in the shallows.

Monday, July 19th

In the summer sales, I bought a pink satin sundress with metal rings around the midriff, a white polo shirt with an iron-on Mickey Mouse transfer, and fashionable platform heel sandals, with leather laces that tie up to the knees. I threw away my worn-out sneakers and wore the sandals for my afternoon shift. Unfortunately, one of the laces snapped, and I had to carry on working, then cycle home barefoot. Mum gave me the usual advice about making wise shopping choices.

Tuesday, July 20th

I took the broken sandals back to the shop and was allowed an exchange of goods to the same value. I chose a pair of pink suede, wedge-heeled lace-ups and wore them home. Mum pulled a face and said they didn't look practical for everyday wear. I replied that it was the best they had and they're very comfortable. After tea, I went potato-picking at Combe Farm. It was a calm evening, with hazy sunshine and softly trilling larks. The simple activity of gathering potatoes from newly-ploughed earth and tossing them into strategically placed boxes was relaxing. That is, until I noticed the PAIN was back. That dreadful pain that's dogged me all my life, and last bothered me two years ago, after the eventful horse ride in the hills.

I struggled on, my knees caked with mud, determined to finish the next row, telling myself the pain would go, but it only got worse. The pointed, terracotta-tiled roof of home was in sight – so close, yet so far. Every second seemed an eternity. At last, I finished. Mr Wilson thanked and paid me, and I went home, the pain now a dull, throbbing ache. I said nothing to anyone. By bedtime, the pain had disappeared as mysteriously as it had come.

Wednesday, July 21st

Dad still has no work. Mum suggested he change the wording on the advert, as ELECTRICAL JOBS DONE AT A PRICE YOU CAN AFFORD! Sounded cheap and tacky.

The new advert reads:

ELECTRICAL INSTALLATIONS BY QUALIFIED, EXPERIENCED LONDON ENGINEER.

'You have to sell yourself, or people will think you're incompetent and you won't get any customers,' Mum told him. Mum's still looking for a better job. There's even talk of selling Edencroft and moving to a smaller place. I don't mind either way.

Thursday, August 5th

Tomorrow we're off to Catford! I can't wait to see Margaret. I'm taking time off my summer jobs, Mayfield Electrics is shut for two weeks, and Dad has told his clients he wants a break. (Dad got work re-wiring a house in Nyehaven).

I finished my shift at Woolworth's at noon, got paid, and went to the bank, which was busy. A mother came in with a pram, so I moved aside for them, and a woman in a smart trouser suit accused me of pushing in. I banked my wages, drew out £20 spending money for the holiday and left, hurt and angry. On the beach. The tide was far out, revealing fresh pools and sandbanks formed by rip currents. A thin strip of water separated shore and the steps at the jetty at the end of the pier – a popular point for strong swimmers. Some, including Alison, boast they can swim AROUND the pier. At very low tide, the distance to the steps was less than I'd swum at the lido. I waded until the water was up to my neck and started swimming, keeping the steps in view. But the steps came no nearer; it seemed I was swimming on the spot. I kept going, but my legs dragged. Deciding to try again another time, I turned round. I kept going, periodically testing the ground, but my feet still floundered. A wave went over my head. I struggled to the surface, gasping for air. I HAD to keep going. The failure to swim to the steps, the stupid incident at the bank, suddenly seemed ludicrous and absurd. As the water rose higher and I sank lower, I wondered what it was really like to die. Perhaps I was about to find out? Yet somehow, I couldn't quite believe I wouldn't see tomorrow. Another wave passed over my head. I called feebly for help to an empty sky. Cold, saltwater filled ears and nose. Fatigue claimed my tired, aching body like a heavy blanket. My legs dropped into the depths... and then my feet touched firm sand.

Panic over, I crossed the wind-rippled sand bar and suddenly remembered the holiday cash. I ran to the crowded sands, frantically searching for the exact spot I'd left my things. I glimpsed my striped beach bag, and dodging lazing sunbathers, I dashed towards it, yanked open the zip and rifled through my belongings like a crazed burglar. The envelope was there, intact, with the four five-pound notes inside. I slumped on the sand and lay still, catching my breath. In the space of minutes, my money and my life were under threat, but now all was well.

Friday, August 6th

Finally, after fifteen years of being a nail-biter, my fingernails are long enough to file and varnish. Keeping busy was the key. Sitting on hands in boring lessons helped. Perish the thought of putting germ-laden fingers in my mouth from where other people had sat.

On the journey, I wore the new dress Mum got me from a catalogue. It's a full-length maxi, in lilac cotton gingham – a bit baggy, but hopefully, I'll grow a bigger bust. I sat admiring the reflection of my manicured hands in the car window, then applied a second coat of lilac nail polish, but Mum complained of the smell, saying it gave her a migraine. The car went over a bump, and I dropped the brush, making an ugly mark on my dress, which won't come off.

Margaret's modern, detached house with big windows is in a quiet cul-de-sac with big back gardens and trees. Margaret's sister Suzanne (an auburn-haired, older version of Margaret) is on University holidays and works at the launderette. Margaret's mum is small and shrew-like, with greying brown hair drawn up into a tight bun. Suzanne admired my dress. Nobody mentioned the hardened smudge of nail varnish. Margaret must have seen it but doesn't care much about clothes anyway.

Mum and Dad stayed to lunch of vegetable soup and rolls, fruit salad and ice cream. Every morsel was eaten, apart from the last pineapple chunk, which everyone was too polite to take. A cup of tea followed, and silences were awkward. At three o'clock, Mum thanked Mrs Pritchard for her hospitality, and my parents left.

Catching up on news, Margaret and I strolled around the streets. A pleasant evening was spent watching TV, looking at photos and diaries.

<u>Saturday, August 7th</u>

Margaret's cat, Charlie, is missing. I told Margaret about Marmie, but she said Charlie was just a year old and had probably gone exploring.

Margaret doesn't have a summer job and says she doesn't want one. She doesn't go on holiday and doesn't spend money on clothes. Her mum sent her to Woolworth's this morning for new underwear and T-shirts. In a small boutique, I bought a cheesecloth shirt, a white bikini joined in the middle, and a midi-length cerise-pink cardigan. The New Seekers' NEVER

ENDING LOVE was playing in the background.

Later, we went swimming at a modern indoor heated pool. I showed off my new swimsuit and my suntan. I imagined I'd be able to swim better, but strangely, my legs felt leaden, and I got tired very quickly. In the evening, while Margaret's mum did embroidery and her dad read the newspaper, Margaret and I watched a war film about a German couple who shot themselves to avoid inevitable capture by the Nazis. It put me in a strange mood all evening. I wish I could learn German!

Worryingly, Charlie, the cat is still missing.

Sunday, August 8th

This morning my comb fell down the back of a heater in Margaret's room. I was concerned it could be a fire hazard, as Miss Hawksworth mentioned having done the same thing a few weeks ago, and she had to call in an engineer to retrieve it. Thankfully, I managed to get it out with a ruler.

Margaret's parents went to church, but Margaret said she didn't mind missing it for once, thank goodness. We went to the park, where we fed bread to the ducks and played on the kids' swings.

Monday, August 9th

Still no sign of Charlie the enigmatic cat of Catford! I wonder if he even exists? Mum and Dad came to collect me after breakfast and declined the offer to stay for coffee and biscuits. I thanked my hosts, and we were on our way. Mum says Marion and Paul's new house is small but very nice, has three bedrooms and a front and back garden. I asked if they were planning to start a family soon. Mum said she didn't dare ask, for fear of offending Marion, but added: "New house, new baby, as the saying goes." I wonder. According to science, everyone's existence is a miracle. The probability of one particular sperm joining one particular egg, forming a unique genetic blueprint for one individual is mega trillions to one. Every person, animal and plant owes their existence to miraculous happenstance.

<u>Tuesday, August 10th</u>

Woolworth's was packed with holidaymakers. I felt quite important, working on the central checkout – until I failed to understand a tourist's heavy accent. I think the customer was asking about kitchen utensils. When I asked her to repeat her question a third time, she retorted, "Can ye no understand the broad Scots?" and stormed off into the crowd. Nobody told me off. The tills were so busy that probably nobody noticed.

Arriving home, I found the brown envelope I'd been dreading. I hid it under the lamp on the sideboard, then showered and changed. Afterwards, I lounged for a while, wearing a purple, swirling dress with a wasp middle – a hand-me-down from Marion and Paul's friend at the American army base. The dress is unusual, unlike anything in British shops... Eventually, I could bear the suspense no longer. I tore open the envelope, read and re-read the information until it sank in.

ENGLISH LANGUAGE	PASS	3
FRENCH	PASS	2
HISTORY	FAIL	8
GEOGRAPHY	PASS	6
ENVIRONMENTAL SCIENCE	FAIL	7

"I HAVE THREE O-LEVELS!" I exclaimed.

"Only THREE?" Mum grumbled.

Dad mumbled, "Shame about the science". Will my parents EVER change?!

<u>Thursday, August 19th</u>

Just like the day Mum brought Marmie home, I came home to a delightful surprise. Without telling me, Mum got two adorable kittens from the Wilsons' farm – a ginger with tiger stripes and a black-and-white. Dad named the black-and-white one Bertie, after Bertie Basset on the Liquorice Allsorts box, and Mum named the ginger Lurcio, after the comic character in the TV series UP POMPEII.

Wednesday, August 25th

Lurcio and Bertie a source of much entertainment. They spring from nowhere, climb curtains, swing on corners of tablecloths, and jump onto forbidden surfaces to steal food. The scampering of tiny paws on floorboards has become a familiar sound. Lurcio's the liveliest – pouncing viciously on cushions, antimacassars and the dog. Dotty is a paragon of patience, sleeping on the floor, while Lurcio stretches out in the dog basket. Bertie has formed a firm attachment to Dad, following him everywhere. He jumps on Dad's lap to snag a morsel of cheese sandwich. Mum doesn't want the kittens under everyone's feet during Arthur and Joan's visit, so she let them out cautiously, fearing they might run back to the farm – but they're quite happy scampering around the garden. Bertie explored the flower border and Lurcio the live-wire dashes down the lawn, looking ludicrous, his tail held high, curled like a question mark.

Saturday, August 29th

The kittens are a hit with Arthur and Anthony, but less so with Joan, who says the cats are a nuisance, the bed too hard, the birds don't sing, and the cornfields aren't golden. Mum seems annoyed, but I'm enjoying a relaxing break from work, looking around town, and spending the afternoon in the garden. Mum and Joan talked about cookery, Dad and Arthur shared gardening tips and reminisced about the war, while Anthony read comics. In the evening we watched a war film – The Dam Busters. Arthur said the aircraft was flying at low level, which I misheard as O-Level. I didn't mention my results and was thankful nobody asked.

Sunday, August 30th

We had a great day out at Salton, a yachting resort ten miles beyond Nyehaven. On the pebbled shore, Dad showed us how to skim stones across flat-calm waters, so they bounced like the Dam Busters bomb. We tried swimming, but I felt my foot strike someone and a voice said, "The sea isn't big enough." It was Dad!

We laughed – a moment of mirth Mum caught on camera with her Box Brownie. Afterwards, we walked around the harbour, picnicked on the crowded esplanade, attracted seagulls, then went to an ice cream parlour for delicious vanilla blackcurrant sundaes.

<u>Monday, August 31st</u>

Bank Holiday – the last balmy day of summer, with milky-blue skies, silken waters, and white sands shimmering in sunshine. On Westcombe beach, Anthony and I went body-boarding. Anthony played a prank on me, saying there were "no decent waves", as a big one was approaching and I was facing the shore. We laughed when cold water smacked against my back. Anthony crooned "Li-lo-li-high-hi-fi" looking ridiculous on his body-board, flapping like an ungainly duck. Anthony stayed in the shallows, while I ventured further out. The first wave approached, dark and mysterious. I stood poised and ready, caught the crest and enjoyed an exhilarating ride on the surf. The next time I let the body-board go. A wall of indigo rushed towards me – I dived through the wave to the other side, while my yellow-and-white body-board bobbed away on the foaming tide. A year ago, I was convinced there was no hope or future for me, but things have changed. Retrieving my body-board, I turned to face the oncoming tide, relishing what was probably the last sea bathe of the season. Catching the next crest, I felt its force-carrying me forward, far away from the painful past and to a future undiscovered.

20: STARRY NIGHT

<u>Thursday, September 9th</u>

Another new school year begins. Morning registration was vibrant with conversations about O-level results. Few gained five passes. Most people failed French, blaming Mr Ross, for not being there when he had other things to deal with. Nobody likes Old Dog, and everyone's sorry Madame Mantes left. Jimmy Murphy sneered at me, saying, "French must be really easy if you can do it." I sensed an atmosphere. At the start of class, I found a drawing pin on my chair, point upwards. I discreetly put it on Jimmy's chair before he returned to it. Mr Conway came in, and Jimmy quickly sat down, then muttered I DIDN'T SIT ON IT!

Mr Conway shouted at him to settle down. I dared to peek and saw Jimmy's freckled face flush scarlet. I smirked silently but soon returned to harsh reality. If maths was difficult before, it's now impossible – logarithms an enigma.

In November, we'll all take Latin and Maths, and re-sit the fails. I'll resit History, but not Environmental Science, because Miss Meadows says we can't resit science if we've opted for arts subjects.

<u>Friday, September 10th</u>

AT LAST I'M LEARNING GERMAN!! The teacher is another Mr Clements (no relation to Paul) a tall, grizzled, forty-something Englishman. Alison and I sat at the back of the top floor classroom overlooking the countryside, but for once I paid attention. German words sound strange and guttural, not how I imagined from reading my phrasebook. The grammar looks complicated, but I'm determined to learn it.

A letter came from Margaret. Charlie the cat came home soon after I left, looking, thinner. It was concluded he'd been shut up in someone's shed for a few days.

Thursday, September 16th

Strong westerly gales hit the hills, stripping trees of summer foliage. It was too windy to cycle, so I walked to school, then regretted it. At the edge of the playing fields, I heard the unmistakable jingle of Dotty's collar. Dad must have let her out too soon. I was furious! He stays at home all day with no job to go to, and he can't even be bothered to keep the dog under control. Arriving at school with Dotty the Dalmatian at my side is NOT an option. I grabbed her by the collar and walked all the way back home. Dad gave me a lift back, but arriving at school, I only just managed to wipe the mud off my tights in time for first lesson. Strangely, nobody commented on my absence in morning registration. Clearly, the register wasn't called, or at least, not properly.

However, the day of pet disasters was far from over. After school, I cleaned the budgie cage as usual, outside on the grass, avoiding mess, a routine chore I've done hundreds of times. As ever, the result was a tidy cage, but NO BIRD! It had happened. The same dreaded thing Marion did a decade ago. All it takes is one unguarded moment and a clever little bird that finds a window of opportunity. A cheerful chirrup alerted me to Buddy's presence in a bush. Creeping close, I tried to catch him, but he evaded my grasp. Literally, a bird in the bush, so near yet so far. I told Dad, and he wasn't angry. Neither was Mum, who came home with a migraine and went straight to bed. I fear for the little bird alone, cold and vulnerable in the dark, autumnal night.

Friday, September 17th

I awoke to the sound of cheerful chirping in the sycamore tree outside the window. We all tried in vain to catch him – he's just too quick.

School buzzed with news. Sandra Bright is leaving, for a job at Dawson's the Drapers. People say she's throwing away her education, but Sandra says she doesn't mind, wants to help her disabled mum, and wait for Mr Right to come along. She has no dad or siblings and lives with her mother in a tiny flat with an outside toilet and no hot water — like Mum's childhood London tenement in the Twenties and Thirties. How could there be such poverty in Britain, in the Seventies?

More gossip: Joanna Strange has undergone a transformation. She's barely recognisable, her hair permed in tight curls and her face like a painted marionette's. There were rude remarks, but Joanna wasn't bothered. She boasted all day about her new-found enjoyment in alcohol, cigarettes and boyfriends. As far as she's concerned, horse-riding is history.

Arriving home, I was sad to find Buddy still flying free. Dad made a fandangled contraption — a length of bamboo attached to the chip-frying basket. Needless to say, it didn't work.

Monday, September 20th

The last sight and sound of Buddy was on Saturday. After school, I took the train to Nyehaven to rectify my mistake. On the journey, I told Jodie the story, but she seemed more interested in her paperback romance. Arriving in Nyehaven, I headed straight for the pet shop, and the route took me past Quay Street. With a shiver, I remember Paul Newton and hurry on.

In the pet store I bought a blue budgie, the closest match I could find. I asked the shopkeeper if there was a guarantee and was told livestock aren't guaranteed. I hope it doesn't die. Dad and I put him in Buddy's cage and hung it in its usual place in the breakfast room. When Mum came home, she wasn't fooled. She suggested I name him. I decided on Philippe — the boy from Hironville — Pip for short. I'll guard him well, especially now we have new cats. Mischievous as ever, Lurcio and Bertie sharpen their claws on chair-legs, leave muddy prints on kitchen worktops, sneak into the bathroom, pull down towels and use them as toilets, much to Mum's annoyance. But they're so cute!

Lurcio purrs like a little motorcycle and Bertie's purr is soft and silken. Placing a finger under their chins, I can feel their purring resonate in their tiny throats.

Friday, September 24th

Today's headline in the Westcombe Herald reads: "PRESTIGIOUS RIDING SCHOOL LOSES REPUTATION"

Miss Crawford faces charges of animal cruelty. Her excuse is "personal difficulties". Horses have been neglected and starved of food and attention. This explains the snarling dogs incident, weeks earlier. Doubtless, the dogs were ravenously hungry. I wonder what has become of Lone Ranger? The stables will either close down or be taken over by someone else. Hopefully the horses have been rescued before winter.

Tonight was clear and frosty. Dad invited me on a dog walk down the lane to view the Milky Way, but I declined. It's too cold, and I wasn't in the mood.

Monday, October 4th

School is unbearable again. Friendships fading, and pressures mounting. This evening I listened to Don Maclean's STARRY STARRY NIGHT – a song about the anguish of Dutch artist Vincent Van Gogh. The lyrics "How you suffered for your sanity" – I can relate to. The artist was also a misfit, at odds with society. Mum keeps telling me to get along with people, but it's not working, however hard I try. Dad says "what they don't understand, they condemn". That makes more sense.

Suddenly Mum burst into the room. I turned the radio off. Mum lectured me saying I WASN'T insane and I should knuckle down and be responsible for my actions. The usual spiel. I know Mum worries and means no harm. For a moment, our eyes met, and I agreed to come out of my room and have supper.

Tuesday, October 12th

School is like a roller-coaster, good days, bad days, and mixed days. In the changing room, after games, Rosemary Richardson said, 'Piss off, you retarded spastic!' because, apparently, I blocked her view of herself in the mirror. During indoor lunch break, 5C's popular extrovert Dora Burke asked me what I was knitting. I showed her the long cardigan, nearly finished, and she admired it. I said knitting helped me stop nail-biting, earning me another compliment for my neat nails with frosted green varnish. Dora spied the diary in my open bag, fished it out and read aloud to her side-kick, Pam Barnes, including the part about Rosemary — who, fortunately, was nowhere nearby. Dora and Pam encouraged me to keep sticking up for myself against a "loud-mouthed show-off."

Wednesday, October 13th

I finished the cardigan and made a matching hat, also with cable-stitch stripes. I wore it to school. Someone yelled "TEA COSY!" from an open window, which gives me an idea for making Christmas presents.

Saturday, October 16th

Nigel Daly phoned, invited me to view his new livestock. In his shed, he showed me Bantam chickens in newly-built cages, and a smaller cage with two budgerigars, one green, one blue — apparently identical to Buddy. I asked Nigel when he got the birds, and he said last month, the chickens from a farm in Combe Ridge and the budgies from the pet shop in Nyehaven. Coincidence? I told Mum afterwards, and she suspects Nigel wasn't telling the truth. Unfortunately, we have no evidence, but if that blue budgie IS Buddy, then at least he is safe and well.

Wednesday, November 10th

Autumn has carpeted the hills in shades of red, green, brown, and gold, a tableau worthy of any artist's appreciation. I'm enjoying practising for Art O-level — a pencil drawing of a still-life arrangement of fruit, flowers, and garden implements and a water-colour painting of a landscape. Revising for other subjects is arduous, especially History, with so many facts to memorise. Maths is a waste of time, likewise Latin, as Miss Hipp's lessons are so badly managed.

Tuesday, November 16th

As expected, the Maths exam was impossible. I guessed practically all the answers and stand less chance of passing it than winning the Football Pools. By contrast, Art was a walk in the park. In the last five minutes, Mr Smith said: "Finish shading in that Wellington boot and you'll be laughing!" I left the exam room on cloud nine.

In the evening, Mum grilled me on my knowledge of the Industrial Revolution. I struggle to remember everything from Mrs Pilkington's lengthy notes. Names like Arkwright and Cartwright are easily confused, and I can't remember who invented what. I'll just hope for the best.

Wednesday, November 17th

In the last lesson before the exam, Mrs Pilkington asked what the driving force was behind the growth of cities in the Industrial revolution. Janet Ford answered, "The needs of growing numbers of peasant families moving from rural to urban areas." That's what I would have said, but Pilchard shook her head. 'NO – it's PROFIT, financial gain.' Money, apparently, is more important than people's health and welfare. The peasants were a commodity – the workforce that yielded bigger profits, strengthening the economy, reducing national debt. (That's something to write in the exam)

Thursday, November 18th

Mum and Dad are discussing Uncle Charles's lost inheritance again. They're convinced the solicitor has embezzled the funds, as we haven't received a penny. Mum is full of wisdom.

"If people can't earn enough they steal it or stay poor!"

"Academic qualifications are the ammunition needed to get good jobs, to prevent poverty."

"Money makes the world go round."

On the way to the History exam, Pilchard passed me in the corridor, gave me a brief smile and wished me luck.

"Thanks, I need it!" I answered. The paper wasn't too bad, and I have a hunch I passed.

Friday, November 19th

All the exams are over! Art was a cinch and Latin a joke. What's done is done. Now I can start to relax and prepare for Christmas. Next week there's a trip to a careers exhibition in London. It'll be an early start and a long day, but Mum says I have to go.

Tuesday, November 23rd

On the coach journey, Jimmy Murphy held a pro-IRA mini-conference at the back of the bus, while Rosemary and Joanna entertained everyone else with bawdy jokes and songs. The exhibition centre was noisy and crowded with scores of schoolchildren. The place wasn't heated, and I froze in my school blazer, regretting wearing the pink suede shoes, as they pinched my toes. I walked past stalls advertising banking, accounting, marketing, engineering... Nothing about becoming a freelance writer or artist. There was even a Police display, with a mounted female officer calmly controlling a fine, black stallion before a gathered crowd.

I sat alone in a picnic area to eat my sandwiches, then walked off, eating an apple. I picked up some leaflets about teacher training, which would please Mum, then tossed the apple core to a nearby bin, unaware it missed.

Suddenly a voice yelled YOU! PICK THAT UP AT ONCE!

A large woman in overalls was glaring at me, asking me what school I was from. Terrified, I pretended I didn't hear and kept walking. All day, nobody else spoke to me – a lone figure in a crowd. Stuff those fancy careers! They're for good, respectable citizens, not complete wasters like me.

The diary entries stopped. Lucy's mood descended to a new nadir, a trend set to continue for a while. After school the next day, Lucy discovered her bicycle pump was gone. She checked her bag. It wasn't there. It was definitely on the bicycle that morning. Ironically, it wouldn't have been any safer in her school bag or desk. Other cyclists left their pumps on their bicycles, so why was hers taken? Lucy boiled with rage, vowing not to dip into her own pocket to replace the pump. It had to be found.

The next morning, Lucy parked her bicycle and searched the cycle shed again, without success. She returned at break, by which time cycle racks were full. Lucy spied a black pump, just like hers. It *was* hers. After school, she would come back to reclaim it. She fretted silently through lessons, then dashed to the cycle sheds, propped her bicycle close to the bike with the pump in question, rummaged in her bag, then deftly dislodged the black pump and packed it away. Later, on closer inspection, Lucy noticed the rim was slightly different. Or was it? On reflection, she couldn't remember what her own pump looked like. Puzzling over it in the same way she had done with Nigel's budgerigar, she decided to forget about it.

During assembly next morning Mr Ross gave an announcement which made Lucy's blood run cold.

'Yesterday a boy lost a bicycle pump. It disappeared from his bicycle at some point during the afternoon. If anyone has any information regarding this matter, please speak to me after assembly.'

Lucy's heart was hammering so heavily she felt sure someone would notice. If her crime were exposed, the results would be disastrous. As far as she was concerned, this was already a disaster. She was a criminal. A common, low-down petty thief, embarking upon a career of crime. No wonder she hadn't wanted to join the Police! And what about the theft of her German dictionary from her desk the previous year? Why hadn't she bothered to report that? Why weren't all the other things that were being stolen in school on a daily basis reported and investigated? And why hadn't she thought of reporting the theft of her own pump? *Because she had no faith that the school could do anything about it!* Most disturbingly of all, why had this anonymous boy reported the theft of his property? Surely he didn't expect an announcement in assembly to help him get it back?

By rights, Lucy knew she should come forward immediately and confess. She could be honest, saying she had taken the pump by mistake, thinking it was hers. But would anyone believe her? Furthermore, her already fragile reputation with staff and pupils would be utterly destroyed.

Lucy was trapped, like a storybook villain. One crime inevitably leads to another, snowballing towards doom. After assembly, trembling, she approached Mr Ross and reported the theft of her own bicycle pump two days earlier.

Mr Ross frowned.

'Describe your pump, Lucy.'

'It was black. Plain black, with thin grooves on the attachment and red blue patterns on the attachment tube.'

Mr Ross's expression darkened. 'The pump which disappeared yesterday was similar. Did your pump have any writing on it, a logo?'

Lucy's mind went blank. 'I can't remember,' she said.

Uncomfortable silence.

'I had a German dictionary taken from my desk last year, too,' Lucy gabbled miserably. 'But I never thought of reporting it because I didn't think I'd ever get it back.'

'All we can do is advise everyone to keep a closer watch on their property. In such a big school, I appreciate this can be difficult.'

'Is there any chance my pump has been handed in as lost property?'

'It's probably worth asking. Now, if you'll excuse me, I have to talk to somebody else. I'll let you know if anything is handed in.'

'Thank you.'

Lucy walked away, downcast and disillusioned. *If there was better supervision around the school in the first place, this wouldn't have happened!* Teachers were too busy to do anything efficiently. At break, Lucy checked the lost property office, but the pump wasn't there. All day, she laboured under the crushing weight of guilt, anger and fear, wondering if the theft was from greed or spite. Without evidence, the culprit – or culprits – would be laughing. And if Hilda discovered Lucy had fallen into crime, she would die of shame. With a cold shudder, Lucy recalled a chilling aside from years before: 'My father told me', Hilda said, 'If you bring shame on this household, I will shoot myself.'

Frozen with remorse, Lucy struggled to the end of the day. Arriving home, she went straight to her room and stayed there for two hours, battling a volatile cocktail of emotions. When Hilda called Lucy to the meal table, Lucy faced her parents, whom she both feared and had the power to hurt. She sat paralysed, refusing to eat, drink or speak, staring motionlessly at her clasped hands on her lap, her swollen eyes brimming with tears.

'Whatever is the matter?' Hilda asked, more anxious than angry.

Lucy neither moved nor spoke. Her parents exchanged worried glances. Lucy's meal remained untouched. Finally, Hilda excused her from the table and watched her withdraw automaton-like to her room.

'Albert, there is something bothering her, and she simply isn't willing to talk about it,'

'We just have to wait. She will tell us when she is ready,' Abert said.

'That could be never,' Hilda sighed.

Not bothering to turn on the light, Lucy buried herself deep in the bedclothes, writhing in raw wounds of terror and remorse. If only she could wind back time and act differently? Slowly and subtly, her darkest secret and deadly plan of the previous year stirred from its long sleep. Was she not a useless waste of space? A year ago, had not that dark design been merely postponed? Blackness descended again upon Lucy's crushed spirit. *Perhaps it's time to reconsider the future?*

Lucy was never caught, her own pump never found, her parents never told. She kept the stolen pump, a constant reminder of her misdemeanour. For days after the incident, Lucy went from task to task, head in a fog, heart as stone. Slowly, her livid conscience began to heal. On crisp, clear frosty nights, she accompanied her father on dog walks in starlit lanes, feeling the blackness of the November night enfold her like a blanket. The night sky was a picture of perspective, the fluid sweep of the Milky Way, the familiar saucepan-like asterism of the Plough plain to see. Countless points of light etched against the vast canopy of space offered escape – escape to a reality far beyond the affairs of man. Stars detected by radio telescope, light-years distant, appeared as they were billions of years before. According to science, they probably no longer existed. Lucy wondered what – if anything – was in their place.

The minutiae of human affairs suddenly seemed triflingly insignificant. Far above this troubled sphere, space stretched to infinity – fearful, and forbidding, filled with mysteries unfathomable, dimensions undiscovered.

Lucy stood in the frost-laden air, drawing comfort from the silvery glow of distant galaxies, trusting in the promise the sun would rise again tomorrow.

21: PINK ENVELOPES

Hilda was teaching Lucy to drive again. The rhythmic throb of the car's engine gave Lucy the impression she was flying a plane. The green Morris sailed effortlessly over the hedge, rising above a line of poplars, skimming past the roof of the Dalys' cottage, veering close to the ground. The sheer slope of High Lea Down rose mistily before her. Lucy floundered, wondering what she was supposed to do next.

'Drink your tea, before it gets cold,' Hilda said.

Released from dream-intoxicated sleep, Lucy remembered it was Saturday.

'I'll go and fetch the mail,' Hilda said, hearing the familiar rumble of the post van. After ten hours of sleep, Lucy took time to surface.

Hilda returned with two letters.

'Post for you, Lucy! From Deutschland! '

Hilda handed Lucy a pink envelope with a German stamp.

'That was quick!' Lucy exclaimed, suddenly wide awake. She opened the envelope, breathless with excitement.

'Well?' Hilda asked.

'I – I can hardly believe it,' Lucy stammered. 'I really will be going to Germany!'

'Of course you'll be going. It'll be a big adventure – a new horizon.'

'The handwriting's terrible. I can't read the girl's name, but I'll read what she says.

'Hallo Lucy! I am your letter-girlfriend of Germany. I am fifteen years old and I am living in south German town that Hildenheim is called. I dwell in a family house with my elders and two brothers. I go in the school Albert Einstein Gymnasium. I am learning mathematics physic and chemistry happily. In my free time I like to reading needlework and especially cooking. I have black hair and I have a glass.

In holidays I was in Austria and Switzerland on skis. That made many fun! I enjoy myself to my holiday in Westcombe. (I have never see the sea.)

Many dear greetings.

Your Beigni'

243

'Her English is terrible! I can't read the name. It begins with B, so I'll call her Bee for now and ask Mr Clements on Monday. I have a glass is a bad translation of ich habe eine Brille, so that must mean she wears glasses. And she has black hair, which is unusual for Germans. Maybe she's of mixed race?'

'She likes cooking,' remarked Hilda. 'She might be overweight?'

Lucy envisaged someone twice her size, who might not even be German.

'She likes Maths, Physics, and Chemistry, so we mightn't have much in common. I don't fancy staying in her house for three whole weeks."

'The letter doesn't tell us much. Staying with complete strangers is always a gamble, but I'm sure they'll do their best to make you welcome. Germans are very hospitable.'

'Gosh, look at the time! I have to go!' Lucy grabbed her bag and jacket and left.

Hilda turned to Albert and said, 'That's our Lucy – the one we know and love.'

Hilda opened the other letter which was addressed to her.

Albert raised an eyebrow.

'I've been invited to an interview,' Hilda said, 'Tuesday morning for the position of wages clerk at Connor Components, a small firm on the same trading estate as Mayfield Electrics. If successful, I'll enjoy better working conditions and more pay. A Godsend, if we're to wait much longer for your inheritance from Uncle Charles!'

Financial matters notwithstanding, Hilda was happy that whatever had troubled Lucy a few weeks before seemed to have blown over for good.

Saturday, December 4th

Today is a PINK LETTER DAY! A pink envelope from Germany – from my new penfriend (whose name I can't decipher) in Hildenheim, Bavaria. In four months I'LL BE THERE!!

At Woolworth's, decorations are up and shelves bursting with Christmas goodies. Much has changed for the better this year. It's time to move on and leave the past behind.

Sunday, December 5th

I spring-cleaned my room, emptying shelves and cupboards of redundant clutter, including clothes I've outgrown, the Guides uniform, and the paperback horror stories, all destined for the bring-and-buy stall at the school Christmas bazaar.

Monday, December 6th

My German penfriend's name is Birgit Schmied. Mr Clements helped me draft a reply to Birgit. German grammar is difficult – much much harder than French. At lunchtime, I posted Birgit's letter, with a Christmas card depicting an English village in the snow. A card came today, from cousin Martha, showing a big Christmas tree laden with candles and decorations. I've heard Christmas in Germany is very atmospheric. This Christmas we're invited to Marion and Paul's.

Tuesday, December 7th

Languages are fascinating. In lunch break today I went to town and bought pocket dictionaries in Spanish, Dutch, Russian and Esperanto – a made-up, universal language used in many countries. Like Latin, it might end up being another "dead" language if people don't speak it enough. I've listed numbers one to ten in seven different languages. I showed Mum the dictionaries, but she just asked how I thought I'd done in the November exams.

Thursday, December 16th

A letter from Birgit already! A colourful postcard of candlelit, frosted fir cones. Also two black-and-white photographs: of Birgit with her two brothers on a summer picnic beside a stream, and the family group under the Christmas tree. All are dark-haired, tall and slender. Birgit wears glasses with big frames and has a wide smile. The Schmieds look a friendly bunch. They have a family house, with grandparents in the downstairs flat. Birgit likes swimming, going for walks, and home baking, trying different recipes. I think we'll get on fine.

Friday, December 17th

Term finished today! Mum and Dad took me to the evening Christmas bazaar. I bought house plants, which Mum and Dad took home, leaving me at the youth club Christmas party. I didn't see anyone I knew. The noise from the disco was deafening. I wandered about the smoky, overheated rooms, picking at snacks and watching the clock until Dad came to pick me up at ten o'clock. I don't think I'll bother coming any more.

Sunday, December 19th

Annoyingly, my hopes for a happy Christmas are ruined by the sudden onset of a heavy, feverish cold – worse than the cold Jodie and I had last February. I blame that stuffy, overcrowded party, and I'm sorry I went. On a brighter note, the tree and decorations look lovely – although we'll be away at Christmas itself. I hope my cold goes away and I don't give it to anyone else.

Monday, December 20th

It's Mum and Dad's 26th wedding anniversary today. Mum showed me the photo of her and Dad on their wedding day– Mum in a dark, pencil-slim skirt, leopard-print jacket and hat with a feather in it, and Dad in an overcoat, a white carnation in the lapel. Mum said they couldn't afford traditional wedding clothes, as the War had not long finished. Today is also the anniversary of the passing of Uncle Charles. He's been gone four years now. "So many things happen around Christmas time," Mum said, with a sigh.

Thursday, December 23rd

All the presents are wrapped and ready. I just need to sew up and wrap the tea cosies I've knitted for Mum and Marion. My cold is getting better, but my nose is still blocked, and I couldn't smell the mince pies Mum was cooking. At this rate, I won't be able to taste the Christmas food.

Friday, December 24th

I had a splitting headache and a blocked nose, but for once, Mum didn't have a headache on the journey. Halfway, we stopped to buy food. Mum wanted to buy a pineapple for Marion, but when she was told it cost 75 new pence, she exclaimed, "That's fifteen shillings! Far too expensive."

246

"But it's been flown in from Kenya, especially for Christmas, Madam!" the shopkeeper argued.

"Well, they can fly it back again, because I'm not paying that!" Mum said, and left the shop.

Marion and Paul's terraced house has bay windows at the front. The front door leads into a tiny hall, and a through lounge leads straight into the kitchen. Up the steep stairs are the master bedroom and two box-rooms, the larger of which has an airing cupboard and a strong smell of gas, noticeable even with a blocked nose. Annoyingly, I smelt none of the mince pies or mulled wine. By nine o'clock, I'd had enough of boring TV, idle chatter and food I couldn't taste, so I went to bed, in the camp-bed, in the gas room. Suddenly, there was a loud rat-tat-tat on the front door, followed by peals of laughter, accordion music, and raucous singing. With no hope of getting to sleep, I dressed and went back downstairs. Opening the door to the lounge, I saw Marion's white kitten on the table, drinking water from the celery jug, and a plump, dark-haired young woman eagerly devouring a plate of pastries.

"Come on, Lucy and have a pew," the girl said, pulling out a chair. "Come and join the fun."

Marion introduced me to Molly and her boyfriend, Patrick. With songs and laughter, food and drink, time passed happily. I had no idea what time the party finished and didn't care.

Saturday, December 25th

For the first time in my life, it's a WHITE CHRISTMAS. By coincidence, Marion already named her white kitten White Christmas. Mum asked me to get the milk in, and when I opened the door, an icy chill greeted me, matching the white haze enveloping the silent street, where rows of houses with bay windows looked quaintly Dickensian under a coat of almost artificial-looking snow. Suddenly the door clicked shut, leaving me locked out, holding the freezing cold milk bottles. I put the bottles down, knocked on the door, but there was no answer. I called through the letterbox, but still, nobody came. By this time, my fingers were blue with cold. I banged the door harder until my frozen knuckles screamed with pain.

Finally, Mum opened the door. Apparently, nobody heard me because everyone was in the kitchen with the door closed and the radio on.

We exchanged presents, and thankful laughter flowed, aided by tea, coffee, or sherry. Socks, underwear, toiletries and chocolate treats were unwrapped in a flurry of coloured paper and polite jokes. It all seemed contrived, devoid of the magic of Christmasses long past, possibly because there was not one child in the house? Peter, John and Sarah came for lunch. Crackers were pulled, dropping worthless plastic trinkets and well-worn jokes that raised feeble laughs and groans. Uncle Peter presided over the lunch table, looking ridiculous in his purple paper hat, telling Irish jokes. Somehow, the conversation degenerated into anecdotes about Hitler and the war, and I stopped listening, wondering how Dotty was doing in kennels, and my head feeling like a pumpkin filled with cement. I can't wait to get home.

Sunday, December 26th

The snow thawed, melting into a typically damp spell of wind and rain. Marion is besotted with her kitten. I wonder how long it will be before she has a baby? I daren't ask, especially since nobody else mentioned the subject all weekend.

I kept busy today with my favourite present – a retractable ball-point pen with six different colours, and a new five-year diary, where I've started filling in the days and dates in different languages.

Monday, December 27th

The return journey was uneventful until we reached the kennels to collect the dog. Dotty has come on heat earlier than expected. Mum is anxious to get her booked with a Dalmatian sire at the earliest opportunity. Mum says this is a last-ditch attempt to make money at Edencroft. Also, Mum is still waiting to hear how she got on at the recent interview at Connor's Components.

Friday, December 31st

Dotty has been booked in at Forest View Farm, fifty miles away, on Tuesday, January 4th, to be mated with a suitable Dalmatian. Meanwhile, Mum's like a cat on hot coals, wondering if she got the new job or not, and what will happen now that the wind has swung round again to the North and snow is forecast for next week. After the accident on the ice, Mum has a horror of road journeys in wintry conditions. Who knows what will happen now, regarding the proposed "canine marriage?"

In conclusion,, 1971 Wasn't A Bad Year. With The German Trip on the horizon, next year promises to be better still.

On the First of January, the Westcombe hills were decked overnight with a blanket of snow. Lucy hunkered down in her room, whiling away the hours, wishing for Spring. Predictably, the canine marriage was cancelled, Dotty's window of fertility missed. No sooner were the lanes clear to traffic, post came for Hilda with the offer of a permanent position of wages clerk at Connor's Components. 'Breeding dogs wasn't meant to be', Hilda reasoned philosophically, 'I sense there are significant changes for us up ahead.'

Lucy had other things on her mind, not least the dreaded O-level results. On Monday morning, she cycled to school in the crisp air, her mind a blank page. On the first descent past the Dalys' cottage, Lucy suddenly found herself surprised and unhurt on the ground – a painless but embarrassing reminder of the fall from Firefly the capricious pony, and her mother's brush with death on black ice. The bicycle lay on its side three feet away, the back wheel spinning round, the briefcase skidding down the slope. Lucy scrambled to her feet, got back on her bicycle and proceeded with caution. Approaching the school campus, Lucy noticed the buildings in darkness and remembered school was supposed to start on Tuesday. She returned home, pleased to have the rest of the day to herself.

The moment of truth was merely postponed.

The next morning, after registration, students reported to the secretary's office. In the queue, Lucy waited tensely, looking at her watch, counting the minutes. Finally, her name was called. Quaking, she walked into the office and was handed a slip of paper:

```
ART       PASS GRADE 2
HISTORY  PASS GRADE 5
MATHEMATICS   FAIL GRADE 8
```

All the history revision paid off, and a good grade for art!

That evening, Lucy showed the results slip to her mother.

Hilda's face darkened. 'You – you didn't pass maths! And you have the gall to just stand there and smile! You just wait until your father hears of this!' Lucy cowered in the doorway.

'But I've got five O-levels now,' she argued.

'Not enough!' Hilda hissed. 'Life is not a continuous round of pleasure. It's all about responsibilities, hardships and work!'

The door slammed in Lucy's face, and the connecting door to the lounge banged a second later. Hilda's raised voice was painfully audible. 'And all she could do was stand there and smile about the whole business, as if it was some kind of joke!'

Lucy stayed in her room for the rest of the evening. The week dragged on. In Friday's art class, Lucy expressed her pent-up tension in a painting. Mr Smith had set up a still-life arrangement of a vase of withered sunflowers against a backdrop of a wooden crate, draped with a blue and white check tea towel. Lucy left out the wooden crate and added more of the cloth. All background noise became silence, as Lucy lost herself in her work.

'That's quite impressive, Lucy,' Mr Smith commented. 'Did Vincent Van Gogh influence you, by any chance?'

'Possibly,' Lucy replied, flattered.

Mr Clements had left at Christmas, replaced by two part-timers; stocky Irishman, Mr Hagin and platinum-blonde, Swedish Mrs Strom, whose daughter Anna joined the class. Anna had already passed German O-level with flying colours. Coincidentally, Alison was learning Swedish in her spare time and had a Swedish penfriend called Anneke. Lucy launched enthusiastically into systematic German study, working alone through extra grammar exercises which Mr Hagin agreed to mark. Anna lent Lucy her German jotter, which Lucy took to work on Saturday. During tea break, Sally said, 'Copying someone else's homework? I used to cheat too.'

Lucy smiled, not bothering to defend herself.

Arriving home, Lucy found her wage-packet was missing from her bag. Surely none of her colleagues was a thief? The spectre of being robbed returned. All through Sunday, Lucy clung to the hope the envelope had fallen out of the bag and been handed in at work. She told her parents nothing, fearing the news would spark endless speculation and no constructive answers.

Tea time was very quiet – until the phone rang.

'It's probably a wrong number,' Hilda grumbled, leaving the table.

Listening hard, Lucy caught snatches of the conversation in the hall.

'Marion! Is anything wrong? Oh, oh!' That is good news. Well, mind you take good care of yourself.'

Hilda stood tall in the doorway and declared proudly, 'We are going to be grandparents, Albert dear – and you, Lucy are going to be an aunt.'

The news carried Lucy through the rest of the day, and all her worries seemed almost trivial. During Monday's lunch break, she went straight to Woolworth's and was delighted to be handed her wage packet. A colleague had found it in her bag on arriving home and was honest enough to return it. Evidently, Lucy had put her wage packet into someone else's plastic carrier bag, with the identical Green Shield Stamps logo. Lucy expressed her thanks and hurried off. Leaving the shop, she paused by the greeting cards stand, a colourful caption catching her eye.

Congratulations on the Birth of your Baby Girl!

The picture showed a cherubic baby in a cradle festooned with cascades of cherry blossom. There was a pink envelope to match. On impulse, Lucy bought it, risking the fifty percent chance Marion's baby might be a boy. Outside, the sun was shining, and Lucy walked back to school feeling lighter than cotton-candy. Life is so good, she sighed, looking up at the sun-kissed hills.

22: HILDENHEIM

A true product of her parents, Lucy oscillated between her father's gentle hesitancy and her mother's fierce determination. Slowly but surely a more assertive, self-confident Lucy was emerging. Was it her imagination, or was she really being targeted less at school? It had been a while since the last unpleasant altercation with the formerly fearsome Abigail – or indeed anyone at all. Nowadays, Lucy walked confidently along the corridors, head held high, a spring in her step.

One morning, on the way to class, Lucy felt a light tap on her shoulder.

'Lucy! Here's your book. Sorry it's been so long. I'd forgotten all about it, and it turned up yesterday when I was tidying my room.'

Alison handed Lucy a battered hardback copy of *Alice Through the Looking Glass*.

'Thanks,' Lucy said. The book's cloth-bound cover was frayed at the edges, the inside page flecked with coffee stains. A toffee wrapper clung to the final page of chapter three. Lucy knew Alison well enough by now and had seen her untidy room. Valuing Alison's friendship more than the book, Lucy didn't complain. At least the book hadn't suffered the same fate as *Alice in Wonderland*, shredded to smithereens by Dotty, four years before.

'Looking forward to Germany?' Alison asked.

'Of course! In a couple of weeks I'll be in Hildenheim, for the entire Easter holidays and longer!'

'That'll be good for you. I'd have gone myself, but I'm needed at the restaurant, so I might go next year.'

'I'm surprised you're not at the station already, with all your luggage,' Jill Simpson sneered – an uncharacteristic response from one of the quiet, polite clique.

Lucy didn't care what people thought. 'Yeah, that's right – I can't wait!'

The lesson bell rang.

'German next!' Lucy screeched with unbridled enthusiasm.

The group trooped to the classroom next to the language lab. Alison and

Lucy sat at the back.

'Pity this room's so overheated – I always end up yawning,' Alison grumbled.

Mr Hagin was seated at his desk, surrounded by paperwork. Barely looking up, he mumbled, 'Good morning, class, this will be a reading lesson.'

Someone groaned quietly. Chairs scraped, students stood up and filed forward to choose a book from the front desk.

Alison whispered to Lucy, 'Let's write to our pen friends. You can write to Birgit, and I'll write to Anneke in Sweden.'

'I've just written to Birgit,' Lucy mumbled, 'but I suppose I could write to Martine. It's French, but Mr Hagin never checks what we're doing.'

Mr Hagin sat statuesque, quietly dozing over a pile of exercise books. The wall clock ticked, pages rustled, voices whispered.

'At least the old codger showed up for this lesson,' Alison snickered.

Lucy wrote the letter, then tried reading a book about a boy on a journey, understanding little of the story. Reading German required much effort. Lucy dropped her dictionary, and Mr Hagin jolted awake. 'Be careful of school property,' he warned tiredly.

The next morning, Mr Kingsley made an unexpected announcement.

'Unfortunately, Mr Hagin has been hospitalised with a heart condition. A temporary replacement has been appointed to teach his classes and to accompany the group to Hildenheim.'

'Good, the trip hasn't been cancelled!' Lucy murmured, earning admonishing glances from those within earshot.

It rained all day, but Lucy's enthusiasm was far from dampened. At break time, she sat in the cloakroom with Alison, practising the German O-level speaking test questions, her self-confidence at a peak. In the corner sat a gaunt, petite third-former, huddling alone on the hard bench, her fringe obscuring her haunted face. Lucy wanted to talk to her, ask her her name and reassure her however hellish form three could be, the time would pass...

The bell rang.

'Art next,' Alison said, jumping to her feet. Lucy's wish to help the enigmatic girl was forgotten. Lucy's sunflowers painting had been finished and was up on the wall. Today she was working on a watercolour seascape depicting rugged coastline and a small ship battling the waves.

'That's quite effective, not your usual style, less exacting and more impressionistic,' Mrs Taylor said.

'It's good – it's very good,' Susan Schofield gasped. Lucy added more brush strokes, basking in the compliments.

'Is the boat the cross-channel ferry?' Alison asked.

'It could be.'

'So when is this wonderful journey happening?' Rosemary asked.

'March 28th, that's also my dog's birthday.'

'Yeah – we all needed to know that!' Jill Simpson scoffed.

'You're away for three weeks! You'll miss the start of the summer term,' Joanna said enviously.

'I've got money saved from my Saturday job, and my mum's giving me extra cash for clothes shopping,' Lucy boasted.

Joanna looked at the ceiling and sighed heavily.

'I'll come shopping with you, if you like?' Alison asked.

'Then come with me Nyehaven after school tomorrow,' Lucy said.

'Okay, good!'

Everything was going so smoothly. Lucy revelled in the joy of inclusion, her happiness levels reaching a record high.

On Nyehaven High Street, Lucy strode forth and bought a midi-length, navy blue wet-look raincoat, a plum-coloured corduroy jacket, two pairs of trousers and three jumpers, spending all the twenty-pounds allowance from her mother. Alison bought lipsticks, skin creams, turquoise eye shadow, lilac tights, and a flimsy, pink blouse which wasn't in the sale.

'There's time before my train, so let's get a bite to eat,' Lucy suggested.

'Good idea!' Alison agreed. 'I'm starving!'"

Over coffee and doughnuts, Lucy contemplated her purchases in quiet content. The doughnut was soft, sweet and quite filling.

Alison ate hers quickly.

'Fattening, but nice,' she said, wiping the jam from her mouth with a paper serviette. *Fattening*? Lucy found the remark redundant since Alison was waif-thin. Since the visit to Cove Cottage, Alison had stretched taller, but no fatter.

'I'm meeting Rosemary and friends now, at the cinema,' Alison said. 'That was good fun, Lucy. See you tomorrow.'

"Bye.' Lucy waved, as Alison disappeared into the crowd.

The next day, Lucy drew thirty pounds from the bank and bought a cassette recorder, an advance on the cumbersome reel-to-reel tape recorder. Feeling a trifle guilty, Lucy resolved to use the new gadget frequently and for educational purposes. Her parents voiced no objection. After supper, Lucy recorded random conversations and played them back.

'It's spooky,' Hilda said, hearing the recorded voices. 'It sounds a bit like us, but different.'

Lucy was as proud as she was on the day she bought the typewriter. At school, she was admired for being one of the first to acquire the latest technology. In the afternoon, Mrs Strom briefed students participating in the exchange, and handed out itinerary sheets. At last, the bell rang for home time. Breathless with excitement, Lucy burst through the main door into bright sunshine and hurtled down the tarmac path. A group of students stood chatting, blocking the way. Lucy dodged past, stepping on the grass.

'YOU THERE!' A voice bellowed.

Lucy walked on, oblivious.

'Yes – you! Didn't you hear me? Where are your manners?'

'Your name and form, please!'

'Me? Er – Lucy Wylie 5K – Sir.'

'Old enough and clever enough to know better! You should be ashamed, setting a bad example in front of younger pupils.'

Lucy squirmed with anger and embarrassment. This teacher now knew her name and would doubtless report her. Old fears reawakened, old wounds re-opened. All excitement vanished. Lucy walked home floundering in a fog of misery. Crossing the bridge, she tore the itinerary sheet to shreds and cast them in the river.

This time, Lucy's welter of woe was short-lived. The altercation on the path was never mentioned and was soon erased from Lucy's mind by escalating events. She apologised to Mrs Strom for mislaying her handout and was given another one.

Hilda bought Lucy a tan coloured suitcase and a red canvas holdall, and the packing began – clothes in the case, confectionery and tea for the Schmieds in the bag, allowing room for food and drink for a twenty-four-hour journey.

The excitement was spine-tingling, almost suffocating.

'It's strange,' said Lucy, staring out at the whisper of green on the branches of Biddlecombe Copse, 'having so much to look forward to.'

'It is strange,' agreed Hilda, 'Strange and rather wonderful.'

The long-awaited day finally came.

'Wakey, wakey, rise and shine!' Hilda called shrilly, on the dot of seven o'clock. Lucy stirred from deep sleep, sprang out of bed and got dressed. The Ben Sherman shirt felt cold and starched, the low-necked striped pullover smelt strange and vaguely oily, but the old red corduroy trousers with red, velvet patches on the knees were comfortable. Fluorescent, turquoise nylon socks and black, plastic slip-on shoes with gold buckles completed the ensemble. After breakfast, Lucy tied her long, auburn hair in two pigtails and glanced in the mirror with a satisfied smile. Then she put on the silver bells ring and the raincoat. The luggage was heavy. Lucy ignored the advice on the handout: luggage should be proportional to the size and physical condition of the owner.

'I can manage these, no problem!' Lucy chuckled, carrying the bags effortlessly to the car. Soon, she was at the station. On the platform stood a few of the Westcombe party, their collars turned up against a sharp, northerly wind. The train arrived punctually. Frau Meyer, the retiree replacing Mr Hagin, did a quick head-count and ordered everyone on board. Students clumped into the reserved carriage, cases bumping, doors slamming.

'Enjoy yourself, love,' Albert said quietly.

'Goodbye, Lucy – and take care!' A brief embrace from Hilda and the leave-taking was done. As the train disappeared from view, Hilda shook her head and said,

'You know, it really feels as if our Lucy is leaving home.'

'Don't be ridicuous,' Albert said, flicking ash over the platform edge. 'She'll be back in three weeks, full of the joys of Spring.'

Everything was going so well – so perfectly. Lucy leaned back, studying the blue-and-green chequered upholstery, the rhythmic clackety-clack of wheels on track lulling her to sleep. But life was too eventful for sleeping.

'We could be in for a rough crossing,' warned the young teacher on a year's work experience from Sydney. She'd jumped at the opportunity to help with the German exchange.

There were a few groans, and someone said, 'I always get sea-sick – it's dreadful!'

'I don't get sea-sick,' Lucy boasted, remembering how well she'd weathered the crossing to France.

'Good!' laughed the Australian. 'That means you'll be able to comfort everyone else.'

Lucy opened her packed lunch and bit into a cheese and pickle sandwich. The name Hildenheim reminded Lucy of her mother's name and German-Dutch ancestry. Filled with an irrepressible thrill, Lucy contemplated the distant destination, still a whole day away. The view from the train was pleasant, a typically English landscape. A familiar landmark came into view, of grey castle turrets above bare branches of deciduous woodland. A subtle shadow fell. Through rain-speckled glass, Lucy saw overcast skies and matt-green fields.

Something was wrong. The pain was back. The same abdominal pain that had dogged her all her life. *Surely not now*? All around, voices babbled in holiday mood. Lucy tried reading, but couldn't concentrate. The train sped on. Lucy's unseen, unwelcome visitor stubbornly refused to move, weighing her down like lead.

At Victoria Station, students were allowed an hour to browse before regrouping at the terminal for the boat-train – an express service to the ferry bound for the Continent. Lucy had long looked forward to this stage of the journey with its thrilling promise of faraway places, but every step was an effort, every moment torture. All the seats in the waiting area were occupied. Lucy perched on her suitcase, then got up and walked around, craving comfort. Dragging her luggage into a shop, she noticed Dora Burke and Pam Barnes. Lucy turned away, avoiding conversation. She looked at magazines, but the pain lodged deep inside like a ten-tonne load of concrete. She hauled herself and her luggage to the cold, noisy concourse and waited, checking her watch, wishing away every minute.

At last, the train was ready. The sound of throbbing engines and happy holidaymakers climbing aboard held no thrill. All Lucy wanted was to crawl into a hole and disappear. She shuffled along, her bags dragging her down, the handles cutting into her hands. The grave-like trench yawned beside her, steel tracks on gravel evoking negative thoughts. Lucy felt stupid, regretting ever having desired pain and death.

The last door slammed, and the guard blew the whistle. As the train pulled away, Lucy leaned back, eyes closed, feigning sleep. The journey seemed eternal, the pain demanding her full attention. Finally, the train slowed down. Lucy looked through a fog of exhaustion at towering chalk cliffs, sheer and forbidding in the afternoon sunlight. The pain tightened its punishing grip – karma for her former, self-destructive melancholy. The train snaked along the undercliff and lurched to a halt. Doors were flung open, and holiday-eager passengers spilt out.

'Keep together! We don't want anyone left behind!' yelled the Australian.

Lucy edged with everyone else through passport control. The ferry was late docking. When passengers finally embarked, daylight was fading. From inside the covered passageway, it was impossible to gauge the weather. An icy wind penetrated the flimsy structures, chasing along the dimly-lit passage, chilling Lucy to the core. After hours of sitting still, she felt frozen and stiff, alienated from her surroundings. She struggled up the gangplank and onto the ferry.

The ship's human cargo resembled a haul of cheek-by-jowl, upright sardines. There were no free seats. Lucy perched awkwardly on her case, opened her packed lunch and stared at the half-eaten sandwich, pork pie, apples, crisps, and chocolate biscuit. *Mum always gives me far too much,* she groaned. *Maybe the chocolate biscuit?* But the familiar sight of a favourite treat failed to entice. Lucy looked longingly at the row of director's style deckchairs, hoping someone would get up and offer her a seat, but no one did. Her clothes felt uncomfortable, gaudy, frivolous, and inadequate against the cold. Right now, a hot water bottle would be ideal.

The forecast was wrong. The crossing was as smooth as silk. No one was sea-sick, and Lucy regretted boasting she was a good sailor. Ironically, she was the one needing comfort. Feet stamped, cases thumped, and the ship's engines rumbled. Every sensation sharpened pain. A cocktail of European languages filled the cabin, dank air hung heavy with the odours of tobacco, packed lunches, and stewed tea. Lucy buried her head in her arms. 'This can't be happening', she muttered, yearning to stretch out, be warm, and pain-free.

Today was Dotty's birthday. Lucy thought of the fireside at home, wishing for a means of contacting her parents, telling them what was happening. Memories of poorly answered exam questions haunted her. *Was this punishment?* She sat motionless, swamped by waves of pain and nausea. If she made the slightest movement she felt she would surely die. *What have I done to deserve this?* she thought desperately.

'I wonder what Lucy's doing now?' Hilda murmured, breaking a long silence.

The firelight danced in her face. 'I just can't get her out of my mind. I do hope she's all right.'

A log hissed and crackled in the grate, and the dozing dog grunted contentedly on the hearth-rug.

'Having the time of her life, I shouldn't wonder,' Albert said, puffing smoke. 'Remember how much she enjoyed France?'

'Yes, I suppose you're right.'

Dusk turned to night. The boat chugged on to Ostend, its occupants heady with cheerful conversations and laughter. The cold, clean harbour lights, the medley of accents, the arrival on foreign shores held no charm for Lucy. The ferry released its passengers in a slow-moving stream through customs and passport control.

Lucy chose a convenient moment to speak to the friendly Australian.

'I hate to say this...' she began.

'Yes dear, what's the problem?'

'I'm afraid – I think I might be ill.'

'Oh, really?'

'It's this pain – I always get it, I mean – I always have done, but this time it's much worse and it hasn't gone away.'

'Time of the month?'

'No, it's not that. I've had this pain on and off all my life.'

'When did this episode start?'

'About an hour after the train left Westcombe.'

The young teacher smiled patronisingly. Clearly a case of holiday nerves!

'Well, let's just get on this train, we'll get you settled for the night, and if things are no better in the morning, we'll get you to a doctor.'

Now that Lucy had actually told someone, it seemed a huge burden had been lifted. She would get on the train, continue the journey, and all would be well. *Perish the thought of being taken to a German doctor!* The bright yellow, smiley brooch on the teacher's lapel seemed to agree.

In the lofty six-berth cabin, Lucy sank gratefully onto a lower bunk and stretched out on the hard, plastic-covered mattress. A linen-covered pillow and rough, woollen blanket were provided. Somewhere along the corridor, raucous laughter resounded, and a door slammed.

'Shhh! Keep the noise down!' the teacher hissed.

The compartment was overheated, cigarette smoke hung in the air, but Lucy was too tired to care. She drew the blanket up over her shoulders.

People were talking, voices fading, melting into a strange, unearthly hushing sound, as the train gathered momentum. Wheels pounded, steel grating against steel, thundering deep into the night.

Lucy blinked hard. Someone pulled up the blind, and the pale glare of early morning invaded the compartment. Aware of a raging thirst, Lucy finished the bottle of flat-tasting lemonade. The pain was gone. Lucy sat up and looked out of the window. Steep terracotta-tiled roofs on white houses flashed by. There was much to take in: tidy lines of trees, rectangular brown fields, box-like buildings, and straight streets lined with tiny cars crawling like insects.

'So this is *Deutschland!*' Lucy exclaimed. The train halted unexpectedly, on an embankment. Not everyone shared Lucy's enthusiasm.

'Stupid train,' grumbled Bridget Barker. 'Why doesn't it get moving!' There were a few badly suppressed yawns. It seemed most of the group hadn't slept well.

The Aussie popped her head round the door and asked, 'How are you all this morning?'

'Fine, thanks,' Lucy replied, her mouth full of pork pie.

'That's good,' the assistant smiled, then stood in the doorway and shouted,

'Gather your belongings now, everyone! We're approaching Heidelberg!'

Modern suburbs melded with a pristine cityscape of cuboid blocks, angular roofs, and church spires. The train slowed down, past bold billboards lining grey concrete walls. An overhead sign read:

Heidelberg
Hauptbahnhof

With a juddering of brakes the train stopped. Lucy grabbed her luggage, was squeezed along the tightly-packed corridor and climbed down to the platform. The party proceeded through the ticket barrier and onto the concourse, stopping near a newsstand.

'Meet here in twenty minutes!' The order was clear. Commuters blended with tourists in movement, colour and noise. German was the predominant language, naturally, but Lucy barely understood a word. At a nearby newsstand, she bought today's *Die Zeit*, thinking it might be like *The Times* – not the easiest of reads. She glanced at it briefly, then rolled it up and stuffed it into her holdall.

The next leg of the journey, a fifty-minute ride through small towns was like a virtual tour of a holiday brochure, as picturesque and quintessentially German as Lucy expected. It was like a dream come true.

At last, the magic words were spoken.

'Nearly there now, folks, so gather all your belongings!'

The Australian was strolling through the carriage, looking as relaxed as a seasoned tourist, her coat open and the smiley badge flapping on the lapel. The sun had risen on the Hildenheim skyline, adorning sharp roofs and the copper cupola of a hilltop church – a golden glow of Easter joy.

The train slowed down. Lucy peered through the window, scanning the crowded platform for a familiar face.

The doors swung open and the party piled out.

Everything was happening quickly. Someone started talking to Lucy in a strange tongue, gesturing to carry her luggage. Their voices were loud but friendly. Birgit looked exactly as she did in the photograph – tall, slim, dark, with big glasses and a wide smile. Lucy was welcomed, fussed over, and ushered through the thronged platform to the car park, where the Schmieds' cream-coloured VW-Beetle stood waiting. Herr Schmied put the bags in the boot. Lucy sat on the back seat with Birgit and eight-year-old Rolf. Birgit's middle brother, Martin sat in the front, smiling through a thatch of jet black hair. Rolf bounced on the seat, chattering like a chimpanzee, his brown eyes wide with enthusiasm.

'*Ja, ja...*' Lucy kept answering, hanging on every word, her mind frantically processing information, too slowly to catch the next word.

Her hesitant '*Wie, bitte?*' resulted in sentences being repeated, but everything sounded like gibberish.

The Schmieds' home was a detached family house with pebble dash walls and white shutters. The front door was set above a brick semicircle of steps and opened into a marble-floored hall. Herr Schmied carried the luggage, and Lucy followed Birgit up the wooden, spiral staircase to the first-floor apartment. Voices and footsteps echoed in the stairwell, the air filled with smells of wax polish and freshly-ground coffee.

In the doorway stood Frau Schmied, open-armed and smiling.

'*Willkommen, Lucy, Herzlich willkommen!*'

Lucy was shown to a bright, airy room with white walls and modern, low-level furniture.

'*Guten Morgen,*' Lucy said shyly.

A flood of incomprehensible German followed.

'*Komm!*' Birgit smiled again, showing braces on her front teeth. '*Ich zeige dir das Haus!*'

She'll... show me the house... Lucy's tired brain slowly translated.

The apartment comprised the upper floor and attic. The girls were to share a large room with white, woodchip walls, sloping roof, and a square window overlooking the town. A huge, concrete bypass dominated the foreground, the roar of traffic deafening. Birgit closed the window, mentioning *Butterbrot* and *Kaffee*. Lucy understood breakfast was next. In the small dining-room, the table was laid with traditional German breakfast on a white cloth. Morning sunshine from a skylight illuminated a spread worthy of a Dutch master's painting: a carafe of orange juice, gleaming crockery, and an array of interesting foods – white, crusty rolls, cold meats, cheeses, and a wicker basket of chestnut-coloured buns twisted into figures-of-eight, sprinkled with white crystals. A cut-glass vase of narcissi completed the picture.

'*Komm, wir essen,*' Birgit said.

Herr Schmied had left for work, but over breakfast, Lucy became better acquainted with taciturn Martin and pert, impish Rolf. Having eaten on the train, Lucy wasn't hungry, but she sampled a little of everything, including one of the brown buns, which Birgit called *Pretzel.* Lucy spread the bun with butter and jam, and cautiously took a bite. The white crystals were salt, not sugar, but tasted good. Frau Schmied kept refilling Lucy's coffee cup. Lucy felt everyone was watching her, but not in a nasty way – not even little Rolf with his sparkling eyes and infectious laugh. Rolf spoke, and the family laughed heartily. Lucy gave a puzzled look.

'*Er spricht Dialekt,*' Birgit explained.

Dialect? Lucy wondered how much proper German she would learn during her stay. After breakfast, Lucy was encouraged to rest. With the curtains closed and the door shut, she lay on the bed, contemplating neat bookshelves, wooden puppets, and Birgit's multicoloured rucksack on the back of a chair. The low bed, the red-and-blue striped covers, and the bolster-like pillow were comfortable. Above the muffled sound of rushing traffic, Lucy heard the solemn resonance of a deeply tolling bell. She rested but didn't sleep. After a while, she got up, keen not to miss anything. She went upstairs to wash, and change into the light blue jeans with the buttons sewn on. The attic bathroom was well-lit by a skylight. It had a large washbasin, bath, shower, toilet, and a bidet. Thick, coloured towels hung over a heated chrome towel rail. The soap was oval, streaked with shades of green, imbued with a scintillating, lingering perfume.

Lucy returned downstairs, eager to unpack, but the lure of lively conversations was stronger. Birgit and Rolf sat watching television. Rolf hopped up like a frog and hid behind the door, sniggering, an echo of her eight-year-old self, always looking for laughs, irrespective of whether others shared her amusement.

Birgit was reading a magazine with a picture of a topless woman on the front cover.

'*Was ist das?*' Lucy asked.

'*Die Fernsehzeitung,*' Birgit answered.

Zeitung meant newspaper and *Fernsehen* meant television. Lucy was relieved to hear Birgit wasn't reading pornography. Germany seemed such a strange place.

Birgit put the magazine back on the shelf.

'*Willst du spazieren?*' she asked.

'*Ja,*' Lucy replied. *Spazieren* meant a walk.

Birgit led the way, under the underpass, towards the town. Everywhere looked clean, uncluttered, and modern.

'*Das ist meine Schule,*' Birgit announced, pointing to a sprawling complex of cuboid buildings. '*Und da ist mein Klassenzimmer.*'

Birgit gestured to the big windows of a ground floor classroom. Beside the school was a miniature golf course. Half a dozen girls in jeans and sweaters were leaning against a wooden fence. Lucy was introduced to the group, retaining only one name – Helene. Everyone was talking at once. Someone handed her a golf club, inviting her to play Minigolf. The un-energetic game involved hitting a ball along asphalt, into small structures, the emphasis on enjoyment more than expertise. Suddenly, Helene spoke, sounding irritated. Birgit pointed to a dark smudge on Lucy's jeans, and to the creosoted fence where she had been leaning. Lucy shrugged. Perhaps Germany wasn't so pristine-clean after all?

Later, Lucy went to the bathroom to change into the lilac cotton trousers. She scrubbed vigorously at the light blue jeans, using the green stripey soap with the fresh fragrance. She removed all but traces of the stain. She hung the jeans on the towel rail and returned downstairs.

'*Ziehst du deine rote Hose nicht gern an?*' Birgit asked.

Don't I like wearing the red trousers? Red clashed with Lucy's hair colour, making her feel as conspicuous as a British letter box. Lucy only wore the trousers because they were a Christmas gift from Marion.

'*Nein,*' Lucy replied, trying to forget the agonising journey and the endless hours staring at red corduroy and suffering untold pain.

'*Komm! Wir gehen in den Garten,*' Birgit said.

The garden comprised a square plot of well-tilled earth, concrete paths, three cherry trees in budding blossom, and a wooden outbuilding with a mesh enclosure housing Bantam hens and cockerel. There was no lawn. An elderly couple pottered about, hoeing and weeding. Birgit introduced them as Opa and Oma, the grandparents. The aroma of fried onions wafted from an upstairs window.

'*Komm! Das Mittagessen ist bald fertig,*'

Birgit said.

Lunchtime already?

While the Schmieds talked and ate, Lucy enjoyed pork cutlets with apple sauce and fried potatoes, followed by home-made plum cake, cherries and fresh cream. Her trousers felt uncomfortably tight. After lunch, a visitor arrived: a tall, iron-grey-haired lady wearing slacks and sweatshirt, spotted neckerchief and beige leather brogues. This was *Tante Ellen* – Aunt Ellen, Frau Schmied's sister. Ellen occupied the corner bench, flanked by her garrulous nephews, while Birgit and her mother baked cakes.

All were talking excitedly, but Lucy barely understood a word.

'*Wie gefällt es dir, hier in Deutschland?*' Ellen asked.

How do you like Germany?

'*Es ist sehr gut,*' Lucy answered. Germany was very good.

For a first day, it seemed she had been here for ages. Cakes safely in the oven, the ladies kept watch, while Lucy and Birgit returned to town, where Lucy mailed a postcard to her parents, telling of her safe arrival, then enjoyed a brief shopping trip. She bought a blue, floral bikini and a small plaque displaying the Hildenheim crest. Birgit browsed, buying nothing. They walked back in time for *Kaffetrinken* – traditional mid-afternoon coffee, with cake and congenial conversation. Strong, filter coffee and English tea were served in the dining room, with vanilla marble cake, plum cake, and chocolate biscuits with cream filling. Ellen, a primary school teacher, talked about her school on the other side of town, and a holiday in Austria. Ellen asked Lucy simple questions about her life in England, listened patiently, correcting her mistakes. Lucy quickly warmed to Ellen's easy-going manner and was glad when she stayed for *Abendbrot* – a modest meal of breads, cold meats, and cheeses. After Ellen left, the boys watched a monochrome Western with cowboys and Indians speaking badly-dubbed German. Lucy smiled from the couch, light-headed with fatigue, but very, very content.

More happy days blended in an extravaganza of activities. On Good Friday, Lucy helped paint the shells of hard-boiled eggs with watercolours. She joined in family games. Birgit laid a set of cards on the floor, face down, explaining the aim was to memorise which cards went where – a useful tool for learning new words. Rolf kept tugging Lucy's sleeve, laughing mischievously. Lucy didn't mind.

After lunch, the family went for a stroll up the hill behind the house. A wide, tarmac path rose steeply to the summit, where a life-size marble crucifix stood overlooking the town. *Appropriate for Good Friday*, Lucy thought. Photographs were taken of the group sitting on a bench. The surrounding slopes were brown and bare, dotted with small huts and rows of sticks, which Lucy learned were *Weinberge* – vineyards. Further along was the Schmieds' own vineyard, a modest plot with a chalet-type hut – currently locked and barred – but a happy weekend retreat in summer. Lucy admired the panorama of mist-shrouded towns, and distant, forested hills, fascinated by this wonderful place and very different way of life.

On Saturday, the Schmieds drove to the local cemetery to visit the graves of Frau Schmied's parents, a tradition Lucy could relate to. However, talk of *Kirche* was unnerving. Evidently, an Easter Sunday church visit was on the agenda. Terrified of a vengeful God, Lucy recalled a reprimand for mistakenly walking the wrong side of the altar rails to collect a posy on Mothering Sunday.

The next morning, Lucy washed and dressed in sober, blue colours – nothing garish. Then, to her horror, she found the bathroom door wouldn't open. Panicking, she repeatedly turned the key, with no success. *They'll be late for church! What if I've broken the lock?*

On the other side of the door, Birgit said *Schlüssel* and *Fenster*. Lucy dropped the key out of the window, heard Rolf clatter downstairs and back again, and then the door was unlocked from the other side.

'*Was habe ich getan?*' Lucy asked, somehow finding the words for what have I done?

Birgit demonstrated the door was unlocked by turning the key twice.

'*Es tut mir Leid,*' Lucy apologised, mortified. Nobody minded.

That Easter morning, Hildenheim's hilltop church was full to bursting. Hundreds of hushed voices and shuffling feet echoed off stone walls. A brief introduction was delivered via a crackly microphone, then silence fell. Lucy stared at the flagstones, wishing she was invisible. Before the altar, a robed priest paced back and fore, chanting in Latin, swaying a sphere that shed clouds of perfumed incense. Lucy sat stiffly, riveted by the rhythmic cadence of rising chants. There was no Bible reading, no hymn, and no sermon. Apparently, nobody in the congregation was obliged to do anything. Afterwards, Lucy stood up with everyone else and followed the crowd out into the sunshine.

At the Schmied house, a roast chicken dinner was followed by the promised egg-hunt. Traditionally, the search for Easter treats hidden by the legendary *Osterhase*, the Easter Hare, takes place in a garden. However, a sudden shower limited the hunt to indoors. Martin and Rolf raced upstairs to search the attic, while Birgit and Lucy looked in the first floor rooms. Birgit pulled out a small basket from under her bed, revealing foil-wrapped chocolate eggs, sugared almonds, and hard-boiled eggs with painted shells. A similar basket was under Lucy's bed. The afternoon was spent in the lounge, eating Easter sweets, Rolf and Martin sprawled on the floor, playing marbles. Lucy wrote postcards, telling family and friends of the wonders of Germany to family.

The next morning, Frau Schmied stayed at home to cook and bake, and the rest of the family piled into the car.

'Where are we going?' Lucy inquired, in German.

'You'll see,' Herr Schmied replied. The Volkswagen rattled off onto the bypass. Beyond vineyard-covered hills stretched verdant pastures, coniferous forests, and villages defined by churches with onion-shaped towers and timber-framed houses. It was hard to believe home was a thousand miles away. Rolf nudged Lucy, offering an open box of chocolates.

'*Danke,*' Lucy said, taking a foil-wrapped chocolate egg. Soon, there was a picnic stop for salami sandwiches and hard-boiled eggs.

'*Er isst ein Ei, und er ist ein Ei!*' Rolf sniggered, as Martin bit into a hard-boiled egg.

'He eats an egg, and he is an egg, sounds the same in German,' Birgit explained.

'I understand,' Lucy said.

The car stopped beside a pine forest and an inn. Feeling full, Lucy anticipated a walk, but everyone headed for the inn. Lucy requested a glass of lemonade. However, when the drinks arrived, so did the crusty bread and the side-salad, followed by pork steaks, *Sauerkraut*, and potatoes. The food was unquestionably good, but Lucy had less than no appetite. She picked fastidiously, pushing forkfuls of food around her plate, playing for time.

'*Ich bin satt!*' Birgit declared she was full, having eaten just a third of her meal.

'*Ich bin satt,*' Lucy echoed, crumpling her serviette and hiding most of her food. She followed the others outside, her stomach as tight as a drum. With the cool breeze in her face, Lucy paced about, taking deep breaths, wishing she understood more German and knew what on earth was happening.

'*Jetzt ein Verdauungsmarsch!*' Birgit announced.

Now a... WHAT?

On the forest walk, Lucy couldn't be bothered asking what the long word meant, but she looked it up later.

Verdauungsmarsch – a walk after a meal, to aid digestion.

Work hard and live well was a way of life. Each day, Lucy felt increasingly at home. This holiday was even better than the French trip, and she wanted it to last forever.

At Hildenheim's indoor pool, Lucy wore the new bikini. The top was tight around the back and the cups too deep, but Birgit was content to swim at a leisurely pace, so it didn't matter.

'It's fun to swim when it's snowing outside,' Birgit said in German. 'The water is warm and you see people outside wearing winter clothes.'

Lucy understood every word.

A man in a rubber bathing cap and heavy rimmed spectacles swam past, spluttering like a porpoise.

'He looks funny,' Birgit said, grinning. 'He's probably trying to lose weight. Also, we're invited to Aunt Ellen's tomorrow, just you and me. There'll be lots of cake.'

'I have another packet of English tea in my suitcase,' Lucy added, excitedly. 'We can bring that, too.'

'That's good. By the way, your German's improving, you can have a proper conversation. We can talk about pretty much anything.'

Lucy's confidence soared. There was nothing about Germany she didn't like. Everything was bigger, faster, tidier, and most importantly, people were friendly.

The next day, Birgit and Lucy took a tram to Ellen's flat on the other side of town. Up two flights of flecked marble stairs in a shared complex, Ellen's apartment was furnished with colourful covers, pictures, and tapestries. Since it was too early for *Kaffeetrinken*, Ellen suggested a drive in the countryside. A short journey in her little red NSU Prinz took them to a forested beauty spot.

Ellen was in cheerful spirits. 'This is the *Speck-weg-Weg!*' she said.

'What's that?' Birgit asked.

'It's a fitness walk. Fat (*Speck*) will be gone (*weg*), on the path (*Weg*), 'but of course, that's not for you girls, it's more for people like me,' Ellen explained, indicating her ample waistline. Walking the five-kilometre, forested path, Lucy was in a buoyant mood. Birds were singing under a cloudless sky, the air laden with the scent of pine needles and wood-smoke.

'I love it here' she said.

'But the hill are so steep,' Birgit complained.

'We'll stop for coffee soon,' Ellen said.

In a log cabin style *Gasthof*, Lucy ordered a slice of English fruit cake, Ellen and Birgit ordered lemon cheesecake. Disappointingly, the fruit cake was very small and very dry. Lucy took small bites, making it last, watching Ellen and Birgit eat their large, creamy portions of cheesecake, wishing she'd had the courage to try something new.

That evening, Birgit baked another *Zwetschgenkuchen* – a sponge-based flan filled with plum preserve.

'We'll pack some of this tomorrow,' Birgit said.

'Why tomorrow?' Lucy asked.

'The trip to Ludwigsburg, of course.'

'I'd forgotten that,' Lucy answered, not anticipating a good day. However, the outing proved better than expected. While others trailed disinterestedly through the castle, Lucy feasted her eyes on aesthetically pleasing décor, furniture and paintings.

'I'm bored,' Dora grumbled.

'My pen friend's so fussy,' Pamela whined. 'She polishes her shoes every day!'

'Green and white! Very nice!' Sadie O'Keefe gushed with her usual enthusiasm. The party shuffled through more opulent rooms.

'I'd like longer to look at the paintings,' Lucy said to Birgit, in German.

Suddenly, she noticed Dora and Pam sniggering and pointing. Lucy bristled nervously. Birgit was quick to notice the negative interaction.

'Last year, a girl in my class was my enemy,' Birgit said. 'I ignored her, and she leaves me alone.'

Bullying goes on in Germany, too? Lucy wondered, her illusions firmly brought to ground. In Birgit, she had found a true friend and ally. Birgit was effectively Lucy's minder on trips to Stuttgart airport and zoo, and Rothenburg-ob-der Tauber with its fairytale, timber-framed houses. At a café, the group ordered lemon tea, adding milk, resulting in dozen dissatisfied customers leaving their glasses of curdled concoction unfinished. Lucy smiled at the memory of the insipid tea served in the hotel in Hironville. In the bathroom queue, two brash extroverts were in floods of tears.

'What's wrong?' Lucy asked cautiously. One of the girls sobbed uncontrollably, the other buried her face on Sadie's ample shoulder.

'They're just missing home,' Sadie said.

Surely things can't be that bad? Lucy wondered. Five more days remained. In Hildenheim, Lucy bought more postcards and souvenirs, plus a blue smock top and cream-coloured corduroys for herself. In the Schmieds' home, excitement was in the air, Martin showed off his new bicycle, an early present for his fifteenth birthday. Rolf hid behind the kitchen door, bombarding Lucy with cushions, imitating her foreign accent in mock derision. Lucy took Rolf's pranks in good part, and they laughed together. Lucy borrowed Birgit's cassette player and filled a thirty-minute cassette with random conversations, radio, television, and the raucous squawking of the budgerigar. Memories to share with family and friends, Lucy thought, packing the cassette safely in her case. On Sunday, Birgit and Lucy slept in till eleven o'clock. The boys were in the garden with Opa and Oma, and the house was quiet. The breakfast table was spread with the usual fare, and Birgit made coffee.

'Where are your parents?' Lucy asked.

'At church, in Regensheim – a village twenty kilometres from here. It's cousin Marianne's White Sunday.'

'White Sunday? What's that?'

'It's a special, Catholic service for children's first Communion.'

'You don't go to church every Sunday?'

'No, just Christmas and Easter. Today, we're invited to Marianne's party. There'll be twenty people in all, and plenty to eat.'

The cousins' small house was crammed with guests. Plump, blonde Marianne was dressed in white taffeta. She posed for photographs, holding a commemorative candle, then scrambled happily on the floor with her younger siblings. A lavish buffet was provided: strong coffee for the adults and fizzy drinks for the children. Marianne's round face was smudged with cream and jam, her dress and tights speckled with crumbs and chocolate. Lucy blended in, feeling at home.

Early next morning, Birgit's alarm clock jangled into the gloom. Daylight filtered through the closed shutters, shedding pale rays of sunrise on the wall. The slumbering teenagers stirred. For a moment, Lucy believed herself to be back in her room at Edencroft. Then she remembered this was the first day of Birgit's new term.

The European school day was a new experience. Lessons were conducted to a strict regime, arts and sciences an integral part of the curriculum. Popular with teachers and students, Birgit was a good all-rounder, a shining star at STEM subjects, and a model student. No teacher arrived late, everything ran like clockwork, and Birgit involved Lucy in conversations and activities, making her welcome. By the end of the morning, Lucy was exhausted from concentrating.

School finished at one o'clock, leaving the rest of the day free, but there were copious amounts of homework.

'We'll do an hour's study after lunch,' Birgit said, settling at her desk with a pile of science books. Lucy was glad to be living in England, where academic life was easier. The notion of both arts and sciences being obligatory was horrendous.

Two days left. The sands of time were slipping inexorably into the funnel of finality. After three magical weeks, it was time to think of home. The Westcombe students' visit concluded with a tea party in the town hall. The mayor of Hildenheim presented everyone with a hardback book about Hildenheim, a monochrome aerial photograph of the town on the front cover. Lucy flicked through the glossy pages. Two photos captured her interest: one of the swimming pool, and the other showing the ruined church in the aftermath of Allied bombings. Hildenheim had recovered, brought from the brink by fierce determination, its centre rebuilt brick-by-brick, its suburbs extended and modernised, to suit today's busy world.

Back at the Schmieds' Lucy found three letters for her on the kitchen table. Rolf watched inquisitively as she opened them. The first, a card depicting a girl leaping up from a chair at the sight of a mouse.

'What's that? Who's it from?' Rolf asked.

'A card from my parents,' Lucy answered. The other cards were from Marion and from Uncle Peter, with pictures of cats and a dog.

'What does that say?' Rolf pestered.

'Nothing,' Lucy answered evasively. She had told no one that tomorrow was her birthday. However, on the breakfast table the next morning she found pink carnations, two cards in white envelopes, and three packages wrapped in coloured paper.

'*Danke... vielen Dank*!' Lucy said, opening gifts of chocolates, notebook and pens, and a leaf shaped pendant. A round of mini-golf filled the morning, followed by home-baking, and afternoon *Kaffeetrinken*. Birgit's friends, Sigrid, Julia and Helene arrived, followed by Tante Ellen, bearing more chocolates, and a handful of children's reading books.

'These are to help you with your German,' Ellen said.

'Thank you – you're very kind,' Lucy said, her happiness rocketing to new levels.

The conversation over coffee, cakes and English tea was lively and amicable. Speaking *Hochdeutsch*, standard German, Ellen regaled the group with amusing anecdotes from her teaching experiences. Lucy learned that Helene's Dachshund had been hit by a car and that Julia had missed a lot of school due to stress. Sigrid described her three cats, four rabbits and talking parrot. Birgit said her budgie didn't talk, then Lucy told the story of Buddy, and mentioned Marion's pregnancy. 'You'll enjoy being an aunt!' Ellen said. Lucy recorded snatches of conversation and played them back, to everyone's amusement. Birgit invited Lucy back next year and suggested Lucy might want to come on a skiing trip to Switzerland. After tea, everyone went to the garden for photographs. Lucy felt happy in the blue smock and cream-coloured corduroys. She stood in the middle, between Birgit and her brothers. Martin leaned proudly on the handlebars of his new bicycle, and Rolf made funny faces at the camera.

Sadly, it was time to pack. Lucy crammed the extra clothes, books and souvenirs into her case and sat on the lid to close the buckles. In town, she spent the last of her German currency on a quartz crystal brooch in the shape of a number seven.

'Why seven?' Megan asked as the train pulled away from Hildenheim.

Lucy shrugged. 'Why not seven?' she answered. Reflecting on the Hildenheim holiday, Lucy couldn't recall ever having felt so welcome anywhere.

By chance, the return journey wasn't entirely uneventful. In Ostend, it was suspected Lucy's passport had been altered. She was shown the line in question: HEIGHT: 5ft 2$^{1/2}$ inches.

Lucy was adamant nothing had been changed. The young Australian raised an eyebrow, as if to say, you again! Mercifully, the official handed back the document and waved the group on. Later, Lucy recalled how, a year ago, in a moment of idleness, she had penned in the extra half-inch to her height detail, for accuracy's sake, unwittingly committing an offence.

A second glitch occurred on the last leg of the journey. The train stopped, for no apparent reason at a rural station. Everyone was obliged to alight on the deserted platform and await the next train. Two tedious hours passed, with no cafeteria or shop nearby. Bridget Barker shared a pack of orange snaps, and Jill Simpson shared her *Lebkuchen*. Dora whined about a new song topping the charts – "Amazing Grace" – played on bagpipes. Lucy was disappointed when Dora turned her transistor off. Then a train came from the opposite direction, and a few commuters got off. Sadie nudged Lucy, pointing to seated passengers, saying, 'Let's make fun of them!' A few fingers pointed randomly at the stationery coach, accompanied by tired sniggering. Sadie's prank brought brief light relief until the train moved off.

Finally, after another twenty minutes, the promised train arrived – a slow, stopping-train that finally trundled into Westcombe at ten o'clock. The forecourt was filled with cars and irate parents, cursing British Rail.

Not caring a jot, Lucy rushed into her mother's ecstatic embrace.

'Hi Mum! I've loads to tell you!'

'We're so glad you're safe!' Hilda cried.

'Good to have you back, love. Trusting you had a lovely time,' Albert said, stubbing out a cigarette.

On arrival at Edencroft, Hilda offered Lucy a light supper and a mug of tea which Lucy gulped gratefully, whilst relating snippets of her three-week absence.

Opening her bedroom door, Lucy was greeted with an unexpected sight. Gone were the ivy-patterned wallpapers, faded curtains and threadbare carpets. Pink, floral curtains matched new wallpaper and a rose-patterned candlewick bedspread. Pastel pink carpet covered the floor, offering light and space. The room smelt fresh and new and was bathed in the soft glow of a bedside lamp made from an old wine carafe, paintballed from the inside.

'How do you like your little surprise?' Hilda asked.

'It's – fantastic!' Lucy gasped.

'Consider it a birthday present,' Hilda said.

Everywhere was quiet. The absence of clamouring voices and thundering trains left a muffled ringing sound in Lucy's ears. She took a shower and dressed in comfortable cotton pyjamas. She stayed up until after midnight, telling of the many good things about the Schmieds, their friends, and Hildenheim. That night, in the silence of her room, Lucy lay awake, taking stock of recent events, until she fell into a deep and dreamless sleep.

23: INFATUATION

Through a chink in the curtains, reflected sunlight pooled brightly on the rose-patterned wallpaper. The fresh smell of new fabrics filled the room; the familiar feel of heavy bedclothes was a comforting cocoon. Lucy leapt out of bed, pulled back the curtains and surveyed sunlit fields. Almost a month ago, she had left on a bleak day under grey skies, but now the countryside flaunted summer colours. Thrilling with joy, Lucy swooped into the breakfast room, where cereals, milk jug and pot of tea stood waiting. In the garden, Hilda was attending to the hens, Dotty darting in and out of bushes, the lawns a lush and brilliant green, flower beds and bushes bursting with blossoms. Biddlecombe Copse was in full foliage, its monster form crouched on the hillside under cloudless skies. 'It's good to be alive', Lucy whispered, trembling with excitement. After breakfast, she went outside and revelled in the idyll of flowers, animals, and birdsong. Edencroft was still a perfect paradise.

On Monday morning, Lucy walked the straight path to the school entrance, her heart feather-light. Swallows screeched overhead, the branches of the white house's boundary hedge overhung the pathway, scattering a cascade of white petals.

All day, Lucy was swept along on a tide of activity, telling everyone all about her wonderful time in Germany. Mr Hagin was back. He didn't comment on Lucy's improved German. Instead, he warned against relying upon linguistic instinct instead of thorough study. He recommended ordering an extra textbook from Nyehaven's bookstore. Ever-keen to advance Lucy's education, Hilda gladly agreed to buy the book and placed an order by telephone. On May Day bank holiday, Lucy took the train Nyehaven to collect it. She met with Jodie on the High Street.

'I like your outfit,' Jodie said.

'German trousers and a jacket I altered myself,' Lucy answered.

Lucy breezed into the bookshop.

'Has my book arrived yet, *Deutsche Sprache und Grammatik?*'

The young man at the till looked puzzled.

'It's German.'

'One moment, please... here we are, Mrs Wylie.'

Lucy's ego rocketed, then she remembered her mother had placed the order.

'You're doing well with German,' Jodie said, as they left the shop.

'You're good at science,' Lucy said.

'Biology is my best subject!' Jodie chortled saucily, the innuendo lost on Lucy. 'Come on, let's buy records!'

Lucy bought three singles reminiscent of recent weeks: Nilsson's "Without You", Colin Blunstone's "Say You Don't Mind", and Les Crane's take on the "Desiderata" poem – haunting tunes, thoughtful lyrics, a mantra for inner peace and contentment. On the train home, Lucy inspected the book. It's cloth-bound, embossed cover, fresh smell of ink on deckle-edged paper, and the black-on-white font screamed quality. Too distracted to read, Lucy allowed the train's rhythmic beat lull her into comfortable euphoria.

As summer approached, Lucy juggled her jobs at Woolworth's and Combe Farm with study, dog walks, beach trips, and meeting with Alison or Jodie. The new textbook was a great asset, but Lucy's attention to other school subjects was minimal, Maths still a major stumbling-block. Latin lessons were ludicrously lax. Miss Hipp routinely shared sweets, lent tuck-shop money, and allowed students to do as they pleased: eat, sleep, read the newspaper, play cards, or listen to the radio. Only a studious few paid attention. Lucy followed the crowd and fell hopelessly behind. On the eve of study leave, she strolled into class five minutes late, eating crisps.

'Wanna crisp, Longjohn?' she asked, offering Arthur the open bag, ignoring Miss Hipp, who was teaching Arthur, Shirley, Janet, and Jonathan, in the front row.

'No!' Arthur squeaked, ducking behind his briefcase.

Lucy slouched to the back and sat beside Alison.

'German's much easier than Latin,' Lucy sighed.

'That model looks ridiculous,' Alison said, reading *Petticoat* magazine. 'I've auburn hair, too, but would never wear those colours.'

'We can't visit ancient Rome to experience the language properly,' Lucy said.

'Unless you're a time-traveller,' Jodie interrupted.

'Or build a time machine?' Lucy said.

'You say weird things, sometimes,' Alison said.

'Yeah, I'd like to fast-forward a month, when exams are over and the summer fun starts,' Jodie winked.

Against advice, many students misused study leave. Lucy frittered away the weeks on fun, spending every fine day at the beach. On the morning of the Latin literature exam, she sat at the breakfast table, reading about Roman soldiers linking shields to protect themselves from advancing enemies. *That's practically all I know*, she sighed, putting the book away.

At ten to nine, students gathered outside the hall. Lucy stared vacantly at the herringbone pattern on the tiled floor. Alison stood tight-lipped and nervous. They briefly exchanged glances.

'Good luck, Lucy,' Alison whispered.

'You too.'

'What we don't know now, we'll never know,' Shirley mumbled apprehensively.

The doors opened. Students took their places in subdued silence. The invigilating teacher handed out papers, chalked the finishing time on a portable blackboard and said, 'You may now begin.'

A hushed rustling like summer rain filled empty time and space. Lucy was pleased to find an opportunity to write about the Roman soldiers' shield-linking stratagem. What little else she wrote was sheer guesswork. Time dragged painfully until the wall clock struck noon.

'Well, that was only absolutely awful!' hooted Joanna, as students left the hall. Alison had disappeared, clearly wishing to avoid a post-mortem on the paper.

'What's the next exam?' Lucy asked Jodie.

'Dunno – Maths, I think.'

'When?'

'Thursday afternoon.'

On Thursday morning, Lucy sat home alone in the breakfast room, knitting a cable-stitch mini-jumper, listening to *Cousin Norman* on the radio. The song evoked a simple, rural way of life, as far removed from exam angst as east is from west. *If only maths were as simple as knitting!*

Suddenly the phone rang. A cultured, female voice asked, 'May I speak to Lucy Wylie?'

This was most mysterious. Lucy practically never received phone calls.

'The school secretary, here. I'm phoning to ask why you're not at your maths exam.'

Lucy's jaw dropped. *A good thing Mum and Dad* are out, she thought.

'B-but it's not till this afternoon,' Lucy stammered. 'Jodie Maitland told me it was this afternoon, and –' Lucy realised she may have landed Jodie into trouble.

'No, it's this morning. Jodie had also been contacted and is on her way. You were both obviously mistaken. It's not too late for you to sit the exam if you come now. You'll be given the allocated time for the paper, from the moment you start.'

'I'll be there in half an hour,' Lucy said.

Arriving at the hall, Lucy was ushered to an empty desk. She opened the question booklet, revealing meaningless numbers, shapes and symbols. She made a start. Minutes later, Jodie arrived and sat in front. Beyond, a sea of concentrating candidates, heads bowed intently writing. Some slouched, twirling their pencils distractedly. The untimely demise of Mr Jenkins and the subsequent stream of ineffectual temporary teachers had left its mark.

When the others were dismissed, Lucy pretended to write, shielding her face. The hall emptied quickly, leaving crooked lines of tables and chairs, the floor dotted with screwed up paper and pink blotting-paper. Forty minutes later, Lucy left the exam room alone and deflated. Jodie would finish later. Lucy left quickly, not wishing to discuss what happened.

The German paper was easy. The only unfamiliar word was *gerettet*, which Lucy discovered afterwards meant rescued, making sense, in the context of shipwreck and lifeboats. In the speaking test, Lucy spoke about *Das Deutsche Familienleben* – German family life, based on recent experience. The last exam was English Literature: two questions on Shakespeare's *Julius Caesar*. Lucy read the questions carefully and found plenty to write.

The exam over, students swarmed out on a tide of excitement, bursting with gossip.

'Guess what!' Joanna exclaimed. 'Miss Forbes is married!'

'You're kidding! She's easily the wrong side of forty, and definitely not good looking,' sneered Abigail. 'Who on earth would want to marry her?'

The air was buzzing with questions.

'When's the wedding?'

'What's his name? Do we know him?'

'He must be strong-willed to marry HER!'

'Maybe she'll be less unbearable from now on,' Lucy added.

Miss Forbes isn't unbearable,' Alison argued. 'I think she's really nice.'

'EXAMS ARE OVER!' Jodie yelled ecstatically as the group dispersed home.

Lessons resumed on Monday, in a heady atmosphere of high summer. Lucy pushed boundaries, flouting regulations. High hemlines, shortened ties and garish colours were the latest trend. Lucy wore orange tights and a purple skirt, the waist rolled up, revealing ten inches of thigh. During lunch hour, students wandered into town, mingling with tourists. Miss Hawksworth made herself scarce, lamenting the fallacy of rules impossible to enforce. In Miss Forbes's absence, the student teacher allowed cross-country running. Taking her bag with her, Lucy invited Alison and Jodie to tea, staying at home afterwards. No questions were asked.

Tuesday's peccadillo was a different matter. Miss Menzies was in a meeting, and Lucy and Alison absconded from the unsupervised English class. However, a prefect came to check the register. Inevitably, Miss Menzies took Lucy and Alison aside, demanding an explanation for their absence.

'We found it too noisy,' Lucy explained. 'We couldn't concentrate.'

'We did the work,' Alison added defensively.

'But you were supposed to be in the classroom, so where were you?'

'The foyer,' Lucy answered, convincing herself since they had walked through the foyer on their way out, that was the truth.

'Very well,' Miss Menzies said. 'But I only have your word for that.'

'That was close,' Alison said afterwards. 'Thanks for getting us out of trouble.'

'It's nothing,' Lucy replied.

Birgit's visit edged closer. Lucy's glowing reports of the Schmied household prompted Hilda to buy new toilet and bath mats, a shower curtain, and an assortment of kitchen gadgets. She recruited Lucy to help spring-clean the spare room and wax the furniture and floor with lavender-scented polish.

'It's so important for the room to smell nice,' Hilda said. 'I would hate to think of Birgit coming here and going back to tell her family that English houses are damp.'

The German students' arrival coincided with a resplendent sunset over Westcombe Bay. Lucy stood with the others on the platform, while Albert waited in the car. Hilda was at home preparing dinner and ensuring the house was shipshape. The train was on time, and the German guests spilt out of the shabby carriage. Birgit looked pale and drawn, her face matching her army-green jacket. Like Lucy, months before, she'd clearly also had a bad journey.

'*Hallo, Birgit! Wie geht's?* You look tired, how was the trip?'

Birgit shook her head and forced a smile. 'Not good journey, boat bad.'

'But that was hours ago! Come, let's go home and I'll make English tea.'

By the time they reached Edencroft it was almost dark. Hilda offered the choice of beef casserole or cold meats and salad. Birgit ate daintily from the cold fare. Slurping her third cup of tea, she declared, 'Za tea ist goot venn you are sirsty!'

Lucy looked at her mother and grinned.

In the morning, Lucy knocked on the spare room door.

'Don't wake her,' Hilda said. 'She'll need to sleep in after travelling.'

Lucy went to school alone, wearing no tie, the purple mini-skirt, shocking-pink tights and white leather clogs. It was the penultimate day of term. At lunchtime, she decided against running home to greet Birgit, as the next lesson was English. Arriving home at four, Lucy found Birgit in the breakfast room, looking refreshed and eating corn flakes. A quiet evening was spent chatting, mostly in German.

The next day was a scorcher – blue skies and sizzling sunshine. Lucy endured school, expecting Birgit to comment on the noise and scruffiness, but Birgit kept smiling, shadowing Lucy like a faithful dog. A week of sun, sea, and sightseeing kept Lucy and Birgit happy until the Hildenheim group's three-day trip to London. Their exchange partners weren't included, but Lucy wasn't disappointed. She resumed her holiday jobs, fewer sessions of strawberry-picking due to pollen levels. Most days were at Woolworth's and the beach. Lucy's favourite spot by the pier was thronged with sun-worshippers. Alison was often there, with Swedish friend Anneke, who was helping at the restaurant, and two bronzed hotel workers – Juan from Madrid, and Roland from Paris. In their presence, Lucy was conscious of her pink, freckled skin, thickening thighs and fat-padded waistline. She stretched out, hiding beneath an open magazine.

'Alison, you are nice girl, very slim – very beautiful,' Juan said.

Alison didn't answer.

'You, er – like sun, it is warm, yes?'

'Yes, I love summer,' Alison said sleepily.

'It is like Spain. Very hot.'

A brief pause.

'You have lovely eyes, Alison, like doves...'

'Thank you.'

'You want to come out with me tonight?'

'No thanks, I'm busy.'

Moments later, Lucy sensed someone sidle up beside her.

'Lucy?' Juan asked.

Lucy put down the magazine and sat up.

'Yes?'

'Lucy, you are nice girl –'

'No, thank you,' Lucy cut Juan short, 'I'm busy tonight, too.'

Juan backed away.

Lucy seethed with indignation. *Of all the nerve! He's like a dirty old dog sniffing after bitches!*

It had been a while since Lucy had thought about boyfriends. Clive had been a friend, Nigel an acquaintance, and Steve a mere nuisance. These boys, however, these men were different. Lucy tried not to stare, suppressing a strange wish to draw closer. *Stuff and nonsense!* Thoughts of Marion in her poky little suburban house, waiting for her baby to be born, and her boring husband to come home, drink beer and gawp at the television were a powerful deterrent. Lucy's mind still wandered. *Marion's good looking, but not academic. Alison has brains AND good looks...* Lucy hid behind her magazine. Suddenly, Alison nudged her.

'Fancy an ice cream? We're all going to have one.'

'Yes please,' Lucy answered. Then she remembered her waistline, instantly regretting the decision.

'How's your German pen-friend getting on?' Alison asked.

'Fine. They're all in London for a few days, and we've already –'

Lucy stopped mid-sentence. Alison seemed more interested in a party of surfers at the water's edge, and then Juan returned with the choc ices.

The next day, Lucy returned to the same place. Juan and Roland were there again, but Alison and Anneke weren't. Lucy spread out her towel and settled down to read. Minutes later, Roland moved closer.

'You, uh – reading a French magazine?' he enquired. His voice had an almost musical quality.

'Yes, I study French at school,' Lucy answered.

'*Paris Match*, ah, *oui*! it is an eenteresting magazine. Uh, you like ice cream?' Anticipation soared in Lucy's breast like a rising lark.

'Yes, please,' she answered, tempted to start speaking French but lacking the nerve. Besides, Roland's command of English was good.

Roland bought two vanilla cornets with chocolate sprinkles. They talked. Lucy learned Roland's full name was Roland Henri Jacques Monet, wasn't related to the famous artist, was ten years her senior, lived in a flat in Paris, had a sister who was married to an architect, and had spent several years on Africa's Ivory Coast. Lucy spoke of Edencroft and visits to Germany and France, slipping in a few phrases in French, which seemed to impress.

Suddenly, she remembered Birgit was due back around tea time. She gave a hurried explanation, wished Roland a hasty *au revoir* and left the beach.

Early next morning, Birgit sipped her tea in the usual noisy way, which Lucy now found irritating. Outside, grey clouds gathered, and the trees of Biddlecombe Copse tossed and bobbed in the breeze.

'Shall we go to the beach this afternoon?' Lucy suggested brightly. Birgit shook her head.

'Venn it is varm,' she said thickly.

Birgit's English was appalling. 'I think the beach is a good plan for today. We'll go there after lunch,' Lucy persisted. 'Cool weather means a less busy beach.'

'But it is too cold for shvimming.'

Lucy smouldered. 'You're used to everything being indoors and heated.'

Albert snorted. Birgit ate her corn flakes in silence.

'We'll go for lunch instead,' Hilda said cheerily. 'I've booked a table at the Bolingbroke Country Hotel.'

'Okay,' Lucy agreed. Roland probably wouldn't be at the beach anyway.

The Bolingbroke Hotel was a low, turreted mansion overlooking Westcombe Bay, set in neatly landscaped grounds. The restaurant was pleasantly quiet. Rows of neatly-laid tables with white linen cloths, folded napkins, floral sprays, and gleaming cutlery filled the opulent dining-room. Hilda gave an approving smile. Two waiters hovered in a doorway, one short and stocky, the other tall, with black sideburns and a Clark Gable moustache. Both looked distinctly Mediterranean. Lucy's heart fluttered.

The waiters swaggered up, gesturing their guests to a table by the window. Two leather-bound menus were casually tossed onto the table. Hilda raised an eyebrow. Lucy couldn't imagine Juan or Roland behaving like this at work.

'Four roast beef, please,' Hilda said, 'and two lagers and two lemonades.'

The tall waiter scribbled on a note pad and put the pencil behind his ear.

The drinks arrived ten minutes later, but after half an hour there was still no food.

'I don't rate the service here,' Hilda grumbled. Albert smoked, Lucy drummed her fingers on the table, and Birgit looked bored.

Finally, the meal appeared. The waiters approached, bearing trays of food to the table with exaggerated panache.

'*Dick und Doof!* Lucy whispered, nudging Birgit.

The girls sniggered.

'What's funny?' Hilda asked.

'Laurel and Hardy – Dick is fat and Doof is daft,' Lucy translated, but Hilda wasn't amused. Four plates of parsimonious portions of leathery-looking roast beef and insipid Yorkshire pudding were set before the hungry guests. Dick waltzed off, returning a minute later, assiduously ferrying a gravy-boat, then proceeded to pour horseradish sauce over Hilda's roast beef.

'STOP!' Hilda protested, but it was too late. Her meagre portion of meat was swamped in sauce.

The little man beetled back to the kitchen door.

'Maybe it's Candid Camera?' Lucy suggested.

'If it is, it's not funny,' Hilda smouldered.

The food was lukewarm and barely edible. Birgit and Lucy exchanged glances and smirked, quietly enjoying the entertainment.

'We won't bother with dessert,' Hilda declared caustically, trying to think of ways to compensate for such a dreadful gastronomic outing. 'We'll make a tea at home, and our own cake, fruit and ice cream.'

'Who needs the Bolingbroke when we have Edencroft?' Lucy smirked.

Arriving home, Hilda handed Lucy the key. 'Lucy, let the dog out, and put the kettle on.'

'Okay, Mum.'

Lucy ran up the path, burst into the porch, and was immediately greeted by the unsavoury sight and smell of regurgitated remains of a fresh kill. The window ledge was strewn with fur and entrails, and in the corner by the geranium pot sat Lurcio, surveying his surroundings with feline complacency. There was no other door into the house. Lucy thought quickly.

She dashed down the slope, calling, 'you gave me the shed key, Mum!'

Hilda looked puzzled. 'Surely I gave you the right key?'

'I'll explain later. Come, Birgit, we'll collect eggs,' Lucy panted, practically dragging Birgit down the garden. Minutes later, they were at the porch door with a basket of seven eggs.

'Be careful not to slip! Mum's just washed the floor,' Lucy warned, pleased to note all was shipshape.

The next day, Lucy introduced Birgit to her beach friends. Roland bought ice creams, and they all talked and swam for two blissful hours. Lucy invited Roland home for the following afternoon, but she had yet to tell her parents. Lucy remembered Marion being reprimanded for bringing home boyfriends unannounced, but that had been late at night, so Lucy didn't envisage a problem.

She broached the subject over supper. 'By the way, Mum, a French student we met at the beach might call by tomorrow. He's a keen cyclist and will be passing by on his bike.'

'All right,' Hilda said. 'We can have tea on the lawn.'

'Thanks, Mum,' Lucy replied, feeling an irrepressible thrill.

Roland came as promised. Hilda served tea, sandwiches and cakes. Lucy, Roland and Birgit lounged on deckchairs and chatted. Roland said he worked long hours in two different hotels and stayed in a tiny, one-man tent on a local campsite. Lucy kept looking at him. Even after he left, she felt light-headed. She snipped a few rambling roses from the patio trellis, their delicate perfume blending with the soothing cooing of doves. She placed the flowers in a vase, in the wicker basket at her bedside. Outwardly serene, she felt inwardly stirred and vibrant. In the small hours she awoke for no apparent reason, her chest tight in the pollen-laden night.

The next day, Roland was back. He was charming, witty and good-humoured. Lucy wore her favourite white dress with the v-neck and red brocade border. She had eyes only for Roland. Albert and Hilda enjoyed his congenial manner, and welcomed him back, several more times, each visit a taste of paradise. The weather stayed fine; refreshments were served *al fresco*, in the sheltered sun-trap between Marmie's grave and the butterfly-festooned buddleia. Roland took photos with his sophisticated camera, discussing with Albert the benefits of a zoom lens, while Birgit snapped shots with her Kodak Instamatic, and Hilda snapped happily with her Box Brownie. Lucy stared at Roland, spellbound by his dancing, dark eyes and the musical quality of his lilting voice.

'Are you having thees smelling all za time?' Roland inquired politely, on the day Mr Biddlecombe spread manure in the next field.

'Only when farmers are muck-spreading and the wind is in the wrong direction,' Albert said.

Roland helped himself to more fruit cake and cheese.

'At least it hasn't put you off your food,' Hilda remarked, looking puzzled at Roland's choice of fare. 'Cake with cheese?'

'*Ah, oui!* Yes, it is what we do in France.'

Roland had many good things to say about Edencroft. He showered compliments like confetti, praising the house and garden, the views, Albert's music, Hilda's cooking, and all the animals. He bent down to Dotty and beckoned her to come and take a biscuit from his mouth – an action Lucy found particularly endearing.

On a group trip to Salton on the last day of Birgit's stay, Lucy felt strangely restless. In a shop, she picked up a birthday card depicting two Dalmatians and the caption "To My Husband With Love".

'You should buy that for your French boyfriend,' Megan said in a small voice.

Lucy glowed inside. She stared at the card for a moment, then put it back on the rack.

'Birgit's a nice girl,' Hilda said the next day, after the Hildenheim group had left.

Lucy nodded. 'She's a good friend.'

Lucy felt exhausted from repeatedly awakening at night, with the same sense of excitement and shortness of breath. Day and night Roland occupied her thoughts. On Sunday, Lucy sat looking out at the misty hills, listening to a cassette recording of Danyel Gerard's "Butterfly", over and over again. August was almost over, time passing too quickly. She bought two pairs of novelty sunglasses with coloured lenses: the yellow pair made the world seem brighter and faster, while the pink pair transformed everything into an extravaganza of joy. *Who needs drugs?* Lucy asked herself, thinking of Jane Haslett, who had fallen into bad company and descended into cocaine addiction. Jane was the last person Lucy would have imagined falling so hard.

Finding Roland at the usual spot, Lucy's heart leapt.

'You want ice cream?' Roland said, his chiselled face smiling perfection.

'Please,' Lucy nodded.

The usual vendor wasn't there, so they walked to the nearest kiosk. Strolling along the promenade hand-in-hand with Roland, eating ice cream, surveying the world through rose-tinted lenses was cotton-candy perfection – a moment Lucy wanted never to end.

Life went on. Hilda arranged a weekend trip to Marion and Paul's before the birth of her first grandchild. On the day before, a plain, brown envelope came for Lucy.

'I got Grade One in German!' Lucy exclaimed, running to tell her mother.

'That's wonderful, dear. I knew you'd do well,' Hilda smiled.

'And a good grade for English literature. I didn't manage Latin and maths, but I will work hard for the resit.'

'Pity about maths. As you say, you'll just have to work at it.'

Fortunately, Hilda was too preoccupied with the imminent prospect of becoming a grandmother to be angry.

At the Clements' home, Hilda did the shopping, cooking and cleaning, and Lucy helped with ironing and the dishes. Tetchy and bored, Marion went for walks, hoping exercise might trigger labour, but nothing happened. Lucy watched her sister lumbering like a laden mule, her long cardigan trailing over her enormous bump. *Will I ever be pregnant?* She wondered. To Hilda's disappointment, the weekend passed, with no baby.

On Monday, Roland wasn't at the beach. Lucy went to the campsite and found a silvery-grey racing bicycle chained to a fence, beside a tiny, one-man tent. Fitting lyrics floated from a nearby caravanette. "I've got a silver machine... I've got a silver machine..." Lucy mused, staring at the bicycle, waiting. Eventually she gave up and went home.

That evening, the doorbell rang. Lucy raced to the door. There stood Roland, perfection in person.

'Come in!' Lucy breathed. Roland was charming as ever, complimenting Hilda on her home baking. After tea, they walked in the garden, speaking a mixture of English and French. In her tiredness, Lucy muddled French and German, but Roland didn't seem to notice. He was busy taking photos of Lucy with the cats and the dog. Lucy recorded snatches of conversation with the cassette-player, preserving the memory of Roland's voice after he had gone.

In humid nights, Lucy slept fitfully, waking tight-chested and breathless. Hilda sent Lucy to the bumbling old doctor in High Lea. Lucy was prescribed pink pills, which had no effect, and after four days, she threw them away, wondering if they contained any medication at all. On the last Sunday of the holidays, mist covered the hills, obscuring the view of Appledore Down. Lucy had made a special effort to look nice, wearing her favourite white dress, leather clogs, and jewellery – the blue bead necklace, number seven brooch, and the silver bells ring. When the doorbell rang, Lucy sprang up from her sewing and ran to greet Roland.

'Eet is nearly time for holidays to feenish,' Roland said over tea. 'Also, za weather is not good.'

'It was raining yesterday,' agreed Hilda.

'I was boring in my tent,' Roland answered.

'The tent must have got wet inside, if you made a hole in it!' laughed Albert.

'Deed I say something wrong?' Roland asked.

'In English, the word boring can mean making a hole in something. It doesn't work like s'ennuyer in French. You were bored, not boring. Boring can also mean ennuyeux- boring – which you are not,' Lucy explained.

'Ah- oui!' Roland responded, 'I understand.'

'Let's go for a drive,' Hilda said. 'That won't be boring.'

Lucy and Roland sat together on the back seat. Roland's hand grasped Lucy's, filling her with irrepressible thrill. At a picture-postcard village with quaint, crooked cottages and ducks and chickens roaming free, Lucy walked hand-in-hand with Roland, beside a chuckling stream.

'Why number seven?' Roland asked, noticing the brooch.

'Why not?' Lucy answered.

Roland said nothing else. Perhaps he doesn't find me attractive? Lucy wondered.

Lucy's parents watched from a distance. Then Hilda shook her head and sighed. 'She's smitten with him, I can tell. But it won't last. The sooner she realises that the better, or she'll get hurt.'

Albert cleared his throat. 'Just like those holiday boyfriends, Marion used to pick up. Five-minute wonders, the lot of 'em.'

At the end of his stay, Roland came with rucksack and panniers packed for the journey to London, on the last train. Hilda laid a lavish spread, and Roland ate heartily, but Lucy had little appetite. Time flowed like sand in an hour-glass.

'Where will you stay tonight?' Hilda asked.

'In za youth hostel, in London,' Roland replied. 'Tomorrow, I return to Paris.'

'Do you have a job?'

'Not yet. I will look.'

Hilda frowned. Lucy prodded her salad and said nothing.

Darkness fell. There were no lights on Roland's bike. Albert agreed to transport Roland and his belongings to the station, the bicycle in the hatchback, Roland sharing the back seat with the protruding bicycle wheel. Lucy sat in the front, her heart like stone.

The parting was short.

'You will write?' Lucy asked.

'Yes, I will write you,' Roland replied, squeezing Lucy's hand. Lucy was afraid to ask if he would return next year. As Roland wheeled his laden bicycle through the station gates, Lucy wondered if she would ever see him again.

On the way home, Lucy's mind was blank. Deep inside, she felt empty and cold, as if a fire had gone out. And then, in the blackness of High Lea Down, a dark shape emerged, a creature crouched at the roadside, eyes gleaming in the headlights.

'Stop!' Lucy shouted, 'I saw an animal – a dog – I think it's hurt!'

The car stopped. Lucy and Albert got out. A black dog was cowering on the grass verge. Together, they carefully lifted the whimpering bundle into the back of the car. The dog snarled with pain but didn't bite. Lucy's clothes were soiled with mud and blood. She didn't care. Albert drove to Westcombe police station, where he was told the dog would be looked after and every effort made to trace its owner.

The incident provided temporary distraction, but the outcome wasn't a happy one. A week later, an officer phoned to say nobody had claimed the dog and asked if the Wylies would like it. But Hilda was adamant she didn't want any more pets, so the dog was destroyed.

24: LOVE AND MARRIAGE

School resumed. Homework was plentiful, but it was fun being a sixth former. Work was more interesting, subjects reduced to favourites, lessons rarely disrupted by bad behaviour. Also, teachers treated students like human beings.

'It seems ages since our summer friends were here,' Alison said over lunch, 'but Roland said he might come back next year.'

Lucy's heart did a somersault. Roland hadn't told her he was coming back. Maybe he assumed Lucy already knew?

'He's really sweet,' Alison continued, picking daintily at her fish finger. 'He asked me out, but I turned him down.'

Lucy's fragile hope took a sharp dip. Ten days had passed since Roland had left. Lucy wondered if she should write to him first. *The man should do the chasing – never the woman*, her mother always said. Lucy ached for Roland, to hear his soft voice, gaze upon his dark features, and feel the gentle, reassuring grasp of his hand. Noticing Lucy's pained expression, Alison shrugged and turned away.

That evening, Lucy rested her elbows on her homework, staring dreamily out of the window. Hilda read her like a book.

'Roland is a charming chap, good-looking, full of fun, and I see why you're attracted to him. But I'm afraid to say he's a fortune-seeker. He's ten years your senior and still without a proper job.'

Lucy looked at the floor.

'You must appreciate the difference between true love and infatuation,' Hilda added weightedly.

'Yes, I suppose so,' Lucy sighed.

She went into the garden and stood at the top of the slope, admiring the sunset over Appledore Down. The wide, azure sky ablaze with trailing purple clouds reminded Lucy of Hironville, a memory fading into the annals of childhood. But memories of Roland were fresh in her mind, festering like unhealed wounds. The sky dimmed, resplendent colours blending with subtle pinks, purples and blues. In the canopy above, early stars twinkled. It was too beautiful a moment to miss: Lucy ran inside for the Box Brownie and captured the scene.

Suddenly, the telephone bell shrilled, shattering the evening calm. Lucy almost dropped the camera. Was this the long-awaited call?

Hilda got to the phone first.

'Paul? How is she? She – what? She's had it?' Hilda sounded frantic.

Lucy strained to listen, but along a hundred miles of cable Paul's voice buzzed like a trapped bumblebee.

'A girl! Oh, How lovely! Sandra, isn't it?'

'Samantha? You're going to call her Samantha?'

Samantha Clements. The name had a good ring to it, Lucy thought.

Hilda was ecstatic. 'Marion's labour was induced – a traumatic experience, by all accounts. Paul was present at the birth, and he didn't faint!'

'I'm an aunt!' Lucy exclaimed, feeling suddenly taller, older, and more grown up. The youngest of her generation, Lucy had in all her sixteen years no close contact with babies. Never having held one, she regarded them as noisy, smelly, squirming bundles over which people constantly fussed. But Samantha was family – a real person, barely an hour old. Lucy couldn't wait to meet her.

A Saturday trip to London was arranged. Lucy cancelled her shift at Woolworth's. During the entire journey, Hilda chirped and clucked, until London's concrete flyovers and suburban sprawl were in view.

'Our little granddaughter has been born into a world of ugly monstrosities such as this! Whatever will she make of it all?' Hilda said.

Soon, surrounded by baby paraphernalia in the Clements' tiny living-room, Lucy and her parents sat sipping mugs of tea.

'Can we open a window?' Lucy asked, feeling stifled.

Marion sounded anxious. 'Shhh!' Don't wake the baby! The window's closed, so she doesn't catch cold.'

A quiet stirring from the carrycot in the corner spring-loaded Marion to action. Lucy watched her sister lift a swaddled bundle and retreat upstairs. A while later, Marion returned and placed her daughter on Hilda's lap. The baby's face was beetroot red, puckered and wrinkled, like a puppy's.

'Isn't she lovely?' Hilda crooned. 'Lucy, come and meet your niece.'

Lucy approached cautiously and placed her little finger in the infant's diminutive hand.

'She's tiny,' Lucy said.

'Yes,' replied Hilda. 'You were that small, once. This baby is the start of a new generation, the first of many grandchildren, God willing.'

Lucy looked unenviously at the pram, carrycot, changing-mat, and bags of creams and nappies occupying most of the room. There was no room to set up the dining-table, so lunch was served on trays, everyone seated on the three-piece suite. Like Marion and Paul, Lucy was happy to use just a fork, spearing chips, sausage and beans, in a manner Hilda always described as slovenly and American. Refusing to use just a fork, the grandparents struggled with knife and fork, beans in sauce slopping off their plates. A piece of sausage jumped onto the carpet.

'Bother!' Hilda growled quietly.

During dessert, a piercing cry like a worried cat came from the corner of the room. Marion jumped up and took the baby upstairs for a breastfeed – a notion Lucy found distasteful. She'd assumed all modern babies were bottle-fed. On an after-dinner perambulation in the park, Albert took photos of each adult holding the swaddled infant. Lucy worried about making the baby cry, or worse still, dropping her. She pushed the pram instead, feeling embarrassed in her tight, red T-shirt with the ironed-on souvenir badge from Paris. She hoped nobody would think she was a teenage mother.

On the return journey, Hilda remained jubilant, but Lucy was subdued.

'Do you think I'll ever get married and have children?' she asked.

'No doubt you will one day,' Hilda said. 'But don't be in a hurry. You've plenty of time yet, and with your prospects, your future looks rosy.'

Unconvinced, Lucy didn't answer. Days passed, and still no word from Roland. Term had begun well, school now practically a pleasure. Perks for sixth formers included the use of a comfortable common room-cum-library during break times and free lessons. Miss Menzies was much less terrifying, small classes an advantage. Prescribed texts were Jane Austen's *Sense and Sensibility*, Shakespeare's *A Winter's Tale*, and the *Poetic Works of William Wordsworth*, and Lucy read them all with interest.

A choice of minor options was on offer. Lucy, Alison and two others signed up for two forty-minute Spanish lessons a week, taught by Mr Ross – a pleasure, with no pressure of exams. Lucy and Alison made Bristol University their goal for studying Modern Languages – a reputable university relatively close to home. However, entry requirements included O-levels in Maths and Latin. After three terms of total slacking in Latin, Lucy, Alison, and a dozen others, had received the bottom grade. Undaunted, Lucy decided to speak to Mr Kingsley, requesting a resit. After assembly, she boldly approached the rostrum, where Mr Kingsley presided like a venerable eagle. Having gained an audience with the Headmaster once before on important business, Lucy wasn't afraid. Alison stood beside her, trembling.

'Sir,' Lucy began, 'Alison and I know our results were poor, because we didn't work hard, but we promise to try hard at the resit, to get into a good university.'

'That's a tall order,' Mr Kingsley said in a low voice.

Alison suppressed a nervous smirk.

'We will work, honestly, Sir, we'll make every effort to catch up,' Lucy pleaded.

'I cannot guarantee that,' Mr Kingsley intoned.

The lesson bell rang, stalling the conversation.

'You may approach Miss Hipp with your request,' Mr Kingsley continued, 'and arrange lessons with her. Depending on your progress and level of commitment, you may or may not be entered for the examination.'

'Thanks, Lucy,' Alison said afterwards. 'That was very brave of you!'

First lesson was games. In the changing rooms, it was obvious marriage had done nothing to mellow flame-haired Miss Forbes, now Mrs Gunning. More dragonish than ever, she snarled commands and remonstrated with reprobates. Lucy cowered behind Alison and Sadie, hoping not to be noticed.

'She's sure gunning for us!' Sadie scoffed.

'I wonder what's got into her?' Shirley said innocently.

'Try looking at her waistline, nitwit!' Rosemary quipped, sniggering.

'EXPLAIN YOURSELF, RICHARDSON!' Mrs Gunning bellowed.

'Whoa! Surnames! She is having a bad day,' Jodie said.

'Ahem – just a sore throat and a tickly cough, Miss – I mean – Mrs Gunning,' Rosemary explained unconvincingly.

'An hour's hockey out in the fresh air will put that right!' Mrs Gunning growled.

As team captain, Alison led the group out into the chill morning air, amid more giggling, and pointing to the games mistress's expanding girth. Today, the short-sighted and overweight girls were picked last; Lucy was one of the first. Mrs Gunning had appointed Alison as this year's hockey captain, replacing Jane Haslett. Lucy relaxed, knowing she wouldn't be on the receiving end of Jane's sharp tongue. Today's game was brisk and evenly balanced, Alison's team defeating their opponents three goals to nil. As goalkeeper, Lucy stopped Joanna's side scoring any goals.

'You played well today,' Alison said, 'Would you like to be a reserve on the team?'

Lucy's self-esteem soared. 'I'd love to,' she answered.

'Good! because we're looking for a replacement goalie next Tuesday, against Nyehaven High.'

This year, Lucy sailed through the seasonal decline with relative ease. South-westerly gales systematically stripped the trees of Biddlecombe Copse, leaving its skeletal monster shape clinging to the horizon of Edencroft's south-facing view. Log fires were lit, summer slipped into the past, leaving photographs, cassette recordings and memories, but still no word from Roland. Lucy looked nostalgically at Roland's picture, his casual stance, sun-tanned visage, and soft, caring eyes. On Monday afternoon, she came home to find a postcard of the Eiffel Tower on her bed. Lucy's legs weakened. Her heart thumped, she could scarcely draw breath.

On the back of the card was a short message:

'Hallo Lucy,

Greetings from Paris- it is cold and raining here·
I am hoping you are well· I am looking for work· I
like to think of my holidays· Perhaps I will see you
again· In Edencroft I was in easy circumstances·
Regards, Roland·

p·s· Greetings to your parents·

Lucy regretted that Roland had neither begun his message with Dear nor signed off with love. Regards sounded empty and formal. Lucy showed the card to her mother.

"Greetings to your parents." Hilda sniffed. 'I don't think much of that. Nor the expression easy circumstances. It's you he should fall in love with, not us or this place.'

Lucy treasured the card with the words, perhaps I will see you again? Along with the photographs and cassette recordings. She clung to hope, quietly identifying with Marianne Dashwood – *Sense and Sensibility's* star-struck teenager, haplessly infatuated with a cad.

Lucy turned her attention to other matters. Never having played on a school team before, she was nervous about the hockey match. At the start of the game, Alison handed Lucy one of the best hockey sticks and said,

'Go for it, Lucy! You can do this.'

On the sunlit field, Lucy found little to do at first, as the ball was mostly at the other end of the pitch, as yet no goals scored. Minutes into the second half, action picked up at Lucy's end of the pitch. She stopped several balls, allowing one in by a whisker, then stopped two more – the end result: One-nil to Nyehaven. Lucy felt a little guilty but was reassured by Alison, Sadie, and Bridget Barker that she did well, as the other team was notoriously difficult to beat.

Arriving home, Lucy found another postcard – of a seafront hotel and a sandy beach. Cousin Sarah was working as a hotel waitress in Barcelona. Lucy was impressed and a little envious. *If only I could be like Sarah*, she thought wistfully; *she is so outgoing, so independent, so strong.* Socially, Lucy was better accepted than ever. Her essay on comparing and contrasting the Dashwood sisters earned a high mark from Miss Menzies, and her essay was read out to the class. Lucy left the lesson in a daze, and stumbled on the stairs, dropping her briefcase, feeling embarrassed, but nobody mocked her.

Autumn morphed into winter. On frosty nights, the silence of the bleak hillsides was rent by the strident bark of foxes. Lucy buried herself in her books. She wasn't needed again as a reserve goalie, but hockey was still fun, and Alison still a friend. Latin coaching began, and with no class clowns to distract, Miss Hipp proved a competent teacher, confident her two candidates – the only entrants for the resit – would do well. As study buddies, Lucy and Alison made good progress. They chanted cassette recordings of *Caesar's Gallic War, Book V*, and Virgil's *The Story of Pallas* – an amusing and effective memory tool. In November, they sat the exam with confidence and calm.

In the run-up to Christmas, Lucy worked extra shifts at Woolworth's, earning extra cash for Christmas presents. She rolled ten pound-notes into a tube, gift-wrapped it, and hung on the Christmas tree, for Marion to buy Sammy's high chair in the January sales. Domestic bliss reigned at Edencroft for two whole days, but on Boxing Day, the wind changed, and storm clouds gathered – literally and figuratively. Rain and gales confined everyone indoors and tempers began to fray. The incessant blaring of Paul's transistor grated on Hilda's nerves, so Albert switched it off, eliciting baleful glances from Marion. At tea time, a row blew up between Marion and Hilda over how to wean the baby onto solids. Hilda claimed she was merely making a suggestion, but Marion interpreted her advice as criticism, glowering venomously through a veil of tears and smudged mascara. Hilda snorted vociferously into her linen handkerchief, while little Sammy fretted in her carrycot, and Lucy kept her distance. Albert took the dog out and hid in the potting-shed, sucking peppermints to relieve indigestion, while Paul lost himself in the newspaper and a can of lager.

Lucy retired to her room early. *If this is what love and marriage does to people then I'm not sure if I want it*, she sighed, burying her head in her pillow to deaden the sound of heated arguments in the next room. Eventually, Marion went into the spare room to feed the baby, and Hilda took to her bed, nursing a headache.

The next morning the Clements family returned to London, and the house was quiet again.

'Has anyone seen Bertie?' Albert asked.

'Not since yesterday,' Hilda said. 'He's probably hiding somewhere. Who can blame him with all that racket going on. He'll turn up soon.'

Sadly, thorough searches and extensive enquiries yielded nothing. Lucy hoped Bertie would appear before new year, but the quiet little cat was nowhere to be seen.

On New Year's Eve, Lucy stayed up late. At the stroke of midnight, Albert poured three glasses of sherry, and Lucy joined her parents in a toast of good health and good fortune. With no perceptible change, a mere moment had passed. The new year had begun.

25: THE APPLE BARREL

Hours later, Lucy sat in the homely disarray of the Rogers' parlour, chatting with Alison over a hot cup of coffee. A daily newspaper lay on the floor, the front page displaying an unflattering caricature of Prime Minister Edward Heath launching into Europe upon a cross-Channel ferry.

Starting the next line of her five-year diary, Lucy wrote:

Britain is in the Common Market! This exciting new political venture will open doors to Continental travel, maybe a job in Germany?

'I can't understand why you keep a diary, I'm much too busy for that.' Alison remarked.

'Maybe I'll be too busy too, this year,' Lucy said.

'Do you have anything planned?'

'Maybe another trip to Germany or France – or both?'

Alison said nothing. A cheerful trilling from the birdcage in the sunny bay window filled the silence.

A week later, Lucy and Alison were delighted with their passes at Latin O-level. Meanwhile, Alison had opted for an easier maths alternative: Certificate of Secondary Education, or CSE, its top grade the equivalent of an O-level pass. Mr Kingsley advised Lucy to try Mathematics O-level once more, offering the tuition himself. Feeling honoured and special, Lucy agreed to two lessons a week, giving up morning breaks on Tuesdays and Thursdays, plus one session with one of Mr Kingsley's fourth form classes. The headmaster's step-by-step teaching method was clear and precise. No textbook was used, just plain paper and a pencil. Every stage of a calculation was explained, with regular checks to see if Lucy had understood. Lucy was surprised by her own progress. Sitting in her old classroom, surrounded by fourteen-year-olds was an odd experience, but she persevered, did the homework, and got most of the answers right.

With the extra workload, Lucy resigned from her job at Woolworth's. She had no regrets: it was time to move on. Studies were now her prime focus. Westcombe School didn't offer a French exchange, but Monsieur Leblanc recommended a national organisation. Lucy applied, and was paired with a Paulette Dumesnil, who lived on a remote farm an hour's drive south of Paris. Lucy wrote to Paulette and looked forward to a three-week Easter visit. Then Mr Hagin suggested Lucy spend the autumn term as a guest student in a German school of her choice.

Lucy's head was spinning. 'I'll think about it,' she said.

That evening, Lucy told her parents.

'What a wonderful idea!' Hilda exclaimed. 'But where will you stay?'

Lucy was pondering the logistics of an extended stay with the Schmieds when Hilda had a different idea.

'What about cousin Martha? She's always kept in touch. It would be *wunderbar* if you could stay with her! I haven't seen Martha since our grandparents' Golden Wedding in 1927. Martha was a teenager then, and I was very young, but I remember Martha was very good to me. She gave Uncle Peter and me a ride in a wheelbarrow and gave us fresh cherries. I remember Martha's quiet manner and kind face.'

'Brilliant idea, Mum! I'll tell Mr Hagin tomorrow!'

'Ask him how much the fare is, so I can budget, and I'll need to send Martha an allowance for your keep,' Hilda said, thinking of the practicalities.

'But we have to write and ask Martha first. Maybe she won't agree?'

'Of course she'll agree. I know my cousin well enough. If only your grandfather had known you! For many years, the extended family was separated by economics and politics. Your grandfather, Gregor Wester, lost the job with his brother Jakob before World War One. He suffered years of discrimination before his death in the last great London smog of 1952. He'd have been proud of you, Lucy, learning German. Martha is his niece. She married Helmut Schumacher just after the war. They have a son. All the relatives are spread across the Rhineland, a few still in Meisenfeld on the Dutch border.'

'Why did you never go back?'

'The Golden Wedding trip was the holiday of a lifetime. My parents saved up hard for that journey and it cost them a pretty penny. Times were hard in the Thirties, then the war came, and no opportunity to return – until now. You have the chance, Lucy, and I'm delighted.'

'I can't wait to go,' Lucy whispered, her heart pounding. This wasn't fanciful fiction; she really was going, on her own, for three months with new people in a new place.

Lucy wrote to Martha in German, outlining the proposal. As ambassador for the family, she was thrilled and honoured. Life suddenly had purpose and direction. So much was happening, and it was still only January.

The next day brought fresh news: Marion phoned, saying Samantha was in hospital with croup, now recovering, the cause thought to be a gas leak in the small bedroom, which Paul was busy repairing. Samantha's Christening was planned for the second Sunday in March. Then Peter phoned and announced Sarah's engagement to a colleague, Terry Fraser. After a whirlwind romance, the couple had returned to London and booked a registry office wedding for mid-February, in time for Valentine's Day.

'She's in too much of a hurry,' Hilda said, 'I hope she's doing the right thing.'

Days passed. Martha replied, saying she would be delighted to welcome Lucy as a *Haustochter* – a house-daughter, for three months in the autumn. Lucy spent Saturday mornings studying, starting with an hour's maths, rewarded by coffee and chocolate biscuits, then language translations and essays. Lucy kept rigidly to her study routine, television now a luxury.

Sarah and Terry's wedding was at half term. The short ceremony was followed by an informal buffet. Sarah wore a cream coloured trouser suit and a scarlet blouse, complementing her shoulder-length auburn hair and round, photogenic face. The tall, lanky groom was dressed unconventionally in purple bell-bottomed trousers and a turquoise silk shirt, unbuttoned almost to the waist, revealing a forest of reddish-brown hair sprouting from his scrawny chest. An unkempt tangle of red hair and bushy sideburns framed a furtive, florid face.

'I do hope he turns out to be better than Anne's Maverick Mick,' Hilda said to Lucy in a low voice. 'He'd better not be Terry the Terrible.'

Lucy grimaced and said nothing, feeling full, her dress uncomfortably tight about the waist.

That week, Albert took Dotty to the vet to be spayed, drawing a line under the dog-breeding proposal.

'I sense a wind of change,' Hilda remarked portentously, 'just wait and see.'

Samantha's Christening was on a blustery Saturday in early March.

'This is the second family event in one month,' Hilda said, on the road trip to London, an edge of intrigue in her voice. 'Things always seem to come in threes. I wonder what's next?'

The pressure of work and family was taking its toll on Hilda, resulting in her worst migraine yet. But the show had to go on. The fact that Paul's ex-girlfriend and her new husband, and not Lucy, had been chosen as Godparents was a bitter pill to swallow.

'I don't mind,' Lucy said. 'We don't live near Sammy, and I'm just happy to be an aunt.'

In truth, the idea of being a Godmother didn't appeal to Lucy. It smacked too much of church, religion, and personal worthiness.

Traffic jams prolonged the journey, and when the Wylies finally arrived,

Marion and Paul were about to leave the house. Baby Samantha was swathed in a white satin robe, her cherubic face framed by a frilly bonnet decorated with satin roses. Hilda shielded her eyes and said nothing. Disappointingly, there was no time for a cup of tea.

The little red-brick church was packed with the Clements clan. Hymns and prayers were followed by a short address, given by a balding cleric with a Cheshire Cat smile. The sleeping infant barely stirred as her forehead was dampened at the baptismal font. Afterwards, everyone trooped outside for photographs. Trees swayed in the stiff breeze and daffodils lay broken on rain-soaked ground. Guests stood shivering; ladies held on to their hats. Albert took a photo of Lucy holding Samantha. Hilda was next. Cradling her first grandchild, she smiled bravely under the brim of her hat, but the occasion was no pleasure. The migraine didn't lift, and Hilda endured the day through a fog of nausea and shards of pain.

A buffet lunch was held at Paul's parents' house, a mile away. Paul's nineteen-year-old sister had recently moved into a council house in the same street, after the birth of her third illegitimate child. The Clements children milled about merrily in the living-room. Lucy sat with her parents in a corner, staring at the crumb-strewn, carpet, where scruffy mongrels sniffed, and runny-nosed infants scampered. Hilda shielded her eyes, hoping nobody would notice her, but Paul's mother, Granny Gladys Clements thought Hilda looked a bit left out, so she proffered a plump baby in a blue romper suit and said, 'Hilda, meet Dean, he's my other new grandchild. Our Sandra had him last Christmas.'

The child's wide eyes matched the cornflower blue of his clothes.

'He's lovely,' Hilda said quietly.

'Yes, he's a bonny boy,' Gladys continued enthusiastically, 'our pride and joy. His older sisters love him to bits, and all. Sandra and Alan are married now. Alan decided to do the honourable thing.'

'That's good,' Hilda whispered wearily, calmed by Gladys's warm-hearted simplicity.

On the journey home, Hilda shook her head and sighed, 'I can't believe this, Peter's getting married again. He's found someone else!'

'Really? I didn't know that,' Albert said.

'Peter told me, after the service. It's so sudden, so soon after dear Rose. She's not been gone four years. Peter says his new lady's on the plump side. Oh, I do hope he's not rushing into anything. It's funny he never mentioned her before. Maybe it's a marriage of convenience?'

'Whose convenience?' Lucy enquired flippantly. 'Anyway, what's her name?'

'Sylvia. Like I said, events always happen in threes. Sarah's wedding, the Christening, and now this.' Hilda paused, fighting back tears. 'It'll be a registry office wedding. No guests – not even close family – and no reception, so we needn't bother going. They'll live in Sylvia's house in Kent. John and his new girlfriend are co-habiting in Peter and Rose's old house, no word of them getting married –'

Hilda stopped, choked with emotion. Arriving home, she took to her bed and stayed there until Monday morning, then rose at the usual time and went straight to work.

Lucy couldn't help worrying. That night she dreamed of Bertie again, one of many similar, recurring dreams. In the dream, Bertie came running through the porch and tapped on the inner door with his front paws, pleading to be let into the house. When Lucy went to open the door the handle was gone. She looked down and found Bertie had disappeared. With every passing day, hope dwindled of ever seeing him again. After fruitless enquiries in the neighbourhood, Hilda attributed Bertie's mysterious disappearance to foxes.

At school, Lucy updated Mr Hagin on cousin Martha's response.

'Excellent!' crowed Mr Hagin, 'Jolly good. Now, have you considered that Alison Rodgers might also like to join you in this venture? She too is a student of some linguistic promise, and you seem to get along together quite well.'

'I'll ask Alison to think it over, and we'll see what my parents say,' Lucy said.

'Lovely!' Mr Hagin beamed.

By evening, Hilda had recovered, looking thinner. After supper, Lucy mentioned Mr Hagin's proposal.

'That's unthinkable!' Hilda protested. 'I couldn't possibly impose upon my cousin in that way. Alison isn't family, not even a close friend. That teacher of yours obviously wants to push things to suit his reputation, and I'm not having it!'

Lucy's face fell. There was no sense arguing. At the same time, she couldn't help feeling relieved.

'Oh, well, never mind,' Alison said, the following morning, 'I expect I'll find something else to do instead.'

And it wasn't long before she did.

On the final Friday of term, Lucy and Alison lounged in the common-room, reading *Paris Match* magazines.

'Pssst!' Alison suddenly whispered. 'There's a dance tonight at the Apple Barrel , and the Miss Westcombe beauty contest. Anyone can enter. Are you coming?'

'Okay,' Lucy agreed. 'I'll come.'

Afterwards, she wasn't sure.

'You should go!' Hilda said, 'doll yourself up, you might win!'

Lucy put on a red tartan mini-dress, pink tights, the pink suede shoes, and a layer of makeup. Just before eight, Albert dropped her off at the Apple Barrel – a cosy little seafront bar. Lucy ordered a grapefruit juice, perched on a barstool, and scanned the dimly-lit room for a familiar face. She stood up and wandered about, feeling conspicuous. Everyone else was wearing "long" or jeans. Lucy looked disparagingly at her reflection in a mirror. Her pale skin and fine features weren't the kind of face that won beauty pageants.

Then Alison entered the room like an elegant swan, radiant and relaxed, a wide smile spreading across her tanned face, her shoulder-length auburn tresses loose and flowing over a long, lilac cheesecloth dress. *If only I'd worn the bridesmaid's dress!* Lucy lamented, wishing the ground would swallow her.

'Sorry I'm late,' Alison said, 'I was at the dentist. My face is still numb after the filling.' Alison's face looked as beautiful as ever, no trace of swelling or pain. Not that Lucy disbelieved Alison. It just seemed, whatever happened to Alison, she always came up smiling, not a hair out of place.

A bushy-haired compère in a glittery trouser suit made an announcement; his words lost to appalling acoustics. The volume was raised to an ear-splitting whistle, then tempered to a crackling invitation for contestants to come forward, one by one. Lucy clung to her mother's encouragement. With deportment and poise, she could walk away with tonight's coveted title, for in the half-light, anyone could pass as beautiful. When her turn came, she stepped forward and calmly gave her name and age, as requested. *So far, so good.*

Then came the next question:

'What made you decide to come to this contest tonight?'

Suddenly Lucy had nothing to say. She could hardly admit she'd been invited by a friend who was a hundred times more beautiful than she was. Suddenly, the short dress seemed to shrink to the size of a shirt. Exposed in the cold glare of the spotlight, Lucy felt naked and ashamed. After an awkward pause, she gabbled the first thing that came into her head.

'Well, I suppose I just wanted to enter into the spirit of the thing, really.'

Her amplified voice sounded thin and unreal. She didn't know why she said this and regretted it instantly.

'Thanking you, Lucy Wylie.'

Polite applause.

'Next contestant, please!'

Alison was next. She lied about her age.

'Well, I am nearly seventeen – well, in a few months,' Alison told Lucy afterwards.

While the judges deliberated, contestants ordered drinks or took to the dancefloor. The atmosphere was electric. Every entrant breathed hope. The crowd had applauded Lucy the same as everyone else, with no hissing or booing. Other contestants were too old, overly made-up, or overweight. Might Lucy be the lucky winner?

Lucy checked the time. Surely the contest would be over by ten? At five to ten, she went outside and found her father already waiting.

'They're just doing the judging, Dad,' Lucy panted. 'I'll only be a few minutes.'

She dashed back to the club, forgetting there was a road to cross, and narrowly missed being struck by a car. More embarrassed than frightened, Lucy hoped her father hadn't noticed, and that nothing would be reported back to Mother. Heart hammering, she returned to the bar and awaited the judges' verdict.

The three winning contestants were announced in reverse order: In third place a heavily made-up, curvy blonde, in second place another blonde, a slim, sophisticated-looking fifth former, also a Londoner. At least they're not prejudiced against outsiders, Lucy thought hopefully, but maybe they just like blondes? Then, with no time to think of anything else, the winner was announced.

'And now, ladies and gentlemen, the moment you've all been waiting for, the prestigious title of Miss Westcombe 1973, goes to... ALISON RODGERS!'

Fresh-faced and beaming, Alison came forward and took her place, amid cheering and applause. Alison shyly brushed a tear from her eye, as cameras flashed and the coveted crown was placed on her head.

This was no surprise. Alison was unquestionably pretty, and Lucy had no reason to doubt the judges' choice. Along with the audience, she smiled and clapped.

Slowly, the truth dawned on her that she had won nothing.

Lucy's steps were light. She walked in a strange, floating fashion towards the end of the garden in bright morning sunshine. Suddenly the sky darkened. A swirling, black fog descended, obliterating all light and encompassing Lucy in a dense, terrifying grip that drained her of her very breath. Then she awoke. In the bright morning light, fragments of the broken dream slowly mingled with the memory of last night.

'It's all cut-and-dried!' Hilda growled. Lucy cupped her hands around her mug. She raised it to her lips, feeling the steam rise in her face. She stared out at the sunlit garden, half expecting to be spirited off to the copse with its monster head and a black cloud suddenly to fall. She toyed with her muesli, then scooped eagerly at the segmented grapefruit. At least that wasn't fattening.

'These beauty contests are all the same,' Hilda went on dryly. 'They decide who's going to win before the contest even starts. Especially if someone's palm has been crossed with silver beforehand!'

Lucy didn't believe there'd been anything corrupt or underhand about last night's decision. She concluded she was just plain, fat and ugly. If she dyed her hair blonde, it would do little to enhance her looks. However, body shape was something she could work on. When the pictures appeared in the newspaper, Hilda commented how plain Alison and the London girl looked, and the plump runner-up was positively obese. At school, Alison was inundated with congratulations. Lucy was too mortified to be jealous. Alison told Lucy, as Miss Westcombe, she was obliged to perform numerous public duties, ruling out the possibility of an extended time away from home.

Lucy hurled herself headlong into her studies, plans for foreign travel, and her new-found project of diet and exercise. If svelte, attractive Alison was calorie-conscious, then lumpy Lucy should certainly get her sack-of-flour figure into shape! From now on there would be smaller portions of potatoes and pastry, no sugar in tea or coffee, no sweets, and very little bread and butter, cakes or biscuits. It wouldn't be easy, but Lucy's mind was made up, and stick to her new regime she would.

26: CHANGES

Paulette sat with her father and sister in a crowded Paris cafe, struggling to evaluate her English guest. This fidgeting, garishly dressed girl made no eye contact, her dishevelled head oscillated like a scarecrow's in the breeze. Beyond a brief *Bonjour*, she had made little effort to converse. The prospect of spending the next three weeks in her company would be challenging. Paulette sat elegant and statuesque, her facial expression unchanged. She watched her guest guzzle the last dregs of coffee and stare around, biting her lip.

Were all English people this weird?

Lucy put down the cup and looked around fascinated, determined to relish every moment. The coffee was a welcome lift after long hours of travelling. In the carefree atmosphere of Paris in spring, Lucy allowed the sounds of accordion music and spoken French to waft over her, enjoying a near-perfect moment so typically French. She pulled a tight-lipped smile, eager to show her hosts her appreciation of their beautiful capital city.

Returning to the hamlet of Les Peupliers, sixty kilometres south of Paris, Paulette and her sister were pleased to note the taciturn English girl was finally making an effort to converse. Her command of French was lively and imaginative. Perhaps the next three weeks wouldn't be so bad after all?

It was almost dark when the little blue Renault drew up alongside the long, low farmhouse, one side of which bordered the main road through the village. The tall, wooden shutters were closed. Lucy wondered whether Paulette and her family lived in a barn, possibly alongside animals? Her fears were allayed when high, iron gates were opened, and the car swung round to the other side of the house. Yellow light shone from traditional French windows onto a cobbled yard. From inside the barn resonated the low menacing bark of a large dog.

'Come,' Paulette spoke to Lucy in clearly enunciated French. 'I will show you your room.'

Lucy was led through the kitchen and lounge, to a room on the right – a high-ceilinged *boudoir* with heavy, oak furnishings and a polished wooden floor.

'Come, we will eat?' Paulette said.

In the farmhouse kitchen, an apron-clad grandmother laboured lovingly over a seething saucepan. Tired from travelling and faint with hunger, Lucy watched the family sit down at the large dining-table. Paulette was petite and picture-perfect, quiet and serious. Her two older sisters were fuller in the face, equally photogenic with chestnut, shoulder-length hair and centre partings, and nine-year-old Sylvie, pert as a bird, sported a straight, black bob. Sylvie clambered onto the bench and switched on the television on a high shelf. The news was on. Lucy struggled to understand. She quietly observed Madame Dumesnil round-faced and talkative, her husband quiet and reticent, Annie loud and brash, Madeleine silent and sullen, dark circles under her eyes, a plethora of pills and medicines beside her. Lucy wondered what on earth was wrong with her.

'*C'est bon*,' Lucy said, eagerly savouring the green salad, trusting the dressing wasn't too rich in calories.

'*Oui! Ce sont des pissenlits*,' the grandmother said, her dark eyes twinkling, her leathery face breaking into a toothless smile.

Dandelions! In shocked surprise, Lucy carved her pork cutlet into tiny cubes, carefully chewing every morsel. The grandmother gave Lucy a puzzled look.

The Dumesnils had two pets: a tabby kitten that pounced on soft furnishings and scampered across the polished floor, a poignant reminder of Lurcio and Bertie. A huge Alsatian dog was kept chained in the yard, presumably a guard dog, for it never came in the house and was said to have bitten its master more than once. Lucy cautiously kept her distance. Paulette and her sisters showed Lucy inside the barn, a towering, wooden structure, each hutch containing a large, plump rabbit. They weren't pets. Sure enough, the next meal was rabbit. At every meal, Lucy sampled a little of everything, even the pigs' brains soup, always making every mouthful last.

Days passed in peaceful, pleasant pursuits. Lucy filled every waking moment with revision, reading, sketching, or walks in hedgeless fields where skylarks soared and trilled in smooth, blue skies. The hamlet of Les Peupliers offered little entertainment, but Lucy wasn't bored. She drew a fluted glass vase, a conch shell, and copied a photo of a smiling toddler, Paulette's niece. Lucy thought of her own niece, whom she hardly ever saw. The sisters admired Lucy's drawing and sat for their own portraits. The Dumesnils treated Lucy well, but she never felt at home, as she had done with the Schmieds. Paulette was distant and aloof, allowing Lucy more time alone. After a week, Lucy felt free to share her concerns about the pressure of school work. Paulette admitted she also found maths difficult and hated having to study arts and sciences for the rest of her school days. A box of books arrived for Madeleine, currently studying at home. Her multiple medications and haunted looks were entirely due to the stress of school.

Or at least, that was what Lucy was led to believe.

On Good Friday, Lucy sat with Paulette, Annie and Madeleine in a country inn, staring out at grey skies and feeling her size twelve skirt tight about the waist. She prodded fastidiously through the *hors d'oeuvres* tureen of goose-liver *pâté* and the main course of *coq-au-vin* but ate every vestige of the *tarte-aux-fraises*. She left the restaurant assailed with guilt, failing to read the disappointment in her host's faces at her lack of response. Tired and drained, Lucy did her best to enjoy the afternoon's brief tour of Rouen. In the car, the sisters listened to European radio. The songs were in English and had nothing to do with Good Friday. Endless lines of mistletoe-festooned poplars flashed past flat fields wreathed in grey mist. It was hard not to compare this Easter holiday with last year's.

Saturday lunch was typically French, each course punctuated with long conversations. There was more food than Lucy could eat, even if she hadn't wanted to diet. She felt left out of the conversation and made no effort to participate, but was pleased to overhear church wasn't on tomorrow's agenda. Paulette said the family were non-practising Catholics, and Lucy didn't ask why. After lunch, the family set off in two cars and drove to a large, walled cemetery. Lucy had no idea whose grave was to be visited, but the mood was clearly subdued. Lucy followed the others past a sea of white, black and grey headstones, looking down at her pink, suede shoes.

The group stopped and gathered around a grave. A plain grey headstone bore a small cameo portrait of the deceased, beside the simple inscription:

MARIE DUMESNIL
1955-1972

Lucy instantly recognised the photo of a smiling, young girl with short, dark hair. An identical photo was on the living-room mantlepiece. Lucy had assumed this was a photo of Annie with a different hairstyle, but there had been a fifth sister. In a moment of silence, the sky hung heavy and dark. A sprinkling of snow settled on the flecked marble. Lucy shivered, her thoughts as bleak as the icy wind that chased mercilessly across the frozen plain.

On the way home, Annie told Lucy about Marie. Annie spoke rapidly, an edge of emotion in her voice. Marie had been Madeleine's twin, tragically killed in a head-on collision a year ago, travelling home for the Easter holidays. Madeleine, who had been at the wheel, sustained minor injuries but blamed herself for her sister's death, although the accident was unquestionably the other driver's fault.

'*Quel dommage. C'est terrible,*' Lucy said, feeling unqualified to empathise.

At tea, Annie asked Lucy about her school friends. Lucy mentioned Alison and her success as a beauty queen. Talking about the Apple Barrel seemed to lift a load. All evening, Lucy remained outwardly congenial and calm, but later, in the privacy of her room, she switched on the radio and worked punishingly at aerobics.

A line from a lively German song was her new mantra:

'*Das weiss der Himmel allein, warum wir beide uns so gut verstehn...*'

Heaven only knows, why we understand each other so well, Lucy fed her soul on the translation, stretching her hip and thigh muscles to their limits, clinging to the hope of future happiness. *Maybe in Germany this autumn, I will find true love?*

In the morning, Lucy helped the sisters paint the iron gates and the wooden shutters. Rousing sounds of Eurovision hits blared from Annie's transistor. Lucy daubed the green gloss paint with deft strokes, lost in thoughts.

'*Tu chantes?*' Annie asked.

'*Non,*' Lucy replied. She didn't sing at all and probably hadn't for years.

'*Tu verr-as, tu te re – con – nai-tras,*' Annie crooned vociferously above the tinny jangling of the radio, her sisters joining in, even Madeleine. Lucy liked the song but kept silent.

After lunch, Annie offered Lucy a turn on her *mobylette* – the simplest of motorcycles not requiring the rider to have a licence. Riding alone on empty lanes, the wind fluttering through her long hair and billowing the blue smock top, Lucy felt as free as a bird. Narrow roads sliced through miles of open fields and isolated farmsteads. Lucy sped onward, onto different colour tarmac, until the fear of running out of petrol prompted her to turn back. Annie expressed surprise Lucy had ridden so far. Apparently, the change in tarmac denoted the boundary between the department of *Seine-et-Marne* and *Le Loiret*. At dinner, the television news reported the passing of the famed painter, Pablo Picasso. The Dumesnils made no comment, which surprised Lucy. *Perhaps they're not interested in art?* Tomorrow would tell, on the day trip to Paris.

Below the high bank by the gnarled oaks of Edencroft, the post van engine throbbed, slowing down for gear change. Hilda listened eagerly for the sound of the slamming door, but with a quiet rumble, the vehicle passed by. Two weeks had passed, and still no word from Lucy. What was going on? With trembling fingers, Hilda dialled 'O' for the operator and requested a direct line to France.

Lucy sat sandwiched between Paulette and Madeleine on the back seat of Annie's little red Renault, listening to this year's Spanish Eurovision entry. The radio presenter gave a French rendering of the lyrics, which Lucy translated in her head into English: *It's you, you are my source of life-giving water... the wheat of my grain... the fire in my hearth...*

The day trip embraced tourist attractions and gourmet restaurants, but disappointingly, the itinerary lacked a visit to the Louvre. Unseasonal chill weather added to Lucy's chagrin. The Eiffel Tower was swathed in fog. Tourists huddled at the base, clicking cameras and cowering from cold winds. Notre Dame cathedral was filled with sightseers, Easter pilgrims shuffling in subdued silence. Lucy paused at a carved wooden crucifix, mesmerised by the tiny points of light from a thousand candles, clenching frozen fingers, feeling cold, empty and alone. By contrast, Montmartre was thronged with artists in smocks and berets. Up on the hill, Sacre Coeur cathedral was bursting with zealous Germans. Returning through Montmartre, Annie called at an apartment block and invited two university friends to a meal at a nearby Pizzeria. Lucy hungrily devoured her larger-than-plate-sized portion, but Paulette and the others left some of theirs, leaving Lucy feeling very greedy and very guilty.

A short metro ride to the *Champs-Elysees* was followed by a tour of a riverside fairground, where Lucy squandered money unnecessarily on tempting side stalls, and narrowly missed having her handbag stolen by groping hands in the ghost train. Next was a cinema trip – a film about four men whizzing around on motorcycles, doing stunts. In the warm, crowded auditorium Lucy dozed off. Annie asked afterwards if she had followed the story. '*Oui*,' Lucy lied, politely.

All day, Roland was never far from Lucy's thoughts. She wondered if, miraculously, fates would allow their paths to meet, but as twilight fell, closure on the Roland romance weighed on Lucy like a leaden cloak. As colourful lights of the *Moulin Rouge* shone optimistically into the young Paris night, the group marched on in search of another eatery. Lucy tagged along. *Not another meal – I'm not even hungry*, she fumed silently. The next restaurant was more expensive than Annie had anticipated, so everyone delved deeper into their own pockets to cover the cost. Lucy was gutted by the obligation to pay for a meal she didn't even want. As twilight deepened into night, wintry showers added to the chill and gloom. Trailing through, glistening, sleet-soaked city streets Lucy floundered in a hollow void of loneliness.

On returning to Les Peupliers, Lucy was told by an agitated Madame Dumesnil that she should telephone her parents immediately. Lucy hurried into the study, wondering what on earth could be wrong. A piece of paper with the UK dialling code was on the desk. Lucy dialled and waited. Then she heard the familiar ringtone and her mother's anxious voice.

'Lucy?'

'Hallo – Mum?'

'Lucy, is that you?'

'Yes, it's me, Mum. What do you want?'

'Thank God you're alive! Your father and I have been so worried about you. Where have you been?'

'We went to Paris for the day.'

'Why didn't you write to us?'

'I sent a postcard on the day I arrived! Didn't you get it?'

'No, not a thing. That was nearly three weeks ago!'

'It must have got lost in the post.'

'Never mind, as long as you're safe. When are you coming home?'

'Thursday.'

'And these people you're with – are they good to you?'

'Of course, Mum. There's nothing wrong!'

Irritated by what she considered unnecessary fuss, Lucy slammed down the phone. She hadn't missed her parents at all. On reflection, ending the conversation so abruptly had doubtless denied her mother the opportunity to wish her happy birthday.

The next day was Lucy's seventeenth birthday. Cards arrived from family, as they had done last year. The Dumesnils gave Lucy a fluted glass vase, similar to the one she had drawn, and a glittery purse, which Lucy doubted she'd ever use. After a two-hour evening meal, Lucy went to her room to pack. Her suitcase was considerably heavier than on the outward journey, chiefly because Madame Dumesnil had given her a large drum of low-fat powdered milk, noticing her preference for it over full-fat milk. Early the next morning, Annie drove Lucy to Paris, Paulette came for the ride. At the *Gare du Nord* Lucy thanked the sisters and promised to write. As the train pulled away, she didn't bother waving goodbye. The carriage was crammed with chattering young Brits. A large, raven-haired girl from South Shields struck up a conversation with Lucy, her accent a reminder of Aunt Rose. Suddenly, a wrapped, boiled bon-bon hurtled from behind and landed in Lucy's lap. She looked around, but nobody claimed it. The dark-haired girl carried on talking, but Lucy wasn't listening. Never mind the calories, she thought, unwrapping the sweet and popping it into her mouth.

Lucy's homecoming seemed oddly surreal. Amid the tranquil beauty of the Westcombe hills lurked an undercurrent of unrest, which Albert summed up as a strange feeling the place belonged to someone else. The past three years had been a journey through highs and lows, with an upward trend. Lucy felt strong, capable, yet in control of her life. Nothing could hurt her again.

This year, there was no trip to Arthur and Joan's. Unbeknown to Lucy, her parents had other plans. Arriving home one Friday, she baked a fruit loaf, prepared a *quiche Lorraine* and salad for dinner, cleared away the dishes, and made a pot of tea.

'Excellent meal, Lucy – and the cake is delicious,' Hilda said. 'Take a break from study tomorrow. We're going to Brighton.'

'Brighton?'

'Yes, Brighton. Dad wants to visit the place he grew up in.'

'To see how much it's changed, and drive around my old cycle routes,'

Albert added.

'Okay,' Lucy agreed. 'a break would be nice.'

Hilda nodded sagely.

The next morning dawned bright and clear. After a smooth journey, Lucy and her parents explored Brighton's historic Lanes, then walked to the shore – a steep, pebbled beach dotted with deckchairs and happy picnickers. Ice cream vans chugged, seagulls screeched, hordes of tourists swarmed the beach, paddling in the shallows.

'It's too crowded,' Albert grumbled, lighting the umpteenth cigarette.

'Time for lunch,' was Hilda's response.

In a side-street pub, Lucy ordered a Ploughman's platter of crusty, white rolls with cheese and pickle; her parents ordered steak pie and chips.

'Don't you want a hot meal?' Hilda inquired anxiously.

'No, thanks. It's a warm day.'

In truth, Lucy was feeling cold and would have preferred the pie and chips. She ate the cheese and chutney, discreetly wrapping the calorie-rich butter and the bread's doughy centre in a serviette. On the esplanade, Lucy bought a German magazine. She declined the offer of ice cream. On a steep street of terraced houses, Albert pointed out the tiny basement where he had lived until he was eighteen, before being called up for active service, and further on, the park he played in as a child. The journey down memory lane continued with a drive to the Devil's Dyke, where Hilda walked the dog, and Albert and Lucy admired the view.

'I cycled along all the roads around here,' Albert said, wistfully.

Cloud shadows passed over the hillside. Lucy recalled family picnics, long ago. Life was better now. After a pleasant day out, she was keen to return to the rigorous routine of study and self-denial.

But the day wasn't over. An unexpected stop was made in a quiet village called Foxfield, down a lane, by a building site. Diggers and cement-mixers stood idle in a sea of dried mud.

'Typical British workmen, taking Saturday off,' Hilda remarked. Lucy recalled a similar visit to a building site in a Buckinghamshire village, ten years earlier. Lucy had hoped her parents would move there and was disappointed to discover they had no such plan.

Lucy followed her parents into what was probably the nicest newbuild on the estate – the last house, which overlooked fields. The front door was unlocked. Inside, footsteps echoed on dusty boards, the smell of new timber and plaster filled the warm air. Upstairs, bright sunshine streamed through putty-smeared windows. Hilda opened a window. Sleepy, summer sounds drifted in – the slow cooing of wood pigeons and the distant whirr of a hand-pushed lawn-mower.

'Do you prefer this room, or the one next to it?' Hilda asked.

'This one's nice,' Lucy said.

'You're standing in your bedroom.'

'What?'

'This is your room, this is our house, Lucy. We bought it.'

'You bought it? When? How?'

'While you were in France, Uncle Charles's money finally came through. All my strongly-worded letters to the MP and to Somerset House finally worked, and that old crook of a solicitor paid up. My boss Mr Connor put a word in for us and made a generous donation to the Conservative party. Dad and I did the sums and planned the move. Lovely as Edencroft is, it'll never work as a business.'

'I suppose not... so this isn't some crazy dream?'

'This is real, Lucy, and to celebrate, we'll go to Lavender Cottage.'

'Where?'

'The last stop on the mystery tour.'

Lavender Cottage was a quaint, rustic tea-room, where Lucy cast aside her calorie-counting principles and enjoyed a pot of Darjeeling and a generous chunk of chocolate cake.

'Edencroft's already on the market,' Hilda said. 'We didn't tell you until you'd seen the new house.'

'So when will we move? What about school?'

'I've thought of all that. You won't have to change schools. We'll probably move in September, when you're at Martha's. I'm keeping my job and renting a holiday flat for us, until you leave school. We'll go home to the new house at weekends.'

'Bristol University will be a long way from home,' Lucy said, thinking ahead. 'London's nearer, but too big for my liking. Maybe Southampton?'

'Oxford or Cambridge?' Hilda winked hopefully.

'The entrance exams are very difficult,' Lucy sighed.

'Canterbury? That's near Peter and Sylvia.'

'What about Blackford?' Albert suggested quietly. 'It's near countryside, where John Constable painted *The Haywain*.'

'There's so much to think about,' Lucy said.

With so much food for thought, she had scarcely any appetite. Sticking to the diet was easy. At school, news of Lucy's impending move to Sussex was added to the list of her interesting attributes. Ironically, now that Westcombe had become a socially comfortable place, it would soon be time to leave it. The Maths O-level was the next significant hurdle, two papers, two days apart. Lucy did her best, enduring a severe attack of hay fever on the day of the second paper. Much depended on this result, but in real life, she would doubtless never need to solve another simultaneous equation nor displacement vector again. The last question was an enigma. Five minutes left! The answer sheet swam before her. Suddenly, in a flash of inspiration, she rubbed out her calculations and started again.

'Time to stop,' The teacher said, but Lucy scribbled on, completing her answer. There was no time to check it. Closing her answer booklet, she left the hall. What was done was done.

Next up was a day trip to London to watch a live performance of Shakespeare's *Anthony and Cleopatra*, for sheer enjoyment, as it wasn't a set text. School uniform wasn't obligatory. Lucy wore a figure-hugging dress, basking in new-found popularity. At the station cafeteria she faced a barrage of questions.

'When are you going to Germany?'

'Where will you stay?'

'Who with?'

'What about school?'

'The dress suits you, have you lost weight?'

'Is it true you're staying a whole term?'

'Wow, you've got guts, Lucy Wylie, I couldn't do that. I'd miss home too much.'

Lucy answered all the questions, then bought another coffee. This time, the cream was past its best, curds floating on the top. Lucy returned to the counter, complained politely and was given a replacement, free of charge. Miss Menzies, the silent observer, smiled at Lucy's new-found ability to speak up for herself.

Hilda sat at her desk, head in hands, anxieties eroding her concentration like persistent rats. Uncle Charles's inheritance awaited equity release. The final payment on the new house was due on September the First, but still no buyer for Edencroft! A temporary flat had to be found, along with an upfront payment to secure a long-term tenancy. Lucy seemed happy with the changes, but her increasing obsession with dieting was disturbing.

Hilda's temples throbbed. Then she felt a firm hand on her shoulder.

'You've worked hard today, Mrs Wylie. You can go home now.'

'Thank you, Mr Connor.'

Hilda went home to rest, but her oasis of calm was short-lived. That evening, Peter rang, inviting himself, Sylvia, and her teenage daughter for the weekend. In the next breath, Peter said Sarah's husband had cheated on her, and Sarah had moved into the old house with John and his girlfriend. Then Lucy refused to give up her bedroom for someone she'd never met. *If only she were less self-centred!* Fortunately, within the hour, Peter phoned again, saying he'd booked a chalet at Sunny Cove Holiday Camp, the venue of many happy holidays in the past.

Lucy took escalating events in her stride. She went with her mother to view The Gables Holiday Flats in Nyehaven. With peeling paintwork and curtains askew, the once grand, Edwardian house had seen better days. Hilda and Lucy were shown a filthy, partitioned room with two single beds, stained mattresses, threadbare, mud-brown carpet, a shared bathroom dark and dank, and a fat-splattered kitchenette reeking with the pungent odour of mice.

'It's good value for money,' the landlady snapped. 'You won't find anything cheaper elsewhere.'

'It's disgusting,' Hilda said curtly. 'We'll see ourselves out.'

Arriving home, Hilda and Lucy found their clothes crawling with fleas.

A local businesswoman seeking a weekend retreat viewed Edencroft, and Hilda's hopes lifted. Unfortunately, the feedback was "rather nice but insufficient room for keeping horses".

'They can stuff their horses!' Hilda huffed indignantly.

Revisiting Sunny Cove Holiday Camp was less than nostalgic. The recreation hall, souvenir shop, and tea-room, once prized as pavilions of paradise now seemed tacky and drab. The adults reminisced over tea and scones, Sylvia's fourteen-year-old daughter read a magazine. Across the trampled rectangle of grass stood the graceless toilet block, marring the view of the sea. Lucy regarded the rows of shabby little chalets, wondering why she had ever liked coming to such a place.

The next day, a quiet couple with four flaxen-haired children viewed Edencroft and were openly smitten with its charm.

'I doubt they'll make an offer,' Hilda said afterwards. 'The house is too small, unless they build an extension or are prepared to live like sardines. Nevertheless, things could happen very quickly, so we must start packing.'

When Paulette came to stay, the bungalow was practically bare, a tower of sealed boxes in the corner of the living room. Hilda organised outings and did her best to make her guest welcome. Paulette smiled politely at everything, like a well-programmed robot. A two-night stay with Marion and Paul offered Paulette a change of scene and the chance to look round London. Marion and Paul squeezed into the airing-cupboard bedroom with Samantha, giving up their bedroom for Albert, Hilda and Lucy, and Paulette was allocated the box-room. On the camp-bed in the corner, Lucy endured traffic noise and her father's snoring. She saw no point complaining. The next day, Lucy took Paulette on the Underground to view Westminster Bridge and Trafalgar Square, before meeting Melanie outside Lyons Corner House for lunch.

'Come on!' Melanie said brusquely. 'Let's eat, I'm famished!'

Melanie ordered sausage, egg and chips, while Paulette and Lucy settled for toasted sandwiches. Lucy felt guilty about the calories but ate every morsel since she had paid for it herself. Melanie talked her way through the afternoon, openly eating chocolate bars in shops and casually casting aside the wrappers.

'I can't understand why you want to go on a diet,' she retorted, 'You're crazy.'

'It's all right for you,' argued Lucy. 'You're thinner than me and eat whatever you like. It's not fair.'

'Don't be so childish!'

'I'm going to Germany next month to stay with my mum's cousin in –' Lucy began. Melanie suddenly stopped at a store window, then barged into the shop and swished a pair of glittery trousers in Lucy's face.

'These are great! A bargain at six pounds!'

Lucy pulled a face. Paulette bought a plain, navy skirt. In the next store, Lucy bought a pink, striped mini-jumper in the sale, for just fifty pence. Suddenly, Paulette tapped Lucy on the arm and said, 'I gave twenty-pound note in the other shop and I did not get enough money.'

'Are you sure?' Lucy asked, checking the receipt. 'Are you sure you gave a twenty pound note and not a ten?'

Paulette nodded. 'I am sure.'

'We'll go back,' Lucy said.

'Well, I'm not going,' snorted Melanie. 'We haven't been to Harrod's yet. If we waste time, the best shops will be closing.'

'We have to ask, so Paulette will get her change.'

'All right, but don't be long,' Melanie grudgingly agreed and waited outside.

'You'll have to wait until we close and cash up,' the assistant said. 'If the till is ten pounds over, you'll get your change. Come back at six o'clock. Someone will open the door for you.'

'Pah!' exploded Melanie, hearing the update.

'What shall we do while we're waiting?' asked Lucy.

'We could have a coffee?' suggested Paulette.

'Stuff that! I'm going!' Melanie retorted, disappearing into the crowd, and out of Lucy's life.

Unwisely, Lucy started to follow. Turning around, she found Paulette had vanished. She spent fifteen minutes systematically searching up and down the street, telling herself not to panic. Crowds of shoppers swarmed past, in both directions. Lucy paced up and down the same stretch of pavement, looking, thinking, hoping. At last, there was Paulette walking calmly, staring trance-like ahead, not a trace of anxiety on her flawless face.

'Paulette! There you are, I thought I'd lost you!' Lucy exclaimed. 'Let's get your change, then we'll go for the train.'

Later, back at Marion and Paul's, with Paulette's change returned, Lucy tried to put the day's events behind her.

'What do you think of Melanie?' she asked Paulette.

'She is alright,' Paulette answered slowly, 'and she has a big mouth.'

'True,' Lucy said.

Lucy slept much better that night. She didn't wake till eleven the next morning. Neither did Paulette. After lunch, Hilda and Albert went to Albert's mother's grave in Ash Farm, while Lucy and Paulette walked around familiar streets. It was strange, seeing her childhood home with red paintwork and Venetian blinds in the windows. The row of conifers was half as high again, making house and garden look smaller. Lucy half expected someone to recognise her and come out to greet her, but nobody did. Walking past the council estate where classmates had lived, Lucy wondered what they were all doing now. The red-bricked, school building stood empty and silent behind locked iron gates. The betting shop, hairdresser's, and launderette were still there; the newsagent's evoking memories of sherbet fountains and sugar mice.

'Let's get some sweets,' Lucy said. Inside the shop, Lucy was surprised to see a familiar face. The petite, dark-haired girl serving at the counter was Susan Quinn.

'Susan!' Lucy exclaimed, 'Meet my French penfriend Paulette. We're just here for the day and going back to Westcombe later, but we're moving to Sussex soon, but I'm going to Germany first –'

Lucy stalled.

'Hi Lucy. Yeah, this is my holiday job. Are you still at Woolworth's? Made any more cardigans lately?' Susan spoke as if Lucy had never left.

'I left Woolworths, and haven't done much knitting lately. I'm looking forward –'

A tinkling of tiny bells interrupted the conversation. A crowd of chattering children had entered the shop. Lucy bought a chocolate bar and promised to write soon. The brief, unemotional meeting was over so quickly that Lucy wondered afterwards whether it had been a dream.

On the return journey, there was a brief stop at Foxfield to view the house, now completed.

'How do you like it?' Lucy asked.

'It is very pleasant,' answered Paulette, in her usual controlled manner.

The journey continued in silence. Trees and hedgerows in summer foliage flashed past.

'Well, we have had a busy time,' Hilda said. Nobody responded.

There was a sudden thud as if a large animal had leapt on the car. Albert pulled over, slamming the brakes. The luggage rack was on the ground; the two suitcases had burst open, their contents scattered across the dual carriageway.

'God love old Ireland!' Hilda gasped – an expletive Lucy hadn't heard in a decade.

'It'll take a while to pick everything up,' Albert said.

Lucy jumped up, ready to lend a hand.

'Lucy! Stay where you are and talk to our guest!' Hilda snapped.

Paulette sat demurely on the back seat, saying nothing, watching her hosts ignominiously retrieve their scattered belongings.

On Saturday, Lucy accompanied Paulette on the morning train to London. After an uneventful parting, Lucy returned alone, closed her eyes, collecting her thoughts. Suddenly she remembered the dreaded Maths result. Lucy arrived home to find a letter from Martha, saying how excited everyone was to meet her. Tickets and passport ready, and cases practically packed, Lucy was poised for the day of departure. But it was too soon to relax.

On Monday, no post came.

On Tuesday morning, one solitary letter was deposited in the mailbox. Hilda fetched it, while Lucy sat indoors embroidering the Hildenheim town crest on a cushion cover. Seeing the plain, brown envelope, Lucy jumped up and tore it open.

Trembling, she unfolded the flimsy sheet.

'Well?' asked Hilda.

'I've passed,' Lucy whispered hoarsely, then shouted, I''VE PASSED!'

Hilda engulfed Lucy in a hearty embrace.

'Well done, Lucy – I knew you could do it!'

Owing a debt of gratitude to Mr Kingsley, Lucy hurled herself happily into her undiscovered future.

27: German Dutch

Achen. 22:05pm. The steely glare of white light flooded the far-reaching expanse of concrete. Lucy stood still, looking around. Not a soul was in sight. Then she glimpsed a woman on a seat, suitcase at her feet. Lucy approached and asked in her best German if the last train to Kochendorf had already left.

'Sorry, luv, I don't speak a word of the lingo. I'm English,' was the unexpected response.

'It's okay, I'm English too,' Lucy answered, cheered by the familiar sound of a Cockney accent. 'Is there a train to Kochendorf tonight?'

'Dunno, dear. Ask the guard over there. He might know.'

'Thanks,' Lucy replied, happy to see a uniformed official.

The Belgian guard spoke English, directed Lucy to the next platform, where after twenty minutes the promised train arrived. Breathless, Lucy climbed aboard and sat in a forward-facing seat, not that there was much to see at night. Excitement clung like a tight band around her chest. Closing her eyes, she revisited the past few hours, spellbound as a child at Christmas.

In the afternoon, the ferry left Dover in bright sunshine, laden with happy holidaymakers, Lucy among them, alone in a crowd, but happy. She felt good. Infinitely better than on the last cross-channel trip. She wandered up on deck and watched the English coastline fade in the afternoon haze. She pulled Martha's crumpled letter from her trouser pocket and re-read it eagerly. Martha asked if the journey was across Nederland, and Lucy wondered why Martha used the Dutch spelling.

The air grew chilly. Lucy draped a cardigan over her shoulders and returned to the cabin. There was no announcement, but the boat was running late. Tourists voiced concerns about missing onward travel. Lucy checked her ticket; it was for the 19:00 express train from Ostend to Essen, changing at Aachen for a direct train to Kochendorf. It was six thirty, but no worries

– everyone's in the same boat!

Afternoon melted into twilight, then to dusk. When the ferry finally docked, no explanation was given for the delay. Lucy hauled her luggage through the queues at customs. On the way to the trains, she stopped often to rest her aching arms.

'Can I help you?' inquired a polite voice.

'Yes, please,' Lucy answered, taxed muscles like rubber, and hands blistered and sore.

'Here, let me carry this for you.'

A well-dressed lady lifted Lucy's case and immediately put it down. 'Good gracious! That case is heavy. Whatever have you got in it , if you don't mind my asking?'

'Books,' Lucy gasped.

'Must dash now – safe travels,' the helpful stranger said and hurried on.

Lucy struggled to a stationary train and found it locked. She shuffled along to ask a guard, who informed her the next train to Aachen was due in an hour. This was a disaster. The train she was booked on had left nearly two hours ago. Would she even reach her destination tonight? She sat down, resigning herself to a long wait. All her packed lunch was gone. She snapped off a corner of a slab of chocolate intended for Martha and Helmut and ate it slowly, reasoning optimistically Martha and Helmut will have been informed of this delay.

Reminiscing scenes from Hildenheim, Lucy marked time until the Aachen train arrived. It was practically empty. Lucy sat back, closed her eyes, and listened to the rhythmic clickety-clack, as the train sped on into the night. What seemed minutes later, the train pulled into Aachen. Doubtless, she had dozed off. Lucy alighted onto the deserted platform. It was ten o'clock – the scheduled time for arrival in Kochendorf. *If only there was a telephone, so I could let Martha know I'll be late...*

And now, at last, the train left Aachen, bound for Kochendorf. Wave upon wave of excitement swept over Lucy, merging with the steady, rhythmic beat of wheels on track. With no desire to read, eat, or reflect, Lucy yearned to reach her destination, each moment bringing her closer to meeting Martha.

Not far now...

It was twenty past midnight when the train rumbled punctually into Kochendorf Hauptbahnhof. Lucy gathered her bags and lumbered down the steps onto a clean, concrete platform.

She looked up and saw a grey-haired lady in a yellow tartan suit hurrying towards her.

'*Luuucy, da bist du endlich!*' Martha swamped her young guest in an exuberant embrace that lifted her off the ground. A spray of wilting, white roses was thrust into Lucy's hands. She understood the first phrase, you're here at last, but didn't catch what was said next. Martha was taller and older than Hilda, but with similar high cheekbones, pale complexion and ice-blue eyes. Lucy sensed a mutual bonding.

'*Na, Fräulein Luuucy, wie geht's?*' Helmut asked, lifting Lucy's suitcase as if it were a foam-filled cushion, '*Komm! Wir gehen nach Hause!*'

Helmut was small and wiry, balding and round-faced, like a cheery gnome.

On the short ride to the suburb of Baumgarten, Lucy did her best to converse, her tired brain processing hybrid sentences of text-book German, South German and French. She apologised for her lack of fluency, but Martha and Helmut insisted her German was good, explaining they spoke a low German dialect *Plattdeutsch* – similar to Dutch. Soon, they arrived at a conifer-lined driveway, beside a chalet bungalow, neat and white in the pearly light of a street lamp. The air was heavy with the scent of flowers. Lucy followed Martha through a small hall to a large kitchen-diner and living-room with a sofa, a glass-fronted cabinet, and a table decked with colourful fabric. A television and a cheese plant occupied one corner, a blackened coal stove the other. Lucy sat at the corner bench in the L-shaped kitchen. Platters of rye bread, cold meats and fresh fruit and cheeses were laid on a chequered, plastic cloth. Too excited to eat, Lucy nibbled at an open sandwich and drank three glasses of mineral water with grape juice. On the wall hung a wooden crucifix, and a plaque bearing the poem:

Hab' Sonne im Herzen, ob es stürmt oder schneit,
Der Himmel voll Wolken, die Erde voll Streit,
Vertraue auf Gott, verlier' nicht den Mut,
Hab' Sonne im Herzen und alles wird gut.

Have sunshine in your heart, in storms or snow
The sky filled with clouds, the world filled with strife
Trust in God, don't lose courage
Have sunshine in your heart, and all will be well.

Lucy could translate it but wasn't sure if she believed in God.

'Come, Lucy,' Martha said. 'It's late. You must be tired. Your room's upstairs, first door on the right.'

A steep staircase led to the first-floor attic. Lucy's room was the smaller of two narrow bedrooms separated by a wooden partition. On the high bed, a voluminous Continental quilt, plumped up and oval-shaped like an air-ship, almost touched the sloping ceiling. The warm air smelt of mothballs.

Lucy thanked Martha and requested a quick shower.

'Bathroom's downstairs, near the front door, I've left you soap and fresh towels,' Martha said.

It was very late when Lucy finally slid under the enormous bulk of duck-down duvet, which despite its size, was extremely light. Feeling the cool texture of brushed cotton sheets, she lay wide awake, listening to the sound of traffic and a distant train whistle. Soon the rhythmic rumblings of Helmut's snores penetrated the thin partition. Lucy sighed contentedly and drifted into dreamless sleep.

Life at the Schumachers' fitted Lucy like a glove. She helped prepare meals, wash dishes, and enjoyed shopping trips and walks. Being here was even better than being at Birgit's. Lucy was more than an honoured guest, she was family. As Martha and Helmut's *Haustochter*, she was treated as the daughter they never had. Roughly the size as Hildenheim, Kochendorf had been restored post-war and extended outwards, its centre a blend of modern architecture and old-world Germanic charm. Baumgarten was prettier than any suburb Lucy had ever seen. Grid-iron streets of neat, white homes with sharp, terracotta roofs in manicured gardens flourished with colourful flowers and shrubs. The Schumachers' back yard comprised a wooden shed, a clothes line, and kitchen garden. Sundays were a day of rest when nobody gardened. On the first Sunday, Lucy was about to hang out washing, but Martha intervened, explaining it wasn't the done thing.

'Uncle Friedrich has invited us next Saturday,' Martha told Lucy. 'They're looking forward to meeting you. Friedrich built the farmhouse himself, between the wars, for his wife Anna and their children. Friedrich's youngest son Wilhelm works the farm now, with his wife Marleen and their teenage children Hubert, Manfred, and Lisa. You'll meet them on Saturday.'

'What kind of farm is it?'

'Pigs, mostly, also grain, fruit and vegetables. Friedrich still bakes bread and cakes, supplying shops in the village.'

'My mother worked on a pig farm in England, during the Second World War,' Lucy said. 'Mother wanted to be near London, so she could visit her father, Gregor Wester, who was retired and German.'

'Gregor was one of Friedrich's brothers, so was my father, Hermann,' Martha said, 'and my mother came from a Dutch farming community, just across the border.'

Lucy felt very connected. Flooded with new German words and phrases, she not only began to think but also dream in German.

The Rhine plains sizzled in a heatwave, so Martha put the feather quilts away. In hot, oppressive nights, Lucy slept heavily, waking each morning with fresh mosquito bites. Martha said to keep windows shut until lights were off, but Lucy still heard the tell-tale, high-pitched whining. She got out of bed, switched on the light and thrashed the walls with a rolled-up magazine, then wiped the red blobs with a cologne tissue. By Saturday, she had lost count of bites and tried hard to ignore them.

In Meisenfeld, Lucy received a hearty welcome. Martha's prior briefing helped put names to faces. Above the corner table in the kitchen hung a faded, monochrome photograph of the Golden Wedding group. At the centre, Johannes and Wilhelmine Wester surrounded by seven surviving adult offspring with their spouses and children. Lucy's grandparents, Gregor and Theresa stood at the right, beside four-year-old Peter and three-year-old Hilda, diminutive and doll-like, clinging to her mother's skirts. On the left, young Friedrich stood tall and dapper, flanked by two small cousins and fifteen-year-old Martha, fair-haired and serene.

'My mother and uncle are the smallest,' Lucy remarked, 'also the boy in the sailor suit. Who is he?'

'Another cousin,' Wilhelm said.

'May I visit him, also?'

'Perhaps. I don't know. He is a very sick man. '

'Come, Lucy,' Lisa said, 'I'll show you around.'

Upstairs were three large bedrooms with heavy oak furniture and Continental quilts, a large modern bathroom with a bidet and shower; downstairs, a large parlour, farmhouse kitchen, cloakroom, and scullery. The garden was vast and lawnless, with rows of vegetables and extensive orchards stretching to arable farmland as flat as a body of water – in every direction, as far as the eye could see, a feature strangely disturbing.

'Where are the pigs?' Lucy asked.

'In the barn.' Lisa said.

'Come! Lunch is ready!' Marleen called from the kitchen door.

At the big kitchen table, Lucy sat in the middle, facing the family photograph. Above the range hung polished pans on a wall of white tiles, some with pictures of Dutch windmills. Warm air wafted from ovens, diffusing the mouth-watering aromas, while dozens of house flies buzzed, landing on surfaces, utensils, tea towels, food, and people. Strangely, nobody seemed bothered, nor by the overpowering stench from the piggery. Lucy flicked a fly off her nose, banishing fears of health risks. She ate pork and vegetables, and the creamy chocolate dessert, vowing she would diet tomorrow.

Friedrich sat at the head of the table, speaking rapidly in *Plattdeutsch* on the rising costs of running the farm and bakery. The cousins asked Lucy about herself and the family in England. Lucy answered, enjoying being the centre of attention. At *Kaffeetrinken* and *Abendbrot* she sampled a little of all the foods, especially Friedrich's home baking, happiness outweighing fears of becoming fat. Helmut called time on the visit at seven o'clock, advising an early night, and an early start in the morning, for the new school year.

Lucy was prepared for the six thirty wake-up call. She got up, washed, and dressed in the lilac slacks, green tank-top with puffed sleeves, and a brown cardigan with white stripes. In the kitchen, Martha was peeling vegetables. The coffee machine rumbled quietly in the background. Helmut sat at the corner bench, resting his elbows on the table, smoking. He regularly ate no breakfast, but Martha had prepared a platter of bread rolls, crackers, cold meats and cheeses. Lucy took a dry crispbread and black coffee and stared at the house plants below the pristine ruff of white net curtain. It was too early for conversation. Helmut finished his cigarette and announced it was time to leave. Lucy watched disgruntled, as Martha packed a greasy salami sandwich and put it into her school bag. Soon, the familiar rattle of the Volkswagen engine sounded on the driveway. Lucy wished Martha goodbye and left.

Rush hour was an assault on the senses: rattling engines, blaring horns, bright lights, a fog of exhaust fumes, and a long wait at a level crossing, allowing two commuter trains to pass. Helmut dropped Lucy by the entrance to Johann Sebastian Bach Gymnasium – an all-girls' secondary school, where a neighbour's daughter, Renate Biedermeier was a pupil. There was no sprawling campus. In its urban setting, the modern three-storey, concrete-and-glass edifice could easily have been an office building, were it not for the scores of teenagers strolling towards it.

Lucy was apprehensive. Rising early for the European school day had been the first hurdle, and now she was about to meet more new people. A lanky girl with short, blonde hair and glasses emerged from the crowd, approaching Lucy with a friendly smile.

'Lucy? '

'Yes, I'm Lucy – Lucy Renate Wylie, Martha Schumacher's cousin from England. You're Renate?'

'That's right. I'll show you around before lessons start. Then, head teacher, Herr Horstmann, will meet you in his office.'

The foyer was filled with the ubiquitous aroma of filter coffee. Two flights of stairs led to a sunlit atrium overlooking a paved inner courtyard, where students congregated around benches, openly smoking.

'They're smoking?' Lucy asked. 'That's forbidden in English schools.'

'That's the designated smoking area,' Renate explained, 'smoking isn't allowed anywhere else in school. By the way, your German is excellent.'

'Thank you.' Lucy blushed, also pleased to have found someone who shared her middle name, which nobody here thought weird.

Herr Horstmann was heavily built, with bushy sideburns and thick-rimmed glasses. His spacious office made Mr Kingsley's office seem like a rabbit hutch. Lucy was given a firm handshake.

'You will be in *Unterprima*, a twelfth year class,' Herr Horstmann said.

'But in England, I'm in *Oberprima* – upper sixth, my last school year, studying A-levels, the *Abitur* equivalent,' Lucy argued.

'I think you'll enjoy twelfth year better,' Herr Horstmann said. 'The atmosphere in *Oberprima* is very intense. In twelfth year, the age range is sixteen to eighteen, so at seventeen you'll fit in. They're a friendly bunch, and you'll be very welcome as their English guest.'

Lucy was shown to a top floor classroom, where a score of students sat at cantilevered tables, awaiting first lesson, which was English. The teacher, Frau Schmidt, asked open questions, students responded accurately, in heavy German accents. Lucy was asked to read from Shakespeare's *Macbeth*. The class hung fascinated by every word. At break, she was fawned over like a celebrity, quizzed on her life in England, and inundated with names, remembering few. Christiane the plump one, Gaby the loud and talkative one, and Eva quirky and eccentric. After break was German, with Draconian Herr Steiff, who instilled fear in everyone. Lucy sat quaking in her shoes, thankful to be ignored. French and History followed, both teachers easy-going, allowing a buzz of working conversation. By the end of the morning, Lucy was faint with hunger, regretting having thrown most of her sandwich to the pigeons at break time. She met Renate, and they walked to the bus stop, talking about their respective school days. Already Lucy felt like a well-seasoned German citizen.

After three days, Lucy had fallen into a steady routine – returning home for lunch, studying upstairs, and dozing off in the stifling heat. In cooler evenings a light meal, a quiet stroll. The nocturnal harassment continued. By Saturday, the mosquito bites had merged to livid patches on Lucy's face, arms and legs.

In the kitchen, Martha and her daughter-in-law Karin were unpacking shopping.

'Are you allergic? Too many tomatoes from the garden, perhaps?' Karin observed.

'I don't think it's the tomatoes,' Lucy answered dismissively. When Helmut came home, Martha served a cold supper. Lucy ate fresh tomatoes, with no adverse effect. She shared English tea and biscuits until Karin's husband Klaus came to take her and Uwe home.

'Come Lucy,' Martha said, 'We'll go for a drive and show you more new places.'

The distraction was welcome. It was too sultry for study.

'This area has been completely rebuilt since the Second World War,' Helmut said, driving past modern homes and office buildings, then to an older part of the town, where a few original buildings remained.

'There's something we want to show you,' Martha said.

The car stopped at an older style, terraced town-house.

'That's the house I inherited from my grandparents who owned many properties,' Martha said. 'We don't live there, as we prefer our little house in Baumgarten. This house has no garden and is divided into flats, which we rent out.'

'Who lives there?' Lucy asked.

'Mostly Greek or Turkish immigrants, known as *Gastarbeiter* – guest workers.'

Lucy listened, struggling against an overwhelming sense of fatigue. That night she slept through the mosquitoes, not waking once.

All morning at school, thunder rumbled ominously in the stifling heat. During break, Lucy was admired for her slim figure, which boosted her confidence, but the tiredness didn't go away. Later, after a light lunch, Lucy went up to her room to rest, too exhausted to study. Suddenly she felt her limbs strangely heavy and stiff. An overwhelming, burning sensation engulfed her. Panicking, she fought for breath. She crept slowly downstairs to the relative coolness of the kitchen and sat down.

Karin was at the table, baby Uwe on her lap.

'Cup of coffee?' Martha asked. Lucy shook her head.

'My goodness, what is the matter? Are you ill?' Karin looked worried. 'Your face is red and your eyes are too bright. Do you have a fever?'

'Go upstairs and lie down,' Martha said. 'I'll get you a glass of water.'

Lucy rested on the bed, hoping the problem would go away. Every breath was an effort. Perhaps Martha and Karin could help? The next few hours – or was it days? – were a nightmarish blur. Fragmented events, snatches of conversations fused with dreams, like scattered puzzle pieces. It was Martha's choir night. Lucy couldn't recall even getting out of bed, fearing her illness was keeping Martha at home, depriving her of an evening out with friends. The sound of singing mingled with Martha's soft voice speaking strange words. It was dark now, perhaps after midnight? Through closed blinds, Lucy discerned the subdued street lighting. Then it was day, with awkward conversations and problems. Should she speak German or English? A pile of muddled photographs needed to be sorted – an impossible task. Lucy fretted with frustration, begging to be left alone. All the while, Martha said, '*Nicht weinen, mein Kind...*' don't cry, my child.

When the fever broke, Lucy went downstairs and sat at the table, feeling light-headed and distant. Was this another dream? Martha and Karin were drinking coffee. Uwe was chuntering quietly on the floor with his toys.

'How do you feel? You look much better. Would you like something to eat?' Martha asked.

Lucy nodded.

Martha fetched the bread-basket and the cold meats and cheeses. Lucy chewed a slice of *Schwarzbrot* – her favourite black rye bread. She drank a glass of water.

'You must eat more,' Karin said. 'You're far too thin. You need more flesh on those bones.'

The comment was unsurprising. Karin's massive frame obscured Lucy's view of the house plants on the window ledge, the white net curtain a backdrop fit for a prima donna.

'More coffee?' Martha said, refilling Lucy's cup. Lucy felt her strength returning. It was good to be up and about again. The peculiar rash had practically disappeared. Karin held fast to the allergy theory.

'You'll need to rest over the weekend, and you should be fit for school on Monday.' Martha said.

Outside, thick clouds were gathering. That evening, a strong wind picked up, releasing a powerful thunderstorm. Torrential rain hammered the little house, cascading down windows, flooding gutters. For three hours, forked lightning tore gloomy skies, and thunder rumbled deep into the night. A cold weather front swept in, banishing mosquitoes into hibernation. The next day, Helmut lit the coal stove.

Suddenly Lucy remembered Samantha's birthday. She went to the local shop, but there wasn't much choice, just postcard-sized pictures that didn't open out – and nothing specifically for a child. Lucy bought a picture-card of a bouquet of lilies tied with a blue ribbon, with the caption *Herzliche Glückwünsche zum Geburtstag* – a long-winded way of saying Happy Birthday.

'I wonder how Lucy's getting on,' mused Hilda, huddling under the canvas of a hired tent on a campsite, a mile from Edencroft, now occupied by the family of flaxen-haired children. The sale had completed earlier than anticipated, leaving Albert and Hilda temporarily homeless.

'Having the time of her life, I shouldn't wonder,' Albert said, puffing smoke. Light rain pattered gently on the canvas.

Hilda sighed. 'I suppose you're right. With Martha, she'll be in good hands. It's only natural for us to worry. Three months is such a long time. I do hope there's no more of that silly, fashion-conscious dieting nonsense.'

The dog grunted, and the budgie chirped cheerfully.

'I'll light the stove and make another cuppa,' Albert said.

Two kilometres from the border, the Dutch market town of Venlo bustled with Saturday shoppers. Quaint streets and gabled houses were a feast for the eyes. Lucy wished she had a camera. On the cobbled market square, Martha bought cheese, and Lucy bought apple-green knitting wool and a puff-sleeved, turquoise pullover. On the stroke of noon, a harmonious carillon of tinkling bell-tones pealed from hidden nooks and crannies, each decorative timepiece jingling its cheerful melody. It was a magical moment. Lucy felt startled and exposed, wishing she hadn't worn such flimsy clothes. She pulled the turquoise pullover on over her halter-neck top and escaped into a little shop. She bought a shoe brush in a wooden clog, a doll in Dutch national costume, and a book of *Snoopy* cartoons. Christmas shopping had begun.

'How do you like Venlo?' Martha asked when they returned to the car.

'It's good.'

'People come across the border for bargains, and Dutch shoopkeepers welcome German currency, as it's worth more.'

The Dutch edition of *Nobody is perfect* – *Niemand is volmaakt* was readable. Lucy decided to keep it for herself.

Sunday's outing was to Cologne, a flagship city that made Kochendorf look like a village. The famed cathedral towered tall and majestic against sunny Autumn skies. Scaffolding was up, on one side.

'Maintenance is ongoing. As soon as one part is restored, another needs attention,' Helmut said. Along the banks of the Rhine, a keen breeze chased fallen leaves. Lucy felt cold inside and strangely depressed. Surely she ought to be cheerful? Today was baby Samantha's first birthday. Lucy wondered what everyone was doing back home. She brushed away an unwelcome tear.

'Are you unhappy, Lucy? What's wrong? Martha asked.

'I'm just tired, that's all.'

At school, Lucy was welcomed back, everyone expressing concern about her health. During break, a small crowd gathered around like bees round a honey pot, asking what she was reading, what was in her packed lunch, what it was like to live in England, and whether she had ever met Cliff Richard or the Queen. A few volunteers read falteringly from *King Lear* and *Sense and Sensibility*, charged with Anglophilic zeal.

Lucy smiled at their efforts.

'You were born in London? How wonderful!' Gaby gasped, reshaping Lucy's opinion on England's capital city and eschewing her parents' critique of London being run-down, filthy, and overcrowded.

Gaby also lived in Baumgarten, and Lucy agreed to go with her to an after-school, amateur athletics club. Lucy was assured no expertise was needed. However, the session amounted to an hour of standing around chatting, with the occasional gentle jog around an asphalt track. There was no instruction, and Lucy quickly became bored. Most participants were overweight, except for two emaciated girls who reminded Lucy of the stick insects in the biology lab. Determined to exercise more, Lucy borrowed Martha's bicycle, exploring Baumgarten's streets and arrow-straight cycle path between forests and railway. In the clattering roar of a passing train, Lucy pedalled faster, the wind in her face, feeling exhilarated, invincible, and free.

Indoors, she helped Martha with chores, as Martha was often tired after cleaning neighbours' houses and babysitting Uwe three mornings a week. Lucy vacuumed the stairs, and was shown how to operate the coffee machine and iron clothes thoroughly – damper items to be ironed twice, then hung to air. Iron for an hour, and you'll have burned the calories of a chocolate biscuit, Gaby had said. Lucy quickly learned to be brisk and efficient, much to Martha's delight.

On the first of October, a letter came:

Flat 7. Trafalgar Villas.
South Esplanade,
Nyehaven.
27.9.73.

Dear Lucy,

Today is your father's birthday, and I'm at work, looking forward to getting home at the weekend! I'm thinking of you a lot and hope you are well. No doubt Martha and Helmut are looking after you well, and you're busy with your studies and learning German. You have a wonderful opportunity, so make the most of it!

Meanwhile, I trust you are eating sensibly. Never take good health for granted.

Work on the new house was delayed, so we camped in old Biddlecombe's field with the dog and the budgie for ten days – which was quite fun, apart from the rain.

The above address is a nice flatlet for us to share on your return. There's a lovely view of the sea. I look forward to when we can be together here and travel home on Friday evenings to Sussex.

The new house is clean and fresh and bright, with a new smell everywhere. We've bought new furniture, carpets and curtains, and a colour television with a 20-inch screen, which you'll see when you come at Christmas.

Little Samantha is growing fast. Marion took photos of her birthday party in the garden. We went for a drive to Chanctonbury Ring, which we all enjoyed, except for Paul, who said the climb was too steep. We had fun arguing over whose turn it was to carry the 'little cherub'.

I'll finish now and pop this letter in the post., Take care of yourself and give my best regards to Martha and all the clan,

Love from your Mum xxxx

Lucy translated. Martha and Helmut seemed surprised, giving the impression that Germans almost never moved house. Helmut had lived in the same little house since it was built thirty years before and had no plans to leave it.

That evening, another visit had been planned. When Helmut came home from work, he stopped the Beetle, left the engine running, and called Martha and Lucy to the car.

'Come, Lucy! Sit at the front and be my co-pilot.'

A World War Two *Luftwaffe* pilot, Helmut spoke little about his active service. If any Nazi footage came on the television, he switched it off immediately.

'We're visiting the Keller family,' Helmut said, lighting a cigarette. 'Franz Keller is a colleague of mine and a good friend.'

Franz and Iris Keller lived with their two small sons in an eighth-floor apartment. Iris was even bigger and rounder than Karin and a devoted mother to her boys, the elder of whom had undergone several surgeries for various health conditions. The Kellers were a cheerful family: the little boys bounced around Lucy on the sofa, showering her with toys and questions. Lucy was pleased to be so well-liked. Iris prepared a lavish supper, with no expense spared, and Lucy was encouraged to eat plenty. However, after three hours indoors, Lucy wasn't hungry. She nibbled daintily at a ham sandwich, making it last.

'*Du musst essen – viel mehr essen!*' Iris urged, offering cake.

'*Danke,*' Lucy said, taking a slice of marble cake. The boys asked about her house, her pets and what she watched on television. Lucy found plenty to say. The more she talked, the less she ate. Franz and Helmut talked about Willi Brandt and the German economy. Lucy overheard Franz saying he longed to afford a house and garden, with space for the children to play.

Apparently, Lucy scored a hit with the Kellers, for she was invited back the following weekend. She was too polite to refuse. Helmut drove Lucy to the flats on Friday evening and stayed for an hour, chatting to Franz over a glass of beer and a game of cards. The boys clambered over Lucy and asked her to play games and do drawings for them. It was wonderful to be wanted, but being in constant demand was tiring work. After an hour, she hid herself behind a book, pleading the need to study.

Once a fortnight, Lucy posted an essay to Miss Menzies, which was returned a few days later, marked and annotated with helpful comments. Lucy's grades were encouraging, allaying her concerns about missing a term's classes. The once daunting Shakespeare texts were easier to understand, Lucy identifying with characters' predicaments, and their mental and emotional struggles. Much had changed in her own life in the past three years. Living in Germany, with a virtually new identity, Lucy felt like a different person.

The start of the Autumn holidays began with a school *Budenfest* – a Booths

Festival and charity fundraiser. Each class hosted an attraction in their classroom, from home-baking and craft sales, raffles, competitions, to games of skill and chance. Class 12A set up a race track for remote control cars, a popular choice, girls enjoying what was considered a boys' activity. Lucy strolled around in the carnival-like atmosphere, visiting stalls, blending in. After the event, Gaby invited the class to a *Stammtisch* – a congenial get-together in a town centre bar, that evening. As an honoured guest, Lucy was obliged to accept. When Helmut dropped her at the venue, Lucy asked to be collected at ten o'clock – partly from habit, but also because she felt dreadfully tired.

The dimly-lit Bierkeller was an uncomfortable reminder of the fateful night at the Apple Barrel. A dozen classmates were talking and laughing over drinks and snacks at a candlelit corner table. Lucy was welcomed into the circle, and the evening passed by pleasantly, Lucy exchanged addresses with a few, promising to stay in touch.

During the *Herbstferien* – Autumn holidays, more socialising was squeezed into Lucy's busy schedule. Martha's friends, the Meyer family had four adopted daughters: eighteen-year-old Dutch twins Miep and Geesje, a toddler from war-ravaged Vietnam, and sixteen-year-old May-Li from Hong Kong, who was fluent in German and keen to learn about life in England. It was strange speaking in German to another foreigner. Lucy realised she hadn't held a single conversation in English for almost two months.

Then Helmut introduced Lucy to Glaswegian colleague, John Mackenzie, who had moved to Kochendorf twenty years ago, married a German, and spoke German like a native. During *Abendbrot* in the Mackenzies' townhouse, Lucy failed to find fault with John's German.

One day, might I be as fluent, and married to a German? Lucy wondered.

'Frau Mackenzie has a hard life,' Helmut said on the way home. 'John drinks a crate of beer every night, swears like a trooper and beats his wife. I don't know how she puts up with it. In her place I'd have left him long ago.'

Lucy was surprised such hardship could hide behind so glossy an exterior.

'You'll meet cousin Margaretha tomorrow,' Martha said, 'She's married to Dutch businessman, Piet Kuyper. They're quite rich and own a luxury apartment in Unterheidenrath. Their son Karl is at teachers' college, and their daughter Anja left home. Margaretha is eager to meet you, and you'll be staying the night.'

'That's nice,' Lucy acquiesced, unsure she could cope with meeting yet more people. She felt more than ever like royalty, kept in luxury, obliged to fulfil public duties.

Soon after arriving at the Kuyper residence, Lucy had the impression Anja had caused the family great sadness and was best not talked about. Lucy also discovered this was the first time the Schumachers had spoken to the Kuypers for three years. Helmut and Martha left politely after lunch, leaving

Lucy alone with her hosts. She offered to help with the dishes, but Margaretha had an automatic dishwasher, a device Lucy had heard of but had never seen. She helped load it enthusiastically.

'By the way, just call me Greta,' Margaretha said. Round-faced and motherly, Greta reminded Lucy of Frau Schmied.

'Could we go for a walk?' Lucy asked, feeling the need to expend energy. 'The weather is nice.'

'All right. Piet is working in the study, but you and I can go to the park. It would be a shame to miss the sunshine.'

From the marble-tiled hallway, they took the lift to the ground floor. The chill air struck cold, and Lucy shivered, wishing she had packed a winter coat. In the park, the setting sun cast long shadows across leaf-strewn gravel paths and rectangular lawns lined with plane trees. Lucy spoke about her home and family in England, while Greta listened with avid interest. In the evening, another large meal was served, which disappointed Lucy, as she was hoping for a cold supper with healthier options. Karl arrived home with his fiancée Inge, making five at the meal table. Lucy talked more about her life in England.

'So you'll go to University?' Greta asked.

'I hope so,' Lucy answered, toying with her vegetables. The white sauce was rich in butter, the peas laced with sugar.

'Which university? Oxford?'

Lucy flushed with pride.

'Probably not, but somewhere not too far from home. Blackford is my first choice, then Reading or Canterbury. I just need to get good grades in my exams.'

'I think you'll do well,' Inge said, sounding wistful, 'I barely noticed you weren't German. I wish my English was as good.'

Dessert was lemon cheesecake – the rich, succulent variety Lucy regretted not ordering at the Speck-Weg-Weg in Bavaria. She took a tiny spoonful and said, 'This is delicious.'

'Eat up then!' Greta insisted. 'You peck like a little bird.'

'I'm watching my weight,' Lucy said.

Piet looked shocked. 'That's ridiculous! When you turn sideways we can hardly see you.'

In her mind's eye, all Lucy could see was pencil-thin Alison.

Karl lit a cigarette.

'I'm thinking of becoming a teacher, too,' Lucy said.

'Then you will teach German, won't you?' Inge asked emphatically. 'You're very good at it.'

'And French, too.' Lucy added, not intending to sound conceited.

Inge's eyebrows shot up. 'French as well? How impressive.'

K was chain-smoking, the ashtray now almost full.

'Do you smoke?' Lucy asked Inge.

'No, I don't like it.'

'Would anyone like coffee?' Greta asked. All but Lucy gave a nod of assent.

'Is German coffee to strong for you?' Greta asked.

'If I drink coffee I can't sleep,' Lucy answered. 'But it smells good.'

'In the evenings I make decaffeinated coffee,' Greta smiled.

'Then I'll have some,' Lucy agreed.

After the meal, Piet withdrew to the lounge to smoke his pipe and read the newspaper, while Karl and Inge went out. Lucy sprang into action, offering to help Greta tidy up.

'You remind me of my daughter,' Greta began. 'Like you, she had fair skin and blue eyes. She was a lovely girl.'

Lucy didn't know what to say.

'She ran away,' Greta continued.

'Why? You have a nice home. You are a nice family.'

'It wasn't about that. It was because of a man.'

'A man?'

'Yes – a boyfriend.'

'But why did she run away?'

Greta hesitated. 'This boyfriend – he was not a good man – he was a – criminal.'

'Doesn't Anja write letters or phone?' Lucy asked.

Greta shook her head. 'She gave no forwarding address or phone number. She said she didn't want to see us again. We haven't heard word from her since the day she left.'

The wall clock ticked. Lucy was touched by Greta's openness about her hidden heartache.

'I often think I'll never be engaged or married, as I'm not good enough or good-looking,' Lucy said, disclosing her own anxieties.

'Rubbish! You're only seventeen!' Greta exclaimed. 'You have your whole life before you, and you have much to offer. There's plenty of time yet.'

That night, Lucy slept well. In the morning, she sauntered into the dining room for breakfast at half past nine. Piet was seated at the table, hidden behind a newspaper. The back page headline was in English:

THE END OF THE WORLD!

England had failed to qualify for the next World Cup football tournament. Piet didn't mention the headline, but Lucy knew Helmut would be interested. She recalled the euphoria in London on that hot afternoon, when England triumphed over Germany in the 1966 World Cup.

'Where's Karl?' Lucy asked.

'Still asleep,' Greta answered. 'He always sleeps late on Sundays.'

Lucy pulled out a chair and sat down. She helped herself to rye bread and jam, carefully avoiding the butter. A song from *Fiddler on the Roof* was on the radio.

If I were a rich man...

Lucy looked out at grey rooftops and bare trees. *The Kuypers are rich,* she thought, *but are they happy?*

28: Denial

School resumed the third week of October. Dark, cheerless mornings and bleak, overcast days heralded the onset of winter. Lucy liked the cosy evenings in the cramped living-room with its faded, threadbare settee and faithful coal stove in the corner. Martha had acquired a bigger table, for Lucy to do homework in the warm, as the bedrooms were unheated. Lucy caught a heavy cold which lingered, aggravated by early starts and walks from school to bus stop in pouring rain. Frau Biedermeier gave Lucy a thick, brown woollen midi-coat, with a fur trim on the hood and cuffs – a hand-me-down from Renate. Lucy was glad of the coat, but her health didn't improve. Abdominal pains, stomach upsets and absence of periods were a mystery. Martha had a theory she chose not to share. Besides, her current concern was visiting cousin Maria in Wiesenbrück, a hundred kilometres north, before the snows came.

'One more weekend visit before winter,' Martha said one evening, over supper.

'Who?' Lucy asked.

'Cousin Maria, in Wiesenbrück. It's a fair way, so an early start on Saturday. The Brauns are friendly and down-to-earth, Maria is very kind. Her husband is Hermann, the children, Detlev and Erika.'

'How old are they?'

'Fourteen and eight.'

'Are there more cousins, apart from the Brauns?' Lucy asked.

'Not exactly.'

'What do you mean?' Lucy asked.

'Nothing, it doesn't matter.'

'Please tell me.'

'Very well. There's another family of Westers in Meisenfeld. But they've said they don't want to meet you, and generally, they don't speak to us.'

'Why not?'

'Because we're on the wrong side of the family.'

'What do you mean?'

'It's about social status. Helmut and I aren't wealthy, but we're content. When your grandfather Gregor and great-uncle Jakob emigrated to England, Jakob was successful, but fell out with his brother and sacked him, and the only work Gregor could find was in a hotel kitchen. That means you're one of the poor relations.'

'If these people don't want to meet me, it's their loss,' Lucy said.

'That's the spirit, girl!' Helmut chuckled.

The next day, Lucy walked from school to the bus stop, a spring in her step. It had been a good morning. In the art class, the task had been to paint geometric shapes, blending two colours. Lucy's painting of tessellating shades of saffron and cobalt blue was praised by most, deemed too gaudy by others. People's negative opinions were of no consequence. Bright colours were good. Chill winds whipped russet-gold leaves in lively eddies along the pavement. The avenue of plane trees and red-bricked houses in this smoky, industrial town was a far cry from the rural beauty and fresh breezes of Edencroft, but Lucy had no regrets. Life was good now, the past in the past.

Wiesenbrück had its own unique character – a blend of old and new, rich and poor, dwellings cheek by jowl. The Brauns' third-floor tenement flat, was small and austere, but its inhabitants were optimistic and upbeat. Hermann Braun was a massive man with a larger-than-life laugh, Maria, a merry, thoughtful soul, with a typical Wester attitude to hospitality. A lunch of sausage, buttered parsley potatoes, and *Sauerkraut* was served at the kitchen table, and conversations flowed in lively exchange of life stories. Detlev grinned behind a mop of straight, blond hair, feeding his broad-shouldered frame and entertaining the family with quips Lucy didn't understand. Erika bonded with Lucy immediately, discovering a common interest in creative crafts and cookery. After lunch, the two families walked and talked through Wiesenbrück's wind-blustered, cobbled streets, in a grand city centre reconstructed in pre-war gabled style. At four o'clock, a joyful carillon of bells pealed from clocks and bell-towers, and as dusk fell, the group hastened home for coffee and Black Forest gateau. Afterwards, Lucy and Erika watched cartoons; then Lucy drew a picture of a house with a red roof and a big garden filled with trees, lawns and colourful flowers. Erika copied it. 'When I grow up, I want to live in a house like that,' she said.

After *Abendbrot*, Maria said to Martha, 'You can sleep in our bedroom and we'll sleep on the living-room couch. Detlev will sleep on the camp-bed in the kitchen and Lucy and Erika can share Detlev's room.'

Nobody complained. The men spent the rest of the evening in the lounge sharing beers and cigars, while the women and girls sat round the kitchen table, enjoying fizzy drinks and *Lebkuchen* – a seasonal speciality of iced, spiced cakes. Lucy's waistband was tight, and the press-stud kept popping open, but she was happy, her pledge to curb the calories on hold. At bedtime, Lucy and Erika lay head-to-toe in Detlev's single bed in the tiny bedroom.

After lights out, Erika said she wasn't tired and continued the conversation until Lucy drifted to a deep sleep.

The time spent with the Brauns lifted Lucy's spirits, and her cheerful demeanour continued for several days. A cold snap descended on the Rhine plains, covering cities, towns and countryside with a white blanket that quickly turned to grey slush on Kochendorf's well-trodden streets. It was time for thick coats, hats, gloves, and boots. The social visits continued. Martha and Lucy were invited to *Kaffeetrinken* in the Biedermeiers' parlour, where Renate's budgerigar was allowed free flight. Lucy thought of the Mayfields' misbehaving avian but told only the saga of Buddy's escape and consequent theft.

'Your German is really improving,' Renate said. 'I would scarcely know you were English.'

Saturday was spent at Meisenfeld. After a busy week, Lucy was exhausted and would have preferred to stay at home. She forked fastidiously at her food and picked at the dessert, scraping the fruit off the flan, leaving the pastry.

Martha was weary of her whims. 'In your letter to us you said you ate everything. But you hardly eat anything!' she protested.

Lucy remembered writing the letter. *But that was before the night at the Apple Barrel!*

'You mentioned the small boy in the photo was a sick man,' Lucy said, changing the subject. There was an awkward silence.

'He doesn't go out. He's mentally handicapped,' Wilhelm explained. 'Besides, he belongs to the side of the family who don't wish to know us.'

Another awkward silence, punctuated by the clatter of cutlery.

Lucy looked down, studying her red corduroy skirt. The colour was too garish and the hemline too short.

After the meal, Lucy helped carry empty lemonade bottles to the cellar. Marleen gave Lucy a bag of home-grown apples and said,

'Take these back to Kochenorf with you. Enjoy them, Lucy. We have plenty to eat in our house, and no one needs to go hungry.'

Lucy looked at the well-stocked shelves laden with jars of pickles, and the wooden barrel filled with dessert apples.

'Thank you,' she answered. Inside, she felt cold, numb and depressed.

Hilda huddled in the gloom, warming her hands at the meagre gas heater. The tension in her neck was working its way from her shoulder to her right temple. Here she was, alone for another week, keeping a place for a daughter who was too busy to write, while fifty miles away her husband spent all day in a comfortable new house with just himself and the dog to care for. Self-pity wasn't in Hilda's religion, but anxiety definitely was. A recently prescribed pack of migraine tablets wasn't working. The doctor had asked if she was worried about anything. Worried? Hilda always worried. Having so much time on her hands in the winter evenings didn't help.

A sudden, soft tap at the door startled her.

'Hello-oo.' A gravelly voice rasped from the other side of the door. 'I know you're in there.'

'Who's there?' Hilda demanded.

'It's me. You remember me, don't you?'

'No, I don't. You're clearly mistaken. Please go away.'

'Oh no, I'm not. I know you'll remember me. Just open the door a tiny bit, you'll see who it is. It'll be a surprise!'

Hilda's spine prickled. 'Go away, or I'll call the police,' she bluffed. The fact that there was no telephone in the flat terrified her.

'But, Lucy, it's me – you know, Steve. I heard you were living here.'

Was this was big, greasy, slimy Steve? What had Lucy been up to years before? Hilda recoiled, shocked, her imagination running wild.

'I am not Lucy! Lucy isn't here, she lives abroad. I'm Lucy's mother. Go now, or I'll call the police,' Hilda answered icily.

'Oh, er – sorry, I d – didn't know it was you, well, g – goodbye.' Steve stammered. Hilda heard him sloping off down the corridor, then the distinctive, dull thud of the heavy front door closing. She sank back in the armchair and sighed heavily.

Lucy sat in the Kochendorf bar, staring sullenly into her glass of lemonade. The residents of Baumgarten were celebrating their win of a coveted national award for the best-kept neighbourhood. There was dancing to a live brass band, and drinks flowed abundantly. Helmut and Martha talked to friends, while Lucy sulked on the sidelines, wishing she'd stayed behind to finish her English essay.

'This one's yours, Lucy, keep it safe,' Helmut said, pressing a raffle ticket into her hand.

'*Danke*,' Lucy mumbled. She put the ticket in her pocket. All this seemed a monumental waste of time. She twiddled her thumbs under the table, seething with frustration. At last, the raffle was drawn, heralding the impending end of the party. Then Helmut came bounding up to Lucy announcing through the noise and clamour that she had won something. Lucy brightened, wondering what the prize could be. A large teddy-bear, perhaps? That would be a bit awkward to carry back home to England. Hopefully not a bottle of drink or a pack of cigars!

'Here you are,' Helmut said, handing Lucy a plain white envelope. Inside was a card:

Kelmer Konditorei - Zitronentorte

'Kelmer's? The confectioner's? A lemon flan?'

'Yes, the cake is the prize,' Martha explained. 'You order it at the shop. They couldn't bring a cake in here and leave it to spoil during the evening, could they? You go to the shop and arrange to collect it.'

'But I can't eat a whole cake,' Lucy protested. A *Torte* was ten times the size of one of her mother's Victoria sponge cakes.

'No problem,' Martha smiled. 'Throw a party!'

But Lucy was in no mood for parties. She just wanted to go home.

The next day, Lucy hoped for news from her mother. Returning from school, she saw Martha's bicycle wasn't in its usual place against the wall. Martha was probably still at her cleaning job, and no doubt had the key with her. Lucy looked in the mail-box. It was empty – and she was locked out in the rain. Exasperated, she stomped off to the Biedermeiers' to ask for the key, but no one was at home. Infuriated, she trudged to the Schneiders', but again, nobody was in. She stormed back to the Schumachers' and rang the bell.

Martha opened the door. 'Where on earth were you? I went to put out the rubbish, and found your school bag on the step. That was half an hour ago. Why didn't you come in?'

'I saw your bicycle was gone, so I looked for you at the Biedermeiers and the Schneiders.'

Martha was extremely annoyed. 'You could have at least knocked! I've been home since eleven o'clock. I put the bicycle away because it was raining. I was at Frau Schneider's this morning and finished early, because Frau Schneider had to go out.'

Lucy was sheepishly silent. On the table was a letter with a British stamp and her mother's bold handwriting. Opening it, Lucy read about the new house, Hilda's colleague Kathy's new baby, and Samantha had learnt to walk.

'Margaretha and Piet have invited you back on Saturday,' Martha said, 'if you want to go, that is.'

Exhausted from all the activities, Lucy was still reluctant to miss anything. 'I'll go,' she agreed.

On Saturday evening, Karl and Inge invited her to a college party. Wearing the cream, crimplene dress she'd worn in France and at Sarah's wedding, Lucy hoped tonight would be special. Disco lights flashed, pop music pounded, in an atmosphere of pre-festive cheer. Karl bought lager for himself and Inge; Lucy requested orange juice. As the dance floor filled, Karl teased Lucy about her typically British, keep-your-distance manner. Lucy accepted one dance, then it was Inge's turn, and Lucy sat down, listening to the beat of British and American pop songs, some evoking memories of Clive and the gang. Lucy had valued his companionship, but now she craved – dare she admit it – love? Surely Karl and Inge were in love? Had her feelings for Roland been true love?

She twirled her silver bells ring nervously.

A young man stood beside her asking,

'*Willst du tanzen?*'

'*Ja – bitte,*' Lucy answered, wondering if this was a dream.

The young lad danced clumsily, then he bought Lucy a drink, insisting she have the same as he did – a brandy. She took a cautious sip, telling herself it had health benefits. The boy swished his glass and downed the shot with panache.

'Tell me about yourself,' he said. Lucy soon grew hoarse from shouting over the din. The boy said nothing, and Lucy wondered if he'd listened to a word she said.

'I'm Frank,' he said.

'Are you a student?'

'I'm in the army. Can't stand it.'

'Oh.' Lucy sipped the brandy, feeling it nip the back of her throat.

'Can I get you another one?'

'*Nein Danke!*' Lucy shook her head.

'You're a sweet girl,' Frank said. In the subdued lighting, Lucy blushed unnoticed.

'You're a sweet girl,' Frank said again. 'I like motor bikes and pizza.'

Lucy stifled a yawn. Though grateful for this boy's attention, she knew nothing about him. Frank reached into his jacket pocket and pulled out a grey, metallic ring of intertwined plaits of steel. He unravelled it and put it back together. 'Here, see if you can do the same.'

He placed the ring in Lucy's hand and went back to the bar. Lucy unravelled the ring and tried reassembling it.

A catchy ABBA song was playing:

> You are the dancing queen...
>
> young and sweet, only seventeen...

'I can't figure this out,' Lucy admitted when Frank returned with another double brandy. He reassembled the ring in seconds and handed it back.

'Keep it. Consider it your first present, from me.'

'Thank you,' Lucy replied. For the next five minutes, the enigmatic ring kept her occupied. She twisted the strands this way and that, but the knack eluded her. She didn't notice Karl and Inge return.

'We're going now, Lucy,' Karl said.

'But –'

'Just leave it there,' Karl said gently.

'This boy – Frank – he gave me the ring –'

'He's asleep, Inge said.

Frank sprawled in the chair, eyes closed and mouth open wide. *Was my company so dull that I bored him to sleep?* Lucy wondered. Leaving her barely-touched glass of brandy and the unravelled ring, Lucy left with Karl and Inge, numb with disappointment.

Returning to the Schumachers', Lucy found a letter from Alison. She had won another beauty contest, had appeared on television and been offered work as a model. Lucy put the letter away and tried to forget about it.

'I collected your cake this morning,' Martha said.

On the worktop was a white cardboard box tied with a ribbon.

'Come and look!' Martha untied the bow and lifted the lid to reveal a circle of smooth white icing and scallops of whipped cream. 'I'll put it the parlour, where it's cooler, and where we'll have the party tomorrow.'

Martha unlocked the converted scullery – a room seldom used, and expensive to heat. There was nothing special to mark this occasion, apart from Lucy's win at the raffle, but Germans needed no excuse to celebrate.

Lucy ate sparingly at lunch, then helped Martha with the dishes and party preparation. A dozen guests were expected, including Karin and Eva and their children, the Meyers, the Biedermeiers, the Schneiders, and two of Martha's choir friends. The buffet began with a selection of sweet and savoury nibbles, served with freshly ground coffee and lashings of whipped cream. The cake graced the centre of the sideboard. For Lucy, it was far too much fuss, just over a silly cake, that would make her even fatter and uglier than she already was. Lemon cheesecake was a favourite indulgence, but curiously, Lucy wasn't hungry. She allowed herself one small slice. After the last guest left, Lucy helped Martha tidy up, then went to her room and spent ten minutes toe-touching and hip-stretching until her sides ached. For supper, Martha served calorie-rich *Reibekuchen* – potato pancakes oozing with butter. Lucy picked sullenly at her portion, tormented by visions of slim, stunningly beautiful Alison beaming blissfully before the television cameras.

A series of solemn festivals and popular traditions marked the countdown to Lucy's return home. November began with *Allerheiligen* – All Saints' Day, a public holiday. Helmut was at home, and school was closed. Lucy accompanied Martha and Helmut to a traditional service at the local Catholic church, a modern building three streets away. For an hour, Lucy mirrored Martha's actions, when to sit and when to rise. A solemn procession followed to Baumgarten Cemetery, where scores of mourners marched in silence in autumn sunshine. Dressed in the long brown coat, Lucy remembered a monotonous dirge from primary school.

> Old Abram Brown is dead and gone
> Alas he is no more
> He used to wear a long brown coat
> That button'd down before...

There was no music or conversation. Lucy found the entire expedition inexpressibly depressing. Days later, a lantern-lit procession in pouring rain marked St. Martin's Day, but Lucy stayed indoors. Next was Armistice Day, and Lucy wondered what the German perspective would be. Helmut drove to town and parked in a side street. A lengthy walk followed. Lucy dragged her feet wearily.

'We're going to the town hall square,' Martha said.

'Why?' Lucy asked, yawning. Martha mentioned *Denkmal* – a word missing from Lucy's vocabulary.

'Do you know what a *Denkmal* is?' Martha asked.

Denken means to think. Lucy took a guess.

'Something you have to think about?'

'Yes, but also a place where people do their thinking.'

In the heart of Kochendorf, hundreds of townsfolk gathered around a stone cenotaph. A silence was held. The crowd stood still as stone, against background traffic sounds. The town hall clock jingled briefly; then, the crowd cheered their corporate joy.

'*Karneval* season has begun,' Martha said, nudging Lucy.

'Carnival season? What's that?'

'From eleven minutes past the eleventh hour on the eleventh day of the eleventh month, we start looking forward to *Karneval* – a big festival in February.'

More partying?

'Oh,' Lucy said tiredly.

'Come,' Martha said, 'let's go shopping.'

In the town's shopping precinct, Lucy's mood lifted at the sight of festive window displays. She bought squared paper, colourful ring-binders in deep orange, magenta and cerise pink, a tree-shaped ornament with luminous plastic balls, and for her mother, a wooden wall plaque bearing a verse.

> **Was uns die Welt auch bieten mag**
> **Mit all' ihren Schätzen,**
> **Ein liebes, treues Mutterherz**
> **Kann niemals sie ersetzen.**

'Your mother will like that,' Martha said. At the travel agent's an open ticket was purchased for the return journey. *This time next month, I'll be home!* Lucy tingled with excitement. Back in her room, Lucy wrote a translation on the back of the plaque:

> *Whatever the world may offer us*
> *With all its joys and pleasures*
> *A loving, caring, mother's heart*
> *Surpasses all these treasures.*

She squeezed everything into her case, leaving little room for anything else. Then Martha gave Lucy a maroon tweed jacket, saying it was too small for her, and a turquoise and gold fabric remnant, suggesting Frau Schneider make her a dress. It was Martha's choir night, and Helmut's took Lucy to an office *Stammtisch* at a rustic hunting lodge with log fire. He bought Lucy a lemonade and a liqueur-glass of *Jägermeister* which was pleasanter to taste than the brandy bought by Frank. Helmut boasted Lucy was a quarter English, a quarter Irish, a quarter Scottish, and a quarter German-Dutch, and that she spoke German like a native. The open fire cast flickering patterns on stag heads and firearms on wood-panelled walls. Lucy relaxed, nibbling peanuts and miniature pretzels. Someone kept mentioning the word *Baummarder*, which Lucy intended to look up in the dictionary but forgot.

That week, post arrived, forwarded from Foxfield – an interview at Reading University in December, and a conditional place and Open Day invitation to Blackford University the week after. Lucy was keen to leave, especially as heavy snow was forecast.

Events escalated, every day distinct.

On Wednesday, Lucy stayed home, informing Frau Schmidt she needed time to finish an English essay. Uwe wandered in and out of the room, banging a toy hammer on the wall, and babbling to a threadbare teddy bear. It was impossible to concentrate. Lucy put the books away and watched the German television coverage of Princess Anne's marriage to Captain Mark Phillips.

On Thursday, Class 12A went swimming in Kochendorf's indoor, heated pool. There was no pressure to compete, just a time of aquatic fun. Lucy planned to swim several lengths, to work up an appetite for cake at *Kaffeetrinken*. Curiously, she stopped halfway through the second length, feeling as if a lead weight was weighing her down. She arrived back to a cold house, the stove unlit. There was no cake, just a few dry cinnamon biscuits. Lucy pulled a face, unprepared for worse news.

'Onkel Friedrich is in hospital,' Martha said, 'He's had a heart attack, not the first one, but a bad one.'

'Is he going to be all right?'

'We hope. If he survives the next few days he'll probably be fine.'

Preoccupied with her pending departure, Lucy wasn't concerned. She wrote to her parents that she'd return on December 2nd, in time for the school party. Martha took Lucy to Frau Schneider's for a dress-fitting, an echo of the run-up to Marion's wedding. The long, halter-neck dress hid Lucy's hips and thighs; the coarse, fibre-glass fabric reminded her of the curtains in the old house in London. The dress was ready on Saturday. Lucy thanked Martha and packed it that night, squeezing it into her case.

Sunday was *Autoloser Sonntag* – a car-less day, a government ploy to save fuel in the current oil crisis. Lucy cycled Baumgarten's empty roads, enjoying fume-free space, feeling conspicuous among youngsters. Surprisingly few adults were taking advantage of the occasion. The atmosphere at *Abendbrot* was subdued. Helmut spoke of the impact of motor vehicles on global oil resources and environmental damage. Lucy wanted to say cars should be used sparingly, people should exercise more, use public transport, and emergency services would operate better on emptier roads, but she was too tired to contribute to the conversation. Martha and Helmut were speaking *Plattdeutsch*. For once, Helmut spoke about the war – his hatred of Hitler and having to fight from obligation, not choice. He mentioned his first wife, who Lucy had been given to understand was killed in an air raid. Now, there was talk of a child, which was news to Lucy. Then she heard words she would never forget: Helmut's young wife had leapt from a bridge with the child.

Friedrich came home the next day and was said to be recovering well.

'We're invited to Sunday lunch,' Martha told Lucy. 'Friedrich especially wants to see you before you leave.'

Upstairs in her room, Lucy continued to pack. For the journey, she would definitely need to wear the hooded jacket and several layers of clothing, freeing up space for last-minute items. With regret, she decided to leave Renate's old winter coat behind until next year.

On Sunday, Friedrich was up and about, occupying his usual seat in the kitchen. He had baked currant bread, especially for Lucy's visit.

'I'll be back again next year,' Lucy told Friedrich.

'If I'm still alive,' Friedrich replied calmly. Lucy took her great-uncle by the hand and said, 'Look after yourself, and of course you'll still be alive.'

'Can I write some verses in your book?' Friedrich asked.

'Of course.' Lucy handed him her diary. Friedrich wrote in bold, deft strokes, then read aloud,

Im Wunderschönen Monat Mai, wo alle Knospen sprangen
Da ist in meinem Herzen, die Liebe aufgegangen!

'Thank you,' Lucy said.

In the wonderful month of May, with all the buds a-bursting,
That was when, in my own heart, the flame of love was kindled...

'I'd like to speak to your mother,' Friedrich said.

Marleen dialled the number and handed Friedrich the phone.

He greeted Hilda for the first time in half a century.

'Your mother wants to speak with you now,'

Lucy struggled to think again in English.

'Hi, Mum...'

'Lucy!' How are you? Are you all right?'

Hilda's voice was faint and anxious.

'Yes, Mum – I'm fine.'

'When are you coming home?'

'December 2nd. There's a letter in the post –'

Then the line went dead.

Later, Lucy noticed her health insurance expired on the last day of

November. The likelihood of anything untoward happening was small, but Lucy wasn't risking anything, since medical treatments abroad were so expensive. Better yet, she could travel a day earlier, walk into the house and give her parents the surprise of their lives?

At school, Frau Schmidt asked Lucy to give a talk in German, describing her home, school, shops, festivals, and the English way of life. The class hung on every word. The moment Lucy finished, they demonstrated their approval by knocking rhythmically in unison on the wooden benches. As a parting gift, Lucy was presented with a card signed by everyone, two textbooks on humanities, and a china coffee-pot with a coffee filter. Lucy was immensely grateful and wondered anew how she was going to carry everything home.

And then Martha gave Lucy yet another present – one she could not refuse.

'Klaus is a keen amateur photographer,' Martha said. 'He developed a copy of the family photograph of the Golden Wedding, for you. It's in cardboard to keep it flat, and it won't be heavy.'

'Thank you – thank you so much,' Lucy responded, envisaging her mother's delight.

The next day brought sad news. Suffering another massive heart attack, Friedrich was rushed to hospital and was pronounced dead on arrival. The funeral was to be next week, and Lucy would miss it. Shocked and disbelieving, Lucy reflected how, at the end of his life, Friedrich had met and spoken with two distant family members.

She felt calm, a sense of closure.

The day of the journey came. Under a heavy sky, Lucy stood with Martha and Helmut on the bleak station platform, flurries of snow swirling thicker and faster, carpeting the ground in bright white. Unsurprisingly, the train was delayed. Time seemed protracted in a wall of silence.

'When do you think the train will come?' Lucy asked tentatively, studying Helmut's thoughtful expression through a veil of falling snow.

'Who can tell?' Helmut replied, looking upwards. 'It's not up to us. These things are determined by Higher Powers.'

The thickening blanket of snow deadened every sound. Then, the distant rhythmic pounding of an approaching train.

'Thank you, thank you for – everything,' Lucy said, scarcely believing her time in Kochendorf was over.

'Take care, my child, take good care of yourself,' Martha said.

Again, a friendly handshake, a brief embrace.

There were no white flowers, just a myriad of swirling snowflakes.

29: LIFE EVENT

In midwinter blackness, the crowded British Rail train rumbled along, each clickety-clack bringing Lucy's homecoming ever closer. Approaching London, the train slowed to snail's pace. Row upon row of terraced homes, uncurtained windows – random rectangles revealing flickering televisions, scampering children, a man sprawled on a couch, reading the newspaper.

Why do English people not bother to close their curtains? Why do English windows not have shutters? Lucy struggled to think in English again. Brakes screeched, the train stopped. Doors slammed, harried voices and hurrying footsteps filled freezing air. Cold, hungry, but thrilled to be back, Lucy bought a hot meat pie. Eagerly she took a bite, then wrapped the pie and put it in her jacket pocket, feeling its warmth against her side. She edged through the crowd to the barrier, dumped her bags impulsively on the nearest trolley – scarcely noticing it was about to be taken by someone else. She apologised briefly, dodged past floods of homeward-bound commuters, and boarded the train just as the guard's whistle blew. She found a seat, closed her eyes, listening to the lackadaisical cadence of colloquial English. A warm, damp object pressed against her chest. She retrieved the half-eaten pie from her pocket and finished it, screwed the wrapper into a tight ball, and stuffed it into a nearby ashtray. Soon, the train juddered to a halt. A hoarse, crackling voice echoed over the tannoy.

'Gatwick Airport, this is Gatwick Airport!' The English accent sounded tinny and strangely foreign. Doors opened and shut, ushering in cold gusts and more people. A stout, American tourist wearing a beige suit and a cowboy hat climbed aboard, pushing two huge cases. Lucy stifled a laugh. The train clattered on into the night, three more stops. The arrival in Millhurst took Lucy by surprise. She jumped up, bundled her baggage out of the train, and stood on the cold platform, catching her breath, her head in a daze. Random ridiculous scenarios crossed her mind. Might her parents be out? What if the dog wouldn't recognise her? *A lot can change in three months*, Lucy thought.

She approached a waiting taxi.

'Where you goin' Miss?' the driver inquired lazily.

'Foxfield!'

'Righty-ho!' The driver lifted Lucy's luggage into the car boot and slammed the door shut. Then a businessman in a trench coat and trilby hat politely requested a cab-share to the other side of town. Lucy agreed, and for a few minutes, they exchanged pleasantries about their respective journeys. The gentleman was returning from a business trip in Düsseldorf – which he pronounced the English way, without the German *Umlaut*, which made Lucy want to laugh.

Beyond the town, the taxi zoomed into pitch-dark, unlit countryside. The journey was longer than expected, but Lucy didn't care about the expense. At last, the taxi purred down the smooth curve of Birchwood Close and stopped in the cul-de-sac, outside number seventeen, where lights shone through drawn curtains.

'That was a long trip, luv,' the driver said, 'but a fiver will do nicely.'

'Thank you,' Lucy said, pressing a crumpled banknote into the driver's hand. 'Thank you, very much.'

Leaving her bags by the front door, Lucy crept through the side gate, planning to enter via the back door and walk in on her unsuspecting parents. Disappointingly, the back door was locked. Lucy went back to the front and rang the bell. Mellow chimes sounded from within, followed by Dotty's sharp bark. A light flicked on in the hall, and through the glass panel on the front door, Lucy discerned the blurred figure of her mother approaching.

The next half hour was a flurry of exclamations, embracings and excited renderings of three months' news. Lucy was ecstatic. The reunion was more joyful than she could imagine, edged with bittersweet, Hilda and Lucy sharing mixed emotions on the fleeting reunion with Friedrich and his sudden passing.

'Fate plays strange tricks,' Hilda said, 'Life is short, and we pass by one another like ships in the night. Take all before you, your great-aunt Miranda always said.'

Upstairs, Lucy's new room was soon strewn with open bags, clothes, books, and gifts. Hilda prepared supper, but Lucy was too excited to eat, with so much to tell and discover. The bright, new home, cosy and carpeted throughout, exuded a warm, refreshing smell of new fabrics. Lucy recognised familiar objects: Uncle Charles's Victorian over-mantle, Albert's favourite lampshades and Art Deco mirror, Hilda's walnut writing-desk... Many things were new: armchairs, dining suite, kitchen equipment, duvets and curtains, bedroom furniture, and a colour television. After supper, a ribald sitcom with canned laughter failed to hold Lucy's attention. She flitted barefoot about the house, feeling the comfort of ducted air heating and the springy texture of new carpets. By bedtime, she could keep the photograph a secret no longer.

She presented it to her delighted mother – the perfect end to a perfect evening.

Deep into the night, Lucy lay awake wide-eyed, gazing into the grey gloom of her new room. The mournful hoot of owls and the hollow rattle of distant trains marked passing time. Lucy's heart was full. In past months she had forged links between two sides of the family, closed a rift caused by time, distance, and international politics. She had gained and spread much happiness. Lucy lay cocooned in the depths of the new duvet, never recalling having felt fulfilled and so serene. She slipped into slumber and awoke to a joyful new day. She sprang out of bed and pulled wide the curtains, revealing a cascade of brightness. Winter sunshine filtered cheerfully through snowy-white nets, dancing on glittering rooftops and frost-tipped conifers. Indoors and outside, everything was fresh and new. Lucy dressed in her favourite smock and corduroys and sauntered downstairs.

After breakfast, Albert and Hilda took Lucy shopping in Brighton. She bought a large German dictionary and Hilda bought Lucy a faux-fur duffel coat. The next day, after lunch, Lucy and Hilda travelled by train to the Nyehaven holiday flatlet, which seemed strangely dark and silent on a winter's night. A warm welcome awaited Lucy at school on Monday: her reputation for being interesting and adventurous a notch higher. Everyone wanted to hear her stories and be her friend. Inundated with compliments, including her obvious weight loss, Lucy no longer cared about dieting, nor about Alison's successes at beauty pageants. She was content to simply be herself.

In her three-month absence, Mr Kingsley had retired, replaced by Mr Mather who wore an ordinary suit and spoke with a Birmingham accent. Assembly was less traditional, without prayers or Bible reading, but with more announcements. Lucy's registration class was U6M, supervised by lanky, dark-haired Hector Morris, who taught Economics and was engaged to the new German assistant, Silke Stoffels. Sixth form girls were permitted to wear dark trousers and blue jumpers, with a white shirt underneath. Ties were optional. The once high-flying academic Fiona Jarvis had dropped two subjects and was applying to a polytechnic. Janet Ford had moved away up north. Enigmatic Arthur Long and studious Jonathan Whitmore had left, reportedly due to stress. Jimmy Murphy had been elected Head Boy but was slacking significantly and being outshone by several unassuming former Beechwood pupils. At break, conversation in the sixth form cloakroom revolved around university applications. Lucy told of her pending interviews, Alison was aiming for Southampton, Jodie for Reading, and Abigail had been accepted at Birmingham Conservatoire. Megan Griffiths was applying to Aberystwyth University, and Susan Schofield had set her sights on Goldsmith's Art College in London. Mr Smith persuaded Lucy to take A-level art, and Mr Hagin suggested she enter for Oxbridge, requiring her to stay an extra term after the summer. Lucy said she would think about it. By

Thursday Lucy was riding high on nervous energy. At four o'clock, she travelled home to Foxfield, happy to have an extra day to unwind before her interview in Reading.

Relaxation was in order. After tea, Lucy took a candlelit bath to relax, partly to save electricity and alleviate the oil crisis, but chiefly because it was atmospheric. Afterwards, she tried on the dress Frau Schneider had made, twirling and posing in front of the mirror. It was too baggy, so Lucy wore the top she had bought in Venlo as a vest, which looked fine. She hung the dress on the edge of the wardrobe, ready to pack on Sunday afternoon. She turned in at ten o'clock and fell into a deep sleep.

The next morning Lucy skipped breakfast. At lunchtime, she still wasn't particularly hungry. Still in her pyjamas, she ate a thin slice of cheese on toast, then went upstairs to change. The trousers felt tight and uncomfortable. Lucy straightened up, breathed in, and hoped for the best.

'Hurry up, Lucy,' Albert called from downstairs. 'It's foggy and it's Friday, so we need to leave now.'

'Coming, Dad!' Lucy picked up her bag and ran downstairs, shrugging into the new coat and fastening the toggles. Chilled to the bone, she wished she didn't have to go out, least of all, to an interview. Thick mist gathered over flat fields and woodlands. Daylight faded into dusk, then darkness. Lights from vehicles and mist-bound towns feebly penetrated freezing fog. Lucy's mind was slow and sluggish. Did she even want to go to this university? Across fog-bound fields, bare branches reached into stony skies. Lucy's mind was blank, empty and free – free enough to feel a subtle intrusion.

It was happening again – that creeping, stealthily invading pain.

After nearly two years, it was back again, like a pantomime demon. The journey dragged, through heavy traffic and thickening fog. They arrived at Reading University campus with twenty minutes to spare.

'See you later, Dad,' Lucy said, trying to sound cheerful. The chill air struck hard, the pain steadily advancing, tightening its grip. Lucy doubted she would perform well. Outside the interview room, she was handed a sheet of paper with a passage of French to read aloud. Across the clinically painted corridor, a bespectacled girl studied her sheet in silence. A lanky boy in bell-bottom jeans and denim jacket slouched in the opposite corner, doodling on his sheet. There was no idle chit-chat. The girl was called in first. Lucy rocked and squirmed upon her chair, trying to keep still. The boy went in next. Nobody else came in. Wylie – almost always the last name on the list.

A door opened, and a thin, grey-haired woman beckoned Lucy in. Standing and walking brought brief relief, but the instant Lucy sat down, the pain surged back with a vengeance, racking her small frame. She shuffled awkwardly, wondering if the anguish could be read in her face. On that unforgettable journey to Hildenheim, the pain had been bad and prolonged, but it eventually stopped. Surely, this time, it would stop?

Lucy read the passage aloud and answered the questions, none of which were difficult except one about the Franco-Prussian war, about which Lucy knew nothing. Afterwards, she walked stiffly out of the room, down a flight of stairs, and through the nearest exit. Soft as a childhood teddy-bear, the coat offered comfort to body and soul, but the sleeves were too short and the cuffs too wide, allowing cold air up her arms. *If only I'd brought Renate's coat*, Lucy thought wistfully. Battling freezing rain, she struggled to find the car park, realising she'd left the building by a different door. Skirting around the building, she finally reached the car, opened the back door and slumped onto the seat.

The notion of sitting upright all the way home was unthinkable.

'It went badly then, did it?' Albert asked, supposing Lucy to have suddenly reverted to childish tantrums.

'No, it didn't go badly. I don't know how it went. I've just got one of those stupid stomach aches.'

'Never mind, dear, I expect it'll soon go away.'

For Lucy, the next hour was an ocean of suffering. She stretched, writhed and changed positioning, bringing no relief. Rest was out of the question; the pain held her in a vice-like grip. Arriving at Millhurst station, Albert got out to meet Hilda. Cold, vulnerable and afraid, Lucy dreaded being left alone, even for a short time. The wait seemed endless, every second an effort. Eventually, her parents returned. Hilda greeted Lucy cheerily and told her not to worry, but Lucy barely heard.

The next few hours were a nightmare. Arriving home, Lucy changed into her pyjamas and went straight to bed, without washing her face or brushing her teeth. This episode was unquestionably the worst yet. The pain raged relentlessly through the night. As a victim on a rack of torture, Lucy begged, pleaded for somebody – anybody – to put her out of her misery. At last, the cold light of morning invaded her room, where the curtains had remained open all night. Realising she must have slept a little, Lucy hoped she hadn't cried out or said anything stupid.

Hilda brought in a cup of tea. 'How's the pain now?'

Lucy drew herself up stiffly and rested on her elbows.

'Thanks, Mum, I think it's gone.' She felt foolish for having made a fuss. Leaving the tea, she put on her dressing-gown and crept downstairs.

'Cereals are on the table, just help yourself.'

Lucy looked at the blue-ringed china and the packets of corn flakes and muesli on the new dining-table. *I'm home, and Christmas is coming*, she thought, trying hard to be happy.

'I'll have something later. I'm not hungry just yet.'

Lucy slouched awkwardly on the chair, looking distractedly at the wall.

'What's the matter? Can't you stand up properly?' Hilda asked,

'Not really,' Lucy replied evasively, 'I'm still a bit stiff after the pain I had yesterday.'

'Then straighten up.'

'I can't. It's too uncomfortable. The pain is still there, but it's different.'

Hilda took a deep breath and said, 'Go back to bed. I'll give you some of my medicine – the stuff I got after that dreadful migraine at Samantha's christening. It's quite effective.'

Lucy dragged herself upstairs and went back to bed, burning with pain and her limbs cold. Hilda brought clear mixture in a sherry glass.

'Cheers,' she smiled, handing Lucy the glass. Lucy took a sip of the bitter liquid.

Hilda left the room quietly. She returned after ten minutes and asked, 'Is it working?'

'I don't know. I didn't drink it all.'

'I'm going to call a doctor.'

'Why? I'm probably not even ill.'

'I just want to make sure.'

'I've been very busy lately,' Lucy argued. 'Maybe I just ate too many mince pies. Don't call a doctor. It'll be so embarrassing if there turns out to be nothing wrong.'

Hilda withdrew quietly, and Lucy lay on her back, studying the patterns on the net curtains and the ripples of pinkish paint on the Artex ceiling. What if this was something serious, potentially fatal? Reports abounded of people dying of undiagnosed illnesses like appendicitis. But this couldn't be true. In the past, doctors always quashed Hilda's theory that Lucy's stomach aches were due to a grumbling appendix. Against the bedside lamp, Lucy had propped a picture of a dog biting a postman's bottom. The caption read, *Vorsicht! Bissiger Hund!*

Beware of the Dog – a whimsical bagatelle, ludicrous and inappropriate in the face of a potentially life-threatening situation. Life-threatening? No, surely not?

With great effort, Lucy hauled herself upright and flipped the card over. She didn't wish any visiting doctor to associate her with such childish kitsch. The feeling of stiffness was spreading, and Lucy felt strangely cold, as though her life were ebbing away.

She didn't want to die.

Not now. Everything was going so well, her life before her.

'When's the doctor coming?' Lucy asked quietly.

Hilda's blood froze. Lucy's words echoed the hoarse whisper of her dying mother, forty years before.

'Not long,' Hilda sighed, 'not long...'

The doctor came an hour later – a tall, young, archetypal Englishman wearing a tweed jacket, grey trousers, and a disarming smile. He checked

Lucy's temperature and pulse.

'It could be your appendix, or maybe an ovarian cyst?' Then, with a curious half-smile, he added, 'There's something I must check.'

Pressing one hand firmly on Lucy's ailing abdomen, he asked, 'How is the pain now?'

'Better,' answered Lucy.

Then he lifted his hand, and Lucy gave a startled cry.

'Well,' the doctor declared quietly, 'I think hospital is the best thing. I'll arrange for an ambulance to arrive within the hour. Have nothing to eat or drink.'

Hospital! Lucy couldn't believe her ears. All she had ever had to do with hospitals involved visits to the elderly or the dying. Wasn't this another of those trivial episodes of pain she'd learned to live with? If she went to hospital now, she would surely be told to pull herself together and stop wasting valuable NHS time.

'What shall I pack for you?' Hilda asked.

'There's no need, I shan't be staying,' Lucy said.

Hilda said nothing. Lucy watched her mother put clothes, washing things and two or three books into her red holdall.

'Get up and come downstairs,' Hilda said. Lucy got up slowly, put on the hooded jacket from Martha and edged her way downstairs. She sat down and waited nervously, staring at the newly-iced Christmas cake on the table.

The minutes ticked by.

'That's an old-fashioned hour, that ambulance should be here by now,' Albert grumbled.

'Here,' Hilda said, handing Lucy the box of decorations. 'Put these on the cake. You've a flair for that sort of thing.' Lucy picked up the tiny ornaments she remembered so well from her childhood: the sprig of plastic holly, the Merry Christmas sign in gold letters, the painted porcelain Santa, and the plaster-of-Paris Christmas pudding. She pressed them into the soft icing.

Finally, the door chimes jangled, and Lucy walked the few steps from the front door to the ambulance. This was embarrassing. She didn't feel particularly unwell. The fifteen-mile journey to the hospital was smooth and quiet, no blaring klaxons and no flashing, blue lights. Lucy concluded her case couldn't be serious. On arrival at the hospital, the paramedics said, 'We can't let you walk, we'd get into trouble. It's a fair way to the ward.'

Lucy understood. She hated being on the wrong side of authorities and didn't want to cause trouble. She was helped onto a trolley, wheeled into a lift, and along a corridor to a ward of frail, elderly ladies huddled in high beds.

Why not a children's ward? Lucy was convinced she'd wake any moment and find this was all a weird dream. Two nurses appeared – one tall with auburn curls, the other blonde and round-faced. Wearing light blue uniforms, white aprons and caps, they looked professional, yet approachable. Lucy was taken to a bed in the middle of the ward. The blonde nurse pulled the curtains around, and the redhead helped Lucy into bed. Lucy said she felt cold. The red-haired nurse fetched an extra blanket.

'The things we do for you,' she said, doubling the white, honeycomb-pattern blanket over, and tucking it under the counterpane.

'We'll be back in a minute. If you need anything, just press the buzzer.'

A call-bell was placed in Lucy's hand. Overwhelmed by the nurses' kindness, Lucy was close to tears. *Tears?* When was the last time she had cried about anything? Years, probably, and then only because she was angry or miserable. This was all new, different, dream-like – a dream her parents were in, her mother fussing, her father hovering nearby, grimacing disdainfully at the foreign doctors.

Lucy wavered between fear of the unknown and of being upbraided for wasting everyone's time.

'Perhaps all this is just due to indigestion and nerves?' Hilda suggested. 'She's been very busy lately.'

'Nothing to do with that,' a young Indian doctor said, 'because that would not raise her temperature.'

The red-haired nurse returned with a syringe tray.

'We need a blood sample from you now. You feel a wee scratch, that's all. It'll only take a couple of seconds.'

Lucy watched the needle go in, and the syringe fill with her life-blood, a dark reminder of mortality. Another nurse appeared, bringing a white cotton cloth cap, open-backed gown, and a loose-fitting cotton socks. She helped Lucy put them on. Then a senior nurse in dark blue ordered the removal of the hat and socks, saying they were unnecessary. Lucy felt sorry for the scolded nurse. A lot was happening, and she was losing track of time.

'We have the blood test result,' the senior nurse told Lucy. 'You'll have your appendix removed, but first you'll sign a consent form.'

'Don't worry, you'll be fine,' the red-haired nurse said, squeezing Lucy's hand. The nurse in navy explained the procedure, handed Lucy a clipboard and pen and showed her where to sign, adding this was a fail-safe policy, in case anything went wrong.

Wrong? What might possibly go wrong?

After that, proddings and pokings, needles and trolleys, a rocky ride down dim corridors, through double doors, the word THEATRE above. Lucy felt like laughing. Wouldn't she much rather be watching a play? A needle was thrust into the back of her hand. There was talking and fussing; then someone gave an injection in her other hand. Hilda was standing close by, her face a blur in the quiet gloom.

'I'm going to have the operation,' Lucy whispered.

Hilda's face melted into a smile.

'I've got news for you, Lucy,' she said, 'you already have.'

Earlier that evening, Hilda had paced about in a daze, complaining about having to come home, make dinner, attend to the dog – when she would rather stay at the hospital, near Lucy. At supper, neither she nor Albert were hungry. Hilda found Lucy's silver bells ring on the bathroom window-ledge and put it on. Soon, she would call the hospital for an update. First, she washed the dishes, the blue-ringed china, spoons, forks, knives... *knives!* A sudden piercing pain stabbed her side.

Hilda caught her breath, went to the lounge and picked up the phone.

'Stop worrying. They'll call us, when there's news,' Albert said from his armchair. The television screen flickered its kaleidoscope of colours, a cigarette smouldered on the over-filled ashtray on the coffee table.

But Hilda was already making the call.

'She's in theatre now? So, we can come back in an hour and see her?'

The call ended. Hilda sank into her chair, staring speechless at the wall.

Lucy's vision of her mother faded. Was this another dream? The night was long. She slept fitfully. The pain in her side was heavy and sharp, hindering movement. She wanted to turn over, but couldn't. The raging thirst was unbearable. The call-bell lay forgotten at her side, but a nurse came anyway and gave an injection to ease the pain. Another nurse was waking her, asking her to swallow tablets. This seemed unfair. Surely, sleep was more important? So was water. The thirst was unbearable. In vain, Lucy looked for a bedside drink, dreaming of shimmering desert mirages, an oasis of cool, fresh water that wasn't there...

A nurse pulled out the back rest and offered Lucy a glass of water – half full, not half empty. Lucy swallowed two white painkillers and a fat, striped capsule, then sank back and slept.

Bright fluorescent lights flashed on, and the ward came to life. Nurses appeared with trolleys, swished curtains around beds and began preparing patients for the day. A nurse brought towels and a bowl of warm water for washing, then helped Lucy out of bed and into a bedside armchair. At nine o'clock Lucy broke her long fast, enjoying corn flakes, toast and marmalade, and a cup of tea.

Breakfast was followed by the doctors' round.

'You had a very nasty appendix,' the Indian surgeon said in grave tones. 'but the operation was successful, and you should make a good recovery.'

'Thank you,' Lucy said. 'When can I go home?'

'As soon as we're satisfied the wound is healing and free of infection.'

All day, Lucy watched the nurses working with quiet dedication. Undeniably, the prompt actions of others had saved her life, giving her faith in her fellow humans. Could she be a people-person? Was her former wish to suffer pain and become a better person finally fulfilled? Uncannily, this was the eighth day of December – the day she had chosen three years earlier to be her last. This startling realisation left Lucy with a unique perspective. She resolved never again to meddle with her destiny.

At visiting time, Lucy heard Hilda's story of the strange stabbing sensation at the kitchen sink.

'So, I wasn't dreaming when I saw you standing nearby?' Lucy asked.

'It wasn't a dream. I was there. All evening, I'd prayed hard you would survive. It was a fraught few hours I'll never forget.'

'I just don't remember anything about it,' Lucy said. 'In primary school, I learned about the missionary doctor Albert Schweitzer, in Africa. His patients said surgery was like being killed, cured, and woken up again. It was exactly like that. They put the needle in, and then I knew nothing, like I was dead, and time stood still.'

'You were very brave,' Hilda said.

All week, Lucy observed the nurses dealing sensitively with fearful and elderly patients, few of whom ever left their beds. Lucy helped a few ladies with jigsaw puzzles in the patients' television lounge. One evening, *Dad's Army* was on, the vicar and verger, dressed as soldiers feebly brandishing bayonets. Lucy laughed. Immediately a razor-sharp pain ripped through her side. Lucy froze, guarding her wound. Seconds later, the pain subsided. *Nobody told me not to laugh*, she thought ruefully.

Later, her parents arrived bringing grapes and letters.

'Arthur and Joan, have invited us for Boxing Day,' Hilda said. 'It's a shorter journey now, so no overnight stay.'

Lucy opened the cards first, from Susan Quinn and Margaret, then the official letter – a flyer from Blackford University with details of Thursday's Open Day.

'I wonder if –' Lucy began.

'I'll call them and explain you can't go,' Hilda said. 'There'll be a chance another time.'

'I'll also miss the school party and won't wear the lovely dress,' Lucy protested feebly. Surely she would be sent home soon? She felt healthier and hungrier than she had for months. That evening, at supper, she ate an extra piece of fish offered by an elderly patient with no appetite. The grapes were almost gone. A grape dropped to the floor and rolled under a radiator, which amused Lucy, but she guarded the urge to laugh. Studying was difficult. A German text given out the previous week was about a tyrannical, nineteenth-century father who rejected his daughter and her illegitimate child. The distraught girl killed the child and herself. Lucy hated the story and put it away. The quiet observer of acts of kindness, Lucy decided against Oxbridge entrance.

Instead, she would take a year off and work at an ordinary job.

On Friday, Lucy went home. The house was filled with festive cheer; the tree sparkled with star-like pinpoints of coloured light dancing on shimmering tinsel on the sideboard covered with cards and goodies. Appetising aromas filled the house, a cassette of Christmas carols played in the background.

Her mother hugged her gingerly. 'Welcome home, Lucy.'

It was a perfect moment – a homecoming even more meaningful than the return from Germany a week before. In her room were bags of presents yet to be wrapped, and more cards to open. Lucy sat on the bed and sighed, deliriously happy.

'You missed a great party!' Alison said on Monday. 'We all missed you.'

'I didn't get to wear my new dress, but perhaps there'll be another time?'

'I thought you'd caught a cold in Reading,' joked Jodie, 'It was pretty chilly there at my interview three weeks ago. So, then, tell us how it went.'

'The interview or the operation?'

'Um – both!' spluttered Jodie.

'What's it like, having your appendix out?' asked Alison. 'It must have been awful. I've never been in hospital. Did the ambulance have flashing lights?'

'No, nothing like that.'

'Oh I do hope you go to Reading.' said Jodie. 'That's where I'm going in October!'

Hector Morris was surprised to see Lucy back at school so soon, and Miss Menzies offered Lucy a front seat in the hall, to watch the Christmas play. While most students admired Lucy's fortitude, there were a few derisory remarks about her being a keenie and a swot. Lucy didn't care a jot.

The holidays passed pleasantly, in an atmosphere of festive cheer. On Christmas Day, Marion, Paul and Samantha arrived for coffee, mince pies, and *Lebkuchen*, and Christmas dinner, after which presents were exchanged. Little Sammy tore the wrapping off her presents, squealing with delight at every surprise and every toy. She scampered around the house, while the adults watched the Queen's Christmas Day speech and sampled the luxury foods from the sideboard. There were no arguments or frayed tempers; nobody had a headache, or a cold, or indigestion. All in all, it was an idyll of peace, harmony, and goodwill.

Boxing Day at Arthur and Joan's was filled with feasting and merriment. Anne had a new close-cropped hairstyle, and Anthony had grown lanky, spotty and bashful. Joan prepared a banquet that lasted until dusk. Last, to sit down, Joan ate twice as much as anyone else, piling her plate with second and third helpings.

'Jolly nice! I'm ready this,' she chuckled, while Lucy's cassette player hummed undetected under the table. Conversations included horticulture, the Common Market, and Lucy's recent adventures.

'You lived in Germany? That's impressive,' Arthur said,

'And you were in hospital, with appendicitis! You're so brave!' exclaimed Anne.

'It wasn't much, after all. Really it wasn't,' Lucy said.

Bravery – that magic word, mentioned again. Her former wish had come true: she had endured great pain and was a better, happier person. Mental anguish is worse than physical pain, Lucy reflected. The words of King Lear rang true:

> '…where the greater malady is fix'd,
> The lesser is scarce felt.'

The brandy sauce was piquant, the Christmas pudding laced with spices.

'This is delicious,' Lucy said, the sharp tastes tickling her throat. She stifled a sneeze. A sudden shard of pain sliced through her wound – no time to move or make a sound. Then, as with the ill-timed laugh in the hospital day-room, the pain faded. Clearly, I still need refining! *Niemand is volmaakt* – nobody is perfect, Lucy smiled philosophically. Her happy mood carried her through the post-Christmas lull. Physically, she grew stronger – in some ways feeling healthier than ever before.

On New Year's Eve, she walked the dog through fields and woodlands and afterwards went straight to her room. The eventful year was over, leaving a hollow anti-climax. Lucy slumped wearily on the bed, burying her head in her hands. This tiny trough of depression seemed oddly superficial. Soon afterwards, Lucy found her period had started – the first since March – explaining the unforeseen mood-swing. Perhaps another positive consequence of the operation?

But what would this new lease of life bring? At the threshold of another new year, Lucy was hopeful. Recent events had shaped her character, moulding her into someone more likeable, more responsible, and more mature.

In theory, at least.

30: THE REAL WORLD

'By the way, Mum,' Lucy asked, 'have you seen my silver bells ring?'

'I'm afraid I've a confession to make,' Hilda said. 'I put it on, the night of your operation – to help me feel closer to you, keep you safe – but later I couldn't find it. I searched the house and car, even rang the hospital to ask if it had been found there. I can only assume I dropped it outside somewhere. I'm sorry, Lucy. I'll get you another one.'

'It doesn't matter, Mum. You never know, it might turn up yet?'

'Let's hope so,' Hilda said, surprised by Lucy's calm reaction. Months earlier, she would have stomped and sulked at far less.

Lucy stood at the ironing board, smoothing out creases in sheets.

'I've been thinking, Mum,' she began.

'What about?'

'About working a year, between school and university. An ordinary job, perhaps in Germany?'

'A year away from studies? An interesting idea. I hadn't thought of that. What kind of ordinary job?'

'Waiting on tables in a posh tea-room?'

'That'll suit you.'

'Auxiliary nursing at Alderbridge?'

It was said. Voiced aloud – the dream conceived that first day in hospital.

'Strange you should want to do nursing,' Hilda said. 'It was my dream too, but I missed the opportunity. What would you rather do – tea-room or nursing?'.

'Nursing,' Lucy replied.

There was a sudden dull thwack, as the morning post landed on the doormat. Lucy dashed into the hall and returned with two letters.

'Both for me,' she panted, tearing the first one open.

'Wow! I can't believe it! I'm offered a conditional place at Reading University, although I was half dead at the interview.'

Hilda smiled. 'And the other letter?'

'It's from Kent University – an interview next Friday – but there's no

349

point going, if I take a year out and get the grades required for Blackford.'

'You might change your mind. Go to Kent on Friday. It'll be a day out, and you'll get home a day earlier.'

On Thursday afternoon Lucy had a strange hunch something would go wrong. Shivering on the platform of Nyehaven station, she wondered what could possibly jinx this interview. Then, from the shadows, a figure emerged. It was Abigail Leuchars. Lucy reasoned there was nothing to fear.

Abigail spoke first. 'Hello, Lucy,' she began, 'What brings you here?'

The past was behind. People at school respected her. She had friends in Westcombe, in London, and in Germany. Recently, complete strangers had saved her life.

'I'm going home to Sussex,' Lucy replied, 'I've an interview in Kent tomorrow.'

'Good luck!' Abigail smiled an honest smile.

'And you?' Lucy asked quickly as her train arrived.

'I was at a concert rehearsal and am heading home. All the best, see you Monday.'

Kent University was on a modern campus, miles from the city of Canterbury. To Lucy, it resembled an overgrown school – or a prison. In a ten-minute interview, Lucy was asked in French and German about her achievements, interests, and plans. She responded fluently and was advised to take a look around campus. Entering one of the box-like buildings, Lucy found bare, brick walls, a concrete staircase, and clouds of cigarette smoke. Students in blue denims loitered around a vending machine, leaned against walls, chatting and smoking. Lucy went upstairs and looked down a narrow, dimly-lit corridor. *This isn't for me*, she thought, returning to the car without a backward glance.

'No good?' Albert asked.

'Yeah, you guessed. Blackford's my best bet. Anyway, let's go home.'

'Roger that! The weather doesn't look promising. Also, it's rush hour and a Friday, so I'm taking a country route. It'll be quicker and quieter.'

Night was falling, the horizon dark with cloud. Soon, torrential rain lashed the windscreen, stray twigs bouncing on the bonnet and roof. Gale-force gusts rocked the car. Along twisting lanes, bare trees loomed ghost-like above high hedges.

Suddenly the brakes slammed. Across the road lay a fallen tree – a terrifying apparition in the headlights. There was no choice but turning back.

'Best to find a main road,' Lucy said quietly.

The storm gathered momentum. A powerful wind thundered, a primaeval predator roaring in thick darkness, twigs and wind-borne debris pelting the car, catapulting onto the windscreen. Around the next bend, another fallen tree lay across the road – another about turn. The fear of being stranded or crushed hovered close. Finally, by miracle or by chance, they reached a main road. Through the storm, Lucy remained calm. She was grateful to arrive home, albeit two hours behind schedule.

'All's well that ends well,' Lucy said, putting the experience behind her.

'Very true,' Hilda agreed. 'Now let's enjoy the weekend.'

The wild weather didn't last. Widening days of hazy sunlight sprinkled Spring over rolling meadows, awakening wildflowers and singing birds. Armed with books and a chocolate bar, Lucy walked the dog along a disused railway beside a meandering river. Lucy shared William Wordsworth's love of wild daffodils and identified with the lively, artistic Marianne Dashwood in *Sense and Sensibility*. The plaintive calls of moorhens and the cheerful trilling of larks were as music to her ears. It was wonderful to be alive.

When a rejection letter arrived from Kent University, Lucy wasn't disappointed. She assumed the outcome was due to her frankness about other university offers. Weekday evenings dragged, with little else to do but study. A sixty-watt light bulb shed a feeble pool of light on the Ercol table where Lucy sat, surrounded by books. The gas fire hissed quietly in the background.

'It'll be nice when spring comes,' Hilda mused over her crossword. 'You'd hardly think we were on the sea front. We might as well be on Mars.'

Lucy hassled over a tricky translation. Outside, driving wind and rain rattled shaky sash windows, the curtains inadequate against draughts.

'Mars?' Lucy sighed. 'I'd really like a Mars bar.'

'I'll buy some tomorrow,' Hilda laughed.

Outside in the carpeted corridor, a floorboard creaked. There was a soft knock at the door. Hilda bristled.

'Hellooo,' a male voice called, 'it's me, Paddy!'

'Wrong flat!' Hilda said in her sternest voice. A floorboard squeaked, and the mysterious caller was gone. Lucy giggled.

Hilda didn't mention the visit from Steve, and it was decades before she did.

The moment of levity did little to lighten Lucy's workload. Study was becoming a relentless chore. On the commute to and from school, Lucy tried to memorise new words and phrases.

sich verlieben mit + ACCUSATIVE CASE – to fall in love with

sich verloben mit + DATIVE CASE – to become engaged to

Fat chance of remembering that, Lucy sighed, closing the book. She fished out *A Pocket Book of French Vocabulary*. Opening it at random, she discovered *Marmite* meant large cooking pot, not Marmite, and *bouvreuil* meant bullfinch, not Bovril. At break, Lucy and Alison sniggered at the words, but Lucy's heavy burden remained. No longer could she depend on existing knowledge. Her essays and translations were peppered with errors – a testimony to Mr Hagin's warning to study diligently and not rely on linguistic ability. Furthermore, an additional hurdle loomed – the Use of English exam – a step up from English language O-level, requiring no revision. It cast gloom over February half term, compounded by a mild dose of 'flu, which affected Hilda and Albert worse. Ironically, Hilda's need for rest curtailed the journey back, and Lucy missed the exam rather than return to Nyehaven alone. Of the exam, Hilda knew nothing.

The unpretentious village of Foxfield was Lucy's new idyll. Here, she could relax in her private bubble, far from the rat-race. People smiled and greeted her in the street, recognising her as the girl with the Dalmatian. At home, Lucy baked cakes and kept house. One day, as she was hanging clothes in the wardrobe, a fur-lined glove fell off the shelf. A small object dropped onto the carpet. Lucy looked under furniture and saw the silver bells ring resting upright by the leg of the dressing-table. Delighted, she put it on and went to tell her mother.

At that moment the post arrived.

'A letter from Alderbridge!' Lucy exclaimed, tearing open the envelope. 'They're offering me a job! As an auxiliary nurse – and there's accommodation available. I just need to be over eighteen, which I will be by the time I leave school.'

'Nursing will give you a window on the real world, Lucy,' Hilda said, 'you'll be doing something useful and practical. A complete change from studying. That's what life's all about.'

'And guess what?' Lucy showed Hilda her hand.

'The ring! Where on earth did you find it?'

'It fell out of your glove.'

'I wore the gloves the night of your operation. The ring must have slipped off my finger and stayed inside the glove.'

'Mystery solved,' Lucy said, trying not to read deeper meaning into the discovery. An exciting new job was on the horizon. Would Mr Right be next?

On Monday the common room was humming with gossip.

'Did you get fed up and decide to go back to Germany?' Alison asked with a wry smile. Lucy shook her head.

'We thought they'd found another appendix in you,' Jodie joked.

'No. Just a mild case of 'flu,' Lucy replied.

'Yeah – some of us have had it, too. Didn't need a whole week off though,' Joanna whinged disdainfully. Lucy began to feel guilty.

'You missed the Use of English exam,' Megan said disapprovingly.

Lucy felt cornered. 'I know. Was it difficult?'

'Not at all. We all expect to pass. You missed a good opportunity to get another qualification,' Jill sneered.

Lucy shrugged and said nothing.

'I got engaged on Saturday,' Jodie said, 'and on Sunday I spent the whole afternoon making a wedding dress on my sewing machine.'

Lucy was too gobsmacked to reply.

'Tell us more,' Alison said.

'Stuff the dress, what about the man? Who is he? What's he like?' Rosemary demanded.

'His name's Gary, and he's a greaser from Combe Ridge.'

Abigail grimaced. Lucy concluded Alfie had been dumped years ago.

'But Gary's so dishy,' Jodie continued. 'We've been together nearly five weeks.'

'That's a miracle, by your standards,' scoffed Abigail.

'Can we see the ring?' Alison asked.

'There isn't one. We don't believe in rings. Gary just asked me to marry him and and I said yes.'

'Just like that?' asked Abigail. 'What brought that on? A few drinks, no doubt.'

Jodie stomped off without replying, leaving a whiff of cheap perfume in the air.

'Any wedding bells for you and Alan yet?' Rosemary asked Alison.

Lucy looked blank. Alison hadn't mentioned anything about a boyfriend.

'Not yet,' Alison smiled shyly, her angelic face a picture of perfection.

Lucy froze, her old insecurities rising. The bell rang, and the group dispersed. Lucy was curious to find out who Alan was, and very soon, she did. At break time, Lucy saw Alison hand-in-hand in the corridor with the new games teacher, Mr Hawkins. At lunchtime, they were together again, in the foyer, staring into each other's eyes, deep in conversation. Lucy's hopes for finding love dwindled again to nil. She went to the library and buried herself in her books.

31: END OF AN ERA

Easter passed by in sunshine, showers and birdsong. Peter phoned to say Sarah was in Canada, where job prospects were better and living standards higher. Her new partner, Sam Cohen, also a Londoner, had moved to Toronto five years ago. Sarah and Sam had no plans to return to England. Meanwhile, John was still living in the old family home with Katie, his childhood sweetheart. Hilda clicked her tongue disapprovingly. 'Nobody bothers to get married these days,' she muttered darkly. 'Whatever is the world coming to?'

'I'll get married though, Mum,' Lucy declared, 'if I ever find anyone who'll have me.'

'Don't rush into anything,' Hilda warned. 'You're an eligible young woman, and men may want to marry you for the wrong reasons. Let your heart and your head judge if you've met your match. You'll know, when the time comes.'

Torn between hope and doubt, Lucy wondered what man on earth could be right for her. A fortnight shy of her eighteenth birthday, she was still single, and with no plans for a party, since her friends lived hundreds of miles apart.

'We'll go to Brighton on Saturday to buy your present. Something special, a ring, perhaps? Or a bicycle?'

'A bicycle would be nice, I haven't been on a bike since I rode Martha's in Kochendorf.'

On Saturday, Lucy was given a bicycle and a ring – a sit-up-and-beg, blue bicycle with a white saddle-bag, and a rolled gold signet ring with a tiger's eye stone inset.

On the morning of her eighteenth birthday, Hilda brought Lucy a cup of tea, a pile of cards, and a small, wrapped package.

'Thanks, Mum,' Lucy yawned sleepily. 'I wasn't expecting another present.'

'This is special. Open it and see.'

There was a soft click, followed by a low whirring sound. Hilda had switched on her cine camera and had begun filming.

Lucy removed the wrapping, revealing a small box with gold edging. Inside was a simple, gold cross on a delicate gold chain. Lucy was speechless. The gift somehow didn't seem appropriate.

'It's a family heirloom, it belonged to Grandma Catherine,' Hilda said.

The necklace gleamed gold in the palm of Lucy's hand.

'But I don't go to church,' Lucy argued quietly.

'That doesn't matter – maybe one day you will,' Hilda said quickly. 'Now open your cards.'

Lucy inclined her head, so her hair fell across her face. She hated being photographed. Being filmed was a hundred times worse. It never occurred to her that her own clandestine cassette recordings might likewise annoy others. The card from her parents was elaborately boxed, with a padded, satin picture of a girl in a flowing, pink dress, fluffy white kitten beside her. The card from Marion and Paul depicted flowers, and a glittery door key, Uncle Peter's greeting was a silvery cardboard key decorated with pink silk flowers. Cards from Susan Quinn and Margaret Pritchard were smaller and floral. There was nothing from Germany or France, which Lucy found disappointing but unsurprising since only a few folk knew when her birthday was. After breakfast, she strolled around the village with Dotty, earning a few cheery greetings from fellow dog-walkers. Hilda made cheese on toast for lunch. Lucy ate one slice and declined the offer of a chocolate cupcake.

'No need to be so strong-willed,' Hilda said. 'After all, it's your birthday!'

'I'll wait till tea time,' Lucy said.

On an afternoon woodland walk, Lucy discovered a clearing filled with fading daffodils and fragrant bluebells. She sat at the foot of an oak tree, leaned against its gnarled, uneven bark, and opened a school book, but her attention wandered, so she returned home. Alison arrived on the four o'clock train, looking radiant in a peach-coloured trouser suit and a crimson bandanna, accentuating her smooth, tanned complexion and immaculate makeup. Lucy ran to greet her.

'Happy birthday, Lucy!' Alison smothered Lucy with an exuberant hug and thrust a package into her hand. 'Congratulations for being eighteen and officially grown up!'

In four-inch platform shoes, Alison towered a head taller than Lucy, who felt small and insignificant in her flat brogues, faded corduroys and smock top from Hildenheim.

'There's so much to show you,' Lucy gabbled as they got into the car, where her father sat engulfed in a veil of cigarette smoke.

'Thanks for the present. Can I open it now?'

'Why not?' Alison glanced upwards, condescendingly. 'It is your birthday, after all.'

'Another necklace!' Lucy exclaimed, putting on the quartz crystal floral pendant. 'That's lovely – thanks, Alison, and it matches my number seven brooch.'

Lucy showed Alison the home, garden and village, talking incessantly like an excited child.

At half past five, tea was served.

'The house is lovely,' Alison said, daintily eating her slice of birthday cake. 'Foxfield is a sweet little place.'

'We're going to the pub later,' Lucy said, forgetting Alison was still seventeen, though her stature and demeanour gave the impression of someone much older.

'Good,' Alison said, clearly willing to flout the law. Lucy remembered the pub crawl with Clive and friends, four years before. Later, at the Rose and Crown in Millhurst, Lucy and Alison sat by the inglenook fireplace, sipping their alcoholic beverages: Lucy's a sherry, Alison's a red wine. Albert had a half-pint of lager.

'Did you have a good journey?' Albert asked.

'I did, thank you, Mr Wylie.'

Albert raised his glass. 'Cheers! Happy birthday Lucy. Here's to success in your exams, both of you.'

They discussed the weather and summer plans. Lucy outlined her proposed trips to Hildenheim and Kochendorf, Alison spoke of her teacher-training plans and part-time modelling. She didn't mention Alan, but tell-tale bruises on her neck were a clear indication they were very much an item.

'I expect you're busy at the restaurant?' Lucy inquired, casually.

'Not really,' Alison replied, 'I'm busy revising, and last weekend I was at Alan's.'

Albert lit another cigarette. Lucy floundered, wondering what to say next. In the awkward silence, Alison sipped her drink.

'Are you looking forward to nursing?' Alison asked.

'Yes, but it's a bit daunting, as I've never done that kind of work before,' Lucy answered truthfully.

'Nursing is one thing I'd never do myself, but admire those who do,' Alison said. Lucy wondered if she had made the right decision. Another silence followed.

'We'd better be going now,' Albert said, 'Mum says to be back by six, as dinner will be ready.'

Hilda's smorgasbord of savoury flans, crusty rolls and healthy salads was appreciated by the figure-conscious females, while Albert grudgingly helped himself to minimal portions, planning to make a cheese and pickle sandwich afterwards. Alison sampled a little of everything, and Lucy allowed herself a sliver of birthday cake and a slice of strawberry flan. A low-key evening was spent watching television and chatting over several cups of tea. Alison stayed the night in the tiny guest room, and in the morning she thanked Lucy's parents for their hospitality and left on the mid-morning train. Waving goodbye, Lucy sensed she and Alison were drifting apart.

Meanwhile, Hilda had a strange suspicion about Lucy's new ring. Its faint scratches and pale, lacklustre, tinny appearance caused her to doubt its authenticity. In spite of the carat labelling, Hilda insisted on complaining. They duly returned to the jeweller's, where a like-for-like exchange was approved – a signet ring with a bevelled edge, heavier, and a deeper shade of gold. Lucy was happy with the swap. This ring was a gift for life.

At the start of summer term, Monsieur Leblanc announced a forthcoming French public speaking competition, organised by Nyehaven Rotary Club, open to local, secondary school pupils. At the back of the hall, Lucy yawned and wasn't listening. Jodie nudged her and whispered, 'You live in Nyehaven, and you're good at French! You should go for it!'

Lucy recoiled immediately, painful memories of the Apple Barrel still raw after more than a year. She looked for excuses not to enter: revision, lack of experience in public speaking, and the fact she was only a temporary resident in Nyehaven. Nobody else met the required entry criteria.

'You're very good at French, Lucy, and it would be foolish not to enter,' Monsieur Leblanc said.

Lucy felt cornered. 'I- I'm not sure I can do this,' she stammered.

'But you can and should, Lucy!' Old Dog declared with a jovial smile, 'In my honest opinion you stand a very good chance of winning!'

'All right then, I will.'

Lucy had no idea what to write. Dismissing popular topics like travel, television, population, and pollution, she racked her brains for something a little different – a topic an audience would like. Maybe add a touch of comedy? But telling jokes to complete strangers was a minefield. Best to stick to a subject of universal appeal. But what? Lucy chewed her pen. The four Ryvitas and cheese lurked tantalisingly in her bag. In this time of tension and image-consciousness, hunger was her constant companion. *That was it – food!* Everyone eats every day. Food is a quintessential feature of life. And aren't the French expert cooks? *La Cuisine en France!* Lucy began her script.

A rough draft won Old Dog's approval, and Lucy set about editing and memorising it, on the train, at the flat, on evening walks, and at school.

'*Tu te parles?* You're talking to yourself. Are you okay?' Alison asked, in the corridor between lessons.

'I'm learning my speech,' Lucy answered, too preoccupied to care what people thought.

Round the next corner, a small crowd gathered at the foyer notice board.

'I must see this!' Alison exclaimed.

Lucy stood aside, reading posters advertising sporting events, a disco, and an Exhibition of the Arts, on which someone had added an F at the beginning of the word Arts. Lucy smirked.

'I passed! Hurrah!' Rosemary rejoiced.

'Passed what?' Lucy asked.

'Use of English, you dummy,' sneered Joanna. 'Great results! I don't think anybody failed.'

'That's another string to my bow,' boasted Abigail, smiling smugly.

Lucy felt a twinge of remorse.

'You didn't pass, Lucy,' Shirley observed dryly, pointing to the blank space beside Lucy's name on the printout.

'I didn't take the exam!' Lucy retorted, through clenched teeth, then went to the art room to work on her sculptures. Two clay models of Dalmatian dogs were due for submission at the end of the week. The entire project had been rushed, the result wooden and lifeless. Mr Smith said the sculptures should be more abstract, lending the dog models a surreal look? Lucy was demotivated by the knowledge the figures would be sent away for assessment, and not returned.

In the evening, Lucy sat in the bay window of the flat, oblivious of the panoramic view of the sapphire sea and the flotilla of bobbing yachts with white sails. Hilda sat at the opposite end of the table, gazing out of the window, reflecting on her own hectic schedule.

'Drink your tea, Lucy, before it gets cold,' she said.

'Yes, Mum,' Lucy answered, thinking about the competition against students from prestigious Salton College and St Bernadette's Convent, where Georgina Mayfield was a pupil. No evening walk tonight. At twilight, she was still reciting her speech under her breath, staring out at the peacock-blue sky and twinkling lights on brooding waters. With a resigned yawn, she got ready for bed. Long after the lights out, she lay listening to the rhythmic glug-glug of a blocked pipe, creaking floorboards, muffled footsteps, and subdued voices as tenants retired to their rooms. Supine and motionless, she stared wide-awake into the darkness, tangled thoughts dancing like fireflies. She relived the final moments before her operation, the descent into painless oblivion. Soon she was fast asleep.

The qualifying heat was held at the White Lion, Nyehaven's upmarket seafront hotel. Lucy hid beneath a veneer of composure, inwardly fraught with nerves. All the contestants looked very young and self-composed. This was like a bad dream. Lucy floundered in self-doubt. *Public speaking! Whatever have I let myself in for?* Terrifyingly, the other speeches were good, considering the age of the entrants. Lucy delivered her speech in a measured, determined manner, then returned to her seat, numb with tension. When the results were announced, she was relieved to be selected for the final. Later, she regretted being chosen, preferring closure. That night, she dreamed the contest was won by a mousy-looking fourteen-year-old convent girl, who spoke about a holiday in Provence. A chilling sense of disappointment lingered all day.

Early on Friday, staff at White Lion prepared for the big event. The first-floor function room furniture was rearranged for a large audience. The panel of judges, Mayor Reginald Middleton, Alderman Charles Wigglesworth, and Messieurs Claude Robert and Jean-Pierre Chevalier, of Framboise-sur-Loire, enjoyed a sumptuous luncheon, then adjourned to the Trafalgar lounge overlooking Nyehaven Bay, for convivial chat over coffee and cigars. Downstairs, students sipped soft drinks and talked nervously amongst themselves. Lucy lingered over her grapefruit juice, putting that fateful night at the Apple Barrel behind her.

Arriving early, Hilda installed herself in the second row, trusting Lucy would do her proud. As contestants filed in, Hilda thought Lucy looked slim and elegant in her navy blue uniform and hair neatly clasped with silver clips, but her face was expressionless and drawn. Momentarily, their eyes met. Hilda gave a customary wink and finger-wave. Lucy flicked a ghost of a smile. Then Alison swept into the lounge-like a movie star, her henna-tinted hair swept back, her photogenic face enhanced with rouge, purple mascara and scarlet lip-gloss. An open-necked, cream silk blouse, figure-hugging skirt, fish-net stockings, and mountainous platform sandals, made her every inch a Seventies supermodel.

Alison likes to be flamboyant, but I'm happy to be a Bluestocking!

In school uniform, black brogues and dark blue tights, Lucy felt at ease.

She reminded herself she'd composed and memorised what was considered an admirable speech. Could she win this contest?

Monsieur Thierry Leblanc, alias Old Dog, rose from his chair.

'Ladies and gentlemen, it is with great pleasure as Rotarian and Head of Modern Languages at Westcombe High School to welcome you here this afternoon. We are about to hear these accompished young people share the treasures of their keen minds, expressed in my mother tongue, French.'

The honoured guests smiled and nodded approvingly.

The head of Nyehaven High School stood up next and droned for five minutes on the friendly links between twin towns and the merits of learning a foreign language. Then two Rotarians each gave a short address. Finally, in alphabetical order, Monsieur Leblanc invited contestants forward to speak. Lucy sat rigid, barely listening.

At last her turn came.

'And now, representing Westcombe is sixth former Lucy Wylie, a hard-working, enthusiastic, and gifted student of languages.'

Stop – stop, now! That's enough! Lucy could bear no more. Letting down herself, her mother, and the school – in a public arena – was not an option. She stood up and walked to the podium, her mind detached and razor-sharp. Absorbed in the delivery of her speech, she enunciated each remark, each word, lending expression to her voice, as if to an imaginary audience.

To focus on the sea of faces would be tantamount to a mountain climber looking down.

Everyone listened intently, laughed in all the right places. As Lucy finished, a deafening, standing ovation rocked the first-floor dining-room and rattled judges' coffee cups in their saucers. Lucy felt numb and distant, relieved it was over.

Two more contestants followed. It was evident from their performance they felt overshadowed by their predecessor. Even the mousy girl from the Convent raised only a mild round of applause. Lucy sat patiently through the Alderman's address, whilst the judges deliberated. Then, with a sharp rap on wood, the chief Rotarian brought the audience to attention.

'Ladies and Gentlemen, it is my pleasure to announce the winners of the Nyehaven Rotary Club French public speaking competition 1974. In third place...'

The voice blended into a haze of palpable excitement. Lucy adjusted her hairgrips. A boy from Nyehaven High School was walking to the front to collect his reward. The applause faded, and a girl from St Bernadette's Convent was called forward to receive second prize. Lucy tried to think about something else. Then she heard the name of her school, and her own name being called. Amid a burst of applause and flashing cameras, she stood up and walked forward to receive a handshake from the Mayor of Nyehaven, a shining silver trophy, and the coveted honour of triumph. Afterwards, Lucy was congratulated and praised by dozens of well-wishers. One of the French judges shook her hand and said, *vous etes tres spirituel!* The compliment was overwhelming. She who had once been dubbed the most miserable, dumb person in school, was now a winner – witty and amusing.

During the buffet, Lucy was showered with congratulations. Hilda stood close by, beaming proudly.

'*La gloire, Lucy – C'est la gloire!* We're both celebrities now!' Alison said.

Fame? Was this Lucy's moment of glory? Or just a dream from which she was about to wake? Across the bay, blue waters shimmered in the glow of high summer. Lucy had reached a pinnacle of personal achievement, from which no person and no circumstance could snatch her away.

On the journey home, Hilda sat silent and serene, as red-gold sunset deepened to the twilight of a summer's night.

'I'm so proud of you, Lucy – more proud than I can say,' she whispered, echoing her exact words after Lucy passed the Eleven Plus examination seven years earlier. Albert met them at Millhurst station. Hilda shared the news, while Lucy basked in her success, feeling so happy she wouldn't have swapped places with anyone else on earth.

'You'll notice a few changes in the house and garden,' Albert said. 'The porch windows are in place, I've painted the car port and laid new turfs, and the tomato plants are thriving. From the side of the house, we now have uninterrupted views across countryside.'

Lucy inspected the porch, where the budgie chirped cheerfully, and potted plants lined the window ledge. Out on the patio, her father stooped down to pick something up.

'Such a shame!'

In his hand was the tiny, limp, lifeless form of a tiny bird – one of the family of tree creepers nesting in the oak tree behind the garden.

'It must have flown straight into the glass – the new pane I put in this afternoon,' Albert said.

In the face of heady, worldly success, Lucy struggled to feel sad about the untimely death of a little bird, an innocent victim of a flawed and fallen world.

One day merged into the next in orchestrated routine – studying, eating, walks along the sunlit esplanade, and revising at twilight, overlooking Nyehaven bay. Marking off each time-tabled exam, Lucy watched her Westcombe days disappear like falling grains of sand in an hourglass. Hilda synchronised her last day at Connor Components with Lucy's last day at school. Lucy attended the short leavers' assembly and joined the group of elated students exiting school for the last time. In the torrid heat, it seemed no one really believed this was happening. Lucy walked the familiar, concrete pathway, past the ramshackle house with the sky-blue window frames and wilder-than-ever garden, still wondering what era had ended for its owner.

Half a lifetime later, in another story, she would find out.

Merging with the crowd, Lucy crossed the sports field to the Railway Hotel, to celebrate the leavers' dubious rite of passage from that infantile institution known as school, to the Big Bad World. At a table in the public bar, Lucy sat with Alison and Alan, Jodie, Rosemary, and Megan, engaging in small talk over a round of drinks. The half-pint of lager tasted lukewarm and flat and smacked of anti-climax. Today marked Lucy's leaving of both school and Westcombe. School had long lost its hellishness. The agony of early teen years seemed part of another life or a convoluted, troubled dream. Reality was now – the cusp of summer holidays, and a future of work and study blossoming like an opening flower. Lucy shared her ideas and plans, exchanging addresses with Alison and Jodie, promising to stay in touch. As the party dispersed into the sultry afternoon, Lucy looked up at the hazy hills at the tiny, brown roof peeping above woodland. Surprisingly, she felt no nostalgia. Edencroft belonged to someone else now. It seemed she had never lived there at all. Quickening her pace, she headed for the station.

Arriving in Nyehaven, Lucy waited. Hilda arrived with military punctuality, carrying a large cardboard box and a bulging bag of belongings from the holiday flat.

'What's in the box?' Lucy asked,

'A table-lamp, a parting gift from Mr Connor,' Hilda answered. 'Stay there and mind the bags while I get the tickets.'

'Okay, Mum.'

A cool breeze stirred the hanging baskets of petunias overhead.

Memories of eight years of life were fading. School, Guides, youth club, horse-riding, summer jobs, Marion and Paul's wedding all seemed like stories that happened to someone else.

'We're actually leaving this place,' Lucy whispered, when Hilda returned.

'In this life, everything has its end,' Hilda said.

Gulls mewed plaintively over the crowded promenade, where multicoloured bunting fluttered, and tourists strolled. The distant outline of Appledore Down shelved like giant steps against iridescent sky remained unchanged. Lucy gazed at the horizon, grasping at closure, wondering when, or if she would ever visit Westcombe again.

32: THE GOLDEN SUMMER

In the heady atmosphere of high summer, Lucy flitted from one activity to another. She booked tickets to Germany, arranging a ten-day stay with Birgit and a week with Martha, after which she would escort Martha and Helmut to England, for a fortnight's holiday in Foxfield. Albert planted a vine under the car-port and diligently watered the garden, while Hilda bustled about the house, dusting and spray-polishing with Germanic zeal.

'I wouldn't want Martha to think we live in a pigsty,' she said.

'We don't.' Lucy smirked, recalling the disarray of the Biedermeiers' parlour with its layer of dust, feathers, and budgerigar droppings.

'Shall we name the new house?' Lucy asked. 'Edencroft was a fitting name, and our old house in Ash Farm was called *Lorelei* after German folklore, so perhaps another German name?'

'*Meisenfeld*,' Hilda said. 'The village of our ancestors.'

'Brilliant! In German it means field of finches, or finchfield,' Lucy said.

'And it goes with Foxfield,' Albert said. 'This time, you can make the sign.'

'Okay, Dad,' Lucy agreed. She meticulously drew the letters on a piece of sandpapered pine, painted them with a fine brush, as her father had demonstrated, years before. The finished work was allowed to dry, then varnished, and hung above the front door.

'Ready for Martha and Helmut's visit,' Hilda said.

Lucy shivered with excitement. With so much to look forward to, this happy phase seemed set to last forever.

In Hildenheim, Lucy reconnected with the Schmieds, watched Germany beat Holland in the World Cup final, visited friends, shopped for bargains, and picnicked on poppy cake beside the open-air lido. It seemed she had never been away.

'*Komm!*' urged Birgit, pointing to the pool, '*Wir gehen schwimmen!*'

Bathers dived and splashed in the azure pool, where choppy waters sparkled invitingly. Lucy hesitated. Even now, the four-inch appendix scar still gave occasional twinges.

'What about my operation?' Lucy asked.

Birgit grinned, showing braces on her front teeth.

'You'll be fine! I went swimming just a month after my appendix operation, when I was ten. Come on!'

Birgit plunged in, creating a shower of glistening droplets in the bright sunshine. Lucy took a deep breath and dived in. Instantly, she felt tingling shock of cold water on her warm skin. She started swimming, sensing a gentle tugging, but no pain. With every stroke, swimming became easier – easier than ever before. Gone was the dead weight that had always slowed her down.

The next morning, Birgit took her driving test: an exacting exam of theory and practice. Lucy went alone to the indoor pool. She began with breaststroke, carefully counting lengths, hoping to break her record of ten. After twenty lengths, she still wasn't tired. She kept going and kept counting. After thirty lengths, her leg muscles ached, so she swam two lengths on her back, continued clock-watching and counting, until she had completed seventy, eighty, ninety – one hundred lengths. She could have swum further, but it was time to leave.

Lunch was a cheerful occasion. Birgit had passed her driving test, and Lucy had achieved a personal record. In the happy, holiday atmosphere, Lucy blended with Birgit's family and friends and was regarded as one of the crowd. Birgit now had a steady boyfriend. Tall, slim, blond, Franz-Josef Paveltish – Franjo for short – was in Birgit's class at school. Unlike Birgit, who loved to talk, Franjo was quiet and unassuming, but they were well matched, and Lucy was happy for them. One afternoon, Lucy found them entwined upon the kitchen corner seat, locked in a passionate embrace. Lucy quickly averted her gaze to the birdcage, where the budgie was making eager overtures to its mirror. Lucy retreated embarrassed into the hallway and was left in no doubt that Birgit had found true love.

A tremor of loneliness shook Lucy's fortress of happiness. She walked alone into town to indulge in retail therapy. The paved precinct thronged with happy families shopping. Lucy bought a gaudy, floral T-shirt, a bright green mini-skirt, cork sandals, and trinkets for family and friends. In three days she would catch up with Martha and Helmut and escort them to England. Finding temporary work in a German hospital was Lucy's dream. She bought paperback *Arztromane* – hospital romances, and lost herself in the stories, dreaming of being swept off her feet by a dashing young doctor.

As Lucy bade farewell to the Schmieds, she was sure she would see them again. The northbound train skirted the banks of the serpentine Rhine, bright and shining, dotted with boats, under a cheerful sky. Lucy stood at the window, gazing fascinated at vistas of vineyard-draped slopes and fairytale castles rising mysteriously from forested hillsides. In every town, ornate buildings with sharply sloping roofs formed an impression of aesthetic order.

Arriving in Kochendorf, Lucy scanned the crowded platform. Soon,

Martha's homely voice was ringing in her ears.

'Ah, Luuuuucy!! You look well! You've gained weight!'

Lucy flung herself into the arms of her cousin, returning the greeting with a heartfelt embrace.

'Schlank ist krank, dicker ist gesunder.' Lucy said. Thin means ill, fatter healthier.

It was a positive and vibrant reunion. Like a fairytale gingerbread house, the little home in Baumgarten was adorned with window-boxes, bursting with colour. Over a cold platter of meats, rye bread and pickles, Lucy eagerly described the Foxfield home, where Martha and Helmut were soon to become honoured guests.

'We're looking forward to this trip so much,' Martha said, 'and meeting the family in England. Will we need to pack coats and umbrellas? I've heard English summers are cold and wet.'

'I don't think so,' Lucy laughed, helping herself to another slice of bread. 'It might be cold enough for umbrellas and raincoats in Scotland, but not in Sussex, in July!'

'You're fuller in the face and with a better colour,' Martha said.

Lucy nodded, her mouth full.

'There's something I didn't tell you last year,' Martha continued, 'when I was about your age, I was also often unwell, until my appendix operation.'

'It's changed my life,' Lucy said.

'Wilhelm and Marleen have invited us to Sunday lunch, so you'd better eat well,' Martha said.

'I will,' Lucy said.

Sure enough, a warm welcome awaited Lucy in Meisenfeld. The conversation at the table was upbeat, but Friedrich's absence was conspicuous, his seat now occupied by Wilhelm, who had taken over management of the farm. Lucy half expected at any moment, to hear Friedrich's strident voice and him to walk into the room. Last November, she had squeezed his hand and promised to return.

Lucy remembered the words of a well-known song, *Ich komme bald wieder, wieder vorbei...* I'll be back again soon. Lucy rued the words she'd spoken days before Friedrich's passing, a week before her own brush with death.

One must never assume there'll be a tomorrow.

On the eve of the journey, Lucy once again found no room for the winter coat.

'I'll take it home next year,' she said, her words dissolving to silence.

'Come,' Martha said, 'we'll eat *Abendbrot* and then early to bed. We've a long day ahead of us tomorrow.'

Everything seemed perfect, surreal as a dream, until the next day, as the ferry docked at Dover, the gangplank was raised, tourists jostled off the ship, shunting heavy cases towards customs.

Suddenly Martha grabbed Lucy's arm.

'Helmut isn't here – he was here just now. Where is he?'

The question fell unanswered in the hubbub. Helmut was nowhere to be seen. Swallowed in a surging crowd – a curious repeat of last year's episode on Oxford Street. That had ended well, but would this? Doubts clouded Lucy's thinking, tendrils of panic clawing the pit of her stomach. Losing time meant missing the connection to London and plans collapsing like a line of dominoes. Seconds passed. Martha had gone quite pale. Lucy took a deep breath and told her not to worry. She related the incident with Paulette, and Martha's expression relaxed. 'At least Helmut has his wallet and papers with him,' she said.

Lucy feared pickpockets and said nothing. A few steps further, standing by a poster advertising Brooke Bond tea, was Helmut, statuesque and serene. Without a word, Martha took his arm, and together they made their way to the train.

Martha and Helmut remarked how different everything looked. Lucy wanted to apologise for the unsightly fly-tipping and graffiti, but her guests were smitten with the quaintness of the villages and the patchwork fields.

'It's like a storybook – a fairytale,' Martha said.

'That's exactly how I see Germany,' Lucy answered. Happy people only see the good things, she thought.

Arriving in Victoria Station, Lucy scanned the crowded platform and soon saw her mother's cheery face. Hilda was wearing the lilac suit she said made her feel like the Queen. In her hand was a small bouquet of wilting, white roses.

The two cousins embraced.

'Here, Martha, white flowers...' Hilda's voice faded, charged with emotion.

Albert and Helmut needed no introduction. Within minutes they struck a common chord of bonhomie, exchanging cigarettes and conversing, each in their own language. Lucy smiled at their misaligned remarks, intervening with an occasional interpretation. The task of interpreting was a brain-taxing, thrilling challenge.

'You need to call it *Haus Meisenfeld*, not just *Meisenfeld*,' Martha said, on arriving at the house. 'Otherwise people might think you own the village.'

'In England, people call their houses anything they want,' Lucy said. 'Our old house was called Edencroft and the one we lived in before was called *Lorelei* – Grandfather Gregor's idea.'

Hilda had baked a cake and iced it with the word *Welcomen* – a mis-spelling of *Willkommen*.

'That's English for Welcome, isn't it?' Martha asked. Lucy didn't bother explaining the error, as the sentiment was appreciated.

A glorious fortnight followed, the friendship between the two families blooming. Views were admired, visits to tea gardens, restaurants, and country inns enjoyed. Albert captured happy moments on two reels of colour film. Martha loved the Jack-and-Jill windmills on the Sussex Downs, as they reminded her of childhood in Meisenfeld. She found their hilltop location interesting. Helmut enthused about practically everything – the house, the food, the landscape, the coast, and the English television programmes – even *Dad's Army*. A day trip included a whistle-stop tour of central London and a visit to Marion and Paul's for afternoon tea. Peter and John were at work, but Sarah and Sam were there, on holiday from Canada. The guests complimented Marion on her home baking, and Martha fawned over Samantha. Hilda's Box Brownie clicked, and the cine camera whirred, as more memories were made. Paul came home at five o'clock, and on went the transistor radio at full volume. It was getting late, and everyone left, reflecting on a highly pleasant afternoon.

Two days later, at Arthur and Joan's homely bungalow, the German visitors enjoyed another round of English hospitality. The next morning, Peter phoned early and invited himself to breakfast.

Hilda shook her head, smiling to herself. 'Typical Peter. Always acting on impulse.'

The doorbell chimed just before nine.

'He's early!' Hilda rushed to the door. Peter swept into the house and promptly swamped first Martha, then Hilda in an exuberant bear hug.

'Nice house, Hilda dear. I like the name – *Meisenfeld*, eh? Very original!'

Peter talked through the full English breakfast. 'Excellent hospitality, my dear sis, and good work on the sign, Lucy! You take after your father for that.'

Lucy smiled and looked at the carpet.

'We've a lot of news to catch up on. About half a century of it, I believe,' Peter told Martha, then related past events, which Lucy translated:

'Peter fought with the British army during the War, but his father Gregor, a German, was imprisoned. My mother Hilda, still a teenager, fought for justice, and Gregor was released and sent home to London, where he took refuge in his austere basement flat, dodging bombs dropped by his native countrymen...'

Shocked, Helmut gave his side of the story. 'I had to fight on the other side, hating Hitler and the Nazis. All men were obliged to fight for their country or be killed, although Hitler's views were generally despised.'

Martha added, 'One member of the less welcoming side of the family married Karl-Heinz Hellmann, a Gestapo officer.'

Lucy interpreted.

Stunned silence was broken by the budgerigar screeching in the sunlit porch.

'We'll visit Westcombe on Saturday,' Hilda said. 'I expect Lucy has told you plenty about it. The countryside and coastline there are very scenic.'

This was unexpected. Lucy had never imagined her parents would want to revisit Westcombe so soon, if indeed ever. She wondered if her parents regretted leaving.

Hilda persuaded Peter to stay for lunch, and Lucy offered to make a chicken casserole. At two o'clock, Lucy lifted the dish from the oven, placed it ready beside the hatch. While fetching the best plates, Lucy heard an ominous crack and a splintering of glass. She ran back to the kitchen, where fragments of dish and dinner lay scattered on the floor and worktop. Initially annoyed at the spoiled meal, the cold truth dawned what would have happened if she'd stood close to the dish. By the time the others returned, Lucy had cleaned up the mess and had prepared a rice salad, served with ham, pork pies, and cheeses.

Lucy told her mother what had happened. Hilda wasn't angry.

'The surface was too cold for the dish,' she explained. 'You should always put hot Pyrex dishes on a mat or cloth that can absorb the heat.'

Lucy agreed, regretting not having paid attention in school science lessons.

Saturday dawned misty, but the fog lifted. In the warm July sunshine, the Westcombe views were as magnificent as ever. At the church where Marion and Paul were married, a hearse drove past, a coffin and floral tributes clearly visible. Martha commented how nice the flowers looked. Numb inside, Lucy realised her once ardent love for Westcombe was dead. On the once familiar lane, Lucy noticed subtle changes to the hedgerows, trees and cottages, indicative of a temporal shift.

'Slow down – here it is – just there, that house with the tiled roof,' Hilda said, as they reached the gates of Edencroft. 'Let's stop, and see if the Campbells are in.'

The silver gates had been repainted green. Hilda and Lucy walked up the slope, feeling like intruders. Every square inch of the two-acre plot, where tangled briars and waist-high weeds had reigned, was filled with a menagerie of hens, ducks and pet rabbits. A donkey grazed lazily at short, parched grass. A stable door had been built into the breakfast room, providing direct access to and from the garden. Toys and children's bicycles were scattered across the grass, where a forlorn conifer marked Marmie's grave.

Mrs Campbell offered her unexpected guests tea and biscuits. Mr Campbell was out with the children, but the place was still a riot of noise and colour, far from its former tranquillity. The kitchen was messy and cluttered; the unit Albert had made replaced by a Welsh dresser, on which presided a large ginger cat. Lucy took a moment to recognise Lurcio. She stroked him. He purred but barely stirred.

The tour ended with a late lunch at a seafront cafeteria. Lucy stared blankly at foam-tipped crests on indigo waters, sensing closure on a significant chapter in her life's story. She doubted she would ever return.

The holiday was over all too quickly. Lucy stood with her parents on the platform at Victoria Station, waving frantically as the boat train pulled away.

On the way home, nobody spoke.

Eventually, Hilda broke the silence. 'I felt strangely hollow and empty, as the train left.'

'But we all had a lovely time,' Lucy said, 'and we will be going to visit Martha and Helmut next summer?'

Hilda didn't answer, her heart as heavy as rock.

Two weeks of glorious summer passed, Lucy busy with cycle rides, cooking, crafts, letter-writing, and reading books of her choice, including a Sue Barton story about a vivacious nurse dramatically rescued from appendicitis, and falling madly in love with a doctor. Lucy felt proud to be on the brink of full-time employment. Hilda drove Lucy to Alderbridge Hospital for a briefing interview. Lucy was met in the foyer by a senior nurse in navy blue uniform and starched, white apron and cap.

'Lucy Wylie?'

'Yes, that's right.'

'I'm Sister Hitchiner. Before showing you round, I'll introduce you to the Nursing Officer, Miss Squires.' Sister Hitchiner's manner was brisk and affable. Lucy was invited into a cosy office with carpets, curtains and padded seats. A smart lady in grey tweed sat at an oak desk with a green telephone, pen pots and notebooks.

'A pleasure to meet you, Miss Wylie. Have a seat. I'm Miss Squires. I always welcome new employees, attend first to formalities, then arrange induction.'

Lucy completed a form, giving the usual personal data, and signed along the dotted line.

'Sister Hitchiner will give you a guided tour,' Miss Squires said, a handshake sealing the deal. Lucy was led through a gloomy walkway to the yard and a line of low prefabricated buildings. Sister Hitchiner indicated an old army Nissen hut. 'That's where you'll be staying. It's the block for auxiliaries and domestics. The trainee nurses' quarters are in the east wing of the main building.'

A covered corridor led past the parallel huts.

'On the right, Bunting Ward – female geriatric – and on our left, Lark Ward – male geriatric. Next are the orthopaedic wards.'

Trolleys rattled past. Doors flapped open and thudded shut, releasing wafts of warm antiseptic-laden air.

'On the right, Fieldfare Ward – female medical ward, where you'll be working.'

'It looks interesting,' Lucy said quietly, 'I think I'll enjoy working here.'

'It's not easy work, you know. It's not like television or paperback fiction. There's a great deal to learn – difficulties that challenge even the most capable, experienced nurses.'

'Yes,' Lucy answered, not daring to ask what kind of difficulties she might face. The temptation to give backword on the job hovered close.

Back in the main building, Lucy was issued with a uniform – two tunics in crisp, white linen, a bundle of white, cardboard caps bearing a thick purple stripe, denoting her rank as an Auxiliary, and a navy blue woollen cape with red lining. Each garment was labelled with Lucy's name and rank.

'Try them on.' Sister said. It sounded like a command. Excited and terrified, Lucy put the tunic on over her blouse and draped the cape over her shoulders.

'But I'm not a nurse yet,' she said. 'I haven't even begun the job. I feel as if I ought to do some training first.'

'The training is on the job,' Sister said, 'There'll be a four-week trial period, during which you'll discover if you like working with us, and we will decide whether or not we want to keep you. Your induction consists of seven days' orientation in other areas. On your first day, you will report to Fieldfare Ward and begin your duties as a ward Auxiliary. Do you have any questions?'

'No, I don't think so,' Lucy replied, her mind suddenly blank.

'Very well. Next, we'll go to the staff canteen.'

As part of protocol, an informal chat over coffee and biscuits was provided for questions.

'What exactly will I be expected to do as an Auxiliary nurse?' Lucy asked.

'A relevant question,' Sister's stare through steel-rimmed spectacles was intimidating. 'A job description will be included in the handout you'll be given today. First, I must ask what you think a nursing Auxiliary does.'

For the winner of a public speaking contest, Lucy was extraordinarily tongue-tied. Memories of her arrival in hospital last year sprang to mind.

'Um – making beds and helping patients?'

'Yes, and how specifically might you want to help a patient?'

'Well, making them comfortable, bringing them things they need?'

'Yes. Basic, bedside nursing skills include making beds, bathing and washing patients, feeding them, taking their pulse and temperature, and – of course – giving them bedpans,' Sister Hitchiner said with a smile.

Lucy smiled back.

'In fact, you will be expected in time to do many of the things a qualified nurse does, apart from for invasive procedures like giving medications, injections, and intravenous drips.'

'I've read the Sue Barton stories, but they're a bit unrealistic, aren't they?' Lucy asked, cautiously.

Sister pealed with laughter. 'Of course they are! We're not like that here. This is real life, not fiction. You'll soon forget all those silly little stories once you start working with us.'

A start date was arranged for early September. Before then, other things occupied Lucy's horizon. Firstly, the A-level results were due any day. When the awaited brown envelope arrived, there were no surprises: grade A* in German, a pass with Merit in the Special Paper, B for French and English, and D for Art – all subjects passed, with good grades, apart from Art, which was predictable, since Lucy had refused to make her work abstract. She had gained the required grades for Blackford University, and that's all that mattered. Hilda ordered a copy of *The Westcombe Herald* to be sent by post. Lucy was surprised to find how well she had done compared with others. A fair few students had gained three A-level passes, but no one else four. After six years, her wish to excel at school had finally come true. Like climbing a mountain, she had toiled up steep and dangerous slopes and was above the clouds, the past's dark valley a distant memory. *Per aspera ad astra.*

Secondly, Lucy's prize holiday in the Loire Valley was due. She regarded it almost as an intrusion. On the eve of departure, she packed a case and handbag. Purse and tickets were ready, but curiously, the passport was nowhere to be found – even after emptying the case and searching the room. Reason told her it must be there. She last recalled seeing it at the bank, whilst collecting travellers' cheques a week ago. Panic gripped her.

Noisy rummaging prompted an irate shout from Hilda.

'Just looking for my passport, Mum,' Lucy panted, flitting from room to room. 'Have you seen it?'

'No, I haven't. Calm down, it can't be far away.'

The car, the garage, the garden, and all rooms were searched, to no avail. The travel agent's and bank were closed. Hilda phoned the police station, but nothing had been handed in. Visions of having to cancel the trip played havoc in Lucy's fuddled brain.

'Maybe you dropped it in the Fox and Hounds?' Albert suggested. 'We went there with Martha and Helmut after you picked up your traveller's cheques.'

'I hadn't thought of that,' Lucy sighed.

A phone call to the pub yielded nothing.

'It could have slipped onto the floor and still be there!' Lucy exclaimed clutching at straw.

'A good excuse to go for a drink,' Albert said. "Get in the car, and we'll go there now.'

Lucy was pleased to find their usual table unoccupied. While Albert bought drinks, Lucy peered under the table, running her hand across the carpet. She found a pork scratching, two cigarette butts and a roasted peanut. Nothing else. Then she heard a faint thud overhead, as Albert placed two half-pint glasses of lager on the table. She got up and sat down, in no mood for drinking.

'If you haven't come across it yet, then it simply isn't there,' Albert said. They finished the drinks in silence and went home for dinner. Hilda insisted

Lucy come to the table and eat immediately. She sat down, still striving to remember if there was anywhere she hadn't searched. She chewed her food dutifully, every mouthful sticking her throat like cement. The moment the meal was over, Hilda reached into the hatch and handed Lucy her passport.

'I found it when you were out,' Hilda said. 'It was on the oak table top, underneath a small package exactly the same size as the passport, so it was completely hidden.'

'Why didn't you tell me you'd found it?' Lucy asked.

'I wanted to see if you'd come to the table and eat your food without fuss,' Hilda replied.

'Well, I'm relieved it's turned up,' Lucy said, knowing she would have enjoyed the meal much more if she had known the good news beforehand. Upstairs, on the bedside table, she discovered what had obscured her passport: a small pack of tampons wrapped in a brown paper bag.

'I don't suppose I'll be needing these anyway,' she muttered morosely, tossing the package into the case. Her last period had been after her appendix operation. Since then, nothing, in spite of her eating a balanced diet. Doubtless, it was due to stress – even positive stress.

Twenty-four hours later, Lucy stared from the train at golden, sun-baked fields under sultry summer skies. In the broiling heat, she longed for the cool splash of water on her face and the chance to change into cool, comfortable clothes. The train bumbled through rural villages: quiet clusters of grey slate roofs and church spires, finally reaching the sleepy little station at Framboise-sur-Loire. Lucy opened the carriage door and carried her cases onto an empty platform.

At the barrier stood a young man with square spectacles, a high forehead and black hair swept back. Beside him, his heavily pregnant partner, a stunning blonde with straight, waist-length hair parted in the middle. Lucy assumed these people must be her hosts, Dr Charpentier and his wife. Lucy had imagined them to be older. The young man introduced himself.

'*Bonjour, Lucy! Je suis le docteur Charpentier.*'

He didn't introduce his partner. He took Lucy's luggage a red Renault – the sole vehicle in the car park.

'Did you have a good journey?' the mother-to-be asked, in French.

'*Oui, merci,*' Lucy replied.

After a short drive to a tall, rambling mansion on the edge of the town, Lucy was introduced to an older Madame Charpentier, a homely woman in her late forties. In conversation, it became clear the man who had met Lucy at the station was the son of Doctor Charpentier senior, a surgeon at a hospital twenty kilometres away. Lucy was pleased to have been placed in a family of medics and looked forward to some interesting conversations. Madame Charpentier offered Lucy light refreshment and said the family would eat at six.

In a lofty, plainly-furnished living-room, Lucy was introduced to sixteen-year-old Caroline, a tall, well-built girl with freckles and reddish-brown hair. The young doctor's name was Jean-Claude, and his pregnant girlfriend, Angelique. A younger brother, Bernard, was following in the family tradition and studying medicine, as was his German girlfriend Ursula. Caroline showed Lucy to her room; a rustic attic with polished, wooden boards and a well-bolstered single bed with iron bedposts. Tall shuttered windows opened onto a wide vista across fertile plains of the Loire Valley. A wild, tangled garden fell away to a huddle of terracotta roofs in the village below. Lucy opened the windows wide, but the air outside was equally warm, humming with insects and heavy with the scent of flowers. A church clock clanged in the still afternoon. Lucy washed and changed in the en-suite bathroom and returned downstairs. Caroline gave her a tour of the neighbourhood. At the post-office, Lucy wrote and mailed a letter – not a postcard – to her parents, informing them of her safe arrival.

The evening meal was relaxed and informal, the family seated at a round table, discussing the day's events. There was no television. Lucy was asked questions about herself and was complimented on her enterprising nature and command of French. Madame Charpentier asked her husband what operations he had performed that day. Lucy strained to listen but understood little. The young couples talked about their futures – Ursula was also pregnant, and she and Bernard were planning their wedding. Both expectant mothers displayed peculiar food fads: Angelique ate plenty of cheese and tomatoes but pushed aside anything containing a mere grain of salt. Ursula picked daintily at a single, dry cracker, her pregnancy too early to show.

The weather stayed sultry all week. Lucy was taken to chateaux, towns, restaurants, shops, and the homes of her hosts' friends and acquaintances. She bought souvenirs, wrote postcards, eagerly looking forward to Alderbridge. One afternoon, she felt strangely tired and out of sorts, with a headache and upset stomach. Anxious about mosquito bites, she feared another allergic reaction. At supper time, she had little appetite. Her concerns about the mosquitoes were dismissed, and the ladies suggested Lucy could be suffering from menstrual troubles, which she denied. Various medications were offered, all of which Lucy refused. She sat hunched at the table, nibbling a dry crispbread and sipping a glass of water. Angelique and Ursula exchanged glances and kept their suspicions to themselves.

The next morning Lucy felt refreshed, so she spent a quiet day around the house and village. She bought a pair of blue, leather moccasins for nursing. In the afternoon, Madame Charpentier showed her the cavernous cellars where wine, fruit and vegetables and tinned and bottled foods were stored. Lucy had offered to help carry up some jars and bottles, but seeing the dark, cobweb-strewn depths, she hesitated, remembering a time she and Alison had been spooked by a spider as they opened a sunshade at Edencroft.

However, once her eyes grew accustomed to the lack of light, curiosity won over fear. The basement contained much more than just food and drink; there were several interconnecting cellars containing coal, bicycles, garden tools, and wooden crates.

'There are even books down here,' Lucy remarked, noticing a shelf of dust-covered paperbacks.

'I need to tidy up and throw a lot of things away,' Madame Charpentier said.

The next day, several boxes of bric-a-brac and books occupied the downstairs hall.

'Help yourself to anything you want,' Madame Charpentier said.

Lucy selected a few decorated glasses showing the different castles in the Loire Valley, a wall-hanging thermometer, and an armful of *livre de poche* paperbacks. She thanked her hosts for their hospitality and apologised for cutting short her stay by two days, in order to start her nursing job – a reason they regarded not only excusable but commendable. The family wished Lucy well in her new venture. Madame Charpentier packed her a generous picnic lunch and gave her a lift to the railway station.

The journey was pleasant and uneventful, with one change – at Le Mans, where Lucy asked a guard for platform directions and caught the next connection by a whisker. She tried reading, but the views of picturesque, quintessentially French towns and parched landscapes were too distracting. The biggest town was Lisieux, where the train stopped for ten minutes in the drab looking station overshadowed by tenement flats. Lucy wondered about the people living there, imagining their lives weren't easy. A platform hoarding showed a cartoon of a man holding a bottle-shaped gun to his head and a bold caption:

**PLUS VOTRE CONSOMMATION DE L'ALCOOL AUGMENTE
PLUS QU'ELLE VOUS DIMINUE...**

The more alcohol you drink, the less you become seemed a powerful message. The train pulled away, slowly gathering momentum. Unzipping her bag, Lucy selected one of the Charpentiers' old paperbacks. Soon she was absorbed in a French translation of A J Cronin's *The Sisters*, while the sun-scorched fields of France disappeared from the landscape of her life.

33: ALDERBRIDGE

In the light, airy room of the former World War Two Nissen hut, Lucy sat on the edge of the bed and looked around. Furniture was sparse and basic: a bedside table, a chair, a chest of four drawers. The curved ceiling and panelled boards were painted pink, matching faded curtains and counterpane. On the cork notice board, Lucy had pinned postcards and maps of France and Germany. The homely tick-tocking of the alarm clock was barely audible above the patter of footfalls and heated arguments among domestics in the corridor. Lucy stood up, looked in the mirror above the washbasin, and adjusted her cap. She donned the long cape, fastening the straps around her waist, then left the room, locked the door, and headed for the first of a row of huts across the yard.

The ward's double doors yielded like massive jaws. Lucy found the cloakroom and hung up her cape, feeling stupid, for apparently, no one else had worn one that morning. It was, after all, still summer. Lucy followed a nurse in light blue uniform to a small office with large, internal windows overlooking the ward. A stout, well-groomed figure in a starched navy uniform introduced herself as Sister Haywood – an archetypal forty-something, awe-inspiring senior nurse. Five other nurses sat on hard, plastic chairs, while the night Sister gave a brief update on each patient; their medical condition and what had been done for them during the shift. Names, facts, figures, and medical jargon went way over Lucy's head. When the night nurse left, Sister Haywood allocated tasks and introduced Lucy to the group.

'This is our new Auxiliary, ladies, Lucy Wylie, joining us for the next few weeks.'

A few nods and smiles.

'Now, Nurse Wylie – your title whilst on duty – meet Staff Nurse Craddock, Senior Auxiliary Pope, Enrolled Nurse Jones, and Pupil Nurses Ho and Engels. Today, Nurse Wylie, you'll work with Nurse Ho. You may also ask a senior member of staff if you have any questions.'

The brisk handover left Lucy little time to put names to faces, but she sensed Sister Haywood would be approachable. Lucy shadowed Nurse Ho –

a petite Oriental in her second year of training. Nurse Ho darted about like a little bird, preparing a trolley with fresh bedding, towels, toiletries and a bowl of warm water.

'Come, Lucy,' she said, 'you may call me Josie. We all use first names when no one is listening. We will help our first patient, Miss Illingworth.'

Josie swished the curtains around the bed of a large lady reclining on three pillows supported by a backrest.

'First we give you wash,' Josie said, pulling back the covers and spreading a towel. The patient removed her spectacles and smiled benignly.

'I wash and you dry,' Josie said, handing Lucy a towel. Josie squeezed the face cloth and carefully washed the patient's face. Lucy patted it dry. Then Josie moved the bedside table for the patient to wash her hands. Lucy handed her the towel.

'Thank you, kind nurses, that was very refreshing,' was the grateful response.

Josie supported the patient's back, while Lucy let down the backrest, and together they removed the hospital gown. Lucy was startled at the sight of the ocean of wobbling, white flesh. She could not recall ever having seen such a big person, apart from Karin Schumacher or Iris Keller, who had, of course, been clothed. The nurses washed one side each, carefully drying the folds of skin and dusting them with talcum powder. Lucy's initial feelings of surprise were overridden by the desire to help and to care. Josie supported the patient while Lucy washed and dried her back.

'You have two clean nighties in here,' Josie said, rummaging in the bedside locker. 'Which one would you like to wear today?'

'The one with the pink flower pattern, please, that's the one my niece gave me for my birthday. She's good to me, and I know she'll look after my cat.'

At handover, it was reported Miss Illingworth was admitted after a heart attack, but facts meant more after meeting the person. Lucy remembered Onkel Friedrich.

'Tell me about your cat,' she said.

'He's black and white and is called Socks.'

Miss Illingworth seemed breathless but happy to talk. 'He has white paws and legs.'

'I've had three cats in the past,' Lucy said. 'Marmie was ginger and white, Lurcio was all ginger with tiger stripes, and Bertie was black and white.'

Chat dovetailed with practical actions. Miss Illingworth was left resting comfortably, with a fresh water jug on her table. Lucy pulled back the curtains and said, 'Breakfast time soon, you're probably looking forward to a cup of tea.'

'Come, Lucy,' Josie said, wheeling away the trolley. 'Time for our next patient.'

In the next bed sprawled mild-mannered grandmother, Mrs Higgs, partially paralysed on one side after a stroke. The task of washing and dressing seemed quicker and easier the second time. Lucy and Josie helped the patient transfer from bed to chair with a Zimmer frame.

Then the breakfast trolley arrived. Conchita the domestic, whose room was next door to Lucy's, poured the teas. Junior nurses brought trays to patients, helped them sit up, and spoon-fed some. Lucy delivered and collected trays. After breakfast, less able patients were helped to the toilet or given a bedpan or commode. Some were bed-bound, with catheters – a tube from the bladder to a plastic bag that collected urine and was clipped to the bed rail. Lucy remembered seeing them last year on the surgical ward. Here too, the ward worked like a well-oiled machine. Sister Haywood did the drugs round; nurses checked patients' pulse, temperature and blood pressure and completed charts. Doctors arrived for the ward round – familiar routines Lucy had observed before. It was weird being the other side of the fence.

By eleven o'clock, half the ward was finished. It was time for coffee in the staff room.

'Today was easy,' Josie said, 'because most patients can walk and wash themselves. It is much harder if no one can get out of bed.'

Afterwards, Josie and Lucy helped three more patient wash and dress, bathed two more, made beds, and measured and recorded patients' temperature, pulse and respirations - observations for short.

At midday, the lunches arrived. Lucy handed out and collected trays. Then Sister Haywood sent her on first break. Lucy went to her room for a light snack of crispbreads, apples and cheese. Other ancillary workers were also on their breaks, or perhaps it was their day off? Somewhere along the corridor, the strains of "Everybody wants Kung Fu fighting" boomed full-blast, swamping all other music from other rooms. Lucy didn't bother putting on her radio. Back on the ward, Lucy unloaded the laundry trolley, helped bed-bound patients drink through plastic beakers, and assisted others to mobilise – tasks requiring strength of body, mind and spirit. Remembering the kindness she had received, Lucy was eager to reciprocate. All afternoon, she moved from one activity to another with philanthropic zeal. Sister Hitchiner was right: An eight-hour shift was hard work. With new names to learn, faces to recognise, and skills to learn, Lucy was stretched to her limits. She returned to her room, exhilarated and exhausted. She took a quick bath in the communal bathroom, made a mug of tea and prepared a cold supper of cheese, crackers and fruit. Conchita's loud singing penetrated the wafer-thin walls. Rousing Spanish folk songs soon became familiar, evoking memories of this phase of Lucy's life.

Conchita went out, slamming the door. Lucy tuned in to a German radio station and dozed off. When she awoke, it was dark, the unfinished supper and mug of cold tea on the bedside table. An ambulance siren wailed close by, its harsh blue light invading the room. Lucy shut the curtains and went to the communal kitchen to heat a pan of soup. The electric hob was slow, so she returned to her room. The Orientation sheet listed her placements: Fieldfare Ward her base, with one-day stints on male geriatric, female orthopaedic, male medical wards, and Casualty. Not Maternity or Surgical wards? Casualty would be interesting...

Suddenly, there was rapid hammering at the door. Lucy sprang up and opened it cautiously.

'You come now in kitchen! It nearly fire!" A tiny, Oriental-looking woman screeched, grabbing Lucy by the sleeve. Lucy dashed down the corridor and was met with the acrid smell of scorched vegetables. She surveyed the charred remains of the soup in the milk pan and tossed the pan and its contents into the bin. This was the first and last time she bothered using the kitchen.

The next morning on Lark Ward, the pace was slow, but the work was no less rewarding. There were patients to wash, clothe, feed, and comfort. Lucy made beds, assisted with meals, emptied catheter bags and urine bottles, and helped patients walk with sticks and Zimmer frames. She helped bath a proud centenarian. Never having seen a naked man before, she averted her gaze when appropriate. The next day, the female geriatric ward was another quiet haven of slowness. Lucy spoon-fed a couple of bed-bound, speechless ladies, discovering how much time and patience was needed. Back on Fieldfare Ward, she reconnected with routines, and patients of all ages walks of life, each personality different, every one an individual. Off shift, Lucy found herself still thinking about them. Miss Illingworth and Mrs Higgs were practically her friends, as were lively Mrs Wilcox, who had lost an arm to diabetes, Mrs Mamie Grant, the American tourist who collapsed at Gatwick airport, Mrs Taylor the delicate mother-to-be, Miss Simpson the retired nurse, and Mrs Middleton, a retired teacher with diabetes and rheumatoid arthritis.

On Thursday, Lucy worked on the female orthopaedic ward in the morning and the male medical ward in the afternoon, meeting more people and learning new skills. She measured urine, completed charts, helped patients in and out of wheelchairs and electric bath seats, and rubbed backs marred by pressure sores. By shift-end, Lucy was exhausted. On Friday, she awoke stiff and aching. One stint remained: Casualty – scheduled for the afternoon, then a weekend at home to recuperate.

That morning, Fieldfare Ward was busier than ever. Two patients had been admitted overnight, and the ward was full. The doctors' round took most of the morning, and Sister Haywood was too occupied to attend to patients, leaving routine tasks to the nurses. At half past eleven, Lucy joined three of her colleagues for second coffee break. The staff room was thick with smoke.

'Fancy a fag, Luce?'

Motherly, peroxide blonde Pat Briggs, offered an open pack of filter tips.

Lucy politely accepted, adding to the smoke wafting down the corridor. After break, there were mixed reactions from patients. Miss Simpson wrinkled her nose disdainfully, Mrs Taylor turned green, and others coughed and spluttered, wishing they had energy and inclination to complain. Mrs Wilcox was the exception.

'I'll have a fag myself,' she rasped, shuffling to the day room.

At twenty past twelve, the lunch trolley was still standing in the corridor. Nurses rushed through the pre-lunch toileting round, and there were still three patients awaiting a wash.

'You ladies will have to wait until this afternoon,' Sister Haywood told them. 'Nurse Engels and Nurse Wylie will attend to you after their lunch breaks.'

'What about my placement at Casualty?' Lucy asked.

'It's been postponed until Monday. We're short staffed and you're needed here. You and Nurse Engels will do the observations, the bedpan round, then help finish the bed baths.'

'Yes, Sister.'

Nurse Engels was a pleasant co-worker, and with plenty to do, the afternoon passed quickly. Afterwards, Lucy collected her bag, locked the door, and hurried to the car park, where Hilda stood waving, beside a small, mint-green car.

'This is my Hillman Imp,' she said. 'A good deal – low mileage and easy on petrol. I'm also looking for a job. Now, tell me about your job! I'm all ears.'

Lucy gave giving a garbled account of the week's activities.

'It all sounds fascinating,' Hilda said. 'I always wanted to be a nurse, but it never happened. After my mother died I left school and started work as an office junior. Then the war broke out. It's different for your generation, with so many career prospects.'

'What's for dinner? I'm starving!'

'Fish and chips. Fish on Fridays, as always.'

'Friday! I forgot to pick up my wage packet. I'll get it on Monday,' Lucy said.

'That's something I wouldn't forget!' Hilda responded.

'But you were a wages clerk, so you'd remember that. Nursing is so fulfilling, it makes you forget everything else.'

That night, Lucy was too stimulated to sleep. She lay awake for hours, listening to the mournful calls of owls. One question burned within her. *Might nursing be a better career than teaching?*

The next day, on the way to Millhurst, Hilda said, 'This car is easy to drive. I could give you driving lessons in it, if you like?'

'I'll think about it,' Lucy said.

In Millhurst she bought a fob watch, a pack of low tar cigarettes, and a bag of russet apples.

'You must manage your money carefully. Those apples are expensive,' Hilda said, 'but at least they're healthy. So many girls of your age waste their money on stupid things like drink and cigarettes.'

And fob watches? Lucy kept silent.

Summer had merged into autumn. Orange, red, and gold tints adorned the mid-Sussex mosaic of fields and forests. Harvests were done, and land lay silent and bare. Trees around Birchwood Close had shed their leaves, and the great oak at the back of the house stood proud, its load of acorns scattered on the ground. A nearby line of elms stood gaunt and forlorn, ravaged by Dutch Elm disease. Lucy recalled the elm's small, rough leaves and ridged bark, and the deep roar of breezes in lofty boughs. Was this venerable tree now history?

On Sunday, Hilda prepared a roast beef dinner.

'I hope you're feeding yourself properly at that place,' she said.

'Of course, Mum.' Lucy sliced through a piece of meat and dipped it in mustard.

Suddenly, she sprang to her feet. The chair thudded to the carpet, the padded seat falling from its frame. Hilda's expression darkened. Would Lucy ever outgrow childish tantrums?

'There's something up my trouser leg,' Lucy hissed, shaking her voluminous trouser leg. A muffled buzzing, a sharp, stabbing pain sent Lucy hopping and screeching the length of the living-room.

'What in heaven's name?' Hilda began.

'A wasp – or bee – I-don't-know-what-it-is-all-I-know is the stupid thing's stinging me!'

'Well don't make such a song and dance about it!' Hilda retorted.

Lucy limped to the bathroom, squashed the offending wasp and flushed it down the toilet. On her left leg was a raised pink area, which Lucy doused with cold water, hoping for the best.

After tea, Hilda drove Lucy back to Alderbridge. Lucy awoke in the morning at seven, worked on Fieldfare for an hour, then reported to Casualty, as instructed. A young staff nurse greeted her at the door and invited her into a well-scrubbed room with trolleys, portable screens and an array of oxygen cylinders and other equipment.

'Monday mornings are usually quiet,' the nurse said. 'We might not even get any patients. A pity you weren't here on Friday. We were so rushed off our feet we had to get extra help.'

'Fieldfare was busy too,' Lucy said. 'That's why I had to stay, and your lady with the heart condition came to us. She's doing okay.'

'That's good. Nursing is like that, very unpredictable – busy days and quiet days, especially on Casualty. If you want to see some action, weekends are best, when more people are out and about and off guard. We get kids falling off bikes, sports injuries, and alcohol-related problems. We don't get many drunks though, not like in the big cities. The road accidents are the worst, and they're more common in winter. But of course, an accident can happen any time.'

Half an hour later, a small boy was brought in with a twisted ankle, then a girl with a gash on her leg from falling off a scooter. The nurse summoned a doctor, and Lucy watched, as the injuries were inspected and dressed, while the young patients winced and were comforted with teddy bears and a lollipop.

Then time dragged. The nurse made milky coffees and offered a tin of fancy biscuits. Lucy took a chocolate Digestive and dunked it in her coffee. Her leg throbbed and burned, and the blue French moccasins pinched her aching feet.

'I don't suppose I could sit down?' she asked, 'My leg's killing me. I was stung by a wasp yesterday.'

'You leg does look swollen. You're in the right place, so I'll ask the medic to come back and look at it.'

Lucy was prescribed antihistamine tablets and calamine lotion. At lunch time she walked to the main building, collected her wage packet and went to the canteen for pie and chips.

Through the week, juggling food, rest and sleep was a challenge. Muscles ached from unaccustomed use, late shifts followed by earlies the hardest. One afternoon, Lucy finished at five, and walked to a local park, seeking rest and solitude. Copper beeches and shrubs were resplendent with autumn colours, reminiscent of last year's walk with cousin Greta in Unterheidenrath, now a fading memory. Lucy continued reading *Deux Soeurs* – the French translation of A J Cronin's *The Sisters*. The tale of a nurse's night vigil for a desperately ill child wasn't easy reading. The nurse chose the wrong moment to make a cup of tea. The child's condition deteriorated, with fatal consequence. Blaming herself, the nurse refused rest or refreshment whilst caring for another child with the same illness. The second patient made a full recovery, but the nurse succumbed to the disease and lost her own battle against it. Lucy put the book down. Falling leaves swirled and danced, and the sun cast long shadows across the grass. She wondered if the story was true.

Lucy sensed a bond developing with her long-stay patients. Some offered sweets and fruit, telling her she was very kind. At every opportunity, she encouraged weaker patients to eat and drink, offering water, squash or tea, diligently completing fluid balance charts. Awkward, cantankerous patients had their endearing ways, like nonagenarian Mrs Blair, who tapped her empty beaker on the bedside table, shouting 'Sis-ter! I want some brrread and butterrr, and nooo marmalade', to whoever happened to be nearby. Eventually, she was moved to a side room where her presence was less obvious.

In spite of her own irregular eating habits, Lucy stayed healthy. Marmite crackers were available on early shifts, but Lucy rarely bothered with a canteen lunch, preferring to snack in her room. One day, she took an open can of marrowfat peas to the ward and hid it in the staff room, planning to eat it during tea break, but the ward clerk found it first and threw it away in disgust. Lucy didn't admit it was hers. Occasionally a free lunch was offered. Unused meals were supposed to be returned to the kitchen for disposal, but Sister Haywood allowed nurses to eat them discretely in the staff room. Once, Conchita snatched Lucy's lunch from the trolley and tossed it into the slop bucket, yelling in Spanish. Bewildered, Lucy went to her room for a light snack, and on returning found Conchita laughing and joking with two porters. Conchita barred Lucy's path. A porter said something in Spanish and asked Lucy to repeat it. She refused, battling unpleasant memories of bullying. Then, thankfully, Sister Haywood intervened, and Lucy returned to her duties, the joy of helping others outweighing the pain of having inadvertently made an enemy.

Thursday, October 10th was Lucy's day off. She went to Foxfield polling station and voted for the first time – Conservative, as her parents had done for decades. At work, she kept political views to herself. Meanwhile, Hilda had found part-time work as a wages clerk on the Foxfield trading estate, and Albert a job at a garden centre. Being an adult seemed to be more about work than anything else.

As winter approached, Fieldfare Ward filled with the frail and elderly, many with cardiovascular and respiratory problems. Nurses were tested to their limits, attending to the needs of the semi-mobile and bed-bound. At shift end, Lucy's legs ached, her feet were sore and her head in a fog. Names, faces, needs and requests flashed before her over and over again like a tape replaying itself. At night she lay awake, reliving the joy of helping others and the pressures of toeing the line. Sister Haywood seemed pleased with Lucy but often rebuked the trainees. The new first-year Pupil Nurse Jackie Fox, confided in Lucy her wish to give up nurse training and become an occupational therapist. Josie and Corrie had the added burden of adapting to a new language and culture. At twenty-five, Corrie looked much younger, and was engaged, to one of the porters. Josie was ever-cheerful and serene, with her own circle of Chinese friends.

On busy days, extra helpers were recruited from elsewhere. One afternoon, Lucy assisted a Ghanaian staff nurse prepare a trolley with draw sheets, incontinence pads, talc, zinc and castor oil, gauze dressings and a washbowl. Eight patients needed two-hourly turns, their backs and bedsores attended to. The nurse worked with efficiency and compassion. Lucy admired her competence but was tempted to mention her long, varnished fingernails to Sister. Lucy was glad she didn't, for that same nurse later upbraided Lucy for entering the dirty utility room with a bedpan in one hand and an empty cup and saucer in the other. Lucy knew she was cutting corners. She accepted the sharp lecture on the dangers of cross-infection. Embarrassed, she tried to think of better ways to multitask. 'Let your head save your legs', Sister Haywood always said.

The next morning, Lucy was busy checking observations, when Miss Simpson, a fragile, straw-like figure, requested help to walk to the toilet.

'Of course,' she answered. She handed Miss Simpson the Zimmer frame and walked with her down the ward.

'Will you fetch me a wheelchair, please?' Miss Simpson whispered faintly.

'Right away,' said Lucy, seeing a spare wheelchair nearby. In the two seconds while Lucy fetched the wheelchair, Miss Simpson collapsed in a crumpled heap upon the floor. Immediately, Sister Haywood and Staff Nurse Craddock were on the scene, helping the patient back to bed. A doctor was summoned. Sister beckoned Lucy into the nurses' station and closed the door.

'You should have asked for help, Nurse Wylie. If there is any doubt whatsoever that a patient can walk, never leave them standing alone!'

'But she had the walking-frame.. I thought –'

'That's not enough!' snapped Sister. 'Anyone with one iota of common sense would know that. We will complete an accident form.'

Lucy felt like a criminal. Fortunately, no adverse effects were reported on Miss Simpson. Lucy continued soberly with her duties.

Three days after the fall, Miss Simpson's condition worsened, and pneumonia was diagnosed. Wave upon wave of dread swept over Lucy. *If Miss Simpson dies, then I shall have killed her*, she reasoned. She scurried quietly at Sister Haywood's heels, seeking an opportune moment to speak.

'Is – is Miss Simpson worse because of me?' Lucy inquired timidly.

'No,' Sister replied curtly. 'Miss Simpson is an extremely ill patient with a serious underlying condition. If the pneumonia had been anything to do with the fall, then we would certainly have told you about it.'

Lucy returned to her work with fresh enthusiasm, and when lunches arrived, she picked up a tray and waited with other staff, as patients' meals were served. Not wishing to stand idle, she folded the paper serviette into a neat cone, as she had done years before at The Merry Teapot. In her mother's book, *The Home Nursing Manual*, Lucy had read about the importance of presenting patients with attractively presented meals.

'Whatever are you doing that for, you stupid girl!' snapped Mavis Pope.

'We don't have time for that sort of thing,' Staff Nurse Craddock added in a low voice. Lucy stared at her feet.

'Go and feed Mrs Blair,' Sister ordered, placing a lunch on Lucy's tray.

'Yes, Sister,' Lucy answered, biting her lip and fighting back tears. Whilst feeding Mrs Blair tiny mouthfuls of mince and mashed potato, she temporarily forgot about the incident. Then, a handful of chocolates offered by a smiling Mrs Wilcox lifted her spirits.

Lucy continued with her afternoon tasks, oblivious of a gathering storm.

The next morning, Lucy was busy with a bed bath, when Sister Haywood parted the curtains and told her to report to Miss Squires in the main building. Corrie was asked to take over Lucy's duties. Lucy knocked briskly on the office door and was invited to come in. Miss Squires eyed Lucy cautiously over the top of her spectacles, her platinum-blonde hair swept up into a tidy bun and her brow furrowed with tension.

'Nurse Wylie, I've been hearing negative reports about you of late.'

Lucy braced herself, expecting to hear more about the Miss Simpson incident.

'There have been complaints from staff about your attitude,' Miss Squires said coldly. 'You are said to be resentful and aloof.'

Lucy couldn't believe she was hearing this.

'B – but I don't understand,' she stammered, recalling the unpleasant encounter with Conchita and the domestics. 'I know I made a big mistake recently, letting a patient fall, and I'm really sorry about that, but hasn't my work otherwise been good enough?' Lucy gabbled defensively.

'No, that's not the issue. You are failing to approach Staff Nurses and Senior Auxiliaries for instructions and advice. You shouldn't always keep running to Sister.'

Lucy stared at the floor. Now, at a time and in a place she least expected, the spectre of bullying was back – in the workplace! The realisation made the pain no less severe.

'Do you enjoy your work?' Miss Squires asked.

Lucy reflected briefly and said, 'Yes. I do – very much'.

'What about the patients?'

'I love the patients!' Lucy replied spontaneously, her optimism rising.

'I see. That's a good attitude, but you have much to learn,' Miss Squires responded evenly. 'Continue working on Fieldfare Ward for a probationary period of two weeks, after which your situation will be reassessed. You may now return to your shift.'

Lucy wondered how her legs carried her back to the ward. This was unreal – a bad dream. Somehow, she finished the shift and returned to her room, wondering what to do. She had practically been sacked from her first full-time job. This was not like the scene in the Sue Barton story, where the young heroine bounces back from a reprimand from a dragonish charge nurse. Again, Sister Hitchiner was right. This wasn't fiction – this was real life. And there would definitely be no dashing, dapper young doctor to sweep Lucy off her feet and carry her into the sunset.

In the evening, exhausted and hungry, Lucy lost her battle with conflicting emotions. Tears flowed uncontrolled down her swollen cheeks, falling on the pages of her open diary, soaking today's short entry: *Unspeakably bleak future...*

Or was it?

Swallowing hard, she grabbed some coins, went to the phone booth in the corridor and called home. Hilda was a sympathetic listener. Lucy remembered many times past, when Hilda had returned from work, stressed and frazzled, with tales of petty criticism and unfairness in the office.

'What should I do, Mum?' Lucy asked. 'Should I leave?'

'No,' answered Hilda. 'That would give them the victory, and you would end on a bad note. My suspicions are they're jealous, because you're educated and possibly they are not. However, they are in authority over you, so you must do as they say. Be polite, and humour them. You have encountered a powerful pecking order and you must respect it.'

Lucy instantly pictured the chickens at Edencroft, then a repetitive bleeping noise signalled the call would end if more coins weren't immediately fed into the machine. Unfortunately, Lucy had run out of change, and the line went dead. But she had heard what she needed to. However, she still felt like running away. She walked into the town, wandering about in a daze until nightfall. Returning to her room, she went straight to bed and hid under the covers, while Conchita's music reverberated through the wall. Lucy blocked her ears and tried to rationalise. Perhaps she should revisit her original plan to work in a tea room? The chink of china, sunlight glinting on pouring tea, a tower of cakes on Willow Pattern plates... *hospitality instead of hospital!* With that comforting thought, Lucy drifted off to sleep.

The next day, Lucy dare not look nurses Craddock or Pope in the face, but she knew avoiding them would make matters worse. Every day, Lucy walked on eggshells, striving to build better working relations with colleagues. The ever-increasing workload kept everyone busy. Corrie confided in Lucy independently she found Staff Nurse Craddock and Sister Haywood unreasonably strict. Listening from her armchair, old Mrs Wilkinson said, 'It seems like you two have a common enemy.'

One day, in a quiet lull before lunch, Sister Haywood's deputy, Sister Barker-Doyle briefed staff on a new admission – nineteen-year-old Sally Parker, a university student of languages, diagnosed with ulcerative colitis. In the afternoon, Lucy found time to chat to Sally, talking mostly about herself, while Sally sat hunched and miserable in her bed. Lucy suddenly stopped. From the corner of her eye, she caught sight of the bustling figure of Mavis Pope.

'I'd better go,' she said quickly, 'I'll come and talk to you later.'

However, Lucy was unable to keep her promise; the heavy workload and hawkish superiors precluded further casual conversations. At shift-end, she swept her cape over her shoulders and walked briskly to her room. Already, Nurses Craddock and Pope seemed friendlier, and with every passing hour, Lucy felt more hopeful that she would keep her job.

On Saturday afternoon, Sister Haywood took her aside in the staff room.

'Well, Nurse Wylie, I shan't keep you long. You'll be pleased to know you've satisfactorily completed your fortnight's probation, and I'll expect you to continue working as hard from now on. Never forget, we all need to work as a team.'

'Yes, Sister, and thank you,' Lucy answered. Once more, she felt accepted and valued and continued her shift feeling lighter than air.

On Lucy's next day off, Marion phoned to say she was pregnant again. To Hilda's relief, Marion asked Lucy to be a godparent. The happy distraction left her unprepared for the ten-day stretch of work ahead. Sally was to go home to convalesce, and she gave Lucy her phone number on a piece of paper, which Lucy put into her tunic pocket, along with some boiled sweets given by Mrs Wilkinson.

'Lucy! Give me a hand with Mrs Middleton!' Pat Briggs ordered.

'Coming,' Lucy answered, pleased to be called by her first name. The patient was helped to her feet and handed a walking stick. Suddenly, the old lady dropped the stick and pitched forwards onto the floor.

'I'm all right, no bones broken!' Mrs Middleton said cheerfully. Lucy quickly bent down and helped her up.

'You did it again!' Pat exploded, face like thunder.

Lucy said nothing, dreading the consequences, but Sister Haywood's reaction was unexpected. 'Mrs Middleton has been examined and is none the worse,' Sister said. 'I saw what happened. You and Nurse Briggs were with her. Patients are encouraged to do as much as possible for themselves, and Mrs Middleton is normally quite capable of walking with her stick unaided. This incident has highlighted the possibility her mobility might be deteriorating. So, continue to be vigilant and report any concerns.'

Lucy returned happily to her tasks. After the shift, she phoned Sally.

'I'm feeling much better and going back to Uni after Christmas,' Sally said.

'What university did you say you're at?' Lucy asked, her mind full of many other things.

'Bath.'

'I've been given an unconditional offer for Blackford and I'm due to start German and French in October,' Lucy said. 'I got good grades –'

A familiar, bleeping tone interrupted the conversation. Lucy fumbled in her pocket and discovered she was out of change – again. Then came the low, plaintive whine of the disconnection tone. After that, the busy-ness of work took over, and sadly, Lucy realised she'd lost the piece of paper with Sally's number on it.

On the ward, Lucy was rapidly earning herself a reputation. After meals, the patients waited for a familiar clanking of the bedpan trolley and the sight of Nurse Wylie, pushing the cumbersome, stainless steel vehicle full of heated bedpans.

'Here she comes!' Mrs Wilkinson cackled joyfully. 'It's Queenie – queen of the bedpans!'

Lucy smiled. Ironically, one of the tasks she imagined would be the most arduous and unpleasant had its rewards.

Christmas was weeks away, and staff were asked to request their preferred days off. On the provisional duty roster, Lucy pencilled in Christmas Eve, Christmas Day, and Boxing Day, but Sister Hitchiner quickly pointed out that everyone was expected to work at least one of those days.

'I suppose I could work Christmas Eve?' Lucy suggested hesitantly.

By chance, Miss Squires appeared. 'But Christmas in hospital is lovely! There's an atmosphere of warmth and goodwill, and if you work on Christmas morning as well, you'll get a free Christmas dinner.'

'All right, I'll work Christmas Eve and Christmas Day,' Lucy agreed.

'That's the spirit,' Sister Haywood smiled. 'You can work early shifts on both days and take the next three days off.'

Lucy made plans to join the carol singers on Christmas Eve, leave after a Christmas dinner at the end of the next shift, and enjoy a family time at home. Meanwhile, she helped decorate the ward between shifts.

'Nurse Wylie looks quite different in her ordinary clothes,' remarked Mrs Wilcox. 'I had no idea her hair was so long.'

'She's very slim,' said another patient. Lucy stood on the ladder, fastening paper chains and tinsel from the light fittings, enjoying the compliments.

'Thank you for helping with the decorations, Nurse Wylie,' Sister Haywood said the following morning. 'However, there's a slight problem. You'll have to take down all the decorations attached to light fittings. It's against fire regulations, according to the new *Health and Safety at Work Act.*' Lucy duly removed the offending paper chains, disappointed that much of her efforts had been wasted.

On the late shift, Corrie took two ladies in wheelchairs to the main hall to watch the Christmas play performed by hospital staff. Lucy expected traditional songs and entertaining sketches, but the curtain rose on a series of disconnected scenes: an unconvincing Santa crooned an off-key "Jingle Bells". Shadowy pantomime cats and three mice pranced around, bemoaning greedy Fat Cats who deprived NHS workers of a decent wage, while a cardboard cut-out, over-fed feline hovered overhead. Four masked figures in scrubs, waving stethoscopes and catheters chanted an embittered lament about nurses' low pay.

Lucy watched the row of heads in front, wondering what the patients were thinking. The performance concluded with polite applause. On the way back to the ward, one of the patients said, 'Well that was a load of crap!'

'Actually, I agree,' Lucy replied, smirking.

Corrie and the other patient declined to comment.

In the morning, a festive mood of good cheer reigned on Fieldfare Ward. Wintry sunshine streamed through windows, highlighting vases of flowers, apple-green bedspreads and green, yellow and blue patterned curtains. Tiny particles of dust danced in the shafts of sunlight, while nurses worked their way up the ward, helping patients up, making beds, and plumping up pillows in time for the doctors' round. At handover, Sister Barker-Doyle reported Mrs Taylor had been moved to a side room for peace and quiet. With a thrill of excitement, Lucy remembered Marion. Niece or nephew? Thoughts of new babies kept her in good spirits through the busy shift. Passing by a side room, Lucy heard a buzzer and went to investigate. Clutching her swollen belly, ashen-faced Mrs Taylor was vomiting violently into a bowl.

'Don't worry – I'll get someone to come,' Lucy said quickly, suddenly feeling awkward. She went to fetch help. She later heard the patient had gone to the Maternity ward.

In the evening, there was a staff party at the nurses' home. It was a cold night, so Lucy dressed casually in slacks, turtleneck sweater and platform shoes. She added a few touches of makeup, put on the silver bells ring and gold cross and chain, then hurried across the courtyard. In the smoke-laden hall, Lucy bought a cola and lit a cigarette, while nurses twisted and gyrated on the dance floor, some of them visibly inebriated. Lucy drew on her cigarette and looked around. Across the room stood Josie with a group of friends. Corrie stood beside her skinny boyfriend, hunched and gaunt in a tight-fitting sweater and flared trousers. Lucy thought they both looked too young to marry. Then the door opened, and a group of doctors sauntered in. Lucy recognised Doctors Major and Crump from Fieldfare Ward, and the young Indian surgeon who had saved her life a year ago. The medics mingled a while, then two of them left – one of them the young surgeon – evidently deciding the party wasn't to their liking. The door opened again, and in swanned three nurses, spearheaded by garishly-dressed Sister Barker-Doyle. *At last – someone to talk to*, Lucy thought, but one glance told her the senior nurse was in no position to hold a coherent conversation. Screeching raucously, the ward Sister swigged audaciously from a gin bottle and took to the dance floor. Lucy looked on in disbelief, then returned to her room.

Unsurprisingly, Sister Barker-Doyle failed to report for duty the following morning. With one worker missing, the difference in the workload was appreciable. Lucy and the other nurses struggled to finish their tasks. At lunchtime, Lucy was happy to be allowed a cooked dinner and to hear that Mrs Taylor had given birth to a baby boy, both doing well.

Remembering the Secret Santa, Lucy hurried to the League of Friends' shop and bought a gold-plated necklace with a rose pink, pearl pendant. She wrapped it, labelled it *To PAT*, and left it in the box in the staff room.

Early the next morning, Lucy was surprised to find eight empty beds.

'We're sending as many people home as possible at Christmas,' Sister Haywood explained, 'as everyone wants to be with their family.'

It was a pleasant, slow-paced morning. Lucy went to the first coffee break at half past ten. In the staff room, nurses were opening their Secret Santa gifts. Lucy's was a small plastic, circular clothes airer with pink pegs attached, suitable for socks and underwear. Lucy pulled a face. She had no idea who had given it, and she never did find out.

In the evening, Lucy joined the nurses for a carol singing tour of the hospital. Coloured lights and candles added to the atmosphere. The last ward was Maternity, where "Once in Royal David's City", "Away in a Manger", and "Silent Night" were rendered with depth and emotion. Lucy's heart thrilled, as she thought of her unborn godchild and Mrs Taylor's baby boy. Halfway through the second carol, a patient began sobbing uncontrollably, burying her head in the pillows. No one came to her. As the carol reached a crescendo, Lucy's voice rose with the others, vibrant notes blending with the tormented sobs of the distraught young mother. Lucy hoped the singing might provide comfort. Afterwards, when the group went to the canteen for sherry and mince pies, she overheard that the child of the crying woman was stillborn.

On the way home the next day, Lucy told Hilda of the delighted faces of the patients as they each opened a small gift on Christmas morning, the turkey dinner, the endless supplies of mince pies and sherry, and how she'd swayed off down the ward to do the observations, dropping two glass thermometers in the process – an action she wasn't proud of. Surprisingly, she was reprimanded neither by nursing staff nor her mother.

That evening, presents were opened by the fireside. Albert and Hilda were delighted with Lucy's gifts; all purchased at Marjoram's stores in Millhurst – a bone china tea service, soup bowls and ceramic hen-shaped egg container, and a gilt-edged, china teapot which Lucy had bought with money Martha had given her last summer to buy her parents a quintessentially English gift.

'It's been a memorable year,' Hilda said solemnly. 'Who'd have imagined, a year ago there'd be so many changes?'

'It's been wonderful,' Lucy whispered, gazing at the coloured lights reflected in sparkling tinsel on the tree.

'We've much to be thankful for,' Hilda sighed.

34: RESPONSIBILITIES

With a sigh, Lucy penned her last diary entry of the year:
Busy shift. I'm exhausted.
She switched off the bedside lamp and hunkered under the covers. Ambulance sirens wailed through the night; blue lights flashed through thin curtains. Lucy lay rigid with tension, awaiting the shrilling of the alarm at six thirty. Eventually, she drifted off, then woke with a strange sense of foreboding.

Would this be a bad year?

The ward was full. Work was relentless. Hope for frail elderly souls awaiting transfer to a geriatric ward or nursing home dwindled by the hour. Some didn't make it that far.

At tea break, all the Marmite crackers were gone. Lucy sank into a chair, poured a coffee and lit a cigarette. Pat Briggs voiced annoyance at such a pathetic present from the Secret Santa and wondered who on earth could have given it. Lucy said nothing. In the afternoon, Sister Haywood sent Lucy on an urgent errand to the pathology lab. Miss Simpson had taken a turn for the worse.

Winchester bottle for a chest aspiration, Winchester bottle for a chest aspiration, Lucy repeated the instruction over and over again, like a mantra. She sped across the yard, anxious to help the patient she had once endangered. The Winchester bottle turned out to be quite large – almost as big as one of Albert's demijohns. Lucy carried it carefully back to the ward, where it was immediately put to use. Hope was fading fast. More pale and drawn than ever, Miss Simpson's emaciated body had shrivelled to skin and bone.

'I feel like a dead-end-kid today,' she murmured. 'I used to weigh eight stone, walk five miles a day, never smoked...'

'I like country walks, too,' Lucy said, straightening the covers. With a deep sense of dread, Lucy knew Miss Simpson would never walk outdoors again.

The next cold snap claimed more lives, among them a young mother of four, whose weight had dropped from twelve stone to less than seven. Her painful symptoms were eventually traced to pancreatic cancer. Remembering

Rose, Lucy still questioned why, even with modern medicine and technology, people still died young. Days later, Miss Simpson passed away peacefully in her sleep, the underlying cause of her debilitating disease unknown. Telling a patient they might have cancer was strictly taboo. Formerly a nurse, Miss Simpson knew the score. A wilting potted plant stood discarded in the utility room after her property was cleared away.

'A pathetic looking plant,' Pat said, 'It belonged to Miss Simpson, didn't it?'

Lucy nodded. The plant reminded her of Miss Simpson – sad, moribund, and alone.

No sooner was one patient discharged; another was admitted. Some were young. One had self harmed with blades, another overdosed on various substances. Some nurses judged them as nuisances and made every effort to get rid of them as quickly as possible to free up beds for the seriously ill. When deemed medically fit, they were sent to the psychiatric ward, which Lucy hadn't been aware even existed.

Pleasant-mannered Bridget stayed a little longer, since bulimia was a condition both psychiatric and physical. A trainee nurse at a convent, Bridget was missing her home in Ireland.

'She's a hopeless case, a time-waster,' Nurse Craddock sneered, during handover. Lucy said nothing. She liked Bridget, not least because Bridget said Lucy would make a good nurse and should do her training.

One lunchtime, Lucy lost track of time. She dashed back to the ward, checked her fob watch, and started the observations three minutes late. Sister Barker-Doyle emerged from the nurses' station.

'Nurse Wylie,' she said icily. 'Can I have a word?'

Lucy received a curt reprimand for her lateness. Her guilty conscience warred with rage. *How dare she – a Sister who should set an example get blind drunk, miss a whole day's work, and still get paid?* Lucy bit her lip, continued working and soon forgot the incident.

Winter dragged on. One afternoon, Lucy spent a quiet half-hour preparing a side room and labelling of crockery and cutlery for an infectious patient, then was asked to remove the labels, because the patient wasn't coming. Instead, another patient came, her skin as yellow as saffron. Lucy stood with her finger on the patient's pulse, her eyes on her fob watch.

The patient was chatty.

'Looks like I've been sunbathing, doesn't it? My skin isn't normally this dark. At this rate, my fat-free diet will have me looking like Twiggy. You can call me Joyce, not Mrs Farmer, as that sounds so formal. What's your name, nurse?'

'Lucy – Lucy Wylie,' Lucy replied, still counting heartbeats.

'Your'e very young. Are you a nursing student?'

'Actually, no...'

Lucy told Joyce about Germany and France, family and friends, and her plans to study. Joyce spoke about her smallholding, two golden retrievers and three sons, the youngest at Southampton University. Then the crisp rustling of a starched apron halted the conversation.

'Nurse Wylie! Come to the nurses' station for a minute before I go off shift,' Sister Haywood said.

'Mrs Farmer has severe jaundice. She has weeks to live, but mention this to no one. Two nurses have phoned in sick, leaving a two-hour gap before the night staff come. I've sent Mrs Parker home, so we've one empty bed. You will be in charge, assisted by an auxiliary from Bunting Ward. Sister on Starling Ward will send in extra help if necessary. Do you have any questions?'

'No, I don't think so,' Lucy answered. This was a golden opportunity to be grown up and responsible.

Two hours. All seemed well. Lucy walked up and down, offering help where required, then preparing the drinks trolley. Leaving the big kettle warming on the stove, she strolled back down the ward, feeling competent and in control.

'Come over here, nurse,' a voice said. Lucy turned to see the familiar, cheery face of Mrs Wiggins. 'Help yourself to chocolates, while it's quiet. You're always so busy, and you deserve a treat!'

'Thanks,' Lucy whispered, dipping her hand into the box.

There was a dull thumping sound. A red light flashed above the door to the nurses' station – the telephone was ringing, on quiet mode. *Bother!* Lucy was looking forward to enjoying chocolates and a nice little chat.

'Just a minute,' she said, and went to the nurses' station to answer the phone.

'Fieldfare Ward, Nurse Wylie speaking.'

'Hello, Nurse Wylie,' drawled the familiar voice of Dr Crump. 'Could I speak to Sister or Staff Nurse?'

'They're both off duty. I'm here with another auxiliary until the night staff come at half past nine.'

'I'm sending you a thirty-year-old with abdominal pain, query cause, high anxiety, hyperventilating, hyperglycaemic. I want you to set up an intravenous drip and prepare an injection tray. Patient in Casualty, due to arrive on the ward in ten minutes.'

'B – but –' Lucy protested, but Dr Crump had hung up.

Surely he knows I'm neither qualified nor allowed to administer drugs or drips? Lucy thought quickly. There was one empty bed, opposite the nurses' station. First, she sent the relief nurse to get help from Starling Ward. Then she fetched a drip stand, observation charts, and a jug of fresh water and a clean glass. The patients were quietly reading, doing crosswords, sipping drinks, or slumbering contentedly, oblivious of a drama about to unfold.

The double doors at the end of the corridor swung open with a dull thwack. An explosion of noise followed: clanking trolleys, raised voices, and an ear-splitting screech. Two porters guided the gurney; two nurses restrained a thrashing, gown-clad figure from hurling herself to the floor. Dr Crump led the procession, fussing and fretting, clipboard in hand. It was like a scene from *Emergency Ward Ten.*

'Nurse Wylie!' Dr Crump snapped. 'Where are the intravenous infusions and injection tray?'

'I requested help immediately,' Lucy answered, glancing anxiously at the door. 'A qualified nurse will be here shortly.'

'But we need these things now!' exploded the doctor. 'Why didn't you prepare them yourself?'

'Because I am not allowed to,' Lucy explained calmly. 'I'm an auxiliary and not a trained nurse.'

Dr Crump stormed off to the treatment room. Lucy pulled the screens. The patient thrashed and screamed, porters eased her onto the bed and raised the bed rails. Quiet whimpering, then a sudden, spine-chilling howl that startled everyone. At last, help arrived – a fleet of four nurses rapidly addressed the task in hand. Lucy showed everyone where relevant equipment was stored and reassured her patients things would soon quieten down.

In the morning Sister Haywood said, 'I hear you coped admirably, last night, Nurse Wylie. You kept your cool and did things right. Well done.'

Lucy flushed with pride.

During handover, it was reported last night's admission had been moved to the gynaecology ward. 'Where she should have been sent in the first place,' Sister Haywood declared.

A new member had joined the team – Ruth Morgan, a mature pupil nurse, who ran the Christian Union and was considered Alderbridge's resident agony aunt. Ruth's room in the nurses' home was an open door for anyone to drop by for a cup of tea and a chat. Ruth kept her views to herself. Nevertheless, Lucy was cautious. Ruth was eccentric but approachable and a good co-worker. Together, they whisked the length of the ward, making beds, blanket-bathing the bedridden, offering words of comfort to the anxious and confused.

Their last patient was a frail ninety-year-old in a side room.

'She won't last another night,' 'Ruth whispered.

'How can you be sure?' Lucy asked.

'I can tell. With cancer, it's obvious. It is the smell of death.'

Ruth was known for her outspokenness. But patients were dying. It was the time of year.

That afternoon, as Lucy checked the observations, she found a patient's wrist cold to touch and her face, grey and expressionless. She had never seen a dead person before. The inadvertent glimpse of Rose's motionless face through the open doorway five Christmases ago didn't really count. This patient, recently admitted, was someone Lucy had never seen alive, and she was the first person to see her dead. The sense of personal responsibility weighed heavily. If she had got there sooner, might the patient still be alive? Lucy drew the curtains around the silent bed. The clipboard and chart still in her hand, she read the details.

NAME: *Edith North*

DATE OF BIRTH: *30· 11· 1897*

ADDRESS: *HONEYSUCKLE COTTAGE*
12, WOODLANDS LANE,
FOXFIELD,
WEST SUSSEX·
BN46 8JQ.

This lifeless body was not the neighbour from around the corner. A spiritless body is like an uninhabited house. Lucy wondered if she'd ever seen Edith North when she was alive, perhaps greeted her in the street? *I must let someone know,* Lucy reasoned, swallowing hard. She found Sister Haywood in the treatment room preparing an injection tray.

'Sorry to bother you, Sister, but I think we have a corpse on our hands,' Lucy said quickly, in a low voice, failing abysmally in her attempt to make light of the grim report.

Sister Haywood bristled.

'Don't say that!' she hissed. 'Just continue with the observations.'

'Yes, Sister,' Lucy answered quietly, the backlash of her own conscience a shock of cold water.

Winter dragged on, every shift as taxing as the one before. On her next day off, Lucy went with her parents to Brighton. It was cold and miserable, and she bought nothing. Returning to the car, Hilda remarked, 'Look, Lucy – that big house must be a home for the elderly. Did you see that nurse in there, going about her duties? She's just helping an old lady with her Zimmer frame...'

'Yes, Mum,' Lucy wished to be spared the running commentary.

'You'll hear from Germany any day now,' Hilda continued, 'from Kochendorf and Hildenheim, regarding your inquiry about work.'

'There probably aren't any jobs.'

'I wouldn't give up just yet.'

A sudden burst of sunlight through a bank of black cloud confirmed Hilda's hopes.

By chance, both responses arrived the following day, after Lucy had returned to Alderbridge. Hilda put the letters unopened in Lucy's room.

Bleak February mornings were still dark, days laden with grey skies and freezing fog.

'A new patient for you to check in,' Sister Haywood told Lucy, handing her the admission paperwork.

'Thanks, Sister.'

Clipboard in hand, Lucy went to the bedside and worked through the list of questions.

'Julie Hale, age 27, divorced, no children, no religious beliefs...'

The robust-looking redhead didn't look particularly ill. Lucy brought her a jug of fresh water and a glass, then moved on to her next task. It had seemed callous and insensitive, prying into a patient's personal circumstances, merely to complete paperwork. She resolved to do better next time, no matter how busy or tired she felt.

'Nurse Wylie!' Sister Haywood called, holding a tray of forms and blood samples. 'Will you take these to the pathology lab for me please? Dr Major wants the results as soon as possible.'

Hope flickered in Lucy's heart at the possibility that prompt action might save someone's life.

'Right away, Sister,' she answered. In the cloakroom, she found her cape had disappeared. Irritated, she crossed the yard in the freezing cold. Suddenly, a van stopped beside her. A long-haired young man rolled down the window and asked, 'Excuse me, can you direct me to Fieldfare Ward?'

'Of course,' Lucy panted. 'I've just come from there. Just past the white building, opposite the Nissen hut, Fieldfare Ward is the first hut on the left.'

'Thanks very much. Where can I can park?'

'The car park's behind the hospital entrance, it's a bit awkward to get to from here, but I'm going past it after taking these to the pathology lab –'

'We'll give you a lift. Jump in the van and you can direct us.'

The wind was bitter and Lucy longed for the warmth of her woollen cape. She climbed into the van and sat between the driver and another young man.

'Stop here first, I have to deliver these,' Lucy said, praying the lads weren't criminals.

'What's in the bottles?' the passenger asked.

'Blood samples,' Lucy said.

'Blood ! Christ! What a job! Sooner you than me.'

Lucy found the remark disquieting.

'Are you visiting someone on Fieldfare Ward?' she asked.

'Yeah, our Mum.'

'Who is she?'

'Joyce Farmer.'

'Joyce is really nice!' Lucy floundered, searching for words of optimism.

'Yeah, that's right. The best. She'll be glad to see us.'

The bottles safely delivered, Lucy directed the lads to the car park.

'Magic!' the driver said, finding the only free space. 'Just the job. Thanks.'

'You're welcome.'

Lucy jumped down and returned to the ward. She looked for a chance to talk to Joyce and her sons, but other tasks took precedence.

The next morning, Julie Hale's bed was occupied by someone else, and Lucy assumed Julie had been sent home. At handover, it was said Julie had been transferred to the intensive care unit during the night. Lucy regretted not having had the chance to make up for the rushed admission. In the busy morning routine she forgot about her.

'Nurse Wylie, you'll assist Nurse Engels with last offices in the side room,' Sister Haywood said.

Last offices? Lucy knew what that was. Corrie fetched gloves, aprons, a plastic bowl, towels, soap, and a bottle of detergent. In the silent room, a motionless figure lay on the bed, covered with a white sheet.

'What do we have to do?' Lucy asked.

'We wash the patient and dress her in a gown,' Corrie answered quietly, drawing back the sheet. She gently washed and dried the blue-grey, expressionless face. Again, the face of a person Lucy had never met alive.

'Now we wash the rest of her.' Corrie said, rinsing and squeezing the flannel. She lifted a lifeless arm and began washing chest and forearms, patting the skin dry. Corrie rinsed and soaped the flannel again, and handed it to Lucy.

'Here – you carry on. The other side.'

Lucy lifted the other arm. It was heavy and cold. This was no routine bed bath. Lucy sensed she was offering no comfort. She said nothing, then stepped back and stared at the wall, feeling distinctly unqualified for the task.

'Why do you look away?' Corrie asked. 'There's nothing to fear.'

'It's okay – I mean, I'm not afraid,' Lucy answered, reddening with embarrassment. They finished the task in silence.

Corrie and Lucy moved to the next side room, to fifty-year-old Mrs Walker, in the final stages of breast cancer – a cancer confirmed after failed surgery. In the darkened room, a waif-like daughter sat at the bedside. The girl moved aside, while Corrie and Lucy began the bed bath. The patient moaned in pain, her bloated body ravaged by the disease soon to claim her life. Beneath iodine-drenched gauze, the blackened flesh was hard and unyielding, oozing fluid.

'I'll get someone to help,' Corrie said quietly.

A long, silent minute passed. Corrie returned with Sister Haywood, who helped turn the patient on her side.

'My goodness, you are heavy, aren't you?' Sister puffed, her sinewy arms supporting the swollen girth. Lucy read the expression on Mrs Walker's face and vaguely discerned a hoarse whisper, 'I'm sorry...'

Sister rubbed the ever-widening, livid bed sores on the patient's back, plumped the pillows said, 'There, that's better for you. Now, Nurse Wylie will get you a cup of tea. Nurse Engels, I need you to help set up a drip...'

The two nurses left, and the door swung shut. Lucy stood for a moment and said nothing. Mrs Walker lay motionless, her eyes half-closed, beads of perspiration forming on her florid brow. Lucy fetched two cups of tea, one each for mother and daughter.

'Thank you,' the girl whispered. Lucy returned later and found the girl in the same place, her eyes closed. The mother lay motionless, staring at the ceiling. Lucy quietly picked up the untouched cup of lukewarm tea and said, 'I'll get you some fresh water.'

Lucy finished at five. After delivering prescriptions to Pharmacy, she headed for the car park, where Hilda sat waiting in her car.

'I've brought some letters for you,' Hilda said, enthusiastically. 'From Germany. They look official.'

Lucy tore the first one open. It was from the Bürgermeister in Kochendorf. The message was simple and direct.

'Well?' Hilda asked.

Lucy translated, 'Thank you for your enquiry but I regret to inform you that currently there are no vacancies for auxiliary nursing staff in and around Kochendorf.'

'And the other letter?' Hilda asked.

Lucy opened it, ready for another refusal. Staring at the page in front of her, her jaw dropped in surprise.

'Guess what? There's a job for me! In a home for the elderly in Hildenheim – starting next month!"

'There you are dear, I said you would get something! I'm always right,' Hilda said.

Three consecutive days off allowed time to plan the next adventure. Lucy wrote to the Altersheim, booked tickets, ordered currency and traveller's cheques, and began packing. Returning to Alderbridge, she handed in a written resignation, wishing she could finish immediately. A fortnight's notice was required. Her missing cape was finally returned, having been found by Mavis Pope in the staff cloakroom on Lark Ward. Someone had probably borrowed it without remembering or bothering to return it. Lucy didn't care. She doubted she'd wear it again. At handover, she was asked to work with trainee Trisha Adams.

'I'll be an Enrolled Nurse soon,' Trisha boasted, adjusting her cap with three green stripes. 'I can't wait!'

Trisha's personal trumpet-blowing was spontaneous and child-like. Trisha made light of almost every situation, staying sensitive to people's feelings. She reminded Lucy of Sue Barton. It was a while since Lucy had thought of the stories which had once so captured her imagination. Lucy and Trisha moved swiftly down the ward, smoothing covers, tidying locker tops and giving cheering words and cups of tea. Noticing an empty side room, Lucy asked, 'Where's Mrs Walker?'

Trisha caught Lucy's eye and glanced upwards.

'Oh. I'm glad the suffering is over.'

Her words sounded empty and hollow. She thought of the quiet daughter and cousin Sarah's stoic response on the day of Rose's funeral.

Working with Trisha raised Lucy's spirits, but later Lucy heard Julie Hale had also died, after failed treatment for a rare cardiac condition. There was no time for emotional responses. New admissions kept coming: frail, emaciated bodies and hollow expressions, dementia patients demanding and unpredictable, needing constant surveillance. One lady climbed over the bed rails, another absconded to Starling Ward and climbed into the bed of an elderly man, before being escorted back by a domestic. Another patient extended a feeble hand during a blanket bath, mumbling Nice nurse, nice nurse, her fingers stealthily groping Lucy's buttocks in a manner that made her shudder. Mrs Walker's bed was now occupied by an anxious fifty-year-old, laid low by a brain haemorrhage. She feared following her sister, who had died a year before. Within days, nurses witnessed this coherent, relatively healthy-looking person suffer a protracted, painful passing.

Lucy learned hospital wasn't just about making patients well but offering the best care and comfort in the circumstances. Staff shortages worsened, workers were run ragged. Lucy kept going, spurred on by thoughts of Hildenheim. On her last day, staff and patients wished her well. Miss Squires handed her three references in sealed, brown envelopes, bearing the typewritten message:

TO WHOM IT MAY CONCERN.

A few patients, including Bridget and Joyce, exchanged addresses with Lucy, saying they'd keep in touch. Dr Major wished Lucy well in her studies at Blackford University, and Mavis urged Lucy to take better care of herself and to eat sensibly. Sister Haywood thanked Lucy for all her hard work, and presented her with a top-of-the-range retractable, ball-point pen, as a parting gift. Lucy handed in her uniforms and keys, carried her four bags of belongings to her mother's car, and didn't look back.

Like a reel of thread on a spool, her time at Alderbridge was over.

35: Death and Life

I n Hildenheim the day was beginning. Cloud clung cobweb-like to bare vineyards, freezing fog hugged the valley, where office blocks rose defiantly to greet the new day. The night train from the North pulled punctually into the Hauptbahnhof at ten to seven. Wide-awake and poised for adventure, Lucy joined the throng of commuters and took a taxi to her destination. Familiar streets looked different. This was no holiday. Places felt different when they were lived and worked in.

'*So, Fräulein – wir sind bald da,*' the driver announced, on the familiar route. We're nearly there! And Ellen lives in the next street!

The taxi stopped by a grim building set close to the pavement. A plain sign read,

STÄDTISCHES ALTERSHEIM

Municipal home for the elderly sounded ominously austere.

'*Danke! Auf Wiedersehen!*' Lucy paid the driver and walked up the steps to the entrance, fraught with hope and fear. She put down her luggage and struggled with the glass door.

Help immediately appeared. A matronly woman with tight, grey curls and owlish spectacles opened the door and introduced herself as deputy manager, Frau Korb.

'Leave your bags in the hall. Come and meet our manager, Frau Muenzel. 'Would you like coffee?' She spoke with the same thick accent as the Schmieds.

'*Ja, bitte.*' Lucy nodded. She was invited into a sunny room filled with books and paintings, where a platinum blonde woman in her fifties smiled from behind a tidy desk.

'Good morning, *Fräulein* Lucy. Did you have a good journey?' Frau Muenzel asked. Her manner was cordial and business-like.

'Yes, thank you.'

'Tell us a bit more about yourself.'

Fuelled by strong coffee, Lucy resurrected her language skills and spoke about Alderbridge, her personal connection with Hildenheim, and her eagerness to begin work at the Altersheim.

'I enjoy working with people and helping them,' Lucy said.

Frau Muenzel seemed impressed. 'You are a very self-motivated young woman. Frau Korb will now give you a brief tour, then show you to your room.'

A panelled corridor led past a hall filled with tables decked with white cloths and chrome cutlery.

'This is the main dining room, where the staff also eat,' Frau Korb said.

The lights were off, the low ceiling and windows overlooked trees, giving a general impression of gloom. Lucy was pleased to note that there was a garden. The silhouette of a large, black bird dominated one of the window panes.

'Why is there a black bird on the window?'

'To prevent small birds from flying into the glass. They see the shape of a large bird and are warned of danger,' Frau Korb replied.

Lucy remembered the tree creeper that flew into the plate glass pane last summer.

'*Guten Morgen, Schwester Elke!*' Frau Korb greeted a tall blonde in a white tunic.

'*Guten Morgen, Frau Korb!*'

'This is Fräulein Lucy. She's just come all the way from England to work with us until August,' Frau Korb said.

'Pleasure to meet you, Lucy,' Elke responded, shaking Lucy's hand.

'My office phone's ringing – perhaps you would show Lucy to Room Four?' Frau Korb asked. 'Here's the key.'

Lucy followed Elke along a corridor of bare walls, grey doors, and a pervading stench of urine.

'You will be working here, the nursing ward,' Elke explained. A door opened, and an older nurse in a white tunic appeared carrying a white plastic bedpan with a lid. *A lot of things are different here*, Lucy noted, remembering Alderbridge's stainless steel bedpans and trolley, and the open-plan ward lined with curtained beds.

'And here's the staff kitchen.' Elke pushed open a door into a narrow room with a gas stove, a row of cupboards and a small refrigerator. A nurse with grey hair and glasses was preparing a beaker of milk and a sandwich for a resident.

'Schwester Helga, meet Lucy, our new assistant from England!'

The nurse looked Lucy up and down.

'Good morning,' she said, then left with the tray.

'Your room's round the next corner,' Elke said, as they left the kitchen.

Low sunshine streamed through French windows overlooking the garden, lifting Lucy's spirits. The T-shaped end of corridor housed window-facing seats. Two teak doors faced each other at each end of the T. Room Four was on the right. Lucy unlocked the door to a spacious, sunlit room with two large windows overlooking wooded grounds.

'You have the best room,' Elke said. 'Room Three opposite overlooks the street.'

Wooden furniture, cream coloured walls, floral tablecloth, curtains and counterpane, and marl-grey linoleum created an overall impression of brightness and warmth.

'It's lovely!' Lucy exclaimed. 'May I put pictures up on the wall?'

'I'm not sure, you'll have to ask. I must go now, so I'll leave you to settle in. We'll speak later. I look forward to working with you.'

Behind the door was a washbasin and mirror, in the opposite corner a television set on a chest of drawers. Lucy unpacked her clothes and put them away, then stowed her empty case and bag in the wardrobe. She wrote Schwester Lucy on a small piece of card and slid it inside the empty brass holder on the door. *This is so much better than I'd imagined*, she thought in German. She opened a window, ushering in a burst of birdsong. There was a knock at the door. Elke announced breakfast was ready.

'*Ich komme sofort!*' Lucy responded with I'm coming right away! Birgit's exact words at meal times last year. The staff table was in the corner, furthest away from the windows. Lucy was introduced to Schwester Magda, a serious lady in her fifties, and several others, but didn't retain their names. Fresh bread rolls with cheese ham and jam satisfied her hunger, and more strong coffee kept her awake. Afterwards, Lucy was issued with four white tunics, which were to be sent weekly to the launderette.

'Today, you must go to the bank to open an account and request a *Lohnsteuerkarte* so you can pay taxes,' Schwester Magda explained, handing Lucy written instructions. 'Tomorrow you'll work an early shift, which starts at a quarter to seven.'

Lucy didn't relish the idea of going into town, just for official business, much less the idea of a very early start in the morning. She took a tram to the town centre, found the *Deutsche Sparkasse*, where she opened an account and completed a form. She asked what to write in the section about what she did in 1937.

'Just leave it blank,' the clerk advised. Lucy smiled and handed back the form.

'You will be paid by cheque at the end of next month,' the clerk continued. 'Good luck with your new job.'

Outside, Lucy found a phone booth, called the Schmied house and heard the familiar tone of a German telephone.

Birgit took the call. 'Lucy! When did you get here?'

'This morning. I start work tomorrow.'

'That's not much time to rest after the journey. Are you free Saturday?'

'Yes, I've the whole day off.'

'Good! We'll pick you up at ten, and you can spend the day with us. But what about tonight? If you're not too tired, I could come over to Tante Ellen's for tea and we could catch up then?'

'Great idea – I'll see you there – about five o'clock?'

'Fine – see you later!'

The colourful bustle of the town centre was tempting, but Lucy decided to put shopping on hold. She returned to the Altersheim for lunch of pork cutlets, parsley potatoes, and *Sauerkraut*, followed by *Erdbeerquark* – a cream cheese, strawberry dessert. The food was excellent and reasonably priced, far better than the stodge at the Alderbridge canteen. Frau Korb wished her a pleasant afternoon. After lunch, Lucy mailed a short letter to her parents. She finished unpacking, showered and changed and was at Ellen's door on the dot of five, bearing tea bags and chocolate. She jabbed the buzzer.

Ellen's face lit up. She crushed Lucy in a welcoming embrace.

'Lucy! What a surprise! Come in!'

A minute later, Birgit and Franjo arrived with flowers and cakes, and lively conversations followed, news and views exchanged. Birgit and Franjo were snowed under with homework. Lucy was glad to be a year ahead of her European counterparts. Two of Ellen's neighbours were Lucy's colleagues Magda and Helga. More coincidences! There was so much to take in.

'I'm staying till August,' Lucy said. 'Then I'm going to Kochendorf to meet my parents at my cousin Martha's, where we'll be staying for two weeks. And guess what? My sister's having another baby in June!'

Everything was going so well. Lucy left after sundown, went to bed early and slept well.

It was still pitch dark when the alarm clock shrilled. Lucy snapped on the bedside lamp, got up and ready, eager to embrace the day. Fluorescent lights in the corridor kick-started her into action. *A whole hour before breakfast*, she sighed, feeling the need for caffeine. Schwester Magda introduced Lucy to a young, bubbly nurse with a mop of blonde curls.

'I'm Liesl,' the girl said. 'I was a domestic, but I've been working on the *Pflegestation* – the nursing floor for a year now. This morning I'll show you the routines with our people.'

Residents were never referred to as patients. They were *Leute* – people. For two hours, Liesl and Lucy worked from room to room, assisting residents with washing, dressing, and getting up – all at varying stages of dementia and mobility loss. Some had bedside commodes – the bedridden and incontinent lay in open-backed gowns.

'This is Frau Weiss,' Liesl told Lucy. 'We wash her but not get her up. We raise the bed rails to keep her safe. She also has a *Lochbett*.'

A *Lochbett* was a hospital-style bed with a plastic-lined hole in the centre, through which bladder and bowel contents passed into a bedpan positioned underneath. The invention worked better for some residents than others. Unsurprisingly, frequent, thorough cleaning was needed. Frau Weiss's morbidly obese roommate Frau Bayer also had a *Lochbett* but was loathe to use it. Instead, she was strapped into a heavy, canvas sling and raised three feet into the air by a *Krankenheber* – a mechanical hoist, operated by turning a handle. This device was used to transfer heavy, immobile residents to and from bed, chair, commode, and bath. Lucy considered the Krankenheber an excellent invention but was less impressed with the *Lochbett*.

The next room was shared by a married couple, Herr and Frau Baumann, who occupied separate beds. The cream-coloured walls were bare, apart from a carved, wooden crucifix.

'Neither of these two get up. They stay in bed all the time,' Liesl said, giving no explanation. The couple showed no signs of dementia and were willing to chat.

'So you're from England?' Herr Baumann asked Lucy. 'How good of you to come all the way here and look after us.'

Clutching her side, Frau Baumann complained of pain.

'Schwester Magda will be here in a minute to give you your tablets,' Liesl said. Pulling back the covers, she revealed a livid wound-like orifice on the patient's side, a pulsating, scarlet circle on ivory-white flesh with a plastic bag over it. Lucy looked puzzled.

'It's a colostomy bag,' Liesl remarked, again without explanation.

'Look,' Herr Baumann said, suddenly, pointing towards the window. '*Ein Eichhörnle.*'

Lucy saw the pert, diminutive form of a red squirrel on the sill, its tufted ears twitching, eyes wide and inquisitive. Schwester Magda brought a white pill which Frau Baumann swallowed with a glass of water. Frau Baumann fixed her eyes on the window and the bird feeder. Liesl began washing her and Lucy dried her face and hands.

'That squirrel is enjoying his food,' Lucy commented.

'Come on, pay attention,' Liesl said. 'We must to attend to the colostomy, change the bag and wash the orifice.'

Liesl washed, and Lucy dried, applying a sprinkling of talc. Then Liesel attached a clean plastic bag inside a rubber ring and clipped it to the belt. Lucy was reminded of her mother's vacuum cleaner bags.

That week, Lucy fell into a routine, building a working relationship with colleagues and a bond of friendship with residents. Lucy admired the Baumanns' openness – their complete lack of bitterness after losing all four of their sons during the Second World War. She wanted to make a difference in their incredibly sad lives.

In the second week, Lucy attended a health check at a clinic in town, Another formality. The balding, black-haired doctor sported sideburns, a pointed beard, and an offhand manner which Lucy found unnerving.

'Do you have any allergies?' the doctor asked.

'Hay fever, in summer.'

'Any serious illnesses?'

Lucy wondered if she should mention the appendix.

'Operations?'

'I had an appendix operation last year,' Lucy said.

'Then you have had a serious illness. Anything else?'

'No.'

'Remove your clothes and shoes and stand on the scales.'

This was unexpected. Lucy stood shivering with embarrassment in pants and non-padded bra. Her weight was exactly fifty kilos. She dressed and sat stiffly, while the doctor scribbled notes. Lucy glanced at the clock.

'Date of last period?' the doctor asked, without looking up.

The question took Lucy by surprise.

'January last year,' she said.

'Last year? 1974?'

'Yes.'

The doctor mumbled about the smallness of her breasts and the possibility of developing masculine features. Dark memories of bullying resurfaced. Her sexuality and fertility were being questioned. Lucy didn't catch the doctor's closing comments. In the next moment, he was politely showing her the door.

Lucy shelved her shopping spree for another day. She went straight back to the Altersheim, her heart as heavy as lead.

Elke met her in the corridor. 'Ah, Lucy! Just the person I wanted to see! You have mail.'

Elke handed Lucy an official-looking envelope with a Hildenheim postmark.

'Thank you,' Lucy said. She opened the letter and glanced across the typewritten page.

'Need any help?' Elke asked.

'No thanks, it's fine.' Lucy gave a puzzled frown.

'Look – this fell out of the envelope.' Elke handed Lucy a small, yellow ticket.

'Thanks,' Lucy said. 'That makes sense now.'

'What's the letter about?'

'It's from the Bürgermeister welcoming me to Hildenheim and inviting me to a symphony concert in the Volkstheater on Thursday.'

'That's lovely! You'll enjoy that, I'm sure.'

Lucy hesitated. 'Come round for a cup of tea or coffee when you've finished your shift, if you like?'

Elke smiled. 'Okay, I finish at four o'clock. See you later.'

Arriving at her door, Lucy found two more letters propped in the brass holder. Then she noticed her Schwester Lucy name card was missing. Perhaps it fell out when the letters were slotted in? It wasn't on the floor, so Lucy assumed it had been swept up when the cleaners came. She opened the letters. The first was from her mother and contained newsy trivia. The second was from Martha, saying how much she was looking forward to the birth of Karin's second child in July, and to welcoming Lucy and her parents in Kochendorf in August. Lucy put the letters on the table and stared at the mist-cloaked garden. The visit to the doctor's office weighed heavily, doubts and fears eclipsed other thoughts.

Later, Lucy went to the kitchen to fetch milk and butter from the fridge. Schwester Helga was in the room, which felt colder than the fridge.

'By the way, I removed the sign from your door. You're not a qualified nurse. You must call yourself Fräulein – not Schwester.'

The words hit like a clip round the ear.

'Yes, Schwester Helga,' Lucy answered, looking at the floor.

Elke arrived, smiling and cheerful. Lucy had laid the round table with a tray of buttered scones, a selection of biscuits, and a pot of English tea. Outside in the garden, bare branches were motionless in the fading afternoon light.

'My goodness, you've made this room so homely!'

'It's a very nice room,' Lucy said.

There was no doubt the pristine room with its flawless furnishings and woodland views ranked with any top hotel. But what use were such things in an unwelcoming atmosphere?

Lucy's lacklustre mood was evident.

'Is there something wrong?' Elke asked.

Fighting a tide of repressed emotion, Lucy buried her face in her hands.

'Do you want to talk about it?' Elke asked softly.

Lucy wiped her eyes and mumbled, 'The doctor at the medical exam this morning – he suggested I wasn't even a girl!'

'What nonsense!' Elke retorted. 'Anyone can see you are a girl, from your appearance and your voice.'

Instantly appeased, Lucy felt stupid for having said too much.

'The tea is very good,' Elke said. 'I really like it with milk.'

'That's good.'

A commotion of rooks fluttering in branches outside the window filled the silence.

'There's also Schwester Helga,' Lucy said. 'She took my name card away and told me I was wrong to call myself Schwester Lucy.'

'Schwester Helga is strict about many things. She's like that with everyone. The word *Schwester* means a trained nurse. Your designation is *Krankenpflegerin* – carer of the sick – or simply *Pflegerin* – female carer. Much of the work nurses and carers do is the same. Qualified nurses perform clinical skills like medications and injections, as you know.'

Elke allayed Lucy's fears and wasn't the kind of person to betray a confidence.

Lucy didn't bother putting another card on the door. Everyone knew who she was by now.

The cold weather continued, shrouding bare vineyards in sparkling gossamer and sprinkling pine trees with frost. On the evening of the concert, it was snowing. Lucy put away the unworn halter-neck gown in favour of corduroy trousers and thick woollens. She set off in the chill, biting wind, her jacket collar turned up. Pavements glistened with melted ice, streets shimmered, falling snow danced in the white glare of headlights. Lucy hunched at the bus stop, the bitter cold penetrating her clothes and prickling the back of her neck. Traffic rushed past, tyres hissing on salted tarmac. The wait and the journey were short, and the bus stopped close to the Volkstheater in the town centre.

In the foyer, Lucy fished in her pocket for the crumpled ticket, feeling conspicuous and alone. Well-dressed people were arriving in tailored suits, glittering ball gowns and fashionable headgear. How could anyone bear to be bare-shouldered and in open-toed sandals on such a freezing night? Doubtless they had all arrived in chauffeur-driven cars and been ferried straight to the door. Lucy took her place in the stalls and sat stiffly through a pleasant Mozart symphony – not one she recognised, as it wasn't in her father's record collection. She regretted not having purchased a programme, but her purse was in her room, and she'd gone out with coins for the bus fare only. During the interval, she wandered around, feeling out of place. It was not evident who the Bürgermeister was, nor indeed if he was even there.

Ellen was amused when Lucy told her about the concert and her inappropriate choice of clothing.

'But you did the right thing to wear warm clothes on a bitterly cold night! Never mind all those posh people arriving in their fancy cars. But you must dress warmly for next weekend's outing. Up in the high hills there's bound to be snow. Is Saturday free for you?'

'No, but Sunday is a day off.'

'Then we'll go on Sunday. All of us. Birgit, Franjo and the family – for a hike and campfire lunch.'

At work, Lucy gained skills and confidence. Schwester Magda showed her how to change duvet covers, aligning quilt tips with corners, holding them firmly, and shaking them with outstretched arms. Footbaths were a favourite, especially with Frau Bayer. Lucy's role involved fewer nursing skills and more domestic ones. Cloth pinafores and rubber gloves were allocated for cleaning. Lucy became adept at removing dust and grime from obscure places, an activity she found rewarding and therapeutic. Schwester Gerda noticed the difference Lucy made and gave her the task of instructing younger domestics how to wash floors efficiently, using a cloth to clean thoroughly in corners.

Sunday dawned frosty and bright. Lucy put on her thickest clothing, and Birgit lent her a pair of walking-boots. The panorama of sunlit valleys and snow-decked pines was a tonic, but in the keen wind, Lucy's fingertips were frozen. Summer was a long way off. Franjo and Martin lit a campfire and sent Rolf to collect wood, while Lucy helped Ellen and Birgit prepare *Bratwurst* – sausages fried on an open fire. Buttered *Pretzels* were followed by chocolate biscuits and cola. Lucy was reminded of hikes with the Guides. It all seemed so long ago.

'You're quiet today, Lucy,' Franjo remarked. 'Don't you like the food?'

'No – I mean – I'm fine,' Lucy answered, snapping out of her daydream. 'The sausage is very good.'

'Would you like another?' Ellen offered.

'No, thanks, I'm full,' Lucy replied distractedly.

'A colleague of mine wondered if you could help her son with English? He's struggling to keep up,' Ellen said.

'Yes, all right,' Lucy agreed.

'Good, I'll give you the details later. Now for photographs!'

The group huddled into a tight knot, against a background of bare woodlands and snow-speckled hills. Birgit and Franjo stood arm-in-arm, Martin hands on hips, Rolf waving his coloured scarf, Lucy in the middle, squinting in the sunlight. Months later, Ellen sent Lucy a copy of the colour snapshot, a treasured keepsake for life.

On the First of March, the weather changed. In the grounds of the Altersheim, early crocuses and daffodils poked through patches of frozen snow. White caps clung persistently to the hilltops like frosted glaze on Christmas buns. In town, shops stocked foil-wrapped chocolate hares, sugar-coated eggs, and *Maikäfer* – chocolate ladybirds. The latter translated as Maybugs, irrespective of Easter never falling in May. Once a week, Lucy gave an hour's tuition to thirteen-year-old Hans-Edgar – a taciturn child who always listened and never argued. Lucy decided she liked teaching, endorsing her vision to train as a languages teacher. Mother would definitely approve.

On days off, Lucy snacked on chocolate and went window-shopping. However, on payday, her salary didn't show in her account. Frau Korb agreed to look into the matter, and Lucy was informed of a clerical error which was being rectified. No time scale was given. The small remuneration from tuition helped a little, but Lucy worried about paying for meals. The school holidays began, and Ellen went on holiday to Austria, leaving Lucy at a loose end. The Schmieds invited her for the day, but things weren't the same. Lucy felt left out. Birgit and Franjo were inseparable and spent most of the day entwined in each other's arms.

A picture postcard of Salzburg came, with the brief message:

> Hallo Lucy!
>
> Weather here is wonderful and scenery breathtaking. By now you'll have been paid and doubtless enjoying the shops and the Easter break. We'll catch up over coffee next week,
>
> Tante Ellen.

The money still wasn't there. If it didn't appear soon, Lucy would have to borrow some. Work kept her occupied. Lucy decorated her window sills with Easter flowers and chocolate hares received from staff and residents. She felt awkward, being unable to reciprocate, but everyone understood.

"It'll be fine,' Frau Korb reassured her, 'and your wages will be backdated.'

On the first working day after Easter, the promised payment finally arrived. Lucy went to town and bought chocolate, summer clothes, and gifts. She pictured the wooden plaque with dried grasses on the stairwell at home, next to the other souvenir plaques from Germany. For her mother's birthday she bought a linen, lace-edged table cover with a cross-stitch template, and red, yellow, and gold silks. Her own birthday would be a workday, which was unimportant since she had no plans to celebrate. Sitting in her room with the windows wide open, she stitched eagerly, envisaging the completed cloth on the round, oak coffee table in the lounge at home in Foxfield. The plaintive sound of a calling bird floated through the open window. On her birthday, Lucy found cards and gifts on the breakfast table: a basket of goodies, a potted plant, a book wrapped in tissue paper, and a colourful, hand-made card signed by her colleagues.

'*Danke, vielen Dank.*' Lucy whispered. She unwrapped the book. It was called *Tipsys Sonderliche Liebesgeschichte*.

'A love story. I think you'll like it,' Frau Korb said.

'It takes place in Estonia,' Lucy remarked, leafing through the first few pages. 'It looks interesting.'

On the *Pflegestation*, the more astute residents knew it was her birthday and wished her well. Blind, ninety-seven-year-old Frau Riemann was keen to know Lucy's age. The old woman sighed nostalgically. "*Neunzehn!* I remember so well being nineteen! How lovely for you, my dear. Enjoy your youth while you can. Time passes so quickly.'

Lucy said nothing. She could not imagine ever being stooped and shrivelled like the pathetic creature before her. After work, she changed into sky-blue jeans and a new turquoise-and-pink striped, velour top. She raced up the steps to Ellen's flat, where Birgit, Franjo, Martin, and Rolf had just arrived. There was a delicious spread of home baking and lemon cheesecake. Lucy was given more cards, flowers, and gifts. Joyful celebrations continued until dusk. Then Lucy headed back to the place she now regarded as her second home. She turned off the light at eleven o'clock and lay awake, listening to shuffling and creaking, as carers assisted centenarian Herr Grindelwald into his bed in the room above. Soon, the old man was snoring. Lucy turned over, listening to the rhythmic clatter and melancholy whistle of a distant train. Then she dropped into dreamless sleep.

At breakfast, the next morning, Liesl was visibly agitated. Her eyes were swollen and red-rimmed, her pale face streaked with tears.

'What's wrong?' Schwester Magda asked.

'*Der ist es nicht wert...*' Liesl muttered, shaking her head. *Der ist es nicht wert...* Lucy wondered who or what was supposed to be not worth it.

She soon found out. One of Liesl's friends was in hospital. Dumped by a boyfriend, the girl took an overdose and was found unconscious by her mother. Lucy vaguely knew the girl in question, a quiet, unassuming domestic who divided her duties between *Pflegestation* and the floor above. All day, Lucy laboured under a pall of gloom, wondering if she herself would ever find a boyfriend, let alone be dumped by one.

A week later, the girl was back at work. The solitary figure mopping grey linoleum in austere corridors seemed no different. Lucy greeted her with the usual, friendly *Grüss Gott!*

The girl looked up briefly and returned the greeting. Lucy wanted to say more – to ask how she was feeling, but the words wouldn't come.

Days passed in clockwork routine, Ellen teaching, Birgit and Franjo cramming for exams. Lucy went for walks in town, swam at the indoor pool and hunkered in her room, sewing, knitting, reading, writing letters. She moved the chocolate hares from the window sill, so they wouldn't melt in the sun, limiting herself to eating just one a week, making them last until the holiday in Kochendorf.

After a ten-day working stretch, Lucy flopped exhausted onto her bed. She began three consecutive days off with a bar of chocolate and an evening of television. She no longer bothered locking the door. No one ever disturbed her, nor came near her secluded corner of the building. Tomorrow was the First of May, a national holiday. Fine weather was forecast, but Lucy had nothing planned. Birgit and Franjo were going out together and hadn't invited Lucy. But then, why should they? Lucy sighed and switched off the light. Herr Grindelwald's heavy snores rumbled overhead, keeping her awake until she drifted fitfully in and out of sleep. Lost in a labyrinth of subconscious meanderings, her overactive mind spun in circles, solving problems, evading danger, struggling for survival in a delirious mix of disquieting dreams.

In the golden light of morning, Lucy woke to the melody of singing birds. She rose slowly, feeling strangely distant. She padded lightly across the linoleum and pulled down the shutter cord. The roller jerked sharply upwards, with an obtrusive rattle. Lucy winced at the harsh sound. She splashed cool water on her face, dressed in light blue jeans and a jaunty, striped T-shirt. She made a cup of tea and wondered how to spend the day. An intangible cloud of heaviness and confusion hung in the air. Lucy tried to think rationally but failed to shake off a pervading sense of impending doom.

In the heart of Hildenheim, practically all shops were closed for the public holiday. The pedestrian precinct was packed with happy walkers and window-shoppers: families and children chatting and laughing in quick-cadenced tempo. Memories of walks with Martha and Helmut filled Lucy with strange nostalgia. She wandered aimlessly through the town, lost and alone, then took refuge in a park, seeking comfort in trees, flowers and birdsong. She sat on a bench and thought, *If meeting someone is a matter of chance, then there is nothing I need to do – the future was written in stone.* At noon, she stood up and walked back to the Altersheim for lunch.

Cheered by the prospect of fried pork steaks and vegetables, Lucy sat at the staff table with on-duty workers. The food tasted good.

Then Schwester Helga said, 'The covers on Frau Weiss's bed were spoiled with drops of coffee yesterday afternoon. I believe you gave her a beaker of coffee after lunch.'

'Yes, I did,' Lucy replied, seeing no reason to lie.

'Just as I thought! This is a disgrace. I've noticed this problem for some time, and now I know who is responsible.'

The brief altercation ended.

Lucy stared at the black bird on the window. Others sitting nearby continued quietly with their conversations and meals. Lucy's inflamed conscience welled up angrily within her, forbidding her from touching another morsel. She muttered a curt apology, rose from the table and left the room, under the curious gaze of bemused colleagues.

In her room, Lucy closed the door behind her, flung herself onto the bed and buried her head in the pillows, for how long she didn't know. Eventually, she got up and made a cup of tea. She opened a carton of long-life milk, not daring to enter the kitchen until Schwester Helga was off shift. A little embroidery might pass the time? Lucy switched on the radio but didn't listen to it.

Just as I thought! This is a disgrace... The meal table conversation replayed itself like an unstoppable machine. Hours passed, and shadows fell. Lucy continued sewing, rankled by the sounds of birds and the distant whistle of trains. Hunger pangs beckoned, Lucy slowly ate one green apple, studiously making each mouthful last, chewing the waxy skin, savouring the sharp sweetness of juice. That was her only food that day.

'Well, my dear?' cackled Frau Riemann the following morning. Lucy's blank, staring expression was lost on the sightless spinster. 'How did you enjoy your wonderful day off?'

Lucy said nothing, relieved to know her tear-stained face wasn't visible. She moved away stealthily, but her presence was detected by the old lady's keen senses.

'Well?' Frau Riemann demanded, groping the air with wizened hands, hoping to grasp Lucy's sleeve. 'Are you still there, Fräulein?'

'It was very nice, thank you,' Lucy replied politely, leaving the room.

In the warmth of advancing summer, birds sang, and trees flourished. White houses on the hillside dazzled in bright sunshine. Shutters were flung open, and the happy scent of summer invaded people's lives. After a harsh winter, the young summer was whole-heartedly embraced by folk who worked hard, played hard, and whose love of life was strong. But Lucy's heart waxed cold. She languished in her tree-shaded room, playing favourite cassettes over and over again. Somewhere within the dark canopy of foliage, the same strange bird call echoed its melancholy note. Lucy gazed enviously at the innocently blooming plant on the windowsill, the solitary, star-like scarlet flower a painful contrast to her own barrenness of body and soul.

Off-shift, Lucy made every effort to be out of the building. In town, it seemed she walked every path in every park and wandered past every shop on every street. She swam at the indoor pool, trawled shops for bargains in summer sales, bought gifts for family and friends back home, and summer clothes – in shades of blue and apple-green, in figure-hugging sizes. Evenings were spent indoors. Birgit was revising for her Abitur and wished to see nobody. Nobody but Franjo and immediate family. On a brief visit to Ellen, Lucy heard all about Birgit's stress, and how she was fading away. Lucy half-listened. She felt no sympathy.

Alone in her room, Lucy tried on different outfits, posing in front of the mirror. All correspondence with England and Germany was up to date, copies of photographs of the hike, the birthday breakfast and tea sent to her mother, along with the embroidered table cloth. There was nothing else to do. Perhaps it was time to begin packing for Kochendorf? Lucy tidied cupboards, dusted and re-arranged the chocolate hares and repeatedly folded her clothes to see how well they would fit into the cases. The reunion in Kochendorf was marked in the diary, still weeks away – a month after Marion's baby was due, and shortly before Karin's. Lucy tried hard to look forward.

Schwester Magda noticed Lucy was missing meals and asked why she was so rarely at the staff dining-table.

'I've been eating out,' Lucy lied coolly.

Eating? Well – drinking plenty of cups of coffee and eating the occasional apple or chocolate bar. Magda eyed Lucy up and down suspiciously, saying nothing.

One afternoon, a young couple came to visit the *Pflegestation*.

'Fräulein Lucy, you must meet Janice – our English helper from two years ago, and her husband, Bertram.'

Must I? Lucy was tired of feigning cheerfulness, especially in the presence of an evidently superior predecessor. Janice had been an excellent worker, full of fun, and had met the man of her dreams in Germany. And here she was, round-faced, radiant and serene. Lucy greeted her pleasantly and returned to her duties.

In the evening, Lucy visited Ellen, who customarily offered cake. Lucy abstained politely, saying she wasn't hungry.

'You look like you've lost weight,' Ellen remarked. 'Are you ill?'

'I'm fine,' Lucy said, silently pleased. There was a pained silence.

'Are you sure there's nothing you want to talk about?' Ellen asked. 'We've plenty of time.'

Lucy longed to reveal her desire to pack up and take the next train home. She swallowed hard and said nothing. The cuckoo-clock on the wall struck the hour. The merry, trifling sound provided momentary distraction, reminding Lucy of a long-forgotten childhood memory. Bullies had teased her during a Christmas concert rehearsal, and her favourite teacher suggested she look at the wall clock and imagine it was a silly clown's face. The idea was so absurd, Lucy immediately forgot her troubles and laughed aloud. Laughed? She was in no mood for laughter now. In the early days at the Altersheim, there had been lighter moments, but now the cold realisation dawned – she hadn't laughed for weeks.

Ellen sat patiently, and for an instant their eyes met.

'I'm not sure how to put this,' Lucy began, struggling for words. 'Things aren't going well at work lately. I've been making mistakes – getting complaints... there's no point staying here.'

'What makes you think that?' Ellen asked.

Biting her lip, Lucy gave an honest account of the coffee stains incident.

'Schwester Helga has had a very hard life. I'm sure she didn't mean to upset you. She can be quite blunt at times – it's just her way. Some unspeakable experiences have left her scarred – emotionally scarred.'

'What things?'

'She was in a concentration camp. One can only imagine what happened there.'

'I had no idea,' Lucy said, remembering Herr and Frau Baumann, on what was certainly their deathbeds, bearing no grudge against anyone. If Helga bore a grudge, Lucy didn't sense it was anything personal. The details of Helga's trauma remained undisclosed. Lucy now viewed the frosty-tempered nurse with new respect.

The days slipped by. Lucy went about her work and made trips to town, grasping at transient distractions. On the spur of the moment, she decided on a new hairstyle. The young hairdresser mentioned Lucy's hair was very greasy, which surprised her, as she always been particular about personal cleanliness. She tried to remember when she last washed her hair. The stylist snipped, Lucy's auburn tresses fell to the floor. Finally, Lucy looked in the mirror. The short bob was similar to the one she had just before the move to Westcombe. It spelt new horizons and new hope. Out in the sunny street, Lucy's steps were lighter. She bought souvenirs small enough to carry home: a silver-plated locket in the shape of a water droplet, matching the silver bells ring, and a book about nursing, which was difficult to understand, but might prove useful one day. For Ellen, she bought a ceramic coffee pot, and for Magda a basket of flowering cacti, chocolates, and meal vouchers, which Lucy would never use.

On returning, Lucy found a card announcing Birgit and Franjo's engagement. Her heart dropped like lead. She had half expected this news, but not so soon. *If I am never to marry, then why can't I be like Tante Ellen – single and happy?* Ellen had said teaching little ones was like caring for a family of her own. The announcement included an invitation to a dance and a reception the next day. Lucy tried on the party gown, but it draped ghoulishly off her bony shoulders, and the turquoise top was at home in England. Lucy packed the dress away, another opportunity to wear it missed.

Ellen and Magda were delighted with their gifts.

'How lovely!'

'You shouldn't have...'

'It's not my birthday!'

'You're very kind...'

At work, the comments flowed. Liesl shouted down the corridor how slim Lucy looked. Schwester Magda said the tear-drop-shaped necklace was fitting for someone who always looked so sad. There were gems of motherly advice from the older nurses. Lucy was offered calcium tablets for a broken fingernail which wouldn't heal, and she was asked if she had a digestive wasting disease. Lucy gave high pollen levels as an excuse for swollen, red eyes, and a fast metabolism for her slenderness. A laundry label in a tunic irritated her back, so she trimmed the edge and was later reprimanded, saying she may have to pay for a new label. Past caring, Lucy said nothing.

Curiously, a strange sense of impending doom remained.

On the next town trip, Lucy bought blue-and-yellow tea service for the happy couple, and magazines, chocolates, cigarettes, and liqueurs for herself. She found a park bench to sit and collect her thoughts. A magazine article about *The Goodies* – a TV show which helped Lucy keep her head above water as a troubled teen caught attention. *When did Lucy last laugh?* She honestly couldn't remember. She left the park and went to the tram stop. A billboard advertising a health spa bore the slogan *Mutti macht Kurlaub* and a group of smiling children. Lucy stared at it for ten minutes. The tram was full, standing room only. Sandwiched between well-presented commuters and satisfied shoppers, Lucy clung to the handrail, detached, unblinking, inwardly frozen, vowing to neglect and starve herself for as long as it took for this feeling – whatever it was – to pass.

After dark, with shutters rolled down, Lucy tried on different clothes, wondering what to wear to the parties, observing her diminishing waistline with silent satisfaction. Birgit had lost weight too, but she was happy and in love – with exams behind and a bright future ahead. Lucy turned on the television, poured a cherry liqueur and sat down. The film was a graphic presentation of a man in hospital, dying of cancer. Lucy switched the television off and put on a cassette.

Griechischer Wein... das ist das Blut der Erde, schenk' nochmal ein...

The liqueur tasted good – rich and mellow, with a slight kick. It wasn't Greek wine, but it seemed the life-blood of the earth – its piquant after-taste reminiscent of cough linctus and her mother's soothing voice at her bedside, long ago. Her senses dulled, Lucy relaxed, her fears and inadequacies melting away.

In the cold light of morning, Lucy pulled up the shutters. The canopy of summer foliage cast dark shadows on the garden. Dresses lay draped across the back of the chair – an agonising reminder of what was to take place that evening. It was too much. Lucy went out and phoned Birgit, pleading an allergy attack, giving backword on tonight's dance. That evening, Lucy imbibed fruit liqueur, its narcotic effect deadening awareness of reality. When sleep eluded her, she shared black coffee and cigarettes with the night staff, telling them about England. Back in her room, she huddled for hours under the sheets, yearning for an unwritten future – for one person who would understand and accept her for who she truly was. Over and over again, she played the same cassettes under the bedclothes, pressing her ear close to the machine, murmuring, how long will this go on? *How long?*

With the morning post, a letter came from Hilda, thanking Lucy for the photos and warning her to eat more and not put her health at risk. Come home, Lucy, Hilda wrote, come home...

How did Mother know? Lucy could only guess.

Today was the Birgit and Franjo's reception. Lucy put on jewellery, platform-heeled sandals, and a beige, calf-length dress, drawn in at the waist with a leather belt. She felt tall and elegant. The earrings were tight, but worth the discomfort. At the party, everyone glowed with happiness. Lucy wore a mask of contentment, smiling through the banquet and the photographs. Birgit looked radiant in a tailored, silk dress and holding a splendid bouquet of matching red, yellow and pink roses. Franjo stood proudly at her side, dressed in a grey suit and multicoloured tie. The impressive array of gifts led Lucy to assume this was the equivalent of a wedding. Sure enough, two suitcases were packed and ready in the foyer. Birgit and Franjo were off to Switzerland that night, for a seven-day vacation.

At work, Lucy's pace slackened. Schwester Magda rebuked her for poor time management. Now, Lucy had an excuse to leave. She wrote a letter of resignation and handed it to Frau Muenzel, giving family matters as the reason for leaving prematurely. With one minute before shift start, there was no time for discussion. An end was in sight, but still, the cloud of gloom didn't lift.

Something didn't feel right.

Logistically, should she go straight to Martha's at the end of the month or go home and then to Kochendorf?

A decision must be made soon.

'*Sie haben Post bekommen!*' Nurse Gottfried Linz greeted Lucy as she returned to the *Pflegestation*. There was nothing unusual in her colleague's facial expression, but his tone of voice betrayed otherwise. *A letter?* Lucy's pulse quickened. *Perhaps Marion's baby had come early?* Reading Lucy's expression, Herr Linz added, 'It looks like bad news, I'm afraid.'

On the staff room table was a white envelope bordered with a heavy, black line, a plain, black cross and the word *Todesanzeige*. Who in Germany, in Lucy's circle of acquaintance, could have died? Friedrich had been the last survivor of the older generation. Had something happened to Karin or her unborn child? Lucy opened the envelope and pulled out a slim, deckel-edged, white card embossed with a plain, black cross. Inside the card, a short message:

Martha Elisabeth Schuhmacher
geboren- 28.7.1910.
gestorben- 4.6.1975.
Requiescat in Pace.

Martha! Lucy read and re-read the simple text, the printed words jarred like shards of shrapnel. *Surely this was a mistake? There had been no reports of illness, and only last week Martha had written to say she was looking forward to Lucy's visit with her parents in August.*

No – this must be a bad dream – the effects of heat, hunger, and a troubled mind. Lucy put the card in her pocket, and took a deep breath, fully expecting to wake up at the start of an ordinary day.

Through the open window, bright sunshine penetrated the dense canopy, where a solitary bird hooted its plaintive note. Lucy opened the card again. The plain words printed black on white danced before her eyes. It was true. Martha was dead.

Slowly, the implications sank in. *A dream holiday cancelled, far greater the loss of a good person. Was this cruel twist of fate punishment? Was the perceived pall of gloom a premonition?* Notwithstanding, Lucy couldn't bear the thought of spending another day in Hildenheim, let alone three weeks. Frau Muenzel's mask of pseudo-cheerfulness was gone, her face dark with disapproval. Lucy was evasive about her personal circumstances and who exactly had died. She booked a one-way ticket home on the first night train north, after her last shift.

Hilda wrote, asking for clarification on how her cousin had died. Lucy still had no idea what had happened. A letter from Frau Meyer explained more. Martha had been the victim of a hit-and-run accident on the way home from choir. She passed away three days later, without regaining consciousness. The drunk-driver faced multiple charges, but nothing could bring Martha back. She had simply been in the wrong place at the wrong time.

Lucy put down the letter. She couldn't bear to read any more. She went out and walked and walked – anywhere – it didn't matter. Amid light, noise, movement and colour, aromas of fresh coffee and frying steaks mingled with summer flowers. Lucy bought a pair of dark sunglasses and hid behind them, stern-faced and stoic, an anonymous, lone figure in the crowd. In a street coffee bar, she allowed herself the pleasure of a cup of espresso. It was the sole, positive moment of the day. Later, in the gaping chasm of the evening, she packed both cases, drank another mini liqueur and went to bed.

Slowly but surely, time was running out. In her diary, Lucy scored a diagonal line through each day. Three days left before the summer solstice, the planned departure date, a telegram arrived. Lucy thanked the nurse on duty and opened the flimsy envelope. The message read:

IT'S A BOY WELL WYLIE

Marion and the baby were safe, thank God. With no intention to visit, Lucy had asked Schwester Magda to leave Birgit's card and present with Ellen. Then she changed her mind.

Loose ends must be tied. After shift, Lucy went to Ellen and told her the truth. Ellen listened patiently to Lucy's account of her apprehension, insecurities, self-neglect, and the recent news of Death and Life.

'You have had a very difficult time,' Ellen said quietly. 'I can understand why you want to go home. You need to be there.'

Ellen refilled two cups with the last of the English tea.

'You are free tomorrow afternoon?' Ellen asked. 'Come up after your shift, and we'll go to the Schmieds' for Birgit's birthday tea.'

'I'll come,' Lucy said, feeling a burden lift. She saw no reason to refuse.

As expected, the visit was a bittersweet experience. The Schmieds tempered their happy mood, while Lucy sat serenely through two hours of happy conversation, sensing closure on her time in Hildenheim.

Saying goodbye at work wasn't difficult. Colleagues wished her a polite farewell, though the residents had poor perception of the situation. Only once did Lucy feel regret. Frau Baumann looked at the crucifix on the wall, and Herr Baumann said, 'We look forward to meeting you again in a better place.'

Everything was packed, Room Four, neat and bare. At seven o'clock Lucy took a taxi to the station. As the train pulled away, she closed the blinds, drank the last of the miniature liqueurs and slept.

36: MOUNTAINS

Weary and deflated, Lucy stood at the door of her parents' home. A large, dark green estate car was parked on the drive. Perhaps there were visitors?

She jabbed her finger on the doorbell. The familiar jingle chimed faintly. *Battery must be flat*, Lucy thought tiredly. Windows were open upstairs and down, net curtains flapping gently in the breeze. One of the nets had caught on the outside wall, where rose-pink brickwork glowed warmly in broad July sunshine. A gentle gust rattled the *Haus Meisenfeld* sign overhead.

The door opened slowly, as if by itself. Lucy looked down and saw the puzzled face of a flaxen-haired child in a blue cotton dress.

'Hello, Samantha,' Lucy whispered. The toddler looked blankly up at the stranger, then clutched anxiously at her grandmother's floral pinafore.

Hilda's arms were outstretched, her face a picture of sadness and relief.

'Welcome home, Lucy. Come in, and let's have a good look at you. I like your hairdo. Well, you don't look as bad as I imagined. I'll put the kettle on.'

Her mother's embrace gave momentary comfort, but Lucy was cold inside. Leaving her luggage in the hall, she followed her mother and niece into the kitchen. Albert came in from the garden with a tray of freshly picked tomatoes.

'She looks like Abby, don't you think?' he said.

'Who?' Lucy looked blank.

'There's a girl called Abby in a new series on the telly,' Hilda said. 'She looks like you, very slim, blue jeans, short hair...'

Lucy was mildly flattered. Hilda served tea and biscuits on the patio while Sammy played on the grass. Lucy translated Frau Meyer's letter. Hilda shook her head, wringing her hands on her pinafore. Lucy tucked the letter inside her diary, and a piece of paper fluttered to the ground. Lucy picked it up and smiled.

'At least there was some good news,' she said, handing Hilda the telegram announcing baby Jamie's birth.

'They could have at least got it right!' sniffed Hilda. They've missed out

417

the word both. It should read It's a boy – both well.'

'It gave me a reason to keep going,' Lucy said.

'I had an inkling you weren't happy working there. I'm glad I sent you that letter, and I'm glad you're home.'

Lucy was relieved her mother held nothing against her for falling short of her intended goal.

'Where's Marion?' she asked.

'At home with baby Jamie. She's tired after the birth, and wants a few days to recuperate. So we have little Sammy with us until the weekend. Our *Thumbelina* – that's her favourite fairy story.'

Hilda winked at her granddaughter. There was no doubt Sammy enjoyed being with her grandparents and the big spotted dog. She loved the sweets, the ice-lollies, the bedtime stories, and all the attention. But now a dark, serious lady had arrived, taking Grandma's attention. The tiny toddler looked on with saucer-like eyes, puzzled and hurt.

After supper, Hilda tucked Sammy into bed and read her a story, while Lucy stayed downstairs. Albert sat in his usual chair, reading the newspaper. A cigarette smouldered on the ashtray.

'I'm going to look for a job,' Lucy said. 'I can't just hang around here until October with nothing to do.'

'You're sure to find something,' Albert said.

'Why did you get a new car?' Lucy asked.

'I part-exchanged the Viva for a Humber Sceptre, with a bigger engine.'

'Oh.' Lucy was unimpressed.

She wrote to Frau Muenzel, thanking her for her hospitality, explaining there had been a family bereavement in tragic circumstances, apologising again for her premature resignation. She mailed the letter, feeling a sense of peace, then cycled around the village in search of work. The potted meat and gummed label factories had no vacancies, neither did the post office. In Marjoram's supermarket, a plump, pink-faced grocer in white overalls said he would ask the manager at Millhurst, and told Lucy to come back in the morning. Returning home, Lucy found the back door locked, so she went to the front and rang the bell. When Hilda answered it, Sammy rushed past and skipped down the driveway.

'Come inside, Samantha!' Hilda ordered. 'You must mind the motor-cars. They could run you over!'

The innocuous remark plunged like a knife in Lucy's heart.

'Motor-car run Aunty Lucy over!' Sammy said.

Lucy froze, went to her room and stayed there until tea time.

Sammy knelt on a cushion on a dining-chair, a plate of salad before her, her face smudged with butter and beetroot juice. A triangle of buttered bread lay face down on the tablecloth.

'Be – bekrook, Gamma,' Sammy stammered happily. Hilda was pleased to note both daughter and granddaughter were eating well.

'I notice you've been raiding the biscuit tin,' Hilda said, winking at Lucy.

'I missed the chocolate Digestives, you can't buy them in Germany,' Lucy said.

'No doubt you missed a few more things while you were there, if I'm not mistaken. Decent meals, home comforts. However posh a place may be, if it doesn't feel like home, then it isn't home.'

The next morning, Lucy returned to the supermarket and was told to report to the Millhurst branch, at three o'clock. Hilda took her in the car and spent an hour with Sammy at the swings. In Mr Marjoram's smoke-filled office, Lucy was interviewed on her qualifications and work experience.

'Well now,' the rotund, middle-aged manager declared, 'we could certainly do with a bit of educated help in our stores. Would you like to start here this afternoon?'

'Well – I, er –' Lucy hesitated, floundering. 'Actually I'm busy this afternoon. Can I start tomorrow?'

'Fine, Miss Wylie. We'll see you here tomorrow. Report to the Foxfield branch at a quarter to nine, and the van driver will bring you here for a full day until half past five.'

It had been quick and easy. Lucy wasn't thrilled, but the job would be a fresh focus from recent events.

'Good work, Lucy,' Hilda said, 'You take after me for finding jobs. I'll be looking for work myself in the autumn, when you go to Blackford.'

At Marjoram's, Lucy's shifts were divided between Millhurst and Foxfield. Keeping herself to herself, Lucy reactivated her old till skills and slipped into a comfortable working routine. The dark days of Hildenheim seemed a million miles away.

At noon on Sunday, there was a screech of tyres, as the Clements' red Ford Cortina swung into the drive. Baby Jamie was wide awake in his carrycot, gurgling happily. Marion embraced Samantha tearfully, saying how much she'd missed her little girl.

'He's simply gorgeous!' Hilda crowed proudly, 'Marion, you're a wonder!'

Paul went into the garden, slumped into a deckchair and opened a copy of *The Sun*, and Albert took refuge in the conservatory, attending to the tomato plants. Lucy hovered beside her little nephew's carrycot. The infant lay on his side, his small, pink head visible above the covers.

'Mum and Lucy, sit down and you can take turns holding him. I'll hand him to you first, Mum,' Marion said.

'Motherhood is such a wonderful thing,' Hilda said, cradling her tiny grandson.

'Yes, Mum,' Marion said, 'but it's so exhausting.'

Then it was Lucy's turn to hold the baby. She sat tensely, cautiously holding the warm, wriggling bundle, fearing Jamie might start to cry.

'He's very cute,' she said. She was glad when Marion took Jamie upstairs for a feed.

After lunch, Hilda insisted on an outing to the coast. On Littlehampton beach, Hilda took photos with her Box Brownie, of Lucy and Samantha building a sandcastle, Marion cuddling the baby, and Albert and Paul eating ice creams. As they were packing to leave, Hilda noticed to her dismay the camera was missing.

'I remember putting it on the breakwater after taking the pictures. That camera was a present from my father. It's served me well for many years and I find it hard to believe it's just – gone. Someone must have stolen it!' she concluded sadly.

About the aborted holiday in Germany, little was said. Hilda described it as a cruel twist of fate and refused to dwell on what might have been. But annual leave had been booked, and Hilda hatched another plan.

After Marion and family had left, Hilda said, 'We're going on holiday to Wales, week after next, Lucy. You'll need to let Marjoram's know.'

Lucy recalled whitewashed cottages with upstairs windows that Hilda said she could clean from standing on a chair, the perfume of pink dog roses, a sandy beach, a caravan site with swings, and people who talked differently.

'Why Wales?' Lucy asked.

'Why not Wales? Wales is lovely. It's been a while since we were there,' Hilda said. 'This time we'll go camping! We have all new equipment, stored in the garage.'

Lucy failed to share her mother's enthusiasm.

On the morning of the holiday, she dressed in her favourite denim jeans and a loose-fitting cheesecloth shirt. The car was crammed full, the roof rack loaded. Travelling light, with just one bag, Lucy watched her mother squeeze into the back seat.

'Come on, Lucy! Sit in front and read the map for us,' Hilda ordered impatiently.

The car was comfortable – the interior smelt of rubber and new upholstery, evoking distant memories of the green Morris. Lucy had been a child then. Everything had been fresh, new, and exciting, but today's outlook seemed dull as the grey fog that hugged damp fields. As the mist slowly lifted, unfurling a mysterious future, Lucy watched the golden sprawl of late summer countryside flash past.

Suddenly Hilda burst into song. In her mezzo-soprano voice, she crooned falteringly,

> We'll keep a welcome in the hillsides,
>
> We'll keep a welcome in the dales...

'I can't remember all the words – but those Welsh land girls had such lovely voices. The Welsh are big-hearted and very welcoming.'

'Like the Pritchards,' Lucy said. 'They made me welcome. I still hear from

Margaret. She wrote to me a few weeks ago, she's at Lancaster University – '

'The Pritchards are an exception,' Hilda interrupted, recalling the pineapple chunk incident and Margaret's sparse remarks after her stay at Edencroft. 'Sometimes poverty makes people reluctant to part with anything – including compliments.'

Lucy found her mother's cynicism ridiculous.

Several picnic stops were made, each an opportunity to admire scenery and walk the dog. Beyond the border were mountains, each mile more breathtaking than the last, a wild, rugged beauty, strangely special. Lucy felt a gathering sense of optimism. Hours later they reached the coast and found a pet-friendly campsite in the lee of Harlech Castle. By sunset, the tent was up, and fried eggs and bacon with crusty, white rolls were on the menu. Lucy ate hungrily, the familiar sounds of the whistling kettle and chinking of enamel mugs making new memories. The night air was warm and damp with the thin whine of mosquitoes, a warning to apply plenty of insect repellent. The tent smelt of new plastic, and the new camp-beds and plump, nylon sleeping bags looked inviting. Snuggling down, Lucy hoped for a peaceful night.

'Hurry up! Quick – get into the car!!' Albert's rasping voice roused Lucy from the depths of sleep. *Or was this part of the dream? What dream?* The tent wall bulged and flapped in a blur of white noise like the rush of passing traffic. A resounding thunderclap catapulted Lucy to consciousness. A brilliant lightning-flash revealed orange canvas and the shadowy form of her mother. The dog whimpered like badly tuned bagpipes. A powerful gust rocked the tent, tugging at the guy ropes. Lucy shuddered, feeling cold canvas against her back. The rain started – loud, thudding, resounding drops – heavy as pebbles.

'Get into the car!" Albert shouted again.

'What in heaven's name is happening?' Hilda screeched, grasping after the trembling dog. 'Hurry up! Put the dog in the car!'

Lucy jumped up and dashed to the car, clutching her cassette recorder under her arm and throwing it on the back seat. She slammed the door behind her. Rhythmic raindrops pummelled the car roof. Her mother was yelling something about the dog. After a fraught few minutes of frantic calling, Dotty returned, cowed and bedraggled, and was bundled into the open hatchback.

Hilda was fuming. Dripping wet, she slid onto the front seat and slammed the door. Turning to Albert, she hissed, 'We almost lost the dog, thanks to you! That tent almost blew away!'

Too stunned to respond, Albert stared through the rain-soaked windshield, half expecting to see it engulfed any second by a flying tent.

'The tent might blow away yet,' Hilda continued, 'and where does that leave us? With rain-soaked bedding for the rest of the holiday!'

'I had no idea a storm was coming,' Albert said sheepishly.

'Didn't you fasten the tent pegs?'

'I put them in as best I could. The ground was hard and dry, and I didn't bring the mallet.'

Another flash of lightning, followed immediately by an ear-splitting thunderclap.

'Right, we'll spend the night in the car,' Hilda said, swallowing her anger.

Not envying her parents, who were unable to stretch out, Lucy curled up on the back seat, refreshing coolness penetrating her damp clothes.

In the cold light of morning, Lucy awoke aching and stiff. On closer inspection of the night's damage, very little was irretrievable. A plastic cup was missing, presumably blown away, and the dog biscuits had been left out and were reduced to mushy pulp. The stove and bedding needed drying out – easily done once the sun was up. Over breakfast, it was decided a trip to Betws-y-Coed was in order.

'The waterfalls will be magnificent in full spate,' Hilda said.

However, at the renowned beauty spot, there was a long queue and a notice displaying car parking tariff and entrance fees.

'Of all the nerve!' Albert exploded. 'It's God's creation, and they're making us pay for it. Let's go and look at another waterfall.'

Swollen by recent rain, other waterfalls may not have been as spectacular, but at least they were free. After an outdoor lunch at a country inn, Lucy was keen to continue sightseeing.

'Can we go up Snowdon?' she asked, envisaging a steep walk up rugged slopes.

'They allow dogs on the mountain railway, so, yes,' Hilda agreed.

'Can't we just walk up?'

'Certainly not! Snowdon is a big mountain. Walking up it would take all day.'

The funicular was packed with tourists. Steep, rocky slopes towered above narrow, winding roads, sheer cliffs of grey slate, and mysterious lakes shimmering in sunshine. The little train toiled noisily upwards. Cameras clicked, sightseers voiced their admiration. Lucy clung to the handrail, gazing at granite peaks and stony slopes that fell sharply away. She remembered the crowded tram journey in Hildenheim and feeling so desperately alone. This was different. Here, she was protected, purpose-driven, strong. Humanly speaking, there was no logical reason. Something else, something intangible and unknown filled her with a powerful sense of direction and belonging.

The train groaned laboriously up the final stretch, grinding to a halt near a cafeteria at Snowdon's stony summit.

'Even up here it's commercialised,' Albert complained, lighting a cigarette.

Lucy wasn't listening. She stared speechless at the ethereal sprawl, where lakes looked like puddles, jagged roads and dry stone walls defined diminutive settlements. On Snowdon's summit, there was no higher ground to gaze upon. All the peaks which had looked so impressive from below seemed smooth and flat. Albert took photos, Hilda and Lucy lamented the lack of a camera. Lucy reasoned it would be nigh impossible to capture the essence of such a panorama.

The downward journey was quick. In the village, a few local boys were playing cricket on the green, exchanging excited shouts in their lilting, guttural tongue. Lucy sensed a peculiar curiosity about the people living in this unique and special place.

That evening, Snowdon's distinctive peak was plain to see from the campsite, the mountain range's ragged skyline dark and forbidding against turquoise skies. Lucy remembered Appledore Down's steep silhouette, an indelible image of another time, another life.

It was still light enough to read. Lucy opened a German book but quickly lost concentration. A *Pocket Book of Welsh Phrases* was more interesting. *Llwybr Cyhoeddus* meant public footpath, *Merched* and *Dynion*, ladies' and gents' toilets, and *Dim Parcio*, No Parking. Alas, Welsh wasn't on the university reading list. However, the Bible was. Lucy's pocket-sized Bible, untouched since school lessons with Mr Jenkins seven years ago, was in the bag. Lucy remembered the sunny afternoon at Peter and Rose's house, ten years ago, when Sarah had given her it, saying, 'You can have my old Bible, Lucy. I've left school now and don't need it.' Sarah's name was written inside the front cover: Sarah Jane Wester.

Somehow, it never seemed right to cross Sarah's name out and write her own. Lucy turned to the book of Revelation, hoping to glean a rough idea of the Bible's message from its conclusion. None of it made sense. The print was small, and by now it was too dark to read.

The next morning, Albert moaned about the site being crowded. Hilda didn't agree, but Albert insisted, so after breakfast, the tent was dismantled, and everything packed away. The next destination was the Cardiganshire fishing village of Aberporth, where Albert was stationed for a while during World War Two. After long hours on the road, Hilda had a headache, and by five o'clock a suitable campsite was yet to be found.

'Let's ask a farmer if we can camp in his field,' Hilda suggested, 'for a small fee. We're all self-contained.'

Albert was sceptical, but the first farmer they asked seized the unforeseen opportunity for business. An hour later, the tent was up. Hilda was peeling potatoes, and Lucy sat nearby, filing her nails.

'Lucy, will you wash the salad for me?' Hilda asked. Lucy got up wearily and dunked the over-ripe tomatoes, and limp lettuce leaves in a bowl of tepid water, feeling tired and jaded. Gone were the sublime thoughts of a few days ago. After a picnic tea of corned beef salad, Lucy accompanied her mother to the farmhouse to buy fresh eggs and milk. The back door was ajar. Two people were conversing rapidly in Welsh. Lucy listened intently, understanding nothing. Hilda knocked. The speakers switched rapidly to

English. A stout, greying woman greeted them at the door.

'Well hello there, do come in! We're just taking a break from working. This is my son, Geraint.'

A raven-haired young man was slouching at the table. Lucy was struck by the musical quality of the woman's Welsh accent.

'We'd like to purchase a pint of milk, and a dozen eggs, please?' Hilda asked.

'Of course. Geraint – get a box of eggs would you, please.'

The boy stood up and went to the pantry.

'We used to keep hens, too. How I miss the lovely, fresh, free-range eggs,' Hilda said wistfully.

Lucy's attention wandered while her mother spoke of bygone days of Edencroft.

'Wales is a beautiful country,' Hilda said, 'Lucy here is learning Welsh. What was your boy's name again?'

'Geraint. He's fifteen. On school holidays, helping on the farm.'

'Ge- raint,' Hilda repeated the name falteringly. To her, it sounded harsh and guttural. 'Lucy, you say it.'

'Geraint,' Lucy said as if it were a German name.

'Lucy is fluent in French and German, you know,' Hilda boasted. 'She's won competitions, lived in Germany, and is going to Blackford University in a few weeks to study languages and become a teacher.'

Lucy wished the ground would swallow her up. At last, Hilda was ready to go.

'Thank you again for your hospitality, and for the eggs and milk, and we'd better go now and cook our meal.'

Returning to camp, Lucy's attention was caught by a song on the car radio, its haunting melody and lyrics stirring unspoken, inner yearnings:

> ...it's gonna be a cold, lonely summer
>
> And I'll send you all my love...every day in a letter...
>
> Sealed with a kiss.

The next morning, her parents seemed content to stay put, but Lucy was restless and bored. Her suggestion of a drive to the coastal town of Cardigan was quashed immediately.

'We're going to Aberporth after lunch. One outing's enough for one day,' Hilda said.

However, Albert was disappointed by Aberporth's modern, seafront restaurants, gaudy gift shops, and hordes of tourists.

'It's not what it used to be,' he grumbled, recalling an empty beach and cluster of unadulterated cottages around the harbour. 'It's far too commercialised.'

Lucy and Hilda found the narrow streets and whitewashed cottages quirky and appealing. In a souvenir shop, Lucy bought a linen tea towel showing an illustrated map of Wales and the heading *Croeso y Gymru* – Welcome to Wales. Lucy asked the shop assistant to read the phrase, which she proudly did. Hilda's attempt to repeat the words was met with a polite smile, and Lucy didn't feel confident to try it herself.

The next day was wet, with more rain forecast. The dampness brought out thick, yellow slugs that trailed revoltingly across the canvas. Even the bedding felt clammy.

'Let's pack up and go home,' Hilda said. 'It's been fun, but enough is enough. North Wales has the dramatic mountain scenery, here is quiet and peaceful. There's not much further south, just coal-mining valleys, and the Gower peninsula, where we've already been.'

In pouring rain, they dismantled the equipment, using twigs to knock slugs off the canvas. Hilda and Lucy traipsed to the farm to thank and pay Mrs Evans. Lucy was hoping to see Geraint again, but he didn't appear. An hour into the return journey, Albert stopped to buy cigarettes. Hilda bought bananas and currant buns, but Lucy stayed in the car. Thoughts of returning to Marjoram's hung over her like heavy clouds. She tried to imagine what Blackford University would be like, but her mind was blank. Night fell, and the rhythmic purring of the car engine lulled her into shallow sleep.

'I hate to say this –' Albert began, clearing his throat.

'Oh, for goodness' sake, what now?' Hilda was hoping for a hitch-free trip home.

'We're running low on petrol, so look out for a garage.'

'Typical!' Hilda snapped. 'I leave the driving to you and you can't even remember to get petrol! It's half past eleven, and all the garages are closed.'

Albert drove on in silence. Torrential rain streamed down the windscreen.

'I'm sure we'll find one, we only need one garage,' Lucy said optimistically. 'I'll look out.'

After passing through numerous villages, all in darkness, Lucy's hopes dwindled. The flashing, orange light on the dashboard shone uninterrupted, indicating critically low fuel levels.

'I'm pulling over at the next lay-by, and we'll wait till morning,' Albert said coldly.

'Another night in the car!' Hilda snorted.

Just then Lucy sat bolt upright.

'Wait a minute – is that a garage there? Better check if it's open!'

A light glowed feebly through the mist, a hundred yards ahead.

At a quarter past midnight, a twenty-four-hour garage was open for business.

'Well, this calls for celebration,' Hilda said, rummaging in the picnic basket. 'We'll have those currant buns now.'

'Good, I'm starving!' Lucy exclaimed.

But the bag of buns was nowhere to be found.

"I must have left them on the counter in the shop,' Hilda sighed.

'Never mind,' Lucy sighed, tiredness outweighing disappointment.

Sleep stole over her.

'My eyes are like organ stops,' Albert said, blinking at the dawn. 'We're almost home now.'

In the hazy half-light of six o'clock, on a Sunday morning, the streets of Foxfield were silent and still. *Haus Meisenfeld* was a welcome sight.

Hilda opened the front door to a pile of post on the mat. 'That lot can wait. Bills, no doubt! Let's get the kettle on, I could murder a cuppa.'

Lucy picked up a postcard of a beach lined with palm trees against a rich, blue sky.

'It's from Alison!' Lucy said aloud. 'She's working on a Kibbutz with a new boyfriend.'

Lucy turned the card over again. There was no sender's address. The other letters included Lucy's provisional driving licence, a card from Karl and Karin announcing the birth of baby Matthias, and an invitation to baby Jamie's Christening in September.

Holiday memories still fresh in her mind, Lucy stuck her favourite postcards of views of the mountains of Gwynedd on her wardrobe door, wondering wistfully when she would visit Wales again. At Marjoram's, she preferred working in the smaller, friendlier Foxfield branch. Pete, the pink-faced manager, never complained or chivvied his staff. Co-worker art student, Anna, was pleasant and chatty, as were the customers, especially Lady Markham, the alcoholic aristocrat, who loved to stop and chat about her cats. The Marjoram daughters, Tess and Anita occasionally made their frosty entrance. Once, sixteen-year-old Anita waltzed in and said, 'Well, hello Mrs Mop!'

'I like cleaning,' Lucy responded meekly, wiping the checkout shelf. Anita breezed off and joined her sister in the Porsche.

'Too high and mighty for her own good, she thinks she's the cat's pyjamas,' said a customer.

'I've yet to hear her say a friendly word,' Lucy agreed.

It was a slack afternoon, hot and airless. Everything was ready for the mid-afternoon rush of schoolchildren. Lucy took a bruised apple from the fruit stall, rubbed it on her skirt and bit into it.

'Standing there doing nothing in the company's time, I see! And have you PAID for that apple?' Anita had returned via the back entrance, carrying boxes of sweets.

'Not yet, but I will,' Lucy lied, afraid to admit Pete allowed her to take substandard fruit.

'Well, make sure you do,' Anita replied loftily, looking at Lucy trembling in the till kiosk like a captive bird. Anita put the boxes of sweets on the lower shelves and strode off.

A small girl bought a bag of dolly mixtures, then lingered by the checkout, as though she'd forgotten something.

'What's the matter?' Lucy asked. The child pointed to the doorway and whispered, 'I can't get past the Al-station!"

Anita's enormous dog lay sprawled across the doorway.

'No problem,' said Lucy, coaxing the dog away and allowing the child to pass. Minutes later, the dog was back, its nose in the box of sherbet dips Anita had just put on the shelf. Lucy chased the dog off and took the contaminated box to Pete, who put it under the counter. Anita was nowhere to be seen.

The next day, in the Millhurst store, Lucy was on the tills all day. At three o'clock, Fred, the deputy manager looked over her shoulder, and Lucy immediately tapped a wrong key – her first mistake of the day. As far as Fred was concerned she could have been making mistakes all day. During afternoon break, Lucy sat exhausted and alone in the staff room over a cup of coffee, drawing on a low tar cigarette. She didn't finish it. She stumped it out in the grimy ashtray and leafed sullenly through a discarded copy of the *Daily Mirror*, clock-watching. *I don't need Marjoram's money...*

She went to Mr Marjoram's office and gave polite, verbal resignation, requesting immediate finish. Time was needed for her nephew's Christening, driving lessons, and university preparation. Fred agreed. A load lifted off her shoulders, Lucy wondered why she hadn't the sense to leave earlier.

Arriving home, Lucy found a letter with a German postmark. It was from Frau Muenzel, acknowledging her letter, which had been delayed in the post for two months. Frau Muenzel thanked Lucy for her work at the Altersheim, emphasising everybody must persevere in difficult circumstances. Lucy sighed, seriously questioning her ability to hold down a long-term job. Long years of study leading to a lifelong career loomed dauntingly on the horizon. Floundering in doubt, Lucy wondered if university was the right choice. She remembered a cartoon in a German magazine, showing two hill-walkers reaching a peak.

The caption read *Jetzt sind wir endlich über den Berg!*

One of the climbers was boasting of finally having climbed the mountain! But behind a cloud lurked a rock face ten times more daunting.

37: THE STUDENT

The day of launching into the fast lane of life's highway had come. The road trip to East Anglia took four hours, evading London conurbation, and factoring in two picnic stops. Lucy sat in front, helping navigate, Hilda sat behind, beside Lucy's suitcases and bags, Dotty sat behind. This was like leaving home properly.

'This is the first day of the rest of your life, so make the most of it, Lucy. Live life to the full. Remember what Aunt Miranda always said? *Carpe Diem!* Take all before you! Miranda's grandmother, your great-great grandmother, was a teacher. You recall the photograph? Don't let this wonderful opportunity slip by. Your studies are a gateway to a lifelong profession.'

'Yes, Mum.' Lucy said, remembering the Daguerrotype of a serious-faced lady in Victorian dress, reputed to be the headteacher of a prestigious London school. The only known family connection with Academia, albeit a very good one.

'Five years of study will lead to a career as a languages teacher, a passport to middle-class citizenship!' Hilda was plainly more excited than Lucy.

The landscape changed. Endless, straight roads dissected a flat-iron tapestry of harvest hues. Mirages danced on warm tarmac, reflecting plush, Indian summer skies. Lucy remembered the road mirages of Brittany. It seemed portentous of exciting, positive times ahead. A distant, subtle skyline sprawled, a grey haze, mysterious on the horizon – ten, twenty miles distant, perhaps further?

'Is that it?' Blackford?'

Lucy whispered the words so softly, no one else heard. For a while, it seemed the car wasn't moving. The view stayed the same, like a latter-day Constable painting. And then, slowly, distant dots took on definition: grey blobs became buildings, trees and church spires took on form.

Breathless with anticipation, Lucy feasted her eyes upon the Fenland town set to be the scene of her foreseeable future. Sharp shafts of low, autumn sunlight penetrated heavy river fog. The veil of sun-steamed smog slowly unfurled like a theatre curtain. Lucy wondered what characters would appear, what events would unfold upon this stage of her life. Noble thoughts were soon swallowed in a sea of traffic noise, exhaust fumes and the confusing one-way systems of a once ancient settlement.

'This is even worse than Oxford,' Albert mumbled. 'We don't have a decent map, just like in France!'

As in a weird dream, all roads seemed to be leading away from the elusive destination, every street clogged with traffic. The University seemed inaccessible – ivory towers enmeshed in an impenetrable force-field. Finally, Brightwell Tower and the tall spire of Blackford Abbey appeared reassuringly close.

'We're almost there,' Lucy said, looking at the brochure. 'We're on Brightwell Road. Brooke House is on Pope Street, first left.'

Minutes later, Lucy stood with her mother in the thronged foyer of Brooke House, Blackford's all-female hall of residence. Cultured voices, clacking footsteps and banging doors echoed in gloomy, wood-panelled corridors laden with the smell of fresh paint and floor polish. Distinguished-looking ladies and gentlemen stood in line with their studious-faced offspring. When Lucy's turn came, she faced a grey-haired warden who presided behind the grille like an overfed arachnid.

'Name?'

'Lucy Wylie.'

'Lucy Wylie,' the fat spider repeated in monotone.

The bespectacled face didn't lookup. Lucy watched a fat finger trace its way down the list of names.

'You're in a double room in one of our annexes, Lomax Lodge. Turn left outside the door, second turning on the right, a one-minute walk.'

A bunch of keys was dangled in front of her. *An annexe? A double room? Sharing with a complete stranger? There had been no such warning. This had to be a crazy dream.*

Typically, Hilda read Lucy's thoughts.

'Sharing a room needn't be a problem,' she said. 'I shared room with girls I didn't know in the Land Army, and we got on well enough.'

'I'm here now, so I'll have to make a go of it, no matter what,' Lucy said.

Hilda smiled. 'That's the spirit, my girl! Let's get back to the car. Dad and I will help you carry your things.'

Off to Lomax Lodge they traipsed, laden with Lucy's cases and bags. In the shabby entrance hall of a once fine Georgian town-house, new arrivals shunted their goods and chattels across scuffed linoleum and up the wooden stairs. Lucy laboured apprehensively up to the top floor. She turned the key of room twelve and pushed open the door.

Someone was already there. On the right, a pair of bare ankles dangling over the edge of the bed. Pink nail varnish adorned neat toes. A voluptuous girl in tight, knee-length jeans and a plaid shirt, open at the top, was reclining on a silk counterpane.

'Hi, I'm Camille, your new roommate. You'll have to introduce yourself.'

Lucy found the girl's open, confident manner disarming.

'I'm Lucy,' she answered, doubting she and Camille would have much in common.

'It's a lovely big room, and you've made it quite homely,' Hilda remarked, nodding towards the rugs, covers, and knick-knacks filling Camille's side of the room.

'Aw yes,' drawled Camille, 'I'm used to all this. Spent all my school days in boarding school, *ectually*.'

Camille spoke as if there was a hot potato in her mouth and she was trying not to burn herself. Lucy had heard people speak like this on radio and television. She wondered if Camille was an actress, but was afraid to pry.

'What do you study?' Lucy asked.

'French and Drama.' Camille smiled flamboyantly, ash-blonde air sweeping across her suntanned face.

'That's nice,' Lucy answered brightly. 'I'm studying French and German.'

'What's that tablecloth doing on the wall?' Albert interrupted, pointing out a square of vibrant fabric covering the chimney piece.

Lucy was conscious of her father's common London accent.

Camille looked puzzled. 'It's an *Efrican* tapestry, given to us by our house boy on my father's estate in Keenya.'

This accent will take some getting used to, Lucy thought. Ethnic artefacts filled the alcove shelves. There was a sharp knock at the bedroom door and in swanned two immaculately dressed girls, who enunciated their vowels in the same distinctive way as Camille. The taller girl introduced herself as Amanda Hunt – which sounded more like *Hant*. Lucy had instant visions of a foxhunt.

Smiling and stone-faced, the smaller girl radiated a subtle air of animosity.

'I am Lucinda Smythe,' she intoned, in finest Queen's English.

A name not dissimilar from Lucy's own, which she didn't find comforting.

'What school did you go to?' Lucinda asked abruptly.

'Westcombe High. I also took a year out working.'

'*Eau, rarely,*' Lucinda drawled, eyeing Lucy up and down. Lucy took a moment to realise Lucinda had said Oh, really?

Five-feet-eleven-inches Amanda towered tall and elegant over Lucy, her face a mask of disdain. Both Camille's visitors seemed reluctant to come right into the room as if an invisible force were keeping them out.

'*Eau-kay* Camille, we'll meet you later at Crispin's,' Amanda said.

Lucy was glad when the duo had gone. She began unpacking and tried to make her meagre space look homely. With her own duvet on the bed, books on the shelves, and Croeso y Gymru tea towel pinned to the corkboard above the bed, the corner was looking a tad more homely.

Hilda paced around uneasily. 'You'd better put away your kitchen things safely,' she said.

The communal kitchen was down four flights of stairs, in an airless semi basement tainted with the odours of burnt toast and escaped gas. Opening her locker, Lucy found Camille had filled the lower shelf, leaving just a narrow ledge above.

Watching Lucy cram her things into the meagre space, Hilda shook her head, wondering how Lucy would cope in the coming months. A large wooden table occupied the centre of the room. The barred window offered little natural light over the double, stainless-steel sink. In one corner stood an overfilled flip-top bin, beside a large refrigerator. Two grease-spattered gas cookers with overhead grills occupied the opposite wall.

Suddenly, the heavy fire door whooshed open. A tall, aristocratic-looking girl made a brief appearance and deposited a tray of dirty dishes on the table, then left the room.

'She clearly has hired domestics to do everything at home,' Hilda said, 'like the family I did cleaning for years ago.'

Moments later, a plump girl in a long, cheesecloth dress came in, put on the fluorescent light and started frying sausages.

'Come on,' Hilda nudged Albert, 'Let's go and get something to eat.'

Soon, in a jaunty little street cafe, Lucy looked out at the hurrying figures in the sunlit street, her thoughts in limbo. The tea was hot and refreshing, the crumpets crisp, oozing butter. Nobody spoke. Hilda chewed mechanically, the crumpets sticking in her throat. She feared for Lucy's safety in this fast-paced environment steeped in the corrupting influences of student life. Later, as Lucy waved goodbye from the steps of Lomax Lodge, Hilda breathed a deep sigh. She watched Lucy disappear into the crowd like a tiny, bobbing cork on a vast ocean.

Early next morning, Lucy woke to the sound of creaking floorboards and the musty odour of old timbers. Autumn sunshine shone through faded curtains. A new day, in a new place, cheek-by-jowl with complete strangers was a challenge. Camille was at her desk. Lucy wished her good morning, got ready quietly, and went out at half past eight. Brooke Road crawled with traffic. Lucy noticed some streets were named after poets, a comforting reminder of Wordsworth Grammar school. Fifty yards up Pope Street, she turned right, into Brightwell Road – beside Brightwell Tower – an imposing, neo-Gothic edifice commissioned by eighteenth-century slaver-turned-philanthropist, Leslie Brightwell.

Inside the building, a hundred voices floated up the vast stairwell. Lucy climbed four flights of concrete stairs to the lecture theatre, a wide room with tiered wooden benches. Lucy sat near the window. The room filled with strangers, a sea of faded denim and cultured voices. The clock struck ten, muffled chimes thundering portentously through thick walls. Upon the tenth stroke, a grizzled gentleman rose phoenix-like from behind the lectern and began speaking about Johann Wilhelm von Goethe. An hour of mumbling blended with whispering within the auditorium and traffic noise outside. Lucy barely wrote half a page of notes, which worried her. When the bell boomed eleven, students stood up and dispersed.

On the landing, a hundred voices echoed. Lucy looked at the glistening quartz crystals on the concrete floor.

'That was Professor Gruber, you know,' a girl in front said.

'Really? That was Professor Gruber? I didn't think much of his lecture.'

'His books are useful though, when he sets the essays,' was the reply.

A group of friends behind Lucy were arranging to meet at a wine bar. Lucy felt isolated and excluded. It seemed all the first years were in ready-made cliques, from public schools and flagship cities across Great Britain.

Further along Brightwell Road, Lucy discovered a small supermarket where she bought a can of ravioli, a can of baked beans, and a few apples. The irresistible aroma of hot food wafted tantalisingly from a nearby shop, where a dozen denim-clad figures waited in line. The sign above read:

Porkie & Best
delicious home-made hot snacks

Lucy joined the queue, bought a hot sausage roll, which she enjoyed in the grounds of Brightwell Tower. She spent most of the afternoon queuing at the Students' Union, a concrete cuboid on the corner of Clare Road and Fenbird Way. After finally obtaining a student card, Lucy wandered about the building, signing up for French and German clubs, Hikers and Ramblers, and Ballroom Dancing – the latter an uncharacteristic choice, a wild card, with the chance of romance. It had worked for Marion and Paul and Birgit and Franjo, so why not Lucy?

A poster caught her attention.

FAFFY DISCO
Friday nite – 8pm
BROOKE HOUSE
Admission 50p
Be There or Be Square!

Lucy decided to go. She returned to Lomax Lodge, grabbed some crackers and cheese and retreated upstairs. Camille was out. Lucy took time over her hair and makeup, dressed in her lilac trousers and blue smock top and went to Brooke House. The disco was deafening, conversation impossible. The dimly-lit function room rocked with noise and reeked of alcohol and tobacco smoke. Lucy joined the dancers on the floor. A scrawny boy moved closer, bouncing, twisting and grinning stupidly, strands of greasy hair falling into his face. Lucy edged away and out of the room. Back at Lomax Lodge, all was quiet. Lucy made herself a cup of tea in the empty kitchen. *It's early days*, she sighed, trudging tiredly up to her room. Other social events would be better, and there was time enough to make friends.

There was no time to feel homesick, lonely or bored. The busy-ness of settling in, attending lectures and seminars for the first time, and finding one's way around taxed practically every student. All the university buildings were situated in the town. Grey, stone Victorian houses, lofty Georgian terraces and cobbled streets with crooked pavements were awe-inspiring, quirky, distinctly Dickensian. Already, Lucy had grown fond of this aesthetically pleasing place.

On Sunday morning, Lucy walked the mile to Cavenfold Forest, where a group of bejeaned, cagoule-clad figures gathered for the Hikers' and Rambers' Club. Lucy sidled into their midst.

As the party set off, a voice said, 'You were in the German poetry lecture, weren't you, if I'm not mistaken?'

The larger-than-life, dark-haired girl spoke with a strident north London accent.

'I was,' Lucy answered, sensing an overture of friendship.

'I'm Abigail Abrahams, but people call me Gail for short. And you are?'

'Lucy Wylie. No one calls me anything for short.'

'I suppose I could call you Loo?" Gail's full-bodied laughter pealed through the fog-laden forest.

Two friends with Lancashire accents were with Gail.

'Lucy, meet Jenny and Katie. They're on my corridor in Brooke House.'

'Hi Lucy, nice to meet you,' they both said together.

Lucy returned the greeting, sensing a cultural difference.

'I'm in Brooke House too – well, sort of,' Lucy said. 'Actually, I'm in Lomax Lodge, in a shared room.'

'You must visit the hall shop,' Gail advised, 'on the ground floor, next to my room, number G4. It sells canned and packet foods, milk and biscuits. very handy.'

'I'll try it. My course is joint French and German. And yours?'

'The same,' Gail replied.

'You're from London too?' Lucy asked.

'Born and raised in Harrow.'

'I was born in Hounslow, lived my childhood in Ash Farm –'

'And we're proud Mancunians,' Katie said.

Down to earth and friendly, like Aunt Rose, Lucy thought.

'My parents and I moved away to the country when I was twelve,' Lucy said, 'but I still have friends and relations in London.'

The leafy pathway narrowed, the two Mancunians walked in front.

'Tell me a bit about yourself,' Gail said.

Lucy spoke of Westcombe, Kochendorf, Sussex, Alderbridge, and Hildenheim, mentioning only the positives.

'So, you were at Wordsworth Grammar before you moved to the back of beyond?' Gail asked.

'That's right, but only for a year.'

'Wordsworth's a good school, as state schools go. I went to Harrow Girls' College. Most of us got in on scholarships, so no empty-headed morons with money, whose parents get them in by the back door – brainless Debs with more money than sense get on my nerves.'

'What are Debs?' Lucy asked, confident enough to show her ignorance.

'Society *Debutantes* – upper-class, young ladies. Their education is paid for by Mummy and *Deddy*, if they fail to make the grade.'

'But some rich kids are clever.'

'Indeed, they're the dangerous ones who become cut-throat lawyers and corrupt politicians,' Gail laughed airily.

Lucy shuddered.

'Did you know Lorna Harrington?' Lucy asked. 'She'd be in the year above you. She was in my class at Macadam Primary. Tall, long hair, glasses? Brainy, popular, good at sports.'

'I've heard of her but don't know her. Also, I never was very sporty. Do you think I look the sporty type?' Gail stuck out her ample bosom and made a lame attempt at jogging. 'Music was my speciality – and languages, of course.'

'What kind of music?'

'Classical. I had piano lessons and was in the school choir. We did productions with Camden College. You've heard of the prestigious conservatoire for boys? They provided the male voices, and because they're all musicians, they were good. Our last joint production was of Handel's "Messiah."'

'My dad likes classical music. I like singing, and was in the school choir at Christmas. Camden College, you said?'

'That's right.'

'We might have a mutual acquaintance. Did you know Danny James?'

'Yes I did meet him. Nice lad, pleasant, unassuming, a lovely voice.'

'I know Danny too! He was in the same class as me for four years and we got on very well.'

Danny was probably Lucy's best friend at school, the kind of person she could both laugh with and share problems with. Danny was extremely intelligent, deeply religious, with no trace of arrogance.

'Danny was quiet, a bit odd, but a good sort,' Gail said.

'We went to the same Sunday School, too,' Lucy added as an afterthought.

'Well, I'm not into that kind of thing. My dad's Jewish, but only Gran goes to the Synagogue. I tried the school Christian Union once, but it was just psychological hype. Religion as a code for living is fine, not as a personal prop or a platform for spouting meaningless claptrap.'

Lucy found Gail's frankness reassuring. 'I'm not a churchgoer either. Too many rules, and they throw the book at you if you make a mistake,' Lucy said.

'Let's talk about something else. Do you like cooking?' Gail asked.

'I do. I never did cookery at school, but I like baking cakes and pastries.'

'Excellent! Then let's plan some in-hall tea parties!'

Lucy sensed a deepening bond of friendship, an effortless connection made in just one hour.

Returning to Lomax Lodge, Lucy was hungry. Finally using the enamel casserole dish her mother had bought for her, she heated a can of steak and kidney with beans, buttered a few crackers, and sat at the empty table. The door creaked open. From the corner of her eye, Lucy discerned the gaunt form of Amanda Hunt.

'That's a nice coat you're wearing,' Lucy said in a small voice.

'*Kate?*' Amanda asked.

Lucy was about to point out her name wasn't Kate, when Amanda said, 'It's not a *kate!* It's a dress!'

'Oh – well, I think it's very nice,' Lucy replied, embarrassed at having failed to identify an article of high fashion, and for misunderstanding Amanda's peculiar accent. As a linguist, Lucy was aware of the vagaries of vowel sounds.

'What's your doll's name?' Aunt Rose had asked.

'Rosebud.'

'Roosebud? That's a nice name.'

'It's ROSEbud, not ROOSEbud!'

Hilda scolded Lucy for being rude. At the time, Lucy had no idea why.

Amanda filled the kettle and put it on the gas.

'Camille says you also took a year off between school and university,' Lucy remarked, attempting polite conversation.

'Yes, I did. Why do you ask?' Amanda inquired diffidently.

'I worked as an auxiliary nurse in a hospital in Sussex for six months, then as a care assistant in a nursing home in Germany,' Lucy said, eager to impress.

'Nursing?' Amanda sniffed disdainfully. 'Ugh! I could never do a thing like that. My job was in an *auffice.*'

At this point the conversation died. Lucy hastily finished her food, cleared away her dishes and left the kitchen.

The next morning, Lucy set off for the German Novelle seminar in the Annexe – an adapted Georgian house in Wilberforce Terrace. A week earlier, she had arrived late for a French language class in the same building, having lost her way. Arriving fifteen minutes early, Lucy found someone else already waiting by the door. A petite girl sporting a stylish trouser suit and a red-and-blue spotted headscarf sat cross-legged on a low window sill, a leather briefcase beside her.

'Hello, I don't believe I've met you before?' The girl's accent was cultured, but not overbearing.

'I'm Lucy Wylie. And you are?'

'Caroline St Clair', the girl answered, pronouncing her name *Sinclair*. 'I'm studying single honours German. How are you settling in?'

'Okay, I suppose,' Lucy answered truthfully. 'Are you in halls?'

'No. I live with my parents in Cavenfold.'

Caroline smiled, radiating confidence and poise. Lucy suddenly missed home. She fought for words.

'Did – didn't you want to leave home and try living in halls anyway?' Lucy asked.

'Blackford's my first choice. I didn't see any point leaving home. I might move out one day, if there's something worth leaving home for.'

Lucy admired Caroline's sound reasoning. In the cramped hallway, other students gathered. On the dot of ten, the door opened, and Lucy was pleased when Caroline invited her to sit beside her.

Today's reading material was Friedrich Schiller's play "Maria Stuart", based on Mary Queen of Scots. While the mild-mannered, balding tutor expounded on the text for a whole hour, Lucy took notes, observing Caroline's ability to write both copiously and in near-perfect, cursive script. As they were leaving, Caroline asked, 'Will you be at the German Society meeting tonight? Eight o'clock at Tiffany's Titbits – the wine bar on Whitefield Way, near the river?'

'I will.'

'Then I look forward to seeing you there,' Caroline replied, and Lucy sensed another embryonic friendship.

Afterwards, Lucy sat disinterestedly through a lecture on Classical French drama, ate a sausage roll from Porkie and Best's for lunch, then doodled her way through another hour of Professor Gruber's ramblings. When the clock bonged its emphatic note at four o'clock, there were audible sighs of relief. Lucy went back to Lomax Lodge for an hour's study. She ate a cheese toastie, then donned her blue jeans and apple-green velour top from Hildenheim, both of which were now uncomfortably tight.

Five minutes' walk across cobbled alleys, Lucy found Tiffany's Titbits – a cosy wine-bar-cum-bistro and popular venue for the German Society Stammtisch. Caroline and Gail were already there. Over a bottle of Liebfraumilch, tongues were loosened and congenial conversation flowed. Lucy was admired for being bold enough to take a gap year. Again, she mentioned only the positives. As fine wine freely flowed, Lucy's insecurities were allayed. It no longer mattered she was a year older than other freshers. Most languages students were female, so competition for boyfriends would be keen. She gazed over her wineglass at the chatting group; Mike Mitchell stood out from the rest. Tall, blond and with a Yorkshire accent, he was the most extrovert and self-assured of all the first-years.

'He's extremely eligible,' Gail drawled, nudging Lucy and grinning.

'Yeah, I suppose so,' Lucy replied nonchalantly, suspecting she would never win his heart.

Days later, the keen knife of disappointment endorsed Lucy's fears. Mike was officially dating bubbly Brummie Clare Hope, whose room was below Lucy's in Lomax Lodge. Mike was now a frequent visitor. Their laughter and cheerful banter were painful reminders of Lucy's singleness. But Lucy wasn't giving up.

A quiet lad from the German course sat next to her in Brightwell Hall, in the queue for immunisation updates.

'It's like musical chairs,' he joked, as the line shuffled forward.

'Yeah, that's right,' Lucy replied, glancing apprehensively, as white-coated medics summoned their next victim behind folding screens.

'But there'll be no prizes for the winner, nor any jelly and ice cream afterwards,' she said. The boy laughed into the din of the crowded hall, the conversation fizzled out.

Afterwards, Lucy went to Brooke House to buy tea bags and milk and to call on Gail. Unexpectedly, the name on the door read ABBY. Lucy knocked on the door. The pain in her knuckles reminded her of when Mrs Pygge, the Macadam Primary dragon, struck her hands with blackboard pegs for daydreaming in class.

'Come in!' Gail's strident voice was unmistakable.

Lucy pushed open the door. 'Who on earth is Abby?' she asked.

Gail poured two mugs of instant coffee and opened a pack of custard creams.

'I am. I wanted a new image. My name is Abigail, but since everyone has called me Gail since I was so-high, I wanted a change.'

'So, we've to call you Abby from now on? That'll take some getting used to.'

'I should have thought of it earlier, but it'll work. Folks back home are going find it harder to get used to.'

'Okay, Abby,' Lucy said, 'I'll do my best to remember.'

Abby dunked a biscuit. 'Were you at that disco on Friday? It was appalling, wouldn't you agree?'

'It was. I only stayed a few minutes. It was too loud.'

'I don't blame you. It was full of first-year squirts. One of them kept prancing in front of me and practically treading on my toes. Then I got talking to a third-year geology student called Dave – tall, dark, and quite eligible – or so I thought. He invited me to his student house for coffee, and in the foyer was a list of names and a grid with ticks. I thought it was a squash ladder until I heard it was an achievement chart for residents' successes at bedding the birds.'

Lucy took another biscuit and said nothing.

'Well, after one cup of coffee,' Abby continued, 'it was obvious what he was after, so I told him where he could sling his hook and I cleared off. When I got back I was so pissed off I pigged half a pound of biscuits.'

Lucy laughed, accustomed by now to Abby's turn of phrase and earthy sense of humour.

'You know Faffy stands for find a friendly first year?' Abby asked.

'I didn't know, but thanks for the clarification.'

'Well, some say the first F stands for another word.'

Lucy sniggered nervously, remembering her mother's warnings about the evils of the outside world.

'So they just use girls and dump them?'

Abby nodded. 'One-night stands.'

'I'm going to ballroom dancing tomorrow, which should be okay. My German friend met her partner at ballroom dancing.'

'Ballroom dancing, eh?' Abby sniffed, 'Mincing around with all those wimps? Not my scene, but you have the figure for it.'

Abby finished her coffee and said, 'Come, let's go food shopping.'

A trip to the local supermarket educated Lucy to Abby's gastronomical tastes. Soon Lucy was adding mayonnaise, olive oil, and peppered mackerel fillets to her shopping basket.

Later, Lucy found the kitchen filled with *debutantes*, and Mike and Clare were at the table, sharing a meal. She took her mackerel, cheese, and crackers upstairs.

Camille was in, sprawled on the bed. 'I've just spent two hours on an essay, so I'm taking a break. How was your day?'

'Good,' Lucy said, 'very good, in fact.'

Camille's eyes flickered.

'Spiffing! Tell me more.'

'Nothing romantic, just a fun afternoon with friends.'

'Excellent. Now, do you fancy an Earl Grey?'

If Lucy hadn't already taken tea with Caroline and Abby, she would have suspected Camille was match-making.

'Yes, please,' she said,

The Earl Grey tea gave incentive to finish a translation and make notes on Molière's "Le Misanthrope". An early night concluded the busy day. The next day, Lucy and Abby had a late lunch at *Koffie en Koek* – a niche Dutch bakery and coffee house at the river end of Brightwell Road. They went Dutch – each paying two pounds fifty – expensive, but the pastries were to die for. Lucy no longer counted calories but was obliged to endure the discomfort of tight trousers through the French poetry seminar.

Les Fleurs du Mal – was predictably dark. The tutor, Dr Masefield, a genteel gentleman in a tweed suit, handled the subject objectively and invited his personal tutees to an informal buffet in the clock tower common room afterwards. Lucy was included. Mingling with four others, Lucy partook modestly from the cheese and wine, feeling everything was going very well. Two bottles of Beaujolais later, the group dispersed merrily. Lucy felt pleasantly light-headed. Out in the twilit street, the air was damp and chill. Lucy quickened her pace. Ballroom dancing tonight! Not bothering with supper, she changed into a colourful, full-length nylon dress, bought on impulse in an expensive Millhurst boutique. Draping a long, oatmeal-coloured cardigan, knitted by her mother, she set off. The cardigan wasn't waterproof and didn't match the dress, but there was nothing else.

In the student union hall, freshers mingled to find partners. Almost immediately, a slim, dark-haired boy with a sallow complexion approached Lucy.

'Hi, I'm Dave Muggeridge,' he said.

'I'm Lucy Wylie.' The flowing gown suddenly seemed magical. Dave seemed shy, definitely not brash. Lucy wondered, *is he the one?*

The instruction began. Fears of making mistakes and giving offence didn't come into the equation. This wasn't school. Nearly everyone was a complete beginner, and there was much giggling and treading on toes. As Dave took Lucy's arms gently for the waltz, they exchanged potted personal profiles. An only child, Dave lived in Surrey with his mum, his dad lost his battle with cancer three years ago. Dave took a gap year, after failing the Oxbridge entrance exam, worked as an office junior for a local pharmaceutical company, saving money to learn to drive and get a car. His hobbies were car maintenance, listening to classical music, country walks, and fly-fishing.

So far, not an awful lot in common, but Lucy was optimistic. *Fishing? Maybe he thinks I'm a good catch?*

Lucy told of her Foxfield home, her niece and nephew, and her gap year jobs. She found Dave's ineptness at dancing and introvert manner endearing. More than once she stood on his feet. Dave sniggered nervously as if trying to suppress a sneeze.

'Can I visit you at Lomax Lodge on Sunday?' he asked at the end of the evening. Lucy startled. Dave definitely didn't seem like the pushy type eager to earn a place on the squash ladder.

'Sorry – not Sunday. I'm booked on a Hikers' and Ramblers' walk,' Lucy answered truthfully.

'Okay, I'll come and see you on Saturday,' Dave said.

Lucy didn't argue.

Alone in her room that night, Lucy wondered what direction this new-found friendship would take. Even if Dave did eventually turn out to be Mr Right, he didn't hold the magical charm of Roland. Lucy went to bed at eleven, pleased that Camille had planned to stay the night elsewhere. The next morning, Lucy slept in till ten o'clock. She made a pot of Earl Grey tea and sat at her desk, looking out across russet-gold treetops and terracotta-tiled roofs to forested plains that melted subtly into the mists, where the River

Wyndham flowed silently through the thriving town.

Reluctantly, Lucy opened "Le Mariage de Figaro", and skim-read the first act. Then there was a soft tap at the door.

'Come in!' Lucy called, guessing the caller wasn't for Camille.

The door opened slowly, and Dave crept in.

He's here early, he's keen.

'Tea?' Lucy asked.

'Yes, please. Milky, two sugars.'

'Sorry, I don't have any sugar.'

'That's okay, I'll have it without.'

Dave talked about fishing and holidays in the Lake District. Lucy spoke about Wales. There were silences, but a common chord was struck, when Dave admired Lucy's reproduction print of Constable's *Haywain*. There was no jovial banter as with Abby, and Lucy sensed tension. Dave looked at his watch and said, 'I have to be going now. Oh – and by the way, I tried to get a late booking for Sunday's hike, but I was too late. Anyway, I'll see you soon.'

After Dave left, Lucy was glad to have time to herself.

Sunday's hike was a disappointment. However spectacular Wyndham Vale may have been, all was enveloped in thick fog. 'Seen a mist, and missed a scene', as her mother would say. Of a choice of three walks, Lucy opted for the middle one, which still proved challenging for all participants. A girl from the German course was on the longest walk. Lankier and leaner than Alison Rodgers, the girl looked fresh-faced and relaxed when the group met afterwards in a pub. Lucy's feet were cold and blistered, the suede boots caked with clay. She drank a half-pint glass of cider and felt her strength return, but talked to no one.

It took her the most of the week to catch up on rest and sleep. By Friday, along with most other students, she went down with a streaming cold, the first one for nearly two years. Dosing herself with Lem-sips, Lucy kept busy. She began a course of driving lessons, which proved more difficult than anticipated, due to Blackford's perplexing network of streets from an era predating motorised transport.

On Sunday, Dave came to see her again.

'I passed my test last year after two courses of six lessons,' he said smugly.

Lucy munched on her Marmite toastie and said nothing.

'Apply for a test now, have a few more lessons, and you'll be driving by Christmas,' Dave said.

Lucy rose to the challenge.

'All right, I'll do it.'

Lucy didn't like the driving school's car. It was a large, dark blue Ford, the seat too far from the pedals, even on the closest setting. A wooden backrest was provided, but it dug into her back, impairing concentration. Never adept at rapid multitasking, Lucy struggled to cope. The instructor, a garrulous man in his early thirties, was full of advice.

'Read the road ahead,' he warned. 'Slow down, change gear in good time.'

Lucy had no idea if the dual control was being used. 'Too much to do at once', she thought, seriously regretting having entered for a test.

In early November, assignment deadlines were set. Lucy's grades dipped, and disillusionment crept in. German tutor, Dr Patricia Ingram, invited personal tutees to an informal lunch at her rambling house on Fenbird Way. A generous buffet was on offer, and feeling hungry, Lucy filled her plate. Society *debutantes* (some of them wistful Oxbridge rejects) gathered in the parlour to watch the live coverage of a rugby match on a twenty-four-inch colour television. Lucy wandered into other rooms, encountering more impenetrable conversations. Everything seemed to be about public schools, country sports, and high society phenomena about which Lucy knew nothing. She chose a quiet moment to tell Dr Ingram about her struggle with eighteenth-century French drama.

'Don't worry,' Dr Ingram replied curtly. 'Everybody finds something difficult.'

Lucy viewed the smooth, self-assured company, doubting anyone present had difficulty with anything. Memories of Martha's kind face and gentle voice dampened her desire to talk about Germany. Battling unwelcome emotions, Lucy rued coming. If only she'd worn jeans and not one of those stupid long, nylon dresses. Other students wore stylish, blue denims, and one of them looked extremely glamorous and startlingly skeletal. Lucy decided to address her poor fashion sense and resume stringent dieting.

The next morning, Lucy slept in until eleven o'clock. Camille was up and about, so Lucy went to the main hall library, intent on serious study. Wearing a long, brown skirt and the oatmeal cardigan, she blended insignificantly with the wood panelling and floor-to-ceiling bookshelves. Every desk overlooking the gardens was occupied. Lucy sat in a dark corner and tried to read, but the sepia pages of German poetry were a blur. The heavy ticking of a grandfather clock filled the airless room, where pages rustled, and students whispered. Lucy returned to her room, pleased to find Camille out. She stayed in, finished a German translation, pleased to have time to herself. After switching off her bedside lamp at eleven o'clock, she lay still, half listening for the sound of footsteps on the wooden stairs and the click of a turning key. Camille didn't return.

Lucy was startled from sleep by shouts and slamming doors. The raised voices continued for a while, and Lucy assumed the drama students downstairs were rehearsing a play. She turned over, pulled the bedclothes over her ears and slept.

The next day, after lectures, Lucy bought a pair of flares with three metal fastenings above the zip, and three lines of stitching down the outside leg. The jeans were expensive and punishingly tight, but Lucy bought them anyway, telling herself they were better than the boned corsets her mother had made her wear years before.

Camille was quick to notice Lucy's new acquisition.

'Very stylish. May I ask, how much?'

'Nine pounds.'

Camille gasped quietly. 'They suit you well.'

'Thanks.' The skin-tight jeans had no back pockets, and Lucy feared looking fat. Pulling her jumper over her hips, she went downstairs for Ryvitas and cottage cheese. In the kitchen, there were hushed whispers, awakening distant recollections of similar conversations at school. Feeling excluded, her back to the group, Lucy rummaged quietly in her locker, overhearing snatches of conversation.

'A nice girl, Karen, a brilliant actress...'

'We were in the choir at school...'

'She sang The Sussex Carol solo – a voice like a nightingale...'

'A shame she got mixed up with that weird group...'

'I hope she'll be okay...'

Apparently, one of the drama students was hospitalised, having suffered a mental breakdown. There was a lot of over-talking, then the volume dipped as if some terrible secret were being disclosed. Morbidly interested, Lucy lingered for a moment, then withdrew quietly. It was later rumoured Karen was sent home to recuperate, last night's disturbance explained.

The atmosphere in Lomax Lodge was deteriorating. Litter, filth in the kitchen, late-night noise were the new norm. Camille and cronies were in as often as they were out. Lucy wished they would simply disappear. Camille's boyfriend spoke with an aristocratic accent, yet swore like a trooper, regularly left brimming ashtrays and dirty crockery in the room, spilt coffee on rugs and furniture, and looked through Lucy like a window-pane. Lucy had practically given up smoking. Dave couldn't stand the smell of cigarette smoke, due to his father's life being cut short by an unbreakable tobacco habit. Dave insisted Lucy visit him at Clare Hall instead. The seedy atmosphere of Lomax Lodge was even too much for Abby. Their chats over coffee took place in Abby's room or in tea rooms in town.

'If I were in your shoes, Lucykins, I'd vote with my feet and get out of that dump right away. It's becoming a proper doss-house,' Abby said.

Lucy gave a hollow, despondent laugh. Abby's throwaway remark had sown the seeds of unrest. Every day, Lucy deferred returning to her room, hating the place more than she had done the Altersheim, where she had at least had a room to herself. Here was nothing – not even a corner she could retreat to undisturbed.

One afternoon, on impulse, she went straight from lectures to a hairdressers, requesting a perm. The new hairstyle was initially pleasing, but on taking a brush to the tight, tidy mop of curls for the first time, Lucy found that her naturally wavy hair had morphed into a hideous ball of fuzz. She applied conditioner, invested in a wide-toothed afro comb and left well alone. Abby admired Lucy's outrageous act, and there were positive comments from others, including Camille.

That evening, Dave drove Lucy to Baring Square, south of the river, to watch the film *Tommy* at the Odeon cinema.

'What do you think of my hair?' Lucy asked.

'Okay, I suppose.'

Without a word, Dave tentatively put his arm around Lucy. Neither uncomfortable nor excited, Lucy knew she wasn't in love. She analysed the film like a prescribed text. *Was it an allegory? If so, what of? What effect would this film have on society?* Lucy looked hard for ideas, knowing that Abby, a film buff, would want to hear all about it.

The next evening, in the Brooke House bar, Abby and Lucy shared a bottle of Hock. The film wasn't even mentioned. Instead, they shared ideas on essay topics.

Then Abby asked, 'How are things with you and Dave?'

'Dave? Oh, well he's not bad.'

'You don't seem enamoured.'

'I'm not.'

'At the end of the day, Lucy, it's your choice. Like whether or not you decide to do anything about Lomax Lodge. Any fresh gossip from there?'

'I got back to find Camille in tears, yesterday. She confided in Amanda Hunt she might be pregnant, and Amanda was comforting her, with her arm around her like a big sister.'

'A right doss-house, just as I said. Hey – I've an idea...' Abby whispered something in Lucy's ear.

'Outrageous!' Lucy spluttered into her wineglass.

'You need more laughs, Lucykins – I'm going to get us all another bottle to share – and celebrate.'

On her way to the bar, Abby was collared by an old school friend and stood talking for what seemed ages. Lucy grew bored and went back to her room, feeling the negative effects of alcohol – not a typical hangover, or *Kater*, as Germans would say, but a sudden mood dip. Without bothering to put on the light, Lucy dwelt morosely on past failures and disappointments. She remembered Martha. She felt cheated, deprived, bereft of a kind, loving friend, who had not deserved to die.

On Saturday night, Camille was out again. Lucy enjoyed a quiet evening in, listening to Beethoven's ninth symphony on the radio, working on a French-to-English translation, and painting a country scene on an old milk bottle. Borrowing an idea from Lynda Miles, an arty law student downstairs, Lucy painted over the embossed lettering, The Cream of Sussex Milk, in dark green, filling in the background with a forested scene.

The next day, Abby's prank was hatched. Lucy stood in the portal of Lomax Lodge, holding up a paper scroll bearing the text DOSS HOUSE midway between the words Lomax and Lodge.

'Smile please!' Abby said, clicking the camera. Laughing was therapeutic, but the levity didn't last. Lucy received a low grade for Saturday evening's translation, her clothes were too tight, she had gained weight – but still no period.

A ten-minute consultation with a lady doctor assured her nothing was wrong.

All along Brightwell Road, festive lights sparkled in shops and quaint, bubble windows sprayed with fake snow. Lucy and Abby joined the French and German Christmas choirs, and assisted with the German Christmas revue. Wearing a green-and-white check *Dirndlkleid* from Hildenheim, Lucy served choice wines with *Bratwurst* and *Sauerkraut*. Dave attended the event, laughing laconically at the slapstick sketches. Well-plied with food and wine, Lucy remained upbeat throughout the evening. Dave took her ice-skating. The rink was filled with the shrieks of scores of happy teenagers skating with ease and expertise. At first, Dave held Lucy's hand, then Lucy broke free, faltering at walking pace, while youngsters whizzed past, dancing free, to the sound of "Bohemian Rhapsody". Dave smiled patronisingly.

The day of Lucy's driving test dawned cold and wet, the streets congested and slippery with sleet. Lucy took her time.

If I deserve to pass, then I will. There was no time to worry. Lucy had no idea if the serious-faced examiner was scribbling good or bad things on his clipboard. Afterwards, when he declared Lucy unfit as a driver, she showed neither emotion nor surprise.

She felt foolish for having listened to Dave.

'Never mind, you can try again,' Dave said when Lucy told him the news.

On the last day of term, the foyer of Lomax Lodge was piled with bags, suitcases and trunks, while students waited eagerly for taxis or lifts. Lucy walked to the station with one bag and one case. On the train, she divided her time between reading and looking out of the window, her mind as blank as the bland landscape stretching to infinity. Suddenly, the train stopped. Five minutes later, it moved at snail's pace, to the displeasure of passengers. The temperature in the carriage plummeted. An announcement informed passengers the train would terminate at Luton. There were disgruntled groans and colourful language. Rumours of worsening weather clouded Lucy's hopes of arriving home today. She immersed herself in Theodor Storm's novella, *Der Schimmelreiter* – a fitting tale for the mysterious mists of Fenland plains. It was dark when Lucy finally reached Waterloo Station and boarded a southbound train. Snow was falling thick and fast, and at Dorking, the train terminated, passengers as good as stranded. Thankfully, gritters and snowploughs were out, carving a navigable passage on main roads. Lucy took a taxi all the way home, using the twenty pounds she'd kept for last-minute Christmas shopping. *Christmas presence is more important than presents*, she told herself.

Seeing Lucy standing on the doorstep, Hilda gave her a meaningful look. Lucy had mentioned she was taking the driving test but hadn't told her the outcome. In a brief embrace, no words were necessary. Gone were the days when Hilda chastised Lucy for not passing an exam.

'Welcome home for Christmas, Lucy! I'm pleased to see you've finally put some flesh on those bones. University life clearly suits you!'

Later, Lucy overheard her mother say, 'Gone is the shrinking violet that came back from that job in Germany, who I left on the doorstep of that hostel, months ago. Is this self-assured young woman with the fancy hair do and posh accent our Lucy?'

'Hmph!' Albert snorted. 'There's sure to be a boyfriend somewhere in the equation.'

'That's what I was thinking,' Hilda sighed. 'I do hope she hasn't made herself cheap.'

A day trip to Marion and Paul's for Christmas Day was a given. The two-up-two-down, terraced house rocked with shouts and laughter. Gifts were unwrapped, dishes clattered, Christmas songs belted out from Paul's transistor radio. The tiny kitchen billowed with steam and smells of turkey roast, Brussels sprouts, and Christmas pudding. Dotty ate the cat's food, the cat broke the gravy-boat, Sammy swam a plastic duck in the animals' water-bowl, and baby Jamie screeched and gurgled from the playpen. Marion fussed, Hilda clucked, Albert went outside to smoke, and Paul went to the shed for cold lager, as there was no room in the fridge. Patrick and Molly and their three children came for tea and mince pies, and a merry sing-song. The group gathered on the patio for photographs – an enduring souvenir of a chaotic, but happy day. Lucy stood holding Jamie, aunt and nephew round-faced and smiling, while Albert and Hilda flanked the Clements family foursome, looking suitably ridiculous in paper hats.

Boxing Day in Foxfield was quiet. While Albert walked the dog and Hilda pottered about in the kitchen, Lucy stood by the fireside, feeling deflated and nostalgic. A line of Christmas cards swayed in the rising heat from the electric fire below. Greetings were from a faithful hard-core of friends and relatives – the ones who never forgot – Marion, Peter, cousin Sarah, Arthur and Joan, and from Hilda's friend Dot who had moved from London to Blackpool after the War. Birgit, Margaret, and Susan Quinn had all remembered. Of course, no card from Martha, a poignant void.

'Christmas is often a sad time,' Hilda said, 'too many memories. People enter our lives and leave again like storybook characters. Fate plays cruel tricks, and this year was no exception.' Hilda clicked her tongue, bitterly.

'It was a terrible thing, Mum.' Lucy said quietly.

'You're young and have your life before you, Lucy. I have many years to look back on, many losses to lament.' Hilda sighed and stared into the fire.

'I'll go and put the kettle on,' Lucy whispered.

The first post after Christmas brought a Christmas card from the cousins in Meisenfeld, and a short letter from Helmut, expressing his anger at Martha's untimely death.

'We'll invite him back and give him a good holiday,' Hilda suggested.

'I'll write the letter,' Lucy said.

'Even if he comes, it won't be the same,' Hilda said.

The phone rang.

Hilda got there first. 'Peter, I expect,' she said.

Lucy said nothing.

'Who?' Hilda asked sternly. 'Dave? I don't know any –'

'It's okay, Mum – it's one of my student friends,' Lucy said.

Hilda handed her the phone, her face crumpled with anxiety.

'Hi Dave, yes, and you. Tomorrow? Eleven o'clock? I'll just check with Mum and Dad.' Lucy cupped her hand over the receiver and said, 'Is it okay if Dave comes for coffee tomorrow morning? He lives in Surrey, so it won't be too far for him to come. He drives and has his own car –'

Lucy paused, conscious of talking quickly.

'Tell him he can stay for lunch,' Hilda said curtly.

'Thanks, Mum.'

'He must be very interested in you.'

'It's not like that, really, Mum – we're just friends.'

Hilda said nothing.

Dave arrived punctually the next morning.

Lucy answered the door. 'Hi, Dave, kettle's on. Coffee?'

Dave was dressed in casual clothes and his hair was greasy and peppered with dandruff. He was quiet, polite, and a little boring, but he wasn't like Steve. Hilda's lurking fears were allayed. Dave gave his usual nervous snigger, which Lucy now found irritating. She handed him a gift – a book about fishing.

'Thanks,' Dave said. 'The book is very nice. I'll be able to get some good tips before next fishing season.' Lucy felt his arm round her waist and detected the smell of stale sweat.

'Um – I've got you a belated Christmas present,' Dave said, handing Lucy a slim, gift-wrapped package, clearly a long-playing, vinyl record. Lucy opened it, revealing "Nana Mouskouri's Greatest Hits" – Sung in German, with a picture of the famed, bespectacled singer. She thanked Dave and said, 'Let's play it now.'

For the next hour, the foursome listened to the nostalgic melodies, Lucy providing occasional translation of lyrics. Dave had brought a sketch-pad and showed Lucy some of his pencil drawings, which she commented on politely.

The drawings were immature and too abstract for her taste. Dinner was roast beef, dessert was lemon meringue pie and custard, Albert's favourite. Dave was meagre with his compliments but quick to remark Hilda's Yorkshire puddings were too crisp, and that he preferred his mother's moister ones. Hilda glanced at Lucy, who was busy eating. Hilda noted Lucy didn't look at Dave once during the entire meal.

'A pleasant chap, there's no denying, but he's not the man for you,' Hilda said after Dave had left.

'You're right,' Lucy said, staring into the electric fire.

38: FRIENDS FOR LIFE

In the heavy grey January morning, Blackford lay blanketed in freezing fog. The 11.45 train from London rumbled into the station, bringing scores of students returning for the new term. In the crowded carriage, Lucy shuffled towards the door, pleased to find it opened onto the platform.

A sudden, muffled buzz sounded from a bag on the floor. There were bewildered stares. The soft, metallic rattle was ominously close. Lucy reddened with embarrassment, realising she was responsible for its source. The alarm clock, tightly packed among her clothes had somehow been activated.

'It's alright – it's only alarm clock,' she said. A gentleman smiled, and nobody seemed bothered. The train juddered to a halt. Lucy lumbered onto the platform and looked for Dave, who'd promised her a lift to halls.

Then someone called her name. She spun round and saw Dave's flatmate.

'Hi, Tony, where's Dave?' Lucy asked.

'At the flat – he's ill.'

'Oh, dear. What's wrong with him?'

'Some kind of stomach trouble. Like 'flu.'

'Oh, that's nasty.' Remembering the long years of the grumbling appendix, Lucy still shuddered at the very mention of such an illness.

'Just drop me off by Lomax Lodge,' Lucy said. 'I've a few things to do today, before lectures tomorrow. Thanks for the lift. Tell Dave I'll come and see him tomorrow.'

Lucy hauled her cases up to the drab, grey door of room twelve. She slowly turned the key, wondering what kind of reception awaited her. Camille was already there, wearing a loose-fitting silk shirt, and reclining on the bed.

'You've gained weight!' Camille exclaimed joyfully. Lucy drew herself in and rued wearing the cheap, brushed cotton jeans which felt distinctly tight around the buttocks. *Another pair of trousers for the charity shop*, she concluded sullenly.

'That's right, plenty of Christmas fare, what?' Lucy tried to regain her pseudo-upper-class accent.

Camille put down her copy of *Tatler* magazine and flashed a cover girl smile. 'Aw, yes, the vac was absolutely ace – relaxing in the sunshine, with freshly squeezed, iced orange juice and fresh pineapple. I just wore a cotton stole about my middle. Hottest time of the year in *Keenya*, you know.'

Lucy tried to forget about her pinkish, pig-like complexion. Camille was the picture of attractiveness and poise. Like a lithe lioness, she tossed a curtain of sun-bleached hair, declaring, 'Grant will hardly recognise me!'

'Hmm,' Lucy responded vaguely, slowly unpacking her bags. She had grown to hate her over-zealous permed curls that resisted all contact with brush and comb. *Definitely a few changes in order, this term*, she told herself.

After shopping for groceries, Lucy called by at Abby's, but she wasn't in. The next morning, Lucy huddled hungrily through lectures, bracing her reluctant brain for forthcoming essays. At noon, dozens of denim-clad students thronged the stairs, feet scuffing on the concrete, excited voices chorusing in cold air. Suddenly, Lucy felt someone nudge her arm.

'Hey, Lucy! How's life?'

'Abby! You're back! How was your Christmas?'

'Yeah, the usual gastronomic extravaganza, which reminds me – Mike and Clare are having a tea party at Mike's on Friday afternoon, so you can expect an invitation.'

'Good!' Lucy was cheered by the thought of something to look forward to. In the evening, Lucy shared spaghetti Bolognese with Abby, then drank tea and listened to records, before a reluctant return to her room at eleven o'clock.

The next day, after lectures, Lucy visited Dave. She sat in his cluttered, airless room, while Dave lounged in bed, on sheets grey with grime. Conversation was stilted. Dave finished a plate of beans on toast, while Lucy stared at the brimming dirty laundry bin and three boxes of baked bean cans in the corner.

'I only eat that brand,' Dave said, 'Mum got them for me. Make yourself a cuppa, and some beans on toast, if you like.'

'No thanks.'

Dave had little else to say, apart from being at death's door. Making an excuse, she left after half an hour, saying she would leave Dave alone to rest.

Wimp! Nothing more off-putting for their relationship – friendship – or whatever it was. Lucy doubted Dave could even be simply a friend.

The next day Professor Gruber began his lecture with the news of the death of Agatha Christie.

A flurry of comments followed.

'What's that got to do with German literature?'

'Agatha Christie was a writer.'

'Everyone reads literature, likes stories...'

'Professor Gruber writes about stories, he doesn't write his own...'

Lost in a fug of essays, translations, and seminar papers, Lucy endured days of mundane routine. By Friday, she still hadn't been invited to Mike and Clare's party. On Saturday evening, she sat alone in her room, listening to cassettes redolent of the past year. Vicious winds rattled the windows, rain lashed against the panes. Not bothering with supper, Lucy filled a hot water bottle, went to bed, and silently cried herself to sleep. Camille didn't return. No doubt she was enjoying a night with the love of her life.

In the raw fog of the next morning, Lucy rose early and trudged to Baring Square shopping precinct. In the crowds, she kept walking, avoiding the advances of charity-tin rattlers and profferers of religious literature. Chilled to the core, she dreaded returning to the room where her voluptuous roommate might suddenly burst in with her boorish beau, filling the room with cigarette smoke and public-school drawl. Lucy had reached her tipping point. *I can't take any more of this*, she concluded. She had literally been pushed into a corner. It was time to move out. *A cardboard box under Baring Bridge arches would be better than this!*

Resorting to retail therapy, Lucy bought a new coat – green, midi-length, tailored at the waist, with duffel toggles, a hood and deep pockets. Lucy felt tall and elegant, cocooned and protected, striding through streets thronged with sophisticated town-dwellers and denim-clad students with frayed, dirt-ingrained flares flapping over platform heels.

Finding accommodation mid-year would be difficult, but Lucy wasn't giving up. *Storm the Bastille!* as her mother would say. Sustained by a hot pasty from Porkie and Best, Lucy trawled the length of Brightwell Road, jotting down details of private lodgings, determined to do the sums. *Anything – anything at all – would be considered.* Then she loped off to Brooke House and tapped on Abby's door.

'Come in!'

Lucy pushed open the door. Abby was lounging in her night attire, surrounded by books and yesterday's dirty crockery.

'Lucykins! Aunty Abby needs a strong cup of coffee, and so do you.'

Abby put the kettle on and picked up a half-eaten pack of Digestive biscuits.

'Here, you'll have to help me eat these.'

'Thanks.'

Lucy sat on the floor cushion, bracing herself for a post-mortem on yesterday's social gathering. Abby's ample bosom bulged behind a turquoise-and-yellow, quilted dressing-gown. A long, cerise-pink nightdress flapped over fluffy, sky-blue slippers.

'It's Saturday today, and I don't care what time it is,' Abby laughed. At two o'clock, she showed no signs of wanting to get dressed.

'I've just come out of the bath: that's always my excuse. Yesterday, when a friend came to give me a lift to the tea party, I was still wearing thisBrentford Nylons regalia. By the way, where were you yesterday?'

'In my room.'

'Did you forget?'

'I wasn't invited.'

'They probably forgot to ask you. You should've come anyway. Just about everyone was there from the department. The food was superb.'

Lucy stared at the wall. The gravelly sound of Roxy Music rumbled from the record player in the corner.

'Are you okay?' Abby asked. 'What's bugging you? Feel free to open up with agony-aunt Abby!'

'I'm moving out.'

'Well, that's no surprise!' Abby dunked her third biscuit. 'You've an awful lot to put up with in that doss-house. Really, Lucykins, you must admit that place just isn't your scene.'

'Then you'll help me find somewhere else – soon?'

Abby was emphatic. 'Absolutely! I'll ask around. Ask Miss Motherwell if there are spaces in the main building.'

Abby's tonic of hope carried Lucy through the afternoon. Leaving her request with the warden, she went to her driving lesson, handled heavy traffic better, and agreed to apply for another test. Back at Lomax Lodge, Lucy opened the door to an unprecedented shambles. An ocean of dirty crockery, discarded food wrappers and brimming ashtrays littered the floor and furniture. Her desk was strewn with crumbs and sticky spoons, her bedspread wrinkled and gritty with ash and crumbs. Despondency turned to anger. *How dare they! I can't stand another minute of this!*

On Camille's bedside table, a scented candle burned, and a whisper of steam rose from a recently boiled kettle. The door clicked open, and in padded Camille, barefoot, wearing one rose-pink towel as a turban, another knotted neatly around her bosom.

'Hi, how was your day?' Camille asked.

'Not bad – until now.' Lucy seethed, in no mood for polite conversation.

'Yah, sorry about the mess. We had a good crowd round. They've only just left. I'll get it cleared up in a minute.'

Lucy was relieved she hadn't arrived earlier, whilst the good crowd was still there.

'Tea?' Camille asked, pouring herself and Lucy a cup of Earl Grey tea.

'Thanks.'

Lucy took off her coat and hung it on the back of the door. She didn't bother mentioning her plan to move out.

'Do anything exciting?' Camille asked.

'Actually, it wasn't a bad day. I went shopping, had lunch, visited a friend in main hall, so I suppose I really ought to get some work done tonight.'

Lucy shook the cover, flopped onto the bed and reached on the bookshelf, her hand closing over *Le Misanthrope*. Anything to take my mind off being stuck here!

Minutes later she put the book away. Her mind was working overtime. *Might she move this week? In which case, she'd better start packing.* Camille sat at her desk, writing, the mess remained. Lucy felt her anger returning. Something, somewhere, even another room share would surely turn up soon?

It had to. Perhaps Dave could help? Lucy hadn't seen him for days. She sprang up and put her coat on.

'Just off out, I've forgotten something,' she said and left quietly.

In the freezing night, she hurried to Clare Hall, a modern edifice overlooking Brightwell Park. Tony was in the communal kitchen making toast.

'Hi, Lucy. Dave's much better and is up and about. He'll be pleased to see you.'

Lucy knocked on Dave's door. She was mildly annoyed to find Dave still in his dressing-gown and pyjamas, lounging on the unmade bed.

'Hello,' Dave said. 'How's life treating you?'

His hair hung limp around his sallow skin, his chin showed a day's growth of dark stubble. In the overheated room, Lucy felt stifled and trapped. She glowered morosely at Dave's cup of lukewarm tea curdling on the cluttered bedside table.

'Make yourself a cup if you want,' Dave said.

'No thanks.'

Lucy perched on the edge of a chair, her mind doing backflips. Two things had to go – Lomax Lodge – and Dave! At least Dave wasn't nasty, he was just plain boring. Lucy knew she'd never fall in love with him. She just hoped he wasn't becoming too fond of her.

'I'm moving out of Lomax Lodge,' she said.

'Can't blame you. Where are you moving to?'

'Don't know, I've only just started looking. Anything's better than staying in that dump.'

'I'm sure something will turn up.'

'I've also applied for another driving test, but I'm dreading it, now that I've so much else to think about.'

'You'll be fine,' Dave said, but Lucy wasn't convinced.

Returning to Miss Motherwell, Lucy was thrilled to be told an empty space was available in a shared room on the first floor. Lucy went there immediately and knocked on the door. There was no reply, so she left a note. Later, at Lomax Lodge, Lucy encountered Amanda Hunt on the stairs.

'A girl was here earlier, looking for you,' Amanda said.

'Who?'

'I *hev neau* idea. She had a *ghaaaastly* Northern accent. I didn't *cetch* what she said.'

Lucy hurried back to Brooke House before the office closed.

'The space is still available,' Miss Motherwell said, 'but you'll need to speak to the other occupant first. She will choose her preferred room mate, and the successful applicant will be informed by Friday.'

'Thank you,' Lucy replied, her hopes sinking. She returned to the room in question. The door was opened by a petite blonde in a plaid shirt and faded jeans.

'H- hi, I've come to ask about the room share,' Lucy stammered.

'Come in.' The girl invited Lucy to a plump floor cushion. 'Coffee?'

'Please, no sugar.'

The walls were plastered with rock star posters, the floor strewn with books, magazines and crumpled clothes. An ironing board piled with clothes presided over the clutter. *I can live with this*, Lucy thought.

Fifteen minutes of chat about cookery, the Beatles, and the weather, left Lucy hopeful. Sharing a space with this humble, untidy pixie-like person would far surpass being stuck with slatternly, bank-balance-in-the-clouds Camille. Lucy unconsciously planned where to put her things: postcards on the corkboard, the Welsh tea towel above the bed, books, radio and spare mugs on the shelves...

'I don't have much stuff – just a few things. I wouldn't get in your way,' Lucy said.

Would that have been better unsaid?

'A few others want to look at the room as well,' the girl concluded with a silken smile.

'I know. Well, I'd better go now. Thanks for the coffee. I enjoyed our chat and hope to see you again.'

Like an exam, the result would be known, in due course. Lucy's optimism lingered. Packing was next on the to-do list. Lucy realised she didn't even know the girl's name. The week passed, and so did the deadline. Alone in her room on Saturday evening, Lucy devoured an entire pack of chocolate biscuits, idling over an essay, listening to music until bedtime. Under the duvet, she pressed her ear close to the cassette recorder, the sounds of Simon and Garfunkel and Gilbert O'Sullivan flooding her mind with memories, and thoughts of what might have been and what might never be.

Sometime later, a note was pushed under the door.

Please turn the music down a little· Yours, a 'non-sleeper·'

Assailed with guilt, Lucy switched off the cassette player, buried her head in tear-soaked pillows and dozed fitfully till dawn.

After Saturday's driving lesson, Lucy met Dave for a walk along Fenbird Way, the main road encircling the town, overlooking open countryside. At Fenbird Bridge, the river flowed ten feet below, through mist-shrouded marshes. Beyond, lay Fenbird Forest, dark and forbidding, like Lucy's future. Dave reassured her everything would go well on the day. *Dave's a good friend*, Lucy told herself, shelving her plans to end their tenuous liaison.

On Monday, Lucy checked her pigeon hole and found a note – another space in a shared room was available. Odds were stacked against anyone willingly inviting a stranger to share their room, even with a rent reduction. Nevertheless, Lucy went to investigate. Far from gloomy, B floor overlooked leafy gardens, and B12 had connotations of healthy diets and Marmite. The room was round a corner, reminiscent of the Altersheim. Lucy wasn't banking on success. She knocked on the door. No answer. She was about to leave when the door was opened by a serious-faced girl with thick glasses and dark hair brushed into a neat bun.

'Yes?'

'Sorry to disturb you,' Lucy began, 'I'm told there's a space in your room, and I was wondering –'

'Come in.'

Lucy wondered what expression lay in the myopic eyes. The room was extremely full, barely a square inch of space to spare.

'I'll make tea,' the girl said, filling the kettle. 'Have a seat.' Shelves, mantlepiece, windowsill and bookcases were crammed with books: flimsy paperbacks, leather-bound Bibles and heavy tomes of Classical mythology. A huge Greek-English lexicon sagged at the centre of a set of shelves on the desk. The tea was hot, strong, and milky. Lucy drank gratefully.

'I'm Hilary Snow, first year Classics. And you?'

'Lucy Wylie, first year French and German.'

'Have some of this, if you like?' Hilary offered a plate of sliced, fruit loaf.

'Thanks.'

'I made it myself. It's marmalade cake.'

'It's very good,' Lucy answered.

'I'll move my books and let you have half the shelf. There's room for your clothes in the chest of drawers and wardrobe.'

Lucy spluttered into her teacup. Hilary was talking as if Lucy had already arrived with all her belongings! Her mind turned somersaults. *No more capricious Camille! Goodbye obnoxious Amanda Hunt!* However eccentric Hilary Snow might be, she would surely be better company than Camille and her cronies.

'So, you are saying, I can actually move in?'

'Well, yes. If you want to, that is.'

'When would it be convenient?'

'Let's see, tomorrow? We can meet at the warden's office in the morning for the formalities.'

Scarcely believing this wasn't a dream, Lucy went straight back to pack. Abby was out. So was Camille. After supper, Lucy completed two translations and an essay with the utmost ease. Scarcely sleeping a wink, she presented herself at the hall office at nine the next morning. Hilary was already waiting. A form was signed, the transaction complete. Lucy was handed a new set of keys, with instructions to return the keys from Brunel lodge when the move was complete.

Her heart as light as thistledown, Lucy ran to break the news to Abby, but she was out. She sped to Brightwell Tower and found Abby in the foyer, cupping her gloved hands around a cup of vending machine coffee.

'Guess what?' Lucy dragged Abby by the sleeve. 'We're celebrating! We're going to Koffie en Koek for cheesecake, and the treat's on me!'

Abby handed her vending machine coffee to a bemused bystander and said, 'I can guess what brought this on!'

Chatting and laughing with Abby in the coffee house, Lucy felt she'd known her for years. *With Abby, I can just be myself,* she pondered, not daring to think where the friendship with Dave was going.

Abby helped Lucy move her things in just three trips.

'Good riddance!' Lucy exclaimed, finally closing the door on Lomax Lodge.

'Now for a new chapter in your life, Lucykins,' Abby said.

Hilary had tea and cakes waiting.

'This is really nice,' Abby concluded, 'A dramatic improvement. You'll be much happier here, and Hilary's such a good cook!'

Hilary offered home-baked butterfly cakes. She looked over the rim of her cup and said, 'Your other room must have been dreadful.'

'No comment,' Abby said.

In her new abode, Lucy felt instantly at home. Coincidentally, Hilary also liked Marmite, usually on toasties at breakfast. She was extremely studious, spending long hours at her desk. Lucy wondered if she too ever felt anxious or lonely.

Dave was one remaining obstacle. Could they just be friends?

Lucy went to tell him about the move. Dave was in the kitchen, discussing Einstein's theory of relativity with Tony.

'The space-time continuum is a strange phenomenon,' Tony said. 'We think time is linear, but it's is curved. As an object approaches the speed of light, time slows down –'

'I imagine,' Lucy cut in, 'that time is like a ball of tangled string.' On the back of her Highway Code booklet, she doodled a complex trajectory. 'Time lines can cross, touching one another, so we might get a glimpse of what is to come.'

'Interesting,' Tony said. 'And you don't study science?'

'Not likely. I was useless at it in school, but I've always been intrigued by space, time, and astronomy.'

'Science doesn't have to be a career, it can be anyone's hobby,' Tony said.

Dave hardly said a word. Perhaps he'd be more talkative on Sunday's hike in the Stour Valley? Dave and Tony had agreed to come.

Sunday dawned misty, but with a good forecast. This time, with a new pair of boots, Lucy strode confidently ahead, trudging through damp meadows, invigorated by fresh air and sunshine. The lads lagged behind. Again, the walk finished in a pub. Dave and Tony played shove-ha'penny with loose change, their sport degenerating to asinine sniggering at the shiny bust of Britannia on one of the coins. Lucy felt like a spare part.

The afternoon of the driving test was strangely surreal. The same bespectacled, black-haired examiner who had failed her in December greeted her with a vague glimmer of recognition. Once more Lucy endured the same route in heavy traffic. Again, the hard backrest was a distraction, and unintentionally, Lucy made similar mistakes. The examiner pronounced the verdict, verbatim to the last occasion, his even-toned voice like a pre-recorded message: 'I'm afraid your ability to drive fails to meet required standards, and therefore I am unable to award you a Pass.'

The entire episode seemed an action replay of a bad dream. Lucy left the test centre, thankful she hadn't told anyone about the test, apart from her mother and Dave.

'You did your best,' Dave said, in his expression a hint of chauvinistic pride.

Caroline's birthday tea provided light relief. Abby told endless jokes and reduced the company to paroxysms of laughter. Caroline dabbed her chin with a serviette and laughed politely, while single honours German students Helen and Charlotte seemed less strait-laced than usual, and Caroline's school chums tittered gleefully from the settee. Lucy sampled a little of everything from the sumptuous buffet, then felt guilty about eating too much. The school chums left early for a prayer meeting, after which Abby voiced her view that church was for brainwashed morons and self-righteous prigs. Caroline looked aghast, and Lucy sat tight-lipped and silent. When she returned to her room, Hilary was out. Suddenly, she felt incredibly miserable and alone. The pleasant afternoon had left a metaphorical gap, which Lucy filled with a Mars bar, guiltily savouring its smoothness whilst staring at her next essay topic. An hour later, Hilary came back, sat at her desk and immersed herself in her books.

'There's an ecumenical tea at St Anselm's vicarage on Saturday,' Hilary said, suddenly. 'Would you like to come?'

'That sounds nice,' Lucy answered, 'but – what's ecumenical?'

'It means people from all church denominations are welcome.'

'But I don't go to church.'

'That doesn't matter. Anyone can come.'

The gas fire hissed faintly.

'All right, I'll come,' Lucy agreed.

St Anselm's Vicarage was a detached Victorian villa in a quiet street, ten minutes' walk from Brooke House. Inside the hallway, the girls took off their coats and threw them over the newel, the coat rack already full. Through an open door, Lucy glimpsed a crowd as loud as a public house. A cassette of hymn music was barely heard.

'Let's go somewhere quieter,' Hilary said, clearly knowing her way around. The back room was filled with armchairs, floor cushions, and rugs on polished floorboards. French doors overlooked a paved patio and lawn littered with children's tricycles and toys. In the front room, someone turned the music off and mumbled a short prayer.

'We'll go through for tea now,' Hilary said.

The buzz of talking started again, and guests wandered to the buffet table.

Lucy filled her plate, and someone came round with a tray of teas. She observed people's clothes and mannerisms, hairstyles and figures, constantly drawing comparisons with herself, wondering how everyone could be so merry without a drop of alcohol. There were many couples, which Lucy found depressing. A door opened. Three children and a Yorkshire terrier scampered in. The smallest boy brandished a Dachshund-shaped draught-stopper at the real dog, until his sister retrieved it, declaring that she didn't want Sausage-Doggie to be ripped to shreds. Two more children rushed in, descending with their siblings into a happy bundle of laughter on the carpet.

The Vicar of St Anselm's was politely moving around the group. Lucy hoped to be passed by, but she was wrong.

'I've not seen you before, have I?' The vicar's voice was disquietingly searching.

Lucy felt trapped. It would be rude to say nothing or get up and walk away.

'I – I'm Lucy Wylie – I'm a first year French and German student – Hilary's new room-m-mate,' she stammered.

'How are you finding university?'

'Oh, it's really good, thank you. I'm enjoying it very much.'

'And you don't have any problems?'

'No, no, none at all,' Lucy replied.

'No, no, none at all,' the cleric echoed. 'It seems you're coping very well.'

There was a rise in intonation at the end of the statement, as with a question. He moved on to the next person.

That brief encounter haunted Lucy for a while to come. The vicar had seen through her like glass, peeled back layers of subterfuge, laid her soul bare. Walking alone in the bracing March breeze, Lucy sought solace. The friendship with Dave had been a sham from the start – a wager for a magical spark to kindle true love. Life wasn't like that. Lucy wasn't ready for marriage. Her life lacked something intangible and extremely important. Was it love? For Dave, she felt not a glimmer of excitement. Had she been in love with Roland, when her feelings ran so high? Lucy floundered in doubt and confusion.

The Students' Union building was a beacon of bright rectangles against the inky-blue sky. Dave would unquestionably be waiting for her in the foyer, like a faithful dog. They would doubtless go up to one of the bars and he would buy her a Cherry B. And then she would be honest and tell him the truth.

After classes on Monday, Lucy went to the foyer of Brooke House to check the post, light-headed and unfettered. The parting with Dave had been easy and amicable, with mutual closure. Lucy leafed through the post in the W pigeonhole. Wilson, Wells, Wilkins... Wylie! Lucy instantly recognised the upright handwriting of Margaret Pritchard, on the back of a postcard of Lancaster. Untypically, Margaret had only written a few words:

Flat 3, 14B Station Terrace,
Minchcombe,
Lancs.
FY47 2BR
March 1st (St. David's Day)1976.

Dear Lucy,

Hope you are well and enjoying uni. I've been busy with essays, clubs and societies, hence the short note. I'd like to invite you to Lancaster for the Ralph McTell concert on February 28th. Looking forward to catching up on news,

Love from,

Margaret xxx

At first, Lucy didn't want to go. She had never heard of Ralph McTell and feared the concert might be an ear-splitting cacophony attended by rowdy and disorderly delinquents – not that Margaret would like that. Maybe Margaret had changed? Lucy began a reply, declining the invitation, then screwed up the letter and tossed it into the bin.

With a complete change of heart, she penned a quick message on the back of a scenic view of Cavenfold Forest.

Room B12,
Brooke House,
Brooke Road,
Blackford,
8.3.76.

Dear Margaret,

Great to hear from you again! Can't wait to catch up on all the news. Must rush to post this card and book my train tickets!

See you soon,
Lucy xxx

Now that life was easier, time sped by. On the day of the trip Lucy made an early start and travelled light. She whiled away the journey reading *Stern* and *Paris Match* magazines and looking out of the window. Beyond Birmingham, the train stopped at a series of towns that filled Lucy with a strange curiosity. She wondered what life was like in such old-fashioned, drab-looking places. She broke her fast with a miniature bottle of egg-nog liqueur – a treat recommended by Abby – which kept hunger at bay and provided the psychoactive effect she secretly craved. Unanswered questions hovered. Would Margaret still be her friend? Would there be religious weirdos? Would Lancaster folk be unfriendly?

The empty train clattered on to the coast. Gulls fluttered in the distance, battling unseen strong winds, apparently going nowhere. A low-level skyline of grey slate roofs and blackened chimneys came into view, and finally, the train reached its terminus in the unsung seaside town of Minchcombe – a strange echo of Westcombe. Margaret was on the platform, wearing different National Health spectacles. Her hair had grown longer and was as lank and greasy as before.

'My flat's just round the corner. I've made a casserole for tea,' Margaret said as if it had been minutes, not years since they last spoke. The flat was above a shop, up an external flight of concrete stone steps.

'Nice place,' Lucy remarked. 'What are your flatmates like?'

'I don't have any. Just me here, living alone.'

'Don't you get lonely?'

'Not really – I'm often on campus, but come here to rest and study.'

'Why didn't you stay in halls?'

'We're only allowed to live in halls for two years out of three, so I'm in a flat for my second year, and I'll back in halls for my final year.'

Over dinner, Lucy told Margaret about her life in Blackford. She didn't bother mentioning Dave. It didn't seem relevant, especially since Margaret didn't have a boyfriend, and to Lucy's knowledge she probably never had.

Afterwards, they went to the corner shop, where Margaret bought a bag of Eccles cakes, a pint of milk, and half a pound of fresh, Lancashire cheese.

'What time are we coming back here tonight?' Lucy asked, suddenly worried about having to stay up late in an unfamiliar social group.

'We're not. The last bus is at five to ten, and the concert doesn't finish till around eleven. So we'll be staying on campus. One of my friends has kindly offered us to share her room.'

'Where will we all sleep?'

'Anna will sleep with her boyfriend, on the floor above, leaving us the bed and the couch.'

Maybe Margaret's become a Hippie? Lucy shuddered, fearing a promiscuous, drug-filled night ahead.

'Do you still write to your penfriends?' Margaret asked.

'Not for about a year, but Birgit keeps in touch. She's living with her fiancé, Franjo. They're both studying to become teachers.'

'I lost touch with my penfriends,' Margaret said. 'That's life. But I'm glad we've stayed in touch!'

On the fifteen-minute bus journey, Lucy stared pensively at forlorn farmsteads and barren pastures weathering the end of winter. Margaret was quiet. As the bus pulled into campus, she said, 'Come, let's meet the gang.'

The shy, ungainly Margaret of bygone years was gone. This Margaret marched boldly into the campus building like a co-owner. On the first floor corridor, she received a cheerful greeting and was tossed a bunch of keys. Margaret unlocked a door into a modern, narrow study-bedroom.

'You can have the bed and I'll sleep on the couch,' Margaret indicated. Lucy put down her bag.

'Let's go over to Jackie's room,' Margaret said. Across the corridor was a room full of people, new faces, new names. Sitting cross-legged on the floor and laughing with her friends, Margaret was part of a social hub. Still a professing Christian, she also identified as a non-militant Socialist. She neither smoked nor did drugs, she was accepted and respected, a modest drinker of cider, and a keen dancer to the cheerful rhythms of popular music. She listened to students' views, shared their vegetarian meals, imitated their accents, and lived among them, detached and free.

Lucy remembered the times she and Melanie mocked Margaret and passed around silly notes and unflattering drawings. Lucy rued the day they cornered Margaret and tried to convince her that small balls of soap were sweets. Margaret had remained unruffled, quietly standing her ground.

Nine years later, Lucy wanted to apologise. She would choose a quiet moment when they were alone.

After coffee, the group set off for the concert. Lucy went with zero expectations. She listened spellbound to Ralph McTell's refreshingly honest, soul-searching songs. The concept of weathering the storm awakened a desire to be strong in the face of adversity. The poignant lyrics on Irish emigration rang true, an echo of Hilda's tales of her maternal ancestors fleeing the potato famine.

Across the songs, alcohol seemed a theme...

> The only time I feel alright is when I'm into drinking,
>
> It can sort of ease the pain of it, and it levels out my thinking...

After two glasses of strong cider, Lucy wondered if the evening would have been as uplifting without alcohol. The concert concluded with standing ovations and encores, the sounds ringing in her ears for hours afterwards. It no longer mattered how late bedtime was. In the wee, small hours, Lucy lay awake listening to the voices and laughter of late revellers returning to their rooms. Eventually, on the cusp of slumber, she heard the strains of a badly played harmonica in the quadrangle below. She turned over and stared into the darkness, thinking of Hilary, and her struggle with insomnia. *So what, if I'm tired tomorrow?* Lucy thought, drifting off to oblivion.

Shafts of light penetrated the gaps above the thick curtains, Margaret, a homely mother-figure, padded about in dressing gown and slippers.

'What time is it?' Lucy asked.

'Midday,' Margaret smiled. 'I'll make tea and toast.'

Lucy stretched and sighed, 'Lovely, just like being at home.'

In the messy, communal kitchen, students came and went. Bins brimmed with empty cans and bottles, the sink was crammed with dirty dishes and the table strewn with crumbs. The tea was hot, the toast warm and crisp, dripping butter and marmalade.

'My train's at one twenty,' Lucy said.

'It's fine, we have time. The bus goes in twenty minutes, from outside the building,' Margaret said, pouring Lucy a mug of tea.

'Did you miss church?' Lucy asked, remembering it was Sunday.

'We meet in the evening, at six o'clock.'

After breakfast, it didn't take long to pack.

'There's something I've been meaning to mention,' Lucy said.

'What's that?'

'It may sound silly, but when we were in school together, I took sides with others and was really nasty to you. I just want to say I'm sorry. I was childish and stupid.'

Margaret smiled and said, 'but you were a child. That was ages ago. I'd quite forgotten. It doesn't matter now, really it doesn't.'

'Thanks, Margaret,' Lucy whispered, close to tears. 'I really appreciate that.'

'Don't mention it. We're still friends. Better than ever. Come, the bus won't wait!'

Another load was lifted, another door closed on murky past. Lucy began her journey, viewing unspoilt countryside and tired urban vistas of the neglected North with new perspective. The local train terminated at

Blackpool. On a spontaneous whim, Lucy decided to seek out her mother's old friend Aunty Dot. Life was short, reconnecting with people important. Lucy's last visit had been when she was five. Hilda and Rose had hired a caravan for a bucket-and-spade holiday with the kids. Lucy smiled at the memory of being kicked out of the bed by Marion and Sarah, rescued by her mother – and Rose's surprise at finding Lucy snuggled between Hilda and Rose in the morning. At Aunty Dot's, the collie dog had puppies and growled at Lucy for coming too close. Then Aunty Dot gave Lucy a black, patent-leather purse with a shiny clasp.

Lucy had no trouble finding Dot's house, a tidy, Edwardian terraced house, with latticed windows and a front garden with rose bushes, like Uncle Charles' home in London. Lucy rang the bell. The door was opened by a tall, middle-aged lady wearing a floral apron and with her curlers in.

'Aunty Dot? I'm Lucy. Hilda's younger daughter."

'Lucy Wylie! What in heaven's name brings you here? Come on in!"

Dot gave Lucy a crushing bear hug and welcomed her into the parlour.

'Well, well, well, this calls for celebration!'

'I've nearly two hours before my train,' Lucy said.

'Angus, put the kettle on! That's my husband. He's a dear. We've been married three years this July. It was such a shock losing Fred, ten years ago this Christmas. It took me a while to get over it.'

Lucy remembered Dot's letter about Fred's sudden death from a burst appendix, once again thankful for her own survival. Dot and Fred had one child, Luke. In later letters, Dot told of her marriage to Angus Lawson from Edinburgh, and Luke's career as a mental health nurse. Dot plied Lucy with tea and ham salad sandwiches with olives, and chocolate biscuits galore. Lucy ate her fill, glad to be wearing her lose-fitting, somewhat theatrical-looking dress. She talked about Edencroft, Alderbridge, her travels and student life, and her parents' new home in Sussex.

'You're so much like your mother,' Dot remarked, 'your confident manner, and you're the spittin' image of Hilda when I worked with her years ago, in London.'

'You remind me of my friend Abby,' Lucy said. 'Quirky, flamboyant, theatrical...'

'Theatrical? Indeed! In Christmas pantomimes I've played Dick Whittington, the fairy godmother, and an ugly sister,'

'I was the grandmother in Wordsworth Grammar School's production of *The Snow Queen*. That's all.'

They reminisced, looking at old photographs. Dot had many of the same black-and-white snapshots of the holiday, fifteen years before.

'It's sad about Rose,' Dot said, 'but you your mum must come and visit us.'

'That would be lovely,' Lucy said.

On the train, Lucy reflected on happy time spent with old friends and how easily distance can separate people, sometimes forever.

Back at Blackford, events were winding down to Easter. Hilary seemed tense, spending long hours studying and baking countless cakes, more than she could possibly eat herself. The girl in the room opposite the kitchen complained about noise in the kitchen at two in the morning. Hilary duly apologised, then told Lucy of her plan to invite everyone on the corridor, plus a few more, to an end-of-term tea party. Lucy and Abby offered to contribute snacks and home baking.

On the day, the kitchen was spread with a wedding-size buffet, kettles, jugs, and mugs filled and ready. Dozens of guests arrived, filling the corridor, study-bedroom and kitchen, the air humming with conversations and laughter. Lucy and Abby replenished kettles, milk jugs, mugs and plates, while Hilary sat in a quiet corner, watching the indoor picnic.

'She's like the *Great Gatsby*,' Abby said, 'hiding away while her guests enjoy her hospitality.'

When the guests had gone, the floor was awash with crumbs and spillages, littered with a flotilla of crockery and paper serviettes. Abby and Caroline helped Hilary tidy up, thanking her for her hospitality.

'It went really well, didn't it?' Lucy said later that evening.

'I think so,' Hilary answered.

'Actually, it was – really good, and your butterfly cakes were heavenly.'

'Thank you.'

That night, Lucy lay awake, stimulated by sugar and caffeine, reflecting on the past weeks and months.

In the theatre of her life, new characters had appeared, old ones had returned. She wondered who would still be on the stage in the final act.

39: NOT ALONE

Apart from the stubborn reverse gear, Hilda's car was easy to drive. Lucy felt comfortable and in control, navigating rural roads and Millhurst's busy streets. Hilda sat beside her, quietly encouraging. Her confidence restored, Lucy applied for a third test.

'I'm looking for jobs in care homes,' Lucy said.

'How will you get there?' Hilda asked. 'I can give you a lift a couple of miles, no further, as I won't have the time.'

'No worries, I have my bicycle,' Lucy said.

Days later, Lucy found work at The Pines – a private nursing home, along a forested drive, on the road to Millhurst. The home was run by matronly Sister Miller and her assistant Sister Brampton. In navy blue uniforms and starched linen caps, they appeared imposing but were fair and approachable. Nurses and auxiliaries wore kingfisher-blue uniform with white collar and cuffs and a white cap. Fifty elderly residents whiled away the hours in lofty, sunlit rooms, chatting, knitting, snoozing, watching television, solving crossword puzzles in timeless ambience. Houseplants and vases of flowers, colourful rugs, cushions and candlewick bedspreads created a homely, domestic scene. Some rooms were shared, others single-bedded, offering more privacy. Residents were from varied backgrounds, from humble farm labourer to eastern potentate.

Lucy approached the work with fresh enthusiasm, regarding residents as individuals approaching life's end, deserving equal treatment. She felt sad for two emaciated ladies languishing in the same armchairs, day in day out, oceans apart from their loved ones. One talked endless nonsense, seeming cheerful, the other slumped, her head bowed into her gaunt shoulders. Whenever an air-mail letter arrived from her only daughter, staff would read it out. The old lady listened with her eyes, but never spoke and never smiled. Across the corridor, a nonagenarian Bishop pottered about his cluttered room like an office gopher, reading, sorting papers, and making telephone calls. Next door, a wrinkled, embittered spinster stared silently at the ceiling, alone and terrified, surrounded by a wealth of valuable antiques.

'It's all about how you stand with Him upstairs,' Sister Brampton remarked, during a handover.

Lucy got on well with practically everyone. A girl who had applied to start mental health nurse training and a young domestic with a speech impediment were the friendliest.

On her twentieth birthday, Lucy took a day off. Chronologically, it seemed a significant milestone, the end of her teenage years. A drive to Chanctonbury Ring for a walk to savour the delights of Spring was celebration enough. Trilling larks and undulating hillsides tinged with the first green of summer filled Lucy with hope. A hedgerow bursting with white hawthorn blossom reminded Lucy of a poem.

'"Now of my threescore years and ten, twenty will not come again..."' Lucy quoted aloud.

'I know that one by heart,' Hilda said.

> "Loveliest of trees, the cherry now,
> Is hung with blossom on the bough,
> And stands about the woodland ride
> Wearing white for Eastertide.
> Now, of my threescore years and ten,
> Twenty will not come again,
> And take from seventy springs a score,
> It only leaves me fifty more.
> And since to look at things in bloom
> Fifty springs are little room,
> About the woodlands I will go
> To see the cherry hung with snow."

We had to learn it at school when I was twelve,' Hilda said.

'Time passes so quickly,' Lucy said.

The holidays were almost over. On her last shift at The Pines, Lucy entered a room and found a resident in tears.

'What's wrong?' she asked.

The frail lady dabbed her face with a handkerchief and said nothing. Then Sister Miller appeared.

'Thank you, Lucy, you can help with the teas now. I need to speak to Mrs Leuchars in private for a moment.'

Later staff were debriefed behind closed doors.

'Mrs Leuchars had a very unpleasant experience this afternoon,' Sister Miller explained. 'Her son and daughter-in-law said some very hurtful things. Our residents rely on us for safe, effective care, but sometimes bad things happen beyond our control. Mrs Leuchars had visitors. Through the intercom, Sister Brampton and I overheard her son calling his mother, I quote, a stupid old cow. He told her hurry up and snuff it.'

'Appalling, absolutely appalling,' someone said.

'Of course, as you all know, nothing of this meeting is to be repeated to anyone outside of these four walls,' Sister concluded.

A few comments were muttered.

'That son just wants to get his clippers the cash!'

'A shame!'

'She's such a sweet old thing.'

'How could anyone be so heartless?'

A possible connection with the Leuchars of Nyehaven was irrelevant. Lucy put the incident behind her but remained aware of how cruel people could be.

Hilda collected Lucy at shift end.

'Post for you!'

A plain brown envelope was waved in Lucy's face.

Lucy ripped it open. 'Brighton Test Centre. Eleven o'clock, July the first. After that, we'll ditch the L-pates and I'll be driving to work,' Lucy said.

'Don't count your chickens before they hatch,' Hilda warned, offering Lucy the driver's seat.

On Monday, back in Blackford, Lucy faced endless essays and revision. Hilary was out. Lucy sat alone at the window desk, memorising a poem by Johann Wolfgang von Goethe.

Über allen Gipfeln
Ist Ruh,
In allen Wipfeln
Spürest du
Kaum einen Hauch:
Die Vögelein schweigen im Walde.
Warte nur, balde
Ruhest du auch.

The words had a rhythmic, calming effect, reminiscent of the view from her room in Foxfield.

"All hill-tops are quiet and still.
In tips of all pine trees barely a zephyr of breeze:
In the woods, the little birds are silent.
Wait now, you too will soon be at peace..."

On that chill, December morning, Lucy had looked through a veil of pain at the lace-curtained window, and at motionless fir trees, wondering if her death was imminent.

Her thoughts were interrupted by bawdy shouts, clanging scaffolding, and the ominous clack of a ladder propped against the windowsill. A noxious odour of gloss paint wafted in. Lucy stood up and closed the window, then up popped a painter, whistling tunelessly. Weary of study, Lucy went out.

Students were quick to voice their opinions, and complaints were lodged about the presence of workmen during exams. Miss Motherwell responded patronisingly that it was in everyone's best interests to have a well-maintained building. Her lame excuses fell on deaf ears.

'Rubbish!' Abby stormed, 'What's she doing about the girls ogled by painters? And the mysterious prowler on the scaffolding during the early hours of Sunday? Someone tried to climb into a girl's room!'

Lucy caught the mood. 'There are rumours it was the girl's ex boyfriend. But having the scaffolding there is inviting trouble.'

'That old bat Miss Motherwell is trying to save cash, hiring a bunch of cowboys in May and June, when rates are cheaper.'

Abby pulled out a chrome whistle from her cleavage. 'This is my dog whistle, which I fully intend to use against any would-be rapists.'

'I still feel safer here than I ever did in Lomax Lodge,' Lucy said.

'That's not surprising!' Abby chortled.

But Lucy's inner anxieties wouldn't go away.

She didn't fear prowlers – just the exams.

With Hilary as roommate, Lucy never lacked a listening ear, a kind word or a cup of tea with cake. It was soon evident Lucy was far from alone. Returning from lectures one morning, she found Hilary red-eyed and tearful, floundering in pre-exam panic. After sleepless nights and long hours of frenzied revision, the harassed Classics undergraduate was teetering on the edge.

'Is there anything I can do?' Lucy asked. Hilary shook her head and said nothing. Lucy felt powerless to help. She tried to read – in one hand French poetry, in the other a book of Welsh folk tales of the supernatural. Lucy sighed, wondering which to look at first. The horror stories harked back to distant days of exam angst and bullying. Lucy put the books down and sighed.

'I need a break. How about a cuppa?' Lucy asked Hilary.

'No, really, Lucy – there's nothing you can do to help. You wouldn't understand,' Hilary said.

Lucy made herself a mug of coffee and carried on reading. Half an hour passed in silence. Then there was a knock at the door, and in strode three long-skirted, spotted-headscarf-sporting stalwarts of the Christian Union.

Lucy hid behind her book.

'Hilary! You must come to the Chaplaincy meeting tonight!' exclaimed the tallest of the headscarf brigade. Hilary left the room to speak with her visitors in the corridor, then returned to pick up her bag.

'I'm going out for a while, I'll see you later,' she said.

'Bye, take care.'

Soon afterwards, Lucy was pleased to be interrupted by Abby. On went the kettle, once again.

'All this swotting's getting me down,' Abby said.

'And me,' Lucy sighed.

'Call me AA, if you like,' Abby said.

'What does AA stand for? Agony Aunt?' Lucy asked.

'You guessed correctly – that's one of my pseudonyms,' Abby grinned. 'Or maybe Automobile Association? or even Alcoholics Anonymous? Actually, I'm thinking of learning to drive as soon as exams are over. Meanwhile, I certainly won't be drowning my sorrows over a bunch of silly bits of paper called exams.'

Abby kicked off her shoes and flounced onto Hilary's bed, showing laddered tights. It was good to have Abby around. She was like a breath of fresh air that swept away cobwebs. However, over coffee and biscuits, congenial chat evolved into discussion on set texts, and a charged argument. Opinions clashed on the whereabouts of the *Wendepunkt* – the turning-point – in a particular novella.

'I don't think the author even knew where it was,' Lucy said.

'Of course he did! It's obvious, just figure it out!'

Realising Abby wasn't going to enlighten her, Lucy panicked.

'That means I'm an ignorant thicko and shouldn't be at this poncy university at all,' she growled, throwing her book to the floor, immediately regretting her action.

'I came here to have a good chat and share ideas – NOT TO HEAR YOU WITTERING ON ABOUT HOW STUPID YOU THINK YOU ARE!' Abby exploded.

She thundered out, slamming the door.

Never before had Lucy seen Abby lose her temper. A good thing Hilary wasn't there, although Lucy wondered if she and Abby might have behaved differently if she had. Lucy sat still for a long time, staring stonily into space. Then she got up and walked to the Abbey grounds, where fresh breezes and uninterrupted views across pastoral plains cleared her clouded mind.

A week went by. Study leave began. Apart from Hilary, Lucy spoke to scarcely anyone. She indulged in chocolate, retail therapy, and reading non-academic material ranging from cheap thrillers to *The Beano*. Workmen continued to disturb daytime revision, so Lucy found quiet places in parks and gardens to read and revise. Returning to her room one afternoon, she found a note pinned to her door.

Dear Lucy – Just to remind you of my existence· Abby·

Opening the door, Lucy was pleased to find Hilary at her desk, looking resfreshed.

'Would you like to come to a Chaplaincy lunch tomorrow?' Hilary asked. 'Anyone can come. Maybe you could ask Abby?'

'All right,' Lucy agreed, 'I'm just going to Abby's now.'

Lucy and Abby spent an hour conversing over tea and biscuits as if nothing had happened. Lucy mentioned the Chaplaincy lunch, and Abby agreed to go, promising she would keep the God-Squad at bay.

As social gatherings went, the Chaplaincy buffet was agreeably low key, and the food was good. Abby encountered an old school chum and talked of the merits of Handel, Bach, and Mozart, while Hilary huddled with the church crowd, and everyone seemed incredibly happy and in control of their life.

Lucy's chest tightened, tears pricked her eyes. Above all, she dreaded the appearance of the jolly vicar of St Anselm's. *I have to get out of here!* Leaving her plate of unfinished food on a table, she slipped out. Returning to her room, she flung herself on the bed and buried her face in the pillow. Memories of Martha resurfaced, painful reminders of happy times past. Anger welled like lava, a frenzied hatred of the person who had killed her and the fact this tragedy had been allowed to happen. What was even the point of her own life-saving surgery? What now? Lost in limbo, Lucy tried to think logically, as if searching for a lost radio signal.

Hilary's clock ticked quietly in the background, marking each second of Lucy's apparently useless existence. And then, something Abby once said surfaced from the depths of Lucy's memory. *I detest being miserable, and there are times when I can't stand my own company...*

Lucy sprang to her feet, grabbed her keys and went out. A westerly wind buffeting her face, she walked alone, skirting the riverbank overlooking Fenbird Marsh. The path was busy with dog-walkers, students, families... Lucy whispered to herself, 'If only I could be more like Abby – single-minded, self-confident, and strong!'

A cloud lifted: the light of reason dawned. So what, if she was sometimes alone in a crowd with no one to talk to? Others might be more lonely? Lucy regretted having walked out. Might it have been better if she'd tried talking to someone new? Time lost cannot be regained.

Lucy returned to find Hilary quietly reading.

'Abby and I couldn't find you when we came back,' Hilary said. 'Where were you? Are you okay?'

"I'm fine,' Lucy answered. 'I just needed some fresh air.'

Hilary smiled and returned to her reading.

Exams came and went, slipping into the sands of time. A sense of anti-climax followed, and Lucy wondered what all the palaver had been about. Abby judiciously avoided post-mortems on exams, and Lucy happily complied. What was done was done. Meanwhile, students enthused about the holidays and made plans for the autumn. Lucy applied for a single room in Brooke House for the next academic year. Securing a position on the Junior Common Room Committee would guarantee a room.

'I've volunteered to be treasurer,' Abby told Lucy. 'Hilary will be librarian. There are still a few vacancies.'

'What vacancies?'

'Babysitting was one. You could do that, couldn't you? After all, you have a niece and nephew.'

'Babysitting? Who in halls has a baby?'

'University staff.'

'I have little to do with my sister's children,' Lucy argued. 'It's geriatrics I have experience with, remember, not kids!'

'Talk to the current rep. You probably only have to lounge on someone's settee, drink coffee and watch telly, while their little darling slumbers in the next room. Quite a doss really.'

'Fine. I'll check it out.'

Miss Motherwell directed Lucy to Grace Bell, who lived on the top floor, where rooms overlooked gardens and countryside. Grace Bell's door was plastered with Smile-Jesus-loves-you stickers, as were several other doors on the corridor. Lucy was sorely tempted to turn back when the sound of footsteps on the stairs prompted her to knock.

The door opened.

Grace was tall and blonde, with owlish glasses.

'Can I help you?' she asked.

'I've come about the babysitting.'

'Do you need a babysitter?'

Lucy blushed, surprised anyone would consider she might have a child of her own. 'No, I'd like to volunteer as babysitting rep. Is the position still available?'

'It is. Come in!'

The room was large and bright, vibrant with colour and warmth.

'There's nothing difficult about the job,' Grace said. 'Basically, there's a list of clients and a list of student babysitters. When someone needs a sitter you find someone to fill the slot. As rep you have first choice. You'll inherit this room, near the corridor telephone. I regularly babysit for a couple with two really nice kids who are never any trouble, I watch TV and there's coffee and biscuits. The pay is fifty pence an hour.'

This was a surprise, as Lucy had expected the service to be voluntary. She half expected to be woken at any moment by the irritating buzz of an alarm clock.

'Your face looks familiar,' Grace said. 'Where are you from?'

'My parents live in Sussex.'

'Alderbridge Hospital – you were an auxiliary.'

'That's right – I worked there in my gap year.'

'I was a canteen assistant, my holiday job. That's where I saw you.'

The coincidence galvanised Lucy's confidence. *This was meant to be.*

Hilary and Abby were delighted with Lucy's news.

'We'll all be back here in October, providing we pass our exams,' Hilary said.

'First years never get thrown out unless they're bone idle and never show up for lectures.' Abby said.

Term finished in a sizzling heatwave. On the last night, in a disused quarry, five miles from Blackford, students sat cross-legged on the dusty ground, enjoying strong cider and barbecued *Bratwurst*. Crickets chirped in dry grass and swifts screeched and swooped in scarlet skies. Fellow first-year, Angharad Jones was entertaining the group with popular songs on an acoustic guitar. A few inebriated voices joined in. Lucy recognised Ralph McTell's "We weather the Storm", and sang along merrily, the effects of the cider lifting her inhibitions. She took off her sandals, tracing circles with her toes in the sand, staying cautiously on the cusp of pleasantly tipsy. Friends and strangers alike exchanged life stories and dreams. Abby spoke of her holiday job as a hospital clerk and mentioned a cousin, a concert pianist. Angharad's brother Dewi talked about the family farm in the Vale of Glamorgan and his degree in Applied Agriculture at Manchester University. Lucy felt connected, rediscovering the joys of Westcombe and Wales. Another flagon of cider was passed around.

Angharad put down her guitar and joined the conversation.

'Any holiday plans, Lucy?' she asked.

'Not sure. Maybe camping with my parents? Last year we went to Snowdonia and Cardiganshire, which was wonderful,' Lucy answered dreamily.

'There's lovely,' Angharad said, in her soft, lilting voice. 'Wales is a beautiful place.'

'I'm glad you like Wales. Wales is the best!' Dewi smiled patriotically.

'I'd love to go back some day,' Lucy sighed wistfully.

'Any other plans? Are you going back to Germany?'

'No. I've a job in a nursing home. Also, I'm taking my driving test –'

Lucy stalled, realising she had given away a closely guarded secret. Somehow it didn't seem to matter any more.

'Good luck with your test,' Dewi said. 'I passed mine in May. I've just got a car. It's parked over there – a Mini.'

I hope he's sober, Lucy thought darkly.

'So that's why I stayed on the orange juice tonight,' Dewi said, knowingly.

'Do you think I will ever pass the driving test?' Lucy murmured, staring into the embers of the camp-fire.

Dewi gently put his arm around Lucy's shoulders, and said, 'A lot depends on you, Lucy. There are some things in life, which you can want so badly, that eventually you will have them.'

Lucy glowed inwardly, filled with optimism and hope.

'I believe you're right,' she whispered.

In the searing heat of sleepy Sussex, hosepipe bans were in force, Foxfield under the threat of a total ban and the use of a communal stand-pipe. Back home Lucy helped water the plants, recycling water previously used for washing dishes or vegetables. The greyish-brown lawn remained unwatered, deep, fractal cracks scoring parched clay. Lucy took advantage of the relatively cool evenings for driving practice. Hilda was optimistic, Lucy less so.

She languished in her room, reading, writing letters, and sewing. She sat on the floor, hand-stitching a pinafore dress, doubting she would ever finish it. The heat was sapping her energy. Lethargy and despondency overwhelmed her. In a fit of frustration, she tossed the unfinished dress to the floor and buried her face in the duvet. 'God give me strength...' she murmured, having no idea what was wrong nor whether she even believed in God.

She wandered downstairs, where her mother sat folding laundry.

'What's wrong?' Hilda asked.

'Nothing.' Lucy answered.

'There is something bothering you, isn't there?' Hilda insisted.

'Everything's fine... well, sometimes I get the feeling – how can I put it? – that I'm only half alive...'

Immediately, Lucy sensed this was a mistake.

Hilda's expression darkened.

'Don't be stupid! In a world filled with troubles, all you can think about is some vague dissatisfaction in your personal life! You have a nerve, telling me you're only half alive! Well, all I can say is you don't know you're alive!'

It had been years since Lucy last kindled her mother's wrath.

'Pull yourself together, for goodness sake!' Hilda hissed 'You know what this is about? It's about sex! You're frustrated because you need a man and you don't have one. The driving force behind every young person is to reproduce.'

Lucy suspected her mother might be at least partly right. At twenty, Hilda had been preparing for marriage. *Fat chance of that happening to me anytime soon* Lucy thought morosely.

But something else was missing from her life – something intangible and immeasurably profound.

She went upstairs and began tidying her room. She took every book off the shelves, dusted and polished, rearranging furniture. She placed the bureau at a right angle to the window, allowing ample light for working. She began replacing the books. In the first pile was the cloth-bound Bible Hilda had bought for her before starting Wordsworth Grammar School. *Another Bible*, Lucy thought. She hadn't looked at it for years. Inside the front cover, her name was written in faded ink and childish handwriting. She opened it at random, to an illustration of a grape-laden vine. From the archaic text, words leapt like lions.

> If the world hate you, ye know that it hated me before it hated you...
>
> If they have persecuted me, they will also persecute you...

Lucy was gobsmacked. *If only I had read this when I was fourteen!* The rite of passage through school was never meant to be painless. In spite of everything, she had survived it. *Anyone can be bullied – even God, apparently*. If Jesus was criticised, mocked, and put to death for no good reason, then what right had she, small, insignificant Lucy Renate Wylie, riddled with shortcomings, to sail through life trouble-free?

Through the snowy veil of net curtain, Lucy discerned the shadowy wall of conifers in the calm evening air. Suddenly convinced she was not alone nor ever had been alone, and there was nothing to fear, Lucy sensed inexpressible joy. Grasping at this moment of clarity, she wanted to keep it forever.

The sense of wellbeing slowly faded. Lucy wondered if her glimpse of inner peace would help her next time anything went wrong. Doubts engulfed her once again. She put the Bible back on the shelf. *This can't be for me*, she sighed, *I'll never become one of those Christian Union weirdos. Besides, they probably wouldn't want me anyway*.

The next morning, the familiar thwack of the letter box lured Lucy downstairs to collect the post. On the mat was a plain, white envelope with a black border. Lucy picked it up, trembling. *What now?* She breathed anxiously. The letter bore a German stamp and was addressed to Familie Wylie.

'It's a Kochendorf postmark,' she said, handing Hilda the letter.

Hilda tore it open. A shadow fell on her face.

'It's Helmut,' she whispered. 'He passed away two weeks ago. Losing Martha was doubtless all too much for him.'

Lucy said nothing. In stunned silence, she read the card, and Karin's note explaining how Helmut had never come to terms with Martha's death. He had finally succumbed to lung cancer, in Karin's words, *das Schlimmste, was es gibt* – the worst thing there is.

Hilda's response was typically philosophical and stalwart. 'Life is short. Always make the most of every opportunity, for we never know what's round the next corner.'

In spite of the heat, Lucy felt cold inside. 'True,' she sighed. 'Some things in life just don't make sense. We have to hold on to the good. Martha and Helmut were a part of our lives, as we were of theirs. Nothing can change that.'

40: Mountain Top

In the sizzling, searing heat of July 1st 1976, Lucy drove across the South Downs, her mother beside her viewing the parched landscape through the scratched lenses of her favourite sunglasses. After months without rain, fields had turned from green to brown, to ashen grey, parched earth cracked and lifeless under the sun's relentless glare. In the distance, Brighton's cityscape shimmered in the torrid haze of an untypical British summer.

The morning's outcome was a mystery yet to unfold. What would be, would be. At the Seven Dials roundabout, Lucy remained serene, calculating each manoeuvre, smoothly manipulating the gears, unruffled by heavy traffic and careless jay-walkers. A man stood on a street corner, conspicuous in a Mexican sombrero.

'Just look at that!'' Hilda's exclamation neither startled nor distracted Lucy.

In a sleeveless cotton dress, she felt comfortable and in control. At the test centre, she rubbed her clammy hands on the cool folds of her dress and drew a deep breath. The airless waiting-room reeked of stale nicotine fumes. Trapped bluebottles droned lazily. Three candidates shuffled apprehensively on sweaty, plastic-backed seats. It was almost too hot to breathe. Even Hilda was disinclined to chat. A glass door opened, and three gaunt, grizzled gentleman emerged, each claiming their respective victim. Lucy wondered if she was to be overlooked. Then, in strode a sandy-haired, clean-shaven, slightly larger dead ringer for Lucy's own father.

'Lucy Wylie?'

Lucy nodded.

'Where are you parked?'

The examiner spoke with a heavy Scots accent.

Hilda squeezed Lucy's hand and whispered 'Good Luck!'

In a trance-like daze, Lucy sat at the wheel and switched on the engine. The silent Scot sat beside her, fanning himself with the clipboard. Lucy wrestled the gear lever into reverse, annoyed for not having had the foresight to reverse into parking space beforehand. Seconds passed. Lucy persevered doggedly, ignoring the examiner's steely stare, her perspiration-drenched palms slipping on the gear lever. She wiped her hands on her dress and tried again. The Scot pushed open the side window – the one Hilda always forbade anyone to use because the catch was faulty. The triangle of toughened glass rocked precariously on its hinges, the bemused examiner muttered under his breath. Lucy winced with embarrassment.

Finally, by chance or by design, the gear stick slipped into reverse, and Lucy drove off. The streets were practically deserted. All the traffic lights were green, and Lucy sailed through them all. The next one was red. Lucy approached slowly, with measured gear changes and glances in the rear mirror. All clear in front and behind. She stopped, waited, then moved on when the light changed, ever sensing the examiner's silent presence. The route led to the seafront, where milling multitudes filled the promenade, pedestrians sauntering casually around a stationary ice cream van. Lucy slowed down to a snail's pace around idle strollers and careless children.

The heat was overpowering. The examiner mopped his brow. Her back glued to the plastic seat, Lucy persevered. Inevitably, the test included a hill-start, a three-point turn, and a few tricky one-way streets. Time was dragging. Lucy reminded herself this was the Driving Test, and this time, she must pass. At last, the test centre building was in sight.

'Turn left into the car park,' the examiner said coldly. Lucy parked neatly and waited nervously. The Highway Code questions were easy. She answered them all correctly, to the best of her knowledge.

'When do you have the right of way at a crossroads?' the examiner asked, his tone argumentative.

'When the light is green.'

'And when else?'

Lucy caught his withering stare and floundered. The desire for a cool bath and a shady place with a chill breeze was overpowering.

'When a major road crosses a minor road, and you're driving on the major road with no road markings on your bit of the junction,' Lucy gabbled nervously.

'And when there are road markings?'

'You always stop at a stop line. At a give way line you pause, then proceed when it's clear.'

'So, at a give way junction, you have the right of way?'

'Yes.'

'NO!!' bellowed the examiner. 'Nobody has the right of way at a crossroads. You may think you have the right of way, but in real life that doesn't guarantee there won't be a vehicle approaching from another direction. It is precisely that kind of attitude that causes accidents – when two motorists each think they have the right of way and neither of them look, when they proceed. Never assume you have the right of way at a crossroads.'

Lucy sat through the tirade, feeling like a whipped schoolgirl. Then she remembered something her mother had said: 'If an examiner is going to pass you, he'll grill you horrendously on the Highway Code, so as a new driver you don't become overconfident.'

Nigel Daly's first outing as a new driver was a prime example of pride preceding a fall.

'Now, I am going to give you a pass,' growled the dour Scot, 'so mind you take care at all times, especially as a new driver. Never forget what you have learned, and always be mindful of other road users. Remember, they can't be trusted. Safe driving!'

Then he handed Lucy the coveted slip of paper, got out of the car and slouched off into the test centre office. Stupefied, Lucy looked at the document in her hand, wondering if she would wake up at any moment, sweltering under too many bedclothes.

The passenger seat door opened, and in hopped Hilda, with a happy smile.

'It's as I dreamed,' she said. 'Over and over again I dreamed you would pass – and now the dream has come true. Well done, Lucy!'

Lucy was speechless.

Hilda removed the L-plates from the bumpers, tossed them onto the back seat and said, 'Now, drive us home.'

Lucy started the engine, engaged reverse gear at first attempt, and drove off.

'You know, now that you've passed,' Hilda said sternly, 'You must always be on your guard. Never get too confident and think that –'

'Don't worry, Mum,' laughed Lucy. 'I had a stern lecture from the examiner – just like you said!'

Suburbs and shops, and then fields and hedgerows flashed by.

'It's Rose's fifty-third birthday today,' Hilda said in a low voice. She spoke as though her sister-in-law were still alive and that she'd forgotten to send a card. 'And the sun is shining on us. It's a lucky day – a day I shall never forget.'

Arriving home, Lucy found her father in the garden, picking tomatoes. Without a word, she held the L-plates triumphantly aloft, just as Hilda had done years before, and snapped them to smithereens. A flurry of broken shreds fluttered to the ground.

'What's that? A nurse's cap?' Albert asked.

Lucy shook her head and laughed.

'She's now a fully-fledged driver,' Hilda said.

Albert nodded and lit a cigarette.

Lucy returned to work, feeling a silent thrill. *I can drive – I drove here, and I will drive home!* The heatwave was set to last. Ever-widening, ever-deepening cracks yawned in sun-baked clay, begging for rain. All day, combine harvesters clanked, gathering what was probably the poorest yield in British history.

A camping trip to the Lake District was scheduled for early August.

'It'll be worth the long journey,' Hilda said. 'There's mountain scenery, and it'll be cooler and more comfortable.'

On the day, heavy traffic and roiling heat necessitated an unscheduled overnight stop at a campsite on the edge of the Peak District. It was a pleasant location, rural and quiet, but the warm air was heavy with the fragrance of newly mown hay, raising the pollen count to unprecedented levels. The anti-histamine tablets had barely any effect. As a distraction, Hilda filmed Lucy pretending to drive a disused tractor, the steering wheel falling off. A picnic supper was at sundown. The tin kettle hissed on the Primus stove, wood pigeons crooned sleepily overhead, but there was nowhere to go to cool down. Hilda and Lucy fanned themselves with magazines, while Dotty panted in the shade.

'The success of camping depends on the weather,' Lucy complained. 'Last year it was too cool and wet, this year it's too hot and dry.'

Albert was enjoying the heat. 'A good, hot cup of tea is what you need, to make you sweat and cool down, and a cigarette to keep insects at bay. That's what we did in Egypt, during the war.'

Hilda and Lucy weren't convinced. Even at night, the heat was stifling. The next morning they packed up and headed for the Lake District.

After a five-hour, sweltering road trip, a suitable spot was found – a quiet corner in a farmer's field, on the western edge of the national park. A simple meal of bacon and eggs was enjoyed in the rain shadow of mountains. Here, it was ten, perhaps twenty degrees cooler. A few yards away, white mist shrouded a river bordered by low trees. On an exploratory walk, Lucy walked close behind her parents, keeping Dotty on a tight leash, conscious of the inquisitive stares of indigenous folk. The narrow lane flanked by dry stone walls petered out into a path through rocky pastures below sheer, granite crags. A farmer and his energetic collie were driving a flock of sheep, the plaintive sound of bleating curiously homely and comforting in the motionless air. Overhead, thick, purple clouds gathered under darkening skies, poised for rain.

'Let's go in that pub over there, before the heavens open and we get soaked,' Hilda said in her loud, London accent.

In the low-beamed, unpretentiously furnished inn, Albert sampled the local ale, while Hilda opted for a lager and lime, and Lucy enjoyed half a pint of Guinness. She shared a pack of pork scratchings with her parents and the dog. A handful of locals huddled round the bar, mumbling. Despite being a tourist and a stranger, Lucy felt strangely connected, as if she belonged in such an environment, in another life.

On the walk back, there was still no sign of rain. The road snaked towards the distant village, under an indigo sky. Surely it would rain soon? But in the sultry air, no storm broke. The following morning dawned bright and warm, with wall-to-wall blue skies above parched, arid ground.

'I like it here,' Hilda said over breakfast. 'I think we'll stay a while.'

Four days passed, without a drop of rain. Outings included visits to Windermere, Ullswater, and Wastwater, where Lucy sketched the scene, enthralled by the vista of misty peaks and forbidding screes that plunged into deep, dark waters.

Disappointingly, the enigmatic Tarn Hows wasn't found, and Lucy was disappointed to find William Wordsworth's Dove Cottage in Grasmere was on a busy road. They didn't bother going inside.

'Let's look for Watendlath instead,' Hilda said. 'Hopefully, that's still unspoilt by the twentieth century.'

The remote hamlet of Watendlath, the setting for the Hugh Walpole novels, was a pilgrimage for Hilda and Lucy. High in the hills and along miles of winding lanes, Watendlath consisted of just one private farmhouse, with a touristy tea room and gift shop. Albert grumbled about the crowds, and Hilda wasn't prepared to wait for a free table in the tea room.

'I prefer to use my imagination when reading a novel,' she said. 'Let's go back and make our own tea,'

'At least we got to see the place,' Lucy said.

Later, at the campsite, the picnic was interrupted by a sudden rustling in the bushes. Dotty gave a startled bark, her ears square.

'We'd better investigate,' Hilda said. 'It might be a dog.'

Footsteps scrunched on pebbles below the river bank. Through the bushes, Lucy saw three boys hurtling along the watercourse.

'Got 'im!' exclaimed one, plunging into the water in a frenzied burst.

'Nooo, be quick – or 'e's goone!'

'Noo – wait! I've got 'im now! In the bag! Huurry!'

Three tousled heads looked up, each pinched, frightened face betraying guilt. The lads stood shivering, the tallest clutching a carrier bag, the tail of a large salmon flapping above the stretched handles.

'What are you doing?' Hilda asked.

'I was lookin' for me doocks.'

Hilda looked blank. The boy repeated, '*Doocks* – you know, they *goo* quack, quack...'

'Ah, ducks! You have ducks, do you?'

The boy nodded.

'And they've swum off down the river?'

'Yeh. An' it's gettin' on a bit. I 'ave to get 'em hoome before dark.'

'What's that? They're getting on a bit?'

'Aye. Must be goin' now.'

The lads loped off upstream, playing aeroplanes with their gawky arms, keeping balance over slippery stones.

Hilda turned to Albert and said, 'Do you think they nicked anything from the tent while we were out? We'd better check.'

Everything was in its place, but Hilda was wary.

The next day, in Keswick, it was raining. Not proper rain, but a misty drizzle that enveloped the small mountain town like cotton candy. Tourists thronged the square, where covered stalls dripped onto grey cobbles. Lucy shivered in the unaccustomed coolness.

'Why are they selling only Bibles and church books here?' she asked.

'This is Keswick!' Hilda retorted, in the way she did when Lucy was a child and asked a question to which she really ought to have known the answer.

'I know that –' Lucy began.

'Well, you must have heard of the Keswick Convention? It's famed for its Bible conferences. People come from far and wide to buy religious literature and hear ecclesiastical speakers.'

'Oh,' Lucy answered, watching the rain drip from an overhanging canopy. She was tempted to look at the stalls but feared someone might try to persuade her to buy something she didn't want. She felt cold, tired and hungry.

Lunch was at a modest inn, deep in the mountains. After a cheese and pickle roll, Lucy was still hungry. Her parents didn't want dessert. Lucy asked Albert for a cigarette, earning a disapproving glance from Hilda. The cigarette was bitter-tasting, and Lucy regretted asking for it. The aroma of her father's freshly-lit cigarettes seemed pleasant in the open air, but not when inhaled. She didn't finish the cigarette and was glad when her mother said it was time to go.

They stopped at a picnic area. The weather was closing in, a whisper of mist now a thick blanket of fog and rain.

'Where are we?' Hilda asked.

'Buttermere,' Lucy said, checking the map, hoping for a glimpse of a village that looked lovely in pictures and was said to be the wettest place in Britain. A good view of it was never guaranteed, not even in the driest summer on record, apparently.

Suddenly, torrents of water cascaded from the sky. The car windows instantly misted over, and shards of cold water lashed in through a tiny gap in the driver's seat window.

'All that lovely scenery and we can't see any of it,' Hilda grumbled.

'We could wait until it clears up?' Lucy suggested.

'We'd be waiting a pretty long time,' Albert growled. With the engine off and windscreen wipers idle, the magnitude of the cloudburst was apparent. Rain drummed deafeningly on the roof, sheets of water lashed terrifyingly on the windscreen. Though hoping for rain, Lucy hadn't bargained for quite so much of it.

'I think it's stopping,' Hilda said.

Hilda and Lucy ventured cautiously out of the car. Suddenly, a cascade descended, and for a moment Lucy wondered if she might be in a lake, rather than near one. Torrents of water dropped out of the sky, drenching every inch of her body, flattening her clothing and filling her shoes.

'I'm not putting up with this!' Hilda shouted, diving back into the car and slamming the door. Lucy stood defiantly, rooted to the spot, unflinching.

'GET BACK IN THE CAR!!' Hilda yelled. Reluctantly, Lucy did as she was told.

'We're leaving one of England's best beauty spots, without actually seeing any of it.' Lucy said sadly.

At the campsite, daisies and buttercups had closed their petals, and the trees along the riverbank tossed and bowed their heads in the westerly wind. The sides of the tent buffeted and billowed in the breeze, and there was not an animal or person in sight.

Then Lucy exclaimed, 'Look! The toilet tent has blown down!'

The little blue tent lay on its side, a pool of rainwater had collected in the canvas.

'Albert, you can put it back up, and I'll get tea ready,' Hilda said.

When the wind dropped, the sun came out again. Dotty suddenly barked, alerting the presence of visitors. Two of the boys were back. The tallest rushed up to Hilda and placed a plastic carrier bag at her feet.

'Me Mam says you're to 'ave this,' he panted.

Hilda felt the weight of the bag, looked inside and saw two filleted portions of fresh salmon.

'Thank you,' she said, and before she could say anything else, the boys had turned on their heels and disappeared down the river bank.

'It's a peace offering,' Hilda said later, as the salmon steamed deliciously on the stove. 'With this gift of yesterday's catch, our silence has been bought. We'd better eat it all up quickly, before anybody thinks we've been poaching.'

'Poached salmon?' Lucy smiled ruefully. Whatever it was, it tasted extremely good.

'Tomorrow, we'll go somewhere different,' Hilda said, 'somewhere north of the Lakes.'

'What's to see there?' Lucy asked.

'Just a few places along the coast,' Hilda replied vaguely.

'Will there be time to go to Scotland? I've never been to Scot-'

'No, there will not,' Hilda replied abruptly. 'It's much further than you think. Just look at the map!'

Lucy didn't bother arguing.

On the journey next morning, Lucy stared silently at windswept moors that stretched to a distant ribbon of blue-grey sea. A grey, coastal town with factory chimneys and rows of stone, slate-roofed cottages resembled Lucy's first impression of Swansea, many years before.

'This is Workington,' Hilda said.

'It doesn't look very touristy.' Lucy said.

The next town was smaller, with similar quaint, cobbled streets, and old-fashioned shops. There were plenty of bicycles but very few cars.

'What's this place?' she asked. 'It looks like a film set of olden days.'

'This is Maryport. Mystery tour over. Aunty Dot's brother lives here, and we're going to visit him.'

Lucy had ceased being surprised by her mother's surprises. Nevertheless, she was intrigued. Even the name of this town seemed old-fashioned, fictitious, positively Dickensian. A cobbled street bore the name Arkwright Terrace, on the wall of a three-storey end-of-terrace house. All front doors opened onto pavement. A black bicycle with a basket in front stood propped against a lamp-post.

'This is it. Number One Arkwright Terrace. Bill and Maggie will make us welcome.'

Hilda rapped sharply on the polished brass door-knocker.

'They're probably out,' Albert said, and then the door opened. A thin woman in a floral pinafore stared blankly at the three strangers on her doorstep.

'Maggie? It is Maggie, isn't it?' Hilda asked.

'Yes, but who are you?'

'You'll remember me, Hilda, from years ago, Bill's sister Dot's old friend from London?'

'You'd better come in,' Maggie said.

The plainly-furnished parlour overlooked the street. An antiquated three-piece suite with floral covers and white antimacassars almost filled the room. Behind the sofa stood an upright piano, its lid up, a music book open at Beethoven's "Moonlight Sonata". Bone china shone from fireplace alcoves, a single sash window was curtained with white lace. The cool air smelt faintly of soot and apples. Lucy sat down, the armchair almost engulfing her, metal springs creaking under the upholstery. Albert and Hilda sat on the couch.

Maggie stood nervously in the doorway.

'Would you like tea?'

'That will be lovely,' Hilda said, and Maggie withdrew to the kitchen.

Through the half-open door, Lucy watched her fill the kettle at the old-fashioned Butler sink. A tabby cat strolled across the cluttered worktop and dipped into the milk jug.

'I do remember you,' Maggie said, returning with a tray of tea and biscuits. 'We lost touch years ago. Our lives carried us away.'

'That's right. Dot introduced me to you and Bill, before she married Fred and before I met Albert again after we were demobbed.'

'Do you still visit Dot?'

'We exchange letters and Christmas cards, but I haven't seen her for fifteen years. Lucy visited Dot earlier this year, and we'll be calling by again on our journey home.'

'You're on holiday here?'

'Camping, in the Lake District. We have a dog, you see.'

'Would you like to bring him in?'

'She's rather big and boisterous. A Dalmatian –'

'It doesn't matter, we don't mind dogs.'

'That's kind of you, thank you.'

Albert fetched Dotty, who sensed the presence of cats and was excited.

'Now sit still, Spotty!' Hilda said.

Albert raised an eyebrow, and Lucy smirked behind her cup.

'You have children, Maggie?' Hilda asked, noting photographs about the room.

'Two sons and a daughter. Our Wendy's eighteen now and has left school. The boys are ten and twelve. Wendy is with her fiancé's family in Workington today, and the boys are at my mother's in Carlisle. How old is your daughter?'

'Lucy's twenty,' Hilda replied. 'We've another daughter, Marion, married with two children and living in London.'

Maggie glanced at Lucy, then back at Hilda.

'Lucy's at Blackford University, studying languages,' Hilda said. Lucy squirmed with pride and embarrassment, assuming Maggie's children weren't well educated. She was wrong.

'Our Wendy did brilliantly at school,' Maggie went on. 'She's very good at music, and went to Durham University last Autumn, but didn't settle. She missed home and the family. She phoned every day, and one day she said, Mam, I can't stand it any longer – I'm coming home. She'd have done really well, I'm sure, but her happiness and wellbeing come first.'

Hilda was silent. Maggie fumbled distractedly with her apron.

'Wendy's happy now. She's got a job at the local supermarket and she and Bobbie are to be married next April. Wendy keeps up with her music, piano and violin, so her talent's not wasted.'

'That's nice.' Hilda sipped her tea politely. Albert reached in his pocket for his lighter and cigarettes, and Lucy took another biscuit.

'Family is important,' Hilda said.

Maggie nodded.'That's very true.'

The mantle clock ticked. These people had found their niche in life. Once again, Lucy was the odd one out, the odd bluestocking, collecting dust on the proverbial shelf of spinsterhood.

A clattering from the kitchen broke the silence – an avalanche of metal pans and the exasperated mewling of cats. Dotty barked, and Albert held her by the collar.

Maggie sat quietly, her hands in her lap.

'Well, thank you for your hospitality,' Hilda said.

'Well, it was very nice of you to call in,' Maggie said, standing up. 'I'll tell Bill you came and give him your best regards.'

On the way back to the campsite, Hilda said, 'Nice people, they were. Very homely, but very impoverished. I couldn't live like that.'

Lucy said nothing. The short time at Maggie's humble home left her with an enduring impression that haunted her for decades and ultimately shaped her future.

On the last day of the holiday, Albert drove deep into the mountains, up Hard Knott Pass. The narrow, winding road grew steeper, reminding Lucy of a recurring dream of being in a vehicle, climbing higher and higher up a steep hill with blind corners and a gradient so sharp, it seemed the car would surely topple and fall to unfathomable depths. It was scary and surreal. The engine whined, toiling in first gear, round yet another bend to a wall of grey tarmac, looming like a tsunami. Albert practically stood, clinging to the steering wheel, peering over the bonnet. Lucy held her breath, praying the car would stay on the ground.

The road suddenly levelled out above a broad vista.

'Let's stop here,' Hilda said.

Grey chunks of granite littered closely-cropped grass. Sheep scattered hap-hazard across the road. On the windswept, dizzy heights, the view was breathtaking. Jagged crags seemed to scratch the sky, their outline a choppy horizon of a restless ocean. The wind blustering in her face, Lucy surveyed the misty vista stretching westwards to the Irish Sea.

'That's the Isle of Man in the distance,' Albert said.

Lucy couldn't see it.

The family trio split up, each lost in their own world.

Hilda sensed peace – a stocktake of long years of life's strife, the holiday a positive hiatus, old acquaintances renewed. At fifty, Hilda had the satisfaction of seeing both daughters grown up, their troubled teen years behind them. Marion, a happy wife and mother, Lucy poised to be an educated, accomplished young woman. Doubtless, in the fullness of time, she too would meet a soul-mate to share her life. And dear Albert, quietly in the background, always there, but for how long? Hilda closed her eyes and prayed to God he would give up smoking for good.

Albert put the cigarettes away. It was too windy. He took photographs, capturing a fraction of Nature's wild beauty, an infinitesimal part of a vast, troubled Universe. The holiday was a brief breathing-space to connect with Creation and spend time with family. Everything passed, all too quickly. Where had the years disappeared? Albert remembered his gentle, caring mother, her patient smile, her kind eyes. His father, truculent, mistrustful, scarred by the Great War, didn't survive long. Then came World War Two, the harrowing conflict in Egypt, best forgotten. After that, marriage and children and the challenge of juggling creativity with necessity. If only life were problem-free and lasted forever.

A year from now, Lucy would have to visit Germany again. Martha's untimely death still weighed heavily. In life, bad things happen. This must be accepted. Pain and change are inevitable. Lucy recalled the views of Westcombe, Hildenheim, Snowdonia, and Blackford, each with a unique perspective, none as far-reaching as this one. At twenty, Lucy had climbed the final rung of the rugged staircase of teen years. Like the valleys below, deep, misty, and mysterious, her future waited, undiscovered and unexplored. The crystallised past, Edencroft's garden idyll, adolescent angst, trips abroad, holiday jobs, university life, were episodes of a story untold. Maggie's family was part of someone else's story. Though envious, Lucy was happy for them. In her own life, hard times awaited, happy times too. Life's events passed as fleeting cloud shadows on hillsides, every person's unique timeline a catalogue of unanswered questions. Some would be resolved this side of eternity, others not.

Beyond the summer sky were countless stars, unseen behind the sun's light. In time, even the stars would pass. Actually, most of them already had. If there was a God, who created such beauty, then surely He must have a plan for her life? All the trivia that had seemed so important was gone, as grass seeds, blown away by the breeze. Exam grades, personal achievements, people's opinions mattered little in the face of the Universe. What was meant to be would surely be engineered by the hand of a Higher Power? And if someone, somewhere, was destined to be her partner-for-life, then the anxious search was over.

On that remote, wind-buffeted hilltop, Lucy embraced her future with fresh hope, thankful to be herself – a unique creation with a part to play, a life to live, in the common confines of Earth and Time.

EPILOGUE

Malchester, 1993.

The dual carriageway ended. The lights changed to red, as they did yesterday and the day before.

Harassed but happy, the mother-of-three glanced in the rearview mirror.

An indefatigable preschooler bounced boisterously on the back seat.

'You'd better still have the seat belt on!' Mother said, sharply.

'Yes, Mum, of course!'

The lights opposite had changed, and traffic swirled across the busy intersection. The infant in the child seat slumbered on. Mother glanced at the dashboard clock. In five minutes, they would be home, with time to put the laundry on and feed the baby before collecting her little boy from school.

Her heart sank at the memory of her son's face as she left him at the classroom door that morning. He wasn't happy. Every day brought more problems. At least a nursery – a private nursery – had been found for her little girl, who learned to talk at nine months and could read and write at three. But that only made things worse for the boy – that brilliant little engineer, who assembled Lego bricks like an adult but barely spoke. Mother stared at the red light, willing it to change.

'Mother! What happened when you were a teenager?'

The little girl chirped cheerfully from the back seat.

The sequence of events was like a temporal loop: every day, the same red traffic light, adding two minutes to the journey, and every day the same question, as if by clockwork. This wasn't the best place for a driver to be quizzed on their past for interesting anecdotes. The filter light had changed, and a new line of traffic swirled across the junction, past a drab terrace of run-down houses. Four more seconds and the lights would change.

It was hard to think of a different story to satisfy the three-year-old's insatiable curiosity. Mother thrummed her fingers on the steering wheel. The requested stories were decades old and probably not worth telling.

'Come on, Mummy! I'm waiting!'

'Be quiet, Sweetie, I am trying to think – but there's nothing you'd really want to hear.'

'Oh, but please! You could tell me about the dog following you to school, or the silly boy who sat on a drawing pin. Or something you haven't told me yet?'

'It would take ages to tell you everything that happened when I was a teenager, and there are things you wouldn't want to know.'

'But Mummy, I want to know!'

'Not everything would be good for you to hear. But one day, I'll write a book, and when you're much older, you can read about my teenage years for yourself.'

About The Author

Cherry-Anna D Law lives in a remote, coastal location – a rugged landscape blessed with the wild beauty of nature. Like several of her family members, Cherry-Anna is a keen artist, musician, and amateur astronomer, and has a formal diagnosis of Autism, which she considers a description of neurotype, not a label of disability.

AUTHOR'S NOTES

Fictional books mentioned in the narrative:
A Pocket Book of French Vocabulary
A Pocket Book of Welsh Phrases
A School English Primer, Book 2
Bonjour la Classe!
Deutsche Sprache und Grammatik
Finding our Way by Annette MacGregor
Logic and Progress
Quantum Star Quest
School Latin Primer, Book 1
The Home Nursing Manual
The Westcombe Herald
Time and Mankind

Fictional Companies/Businesses:
The Apple Barrel
Astroguides Ltd
The Bolingbroke Country Hotel
Clarissa Mainwaring's Canine Academy
Connor Components
Cove Cottage Tea Room
Dawson's the Drapers
High Lea Riding School
Koffie en Koek
Hotel au Lapin Blanc
Lavender Cottage Tea Room
Marjoram's Stores
Maverick and Co. (Solicitors)
Morton and Gordon-Smythe (Solicitors)
Porkie and Best
The Merry Teapot Restaurant
Tiffany's Titbits Tearoom
Westcombe Riding School
The White Lion Hotel

Fictional Celebrities:
Leslie Brightwell
Suzy Munro

Foreign Language words and phrases are understandable from context, self explanatory, or a translation is given within the narrative.

Exception: Baummarder: pine marten (a Leitmotiv for plot purposes in Fields of our Hearts, a later novel in the Lucy quintilogy)

Artistic works not referenced within the text and not in the wider public domain (such as Shakespeare or the Bible):

All Fools' Day is a 1966 sci-fi novel, set in 1971, by Edmund Cooper. Published by AbeBooks.

Sue Barton: Student Nurse is the first novel in a series by Helen Dore Boylston (published by Little, Brown & Co, New York, 1936)

Teahouse of the August Moon is a 1953 comedy drama for stage theatre, by John Patrick, adapted from the original 1951 novel by Vern. J. Sneider. The play is about the US army in occupied Okinawa in the aftermath of World War II.

Through the Tunnel is a short story by Doris Lessing, featuring in Short Stories of Our Time, a collection of twentieth century works by various authors, published by Harrap 1963 (Edited by DR Barnes)

"four men whizzing around on motorcycles doing stunts" is Lucy's impression of *Quelques Messieurs trop tranquilles* – a 1973 action film by Georges Lautner, in which a group of Hippie motorcyclists arrive in a French village and are implicated in a local murder.

Abby is a character in *Survivors* – a 1973 post-apocalyptic drama series by Terry Nation, first aired on BBC 1 in 1973.

Ralph McTell staged an informal gig at Lancaster University, early in 1976, featuring the song "Weather the Storm", from the album *Right Side Up*.

"Amazing Grace": 1971 played by the Military Band of the Royal Scots Dragoon Guards

"Cousin Norman": 1969 song by The Marmalade in: *Reflections of My Life*

"*Das weiss der Himmel allein*": (Heaven only knows) 1973 song by Ramona Wulf

"*Eres Tu*": (You're the One) runner-up to the 1973 Eurovision song contest, sung by Mocedades, representing Spain.

"*Griechischer Wein*": (Greek Wine) 1971 song by Udo Juergens

"*Ich komm'bald wieder*": (I'll be back soon) 1973 song by Cindy & Bert

"Kung Fu Fighting": 1974 song by Karl Douglas

"Sad, Sweet Dreamer": 1975 song by Sweet Sensation

"Sealed with a Kiss": 1962 song by Brian Hyland

"Silver Machine": 1971 song by Hawkwind

"*Tu te reconnaitras*": (You'll recognise yourself) 1973 Eurovision winning song by Anne-Marie David, representing Luxembourg.

"When will I see you again?": 1975 song by The Three Degrees

1896 poem by A E Housman

Loveliest of Trees; 1859 poem by A E Housman

Short Stories of Our Time. Ed: Douglas R Barnes. Publ Harrap

Tipsy's sonderliche Liebesgeschichte: 1973 by Else Hueck-Dehio, Heilbronn 1973 – a Romantic Idyll set in Estonia.

Printed in Great Britain
by Amazon